UNITED STATES GOVERNMENT

# Policy and Supporting Positions

Committee on Oversight and Reform

U.S. House of Representatives

116th Congress, 2d Session

DECEMBER 2020

ISBN: 978-1-63671-031-0

# COMMITTEE ON OVERSIGHT AND REFORM

CAROLYN B. MALONEY, New York, *Chairwoman*

ELEANOR HOLMES NORTON, District of Columbia
WM. LACY CLAY, Missouri
STEPHEN F. LYNCH, Massachusetts
JIM COOPER, Tennessee
GERALD E. CONNOLLY, Virginia
RAJA KRISHNAMOORTHI, Illinois
JAMIE RASKIN, Maryland
HARLEY ROUDA, California
RO KHANNA, California
KWEISI MFUME, Maryland
DEBBIE WASSERMAN SCHULTZ, Florida
JOHN P. SARBANES, Maryland
PETER WELCH, Vermont
JACKIE SPEIER, California
ROBIN L. KELLY, Illinois
MARK DESAULNIER, California
BRENDA L. LAWRENCE, Michigan
STACEY E. PLASKETT, Virgin Islands
JIMMY GOMEZ, California
ALEXANDRIA OCASIO-CORTEZ, New York
AYANNA PRESSLEY, Massachusetts
RASHIDA TLAIB, Michigan
KATIE PORTER, California

JAMES COMER, Kentucky, *Ranking Minority Member*
JIM JORDAN, Ohio
PAUL A. GOSAR, Arizona
VIRGINIA FOXX, North Carolina
THOMAS MASSIE, Kentucky
JODY B. HICE, Georgia
GLENN GROTHMAN, Wisconsin
GARY PALMER, Alabama
MICHAEL CLOUD, Texas
BOB GIBBS, Ohio
CLAY HIGGINS, Louisiana
RALPH NORMAN, South Carolina
CHIP ROY, Texas
CAROL D. MILLER, West Virginia
MARK E. GREEN, Tennessee
KELLY ARMSTRONG, North Dakota
W. GREGORY STEUBE, Florida
FRED KELLER, Pennsylvania

DAVID RAPALLO, *Staff Director*
ELISA LANIER, *Chief Clerk*
AMY STRATTON, *Clerk*
CONTACT NUMBER: 202-225-5051
MARK MARIN, *Minority Staff Director*

# FOREWORD

Every four years, just after the Presidential election, the "United States Government Policy and Supporting Positions," commonly known as the *Plum Book*, is published, alternately, by the Senate Committee on Homeland Security and Governmental Affairs and the House Committee on Oversight and Reform.

This publication contains data (as of June 30, 2020) on over 9,000 Federal civil service leadership and support positions in the legislative and executive branches of the Federal Government that may be subject to noncompetitive appointment (e.g., positions such as agency heads and their immediate subordinates, policy executives and advisors, and aides who report to these officials). The duties of many such positions may involve advocacy of Administration policies and programs and the incumbents usually have a close and confidential working relationship with the agency head or other key officials.

Following are the major categories of positions listed:

- Executive Schedule and salary-equivalent positions paid at the rates established for levels I through V of the Executive Schedule;

- Senior Executive Service (SES) "General" positions;

- Senior Foreign Service positions;

- Schedule C positions excepted from the competitive service by the President, or by the Director, Office of Personnel Management, because of the confidential or policy-determining nature of the position duties; and

- Other positions at the GS–14 and above level excepted from the competitive civil service by law because of the confidential or policy-determining nature of the position duties.

See Appendix 2 for more details on SES appointments and Appendix 3 for more details on Schedule C appointments. Additional information on the positions listed and the Federal salary schedules under which they are paid is provided in the appendices. The Legend on the following page shows the codes and acronyms used in this publication.

## DISCLAIMER

**The information for this committee print was provided by the U.S. Office of Personnel Management [OPM].**

# LEGEND

**Position Location (Column 1)**

Listed are the cities, States/Provinces and foreign countries in which the positions are located. Countries and cities (or other subdivisions) are shown for overseas posts. Note that "Washington, DC" includes positions in the entire metropolitan area and therefore may include certain cities and counties in the States of Maryland and Virginia.

**Position Title (Column 2)**

Listed are the position titles and the names of the organizations in which they are located.

**Name of Incumbent (Column 3)**

Listed are the names of individuals serving under other than career appointments. The phrase "Career Incumbent" is shown for positions incumbered by career appointees. The term "Vacant" is shown for positions that were not occupied on June 30, 2020, the "as of" date of this publication.

Note the law requires "member" positions in certain agencies (e.g., boards, committees, and commissions) be filled on a bipartisan basis. For such positions, the following letter codes are shown in parentheses following the name of the incumbent:

(D) = Democrat      (I) = Independent      (R) = Republican

**Type of Appointment (Column 4)**

Listed are letter codes that denote the type of appointment under which the position incumbent is serving. Note that several categories of positions can be filled by more than one type of appointment, e.g., SES positions listed in this publication may be filled by using career, noncareer, limited emergency, or limited term appointment authorities. Therefore, no "Type of Appointment" is shown for such positions when they are vacant.

| | | |
|---|---|---|
| PAS | = | Presidential Appointment with Senate Confirmation |
| PA | = | Presidential Appointment (without Senate Confirmation) |
| CA | = | Career Appointment |
| NA | = | Noncareer Appointment |
| EA | = | Limited Emergency Appointment |
| TA | = | Limited Term Appointment |
| SC | = | Schedule C Excepted Appointment |
| XS | = | Appointment Excepted by Statute |

## Pay Plan (Column 5)

Listed are letter codes that denote the Federal salary schedule or pay system under which the position incumbents are going to be paid. Tables showing the salary range for major pay systems are contained in Appendix 4.

| | | |
|---|---|---|
| AD | = | Administratively Determined Rates |
| ES | = | Senior Executive Service |
| EX | = | Executive Schedule |
| FA | = | Foreign Service Chiefs of Mission |
| FE | = | Senior Foreign Service |
| FP | = | Foreign Service Specialist |
| GS | = | General Schedule |
| PD | = | Daily Pay Rate* (per diem) |
| SL | = | Senior Level |
| TM | = | Federal Housing Finance Board Merit Pay |
| VH | = | Farm Credit Administration Pay Plan |
| WC | = | Without Compensation* |
| OT | = | Other Pay Plan* (all those not listed separately) |

* Although not pay plans, these codes are shown for information purposes.

## Level, Grade, or Pay (Column 6)

Listed are numerical and letter codes that denote the level, grade or salary of the position incumbered:

Levels I through V of the Executive Schedule

Grades 1 through 15 of the General Schedule

Annual Salary in Dollars

Daily Pay Rate in Dollars

If there is no entry in this column, the position does not have an established level, grade, or pay rate. For example, the pay rate for Senior Executive Service and Senior Level positions is "personal," i.e., attached to the incumbent, not the position. The pay rate for each new appointee is set by the appointing authority (usually the agency head) on a case-by-case basis. Annual salary schedules and pay ranges for such positions are shown in Appendix 4.

## Tenure (Column 7)

Listed are the terms or durations of the appointment in years. If there is no entry in this column, the appointment has no fixed term.

## Expires (Column 8)

Listed are the expiration dates for time-limited appointments. If there is no entry in this column, the incumbent is not serving under a time-limited appointment. However, many member positions on agency advisory boards, councils, and commissions are filled initially for a fixed term, but the incumbents may (and often do) serve beyond the expiration date until they are replaced. In such cases, no expiration date is shown.

# CONTENTS

viii

## APPENDICES

# LEGISLATIVE BRANCH

## ARCHITECT OF THE CAPITOL

| Location | Position Title | Name of Incumbent | Type of Appt. | Pay Plan | Level, Grade, or Pay | Tenure | Expires |
|---|---|---|---|---|---|---|---|
| Washington, DC ...... | Architect of the Capitol ..................................... | Brett Blanton........................ | PAS | OT | $172,500 | 10 Years | 05/12/20 |

## GOVERNMENT ACCOUNTABILITY OFFICE

| Location | Position Title | Name of Incumbent | Type of Appt. | Pay Plan | Level, Grade, or Pay | Tenure | Expires |
|---|---|---|---|---|---|---|---|
| Washington, DC ...... | **OFFICE OF THE COMPTROLLER GENERAL** Comptroller General............................................ | Gene Dodaro .......................... | PAS | OT | $183,100 | ................ | |
| Do ..................... | Deputy Comptroller General............................. | Vacant ................................... | PAS | OT | ................ | ................ | |

## GOVERNMENT PUBLISHING OFFICE

| Location | Position Title | Name of Incumbent | Type of Appt. | Pay Plan | Level, Grade, or Pay | Tenure | Expires |
|---|---|---|---|---|---|---|---|
| Washington, DC ...... | Director........................................................... | Hugh Nathanial Halpern..... | PAS | EX | II | ................ | |
| Do ..................... | Deputy Director ............................................. | Patty Collins ........................ | XS | EX | III | ................ | |
| Do ..................... | Superintendent of Documents ....................... | Laurie B. Hall ...................... | XS | OT | ................ | ................ | |
| Do ..................... | Executive Assistant to the Director.................. | Vacant ................................... | SC | OT | ................ | ................ | |
| Do ..................... | Inspector General ........................................... | Michael P. Leary................... | XS | OT | ................ | ................ | |

## LIBRARY OF CONGRESS

| Location | Position Title | Name of Incumbent | Type of Appt. | Pay Plan | Level, Grade, or Pay | Tenure | Expires |
|---|---|---|---|---|---|---|---|
| Washington, DC ...... | **OFFICE OF THE LIBRARIAN** Librarian of Congress...................................... | Carla Hayden ....................... | PAS | EX | II | 10 Years | |
| Do ..................... | **AMERICAN FOLKLIFE CENTER BOARD OF TRUSTEES** Ex Officio Member, Chairman, National Endowment for the Humanities. | Jon Parrish Peede................. | XS | WC | ................ | ................ | 01/20/17 |
| Do ..................... | Ex Officio Member, Chairman, National Endowment for the Arts. | Mary Anne Carter ................ | XS | WC | ................ | ................ | |
| Do ..................... | Board Member ................................................ | Vacant ................................... | PA | WC | ................ | 6 Years | |
| Do ..................... | ......do ........................................................... | ......do ................................... | PA | WC | ................ | 6 Years | |
| Do ..................... | ......do ........................................................... | ......do ................................... | PA | WC | ................ | 6 Years | |
| Do ..................... | ......do ........................................................... | ......do ................................... | PA | WC | ................ | 6 Years | |
| Do ..................... | **LIBRARY OF CONGRESS TRUST FUND BOARD** Ex Officio Member, Secretary of the Treasury... | Jacob J. Lew ......................... | XS | WC | ................ | ................ | 01/20/17 |
| Do ..................... | Board Member ................................................ | Joan W. Harris ..................... | PA | WC | ................ | 5 Years | 12/02/16 |
| Do ..................... | ......do ........................................................... | Sally Sussman ...................... | PA | WC | ................ | 5 Years | 09/02/18 |
| Do ..................... | **PERMANENT COMMITTEE FOR THE OLIVER WENDELL HOLMES DEVISE** Committee Member ......................................... | Michael Les Benedict........... | PA | WC | ................ | 8 Years | 04/30/19 |
| Do ..................... | ......do ........................................................... | Linda K. Kerber.................... | PA | WC | ................ | 8 Years | 06/30/19 |
| Do ..................... | ......do ........................................................... | Rachel F. Moran................... | PA | WC | ................ | 8 Years | 09/30/19 |
| Do ..................... | ......do ........................................................... | Vacant ................................... | PA | WC | ................ | 8 Years | |

# EXECUTIVE BRANCH

## EXECUTIVE OFFICE OF THE PRESIDENT

| Location | Position Title | Name of Incumbent | Type of Appt | Pay Plan | Level, Grade, or Pay | Tenure | Expires |
|---|---|---|---|---|---|---|---|
| | **EXECUTIVE OFFICE OF THE PRESIDENT** | | | | | | |
| | *WHITE HOUSE OFFICE* | | | | | | |
| Washington, DC ...... | Assistant to the President and Chief of Staff .... | Mark R. Meadows................. | PA | AD | ............. | ............. | |
| Do ..................... | Assistant to the President and National Security Advisor. | Robert C. O'Brien ............... | PA | AD | ............. | ............. | |
| Do ..................... | Assistant to the President and Special Representative for International Negotiations. | Avrahm J. Berkowitz............ | PA | AD | ............. | ............. | |
| Do ..................... | Counsel to the President ..................................... | Pasquale A. Cipollone........... | PA | AD | ............. | ............. | |
| Do ..................... | Assistant to the President and Senior Counselor. | Kellyanne E. Conway ........... | PA | AD | ............. | ............. | |
| Do ..................... | Assistant to the President and Deputy Chief of Staff for Policy to the First Lady. | Emma K. Doyle.................... | PA | AD | ............. | ............. | |
| Do ..................... | Deputy Counsel to the President for National Security Affairs and Legal Advisor to the National Security Council. | John A. Eisenberg ............... | PA | AD | ............. | ............. | |
| Do ..................... | Assistant to the President and Director of Strategic Communications. | Alyssa A. Farah ................... | PA | AD | ............. | ............. | |
| Do ..................... | Assistant to the President and Press Secretary. | Kayleigh M. Gilmartin........ | PA | AD | ............. | ............. | |
| Do ..................... | Assistant to the President and Chief of Staff to the First Lady and Spokesperson. | Stephanie A. Grisham.......... | PA | AD | ............. | ............. | |
| Do ..................... | Assistant to the President and Counselor to the President. | Hope C. Hicks ....................... | PA | AD | ............. | ............. | |
| Do ..................... | Assistant to the President for Economic Policy . | Lawrence A. Kudlow ............ | PA | AD | ............. | ............. | |
| Do ..................... | Assistant to the President and Director of Oval Office Operations. | Nicholas F. Luna.................. | PA | AD | ............. | ............. | |
| Do ..................... | Assistant to the President and Counselor to the President. | Derek S. Lyons..................... | PA | AD | ............. | ............. | |
| Do ..................... | Assistant to the President and Director of Presidential Personnel. | John D. McEntee, II ............ | PA | AD | ............. | ............. | |
| Do ..................... | Assistant to the President and Senior Advisor to the President for Policy. | Stephen Miller..................... | PA | AD | ............. | ............. | |
| Do ..................... | Assistant to the President for Trade and Manufacturing Policy. | Peter K. Navarro ................. | PA | AD | ............. | ............. | |
| Do ..................... | Assistant to the President and Cabinet Secretary. | Kristan K. Nevins............... | PA | AD | ............. | ............. | |
| Do ..................... | Assistant to the President and Deputy National Security Advisor. | Matthew F. Pottinger .......... | PA | AD | ............. | ............. | |
| Do ..................... | Assistant to the President and Acting Director of the Domestic Policy Council. | Brooke L. Rollins................. | PA | AD | ............. | ............. | |
| Do ..................... | Assistant to the President and Deputy Chief of Staff for Communications. | Daniel J. Scavino ................. | PA | AD | ............. | ............. | |
| Do ..................... | Assistant to the President and Acting Director of the Office of Legislative Affairs. | Amy H. Swonger.................... | PA | AD | ............. | ............. | |
| Do ..................... | Director of Records Management ....................... | Philip C. Droege................... | XS | AD | ............. | ............. | |
| Do ..................... | Executive Clerk.................................................... | David E. Kalbaugh ............. | XS | AD | ............. | ............. | |
| Do ..................... | Deputy Assistant to the President and Director of White House Management and Administration and Director of the Office of Administration. | Monica J. Block.................... | PA | AD | ............. | ............. | |
| Do ..................... | Deputy Assistant to the President and Principal Deputy Press Secretary. | John H. Gidley..................... | PA | AD | ............. | ............. | |
| Do ..................... | Deputy Assistant to the President for Presidential Scheduling and Advance. | Michael B. Haidet................ | PA | AD | ............. | ............. | |
| Do ..................... | Deputy Assistant to the President and Advisor for Policy, Strategy, and Speechwriting. | Vincent M. Haley................. | PA | AD | ............. | ............. | |
| Do ..................... | Depury Assistant to the President for Operations. | Williams B. Harrison .......... | PA | AD | ............. | ............. | |
| Do ..................... | Deputy Assistant to the President and Director of Intergovernmental Affairs. | Douglas L. Hoelscher .......... | PA | AD | ............. | ............. | |
| Do ..................... | Deputy Assistant to the President and Chief of Staff to the Senior Counselor. | Hope R. Hudson.................... | PA | AD | ............. | ............. | |
| Do ..................... | Deputy Assistant to the President and Director of Political Affairs. | Brian T. Jack........................ | PA | AD | ............. | ............. | |

## EXECUTIVE OFFICE OF THE PRESIDENT—Continued

| Location | Position Title | Name of Incumbent | Type of Appt. | Pay Plan | Level, Grade, or Pay | Tenure | Expires |
|---|---|---|---|---|---|---|---|
| Washington, DC ...... | Deputy Assistant to the President and Deputy Staff Secretary. | Catherine B. Keller .............. | PA | AD | ............... | ............... | |
| Do .................... | Deputy Assistant to the President and Director of Presidential Advance. | Max L. Miller...................... | PA | AD | ............... | ............... | |
| Do .................... | Deputy Assistant to the President and Social Secretary. | Anna C. Niceta .................... | PA | AD | ............... | ............... | |
| Do .................... | Deputy Assistant to the President and Director of the Office of Public Liaison. | Timothy A. Pataki ............... | PA | AD | ............... | ............... | |
| Do .................... | Deputy Counsel to the President........................ | Patrick F. Philbin.................. | PA | AD | ............... | ............... | |
| Do .................... | Depury Counsel to the President........................ | Michael M. Purpura ............. | PA | AD | ............... | ............... | |
| Do .................... | Deputy Assistant to the President for Strategic Initiatives. | John N. Rader...................... | PA | AD | ............... | ............... | |
| Do .................... | Depury Assistant to the President and Chief of Staff to the Advisor. | Julie T. Radford ................... | PA | AD | ............... | ............... | |
| Do .................... | Deputy Assistant to the President and Director of Presidential Correspondence. | Desiree T. Sayle ................... | PA | AD | ............... | ............... | |
| Do .................... | Deputy Assistant to the President and Deputy Director of the Office of American Innovation. | Ja'Ron K. Smith................... | PA | AD | ............... | ............... | |
| Do .................... | Deputy Assistant to the President and Director of White House Information Technology. | Roger L. Stone .................... | PA | AD | ............... | ............... | |
| Do .................... | Deputy Assistant to the President and Deputy Counsel to the President. | Kathryn L. Todd .................. | PA | AD | ............... | ............... | |
| Do .................... | Deputy Assistant to the President and Senior Advisor to the Chief of Staff and Senior Communications Advisor. | Benjamin D. Williamson ...... | PA | AD | ............... | ............... | |
| Do .................... | Deputy Assistant to the President and Deputy Policy Coordinator. | Nicholas W. Butterfield ........ | PA | AD | ............... | ............... | |
| Do .................... | Deputy Assistant to the President for Legislative Affairs and House Liaison. | Christopher C. Cox.............. | PA | AD | ............... | ............... | |
| Do .................... | Deputy Assistant to the President and Director of Operations for the Office of the First Lady. | Hayley L. D'Antuono............ | PA | AD | ............... | ............... | |
| Do .................... | Depury Assistant to the President and Advisor to White House Counsel. | Sylvia M. Davis ................... | PA | AD | ............... | ............... | |
| Do .................... | Deputy Assistant to the President and Advisor to the Senior Advisor. | Cassidy M. Dumbauld.......... | PA | AD | ............... | ............... | |
| Do .................... | Deputy Counsel to the President........................ | Scott F. Gast....................... | PA | AD | ............... | ............... | |
| Do .................... | Deputy Assistant to the President and Deputy Director of Communications. | Julia A. Hahn...................... | PA | AD | ............... | ............... | |
| Do .................... | Deputy Assistant to the President and Deputy Director of the Office of Public Liaison. | Jennifer S. Korn .................. | PA | AD | ............... | ............... | |
| Do .................... | Deputy Assistant to the President and Executive Assistant to the President. | Molly A. Michael.................. | PA | AD | ............... | ............... | |
| Do .................... | Deputy Assistant to the President and Advisor for Policy, Strategy, and Speechwriting. | Ross P. Worthington ............ | PA | AD | ............... | ............... | |
| Do .................... | Deputy Assistant to the President and Advisor for Policy. | John A. Zadrozny................. | PA | AD | ............... | ............... | |
| Do .................... | Deputy Director and Senior Advisor for Records Management. | Paul S. Raizk ...................... | XS | AD | ............... | ............... | |
| Do .................... | Senior Associate Counsel to the President........ | Mark A. Grider .................... | PA | AD | ............... | ............... | |
| Do .................... | Special Assistant to the President and Deputy Director of Advance. | Craig E. Handzlik................. | PA | AD | ............... | ............... | |
| Do .................... | Associate Counsel to the President ................... | Tara J. Helfman................... | PA | AD | ............... | ............... | |
| Do .................... | Senior Associate Counsel to the President........ | David M. Jones .................... | PA | AD | ............... | ............... | |
| Do .................... | Special Assistant to the President and Director of Domestic Initiatives. | Rosemary A. Lahasky .......... | PA | AD | ............... | ............... | |
| Do .................... | Special Assistant to the President and Deputy Director of White House Information Technology. | David J. Lambrecht.............. | PA | AD | ............... | ............... | |
| Do .................... | Special Assistant to the President and Director of Hispanic Outreach. | Andrea R. Ramirez.............. | PA | AD | ............... | ............... | |
| Do .................... | Assistant Executive Clerk................................. | Thomas R. Edwin, III.......... | XS | AD | ............... | ............... | |
| Do .................... | Special Assistant to the President and Speechwriter. | Brittany L. Baldwin ............. | PA | AD | ............... | ............... | |
| Do .................... | Special Assistant to the President and Associate Director of Presidential Personnel. | Matthew A. Buckham .......... | PA | AD | ............... | ............... | |
| Do .................... | Special Assistant to the President and Deputy Press Secretary. | Judson P. Deere ................... | PA | AD | ............... | ............... | |
| Do .................... | Special Assistant to the President for Legislative Affairs. | Jeffrey K. Freeland.............. | PA | AD | ............... | ............... | |
| Do .................... | Special Assistant to the President and Director of the Office of the Senior Advisor for Policy. | Robert Gabriel, Jr. ................ | PA | AD | ............... | ............... | |

## EXECUTIVE OFFICE OF THE PRESIDENT—Continued

| Location | Position Title | Name of Incumbent | Type of Appt. | Pay Plan | Level, Grade, or Pay | Tenure | Expires |
|---|---|---|---|---|---|---|---|
| Washington, DC | Special Assistant to the President and Assistant Communications Director for Strategic Messaging. | Katherine A. Henning | PA | AD | | | |
| Do | Special Assistant to the President and Deputy Director of Political Affairs for Outreach | Alexander S. Latcham | PA | AD | | | |
| Do | Special Assistant to the President for Legislative Affairs. | Virginia D. McMillin | PA | AD | | | |
| Do | Special Assistant to the President and Director of White House Personnel. | Joe E. Otaño | PA | AD | | | |
| Do | Special Assistant to the President for Legislative Affairs. | Sean M. Riley | PA | AD | | | |
| Do | Special Assistant to the President and Speechwriter. | Theodore M. Royer | PA | AD | | | |
| Do | Special Assistant to the President and Assistant Staff Secretary. | Douglas C. Sellers, Jr. | PA | AD | | | |
| Do | Special Assistant to the President and Deputy Director of White House Management and Administration. | Alexandra E. Stone | PA | AD | | | |
| Do | Special Assistant to the President for Legislative Affairs. | Adam R. Telle | PA | AD | | | |
| Do | Associate Counsel to the President | Andrew R. Varcoe | PA | AD | | | |
| Do | ......do | Mitchell D. Webber | PA | AD | | | |
| Do | Assistant Executive Clerk | William W. McCathran | XS | AD | | | |
| | *OFFICIAL RESIDENCE OF THE VICE PRESIDENT* | | | | | | |
| Do | Deputy Social Secretary | Megan Schray | SC | GS | 11 | | |
| | *OFFICE OF POLICY DEVELOPMENT* | | | | | | |
| Do | Deputy Assistant to the President for Domestic Policy. | Jennifer B. Lichter | PA | AD | | | |
| Do | Deputy Assistant to the President for Economic Policy and Deputy Director of the National Economic Council. | Francis J. Brooke Jr. | PA | AD | | | |
| Do | Deputy Assistant to the President for Domestic Policy. | Theodore J Wold | PA | AD | | | |
| Do | Special Assistant to the President and Senior Director for International Trade and Investment. | Katherine R Kalutkiewicz | PA | AD | | | |
| Do | Special Assistant to the President for Domestic Policy. | James S Baehr | PA | AD | | | |
| Do | ......do | James Sherk | PA | AD | | | |
| Do | Special Assistant to the President and Chief of Staff to the Director of the National Economic Council. | Susan C Varga | PA | AD | | | |
| | *OFFICE OF ADMINISTRATION* | | | | | | |
| Do | Deputy Assistant to the President and Director, Office of Administration. | Monica J. Block | PA | AD | | | |
| Do | Special Assistant to the President and Deputy Director and Chief Administrative Officer. | Zaina A. Shaath | PA | AD | | | |
| Do | General Counsel | Andrew C. Proyect | PA | AD | | | |
| Do | Chief Financial Officer | Heather D. Martin | PA | EX | IV | | |
| Do | Senior Advisor and Counselor | Kathleen H. Shannon | PA | AD | | | |
| Do | Chief of Operations | Samuel T. Price II | PA | AD | | | |
| Do | Senior Advisor | William A. Wetzel | PA | AD | | | |
| Do | Special Assistant to the President and Technical Advisor. | Gabriel E. Perez | PA | AD | | | |
| Do | ......do | Evan B. Torrens | PA | AD | | | |
| Do | Associate Director of Operations and Facilities. | Thomas J. Tsaveras | PA | AD | | | |
| Do | Staff Assistant | Chamberlain R. Harris | PA | AD | | | |
| | *OFFICE OF MANAGEMENT AND BUDGET* | | | | | | |
| | *Office of the Director* | | | | | | |
| Washington, DC | Director Office of Management and Budget | Vacant | PAS | EX | I | | |
| Do | Deputy Director Office of Management and Budget. | Russell Thurlow Vought | PAS | EX | II | | |
| Do | Deputy Director for Management | Vacant | PAS | EX | II | | |
| Do | Chief of Staff | ......do | | ES | | | |
| Do | Deputy Chief of Staff | Ashlea Nicole Frazier | NA | ES | | | |
| Do | Senior Advisor to the Deputy Director for Management. | Patrick Corrigan | SC | GS | 15 | | |
| Do | Senior Advisor | Nathan Uldricks | SC | GS | 15 | | |
| Do | ......do | Michael Williams | NA | ES | | | |
| Do | Special Assistant | Ann Conant | SC | GS | 11 | | |
| Do | Special Assistant to the Director | Mark Christopher Bigley | SC | GS | 11 | | |

## EXECUTIVE OFFICE OF THE PRESIDENT—Continued

| Location | Position Title | Name of Incumbent | Type of Appt. | Pay Plan | Level, Grade, or Pay | Tenure | Expires |
|---|---|---|---|---|---|---|---|
| Washington, DC ...... | Confidential Assistant ........................................ | Jason Miles Hoffman ........... | SC | GS | 7 | ................ | |
| Do .................... | ......do ................................................. | Austin Brittany Hoffman..... | SC | GS | 7 | ................ | |
| Do .................... | Senior Advisor.................................................... | Vacant ................................ | | ES | ................ | ................ | |
| Do .................... | ......do ......................................... | ......do ................................ | | ES | ................ | ................ | |
| Do .................... | Executive Associate Director............................ | Derek Tai Ching Kan ........... | NA | ES | ................ | ................ | |
| | *Legislative Affairs* | | | | | | |
| Do .................... | Associate Director for Legislative Affairs .......... | Jason Alan Yaworske ........... | NA | ES | ................ | ................ | |
| Do .................... | Deputy to the Associate Director for Legislative Affairs (Appropriations). | James Carlin Braid ............. | SC | GS | 14 | ................ | |
| Do .................... | Deputy to the Associate Director for Legislative Affairs (House). | Hugh Davis Fike ................. | SC | GS | 13 | ................ | |
| Do .................... | Deputy to the Associate Director for Legislative Affairs (Senate). | Natalie Michelle Mcintyre ... | SC | GS | 13 | ................ | |
| | *General Counsel* | | | | | | |
| Do .................... | Deputy General Counsel ..................................... | Hallee Katherine Morgan .... | NA | ES | ................ | ................ | |
| Do .................... | Associate General Counsel................................... | Joseph Anthony Gammello .. | SC | GS | 14 | ................ | |
| Do .................... | Special Counsel.................................................... | Kenneth Alan Klukowski..... | SC | GS | 15 | ................ | |
| Do .................... | Deputy General Counsel for Oversight ............. | Jessica Lea Donlon.............. | NA | ES | ................ | ................ | |
| Do .................... | General Counsel.................................................... | Mark Richard-Alan Paoletta. | NA | ES | ................ | ................ | |
| Do .................... | Deputy General Counsel ..................................... | Career Incumbent ............... | CA | ES | ................ | ................ | |
| Do .................... | Confidential Assistant ........................................ | James Milam Johnson ......... | SC | GS | 9 | ................ | |
| | *Communications* | | | | | | |
| Do .................... | Associate Director for Communications and Strategy. | Rachel Kay Semmel ............. | NA | ES | ................ | ................ | |
| Do .................... | Deputy to the Associate Director for Communications. | Chase William Jennings ...... | SC | GS | 13 | ................ | |
| Do .................... | Press Secretary ................................................... | Robert Neil Kuhlman........... | SC | GS | 13 | ................ | |
| Do .................... | Deputy Press Secretary ...................................... | Edie Marie Heipel ............... | SC | GS | 9 | ................ | |
| | *General Government Programs* | | | | | | |
| Do .................... | Associate Director, General Government Programs/Transportation, Homeland Security, Justice Services. | Thomas Anthony Alexander. | NA | ES | ................ | ................ | |
| Do .................... | Associate Director, General Government Program/Housing, Commerce, and Treasury. | Vacant ................................ | | ES | ................ | ................ | |
| Do .................... | Confidential Assistant ........................................ | Nicole Reeves...................... | SC | GS | 7 | ................ | |
| | *Education, Income, Maintenance and Labor Programs* | | | | | | |
| Do .................... | Associate Director for Education, Labor, and Income Maintenance. | Denzel Ellyn Mcguire........... | NA | ES | ................ | ................ | |
| Do .................... | Special Assistant................................................. | Madison Biedermann........... | SC | GS | 11 | ................ | |
| Do .................... | Confidential Assistant ........................................ | Katherine Anne Trout.......... | SC | GS | 7 | ................ | |
| | *Office of Information and Regulatory Affairs* | | | | | | |
| Do .................... | Administrator, Office of Information and Regulatory Affairs. | Paul J Ray.......................... | PAS | EX | III | ................ | |
| Do .................... | Associate Administrator, Office of Information and Regulatory Affairs. | Rosario Anthony Palmieri.... | NA | ES | ................ | ................ | |
| Do .................... | Deputy Administrator.......................................... | Career Incumbent ............... | CA | ES | ................ | ................ | |
| Do .................... | Chief, Transportation and Security Branch....... | ......do ................................ | CA | ES | ................ | ................ | |
| Do .................... | Counselor to the Office of Information and Regulatory Affairs Administrator. | Satya Thallam ..................... | SC | GS | 15 | ................ | |
| Do .................... | Confidential Assistant ........................................ | Taylor Marie Chaffetz .......... | SC | GS | 7 | ................ | |
| | *Health Division* | | | | | | |
| Do .................... | Program Associate Director for Health Programs. | Gregory Brian Dangelo........ | NA | ES | ................ | ................ | |
| Do .................... | Confidential Assistant ........................................ | Grace Ann Bruno.................. | SC | GS | 9 | ................ | |
| | *Office of Federal Financial Management* | | | | | | |
| Do .................... | Controller, Office of Federal Financial Management. | Vacant ................................ | PAS | EX | III | ................ | |
| Do .................... | Deputy Controller................................................ | Career Incumbent ............... | CA | ES | ................ | ................ | |
| Do .................... | Chief, Management Controls and Assistance Branch. | ......do ................................ | CA | ES | ................ | ................ | |
| | *Office of Federal Procurement Policy* | | | | | | |
| Do .................... | Administrator Office of Federal Procurement Policy. | Michael Wooten ................... | PAS | EX | III | ................ | |
| Do .................... | Special Assistant................................................. | Michelle Balch Kelley .......... | SC | GS | 11 | ................ | |
| | *Staff Offices* | | | | | | |
| Do .................... | Associate Director for Economic Policy ............. | Vacant ................................ | | ES | ................ | ................ | |

## EXECUTIVE OFFICE OF THE PRESIDENT—Continued

| Location | Position Title | Name of Incumbent | Type of Appt. | Pay Plan | Level, Grade, or Pay | Tenure | Expires |
|---|---|---|---|---|---|---|---|
| Washington, DC ...... | Associate Director for Performance Management. | Peter Warren.................... | NA | ES | .............. | .............. | |
| | *Office of E-Government and Information Technology* | | | | | | |
| Do .................. | Federal Chief Information Security Officer ...... | Career Incumbent ............... | CA | ES | .............. | .............. | |
| Do .................. | Special Assistant.................... | Haley Zoey Friedman........... | SC | GS | 11 | .............. | |
| Do .................. | Senior Advisor and Interagency Coordinator for Artificial Intelligence Information Technology Policy. | Camilo Jaime Sandoval ....... | NA | ES | .............. | .............. | |
| Do .................. | Deputy Federal Chief Information Officer ........ | Career Incumbent ............... | CA | ES | .............. | .............. | |
| Do .................. | Administrator, E-Government and Information Technology. | Suzette Kuhlow Kent........... | PAS | EX | III | .............. | |
| | COUNCIL OF ECONOMIC ADVISERS | | | | | | |
| Do .................. | Chairman, Council of Economic Advisers ......... | Vacant ..................... | PAS | EX | II | .............. | |
| Do .................. | Member (Council for Economic Advisers) .......... | Tyler Goodspeed ................... | PAS | EX | IV | .............. | |
| Do .................. | ......do ..................... | Vacant ..................... | PAS | EX | IV | .............. | |
| Do .................. | Chief of Staff .................... | Rachael Seidenschnur Slobodien. | XS | AD | .............. | .............. | |
| Do .................. | Director for Macroeconomic Forecasting........... | Career Incumbent ............... | CA | ES | .............. | .............. | |
| | COUNCIL ON ENVIRONMENTAL QUALITY | | | | | | |
| Do .................. | Chairman (Council on Environmental Quality). | Mary B Neumayr.................. | PAS | EX | II | .............. | |
| Do .................. | Member (Council on Environmental Quality) ... | Vacant ..................... | PAS | EX | IV | .............. | |
| Do .................. | ......do ..................... | ......do ..................... | PAS | EX | IV | .............. | |
| Do .................. | Deputy Director ..................... | ......do ..................... | PAS | EX | IV | .............. | |
| Do .................. | General Counsel and Chief of Staff.................. | Viktoria Ziebarth Seale........ | XS | AD | .............. | .............. | |
| Do .................. | Principal Deputy General Counsel.................... | Lamar N Echols III .............. | XS | AD | .............. | .............. | |
| Do .................. | Associate Director for Legislative and Regulatory Affairs. | Theresa Lavery Pettigrew ... | XS | AD | .............. | .............. | |
| Do .................. | Associate Director for Communications............ | Daniel Joseph Schneider...... | XS | AD | .............. | .............. | |
| Do .................. | Associate Director for Natural Resources.......... | Melanie Ann Steele .............. | SC | GS | 14 | .............. | |
| Do .................. | Special Assistant.................... | Kelly Murphy Collins........... | XS | AD | .............. | .............. | |
| | OFFICE OF THE UNITED STATES TRADE REPRESENTATIVE | | | | | | |
| Do .................. | Assistant United States Trade Representative for Western Hemisphere. | Vacant ..................... | | ES | | | |
| | *Office of the Ambassador* | | | | | | |
| Do .................. | United States Trade Representative ................. | Robert E Lighthizer ............ | PAS | EX | I | .............. | |
| Do .................. | Chief of Staff.................... | Kevin Garvey........................ | NA | ES | .............. | .............. | |
| Do .................. | Counselor to the United States Trade Representative. | Vacant ..................... | | ES | | | |
| Do .................. | Senior Advisor.................... | ......do ..................... | | ES | | | |
| Do .................. | ......do ..................... | ......do ..................... | | ES | | | |
| Do .................. | ......do ..................... | Michael Nemelka.................. | NA | ES | | | |
| Do .................. | Attorney-Advisor.................... | Joseph Leo Barloon ............ | NA | ES | | | |
| Do .................. | Director of Scheduling and Advance Coordinator. | Jaclyn Cecilia Knight........... | XS | AD | .............. | .............. | |
| Do .................. | Executive Secretary.................... | Andrew Edward Eilts........... | SC | GS | 14 | .............. | |
| Do .................. | Senior Director for Policy .................... | Dereck Christopher Chapman. | XS | AD | .............. | .............. | |
| Do .................. | ......do ..................... | Haley Marissa Dorval .......... | XS | AD | .............. | .............. | |
| Do .................. | Correspondence Analyst .................... | Mark Diplacido.................. | XS | AD | .............. | .............. | |
| Do .................. | Confidential Assistant .................... | South Trimble Patterson...... | XS | AD | .............. | .............. | |
| Do .................. | ......do ..................... | Jodi Elizabeth Davis ............ | XS | AD | .............. | .............. | |
| Do .................. | Special Assistant.................... | Aaron Michael Bernasconi... | XS | AD | .............. | .............. | |
| | *Deputy United States Trade Representative (1)* | | | | | | |
| Do .................. | Deputy United States Trade Representative..... | Jeffrey David Gerrish........... | PAS | EX | III | .............. | |
| Do .................. | Confidential Assistant .................... | Emily Helen Jensen ............ | XS | AD | .............. | .............. | |
| | *Deputy United States Trade Representative (2)* | | | | | | |
| Do .................. | Deputy United States Trade Representative..... | Curtis Joseph Mahoney ....... | PAS | EX | III | .............. | |
| | *Chief Agricultural Negotiator* | | | | | | |
| Do .................. | Chief Agricultural Negotiator.................... | Gregory Fay Doud .............. | PAS | EX | III | .............. | |
| Do .................. | Special Assistant to the Deputy.................... | Trey Michael Forsyth........... | XS | AD | .............. | .............. | |
| | *Geneva* | | | | | | |
| Geneva, Switzerland. | Deputy United States Trade Representative..... | Dennis Shea........................ | PAS | EX | III | .............. | |
| Do .................. | Deputy Chief of Mission-Geneva .................... | Career Incumbent ............... | CA | ES | | | |
| | *General Counsel* | | | | | | |
| Washington, DC ...... | General Counsel.................... | Vacant ..................... | | ES | | | |

| Location | Position Title | Name of Incumbent | Type of Appt. | Pay Plan | Level, Grade, or Pay | Tenure | Expires |
|---|---|---|---|---|---|---|---|
| Washington, DC ...... | Deputy General Counsel ...................................... | Vacant ................................ | ............ | ES | ............... | ............... | |
| Do ..................... | ......do ................................................. | Career Incumbent ............... | CA | ES | ............... | ............... | |
| | *Public and Media Affairs* | | | | | | |
| Do ..................... | Assistant United States Trade Representative for Public and Media Affairs. | Vacant ................................ | ............ | ES | ............... | ............... | |
| Do ..................... | Assistant United States Trade Representative for Public Affairs. | Jeffrey Wade Emerson ......... | NA | ES | ............... | ............... | |
| | *Congressional Affairs* | | | | | | |
| Do ..................... | Assistant United States Trade Representative for Congressional Affairs. | Christopher L Jackson ......... | NA | ES | ............... | ............... | |
| Do ..................... | Senior Director for Congressional Affairs ......... | Kimberly Ekmark................. | SC | GS | 14 | ............... | |
| Do ..................... | Director of Congressional Affairs........................ | Kerrie Lynn Carr ................. | SC | GS | 13 | ............... | |
| Do ..................... | Deputy United States Trade Representative for Congressional Affairs. | Cameron Bishop ................... | XS | AD | ............... | ............... | |
| | *Intergovernment Affairs and Public Liaison* | | | | | | |
| Do ..................... | Assistant United States Trade Representative for Intergovernmental Affairs and Public Engagement. | Vacant ................................ | ............ | ES | ............... | ............... | |
| Do ..................... | Deputy Assistant United States Trade Representative for Intergovernmental Affairs and Public Engagement. | Samuel Austin Scales........... | SC | GS | 15 | ............... | |
| Do ..................... | Director, Intergovernmental Affairs and Public Engagement. | Joseph Maybank Howell...... | XS | AD | ............... | ............... | |
| Do ..................... | Confidential Assistant ......................................... | Dallas Quin Mcclendon........ | XS | AD | ............... | ............... | |
| | *China Affairs* | | | | | | |
| Do ..................... | Assistant United States Trade Representative for China Affairs. | Career Incumbent ............... | CA | ES | ............... | ............... | |
| Do ..................... | Senior Trade Representative (Minister Counselor for Trade Affairs). | Vacant ................................ | ............ | ES | ............... | ............... | |
| | *Japan, Korea and Asia Pacific Economic Cooperation Affairs* | | | | | | |
| Do ..................... | Assistant United States Trade Representative for Japan, Korea, and Asia Pacific Economic Cooperation. | Career Incumbent ............... | CA | ES | ............... | ............... | |
| | *Southeast Asia and Pacific* | | | | | | |
| Do ..................... | Assistant United States Trade Representative for Southeast Asia and Pacific. | ......do ................................ | CA | ES | ............... | ............... | |
| | *African Affairs* | | | | | | |
| Do ..................... | Assistant United States Trade Representative for Africa. | ......do ................................ | CA | ES | ............... | ............... | |
| | *Environment and Natural Resources* | | | | | | |
| Do ..................... | Assistant United States Trade Representative for Environment and Natural Resources. | Vacant ................................ | ............ | ES | ............... | ............... | |
| | *World Trade Organization and Multilateral Affairs* | | | | | | |
| Do ..................... | Assistant United States Trade Representative for World Trade Offices and Multilateral Affairs. | Career Incumbent ............... | CA | ES | ............... | ............... | |
| | *Agricultural Affairs* | | | | | | |
| Do ..................... | Assistant United States Trade Representative for Agricultural Affairs. | ......do ................................ | CA | ES | ............... | ............... | |
| | *Administration* | | | | | | |
| Do ..................... | Assistant United States Trade Representative for Administration. | ......do ................................ | CA | ES | ............... | ............... | |
| | *Services, Investment* | | | | | | |
| Do ..................... | Assistant United States Trade Representative for Services and Investment. | ......do ................................ | CA | ES | ............... | ............... | |
| | *Monitoring and Enforcement* | | | | | | |
| Do ..................... | Assistant United States Trade Representative for Monitoring and Enforcement. | ......do ................................ | CA | ES | ............... | ............... | |
| | *Economic Affairs* | | | | | | |
| Do ..................... | Assistant United States Trade Representative for Trade Policy and Economics. | ......do ................................ | CA | ES | ............... | ............... | |
| | *Innovation and Intellectual Property* | | | | | | |
| Do ..................... | Chief Innovation and Intellectual Property Negotiator. | Vacant ................................ | PAS | EX | III | ............... | |

## EXECUTIVE OFFICE OF THE PRESIDENT—Continued

| Location | Position Title | Name of Incumbent | Type of Appt. | Pay Plan | Level, Grade, or Pay | Tenure | Expires |
|---|---|---|---|---|---|---|---|
| Washington, DC ...... | Assistant United States Trade Representative for Intellectual Property and Innovation Rights. | Vacant ................................. | ............ | ES | ................ | ................ | |
| | *Europe and the Middle East* | | | | | | |
| Do .................... | Assistant United States Trade Representative for Europe and the Middle East. | Career Incumbent ............... | CA | ES | ................ | ................ | |
| | *Textiles* | | | | | | |
| Do .................... | Assistant United States Trade Representative for Textiles. | ......do ........................... | CA | ES | ................ | ................ | |
| | *South Asian Affairs* | | | | | | |
| Do .................... | Assistant United States Trade Representative for Central and South Asia. | ......do ........................... | CA | ES | ................ | ................ | |
| | OFFICE OF SCIENCE AND TECHNOLOGY POLICY | | | | | | |
| Do .................... | Assistant to the President for Science and Technology. | Vacant ................................. | PAS | EX | II | ................ | |
| Do .................... | Director, Office of Science and Technology Policy. | Kelvin Kay Droegemeier...... | PAS | EX | II | ................ | |
| Do .................... | United States Chief Technology Officer and Associate Director of the Office of Science and Technology. | Michael John Kotsakas Kratsios. | PAS | EX | ................ | ................ | |
| Do .................... | Associate Director, Science................... | Vacant ................................. | PAS | EX | III | ................ | |
| Do .................... | Associate Director, Technology................ | ......do ...... | PAS | EX | III | ................ | |
| Do .................... | Associate Director for Environment ...... | ......do ...... | PAS | EX | III | ................ | |
| Do .................... | Chief Technology Officer ...................... | ......do ...... | PA | EX | III | ................ | |
| Do .................... | Chief of Staff .................................... | Sean Christopher Bonyun ... | NA | ES | | | |
| Do .................... | Deputy Chief of Staff and Assistant Director ... | Vacant ................................. | ............ | ES | | | |
| Do .................... | General Counsel.................................. | ......do ...... | ............ | ES | | | |
| Do .................... | Deputy Assisant to the President for Technology Initiatives and Deputy United States Chief Technology Officer. | ......do ...... | ............ | ES | | | |
| Do .................... | Deputy Chief Technology Officer ............. | ......do ...... | ............ | ES | ................ | ................ | |
| Do .................... | Press Secretary ................................. | Jordan Chrystine Hunter .... | SC | GS | 11 | ................ | |
| Do .................... | Confidential Assistant ......................... | Jacqueline Collie ................. | SC | GS | 7 | ................ | |
| Do .................... | Associate Director, National Security and International Affairs. | Vacant ................................. | PAS | EX | III | ................ | |
| | NATIONAL SECURITY COUNCIL | | | | | | |
| Do .................... | Executive Secretary............................ | ......do ...... | PA | EX | IV | ................ | |
| | NATIONAL SECURITY PROGRAMS | | | | | | |
| Do .................... | Associate Director for National Security Programs. | Michael Patrick Duffey ........ | NA | ES | ................ | ................ | |
| Do .................... | Special Assistant................................ | Bryn Woollacott ................. | SC | GS | 13 | ................ | |
| Do .................... | Confidential Assistant ......................... | Laura Dennehy.................... | SC | GS | 11 | ................ | |
| | NATIONAL SPACE COUNCIL | | | | | | |
| Do .................... | Deputy Assistant to the President and Executive Secretary of the National Space Council. | Scott N. Pace ...................... | PA | AD | ................ | ................ | |
| Do .................... | Senior Advisor for Space Policy ........... | Peter J. Marquez ................. | XS | AD | ................ | ................ | |
| Do .................... | Chief of Staff for the National Space Council.... | Kathryn E. Wall................... | XS | AD | ................ | ................ | |
| Do .................... | Special Assistant to the Executive Secretary of the National Space Council. | Hilda V. Esquivel ................. | XS | AD | ................ | ................ | |
| | NATURAL RESOURCE PROGRAMS | | | | | | |
| Do .................... | Associate Director for Natural Resource Programs. | Brian Vaughan Mccormack.. | NA | ES | ................ | ................ | |
| Do .................... | Confidential Assistant ......................... | Ansley Marie Schoen............ | SC | GS | 7 | ................ | |
| | OFFICE OF NATIONAL DRUG CONTROL POLICY | | | | | | |
| .................... | *Office of the Director* | ................................. | ............ | ............ | ................ | ................ | |
| Washington, DC ...... | Director................................................ | James William Carroll Jr..... | PAS | EX | I | ................ | |
| Do .................... | Deputy Director, Office of National Drug Control Policy. | Vacant ................................. | PA | EX | II | ................ | |
| Do .................... | Chief of Staff........................................ | Kristin Shelby Skrzycki...... | NA | ES | ................ | ................ | |
| Do .................... | Deputy Chief of Staff............................. | Vacant ................................. | ............ | ES | ................ | ................ | |
| Do .................... | Senior Advisor for Rural Affairs ............ | Anne Catherine Hazlett...... | NA | ES | ................ | ................ | |
| Do .................... | Assistant Director for Public Health, Education and Treatment Task Force. | Saibatu Isat Mansaray ........ | TA | ES | ................ | ................ | 08/03/22 |
| Do .................... | Special Advisor to the Director and Director of Operations. | Hayley Catherine Conklin ... | SC | GS | 13 | | |

## EXECUTIVE OFFICE OF THE PRESIDENT—Continued

| Location | Position Title | Name of Incumbent | Type of Appt. | Pay Plan | Level, Grade, or Pay | Tenure | Expires |
|---|---|---|---|---|---|---|---|
| Washington, DC ...... | Assistant Director for the National Opioids and Synthetics Coordination Group. | Career Incumbent ................ | CA | ES | ............... | ............... | |
| Do ..................... | Assistant Director for the National Cocaine Coordination Group. | ......do ................................... | CA | ES | ............... | ............... | |
| | *OFFICE OF LEGISLATIVE AFFAIRS* | | | | | | |
| Do ..................... | Assistant Director, External and Legislative Affairs. | Kayla Munro Tonnessen ...... | NA | ES | ............... | ............... | |
| Do ..................... | Deputy Assistant Director, Office of Legislative Affairs. | Natasha Yenny Eby.............. | SC | GS | 13 | ............... | |
| Do ..................... | Public Affairs Specialist ...................................... | Gregory Thomas Angelo....... | SC | GS | 12 | ............... | |
| Do ..................... | Public Affairs Specialist (Program Support)...... | Gabriella Maria Uli.............. | SC | GS | 11 | ............... | |
| | *OFFICE OF LEGAL COUNSEL* | | | | | | |
| Do ..................... | General Counsel.................................................. | Vacant ................................... | ............ | ES | ............... | ............... | |
| | *OFFICE OF PERFORMANCE AND BUDGET* | | | | | | |
| Do ..................... | Deputy Assistant Director for Performance and Interagency Budget. | Career Incumbent ................ | CA | ES | ............... | ............... | |
| Do ..................... | Deputy Assistant Director for Budget................ | ......do ................................... | CA | ES | ............... | ............... | |

# DEPARTMENTS

## DEPARTMENT OF AGRICULTURE

| Location | Position Title | Name of Incumbent | Type of Appt. | Pay Plan | Level, Grade, or Pay | Tenure | Expires |
|---|---|---|---|---|---|---|---|
| | **OFFICE OF THE SECRETARY** | | | | | | |
| Washington, DC | Secretary | George Ervin Perdue III | PAS | EX | I | | |
| Do | Chief of Staff | Joby Freeman Young | NA | ES | | | |
| Do | .....do | Vacant | | ES | | | |
| Do | Deputy Chief of Staff | Andrew Blake Rollins | NA | ES | | | |
| Do | Senior Advisor to the Secretary | Kristi Boswell | NA | ES | | | |
| Do | Senior Advisor | Dudley Hoskins | NA | ES | | | |
| Do | .....do | Rebeckah Adcock | NA | ES | | | |
| Do | Executive Secretary to the Department | Arthur Harding | NA | ES | | | |
| Do | Senior Policy Advisor | Elizabeth Bennett | NA | ES | | | |
| Do | Special Assistant to the Secretary | Hailey Ghee | SC | GS | 13 | | |
| Do | Senior Advisor | Mary Beal | SC | GS | 13 | | |
| Do | .....do | Campbell Eileen Shuford | SC | GS | 13 | | |
| Do | .....do | Kyle Liske | SC | GS | 15 | | |
| Do | Special Assistant and Advisor | Charles Taylor Crowe | SC | GS | 11 | | |
| Do | Confidential Assistant | Sally Lindsay | SC | GS | 11 | | |
| Do | .....do | Ashley Smith | SC | GS | 9 | | |
| Do | Director of Operations | Lauren Elizabeth Sullivan | SC | GS | 14 | | |
| Do | Deputy Director of Scheduling | Margot Adams | SC | GS | 11 | | |
| Do | .....do | Samuel Justin Barke | SC | GS | 11 | | |
| Do | Deputy Director of Advance | Nicholas Matteo Westcott | SC | GS | 12 | | |
| Do | Advance Lead | Matthew Ziegler | SC | GS | 9 | | |
| Do | Advance Associate | Henry Miller | SC | GS | 7 | | |
| Do | White House Liaison | Matthew Christianson | SC | GS | 11 | | |
| Do | Senior Advisor to the Secretary | Vacant | | ES | | | |
| Do | Senior Advisor | .....do | | ES | | | |
| Do | Legislative Analyst | .....do | XS | GS | | | |
| Do | Senior Advisor to the Secretary | .....do | | ES | | | |
| Do | Senior Advisor | .....do | | ES | | | |
| Do | Director, Office of Partnerships and Public Engagement. | .....do | | ES | | | |
| Do | Senior White House Advisor | .....do | | ES | | | |
| Do | Senior Advisor to the Secretary | .....do | | ES | | | |
| Do | Deputy Chief of Staff for Operations | .....do | | ES | | | |
| Do | Assistant to the Secretary for Rural Development. | .....do | | ES | | | |
| Do | Deputy Chief of Staff for Outreach | .....do | | ES | | | |
| Do | Principal Deputy Assistant Secretary | .....do | | ES | | | |
| Do | Senior Advisor | .....do | | ES | | | |
| Do | Senior Advisor of Rural Infrastructure | .....do | | ES | | | |
| Do | Advisor to the Secretary | .....do | | ES | | | |
| Do | Legislative Correspondent | Bethanny Lawson | SC | GS | 7 | | |
| Do | Legislative Correspondent | Susan Lester | SC | GS | 9 | | |
| | *Office of the Deputy Secretary* | | | | | | |
| Do | Deputy Secretary of Agriculture | Stephen L Censky | PAS | EX | II | | |
| Do | Chief of Staff to the Deputy Secretary | Vacant | | ES | | | |
| Do | Senior Advisor | .....do | | ES | | | |
| Do | Chief of Staff | Kailee Marie Tkacz | NA | ES | | | |
| | *Office of the Assistant Secretary for Congressional Relations* | | | | | | |
| Do | Assistant Secretary for Congressional Relations. | Kenneth Barbic | PAS | EX | IV | | |
| Do | Chief of Staff | Vacant | | ES | | | |
| Lubbock, TX | Senior Advisor | .....do | | ES | | | |
| Washington, DC | Chief of Staff | Evan Lee | SC | GS | 13 | | |
| Do | Director Congressional Relations | Veronica Wong | SC | GS | 15 | | |
| Do | Deputy Director, External & Intergovernmental Affairs. | Ashley Willits | SC | GS | 9 | | |
| Do | Policy and Congressional Advisor | Zellie Duvall | SC | GS | 11 | | |
| Do | Congressional and Policy Advisor | Victoria Ness | SC | GS | 9 | | |
| Do | Legislative Analyst | Ronald Jacobs | SC | GS | 7 | | |
| Do | .....do | Noah Jackson | SC | GS | 7 | | |
| Do | .....do | Leon Striker | SC | GS | 9 | | |

## DEPARTMENT OF AGRICULTURE—Continued

| Location | Position Title | Name of Incumbent | Type of Appt. | Pay Plan | Level, Grade, or Pay | Tenure | Expires |
|---|---|---|---|---|---|---|---|
| | *Office of the Assistant Secretary for Civil Rights* | | | | | | |
| Washington, DC ...... | Assistant Secretary for Civil Rights................. | Vacant .......................... | PAS | EX | IV | .............. | |
| Do .................... | Deputy Assistant Secretary for Civil Rights...... | Devon Westhill...................... | NA | ES | .............. | .............. | |
| Do .................... | Associate Assistant Secretary for Civil Rights .. | Career Incumbent ................ | CA | ES | .............. | .............. | |
| Do .................... | Chief of Staff ............................... | Vacant .......................... | | ES | .............. | .............. | |
| | *Office of Civil Rights* | | | | | | |
| Do .................... | Director, Compliance, Policy, Training and Cultural Transformation. | ......do ...................... | | ES | .............. | .............. | |
| Do .................... | Director, Outreach and Diversity...................... | ......do ...................... | | ES | .............. | .............. | |
| | *Office of Communications* | | | | | | |
| Do .................... | Director of Communications ............................. | Michawn Marie Rich............ | NA | ES | .............. | .............. | |
| Do .................... | Deputy Director of Communications ................ | Vacant .......................... | | ES | .............. | .............. | |
| Do .................... | ......do ...................... | Meghan Rose Rodgers.......... | SC | GS | 15 | .............. | |
| Do .................... | Director of Communications ............................. | Vacant .......................... | | ES | .............. | .............. | |
| Do .................... | ......do ...................... | ......do ...................... | | ES | .............. | .............. | |
| Do .................... | Director of Scheduling and Advance ................ | ......do ...................... | | ES | .............. | .............. | |
| Do .................... | Senior Advisor Internal Comms ...................... | Ryann Durant...................... | SC | GS | 13 | .............. | |
| Do .................... | Deputy Press Secretary ................................ | Alecsandar Varsamis............ | SC | GS | 11 | .............. | |
| Do .................... | Press Assistant.......................................... | Audra Weeks...................... | SC | GS | 9 | .............. | |
| | *Office of the Chief Economist* | | | | | | |
| Do .................... | Chief Economist ........................................ | Career Incumbent ............... | CA | ES | .............. | .............. | |
| | *Office of Budget and Program Analysis* | | | | | | |
| Do .................... | Director of Budget and Program Analysis ......... | Vacant .......................... | | ES | .............. | .............. | |
| Do .................... | Deputy Director for Program Analysis............... | Career Incumbent ............... | CA | ES | .............. | .............. | |
| Do .................... | Deputy Director, Budget, Legislative and Regulation Systems. | ......do ...................... | CA | ES | .............. | .............. | |
| Do .................... | Associate Director........................................ | ......do ...................... | CA | ES | .............. | .............. | |
| Do .................... | Director, Budget Control and Analysis Division. | ......do ...................... | CA | ES | .............. | .............. | |
| | *Office of the Chief Information Officer* | | | | | | |
| Do .................... | Chief Information Officer............................... | ......do ...................... | CA | ES | .............. | .............. | |
| Do .................... | Deputy, Chief Information Officer ................... | Vacant .......................... | | ES | .............. | .............. | |
| Do .................... | Associate Chief Information Officer ................ | Career Incumbent ............... | CA | ES | .............. | .............. | |
| Do .................... | Associate Chief Information Officer for Policy, E-Government and Fair Information Practices. | ......do ...................... | CA | ES | .............. | .............. | |
| Do .................... | Associate Chief Information Officer, Client Technology Services. | Vacant .......................... | | ES | .............. | .............. | |
| Do .................... | Associate Chief Information Officer, International Security Operations Center, Cyber. | Career Incumbent ............... | CA | ES | .............. | .............. | |
| Do .................... | Executive Director of IT Modernization............. | ......do ...................... | CA | ES | .............. | .............. | |
| Do .................... | Executive Officer, Enterprise Management ....... | Vacant .......................... | | ES | .............. | .............. | |
| Do .................... | Chief Technology Officer ............................. | ......do ...................... | | ES | .............. | .............. | |
| | *Office of the General Counsel* | | | | | | |
| Do .................... | General Counsel.......................................... | Stephen Alexander Vaden.... | PAS | EX | IV | .............. | |
| Do .................... | Deputy General Counsel (Principal)................... | Richard William Goeken...... | NA | ES | .............. | .............. | |
| Do .................... | Deputy General Counsel .............................. | Tyler Clarkson...................... | NA | ES | .............. | .............. | |
| Do .................... | ......do ...................... | Vacant .......................... | | ES | .............. | .............. | |
| Do .................... | ......do ...................... | Career Incumbent ............... | CA | ES | .............. | .............. | |
| Do .................... | ......do ...................... | Vacant .......................... | | ES | .............. | .............. | |
| Do .................... | Deputy General Counsel for Special Projects .... | ......do ...................... | | ES | .............. | .............. | |
| Do .................... | Associate General Counsel, Civil Rights Litigation. | Career Incumbent ............... | CA | ES | .............. | .............. | |
| Do .................... | Associate General Counsel, International Affairs, Food Assistance, and Farm and Rural Programs Division. | Vacant .......................... | | ES | .............. | .............. | |
| Do .................... | Associate General Counsel, Regulatory and Marketing. | Career Incumbent ............... | CA | ES | .............. | .............. | |
| Do .................... | Associate General Counsel, International Affairs and Commodity Programs and Food Assistance. | ......do ...................... | CA | ES | .............. | .............. | |
| Do .................... | Assistant General Counsel, Civil Rights, Labor and Employment Law Division. | ......do ...................... | CA | ES | .............. | .............. | |
| Do .................... | Assistant General Counsel, International Affairs, Food Assistance, and Farm and Rural Programs Division. | Vacant .......................... | | ES | .............. | .............. | |

## DEPARTMENT OF AGRICULTURE—Continued

| Location | Position Title | Name of Incumbent | Type of Appt. | Pay Plan | Level, Grade, or Pay | Tenure | Expires |
|---|---|---|---|---|---|---|---|
| Washington, DC ...... | Assistant General Counsel, International Affairs, Food Assistance and Farm and Rural Programs Division. | Career Incumbent ................ | CA | ES | .............. | .............. | |
| Do ................... | Assistant General Counsel, Marketing, Regulatory and Food Safety Division. | ......do ...................... | CA | ES | .............. | .............. | |
| Do ................... | Assistant General Counsel, General Law and Research Division. | ......do ...................... | CA | ES | .............. | .............. | |
| Do ................... | Assistant General Counsel, Marketing, Regulatory and Food Safety Programs Division. | ......do ...................... | CA | ES | .............. | .............. | |
| Do ................... | Director, Office of Ethics.................................. | ......do ...................... | CA | ES | .............. | .............. | |
| San Francisco, CA ... | Regional Attorney ........................................ | ......do ...................... | CA | ES | .............. | .............. | |
| Kansas City, MO .... | ......do ...................... | ......do ...................... | CA | ES | .............. | .............. | |
| Denver, CO ............ | ......do ...................... | ......do ...................... | CA | ES | .............. | .............. | |
| Atlanta, GA ............ | ......do ...................... | ......do ...................... | CA | ES | .............. | .............. | |
| Washington, DC ...... | Senior Advisor to the General Counsel ............. | Vacant ...................... | .......... | ES | .............. | .............. | |
| Do ................... | Advisor to the General Counsel.......................... | Rachel Helen Pick ............ | SC | GS | 13 | .............. | |
| | **OFFICE OF THE ASSISTANT SECRETARY FOR ADMINISTRATION** | | | | | | |
| Do ................... | Assistant Secretary for Administration ............ | Vacant ...................... | PA | EX | IV | .............. | |
| Do ................... | Deputy Assistant Secretary for Administration. | ......do ...................... | .......... | ES | .............. | .............. | |
| Do ................... | Principal Deputy Assistant Secretary for Administration. | David Wu ...................... | NA | ES | .............. | .............. | |
| Do ................... | Deputy Assistant Secretary for Administration. | Vacant ...................... | .......... | ES | .............. | .............. | |
| Do ................... | Chief of Staff ............................................. | Courtney Knupp.............. | NA | ES | .............. | .............. | |
| Do ................... | Director, Office of Small and Disadvantaged Business Utilization. | Vacant ...................... | .......... | ES | .............. | .............. | |
| Do ................... | Director, Secretarys Office of Customer Experience. | ......do ...................... | .......... | ES | .............. | .............. | |
| Do ................... | Senior Advisor and Director Aapi Affairs........... | ......do ...................... | .......... | ES | .............. | .............. | |
| Do ................... | Senior Advisor......................................... | Maureen Gardner................ | SC | GS | 14 | .............. | |
| Do ................... | Interim Deputy Director, Secretarys Office of Customer Experience. | Vacant ...................... | .......... | ES | .............. | .............. | |
| Do ................... | Interim Director, Secretarys Office of Customer Experience. | ......do ...................... | .......... | ES | .............. | .............. | |
| | *Departmental Administration* | | | | | | |
| Do ................... | Director, Office of Property and Fleet Management. | Career Incumbent ................ | CA | ES | .............. | .............. | |
| Do ................... | Chief Learning Officer.................................... | Vacant ...................... | .......... | ES | .............. | .............. | |
| | **OFFICE OF THE CHIEF FINANCIAL OFFICER** | | | | | | |
| Do ................... | Chief Financial Officer ................................. | ......do ...................... | PAS | EX | IV | .............. | |
| Do ................... | Principal, Deputy Chief Financial Officer.......... | George Soles ................ | NA | ES | .............. | .............. | |
| Do ................... | Associate Chief Financial Officer, Financial Operations/Controllor. | Career Incumbent ................ | CA | ES | .............. | .............. | |
| Do ................... | Senior Advisor to the Chief Financial Officer.... | Vacant ...................... | .......... | ES | .............. | .............. | |
| Do ................... | Chief of Staff ............................................. | ......do ...................... | .......... | ES | .............. | .............. | |
| | *National Finance Center* | | | | | | |
| New Orleans, LA ..... | Director, National Finance Center.................... | Career Incumbent ................ | CA | ES | .............. | .............. | |
| Do ................... | Director, Government Employee Services Division. | Vacant ...................... | .......... | ES | .............. | .............. | |
| | *Office of Homeland Security and Emergency Coordination* | | | | | | |
| Washington, DC ...... | Director, Office of Homeland Security and Emergency Coord. | Career Incumbent ................ | CA | ES | .............. | .............. | |
| | *Office of Advocacy and Outreach* | | | | | | |
| Do ................... | Deputy Director, Office of Advocacy and Outreach. | Vacant ...................... | .......... | ES | .............. | .............. | |
| | *Office of Partnerships and Public Engagement* | | | | | | |
| Do ................... | Director Office of Partnerships and Public Engagement. | Michael Beatty ............... | NA | ES | .............. | .............. | |
| Do ................... | Director, Office of Tribal Relations .................... | Diane L Cullo ............... | NA | ES | .............. | .............. | |
| Do ................... | Chief of Staff............................................. | Riley Pagett ................ | SC | GS | 15 | .............. | |
| Do ................... | Special Initiatives Advisor ............................. | Kelsey Barnes................ | SC | GS | 11 | .............. | |
| Do ................... | Confidential Assistant ................................... | Mitchell Baker................ | SC | GS | 7 | .............. | |
| | **OFFICE OF HUMAN RESOURCES MANAGEMENT** | | | | | | |
| Do ................... | Chief Human Capital Officer............................ | Career Incumbent ................ | CA | ES | .............. | .............. | |

## DEPARTMENT OF AGRICULTURE—Continued

| Location | Position Title | Name of Incumbent | Type of Appt. | Pay Plan | Level, Grade, or Pay | Tenure | Expires |
|---|---|---|---|---|---|---|---|
| Washington, DC ...... | Deputy Chief Human Capital Officer................ | Career Incumbent ............... | CA | ES | ............... | ............... | |
| | *Office of Small and Disadvantaged Business Utilization* | | | | | | |
| Do ..................... | Director, Office of Small and Disadvantaged Business Utilization. | Vacant .................................. | ............... | ES | ............... | ............... | |
| | **OFFICE OF THE UNDER SECRETARY FOR RURAL DEVELOPMENT** | | | | | | |
| Do ..................... | Under Secretary for Rural Development ......... | ......do ............................... | PAS | EX | III | | |
| Do ..................... | Deputy Under Secretary for Rural Development. | ......do ............................... | ............... | ES | ............... | ............... | |
| Do ..................... | Chief of Staff.......................................... | Giles Misty............................ | NA | ES | ............... | ............... | |
| Do ..................... | .....do ..................................................... | Vacant .................................. | ............... | ES | ............... | ............... | |
| Do ..................... | Chief Risk Officer ................................... | ......do ............................... | ............... | ES | ............... | ............... | |
| Do ..................... | Senior Advisor for Rural Development ............ | ......do ............................... | ............... | ES | ............... | ............... | |
| Do ..................... | Senior Advisor........................................ | Kathryn Boots ..................... | SC | GS | 15 | ............... | |
| Do ..................... | .....do ..................................................... | Vacant .................................. | ............... | ES | ............... | ............... | |
| Do ..................... | .....do ..................................................... | ......do ............................... | ............... | ES | ............... | ............... | |
| Do ..................... | Confidential Assistant ............................. | Alexandra Lavy ..................... | SC | GS | 7 | ............... | |
| Do ..................... | .....do ..................................................... | Robert Gallagher .................. | SC | GS | 11 | ............... | |
| | *Rural Development* | | | | | | |
| Do ..................... | Deputy Chief Operating Officer.................... | Career Incumbent ............... | CA | ES | ............... | ............... | |
| Do ..................... | Confidential Assistant .............................. | Mikayla Athey ..................... | SC | GS | 7 | ............... | |
| | *Rural Housing Service* | | | | | | |
| Do ..................... | Administrator, Rural Housing Service ............ | Bruce Lammers ..................... | NA | ES | ............... | ............... | |
| Do ..................... | Associate Administrator ............................ | Vacant .................................. | ............... | ES | ............... | ............... | |
| Do ..................... | Chief of Staff........................................... | ......do ............................... | ............... | ES | ............... | ............... | |
| Do ..................... | .....do ..................................................... | Justin Domer ....................... | SC | GS | 15 | ............... | |
| Do ..................... | Deputy Administrator, Community Programs... | Career Incumbent ............... | CA | ES | ............... | ............... | |
| Do ..................... | Deputy Administrator for Single-Family Housing. | ......do ............................... | CA | ES | ............... | ............... | |
| Do ..................... | Chief Operating Officer............................. | ......do ............................... | CA | ES | ............... | ............... | |
| Do ..................... | Chief Information Officer........................... | ......do ............................... | CA | ES | ............... | ............... | |
| Do ..................... | Deputy Chief Financial Officer.................... | ......do ............................... | CA | ES | ............... | ............... | |
| Do ..................... | Director, Budget ...................................... | Vacant .................................. | ............... | ES | ............... | ............... | |
| Do ..................... | Director, Compliance Operations.................. | Career Incumbent ............... | CA | ES | ............... | ............... | |
| Do ..................... | Executive Director ................................... | ......do ............................... | CA | ES | ............... | ............... | |
| Do ..................... | Senior Advisor........................................ | Lori A. Urban....................... | SC | GS | 15 | ............... | |
| Do ..................... | .....do ..................................................... | Vacant .................................. | ............... | ES | ............... | ............... | |
| Do ..................... | Policy Advisor......................................... | Brandon Donald Sapala....... | SC | GS | 11 | ............... | |
| Do ..................... | Congressional Advisor .............................. | Helen Langfeldt.................... | SC | GS | 12 | ............... | |
| Montgomery, AL ...... | State Director - Alabama............................ | Chris Beeker ....................... | SC | GS | 15 | ............... | |
| Little Rock, AR ...... | State Director - Arkansas........................... | David Branscum................... | SC | GS | 15 | ............... | |
| Gainesville, FL ........ | State Director - Florida ............................. | Philip Leary ........................ | SC | GS | 15 | ............... | |
| Hilo, HI .................. | State Director - Hawaii ............................. | Brenda Iokepa-Moses........... | SC | GS | 15 | ............... | |
| Champaign, IL ........ | State Director - Illinois ............................. | Douglas A Wilson ............... | SC | GS | 15 | ............... | |
| Indianapolis, IN ...... | State Director - Indiana ............................ | Michael Dora ...................... | SC | GS | 15 | ............... | |
| Des Moines, IA ........ | State Director - Iowa ................................ | Grant Menke ...................... | SC | GS | 15 | ............... | |
| Lexington, KY ......... | State Director - Kentucky .......................... | Hilda G Legg ...................... | SC | GS | 15 | ............... | |
| Alexandria, LA ........ | State Director - Louisiana.......................... | Roy Holleman ..................... | SC | GS | 15 | ............... | |
| Bangor, ME............. | State Director - Maine .............................. | Timothy Hobbs .................... | SC | GS | 15 | ............... | |
| Amherst, MA ........... | State Director - Massachusetts ................... | George Krivda Jr. ................. | SC | GS | 15 | ............... | |
| St. Paul, MN ........... | State Director - Minnesota ......................... | Bradley Finstad ................... | SC | GS | 15 | ............... | |
| Columbia, MO ........ | State Director - Missouri ........................... | Jeffrey Case ....................... | SC | GS | 15 | ............... | |
| Lincoln, NE............. | State Director - Nebraska .......................... | Karl Elmshaeuser ................ | SC | GS | 15 | ............... | |
| Raleigh, NC ............ | State Director - North Carolina ................... | Robert Hosford .................... | SC | GS | 15 | ............... | |
| Bismarck, ND ......... | State Director - North Dakota ..................... | Clare Carlson...................... | SC | GS | 15 | ............... | |
| Columbus, OH ........ | State Director - Ohio ................................ | David Hall .......................... | SC | GS | 15 | ............... | |
| Stillwater, OK ......... | State Director - Oklahoma ......................... | Lee Denney ........................ | SC | GS | 15 | ............... | |
| Portland, OR........... | State Director - Oregon ............................. | John Huffman...................... | SC | GS | 15 | ............... | |
| Columbia, SC.......... | State Director - South Carolina ................... | Debbie Turbeville ................ | SC | GS | 15 | ............... | |
| Huron, SD............... | State Director - South Dakota ..................... | Julie Gross ......................... | SC | GS | 15 | ............... | |
| Nashville, TN.......... | State Director - Tennessee ......................... | Jim Tracy ........................... | SC | GS | 15 | ............... | |
| Salt Lake City, UT .. | State Director - Utah ................................ | Randall Parker .................... | SC | GS | 15 | ............... | |
| Richmond, VA ......... | State Director - Virginia ............................ | Elizabeth Green ................... | SC | GS | 15 | ............... | |
| Casper, WY ............ | State Director - Wyoming .......................... | Francis Wolski ..................... | SC | GS | 15 | ............... | |
| Morgantown, WV .... | State Director - West Virginia ..................... | Kristian Warner.................... | SC | GS | 15 | ............... | |
| Syracuse, NY .......... | State Director.......................................... | Richard Mayfield .................. | SC | GS | 15 | ............... | |
| Lakewood, CO ........ | State Director.......................................... | Sallie Clark ........................ | SC | GS | 15 | ............... | |
| Palmer, AK ............. | State Director - Alaska .............................. | Jerry Ward ......................... | SC | GS | 15 | ............... | |
| Topeka, KS.............. | State Director - Kansas ............................. | Lynne Hinrichsen................. | SC | GS | 15 | ............... | |
| East Lansing, MI..... | State Director - Michigan.......................... | Jason E Allen ...................... | SC | GS | 15 | ............... | |

## DEPARTMENT OF AGRICULTURE—Continued

| Location | Position Title | Name of Incumbent | Type of Appt. | Pay Plan | Level, Grade, or Pay | Tenure | Expires |
|---|---|---|---|---|---|---|---|
| Carson City, NV | State Director - Nevada | Vincent Cowee | SC | GS | 15 | | |
| Mt Holly, NJ | State Director - New Jersey | Michael Thulen Jr. | SC | GS | 15 | | |
| Albuquerque, NM | State Director - New Mexico | Blake Curtis | SC | GS | 15 | | |
| Harrisburg, PA | State Director - Pennsylvania | Curt Coccodrilli | SC | GS | 15 | | |
| Hato Rey, Puerto Rico. | State Director - Puerto Rico | Josue Rivera-Castro | SC | GS | 15 | | |
| Temple, TX | State Director - Texas | Edward E Hargett | SC | GS | 15 | | |
| Olympia, WA | State Director - Washington | Kirk Pearson | SC | GS | 15 | | |
| Stevens Point, WI | State Director - Wisconsin | Frank Frassetto | SC | GS | 15 | | |
| Davis, CA | State Director - California | Kimberly Dolbow Vann | SC | GS | 15 | | |
| Phoenix, AZ | State Director - Arizona | Jack Smith | SC | GS | 15 | | |
| Washington, DC | State Director | Carla Joyce White | SC | GS | 15 | | |
| Montpelier, VT | State Director, Vermont/New Hampshire | Anthony Linardos | SC | GS | 15 | | |
| Havre, MT | State Director | Charles Robison | SC | GS | 15 | | |
| Dover, DE | ......do | Denise Lovelady | SC | GS | 15 | | |
| | *Rural Business Service* | | | | | | |
| Washington, DC | Administrator, Rural Business Cooperative Service. | Vacant | | ES | | | |
| Do | ......do | Bette Brand | NA | ES | | | |
| Do | Deputy Administrator, Cooperative Services Programs. | Vacant | | ES | | | |
| Do | Chief Enterprise Officer | Career Incumbent | CA | ES | | | |
| Do | Confidential Assistant | Trent Allard | SC | GS | 11 | | |
| | *Rural Utilities Service* | | | | | | |
| Do | Administrator, Rural Utilities Service | Chad Rupe | PA | EX | IV | | |
| Do | Deputy Administrator, Rural Utilities Service | Vacant | | ES | | | |
| Do | Chief of Staff | Curtis M Anderson | NA | ES | | | |
| Do | ......do | Vacant | | ES | | | |
| Do | Deputy Administrator | ......do | | ES | | | |
| Do | Assistant Administrator - Telecommunications. | ......do | | ES | | | |
| Do | Assistant Administrator, Water and Environmental Programs. | Career Incumbent | CA | ES | | | |
| Do | Assistant Administrator - Electric Program | ......do | CA | ES | | | |
| St. Louis, MO | Deputy Director, National Financial and Accounting Operations Center. | Vacant | | ES | | | |
| Washington, DC | Policy Advisor | Taylre Beaty | SC | GS | 11 | | |
| Do | ......do | Vacant | | ES | | | |
| | **OFFICE OF THE UNDER SECRETARY FOR MARKETING AND REGULATORY PROGRAMS** | | | | | | |
| Do | Under Secretary for Marketing and Regulatory Programs. | Gregory Ibach | PAS | EX | III | | |
| Do | Deputy Under Secretary for Marketing and Regulatory Programs. | Vacant | | ES | | | |
| Do | ......do | ......do | | ES | | | |
| Do | ......do | ......do | | ES | | | |
| Do | Chief of Staff | Lorren Walker | NA | ES | | | |
| Do | Senior Advisor | Vacant | | ES | | | |
| | *Animal and Plant Health Inspection Service* | | | | | | |
| Do | Administrator, Animal and Plant Health Inspection Service. | Career Incumbent | CA | ES | | | |
| Do | Associate Administrator | ......do | CA | ES | | | |
| Do | ......do | ......do | CA | ES | | | |
| Do | Associate Administrator (Economics) | ......do | CA | ES | | | |
| Do | Associate Deputy Administrator, Wildlife Services. | ......do | CA | ES | | | |
| Do | Associate Deputy Administrator, International Services. | ......do | CA | ES | | | |
| Riverdale, MD | Associate Deputy Administrator, Field Operations. | Vacant | | ES | | | |
| Washington, DC | Associate Deputy Administrator for International Services. | Career Incumbent | CA | ES | | | |
| Do | Deputy Administrator, Policy and Program Development. | ......do | CA | ES | | | |
| Do | Senior Invasive Species Coordinator | Vacant | | ES | | | |
| Do | Executive Director, Strategy & Policy | Career Incumbent | CA | ES | | | |
| Do | Senior Advisor | Caleb Crosswhite | SC | GS | 15 | | |
| | *Plant Protection and Quarantine Service* | | | | | | |
| Do | Deputy Administrator, Plant Protection and Quarantine. | Career Incumbent | CA | ES | | | |

## DEPARTMENT OF AGRICULTURE—Continued

| Location | Position Title | Name of Incumbent | Type of Appt. | Pay Plan | Level, Grade, or Pay | Tenure | Expires |
|---|---|---|---|---|---|---|---|
| Washington, DC ...... | Associate Deputy Administrator, Plant Protection and Quarantine. | Career Incumbent ............... | CA | ES | ............... | ............... | |
| Do ................... | Assistant Deputy Administrator, Plant Protection and Quarantine. | Vacant ..................... | ............ | ES | ............... | ............... | |
| Do ................... | Executive Director Emergency and Domestic Programs. | Career Incumbent ............... | CA | ES | ............... | ............... | |
| | *Veterinary Services* | | | | | | |
| Do ................... | Deputy Administrator, Veterinary Services ....... | ......do ............... | CA | ES | ............... | ............... | |
| Do ................... | Associate Deputy Administrator, Regional Programs. | Vacant ..................... | ............ | ES | ............... | ............... | |
| Fort Collins, CO....... | Associate Deputy Administrator (Strategy & Policy). | Career Incumbent ............... | CA | ES | ............... | ............... | |
| Ames, IA ................. | Director National Veterinary Services Laboratories. | Vacant ..................... | ............ | ES | ............... | ............... | |
| | *Agricultural Marketing Service* | | | | | | |
| Washington, DC ...... | Administrator, Agricultural Marketing Service. | Career Incumbent ............... | CA | ES | ............... | ............... | |
| Do ................... | Associate Administrator ..................... | ......do ............... | CA | ES | ............... | ............... | |
| Do ................... | Deputy Administrator, Federal Grain Inspection. | ......do ............... | CA | ES | ............... | ............... | |
| Do ................... | Deputy Administrator, Commodity Procurement Program. | ......do ............... | CA | ES | ............... | ............... | |
| Do ................... | Deputy Administrator, National Organic Program. | Vacant ..................... | ............ | ES | ............... | ............... | |
| Do ................... | Chief of Staff ..................................... | Anna Osterlind ..................... | SC | GS | 15 | ............... | |
| Do ................... | ......do ..................................... | Vacant ..................... | ............ | ES | ............... | ............... | |
| Do ................... | Special Assistant..................................... | Christopher Paul O'Hagan .. | SC | GS | 12 | ............... | |
| | *Grain Inspection, Packers and Stockyards Administration* | | | | | | |
| Do ................... | Administrator..................................... | Vacant ..................... | ............ | ES | ............... | ............... | |
| Do ................... | Deputy Administrator for Packards Stockyards Programs. | ......do ............... | ............ | ES | ............... | ............... | |
| Kansas City, KS ..... | Director, Technical Services Division................. | ......do ............... | ............ | ES | ............... | ............... | |
| | **OFFICE OF THE UNDER SECRETARY FOR FOOD SAFETY** | | | | | | |
| Washington, DC ...... | Under Secretary for Food Safety ..................... | Mindy Brashears.................. | PAS | EX | III | ............... | |
| Do ................... | Deputy Under Secretary for Food Safety .......... | Vacant ..................... | ............ | ES | ............... | ............... | |
| Do ................... | Chief of Staff ..................................... | Shawna Newsome ............... | NA | ES | ............... | ............... | |
| Do ................... | ......do ..................................... | Vacant ..................... | ............ | ES | ............... | ............... | |
| Do ................... | Staff Assistant..................................... | Margaret Laing ..................... | SC | GS | 7 | ............... | |
| | *Food Safety and Inspection Service* | | | | | | |
| Do ................... | Administrator..................................... | Career Incumbent ............... | CA | ES | ............... | ............... | |
| Do ................... | Deputy Assistant Administrator, Office of Planning, Analysis and Risk Management. | Vacant ..................... | ............ | ES | ............... | ............... | |
| Do ................... | Executive Associate for Regulatory Operations. | ......do ............... | ............ | ES | ............... | ............... | |
| | **OFFICE OF THE UNDER SECRETARY FOR FOOD, NUTRITION AND CONSUMER SERVICES** | | | | | | |
| Do ................... | Under Secretary for Food, Nutrition, and Consumer Services. | ......do ............... | PAS | EX | III | ............... | |
| Do ................... | Deputy Under Secretary, Food, Nutrition and Consumer Services. | Brandon Ray Lipps ............... | NA | ES | ............... | ............... | |
| Do ................... | Administrator..................................... | Pamilyn Miller.................. | NA | ES | ............... | ............... | |
| Do ................... | Chief of Staff ..................................... | Vacant ..................... | ............ | ES | ............... | ............... | |
| Do ................... | ......do ..................................... | ......do ............... | ............ | ES | ............... | ............... | |
| Do ................... | Director of Regulatory and Policy Coordination. | Anne Decesaro..................... | TA | ES | ............... | ............... | 09/28/22 |
| Do ................... | Chief of Staff-Director of Policy ..................... | Vacant ..................... | ............ | ES | ............... | ............... | |
| Do ................... | Confidential Assistant ..................................... | Wesley Gwinn ..................... | SC | GS | 9 | ............... | |
| | *Food and Nutrition Service* | | | | | | |
| Do ................... | Associate Administrator..................................... | Vacant ..................... | ............ | ES | ............... | ............... | |
| Alexandria, VA ....... | Associate Administrator for Supplemental Nutrition Assistance Program. | Career Incumbent ............... | CA | ES | ............... | ............... | |
| Do ................... | Deputy Administrator, Center for Nutrition Policy and Programs. | ......do ............... | CA | ES | ............... | ............... | |
| Do ................... | Deputy Administrator for Supplemental Nutrition and Safety Programs. | ......do ............... | CA | ES | ............... | ............... | |
| Do ................... | Deputy Administrator, Child Nutrition Programs. | ......do ............... | CA | ES | ............... | ............... | |
| Washington, DC ...... | Deputy Administrator, Center Nutrition and Programs. | ......do ............... | CA | ES | ............... | ............... | |
| Do ................... | Deputy Administrator, Policy Support ............... | ......do ............... | CA | ES | ............... | ............... | |

## DEPARTMENT OF AGRICULTURE—Continued

| Location | Position Title | Name of Incumbent | Type of Appt. | Pay Plan | Level, Grade, or Pay | Tenure | Expires |
|---|---|---|---|---|---|---|---|
| Washington, DC ...... | Chief Information Officer | Career Incumbent | CA | ES | | | |
| Atlanta, GA ............ | Regional Administrator, Atlanta, Georgia | ......do | CA | ES | | | |
| Robbinsville, NJ ...... | Regional Administrator - Robbinsville, New Jersey. | ......do | CA | ES | | | |
| San Francisco, CA ... | Regional Administrator, San Francisco, California. | ......do | CA | ES | | | |
| Dallas, TX ............ | Regional Administrator, Dallas, Texas | ......do | CA | ES | | | |
| Chicago, IL............. | Regional Administrator (Chicago), Food and Nutrition Service. | ......do | CA | ES | | | |
| Denver, CO ............ | Regional Administrator (Denver), Food and Nutrition Service. | ......do | CA | ES | | | |
| Boston, MA ............ | Regional Administrator - Northeast Region ..... | ......do | CA | ES | | | |
| Washington, DC ...... | Director of Intergovernmental Affairs | Joseph Tvrdy | SC | GS | 13 | | |
| Do ................. | Associate Executive Director | Vacant | | ES | | | |
| Alexandria, VA ....... | Program Manager | ......do | | ES | | | |
| Washington, DC ...... | Senior Advisor | ......do | | ES | | | |
| Do ................. | Senior Advisor for Snap Access | ......do | | ES | | | |
| Do ................. | Senior Policy Advisor | Lindsay Datlow | SC | GS | 14 | | |
| Do ................. | Confidential Assistant | Laura Stagno | SC | GS | 9 | | |
| Alexandria, VA ....... | ......do | Maria Rey | SC | GS | 11 | | |
| | **OFFICE OF THE UNDER SECRETARY FOR TRADE AND FOREIGN AGRICULTURAL AFFAIRS** | | | | | | |
| Washington, DC ...... | Under Secretary for Trade and Foreign Agricultural Affairs. | Mckinney Ted | PAS | EX | | | |
| Do ................. | Deputy Under Secretary for Trade and Foreign Agricultural Affairs. | Vacant | | ES | | | |
| Do ................. | Deputy Under Secretary for Farm and Foreign Agricultural Services. | ......do | | ES | | | |
| Do ................. | ......do | ......do | | ES | | | |
| Do ................. | Deputy Under Secretary for Farm and Foreign Agricultural Service. | ......do | | ES | | | |
| Do ................. | Chief of Staff | ......do | | ES | | | |
| Do ................. | Senior Advisor | ......do | | ES | | | |
| | *Foreign Agricultural Service* | | | | | | |
| Do ................. | Administrator, Foreign Agricultural Service...... | Kenneth Isley | NA | ES | | | |
| Do ................. | Associate Administrator, Foreign Agricultural Service. | Vacant | | ES | | | |
| Do ................. | Associate Administrator | Career Incumbent | CA | ES | | | |
| Do ................. | Deputy Administrator for Capacity Building .... | Vacant | | ES | | | |
| Do ................. | Deputy Administrator, Trade Programs | Career Incumbent | CA | ES | | | |
| Do ................. | Deputy Administrator, Agreements and Scientific Affairs. | Vacant | | ES | | | |
| Do ................. | ......do | ......do | | ES | | | |
| Do ................. | Senior Advisor | Allison Beach | SC | GS | 13 | | |
| Do ................. | Policy Analyst | Jordan Bonfitto | SC | GS | 11 | | |
| | **OFFICE OF THE UNDER SECRETARY FOR RESEARCH, EDUCATION, AND ECONOMICS** | | | | | | |
| Do ................. | Under Secretary for Research, Education and Economics. | Vacant | PAS | EX | III | | |
| Do ................. | Deputy Under Secretary for Research, Education and Economics. | Scott Hutchins | NA | ES | | | |
| Do ................. | Deputy Under Secretary, Research, Education and Economics. | Vacant | | ES | | | |
| Do ................. | Chief of Staff | ......do | | ES | | | |
| Do ................. | Senior Advisor (Scientific Integrity) | ......do | | ES | | | |
| Do ................. | Senior Advisor | ......do | | ES | | | |
| Do ................. | Policy Advisor | Brock Andrew Densel | SC | GS | 12 | | |
| Do ................. | Staff Assistant | Elizabeth Edmunds | SC | GS | 7 | | |
| | *Agricultural Research Service* | | | | | | |
| Do ................. | Administrator, Agricultural Research Service ... | Career Incumbent | CA | ES | | | |
| Beltsville, MD........ | Director, National Agricultural Library | ......do | CA | ES | | | |
| Manhattan, KS........ | Director, National Bio and Agro-Defense Facility. | ......do | CA | ES | | | |
| Washington, DC ...... | Chief, Cyber Security Operations Officer | ......do | CA | ES | | | |
| | *National Institue of Food and Agriculture* | | | | | | |
| Do ................. | Director | Jay Angle | PA | EX | II | | |
| Do ................. | Associate Director for Programs | Career Incumbent | CA | ES | | | |
| Do ................. | Associate Director for Operations | Vacant | | ES | | | |

## DEPARTMENT OF AGRICULTURE—Continued

| Location | Position Title | Name of Incumbent | Type of Appt. | Pay Plan | Level, Grade, or Pay | Tenure | Expires |
|---|---|---|---|---|---|---|---|
| Washington, DC ....... | Deputy Director, Institute of Youth, Family and Community. | Vacant ................................. | ............. | ES | ................ | ................ | |
| Do .................... | Deputy Director, Institute of Food Production and Sustainability. | ......do .......... | ............. | ES | ................ | ................ | |
| Do .................... | Policy Advisor................................................ | Laney Copeland.................... | SC | GS | 11 | ................ | |
| | **OFFICE OF UNDER SECRETARY FOR NATURAL RESOURCES AND ENVIRONMENT** | | | | | | |
| Do .................... | Under Secretary for Natural Resources and Environment. | James Edward Hubbard ...... | PAS | EX | III | ................ | |
| Do .................... | Deputy Under Secretary for Natural Resources and Environment. | Vacant ................................. | ............. | ES | ................ | ................ | |
| Do .................... | ......do | ......do .......... | ............. | ES | ................ | ................ | |
| Do .................... | Chief of Staff .................................................. | Christopher Marklund ......... | NA | ES | ................ | ................ | |
| Do .................... | Senior Policy Advisor..................................... | Robert Macgregor................ | SC | GS | 13 | ................ | |
| Do .................... | Staff Assistant................................................ | William Guy........................ | SC | GS | 7 | ................ | |
| | *Forest Service* | | | | | | |
| Do .................... | Chief Forester ............................................... | Career Incumbent ............... | CA | ES | ................ | ................ | |
| Do .................... | Associate Chief............................................... | Vacant ................................. | ............. | ES | ................ | ................ | |
| Do .................... | Chief of Staff .................................................. | Career Incumbent ............... | CA | ES | ................ | ................ | |
| Do .................... | Associate Deputy Chief, Business Operations ... | ......do .......... | CA | ES | ................ | ................ | |
| Do .................... | Associate Deputy Chief, Business Operations, Policy. | Vacant ................................. | ............. | ES | ................ | ................ | |
| Do .................... | Associate Deputy Chief, Research and Development. | ......do .......... | ............. | ES | ................ | ................ | |
| Do .................... | Deputy Chief for State and Private Forestry..... | Career Incumbent ............... | CA | ES | ................ | ................ | |
| Do .................... | Director, Human Resources Management.......... | ......do .......... | CA | ES | ................ | ................ | |
| Do .................... | Chief Information Officer ............................... | ......do .......... | CA | ES | ................ | ................ | |
| Do .................... | Assistant Chief Information Officer ................. | ......do .......... | CA | ES | ................ | ................ | |
| Do .................... | Director, Senior Youth and Volunteer Programs. | Vacant ................................. | ............. | ES | ................ | ................ | |
| Albuquerque, NM.... | Director, Albuquerque Service Center-Budget and Finance. | Career Incumbent ............... | CA | ES | ................ | ................ | |
| Washington, DC ...... | Director, Strategic Planning and Budget Accountability. | Vacant ................................. | ............. | ES | ................ | ................ | |
| Do .................... | Director Work Environment and Performance .. | Career Incumbent ............... | CA | ES | ................ | ................ | |
| Do .................... | Director, Civil Rights Staff............................. | ......do .......... | CA | ES | ................ | ................ | |
| Do .................... | Director, Sustainability and Climate Change.... | ......do .......... | CA | ES | ................ | ................ | |
| Lakewood, CO ........ | Director, National Job Corps........................... | Vacant ................................. | ............. | ES | ................ | ................ | |
| Washington, DC ...... | Director, Emergency Medical Services .............. | Career Incumbent ............... | CA | ES | ................ | ................ | |
| | *National Forest System* | | | | | | |
| Do .................... | Deputy Chief, National Forest System................ | ......do .......... | CA | ES | ................ | ................ | |
| Do .................... | Associate Deputy Chief, National Forest System. | ......do .......... | CA | ES | ................ | ................ | |
| Do .................... | ......do | ......do .......... | CA | ES | ................ | ................ | |
| Do .................... | ......do | Vacant ................................. | ............. | ES | ................ | ................ | |
| Do .................... | Director, Recreation and Heritage Resources .... | ......do .......... | ............. | ES | ................ | ................ | |
| | *International Forest System* | | | | | | |
| Do .................... | Director of International Programs.................... | Career Incumbent ............... | CA | ES | ................ | ................ | |
| | *State and Private Forestry* | | | | | | |
| Do .................... | Associate Deputy Chief, State and Private Forestry. | Vacant ................................. | ............. | ES | ................ | ................ | |
| Do .................... | ......do | Career Incumbent ............... | CA | ES | ................ | ................ | |
| | *Field Units* | | | | | | |
| Missoula, MT.......... | Regional Forester, Region 1, Northern Region, Missoula. | ......do .......... | CA | ES | ................ | ................ | |
| Lakewood, CO ........ | Regional Forester, Rocky Mountain Region ....... | ......do .......... | CA | ES | ................ | ................ | |
| Albuquerque, NM.... | Regional Forester, Region 3, Southwest Region, Albuquerque. | ......do .......... | CA | ES | ................ | ................ | |
| Ogden, UT .............. | Regional Forester, Region 4, Intermountain Region, Ogden. | Vacant ................................. | ............. | ES | ................ | ................ | |
| San Francisco, CA... | Regional Forester, Region 5, Pacific Southwest Region, Vallejo. | Career Incumbent ............... | CA | ES | ................ | ................ | |
| Portland, OR........... | Regional Forester, Region 6, Pacific Northwest Region, (Portland). | ......do .......... | CA | ES | ................ | ................ | |
| Atlanta, GA ............ | Regional Forester, Region 8,Southern Region, Atlanta. | ......do .......... | CA | ES | ................ | ................ | |
| Milwaukee, WI ....... | Regional Forester, Region 9, Eastern Region ..... | Vacant ................................. | ............. | ES | ................ | ................ | |
| Juneau, AK............. | Regional Forester, Region 10, (Juneau)............. | ......do .......... | ............. | ES | ................ | ................ | |

## DEPARTMENT OF AGRICULTURE—Continued

| Location | Position Title | Name of Incumbent | Type of Appt. | Pay Plan | Level, Grade, or Pay | Tenure | Expires |
|---|---|---|---|---|---|---|---|
| | *Research* | | | | | | |
| Washington, DC ...... | Deputy Chief, Research and Development........ | Vacant ............................... | ............ | ES | .............. | .............. | |
| | **OFFICE OF THE UNDER SECRETARY FOR FARM PRODUCTION AND CONSERVATION** | | | | | | |
| Do .................... | Under Secretary for Farm Production and Conservation. | William Northey.................. | PAS | EX | .............. | .............. | |
| Do .................... | Chief of Staff-Advisor to the Under Secretary... | Jamie Clover Adams ........... | NA | ES | .............. | .............. | |
| Spokane, WA............ | Regional Director ................................... | Brian Ross Dansel.............. | NA | ES | .............. | .............. | |
| Bismarck, ND ........ | ......do ......................................... | Vacant ............................... | ............ | ES | .............. | .............. | |
| Escondido, CA........ | ......do ......................................... | Thomas Schultz.................. | NA | ES | .............. | .............. | |
| Taloga, OK.............. | ......do ......................................... | Jimmy Emmons.................. | NA | ES | .............. | .............. | |
| Des Moines, IA ...... | ......do ......................................... | Jeremy Davis ..................... | NA | ES | .............. | .............. | |
| Huntsville, AL ........ | ......do ......................................... | William Bailey Jr................ | NA | ES | .............. | .............. | |
| Bangor, ME............. | ......do ......................................... | Walter Whitcomb................ | NA | ES | .............. | .............. | |
| Lafayette, LA .......... | ......do ......................................... | Carrie Castille ................... | NA | ES | .............. | .............. | |
| Englewood, OH....... | ......do ......................................... | Marissa Walters................. | NA | ES | .............. | .............. | |
| Hillsboro, OH.......... | Regional Coordinator ........................... | Vacant ............................... | ............ | ES | .............. | .............. | |
| Washington, DC ...... | Chief Operating Officer ........................ | Career Incumbent .............. | CA | ES | .............. | .............. | |
| Do .................... | Deputy Chief Operations Officer .............. | Vacant ............................... | ............ | ES | .............. | .............. | |
| Do .................... | Deputy, Chief Operating Officer (Enterprise Services). | Career Incumbent .............. | CA | ES | .............. | .............. | |
| Do .................... | Chief Human Capital Officer ................... | ......do ......................... | CA | ES | .............. | .............. | |
| Do .................... | Deputy Chief Human Capital Officer......... | ......do ......................... | CA | ES | .............. | .............. | |
| Do .................... | Assistant Director, Homeland Security & Emergency Management. | ......do ......................... | CA | ES | .............. | .............. | |
| Do .................... | Chief Financial Officer ......................... | ......do ......................... | CA | ES | .............. | .............. | |
| Do .................... | Chief Financial Operations .................... | Vacant ............................... | ............ | ES | .............. | .............. | |
| Do .................... | Chief Economist .................................. | Career Incumbent .............. | CA | ES | .............. | .............. | |
| Do .................... | Deputy Director, Legislative Liaison ........ | ......do ......................... | CA | ES | .............. | .............. | |
| Do .................... | Deputy Director for Communications ........ | ......do ......................... | CA | ES | .............. | .............. | |
| Do .................... | Assistant Chief Information Officer .......... | ......do ......................... | CA | ES | .............. | .............. | |
| Do .................... | Director Management Services.................. | ......do ......................... | CA | ES | .............. | .............. | |
| Do .................... | Director, Office of Acquisition ................ | ......do ......................... | CA | ES | .............. | .............. | |
| Do .................... | Director, External Affairs ...................... | David Warner...................... | NA | ES | .............. | .............. | |
| Do .................... | Director, Environmental Activities ........... | Career Incumbent .............. | CA | ES | .............. | .............. | |
| Do .................... | Director, Performance, Accountability and Risk. | ......do ......................... | CA | ES | .............. | .............. | |
| Do .................... | Budget Officer.................................... | ......do ......................... | CA | ES | .............. | .............. | |
| Do .................... | Chief Information Solutions Services Del Ops .. | Vacant ............................... | ............ | ES | .............. | .............. | |
| Do .................... | Policy Advisor.................................... | Joshua Storey ..................... | SC | GS | 9 | .............. | |
| Do .................... | Confidential Assistant .......................... | Andrew Shaeffer.................. | SC | GS | 9 | .............. | |
| | *Farm Service Agency* | | | | | | |
| Do .................... | Administrator...................................... | Richard Fordyce.................. | NA | ES | .............. | .............. | |
| Do .................... | Associate Administrator ......................... | Vacant ............................... | ............ | ES | .............. | .............. | |
| Do .................... | Associate Administrator for Operations and Management. | ......do ......................... | ............ | ES | .............. | .............. | |
| Do .................... | Chief of Staff ..................................... | Dana Peterson .................... | NA | ES | .............. | .............. | |
| Do .................... | Deputy Administrator for Field Operations....... | Browne Peggy ...................... | NA | ES | .............. | .............. | |
| Do .................... | Deputy Administrator for Farm Programs ........ | William Beam ...................... | NA | ES | .............. | .............. | |
| Do .................... | Deputy Administrator, Management ............ | Vacant ............................... | ............ | ES | .............. | .............. | |
| Do .................... | Deputy Administrator for Commodity Operations. | ......do ......................... | ............ | ES | .............. | .............. | |
| Do .................... | Director, Economic and Policy Analysis Staff .... | ......do ......................... | ............ | ES | .............. | .............. | |
| Do .................... | Director, Production, Emergencies and Compliance Division. | ......do ......................... | ............ | ES | .............. | .............. | |
| Do .................... | Director, Information Technology Services Division. | ......do ......................... | ............ | ES | .............. | .............. | |
| Do .................... | Special Assistant.................................. | David Warren Matthews...... | SC | GS | 12 | .............. | |
| Do .................... | Confidential Assistant........................... | Gabrielle Rossi.................... | SC | GS | 12 | .............. | |
| Bozeman, MT ......... | State Executive Director ........................ | Michael Foster .................... | SC | GS | 15 | .............. | |
| Tolland, CT ............ | ......do ......................................... | Clark Chapin ...................... | SC | GS | 15 | .............. | |
| Amherst, MA .......... | ......do ......................................... | Edward Davidian ................ | SC | GS | 15 | .............. | |
| Lakewood, CO ........ | ......do ......................................... | Clarice Ratzlaff................... | SC | GS | 15 | .............. | |
| College Station, TX . | ......do ......................................... | Gary Six ............................ | SC | GS | 15 | .............. | |
| Montgomery, AL ...... | State Executive Director - Alabama ................ | David McCurdy ................... | SC | GS | 15 | .............. | |
| Palmer, AK............. | State Executive Director - Alaska ................ | Brian Scoresby.................... | SC | GS | 15 | .............. | |
| Little Rock, AR ....... | State Executive Director - Arkansas ................ | David Curtis ....................... | SC | GS | 15 | .............. | |
| Dover, DE............... | State Executive Director - Delaware ............ | Sean Mckeon....................... | SC | GS | 15 | .............. | |
| Honolulu, HI........... | State Executive Director - Hawaii ................ | Allen Frenzel ...................... | SC | GS | 15 | .............. | |
| Springfield, IL ........ | State Executive Director - Illinois .................... | William Graff...................... | SC | GS | 15 | .............. | |

# DEPARTMENT OF AGRICULTURE—Continued

| Location | Position Title | Name of Incumbent | Type of Appt. | Pay Plan | Level, Grade, or Pay | Tenure | Expires |
|---|---|---|---|---|---|---|---|
| Indianapolis, IN | State Executive Director - Indiana | Steven Brown | SC | GS | 15 | | |
| Des Moines, IA | State Executive Director - Iowa | Amanda Dejong | SC | GS | 15 | | |
| Manhattan, KS | State Executive Director - Kansas | David Schemm | SC | GS | 15 | | |
| Lexington, KY | State Executive Director - Kentucky | Brian Lacefield | SC | GS | 15 | | |
| Bangor, ME | State Executive Director - Maine | David Lavway | SC | GS | 15 | | |
| East Lansing, MI | State Executive Director - Michigan | Joel Johnson | SC | GS | 15 | | |
| Lincoln, NE | State Executive Director - Nebraska | Nancy Montanez Johner | SC | GS | 15 | | |
| Reno, NV | State Executive Director - Nevada | Janice Kolvet | SC | GS | 15 | | |
| Syracuse, NY | State Executive Director - New York | Clark Putman | SC | GS | 15 | | |
| Fargo, ND | State Executive Director - North Dakota | Bradley Thykeson | SC | GS | 15 | | |
| Columbus, OH | State Executive Director - Ohio | Leonard Hubert | SC | GS | 15 | | |
| Nashville, TN | State Executive Director - Tennessee | James Mayfield | SC | GS | 15 | | |
| Burlington, VT | State Executive Director - Vermont | Wendy Wilton | SC | GS | 15 | | |
| Spokane, WA | State Executive Director - Washington | Jon Wyss | SC | GS | 15 | | |
| Casper, WY | State Executive Director - Wyoming | Lois Van Mark | SC | GS | 15 | | |
| Raleigh, NC | State Executive Director, North Carolina | Edwin Woodhouse Jr. | SC | GS | 15 | | |
| Gainesville, FL | State Executive Director | Sherry Mccorkle | SC | GS | 15 | | |
| Morgantown, WV | State Executive Director - West Virginia | Roger Dahmer | SC | GS | 15 | | |
| Annapolis, MD | State Executive Director | James Eichhorst | SC | GS | 15 | | |
| New Mexico, NM | ......do | Michael White | SC | GS | 15 | | |
| Salt Lake City, UT | State Executive Director - Utah | Bruce Richeson | SC | GS | 15 | | |
| Phoenix, AZ | State Executive Director - Arizona | James Mago Jr. | SC | GS | 15 | | |
| Boise, ID | State Executive Director, Idaho | Thomas Dayley | SC | GS | 15 | | |
| Davis, CA | State Executive Director - California | Connie Conway | SC | GS | 15 | | |
| Richmond, VA | State Executive Director - Virginia | Nivin Elgohary | SC | GS | 15 | | |
| Concord, NH | State Executive Director - New Hampshire | Jeffrey Holmes | SC | GS | 15 | | |
| Warwick, RI | State Executive Director - Rhode Island | William Sullivan | SC | GS | 15 | | |
| Columbia, SC | State Executive Director | Boone Peeler | SC | GS | 15 | | |
| Alexandria, LA | State Executive Director - Louisiana | Craig A Mccain | SC | GS | 15 | | |
| Stillwater, OK | State Executive Director - Oklahoma | Scott Biggs | SC | GS | 15 | | |
| Madison, WI | State Executive Director - Wisconsin | Sandra Chalmers | SC | GS | 15 | | |
| Jackson, MS | State Executive Director - Mississippi | Robert Carson | SC | GS | 15 | | |
| Harrisburg, PA | State Executive Director - Pennsyvlania | Gary Groves | SC | GS | 15 | | |
| St. Paul, MN | State Executive Director | Joseph Martin | SC | GS | 15 | | |
| Hamilton Square, NJ. | State Director - New Jersey | Barry Calogero | SC | GS | 15 | | |
| | *Risk Management Agency* | | | | | | |
| Washington, DC | Administrator, Risk Management Agency | Martin Barbre | NA | ES | | | |
| Do | Associate Administrator | Vacant | | ES | | | |
| Do | ......do | ......do | | ES | | | |
| Do | Chief of Staff | Gregory Gray | NA | ES | | | |
| Do | Chief Financial Officer | Vacant | | ES | | | |
| Do | Deputy Administrator for Compliance | Career Incumbent | CA | ES | | | |
| Do | Chief Information Officer | Vacant | | ES | | | |
| Do | Policy Advisor | Rudolph Layher Jr. | SC | GS | 12 | | |
| | *Natural Resources Conservation Service* | | | | | | |
| Do | Chief, Natural Resources Conservation Service. | Matthew Lohr | NA | ES | | | |
| Do | Chief of Staff | Christopher Hess | NA | ES | | | |
| Do | ......do | Eric Ventimiglia | SC | GS | 14 | | |
| Do | Deputy Chief for Science and Technology | Vacant | | ES | | | |
| Do | Deputy Chief, Management and Strategy | Career Incumbent | CA | ES | | | |
| Beltsville, MD | Deputy Chief Soil Survey and Resource Assessment. | ......do | CA | ES | | | |
| Washington, DC | Associate Chief for Conservation | ......do | CA | ES | | | |
| Do | Chief Information Officer | Vacant | | ES | | | |
| Do | Regional Conservationist, South East | Career Incumbent | CA | ES | | | |
| Do | Regional Conservationist, Central | ......do | CA | ES | | | |
| Do | Regional Conservationist, West | ......do | CA | ES | | | |
| Davis, CA | State Conservationist, California | ......do | CA | ES | | | |
| Temple, TX | State Conservationist, Temple, Texas | Vacant | | ES | | | |
| Washington, DC | Director Resource Inventory and Assessment Division. | Career Incumbent | CA | ES | | | |
| Madison, MS | Director, Gulf of Mexico Ecosystem Restoration Team. | ......do | CA | ES | | | |
| Washington, DC | Senior Advisor | Vacant | | ES | | | |
| Do | ......do | ......do | | ES | | | |
| Do | Policy Advisor | Faith Burns | SC | GS | 14 | | |

# DEPARTMENT OF COMMERCE

| Location | Position Title | Name of Incumbent | Type of Appt. | Pay Plan | Level, Grade, or Pay | Tenure | Expires |
|---|---|---|---|---|---|---|---|
| Washington, DC ...... | Secretary .................................................... | Wilbur Lewis Ross Jr. .......... | PAS | EX | I | ............... | |
| Do .................. | Chief of Staff ............................................. | Vacant ............................ | ............... | ES | ............... | ............... | |
| Do .................. | Senior Advisor to the Secretary...................... | ......do .............................. | ............... | ES | ............... | ............... | |
| Do .................. | ......do ...................................................... | ......do .............................. | ............... | ES | ............... | ............... | |
| Do .................. | Senior White House Advisor ........................... | ......do .............................. | ............... | ES | ............... | ............... | |
| Do .................. | Special Advisor............................................. | Talat Goudarzi..................... | SC | GS | 11 | ............... | |
| | **OFFICE OF THE DEPUTY SECRETARY** | | | | | | |
| Do .................. | Deputy Secretary .......................................... | Karen Dunn Kelley ............... | PAS | EX | II | ............... | |
| Do .................. | Chief of Staff to the Deputy Secretary............. | Vacant ............................ | ............... | ES | ............... | ............... | |
| Do .................. | Senior Advisor for Policy and Program Integration. | Career Incumbent ................ | CA | ES | ............... | ............... | |
| Do .................. | Chief Data Officer ........................................ | Vacant ............................ | ............... | ES | ............... | ............... | |
| Do .................. | Executive Director for Shared Services............. | ......do .............................. | ............... | ES | ............... | ............... | |
| Do .................. | Interim Executive Director ............................. | ......do .............................. | ............... | ES | ............... | ............... | |
| Do .................. | Director of Information Technology for Enterprise Services. | Career Incumbent ................ | CA | ES | ............... | ............... | |
| Do .................. | Director of Business Operations for Shared Services. | Vacant ............................ | ............... | ES | ............... | ............... | |
| Do .................. | Deputy Director, Information Systems for Shared Services (Phase III). | ......do .............................. | ............... | ES | ............... | ............... | |
| Do .................. | Project Lead for Service Management Implementation. | ......do .............................. | ............... | ES | ............... | ............... | |
| Do .................. | Senior Advisor ............................................. | ......do .............................. | ............... | ES | ............... | ............... | |
| Do .................. | ......do ...................................................... | Nathaniel Cogley.................. | SC | GS | 15 | ............... | |
| Do .................. | ......do ...................................................... | Anthony M Paranzino .......... | SC | GS | 13 | ............... | |
| Do .................. | ......do ...................................................... | Beeta Christine Rafiekian ... | SC | GS | 13 | ............... | |
| Do .................. | Special Advisor ............................................. | Beatrice Elizabeth Brooke ... | SC | GS | 9 | ............... | |
| Do .................. | Special Assistant.......................................... | Nicole Martin..................... | SC | GS | 9 | ............... | |
| | **OFFICE OF THE SECRETARY** | | | | | | |
| Do .................. | Chief of Staff ............................................. | Vacant ............................ | ............... | ES | ............... | ............... | |
| Do .................. | Senior Advisor ............................................. | ......do .............................. | ............... | ES | ............... | ............... | |
| Do .................. | Senior Advisor to the Secretary for International Trade. | ......do .............................. | ............... | ES | ............... | ............... | |
| Do .................. | Senior Advisor to the Secretary for Economic Affairs. | ......do .............................. | ............... | ES | ............... | ............... | |
| | **OFFICE OF THE CHIEF OF STAFF** | | | | | | |
| Do .................. | Chief of Staff and Senior Advisor to the Secretary. | ......do .............................. | ............... | ES | ............... | ............... | |
| Do .................. | ......do ...................................................... | ......do .............................. | ............... | ES | ............... | ............... | |
| Do .................. | Director, Center for Faith and Opportunity Initiatives. | John Pughe ......................... | SC | GS | 13 | ............... | |
| Do .................. | Chief of Staff to the Secretary of Commerce...... | Michael Walsh Jr. ................ | NA | ES | ............... | ............... | |
| Do .................. | Deputy Chief of Staff and Senior Advisor to the Secretary. | Vacant ............................ | ............... | ES | ............... | ............... | |
| Do .................. | ......do ...................................................... | ......do .............................. | ............... | ES | ............... | ............... | |
| Do .................. | Deputy Chief of Staff and Senior Advisor.......... | Garth Robin Van Meter ....... | NA | ES | ............... | ............... | |
| Do .................. | Senior Advisor to the Chief of Staff................. | David Richard Dorey............ | NA | ES | ............... | ............... | |
| Do .................. | Deputy Chief of Staff for Strategic Initiatives... | James Rockas ...................... | SC | GS | 14 | ............... | |
| Do .................. | Deputy Director of Advance ........................... | Eric Philipkosky ................. | SC | GS | 13 | ............... | |
| Do .................. | Confidential Assistant to the Secretary ............ | Steven Barranca.................. | SC | GS | 9 | ............... | |
| Do .................. | Confidential Assistant ................................... | David Mikell Hay Jr............. | SC | GS | 7 | ............... | |
| | *Office of Advance, Scheduling and Protocol* | | | | | | |
| Do .................. | Deputy Director of Advance ........................... | Daniel Risko ...................... | SC | GS | 13 | ............... | |
| Do .................. | Advance Representative ................................. | William Smith III................. | SC | GS | 7 | ............... | |
| Do .................. | Advance Assistant ........................................ | Adam Hageman.................... | SC | GS | 9 | ............... | |
| Do .................. | Special Assistant.......................................... | Chelsey Neuhaus................. | SC | GS | 11 | ............... | |
| | *Office of White House Liaison* | | | | | | |
| Do .................. | Director of the Office of White House Liaison and Senior Advisor to the Secretary. | Vacant ............................ | ............... | ES | ............... | ............... | |
| Do .................. | Director, Office of White House Liaison ............ | ......do .............................. | ............... | ES | ............... | ............... | |
| Do .................. | ......do ...................................................... | Ryan Leppert....................... | SC | GS | 15 | ............... | |
| Do .................. | Deputy White House Liaison ........................... | Anthony Damiano Labruna . | SC | GS | 9 | ............... | |
| Do .................. | White House Liaison ...................................... | Sean Mclean ....................... | SC | GS | 15 | ............... | |
| Do .................. | Confidential Assistant ................................... | Sloane Reid ........................ | SC | GS | 7 | ............... | |
| Do .................. | ......do ...................................................... | Alexandra Oscarson ............ | SC | GS | 7 | ............... | |
| | *Office of Policy and Strategic Planning* | | | | | | |
| Do .................. | Director, Office of Policy and Strategic Planning. | Robert Blair ....................... | NA | ES | ............... | ............... | |
| Do .................. | Senior Advisor .................................... | Virginia Mckay Boney.......... | SC | GS | 15 | ............... | |

## DEPARTMENT OF COMMERCE—Continued

| Location | Position Title | Name of Incumbent | Type of Appt. | Pay Plan | Level, Grade, or Pay | Tenure | Expires |
|---|---|---|---|---|---|---|---|
| Washington, DC | Director, Office of Policy and Strategic Planning. | Vacant | | ES | | | |
| Do | Senior Advisor | Edward D Hearst | NA | ES | | | |
| Do | Strategic Advisor | Michael Ding | SC | GS | 15 | | |
| Do | Special Assistant | Willam Sleiman | SC | GS | 9 | | |
| | *Office of Executive Secretariat* | | | | | | |
| Do | Director, Executive Secretariat | Vacant | | ES | | | |
| Do | ......do | ......do | | ES | | | |
| Do | Special Assistant | Samuel Pepper | SC | GS | 9 | | |
| | *Office of Business Liaison* | | | | | | |
| Do | Director, Office of Business Liaison | Vacant | | ES | | | |
| Do | ......do | William Patrick Wilson | NA | ES | | | |
| Do | Deputy Director, Office of Business Liaison | Kelly Rzendzian | SC | GS | 14 | | |
| Do | Senior Advisor for Policy and Engagement | Grant Gardner | SC | GS | 13 | | |
| | *Office of Public Affairs* | | | | | | |
| Do | Director of Public Affairs | Meghan Burris | NA | ES | | | |
| Do | Director of Speechwriting and Senior Advisor | Richard McCormack | SC | GS | 15 | | |
| Do | Deputy Press Secretary | Caitlin Jean Davis | SC | GS | 13 | | |
| Do | Press Assistant | Caroline Tucker | SC | GS | 7 | | |
| | *Office of the Chief Information Officer* | | | | | | |
| Do | Chief Information Officer | Career Incumbent | CA | ES | | | |
| | *Office of Legislative and Intergovernmental Affairs* | | | | | | |
| Do | Assistant Secretary for Legislative and Intergovernmental Affairs. | Vacant | PAS | EX | IV | | |
| Do | Director of Intergovernmental Affairs | Anthony Foti | SC | GS | 15 | | |
| Do | Deputy Director of Legislative Affairs | Lawson Kluttz | SC | GS | 13 | | |
| Do | Associate Director for Legislative Affairs | Harry Kumar | SC | GS | 12 | | |
| Do | Legislative Affairs Specialist | Eileen M Dombrowski | SC | GS | 9 | | |
| Do | Intergovernmental Affairs Specialist | Diego-Christopher Lopez | SC | GS | 7 | | |
| Do | Confidential Assistant | Duncan McGaan | SC | GS | 7 | | |
| | *Office of Deputy Assistant Secretary for Legislative and Intergovernmental Affairs* | | | | | | |
| Do | Deputy Assistant Secretary for Legislative and Intergovernmental Affairs. | Vacant | | ES | | | |
| | *Office of the General Counsel* | | | | | | |
| Do | General Counsel | ......do | PAS | EX | IV | | |
| Do | Deputy General Counsel | ......do | | ES | | | |
| Do | Deputy Assistant General Counsel for Administration and Transactions. | ......do | | ES | | | |
| Do | Assistant General Counsel for Administration and Transactions. | Career Incumbent | CA | ES | | | |
| Do | Chief, Employment and Labor Law Division | Vacant | | ES | | | |
| Do | Assistant General Counsel for Employment, Litigation, and Information Law. | ......do | | ES | | | |
| Do | Assistant General Counsel for Legislation and Regulation. | Career Incumbent | CA | ES | | | |
| Do | Assistant General Counsel for Litigation, Employment, and Oversight. | ......do | CA | ES | | | |
| Do | Chief Counsel for Trade Enforcement and Compliance. | ......do | CA | ES | | | |
| Do | Chief, General Law Division | Vacant | | ES | | | |
| Do | Chief Counsel for Commercial Law Development Program. | Career Incumbent | CA | ES | | | |
| Do | Chief Counsel for International Commerce | ......do | CA | ES | | | |
| Do | Chief Counsel for Economic Affairs | ......do | CA | ES | | | |
| Do | Chief Counsel for Industry and Security | ......do | CA | ES | | | |
| Do | Senior Counsel for Special Projects | Stephanie Herbert | SC | GS | 15 | | |
| Do | ......do | Sean Brebbia | SC | GS | 15 | | |
| Do | Senior Counsel | Stephanie Olson | SC | GS | 15 | | |
| Do | Director of Operations for Special Projects | Meredith Glacken | SC | GS | 14 | | |
| Do | Counsel | Paul Zimmerman | SC | GS | 13 | | |
| Do | ......do | Aristidis Kourkoumelis | SC | GS | 14 | | |
| Do | ......do | Ethan Meredith | SC | GS | 14 | | |
| Do | ......do | Benjamin Mehr | SC | GS | 13 | | |
| Do | ......do | Lucy Kelly | SC | GS | 13 | | |
| Do | Special Advisor | Mary Cannon | SC | GS | 12 | | |
| Do | Special Assistant | Robert Burkett | SC | GS | 11 | | |
| Do | Confidential Assistant | Tristan Youngstrom | SC | GS | 9 | | |
| Do | ......do | Nicholas Laios | SC | GS | 7 | | |

## DEPARTMENT OF COMMERCE—Continued

| Location | Position Title | Name of Incumbent | Type of Appt. | Pay Plan | Level, Grade, or Pay | Tenure | Expires |
|---|---|---|---|---|---|---|---|
| | *Office of the Chief Finanical Officer and Assistant Secretary for Administration* | | | | | | |
| Washington, DC | Chief Financial Officer and Assistant Secretary for Administration. | Thomas F Gilman | PAS | EX | IV | | |
| Do | Senior Advisor to the Chief Financial Officer and Assistant Secretary for Administration. | Vacant | | ES | | | |
| Do | Deputy Assistant Secretary for Intelligence and Security. | ......do | | ES | | | |
| Do | Director of Human Resources for Shared Services. | ......do | | ES | | | |
| Do | Director of Acquisitions for Shared Services | ......do | | ES | | | |
| Do | Deputy Project Director, Human Resources Shared Services (Phase III). | ......do | | ES | | | |
| Do | Senior Advisor for Bureau Relations | ......do | | ES | | | |
| Do | Chief of Staff to the Chief Financial Officer and Assistant Secretary for Administration. | Kevin Preskenis | SC | GS | 15 | | |
| Do | Special Assistant | Katherine Kline | SC | GS | 9 | | |
| Do | Confidential Assistant | Caroline Zuchold | SC | GS | 7 | | |
| | **OFFICE OF THE DEPUTY CHIEF FINANCIAL OFFICER FOR FINANCIAL MANAGEMENT** | | | | | | |
| Do | Director, Financial Management Systems | Career Incumbent | CA | ES | | | |
| | **OFFICE OF PRIVACY AND OPEN GOVERNMENT** | | | | | | |
| Do | Chief Privacy Officer and Director of Open Government. | ......do | CA | ES | | | |
| | **OFFICE OF CIVIL RIGHTS** | | | | | | |
| Do | Director, Office of Civil Rights | ......do | CA | ES | | | |
| | **OFFICE OF THE DEPUTY ASSISTANT SECRETARY FOR ADMINISTRATION** | | | | | | |
| Do | Deputy Assistant Secretary for Administration. | ......do | CA | ES | | | |
| | **TECHNOLOGY ADMINISTRATION** | | | | | | |
| Do | Director Office Air and Space Commercialization and Special Assistant to the Under Secretary. | Vacant | | ES | | | |
| | **ECONOMICS AND STATISTICS ADMINISTRATION** | | | | | | |
| Do | Deputy Under Secretary for Economic Affairs | ......do | | ES | | | |
| Do | Chief Economist | ......do | | ES | | | |
| Do | Counselor for Economic Affairs | ......do | | ES | | | |
| Do | Director for External Affairs | ......do | | ES | | | |
| | *Office of the Under Secretary for Economic Affairs* | | | | | | |
| Do | Chief Economist | ......do | | ES | | | |
| Do | Under Secretary for Economic Affairs | ......do | PAS | EX | III | | |
| Do | Senior Advisor | ......do | | ES | | | |
| Do | Confidential Assistant | Kelsey Kilgore | SC | GS | 9 | | |
| | *Office of the Director* | | | | | | |
| Suitland, MD | Chief of Communications | Career Incumbent | CA | ES | | | |
| | *Office of the Chief Economist* | | | | | | |
| Washington, DC | Deputy Chief Economist | Vacant | | ES | | | |
| | *Bureau of the Census* | | | | | | |
| Do | Deputy Director for Policy | ......do | | ES | | | |
| Atlanta, GA | Regional Director, Atlanta Regional Office | ......do | | ES | | | |
| Boston, MA | Regional Director, Boston Regional Office | ......do | | ES | | | |
| Charlotte, NC | Regional Director, Charlotte Regional Office | ......do | | ES | | | |
| Chicago, IL | Regional Director, Chicago Regional Office | ......do | | ES | | | |
| Denver, CO | Regional Director, Denver Regional Office | ......do | | ES | | | |
| Detroit, MI | Regional Director, Detroit Regional Office | ......do | | ES | | | |
| Kansas City, MO | Regional Director, Kansas City Regional Office. | ......do | | ES | | | |
| Los Angeles, CA | Regional Director, Los Angeles Regional Office. | ......do | | ES | | | |
| New York New York, NY. | Regional Director, New York Regional Office. | ......do | | ES | | | |
| Seattle, WA | Regional Director, Seattle Regional Office | ......do | | ES | | | |
| | **OFFICE OF THE DIRECTOR** | | | | | | |
| Suitland, MD | Director of the Census | Steven D Dillingham | PAS | EX | IV | | |
| Do | Deputy Director | Career Incumbent | CA | ES | | | |

## DEPARTMENT OF COMMERCE—Continued

| Location | Position Title | Name of Incumbent | Type of Appt. | Pay Plan | Level, Grade, or Pay | Tenure | Expires |
|---|---|---|---|---|---|---|---|
| Suitland, MD | Chief of Staff | Career Incumbent | CA | ES | | | |
| Do | Senior Advisor to the Deputy Director | ......do | CA | ES | | | |
| Do | Associate Director for Communications | Ali Ahmad | NA | ES | | | |
| Do | Assistant Director for Communications (Operations and Management). | Career Incumbent | CA | ES | | | |
| Do | Assistant Director for Communications (Digital, Marketing, and Strategic Communications). | ......do | CA | ES | | | |
| Do | Director of Strategic Initiatives | Kevin Quinley | SC | GS | 15 | | |
| Do | Chief of Congressional Affairs | Chris Stanley | SC | GS | 15 | | |
| | *Associate Director for Field Operations* | | | | | | |
| Atlanta, GA | Regional Director, Atlanta | George Grandy Jr. | TA | ES | | | 01/06/21 |
| Chicago, IL | Regional Director, Chicago | Marilyn Sanders | TA | ES | | | 01/06/21 |
| Dallas, TX | Regional Director, Dallas Regional Office | Vacant | | ES | | | |
| Denver, CO | Regional Director, Denver | Cathy Lacy | TA | ES | | | 01/06/21 |
| Los Angeles, CA | Regional Director, Los Angeles | Julie A Lam | TA | ES | | | 04/28/21 |
| Do | ......do | James T Christy | TA | ES | | | 01/06/21 |
| New York, NY | Regional Director, New York | Jeff Behler | TA | ES | | | 01/06/21 |
| Philadelphia, PA | Regional Director, Philadelphia Regional Office. | Vacant | | ES | | | |
| Do | Regional Director, Philadelphia | Fernando E Armstrong | TA | ES | | | 01/06/21 |
| **BUREAU OF INDUSTRY AND SECURITY** | | | | | | | |
| Washington, DC | Under Secretary of Commerce for Industry and Security. | Vacant | PAS | EX | III | | |
| Do | Deputy Under Secretary for Industry and Security. | Cordell Hull | NA | ES | | | |
| Do | Chief of Staff for Bureau of Industry and Security. | Prentiss Lee Smith Jr. | NA | ES | | | |
| Do | Director of Congressional and Public Affairs | Michael Cys | SC | GS | 15 | | |
| Do | Policy Advisor | Anne C Teague | SC | GS | 12 | | |
| Do | Senior Advisor | Donna Ganoe | SC | GS | 14 | | |
| **OFFICE OF THE ASSISTANT SECRETARY FOR EXPORT ENFORCEMENT** | | | | | | | |
| Do | Assistant Secretary for Export Enforcement | Vacant | PAS | EX | IV | | |
| Do | Assistant Secretary for Export Administration. | Richard Ashooh | PAS | EX | IV | | |
| Do | Deputy Assistant Secretary for Export Administration. | Career Incumbent | CA | ES | | | |
| Do | Director, Office of Nonproliferation and Treaty Compliance. | ......do | CA | ES | | | |
| Do | Director Office of Exporter Services | ......do | CA | ES | | | |
| Do | Director, Office of National Strategic and Technology Transfer Controls. | ......do | CA | ES | | | |
| Do | Director, Office of Strategic Industries and Economic Security. | Vacant | | ES | | | |
| Do | Special Advisor | Jessica Curyto | SC | GS | 14 | | |
| **ECONOMIC DEVELOPMENT ADMINISTRATION** | | | | | | | |
| Do | Chief of Staff | Dana Gartzke | NA | ES | | | |
| Do | Director of Recovery Communications | Lauren Elizabeth Gorey | NA | ES | | | |
| | *Office of the Assistant Secretary for Economic Development* | | | | | | |
| Do | Assistant Secretary of Commerce for Economic Development. | John Calvin Fleming Jr. | PAS | EX | IV | | |
| Do | Senior Advisor | Randall Gentry | SC | GS | 15 | | |
| Do | Special Advisor | Clayton Tufts | SC | GS | 12 | | |
| Do | Director of External Affairs | Joel Frushone | SC | GS | 15 | | |
| | *Office of the Deputy Assistant Secretary* | | | | | | |
| Do | Deputy Assistant Secretary for Economic Development. | Career Incumbent | CA | ES | | | |
| Do | Special Assistant | Mary Hoernig | SC | GS | 11 | | |
| | *Office of Regional Affairs* | | | | | | |
| Do | Deputy Assistant Secretary for Regional Affairs. | Vacant | | ES | | | |
| | *Philadelphia Regional Office* | | | | | | |
| Philadelphia, PA | Philadelphia Regional Director | Career Incumbent | CA | ES | | | |
| | *Chicago Regional Office* | | | | | | |
| Chicago, IL | Chicago Regional Director | Vacant | | ES | | | |

## DEPARTMENT OF COMMERCE—Continued

| Location | Position Title | Name of Incumbent | Type of Appt. | Pay Plan | Level, Grade, or Pay | Tenure | Expires |
|---|---|---|---|---|---|---|---|
| | *Austin Regional Office* | | | | | | |
| Austin, TX | Austin Regional Director | Career Incumbent | CA | ES | | | |
| | *Atlanta Regional Office* | | | | | | |
| Atlanta, GA | Atlanta Regional Director | ......do | CA | ES | | | |
| | *Seattle Regional Office* | | | | | | |
| Seattle, WA | Regional Director | ......do | CA | ES | | | |
| | *Denver Regional Office* | | | | | | |
| Denver, CO | Denver Regional Director | ......do | CA | ES | | | |
| | **INTERNATIONAL TRADE ADMINISTRATION** | | | | | | |
| Washington, DC | Deputy Chief of Staff for Strategic Initiatives | Vacant | | ES | | | |
| Do | Executive Director for Europe | ......do | | ES | | | |
| Do | Senior Advisor for Administrative Modernization. | Career Incumbent | CA | ES | | | |
| Do | Chief of Staff | Bradley Mckinney | SC | GS | 15 | | |
| Do | Director, Office of Legislative Affairs | Alexander Stoddard | SC | GS | 15 | | |
| Do | Advisor | Austin James Sprenger | SC | GS | 11 | | |
| | **OFFICE OF UNDER SECRETARY** | | | | | | |
| Do | Under Secretary Oceans and Atmosphere (Administrator National Oceanic and Atmospheric Administration). | Vacant | PAS | EX | III | | |
| Do | Assistant Secretary of Commerce for Oceans and Atmosphere. | Timothy Gallaudet | PAS | EX | IV | | |
| Do | Assistant Secretary of Commerce for Environmental Observation and Prediction. | Neil A Jacobs | PAS | EX | IV | | |
| Do | Chief Scientist | Vacant | PA | EX | V | | |
| Do | Deputy Chief of Staff and Senior Advisor | Julie Roberts | NA | ES | | | |
| Do | Deputy Chief of Staff for Policy | Vacant | | ES | | | |
| Do | Director of Policy/Senior Policy Advisor | ......do | | ES | | | |
| Seattle, WA | Senior Advisor to the Under Secretary National Oceanic Atmospheric Administration. | ......do | | ES | | | |
| Washington, DC | Senior Advisor on Climate to the Under Secretary. | ......do | | ES | | | |
| Do | Director of Communications | ......do | | ES | | | |
| Do | Deputy Director, Office of Communications | Career Incumbent | CA | ES | | | |
| Do | Deputy Assistant Secretary for International Fisheries. | Andrew Lawler | NA | ES | | | |
| Do | Chief of Staff for National Oceanic and Atmospheric Administration. | Stuart Levenbach | NA | ES | | | |
| Do | Senior Advisor | Taylor Jordan | SC | GS | 15 | | |
| Do | ......do | Erik Noble | SC | GS | 15 | | |
| Do | Policy Advisor | Brandon Elsner | SC | GS | 13 | | |
| Do | ......do | Nicholas Flocken | SC | GS | 13 | | |
| | **OFFICE OF THE DEPUTY UNDER SECRETARY** | | | | | | |
| Do | Deputy Under Secretary for International Trade. | Joseph C Semsar | NA | ES | | | |
| Do | Chief Information Officer | Career Incumbent | CA | ES | | | |
| | *Assistant Secretary for Enforcement and Compliance* | | | | | | |
| Do | Assistant Secretary for Enforcement and Compliance. | Jeffrey Kessler | PAS | EX | IV | | |
| Do | Deputy Assistant Secretary for Enforcement and Compliance. | Vacant | | ES | | | |
| Do | Special Assistant | Alex Rankin | SC | GS | 11 | | |
| | *Deputy Assistant Secretary for AD/CVD Operations* | | | | | | |
| Do | Deputy Assistant Secretary for Antidumping and Countervailing Duty Operations. | Career Incumbent | CA | ES | | | |
| | *Deputy Assistant Secretary for Policy and Negotiations* | | | | | | |
| Do | Director, Office of Policy | ......do | CA | ES | | | |
| Do | Deputy Assistant Secretary for Policy and Negotiations. | Vacant | | ES | | | |
| Do | Executive Director for Trade Agreements Policy and Negotiations. | Career Incumbent | CA | ES | | | |
| | *Assistant Secretary for Industry and Analysis* | | | | | | |
| Do | Assistant Secretary for Industry and Analysis | Nazakhtar Nikakhtar | PAS | EX | IV | | |

## DEPARTMENT OF COMMERCE—Continued

| Location | Position Title | Name of Incumbent | Type of Appt. | Pay Plan | Level, Grade, or Pay | Tenure | Expires |
|---|---|---|---|---|---|---|---|
| Washington, DC ...... | Deputy Assistant Secretary for Industry and Analysis. | Career Incumbent ............... | CA | ES | .............. | .............. | |
| Do .................. | Deputy Assistant Secretary for Manufacturing. | Brian Lenihan ...................... | NA | ES | .............. | .............. | |
| Do .................. | Deputy Assistant Secretary for Services............ | Vacant ................................ | ............ | ES | .............. | .............. | |
| Do .................. | ......do ......... | ......do ................. | ............ | ES | .............. | .............. | |
| Do .................. | Deputy Assistant Secretary for Europe............ | Career Incumbent ............... | CA | ES | .............. | .............. | |
| Do .................. | Executive Director, Office of Trade Programs and Strategic Partnerships. | Vacant ................................ | ............ | ES | .............. | .............. | |
| Do .................. | Director, Office of Supply Chain, Professional and Business Service. | ......do ................. | ............ | ES | .............. | .............. | |
| Do .................. | Deputy Chief of Staff for Bureau of Industry and Security. | ......do ................. | ............ | ES | .............. | .............. | |
| Do .................. | Senior Director for Industry and Analysis......... | James Sullivan Jr. ................ | NA | ES | .............. | .............. | |
| Do .................. | Director, Office of Industry Engagement ........... | Kirt Gallatin ...................... | SC | GS | 15 | .............. | |
| Do .................. | Senior Advisor .......................................... | Jane Kotlarski ...................... | SC | GS | 15 | .............. | |
| Do .................. | ......do ......... | Christopher Moritz............. | SC | GS | 15 | .............. | |
| | *Deputy Assistant Secretary for Textiles and Apparel* | | | | | | |
| Do .................. | Deputy Assistant Secretary for Textiles, Consumer Goods, and Materials. | Lloyd Wood III ...................... | NA | ES | .............. | .............. | |
| | *Deputy Assistant Secretary for Trade, Policy and Analysis* | | | | | | |
| Do .................. | Director, Office of Trade and Economic Analysis. | Career Incumbent ............... | CA | ES | .............. | .............. | |
| Do .................. | Deputy Assistant Secretary for Trade Policy and Analysis. | ......do ................. | CA | ES | .............. | .............. | |
| | **NATIONAL TRAVEL AND TOURISM OFFICE** | | | | | | |
| Do .................. | Deputy Assistant Secretary and Executive Director. | Philip Lovas .......................... | NA | ES | .............. | .............. | |
| | **DIRECTOR GENERAL OF THE U.S. AND FOREIGN COMERCIAL SERVICE AND ASSISTANT SECRETARY FOR GLOBAL MARKETS** | | | | | | |
| Do .................. | Director General of the United States and Foreign Commercial Service and Assistant Secretary for Global Markets. | Ian Steff ................................ | PAS | EX | IV | .............. | |
| Do .................. | Senior Advisor for Trade Initiatives Implementation. | Vacant ................................ | ............ | ES | .............. | .............. | |
| Do .................. | Deputy Assistant Secretary for Global Markets. | Career Incumbent ............... | CA | ES | .............. | .............. | |
| Do .................. | Executive Director of Select USA ...................... | Vacant ................................ | ............ | ES | .............. | .............. | |
| Do .................. | Senior Advisor for U.S. and Foreign Commercial Service. | Sally Leach .......................... | SC | GS | 14 | .............. | |
| Do .................. | Senior Advisor and Director of Outreach........... | Steven Meyers ...................... | SC | GS | 15 | .............. | |
| Do .................. | Senior Advisor for External Affairs .................. | Kelly Ilagan ...................... | SC | GS | 13 | .............. | |
| Do .................. | Senior Director........................................... | Jonathan David Lang.......... | SC | GS | 15 | .............. | |
| Do .................. | Senior Advisor............................................. | Ned Rauch-Mannino ............ | SC | GS | 15 | .............. | |
| Do .................. | ......do ......... | John M. Cooney III.............. | NA | ES | .............. | .............. | |
| | *Deputy Assistant Secretary for U.S. Field* | | | | | | |
| Do .................. | Deputy Assistant Secretary for U.S. Field ........ | Ana Maria Guevara ............. | NA | ES | .............. | .............. | |
| Do .................. | National Field Director ................................. | Career Incumbent ............... | CA | ES | .............. | .............. | |
| | *Advocacy Center* | | | | | | |
| Do .................. | Director, Advocacy Center ............................. | Jose Cunningham.................. | NA | ES | .............. | .............. | |
| | *Deputy Assistant Secretary for Western Hemisphere* | | | | | | |
| Do .................. | Deputy Assistant Secretary for Western Hemisphere. | Career Incumbent ............... | CA | ES | .............. | .............. | |
| | *Deputy Assistant Secretary for Asia* | | | | | | |
| Do .................. | Deputy Assistant Secretary for Asia ................ | ......do ................. | CA | ES | .............. | .............. | |
| | *Deputy Assistant Secretary for Europe* | | | | | | |
| Do .................. | Executive Director for Europe ......................... | Vacant ................................ | ............ | ES | .............. | .............. | |
| Do .................. | Deputy Assistant Secretary for Middle East and Africa. | ......do ................. | ............ | ES | .............. | .............. | |
| | *Assistant Secretary and Director General for United States and Foreign Commercial Service* | | | | | | |
| Do .................. | Senior Advisor................................................. | Barbara Yankasky-Norton ... | SC | GS | 14 | .............. | |

## DEPARTMENT OF COMMERCE—Continued

| Location | Position Title | Name of Incumbent | Type of Appt. | Pay Plan | Level, Grade, or Pay | Tenure | Expires |
|---|---|---|---|---|---|---|---|
| | **MINORITY BUSINESS DEVELOPMENT AGENCY** | | | | | | |
| Washington, DC ...... | Associate Director of Whiaapi.......................... | Amy Cheng .......................... | SC | GS | 12 | .............. | |
| Do .................... | Executive Director of Whiaapi.......................... | Yu-Ting Tina Wei Smith ...... | SC | GS | 12 | .............. | |
| Do .................... | Senior Advisor.......................... | Holly Ham.......................... | SC | GS | 15 | .............. | |
| Do .................... | Special Assistant.......................... | Ashley R. Morgan .......................... | SC | GS | 9 | .............. | |
| Do .................... | ......do .......................... | Ryan Sun .......................... | SC | GS | 9 | .............. | |
| Do .................... | Confidential Assistant .......................... | Melanee Thomas.................. | SC | GS | 9 | .............. | |
| | **OFFICE OF THE UNDER SECRETARY OF COMMERCE FOR STANDARDS AND TECHNOLOGY** | | | | | | |
| Gaithersburg, MD ... | Under Secretary of Commerce for Standards and Technology. | Walter Copan.......................... | PAS | EX | IV | .............. | |
| | **OFFICE OF TECHNOLOGY POLICY** | | | | | | |
| Washington, DC ...... | Deputy Assistant Secretary for Technology Policy. | Vacant .......................... | .............. | ES | .............. | .............. | |
| | **OFFICE OF THE DIRECTOR** | | | | | | |
| Bethesda, MD.......... | Director, National Technical Information Service. | Career Incumbent .......................... | CA | ES | .............. | .............. | |
| Washington, DC ...... | National Director, Minority Business Development Agency. | Vacant .......................... | .............. | ES | .............. | .............. | |
| Do .................... | Deputy Director, Minority Business Development Agency. | David John Byrd .................. | NA | ES | .............. | .............. | |
| Do .................... | Senior Advisor.......................... | Vacant .......................... | .............. | ES | .............. | .............. | |
| | **NATIONAL OCEANIC AND ATMOSPHERIC ADMINISTRATION** | | | | | | |
| Silver Spring, MD ... | Senior Advisor for Human Resources.................. | ......do .......................... | | ES | .............. | .............. | |
| Do .................... | Big Data Project Director .......................... | ......do .......................... | | ES | .............. | .............. | |
| | **OFFICE OF THE UNDER SECRETARY** | | | | | | |
| Washington, DC ...... | Under Secretary for International Trade.......... | ......do .......................... | PAS | EX | III | .............. | |
| Do .................... | Senior Advisor.......................... | Peter Barrett.......................... | NA | ES | .............. | .............. | |
| Do .................... | Chief of Staff for International Trade Administration. | Vacant .......................... | .............. | ES | .............. | .............. | |
| Do .................... | Director of Policy.......................... | Joseph A Laroski Jr............... | NA | ES | .............. | .............. | |
| Do .................... | Deputy Director General.......................... | Vacant .......................... | .............. | ES | .............. | .............. | |
| Do .................... | Senior Advisor to the Chief of Staff for International Trade Administration. | Dina Beaumont .................. | SC | GS | 15 | .............. | |
| Do .................... | Deputy Director of Public Affairs .................. | Vanessa Ambrosini .................. | SC | GS | 13 | .............. | |
| Do .................... | Special Advisor.......................... | Christina Delgado .................. | SC | GS | 12 | .............. | |
| | **OFFICE OF LEGISLATIVE AFFAIRS** | | | | | | |
| Do .................... | Director of Legislative Affairs.......................... | Vacant .......................... | .............. | ES | .............. | .............. | |
| | **OFFICE OF DEPUTY UNDER SECRETARY** | | | | | | |
| Do .................... | Deputy Under Secretary for Operations .......... | Career Incumbent .................. | CA | ES | .............. | .............. | |
| Do .................... | Assistant Administrator, Office of Program Planning and Integration. | Vacant .......................... | .............. | ES | .............. | .............. | |
| | **OFFICE OF GENERAL COUNSEL** | | | | | | |
| Do .................... | General Counsel .......................... | John Seely Luce Jr............... | NA | ES | .............. | .............. | |
| Silver Spring, MD ... | Deputy General Counsel .......................... | Career Incumbent .................. | CA | ES | .............. | .............. | |
| Washington, DC ...... | Associate Deputy General Counsel.................... | ......do .......................... | CA | ES | .............. | .............. | |
| Do .................... | Assistant General Counsel for Fisheries.......... | ......do .......................... | CA | ES | .............. | .............. | |
| Do .................... | Senior Advisor.......................... | Vacant .......................... | .............. | ES | .............. | .............. | |
| | **DEPUTY GENERAL COUNSEL FOR ATMOSPHERIC AND OCEAN RESEARCH AND SERVICES** | | | | | | |
| Do .................... | Deputy General Counsel for Atmospheric and Ocean Research and Services. | Career Incumbent .................. | CA | ES | .............. | .............. | |
| | **OFFICE OF PROGRAM EVALUATION AND RISK MANAGEMENT** | | | | | | |
| Do .................... | Director for Program Evaluation and Risk Management. | Vacant .......................... | .............. | ES | .............. | .............. | |
| | **NATIONAL MARINE FISHERIES SERVICE** | | | | | | |
| Silver Spring, MD ... | Director, International Affairs and Seafood Inspection. | Career Incumbent .................. | CA | ES | .............. | .............. | |
| Do .................... | Deputy Assistant Administrator for Regulatory Programs. | ......do .......................... | CA | ES | .............. | .............. | |
| Do .................... | Assistant Administrator for Marine Fisheries... | Christopher Wayne Oliver ... | NA | ES | .............. | .............. | |

## DEPARTMENT OF COMMERCE—Continued

| Location | Position Title | Name of Incumbent | Type of Appt. | Pay Plan | Level, Grade, or Pay | Tenure | Expires |
|---|---|---|---|---|---|---|---|
| | *Northwest Region, National Marine Fisheries Service* | | | | | | |
| Seattle, WA ............. | Regional Administator Northwest Region ......... | Vacant ................................... | ............ | ES | ............... | ............... | |
| | *Office of Protected Resources* | | | | | | |
| Washington, DC ...... | Director Office of Protected Resources .............. | Career Incumbent ................ | CA | ES | ............... | ............... | |
| | *National Ocean Service* | | | | | | |
| Do ..................... | Assistant Administrator for Ocean Services and Coastal Zone Management. | Vacant ................................... | ............ | ES | ............... | ............... | |
| | *Office of National Marine Sanctuaries* | | | | | | |
| Silver Spring, MD ... | Director, Office of National Marine Sanctuaries. | Career Incumbent ................ | CA | ES | ............... | ............... | |
| | *Office of Assistant Administrator, Ocean and Atmospheric Research* | | | | | | |
| Rockville, MD .......... | Chief, Marine Advisory Service............................ | Vacant ................................... | ............ | ES | ............... | ............... | |
| Washington, DC ...... | Assistant Administrator for Oceanic and Atmospheric Research. | Career Incumbent ................ | CA | ES | ............... | ............... | |
| Silver Spring, MD ... | Deputy Assistant Administrator for Programs and Administration. | ......do ................................. | CA | ES | ............... | ............... | |
| | *Office of the Assistant Administrator for Weather Services* | | | | | | |
| Do ..................... | Assistant Administrator for Weather Services .. | ......do ................................. | CA | ES | ............... | ............... | |
| Washington, DC ...... | Deputy Assistant Administrator for Weather Services. | ......do ................................. | CA | ES | ............... | ............... | |
| | *Office - Federal Coordinator - Meteorology* | | | | | | |
| Do ..................... | Confidential Assistant ........................................ | Rose Stevens ...................... | SC | GS | 7 | ............... | |
| | *Office of Satellite and Product Operations* | | | | | | |
| Suitland, MD .......... | Director, Office of Satellite and Product Operations. | Career Incumbent ................ | CA | ES | ............... | ............... | |
| | *Office of Air and Space Commercialization* | | | | | | |
| Washington, DC ...... | Director, Office of Space Commerce.................... | Kevin M O'Connell .............. | NA | ES | ............... | ............... | |
| | *Office of Assistant Administrator Satellite, Data Information Service* | | | | | | |
| Do ..................... | Assistant Administrator for National Environmental Satellite Data and Information Services. | Career Incumbent ................ | CA | ES | ............... | ............... | |
| Silver Spring, MD ... | Deputy Assistant Administrator, National Environmental Satellite, Data, and Information Service. | ......do ................................. | CA | ES | ............... | ............... | |
| | *Regional Offices* | | | | | | |
| Juneau, AK ............. | Regional Administrator, Alaska Region ............. | ......do ................................. | CA | ES | ............... | ............... | |
| Gloucester, MA ....... | Regional Administrator, Greater Atlantic Region. | ......do ................................. | CA | ES | ............... | ............... | |
| Honolulu, HI............ | Regional Administrator, Pacific Island Region .. | ......do ................................. | CA | ES | ............... | ............... | |
| St. Petersburg, FL ... | Regional Administrator Southeast Region........ | ......do ................................. | CA | ES | ............... | ............... | |
| Seattle, WA ............. | Regional Administrator, West Coast Region ...... | ......do ................................. | CA | ES | ............... | ............... | |
| Washington, DC ...... | **NATIONAL TELECOMMUNICATIONS AND INFORMATION ADMINISTRATION** Deputy Assistant Secretary to National Telecommunications and Information Administration. | David Candeub...................... | NA | ES | ............... | ............... | |
| Do ..................... | Senior Advisor to National Telecommunications and Information Administration. | Carolyn Roddy ...................... | SC | GS | 15 | ............... | |
| Do ..................... | Senior Advisor........................................................ | James Medica ....................... | SC | GS | 15 | ............... | |
| Do ..................... | **OFFICE OF THE ASSISTANT SECRETARY FOR COMMUNICATIONS AND INFORMATION** Assistant Secretary of Commerce for Communications and Information. | Vacant ................................... | PAS | EX | ............... | ............... | |
| Do ..................... | Assistant Secretary for Communications and Information. | ......do ................................. | PAS | EX | IV | ............... | |
| Do ..................... | Deputy Assistant Secretary for Communications and Information. | Diane Rinaldo...................... | NA | ES | ............... | ............... | |
| Do ..................... | Director for Digital Economy ............................ | Vacant ................................... | ............ | ES | ............... | ............... | |
| Do ..................... | **OFFICE OF THE CHIEF COUNSEL** Chief Counsel ........................................................ | Career Incumbent ................ | CA | ES | ............... | ............... | |

## DEPARTMENT OF COMMERCE—Continued

| Location | Position Title | Name of Incumbent | Type of Appt. | Pay Plan | Level, Grade, or Pay | Tenure | Expires |
|---|---|---|---|---|---|---|---|
| | **OFFICE OF POLICY ANALYSIS AND DEVELOPMENT** | | | | | | |
| Washington, DC ...... | Deputy Associate Adminstrator for Policy Analysis and Development. | Career Incumbent ................ | CA | ES | ................ | ................ | |
| Do .................... | Associate Administrator for Policy Analysis and Development. | ......do ...................... | CA | ES | ................ | ................ | |
| | **OFFICE OF SPECTRUM MANAGEMENT** | | | | | | |
| Do .................... | Deputy Associate Administrator for Spectrum Planning and Policy. | ......do ...................... | CA | ES | ................ | ................ | |
| Do .................... | Deputy Associate Administrator for Spectrum Management. | ......do ...................... | CA | ES | ................ | ................ | |
| Do .................... | Associate Administrator Spectrum Management. | Vacant ...................... | | ES | ................ | ................ | |
| | **OFFICE OF TELECOMMUNICATIONS AND INFORMATION APPLICATIONS** | | | | | | |
| Do .................... | Associate Administrator for Telecommunications and Information Applications. | Career Incumbent ................ | CA | ES | ................ | ................ | |
| | **OFFICE OF PUBLIC SAFETY COMMUNICATIONS** | | | | | | |
| Do .................... | Associate Administrator for Public Safety Communications. | ......do ...................... | CA | ES | ................ | ................ | |
| | **FIRST RESPONDER NETWORK AUTHORITY** | | | | | | |
| Reston, VA .............. | Executive Director, First Responder Network Authority. | ......do ...................... | CA | ES | ................ | ................ | |
| Do .................... | Deputy Executive Director, First Responder Network Authority. | ......do ...................... | CA | ES | ................ | ................ | |
| Washington, DC ...... | Interim Deputy General Manager ...................... | Vacant ...................... | | ES | ................ | ................ | |
| Do .................... | Chief Counsel, First Responder Network Authority. | ......do ...................... | | ES | ................ | ................ | |
| Reston, VA .............. | Chief Customer Officer............................ | Career Incumbent ................ | CA | ES | ................ | ................ | |
| Do .................... | Director, Nationwide Public Safety Broadband Network Program Office. | Vacant ...................... | | ES | ................ | ................ | |
| | **OFFICE OF INSPECTOR GENERAL** | | | | | | |
| Washington, DC ...... | Inspector General ........................ | Peggy Gustafson .................. | PAS | EX | IV | ................ | |
| Do .................... | Deputy Inspector General .................... | Vacant ...................... | | ES | ................ | ................ | |
| | **PATENT AND TRADEMARK OFFICE** | | | | | | |
| Alexandria, VA ........ | Special Advisor for Communications................ | Michael Burgess .................. | SC | GS | 12 | ................ | |
| Do .................... | Senior Legislative Advisor .................... | Peter Krug .................... | NA | ES | ................ | ................ | |
| Do .................... | Chief Communications Officer.................... | Timothy Clark .................. | NA | ES | ................ | ................ | |
| Do .................... | Senior Legal Advisor .................... | Branden Ritchie .................. | NA | ES | ................ | ................ | |
| Do .................... | ......do .................... | Nicholas T Matich .............. | NA | ES | ................ | ................ | |
| Do .................... | Special Assistant .................... | Nicole Grove .................. | SC | GS | 13 | ................ | |
| Do .................... | Deputy Chief Communications Officer............ | Christos J Katopis.............. | SC | GS | 15 | ................ | |
| | **OFFICE OF THE UNDER SECRETARY** | | | | | | |
| Do .................... | Under Secretary and Director of United States Patent and Trademark Office. | Andrei Iancu ........................ | PAS | EX | III | ................ | |
| Do .................... | Deputy Under Secretary and Deputy Director of the United States Patent and Trademark Office. | Laura Peter.......................... | XS | AD | ................ | ................ | |
| Do .................... | Chief of Staff.................... | Christopher Shipp .............. | NA | ES | ................ | ................ | |
| Washington, DC ...... | Senior Advisor.......................... | Kathleen Cooney-Porter....... | SC | GS | 15 | ................ | |
| Alexandria, VA ........ | ......do .................... | Jason Clark.......................... | SC | GS | 15 | ................ | |
| | **OFFICE OF POLICY AND INTERNATIONAL AFFAIRS** | | | | | | |
| Do .................... | Chief Policy Officer and Director for International Affairs. | Career Incumbent ................ | CA | ES | ................ | ................ | |
| | **OFFICE OF THE GENERAL COUNSEL** | | | | | | |
| Do .................... | General Counsel.......................... | ......do ...................... | CA | ES | ................ | ................ | |
| | **OFFICE OF THE CHIEF ADMINISTRATIVE OFFICER** | | | | | | |
| Do .................... | Chief Administrative Officer.......................... | ......do ...................... | CA | ES | ................ | ................ | |
| Do .................... | Senior Advisor to the Chief Administrative Officer. | ......do ...................... | CA | ES | ................ | ................ | |
| | **OFFICE OF THE COMMISSIONER FOR PATENTS** | | | | | | |
| Arlington, VA............ | Commissioner for Patents ...................... | Andrew H Hirshfeld.............. | XS | AD | ................ | ................ | |

## DEPARTMENT OF COMMERCE—Continued

| Location | Position Title | Name of Incumbent | Type of Appt. | Pay Plan | Level, Grade, or Pay | Tenure | Expires |
|---|---|---|---|---|---|---|---|
| | **OFFICE OF THE COMMISSIONER FOR TRADEMARKS** | | | | | | |
| Arlington, VA........... | Commissioner for Trademarks ........................... | David S Gooder...................... | XS | AD | ............... | ............... | |
| | **OFFICE OF THE CHIEF INFORMATION OFFICER** | | | | | | |
| Alexandria, VA ........ | Office Director- Application Engineering and Development. | Vacant .................................... | ............. | ES | ............... | ............... | |
| Do .................... | Chief Information Officer.................................... | Career Incumbent ................ | CA | ES | ............... | ............... | |

## DEPARTMENT OF COMMERCE OFFICE OF THE INSPECTOR GENERAL

| Location | Position Title | Name of Incumbent | Type of Appt. | Pay Plan | Level, Grade, or Pay | Tenure | Expires |
|---|---|---|---|---|---|---|---|
| | **OFFICE OF AUDIT AND EVALUATION** | | | | | | |
| Washington, DC ...... | Assistant Inspector General................................ | Career Incumbent ................ | CA | ES | ............... | ............... | |

# DEPARTMENT OF DEFENSE

## DEPARTMENT OF THE AIR FORCE

| Location | Position Title | Name of Incumbent | Type of Appt. | Pay Plan | Level, Grade, or Pay | Tenure | Expires |
|---|---|---|---|---|---|---|---|
| | **OFFICE OF THE SECRETARY** | | | | | | |
| Washington, DC ...... | Special Assistant and Deputy Chief of Staff...... | Justin Glenn Veillon.............. | SC | GS | 15 | ................ | |
| | *Department of the Air Force* | | | | | | |
| Arlington, VA........... | Deputy Assistant Secretary for Strategic Diversity Integration. | Vacant ................................... | ............ | ES | ................ | ............ | |
| | **OFFICE OF THE SECRETARY** | | | | | | |
| Do ................... | Secretary of the Air Force ..................... | Barbara M Barrett .............. | PAS | EX | II | ............ | |
| Do ................... | Deputy Chief Management Officer.................... | Career Incumbent ................ | CA | ES | ................ | ............ | |
| | *Department of the Air Force* | | | | | | |
| Do ................... | Senior Advisor to the Secretary and Under Secretary of the Air Force. | Jamie Brooke Forseth .......... | NA | ES | ................ | ............ | |
| Do ................... | Assistant Deputy Chief of Staff, Logistics, Engineering and Force Protection. | Career Incumbent ................ | CA | ES | ................ | ............ | |
| | **OFFICE OF THE SECRETARY** | | | | | | |
| Do ................... | Special Assistant/Chief of Staff to the Secretary of the Air Force. | Vacant ................................... | ............ | ES | ................ | ............ | |
| | *Department of the Air Force* | | | | | | |
| Washington, DC ...... | Deputy Director Sexual Assault Prevention and Response Office. | ......do ............................... | ............ | ES | ................ | ............ | |
| | **OFFICE OF THE SECRETARY** | | | | | | |
| Arlington, VA........... | Special Assistant/Chief of Staff......................... | Benjamin Schramm............... | NA | ES | ................ | ............ | |
| | *Department of the Air Force* | | | | | | |
| Scott Air Force Base, IL. | Senior Advisor, Department of Defense Commercial Airlift Programs. | Vacant ................................... | XS | SL | ............ | ............ | |
| | **OFFICE OF THE SECRETARY** | | | | | | |
| Arlington, VA........... | Special Assistant................................................ | Daniel Tomanelli .................. | SC | GS | 12 | ............ | |
| Do ................... | Deputy General Counsel (Fiscal, Ethics and Administrative Law). | Career Incumbent ................ | CA | ES | ................ | ............ | |
| | **OFFICE OF ASSISTANT SECRETARY AIR FORCE FOR ACQUISITION** | | | | | | |
| Do ................... | Director of Transformational Innovation.......... | Vacant ................................... | ............ | ES | ................ | ............ | |
| Do ................... | Assistant Secretary of the Air Force (Acquisition). | William Bruce Roper Jr. ...... | PAS | EX | IV | ............ | |
| Do ................... | Principal Deputy Assistant Secretary (Aquisition, Technology and Logistics). | Career Incumbent ................ | CA | ES | ................ | ............ | |
| Do ................... | Personal and Confidential Assistant ................ | James Hickey....................... | SC | GS | 15 | ............ | |
| | **OFFICE OF ASSISTANT SECRETARY AIR FORCE FOR FINANCIAL MANAGEMENT AND COMPTROLLER** | | | | | | |
| Do ................... | Principal Deputy Assistant Secretary Financial Management and Comptroller. | Career Incumbent ................ | CA | ES | ................ | ............ | |
| | **OFFICE OF THE UNDER SECRETARY** | | | | | | |
| Do ................... | Under Secretary of the Air Force...................... | Vacant ................................... | PAS | EX | III | ............ | |
| Washington, DC ...... | Headquarters Air Force Chief Data Officer ....... | Career Incumbent ................ | CA | ES | ................ | ............ | |
| | **OFFICE OF ASSISTANT SECRETARY AIR FORCE FOR FINANCIAL MANAGEMENT AND COMPTROLLER** | | | | | | |
| Arlington, VA........... | Assistant Secretary of the Air Force (Financial Management and Comptroller). | John P Roth ......................... | PAS | EX | IV | ............ | |
| | **OFFICE OF THE UNDER SECRETARY** | | | | | | |
| Do ................... | Special Advisor (Invisible Combat Wounds Initiative). | Vacant ................................... | ............ | ES | ................ | ............ | |
| Do ................... | Deputy Director for Business Transformation... | Career Incumbent ................ | CA | ES | ................ | ............ | |
| | **OFFICE OF THE GENERAL COUNSEL** | | | | | | |
| Do ................... | Deputy General Counsel (National Security and Military Affairs). | Vacant ................................... | ............ | ES | ................ | ............ | |
| Do ................... | Deputy General Counsel (Contractor Responsibility). | Career Incumbent ................ | CA | ES | ................ | ............ | |
| Do ................... | Principal Deputy General Counsel..................... | ......do ............................... | CA | ES | ................ | ............ | |
| Do ................... | Deputy General Counsel (Intelligence, International and Military Affairs). | Vacant ................................... | ............ | ES | ................ | ............ | |
| Washington, DC ...... | Deputy General Counsel (Acquisition)............. | Career Incumbent ................ | CA | ES | ................ | ............ | |
| Arlington, VA........... | General Counsel................................................ | Thomas E Ayres .................. | PAS | EX | IV | ............ | |
| Washington, DC ...... | Deputy General Counsel (Installations, Energy and Environment). | Career Incumbent ................ | CA | ES | ................ | ............ | |

# DEPARTMENT OF DEFENSE—Continued

## DEPARTMENT OF THE AIR FORCE—Continued

| Location | Position Title | Name of Incumbent | Type of Appt. | Pay Plan | Level, Grade, or Pay | Tenure | Expires |
|---|---|---|---|---|---|---|---|
| | **OFFICE OF ASSISTANT SECRETARY AIR FORCE, INSTALLATIONS, ENVIRONMENT, AND ENERGY** | | | | | | |
| Arlington, VA | Special Assistant | Corbett D Ekonomou | SC | GS | 9 | | |
| Do | Deputy Assistant Secretary (Environment, Safety and Occupational Health). | Career Incumbent | CA | ES | | | |
| Do | Deputy Assistant Secretary (Energy) | ......do | CA | ES | | | |
| Do | Assistant Secretary of the Air Force (Installations, Environment and Energy). | John W Henderson | PAS | EX | IV | | |
| Do | Principal Deputy Assistant Secretary (Installations, Environment and Logistics). | Career Incumbent | CA | ES | | | |
| | **OFFICE OF ASSISTANT SECRETARY OF THE AIR FORCE FOR MANPOWER AND RESERVE AFFAIRS** | | | | | | |
| Do | Assistant Secretary of the Air Force (Manpower and Reserve Affairs). | Shon Manasco | PAS | EX | IV | | |
| Do | Deputy Assistant Secretary for Force Management and Integration. | Vacant | | ES | | | |
| Do | Principal Deputy Assistant Secretary (Manpower and Reserve Affairs). | Career Incumbent | CA | ES | | | |
| Do | Deputy Assistant Secretary for Force Management and Integration. | ......do | CA | ES | | | |
| Do | Deputy Assistant Secretary for Strategic Diversity Integration. | Tamera Jo Nelson | NA | ES | | | |
| | **DEPUTY CHIEF OF STAFF, PERSONNEL** | | | | | | |
| Do | Program Manager, National Security Personnel System (NSPS) Program Management Office. | Vacant | | ES | | | |
| | **OFFICE DEPUTY ASSISTANT SECRETARY INSTALLATIONS** | | | | | | |
| Washington, DC | Deputy Assistant Secretary (Installations) | ......do | | ES | | | |
| | **OFFICE OF ADMINISTRATIVE ASSISTANT TO THE SECRETARY** | | | | | | |
| Arlington, VA | Special Assistant | Savannah Jolly | SC | GS | 13 | | |
| | **DEPUTY UNDER SECRETARY (SPACE)** | | | | | | |
| Do | Director, Principal Dod Space Advisor Staff | Vacant | | ES | | | |
| | **OFFICE DEPUTY ASSISTANT SECRETARY RESERVE AFFAIRS** | | | | | | |
| Do | Deputy Assistant Secretary for Reserve Affairs. | ......do | | ES | | | |
| | **DEPUTY UNDER SECRETARY (INTERNATIONAL AFFAIRS)** | | | | | | |
| Washington, DC | Deputy Under Secretary (International Affairs). | ......do | | ES | | | |

## DEPARTMENT OF DEFENSE—Continued

### DEPARTMENT OF THE ARMY

| Location | Position Title | Name of Incumbent | Type of Appt. | Pay Plan | Level, Grade, or Pay | Tenure | Expires |
|---|---|---|---|---|---|---|---|
| | **OFFICE OF THE SECRETARY** | | | | | | |
| Arlington, VA | Secretary of the Army | Ryan D McCarthy | PAS | EX | II | | |
| Do | Chief of Staff to the Secretary of the Army | Vacant | | ES | | | |
| Washington, DC | Director, DC National Guard | William J Walker | NA | ES | | | |
| Arlington, VA | Deputy Director, DC National Guard | Aaron R Dean II | NA | ES | | | |
| Do | Under Secretary of the Army | James E McPherson | PAS | EX | III | | |
| | **OFFICE DEPUTY UNDER SECRETARY OF ARMY** | | | | | | |
| Do | Deputy Under Secretary of the Army | Thomas E Kelly III | NA | ES | | | |
| Do | Special Assistant to Deputy Under Secretary of the Army. | Natalie S. Bosse | SC | GS | 13 | | |
| | **OFFICE OF SMALL AND DISADVANTAGED BUSINESS UTILITILIZATION** | | | | | | |
| Do | Director of Small Business Programs | Career Incumbent | CA | ES | | | |
| | **OFFICE ASSISTANT SECRETARY ARMY (ACQUISITION, LOGISTICS AND TECHNOLOGY)** | | | | | | |
| Do | Assistant Secretary of the Army (Acquisition, Logistics and Technology). | Bruce D Jette | PAS | EX | IV | | |
| Do | Principal Deputy Assistant Secretary of the Army (Acquisition, Logistics and Technology). | Jeffrey S White | NA | ES | | | |
| Do | Deputy Director, Hypersonic, Directed Energy, Space & Rapid Acquisition Office. | Robert K Strider | TA | ES | | | 07/06/22 |
| Do | Deputy Assistant Secretary of the Army (Strategy Acquisition Reform). | Vacant | | ES | | | |
| Do | Special Assistant to the Deputy Assistant Secretary of the Army (Strategy and Acquisition Reform). | Robert James Swope | SC | GS | 15 | | |
| | **OFFICE ASSISTANT SECRETARY ARMY (CIVIL WORKS)** | | | | | | |
| Do | Assistant Secretary of the Army (Civil Works).. | Rickey Dale James | PAS | EX | IV | | |
| Do | Principal Deputy Assistant Secretary of the Army (Civil Works) / Deputy Assistant Secretary of the Army (Legislation). | Ryan Andrew Fisher | NA | ES | | | |
| Do | Deputy Assistant Secretary of the Army (Project Planning and Review). | Career Incumbent | CA | ES | | | |
| Do | Deputy Assistant Secretary of the Army (Policy and Legislation). | Deana Young Funderburk | NA | ES | | | |
| Do | Special Assistant to the Principal Deputy Assistant Secretary of the Army (Civil Works). | Katherine J Krause | SC | GS | 9 | | |
| Do | Special Assistant to the Assistant Secretary of the Army (Civil Works). | Darren K Lingle | SC | GS | 14 | | |
| | **OFFICE ASSISTANT SECRETARY ARMY (FINANCIAL MANAGEMENT AND COMPTROLLER)** | | | | | | |
| Do | Assistant Secretary of the Army (Financial Management and Comptroller). | John E Whitley | PAS | EX | IV | | |
| Do | Principal Deputy Assistant Secretary of the Army (Financial Management and Comptroller). | Jonathan Moak | NA | ES | | | |
| Do | Special Advisor Assistant Security of the Army (Financial Management and Comptroller). | Eric Buller | SC | GS | 15 | | |
| Do | Special Assistant to the Assistant Secretary of the Army (Financial Management and Comptroller). | Jay Brooks | SC | GS | 11 | | |
| | **OFFICE ASSISTANT SECRETARY ARMY (INSTALLATIONS, ENERGY AND ENVIRONMENT)** | | | | | | |
| Do | Assistant Secretary of the Army (Installations and Environment). | Alex A Beehler | PAS | EX | IV | | |
| Do | Principal Deputy Assistant Secretary (Installations and Environment). | Bryan M Gossage | NA | ES | | | |
| Do | Deputy Assistant Secretary of the Army (Installations and Housing). | Career Incumbent | CA | ES | | | |
| Do | Deputy Assistant Secretary of the Army (Energy and Sustainability). | Vacant | | ES | | | |

# DEPARTMENT OF DEFENSE—Continued

## DEPARTMENT OF THE ARMY—Continued

| Location | Position Title | Name of Incumbent | Type of Appt. | Pay Plan | Level, Grade, or Pay | Tenure | Expires |
|---|---|---|---|---|---|---|---|
| Arlington, VA............ | Confidential Assistant to the Assistant Secretary of the Army (Installations, Energy and Environment). | Lisa M Hamar ...................... | SC | GS | 15 | ................ | |
| Do ..................... | Special Assistant to the Deputy Assistant Secretary of the Army (Energy and Sustainability). | Bret M Strogen ...................... | SC | GS | 15 | ................ | |
| | **OFFICE ASSISTANT SECRETARY ARMY (MANPOWER AND RESERVE AFFAIRS)** | | | | | | |
| Do ..................... | Assistant Secretary of the Army (Manpower and Reserve Affairs). | Eugene C Wardynski Jr. ...... | PAS | EX | IV | ................ | |
| Do ..................... | Principal Deputy to the Assistant Secretary of the Army (Manpower and Reserve Affairs). | Marshall D Williams ............ | NA | ES | ................ | ................ | |
| Do ..................... | Deputy Assistant Secretary of the Army (Training, Readiness and Mobilization). | Career Incumbent ................ | CA | ES | ................ | ................ | |
| Do ..................... | Special Assistant to the Assistant Secretary of the Army (Manpower and Reserve Affairs). | Peter Knickerbocker............ | SC | GS | 14 | ................ | |
| Do ..................... | Special Assistant to the Principal Deputy Assistant Secretary of the Army (Manpower and Reserve Affairs). | Brian L Scarlett.................... | SC | GS | 13 | ................ | |
| | **OFFICE OF THE GENERAL COUNSEL** | | | | | | |
| Do ..................... | General Counsel............................................ | Vacant ...................................... | PAS | EX | IV | ................ | |
| Do ..................... | Principal Deputy General Counsel.................... | Michele Pearce...................... | NA | ES | ................ | ................ | |
| Do ..................... | Deputy General Counsel (Acquisition)............. | Career Incumbent ................ | CA | ES | ................ | ................ | |
| Do ..................... | Deputy General Counsel (Operations and Personnel). | ......do ...................................... | CA | ES | ................ | ................ | |
| Do ..................... | Deputy General Counsel (Installations, Environment and Civil Works). | ......do ...................................... | CA | ES | ................ | ................ | |
| Do ..................... | Senior Intellectual Property Law Attorney....... | Charles H Harris.................... | XS | SL | ................ | ................ | |
| Do ..................... | Deputy General Counsel (Ethics and Fiscal)..... | Career Incumbent ................ | CA | ES | ................ | ................ | |
| | **OFFICE OF LEGISLATIVE LIAISON** | | | | | | |
| Do ..................... | Principal Deputy Chief of Legislative Liaison ... | ......do ...................................... | CA | ES | ................ | ................ | |
| | **CHIEF INFORMATION OFFICER/G-6** | | | | | | |
| Do ..................... | Director, Enterprise Cloud Management Office, Chief Information Officer/G6. | Paul B Puckett III ................ | TA | ES | ................ | ................ | 11/24/22 |
| | **OFFICE, CHIEF OF STAFF** | | | | | | |
| Washington, DC ...... | Director of Management/Vice Director of the Army Staff. | Career Incumbent ................ | CA | ES | ................ | ................ | |
| | **OFFICE, DEPUTY CHIEF OF STAFF, G-8** | | | | | | |
| Arlington, VA............ | Deputy Director, Program Analysis and Evaluation Directorate. | ......do ...................................... | CA | ES | ................ | ................ | |
| | **CENTER FOR ARMY ANALYSIS (CENTER FOR ARMY ANALYSIS)** | | | | | | |
| Fort Belvoir, VA ...... | Director, Center for Army Analysis ................... | ......do ...................................... | CA | ES | ................ | ................ | |
| Do ..................... | Technical Director........................................... | Vacant ...................................... | ........... | ES | ................ | ................ | |
| | **OFFICE OF THE SURGEON GENERAL** | | | | | | |
| Falls Church, VA ..... | Chief of Staff, U.S. Army Medical Command ..... | Richard Roland Beauchemin. | TA | ES | ................ | ................ | 02/02/22 |
| | **OFFICE OF THE JUDGE ADVOCATE GENERAL** | | | | | | |
| Arlington, VA............ | Director, Civilian Personnel, Labor and Employment Law. | Career Incumbent ................ | CA | ES | ................ | ................ | |
| Rosslyn, VA............. | Director, Soldier and Family Legal Services ...... | ......do ...................................... | CA | ES | ................ | ................ | |
| | **OFFICE OF THE PROVOST MARSHALL GENERAL** | | | | | | |
| Arlington, VA............ | Director, Forensics and Biometrics Field Operating. | ......do ...................................... | CA | ES | ................ | ................ | |
| | **U.S. ARMY TEST AND EVALUATION COMMAND** | | | | | | |
| Falls Church, VA ..... | Executive Technical Director/Deputy to the Commander. | ......do ...................................... | CA | ES | ................ | ................ | |
| | **AFC, UNITED STATES ARMY MEDICAL RESEARCH AND MATERIEL COMMAND** | | | | | | |
| Fort Detrick, MD ..... | Principal Assistant for Research and Technology. | Vacant ...................................... | ........... | ES | ................ | ................ | |
| | **UNITED STATES ARMY MATERIEL COMMAND** | | | | | | |
| Washington, DC ...... | Chief, Supply, Production and Distribution ........ | Paul P Ostrowski.................. | TA | ES | ................ | ................ | 06/08/21 |

# DEPARTMENT OF DEFENSE—Continued

## DEPARTMENT OF THE ARMY—Continued

| Location | Position Title | Name of Incumbent | Type of Appt. | Pay Plan | Level, Grade, or Pay | Tenure | Expires |
|---|---|---|---|---|---|---|---|
| | **OFFICE OF COMMAND COUNSEL** | | | | | | |
| Redstone Arsenal, AL. | Command Counsel | Career Incumbent | CA | ES | | | |
| Do | Deputy Command Counsel | ......do | CA | ES | | | |
| | **TANK-AUTOMOTIVE AND ARMAMENTS COMMAND (TANK-AUTOMOTIVE AND ARMAMENTS COMMAND)** | | | | | | |
| Warren, MI | Chief Counsel | ......do | CA | ES | | | |
| | **UNITED STATES ARMY AVIATION AND MISSILE COMMAND (ARMY MATERIEL COMMAND)** | | | | | | |
| Redstone Arsenal, AL. | ......do | ......do | CA | ES | | | |
| | **UNITED STATES ARMY SUSTAINMENT COMMAND** | | | | | | |
| Rock Island, IL | ......do | ......do | CA | ES | | | |
| | **U.S. ARMY COMMUNICATIONS ELECTRONICS COMMAND** | | | | | | |
| Aberdeen Proving Ground, MD. | ......do | ......do | CA | ES | | | |
| | **UNITED STATES ARMY CONTRACTING COMMAND** | | | | | | |
| Redstone Arsenal, AL. | Chief Counsel, Army Contracting Command | Vacant | | ES | | | |
| | **UNITED STATES ARMY CORPS OF ENGINEERS** | | | | | | |
| Washington, DC | Chief Counsel | Career Incumbent | CA | ES | | | |
| Do | Deputy Chief Counsel | ......do | CA | ES | | | |
| | **HEADQUARTERS, UNITED STATES ARMY, EUROPE** | | | | | | |
| Wiesbaden, Germany. | Assistant Chief of Staff, Strategy and Plans U.S. Army Europe. | ......do | CA | ES | | | |
| | **UNITED STATES EUROPEAN COMMAND** | | | | | | |
| Stuttgart, Germany. | Civilian Deputy / Foreign Policy Advisory to the Commander European Command. | Adam H Sterling | | ES | | | 08/03/22 |
| Do | Director, Russia Strategic Initiative | Vacant | | ES | | | |
| | **UNITED STATES AFRICA COMMAND** | | | | | | |
| Do | Deputy to the Commander for Civil-Military Activities, U.S. Africa Command. | ......do | | ES | | | |
| Do | Advisor, Development and Humanitarian Assistance, U.S. Africa Command. | Barbara Hughes | TA | ES | | | 08/09/21 |
| | **NORTH ATLANTIC TREATY ORGANIZATION** | | | | | | |
| Brussels, Belgium | Director, Defense Operations and Plans | Career Incumbent | CA | ES | | | |
| Do | Administrative Advisor to United States Ambassador to North Atlantic Treaty Organization. | ......do | CA | ES | | | |
| Do | Director, Resources and Logistics | ......do | CA | ES | | | |
| Do | Managing Director Defense Armaments, Communications Electronics and Investments Division. | ......do | CA | ES | | | |
| Rome, Italy | Dean, North Atlantic Treaty Organization Defense College. | Stephen J. Mariano | TA | ES | | 3 Years | 01/05/22 |

## DEPARTMENT OF DEFENSE—Continued

### DEPARTMENT OF THE NAVY

| Location | Position Title | Name of Incumbent | Type of Appt. | Pay Plan | Level, Grade, or Pay | Tenure | Expires |
|---|---|---|---|---|---|---|---|
| | **OFFICE OF THE SECRETARY OF THE NAVY** | | | | | | |
| Arlington, VA........... | Secretary of the Navy ........................................ | Kenneth Braithwaite III ...... | PAS | EX | II | .............. | |
| Do .................... | Chief of Staff .................................................... | Vacant ................................ | ............. | ES | .............. | .............. | |
| Do .................... | ......do ............................................................ | ......do ................................ | ............. | ES | .............. | .............. | |
| Do .................... | Deputy Chief of Staff to the Secretary of the Navy. | ......do ................................ | ............. | ES | .............. | .............. | |
| Do .................... | Special Assistant to the Secretary of the Navy . | ......do ................................ | ............. | ES | .............. | .............. | |
| Washington, DC ...... | Special Assistant to the Secretary for Information Management/Chief Information Officer. | ......do ................................ | ............. | ES | .............. | .............. | |
| Arlington, VA........... | Deputy Director, Office of Program Appraisal ... | ......do ................................ | ............. | ES | .............. | .............. | |
| Do .................... | Deputy Chief Learning Officer for Naval Education. | ......do ................................ | ............. | ES | .............. | .............. | |
| Do .................... | Special Assistant for Strategic Readiness Review. | ......do ................................ | ............. | ES | .............. | .............. | |
| | *Office of the Under Secretary of the Navy* | | | | | | |
| Do .................... | Under Secretary of the Navy ............................. | ......do ................................ | PAS | EX | III | .............. | |
| Washington, DC ...... | Deputy Under Secretary of the Navy ................. | Career Incumbent ................ | CA | ES | .............. | .............. | |
| Arlington, VA........... | Senior Advisor.................................................... | Vacant ................................ | ............. | ES | .............. | .............. | |
| Washington, DC ...... | Director, Small Business Programs .................... | Career Incumbent ................ | CA | ES | .............. | .............. | |
| Arlington, VA........... | Chief of Staff to the Unsecnav ......................... | Vacant ................................ | ............. | ES | .............. | .............. | |
| Do .................... | Chief Learning Officer for Naval Education...... | ......do ................................ | ............. | ES | .............. | .............. | |
| Do .................... | Director for Data Strategy ................................ | Career Incumbent ................ | CA | ES | .............. | .............. | |
| Washington, DC ...... | Residence Director ............................................ | Cynthia Andrade ................ | SC | GS | 14 | .............. | |
| Arlington, VA........... | Special Assistant and Director of Staff ............. | Vacant ................................ | ............. | ES | .............. | .............. | |
| Washington, DC ...... | Senior Director (Policy and Strategy)................ | Career Incumbent ................ | CA | ES | .............. | .............. | |
| | *Office of the Assistant Secretary of Navy (Manpower and Reserve Affairs)* | | | | | | |
| Arlington, VA........... | Assistant Secretary of the Navy (Manpower and Reserve Affairs). | Gregory Joseph Slavonic...... | PAS | EX | IV | .............. | |
| Do .................... | Special Assistant..................................... | Dino Sandeep Teppara ......... | SC | GS | 15 | .............. | |
| Do .................... | Special Assistant to the Assistant Secretary of the Navy (Manpower and Reserve Affairs). | Brendan O'Toole .................. | SC | GS | 9 | .............. | |
| Do .................... | Special Assistant to the Under Secretary of the Navy. | Eric Wiese ............................ | SC | GS | 15 | .............. | |
| | *Office of the Assistant Secretary of Navy (Energy, Installations and Environment)* | | | | | | |
| Do .................... | Assistant Secretary of the Navy (Energy, Installations and Environment). | Charles Arthur Williams Jr.. | PAS | EX | IV | .............. | |
| Do .................... | Deputy Assistant Secretary of the Navy (Environment). | Career Incumbent ................ | CA | ES | .............. | .............. | |
| Washington, DC ...... | Deputy Assistant Secretary of the Navy (Infrastructure, Facilities and Basing). | Vacant ................................ | ............. | ES | .............. | .............. | |
| | *Office of the Assistant Secretary of the Navy (Research, Development and Acquisition)* | | | | | | |
| Arlington, VA........... | Assistant Secretary of the Navy (Research Development and Acquisition). | James F Geurts ..................... | PAS | EX | IV | .............. | |
| Do .................... | Research and Development Investment Executive. | Jennifer Santos..................... | NA | ES | .............. | .............. | |
| Do .................... | Deputy Assistant Secretary of the Navy (Unmanned Systems). | Vacant ................................ | ............. | ES | .............. | .............. | |
| | *Office of the Assistant Secretary of Navy (Financial Management and Comptroller)* | | | | | | |
| Do .................... | Assistant Secretary of the Navy (Financial Management and Comptroller). | Thomas Wesley Harker........ | PAS | EX | IV | .............. | |
| Do .................... | Deputy Director, Financial Operations ............. | Career Incumbent ................ | CA | ES | .............. | .............. | |
| | *Office of the General Counsel* | | | | | | |
| Do .................... | General Counsel.................................................. | Robert J Sander.................... | PAS | EX | IV | .............. | |
| | *Chief of Naval Operations* | | | | | | |
| Washington, DC ...... | Director, Shore Readiness Division ................... | Career Incumbent ................ | CA | ES | .............. | .............. | |
| | *Bureau of Medicine and Surgery* | | | | | | |
| Falls Church, VA ..... | Director, Total Force............................................ | ......do ................................ | CA | ES | .............. | .............. | |
| | *Commander, Naval Expeditionary Combat Command* | | | | | | |
| Virginia Beach, VA.. | Executive Director, Navy Expeditionary Combat Command. | Vacant ................................ | ............. | ES | .............. | .............. | |

# DEPARTMENT OF DEFENSE—Continued

## DEPARTMENT OF THE NAVY—Continued

| Location | Position Title | Name of Incumbent | Type of Appt. | Pay Plan | Level, Grade, or Pay | Tenure | Expires |
|---|---|---|---|---|---|---|---|
| | *Office of the Commander, United States Pacific Command* | | | | | | |
| Camp Hm Smith M Corp B, HI. | Director, Center for Excellence ........................... | Career Incumbent ................ | CA | ES | ................ | ................ | |
| | *Office of Commander, United States Fleet Forces Command* | | | | | | |
| Naples, Italy ............ | Executive Director, Commander U.S. Naval Forces/Africa. | Vacant .................................. | ............ | ES | ................ | ................ | |
| | *Naval Supply Systems Command Headquarters* | | | | | | |
| Mechanicsburg, PA.. | Executive Strategic Initiatives ........................... | Career Incumbent ................ | CA | ES | ................ | ................ | |
| | *United States Marine Corps Headquarters Office* | | | | | | |
| Washington, DC ...... | Deputy Director, Command, Control, Communication, and Computers/Deputy Chief Information Officer-Marine Corps. | ......do .................................. | CA | ES | ................ | ................ | |

# DEPARTMENT OF DEFENSE—Continued

## OFFICE OF THE SECRETARY OF DEFENSE

| Location | Position Title | Name of Incumbent | Type of Appt. | Pay Plan | Level, Grade, or Pay | Tenure | Expires |
|---|---|---|---|---|---|---|---|
| | *Office of the Secretary* | | | | | | |
| Arlington, VA | Secretary of Defense | Mark T Esper | PAS | EX | I | | |
| Do | Special Assistant to the Secretary of Defense for Protocol. | Vacant | | ES | | | |
| Do | Deputy Chief of Staff to the Secretary of Defense. | Alexis L Ross | NA | ES | | | |
| Do | Defense Fellow | Peter O'Rourke Jr. | SC | GS | 9 | | |
| Do | Confidential Assistant | Anne F Powers | SC | GS | 15 | | |
| Do | Special Assistant | Gregory Pejic | SC | GS | 15 | | |
| Do | ......do | Marielle E Pavek | SC | GS | 9 | | |
| Do | Protocol Officer | Bryce Goodwin | SC | GS | 9 | | |
| Do | Deputy Secretary of Defense | David L Norquist | PAS | EX | II | | |
| Do | Special Assistant | Hannah Gonzalez | SC | GS | 7 | | |
| | *Office of the Secretary of Defense* | | | | | | |
| Do | Deputy White House Liaison | Sara Lynn Colley | SC | GS | 13 | | |
| Do | Speechwriter | Alissa Tabirian | SC | GS | 13 | | |
| Fort Meade, MD | Inspector General of the Nsa | Robert P Storch | PAS | EX | | | |
| Arlington, VA | Senior Advisor to the Secretary of Defense | Anthony Tata | NA | ES | | | |
| Do | Chief of Staff to the Secretary of Defense | Jennifer M Stewart | NA | ES | | | |
| Do | Deputy Chief of Staff to the Secretary of Defense. | Vacant | | ES | | | |
| Do | Advance Officer | Kipp Mcguire | SC | GS | 11 | | |
| Do | Director, Travel Operations | Coleman Lapointe | SC | GS | 15 | | |
| Do | Special Assistant | Caroline Vik | SC | GS | 13 | | |
| Do | Protocol Officer | Kelly L. Shaul | SC | GS | 12 | | |
| Do | Special Assistant | Rebecca Wostenberg | SC | GS | 13 | | |
| Do | Director, National Reconnaissance Office | Christopher Scolese | PAS | EX | | | |
| Do | Defense Fellow | Audrey B Anderson | SC | GS | 9 | | |
| Do | Advance Officer | Randall Caroline Engeman | SC | GS | 13 | | |
| Do | ......do | Natalie Boyse | SC | GS | 13 | | |
| Do | Speechwriter | Alexandra Jane Seymour | SC | GS | 11 | | |
| Do | Advance Officer | Sarah Jane Dwyer | SC | GS | 12 | | |
| Do | Defense Fellow | Mary Allen | SC | GS | 12 | | |
| Do | Special Assistant to the Secretary of Defense for White House Liaison. | Macon Dean Hughes | NA | ES | | | |
| Do | Deputy Chief of Staff | Career Incumbent | CA | ES | | | |
| Do | Director, Strategic Capabilities Office | ......do | CA | ES | | | |
| Chantilly, VA | Inspector General of the Nro | Susan Gibson | PAS | EX | | | |
| Fort Meade, MD | Director of the National Security Agency (NSA). | Vacant | PAS | EX | | | |
| Arlington, VA | Chief of Staff to the Deputy Secretary of Defense. | Robert J Henke | NA | ES | | | |
| | *Office of the Joint Chiefs of Staff* | | | | | | |
| Do | Director for Joint History | Career Incumbent | CA | ES | | | |
| Do | Principal Deputy Director for Logistics | ......do | CA | ES | | | |
| Do | Principal Deputy Director for Strategic Plans and Policy. | ......do | CA | ES | | | |
| Do | Deputy Director, Strategic Stability | ......do | CA | ES | | | |
| Suffolk, VA | Deputy Director Cyber and Command Control Communications and Computers (C5) Integration. | ......do | CA | ES | | | |
| Arlington, VA | Director, Directorate of Management | ......do | CA | ES | | | |
| Do | Vice Director for Force Structure, Resources and Assessment. | ......do | CA | ES | | | |
| Do | Deputy Director for Simulations and Analysis | ......do | CA | ES | | | |
| | *Office of the Chief Management Officer* | | | | | | |
| Do | Deputy Director, Defense Business Systems | Anthony B Murphy | SC | GS | 15 | | |
| Do | Special Assistant to the Deputy Chief Management Officer. | Charles David Burke | SC | GS | 15 | | |
| Do | Deputy Director, Defense Business Systems | Anthony B Murphy | SC | GS | 15 | | |
| Do | Special Assistant | Patrick Nevins | SC | GS | 14 | | |
| Do | Director, Transformation and Reform | Career Incumbent | CA | ES | | | |
| Do | Deputy Chief Management Officer | Vacant | | ES | | | |
| Do | Chief of Staff | Andrew Mapes | NA | ES | | | |
| Do | Senior Advisor to the Chief Management Officer. | Kirk Ryan Marshall | NA | ES | | | |
| Do | Military Commission Appellate Judge | Lisa Schenck | PAS | AD | | | |
| Do | Director, Category Management Reform | Steven Benson | TA | ES | | | 06/20/21 |
| Do | Senior Advisor, Defense-Wide Program Office | Vacant | | ES | | | |

# DEPARTMENT OF DEFENSE—Continued

## OFFICE OF THE SECRETARY OF DEFENSE—Continued

| Location | Position Title | Name of Incumbent | Type of Appt. | Pay Plan | Level, Grade, or Pay | Tenure | Expires |
|---|---|---|---|---|---|---|---|
| Arlington, VA | Military Commission Appellate Judge | William Pollard | PAS | AD | | | |
| Do | Director, 4th Estate IT Optimization | Career Incumbent | CA | ES | | | |
| Do | Military Commission Appellate Judge | Scott Silliman | PAS | AD | | | |
| Do | Chief Management Officer | Lisa Hershman | PAS | EX | II | | |
| | **Washington Headquarters Services** | | | | | | |
| Do | Defense Fellow | Christopher Grisafe | SC | GS | 15 | | |
| Do | Deputy Director, Washington Headquarters Services. | Vacant | | ES | | | |
| Do | General Counsel | Career Incumbent | CA | ES | | | |
| Do | Director, Financial Management Directorate and Chief Financial Executive. | Vacant | | ES | | | |
| Washington, DC | Deputy Director, White House Military Office | Career Incumbent | CA | ES | | | |
| Arlington, VA | Deputy General Counsel, Washington Headquarters Services and Pentagon Force Protection Agency. | ......do | CA | ES | | | |
| Do | Director, Executive Services Directorate | Vacant | | ES | | | |
| Do | Assistant Director Manpower and Personnel | Career Incumbent | CA | ES | | | |
| Do | Defense Fellow | James A Brooks III | SC | GS | 9 | | |
| Alexandria, VA | Director, Whs Erpt Expansion and Reform Initiative. | Jae Lee | TA | ES | | | 04/13/22 |
| Do | Senior Advisor for Human Resources Operations. | Mary C Byers | TA | ES | | | 01/20/22 |
| Arlington, VA | Special Assistant to the Director, Executive Services Directorate. | Darren Irvine | TA | ES | | | 05/26/21 |
| Do | Defense Fellow | Reagan P Hedlund | SC | GS | 14 | | |
| Do | ......do | Samuel Lehardy | SC | GS | 7 | | |
| Do | Chief Counsel National Guard Bureau | Career Incumbent | CA | ES | | | |
| Do | Defense Fellow | Andrew Galkowski | SC | GS | 14 | | |
| Do | ......do | Sean Patrick Carney | SC | GS | 12 | | |
| Washington, DC | Director, White House Military Office | Vacant | | ES | | | |
| Do | Special Advisor | Thomas Cluff | SC | GS | 15 | | |
| Arlington, VA | Attorney-Advisor (General) | Mary Sydney Leach | SC | GS | 15 | | |
| Washington, DC | Special Assistant | Joy Ruiz | SC | GS | 9 | | |
| Arlington, VA | Defense Fellow | Kirk Harris | SC | GS | 15 | | |
| Do | Director, Washington Headquarters Services | Career Incumbent | CA | ES | | | |
| Do | Director Programs and Resources/Comptroller - National Guard Bureau. | ......do | CA | ES | | | |
| Alexandria, VA | Special Assistant to the Director, Washington Headquarters Services. | ......do | CA | ES | | | |
| Arlington, VA | Chief Information Officer (National Guard Bureau) and Director National Guard Bureau J6. | ......do | CA | ES | | | |
| | *Office of the Under Secretary of Defense (Research and Engineering)* | | | | | | |
| Do | Deputy Director, Defense Laboratory Programs. | ......do | CA | ES | | | |
| Alexandria, VA | Principal Deputy Director, Test Resource Management Center. | ......do | CA | ES | | | |
| Arlington, VA | Principal Deputy Director, Emerging Capability and Prototyping. | ......do | CA | ES | | | |
| Alexandria, VA | Deputy Director, Portfolio Management and Outreach. | Vacant | | ES | | | |
| Arlington, VA | Director, Human Systems | Career Incumbent | CA | ES | | | |
| Do | Director of Defense Research and Engineering for Modernization. | Mark Lewis | NA | ES | | | |
| Do | Deputy Director, Strategic Technology Protection and Exploitation. | Vacant | | ES | | | |
| Do | Director, Maintaining Technology Advantage | Career Incumbent | CA | ES | | | |
| Do | Director, Developmental Test and Evaluation (D,DT&E). | ......do | CA | ES | | | |
| Do | Director of Defense Research and Engineering for Research and Technology. | Vacant | | ES | | | |
| Do | Special Assistant | John Troup Calhoun Hemenway. | SC | GS | 13 | | |
| Do | Chief Space Transport Cell | Vacant | | ES | | | |
| Do | Deputy Director, Research Technology and Laboratories. | ......do | | ES | | | |
| Do | Special Assistant | Matthew A Lytwyn | SC | GS | 14 | | |
| Do | ......do | Colin M MacDermott | SC | GS | 13 | | |
| Do | Deputy Director Engineering | Sandra Magnus | NA | ES | | | |

# DEPARTMENT OF DEFENSE—Continued

## OFFICE OF THE SECRETARY OF DEFENSE—Continued

| Location | Position Title | Name of Incumbent | Type of Appt. | Pay Plan | Level, Grade, or Pay | Tenure | Expires |
|---|---|---|---|---|---|---|---|
| Arlington, VA | Director, Business Operations | Career Incumbent | CA | ES | | | |
| Do | Director, Technology and Manufacturing Industrial Base. | ......do | CA | ES | | | |
| Do | Deputy Under Secretary of Defense (Research and Engineering). | Lisa J Porter | PAS | EX | | | |
| Do | Director for Strategic Communications for Office of the Under Secretary of Defense for Research and Engineering. | Samuel Amber | NA | ES | | | |
| Do | Director, Space Development Agency | Derek M Tournear | TA | ES | | | 10/26/22 |
| Do | Director, Small Business and Technology Partnerships. | Molly L Walsh | NA | ES | | | |
| Do | Director, Engineering Policy and Systems | Career Incumbent | CA | ES | | | |
| Do | Director Platforms and Weapons Technologies | ......do | CA | ES | | | |
| Do | Director Resilient Systems | ......do | CA | ES | | | |
| Do | Director Mission Integration | Vacant | | ES | | | |
| Do | Director, Prototypes and Experiments | Career Incumbent | CA | ES | | | |
| Do | Director Basic Research | ......do | CA | ES | | | |
| Do | Director Defense Research and Enginerring for Advanced Capabilities / Director, Test Resource Management Center. | James A Faist | NA | ES | | | |
| Do | Deputy Director Space Development Agency | Vacant | | ES | | | |
| Do | Principal Deputy to the Director Defense Research and Engineering for Advanced Capabilities. | Career Incumbent | CA | ES | | | |
| Do | Under Secretary of Defense (Research and Engineering). | Michael D Griffin | PAS | EX | | | |
| Do | Principal Deputy to the Director of Defense Research and Engineering for Research and Technology. | Career Incumbent | CA | ES | | | |
| Alexandria, VA | Administrator, Defense Technical Information Center. | ......do | CA | ES | | | |
| Arlington, VA | Deputy Director, Developmental Test Evaluation & Prototyping. | Timothy Dare | NA | ES | | | |
| | *Defense Advanced Research Projects Agency* | | | | | | |
| Do | Director, Defense Advanced Research Project Agency. | Vacant | | ES | | | |
| Do | Comptroller | Career Incumbent | CA | ES | | | |
| | *Missile Defense Agency* | | | | | | |
| Do | General Counsel, Missile Defense Agency | ......do | CA | ES | | | |
| Huntsville, AL | Program Director, Ballistic Missile Defense (Bmd) Sensors. | ......do | CA | ES | | | |
| Fort Belvoir, VA | Comptroller/Chief Financial Officer | Vacant | | ES | | | |
| Redstone Arsenal, AL. | Director for Mission Support | ......do | | ES | | | |
| Arlington, VA | Executive Director | ......do | | ES | | | |
| Huntsville, AL | Deputy Director for Test | Career Incumbent | CA | ES | | | |
| | *Office of the Under Secretary of Defense (Acquisition and Sustainment)* | | | | | | |
| Alexandria, VA | President, Defense Acquisition University | ......do | CA | ES | | | |
| Arlington, VA | Executive Director, International Cooperation | ......do | CA | ES | | | |
| Do | Executive Director, Joint Rapid Acquisition Cell. | ......do | CA | ES | | | |
| Do | Deputy Director, Planning, Programs and Analysis. | ......do | CA | ES | | | |
| Fort Belvoir, VA | Strategic Advisor, Under Secretary of Defense for Acquisition and Technology. | Vacant | | ES | | | |
| Aberdeen Proving Ground, MD. | Dpeo, Assembled Chemical Weapons Alternatives. | Nicholas Stamatakis III | TA | ES | | | 06/21/22 |
| Arlington, VA | Strategic Adviser to the Under Secretary of Defense. | Lucian Niemeyer | PAS | EX | | | |
| Do | Special Assistant | Joseph Sevage | SC | GS | 9 | | |
| Do | Director, DOD Committee on Foreign Investment in the United States. | Vacant | | ES | | | |
| Do | Special Assistant | Abigail Welborn | SC | GS | 9 | | |
| Do | Under Secretary of Defense (Acquisition and Sustainment). | Ellen Lord | PAS | EX | III | | |
| Alexandria, VA | Director Small Business Programs | Amy Murray | NA | ES | | | |
| Arlington, VA | Deputy Under Secretary of Defense (Acquisition & Sustainment). | Alan R Shaffer | PAS | EX | IV | | |

# DEPARTMENT OF DEFENSE—Continued

## OFFICE OF THE SECRETARY OF DEFENSE—Continued

| Location | Position Title | Name of Incumbent | Type of Appt. | Pay Plan | Level, Grade, or Pay | Tenure | Expires |
|---|---|---|---|---|---|---|---|
| Alexandria, VA ........ | Director, International Armaments Cooperation. | Career Incumbent ................ | CA | ES | ................ | ................ | |
| Arlington, VA........... | Special Assistant to the Deputy Assistant Secretary of Defense (Manufacturing and Industrial Base Policy). | Christopher Lehman............ | SC | GS | 15 | ................ | |
| Do .................... | Deputy Assistant Secretary of Defense (Industrial Policy). | Vacant ................................. | ............ | ES | ................ | ................ | |
| Do .................... | Executive Director, Human Capital Initiatives . | ......do ............................... | ............ | ES | ................ | ................ | |
| Do .................... | Principal Director, Manufacturing and Industrial Base Policy. | Career Incumbent ................ | CA | ES | ................ | ................ | |
| Do .................... | Chief of Staff ........................................... | Vacant ................................. | ............ | ES | ................ | ................ | |
| | *Office of the Assistant Secretary of Defense (Acquisition)* | | | | | | |
| Do .................... | Director, Office of Economic Adjustment............ | Career Incumbent ................ | CA | ES | ................ | ................ | |
| Washington, DC ...... | Deputy Assistant Secretary of Defense (Information & Integration Portfolio Mgmt). | ......do ............................... | CA | ES | ................ | ................ | |
| Arlington, VA........... | Director, Surface Warfare ............................... | ......do ............................... | CA | ES | ................ | ................ | |
| Do .................... | Principal Deputy Assistant Secretary of Defense for Acquisition. | Vacant ................................. | ............ | ES | ................ | ................ | |
| Washington, DC ...... | Director, Electronic Warfare............................. | Career Incumbent ................ | CA | ES | ................ | ................ | |
| Arlington, VA........... | Principal Deputy Director, Performance Assessment & Root Cause Analyses/Deputy Director Root Cause Analyses. | ......do ............................... | CA | ES | ................ | ................ | |
| Do .................... | Director, Cyber ........................................... | ......do ............................... | CA | ES | ................ | ................ | |
| Do .................... | Assistant Secretary of Defense (Acquisition)..... | Kevin M Fahey .................... | PAS | EX | IV | ................ | |
| Do .................... | Special Assistant ........................................ | Adam David Garnica............ | SC | GS | 15 | ................ | |
| | *Office of the Assistant Secretary of Defense (Nuclear, Chemical and Biological Defense Programs)* | | | | | | |
| Do .................... | Deputy Assistant Secretary of Defense (Threat Reduction and Arms Control). | Charles Ball......................... | NA | ES | ................ | ................ | |
| Do .................... | Deputy Assistant Secretary of Defense (Chemical and Biological Defense). | Career Incumbent ................ | CA | ES | ................ | ................ | |
| Do .................... | Assistant Secretary of Defense (Nuclear, Chemical and Biological Defense). | Vacant ................................. | PAS | EX | IV | ................ | |
| | *Office of the Assistant Secretary of Defense (Sustainment)* | | | | | | |
| Alexandria, VA ........ | Executive Director, Department of Defense Siting Clearinghouse. | Career Incumbent ................ | CA | ES | ................ | ................ | |
| Arlington, VA........... | Assistant Secretary of Defense (Sustainment) .. | William J Gillis ................... | PAS | EX | | ................ | |
| Do .................... | Deputy Assistant Secretary of Defense (Facilities Management). | Career Incumbent ................ | CA | ES | ................ | ................ | |
| Do .................... | Deputy Assistant Secretary of Defense (Logistics). | ......do ............................... | CA | ES | ................ | ................ | |
| Do .................... | Deputy Assistant Secretary of Defense (Materiel Readiness). | ......do ............................... | CA | ES | ................ | ................ | |
| Do .................... | Deputy Assistant Secretary of Defense for Product Support. | Vacant ................................. | ............ | ES | ................ | ................ | |
| | *Defense Logistics Agency* | | | | | | |
| Fort Belvoir, VA ....... | Special Assistant to the Director, Dla Logistics Operations. | Kevin K Kachinski ............... | TA | ES | ................ | ................ | 02/15/21 |
| | *Defense Threat Reduction Agency* | | | | | | |
| Do .................... | Vice Director-Mission Integration ...................... | Career Incumbent ................ | CA | ES | ................ | ................ | |
| Do .................... | Director, Defense Threat Reduction Agency....... | Vayl S Oxford...................... | NA | ES | ................ | ................ | |
| | *Office of the Under Secretary of Defense (Policy)* | | | | | | |
| Arlington, VA........... | Special Assistant........................................... | Matthew Costlow.................. | SC | GS | 11 | ................ | |
| Do .................... | ......do ...................................................... | Anthony Holmes.................. | SC | GS | 14 | ................ | |
| Do .................... | ......do ...................................................... | Cailin Schmeer .................... | SC | GS | 13 | ................ | |
| Do .................... | ......do ...................................................... | Leah Scheunemann............... | SC | GS | 14 | ................ | |
| Do .................... | Under Secretary of Defense for Policy............... | Vacant ................................. | PAS | EX | III | ................ | |
| Do .................... | Deputy Principal Cyber Advisor ....................... | ......do ............................... | ............ | ES | ................ | ................ | |
| Do .................... | Director, Defeat Isis Task Force ....................... | Christopher P Maier ............ | NA | ES | ................ | ................ | |
| Do .................... | Special Assistant to the Deputy Assistant to the Secretary of Defense (Asia). | Benjamin S. Kutler............... | SC | GS | 15 | ................ | |
| Do .................... | Special Assistant........................................... | Rafael Leonardo .................. | SC | GS | 14 | ................ | |
| Do .................... | Deputy Chief of Staff..................................... | Mark Tomb.......................... | NA | ES | ................ | ................ | |
| Do .................... | Special Assistant / Career Broadening............... | Career Incumbent ................ | CA | ES | ................ | ................ | |
| Do .................... | Special Assistant........................................... | Emma Hamilton.................... | SC | GS | 11 | ................ | |

# DEPARTMENT OF DEFENSE—Continued

## OFFICE OF THE SECRETARY OF DEFENSE—Continued

| Location | Position Title | Name of Incumbent | Type of Appt. | Pay Plan | Level, Grade, or Pay | Tenure | Expires |
|---|---|---|---|---|---|---|---|
| Arlington, VA | Special Assistant | James Thomas Ward | SC | GS | 14 | | |
| Do | ......do | Barry Smith | SC | GS | 14 | | |
| Do | ......do | Dominique Yantko | SC | GS | 14 | | |
| Do | ......do | James Skinner | SC | GS | 11 | | |
| Do | Chief Operating Officer | Career Incumbent | CA | ES | | | |
| Do | Special Assistant | Morgan Vina | SC | GS | 15 | | |
| Do | Special Assistant to the Deputy Assistant to the Secretary of Defense (East Asia). | Jordan C Wilson | SC | GS | 14 | | |
| Do | Special Assistant | Samuel Spector | SC | GS | 15 | | |
| Do | ......do | Hilton S Beckham | SC | GS | 12 | | |
| Do | ......do | Andrew Cote | SC | GS | 13 | | |
| Do | ......do | Joshua James Young | SC | GS | 13 | | |
| Do | ......do | Madeline Wilczewski | SC | GS | 15 | | |
| Do | ......do | Brian Slattery | SC | GS | 14 | | |
| Do | Us Chairman of the Us-Russia Joint Commission on Pow/Mia. | Vacant | PA | AD | | | |
| Do | Senior Advisor and Director for Analytics and Acquisition. | Daniel E Folliard | TA | ES | | | 08/31/21 |
| Do | Deputy Under Secretary of Defense (Policy) | James Anderson | PAS | EX | IV | | |
| | *Office of the Deputy Under Secretary of Defense (Policy)* | | | | | | |
| Do | Director, Dtsa | Vacant | | ES | | | |
| Do | Director, Defense Prisoner of War/Missing in Action Accounting Agency. | Career Incumbent | CA | ES | | | |
| Do | Foreign Relations and Defense Policy Manager. | ......do | CA | ES | | | |
| Do | Principal Director for Washington Operations, Defense Prisoner of War / Missing in Action Accounting Agency. | ......do | CA | ES | | | |
| Do | Senior Advisor | David V Trulio | NA | ES | | | |
| Do | Special Assistant | Rebecca Ulrich | SC | GS | 15 | | |
| Do | ......do | Tres Smith | SC | GS | 15 | | |
| Do | ......do | Lauren Michelle Davis | SC | GS | 12 | | |
| Do | ......do | Paul W Mandelson | SC | GS | 14 | | |
| Do | ......do | Aaron Kenneth Bailey | SC | GS | 15 | | |
| Do | Deputy Assistant Secretary of Defense China | Luke Burke | SC | GS | 13 | | |
| Do | Special Assistant (Career Broadening) | Career Incumbent | CA | ES | | | |
| Do | Deputy Director, Defense Technology Security Administration. | ......do | CA | ES | | | |
| | *Office of the Assistant Secretary of Defense (Homeland Defense and Global Security )* | | | | | | |
| Do | Assistant Secretary of Defense (Homeland Defense & Global Security). | Kenneth Rapuano | PAS | EX | IV | | |
| Do | Principal Deputy Assistant Secretary of Defense for Global Strategic Affairs. | Career Incumbent | CA | ES | | | |
| Do | Deputy Assistant Secretary of Defense Homeland Defense Integration and Defense Support of Civil Authorities and Chief of Staff. | ......do | CA | ES | | | |
| Do | Principal Director, Countering Weapons of Mass Destruction. | ......do | CA | ES | | | |
| Do | Deputy Assistant Secretary of Defense for Space Policy. | Stephen Kitay | NA | ES | | | |
| Do | Principal Director, Space Policy | Career Incumbent | CA | ES | | | |
| Do | Principal Deputy Assistant Secretary of Defense (Homeland Defense & Global Security). | ......do | CA | ES | | | |
| Do | Deputy Assistant Secretary of Defense (Defense Continuity & Mission Assurance). | Derek J Maurer Esq | NA | ES | | | |
| Do | Deputy Assistant Secretary of Defense (Countering Weapons of Mass Destruction). | David Lasseter | NA | ES | | | |
| Do | Deputy Assistant Secretary of Defense (Cyber Policy). | Thomas Wingfield | NA | ES | | | |
| | *Office of the Assistant Secretary of Defense (Indo-Pacific Security Affairs)* | | | | | | |
| Do | Assistant Secretary of Defense (Indo-Pacific Security Affairs). | Vacant | PAS | EX | IV | | |
| Do | Principal Deputy Assistant Secretary of Defense (Asian and Pacific Security Affairs). | Career Incumbent | CA | ES | | | |

# DEPARTMENT OF DEFENSE—Continued

## OFFICE OF THE SECRETARY OF DEFENSE—Continued

| Location | Position Title | Name of Incumbent | Type of Appt. | Pay Plan | Level, Grade, or Pay | Tenure | Expires |
|---|---|---|---|---|---|---|---|
| Arlington, VA | Deputy Assistant Secretary of Defense (China). | Chad Lawrence Sbragia | NA | ES | | | |
| Do | Deputy Assistant Secretary of Defense (Afghanistan, Pakistan and Central Asia). | Thomas Dominick Croci | NA | ES | | | |
| Do | Deputy Assistant Secretary of Defense for East Asia. | Heino Klinck | NA | ES | | | |
| Do | Deputy Assistant Secretary of Defense for South and Southeast Asia. | Reed Werner | NA | ES | | | |
| | *Office of the Assistant Secretary of Defense (International Security Affairs)* | | | | | | |
| Do | Assistant Secretary of Defense (International Security Affairs). | Vacant | PAS | EX | IV | | |
| Do | Principal Deputy Assistant Secretary of Defense (International Security Affairs). | Kathryn L Wheelbarger | NA | ES | | | |
| Do | Deputy Assistant Secretary of Defense (African Affairs). | Peter Marocco | NA | ES | | | |
| Do | Deputy Assistant Secretary of Defense (Western Hemisphere Affairs). | Sergio De La Pena | NA | ES | | | |
| Do | Deputy Assistant Secretary of Defense (Europe and North Atlantic Treaty Organization Policy). | Michael C Ryan | NA | ES | | | |
| Do | Principal Director for Middle East Policy | Career Incumbent | CA | ES | | | |
| Do | Deputy Assistant Secretary of Defense (Russia, Ukraine and Eurasia Policy). | ......do | CA | ES | | | |
| Do | Principal Director (Russia, Ukraine, and Eurasia Policy). | Catherine E Sendak | NA | ES | | | |
| Do | Special Assistant to the Deputy Assistant Secretary of Defense for Middle East. | Peter Todd Metzger II | SC | GS | 15 | | |
| Do | Deputy Assistant Secretary of Defense (Middle East). | Simone A Ledeen | NA | ES | | | |
| | *Office of the Assistant Secretary of Defense (Special Operations / Low Intensity Conflict)* | | | | | | |
| Do | Deputy Assistant Secretary of Defense (Counternarcotics and Global Threats). | Ezra Miller | NA | ES | | | |
| Do | Deputy Assistant Secretary of Defense for Special Operations and Combating Terrorism. | Christopher C Miller | NA | ES | | | |
| Do | Deputy Assistant Secretary of Defense for Strategy and Force Development. | Daniel Green | NA | ES | | | |
| Do | Special Advisor to Assistant Secretary of Defense (Special Operations/Low Intensity Conflict). | Career Incumbent | CA | ES | | | |
| Do | Deputy Assistant Secretary of Defense for Special Operations Policy and Programs. | Vacant | | ES | | | |
| Do | Principal Deputy Assistant Secretary of Defense (Special Operations/Low Intensity Conflict). | ......do | | ES | | | |
| Do | Special Assistant to Deputy Assistant Secretary of Defense Special Operations and Combating Terrorism. | Matthew Aquino | SC | GS | 11 | | |
| Do | Principal Director (Counternarcotics and Global Threats). | Career Incumbent | CA | ES | | | |
| Do | Principal Director, Stability and Humanitarian Affairs. | Stephanie L. Hammond | SC | GS | 14 | | |
| Do | Assistant Secretary of Defense (Special Operations/Low Intensity Conflict). | Vacant | PAS | EX | IV | | |
| Do | Principal Director for Special Operations and Combating Terrorism. | ......do | | ES | | | |
| | *Office of the Assistant Secretary of Defense (Strategy, Plans and Capabilities)* | | | | | | |
| Do | Deputy Assistant Secretary of Defense (Nuclear and Missile Defense Policy). | Robert Mark Soofer | NA | ES | | | |
| Do | Senior Advisor to the Assistant Secretary of Defense (Strategy, Plans, and Force Development). | Thomas Mackin Williams | SC | GS | 15 | | |
| Do | Principal Director (Plans) | Career Incumbent | CA | ES | | | |
| Do | Special Assistant | Caroline T Ingram | SC | GS | 15 | | |
| Do | Assistant Secretary of Defense (Strategy, Plans & Capabilities). | Victorino G. Mercado | PAS | EX | IV | | |
| Do | Deputy Assistant Secretary of Defense for Plans and Posture. | Vacant | | ES | | | |

# DEPARTMENT OF DEFENSE—Continued

## OFFICE OF THE SECRETARY OF DEFENSE—Continued

| Location | Position Title | Name of Incumbent | Type of Appt. | Pay Plan | Level, Grade, or Pay | Tenure | Expires |
|---|---|---|---|---|---|---|---|
| Arlington, VA | Deputy Assistant Secretary of Defense for Security Cooperation. | Michael Cutrone | NA | ES | | | |
| Do | Principal Deputy Assistant Secretary of Defense (Strategy, Plans and Capabilities). | Vacant | | ES | | | |
| | *Defense Security Cooperation Agency* | | | | | | |
| Do | Deputy Director, Defense Security Cooperation Agency. | ......do | | ES | | | |
| Do | Principal Director, Business Operations | Career Incumbent | CA | ES | | | |
| Do | Principal Director for Security Assistance Management. | ......do | CA | ES | | | |
| Do | Principal Director for Building Partner Capacity. | ......do | CA | ES | | | |
| | **UNITED STATES MISSION TO THE NORTH ATLANTIC TREATY ORGANIZATION** | | | | | | |
| Washington, DC | Defense Advisor to the Us Ambassador to North Atlantic Treaty Organization (NATO). | Richard Landolt | NA | ES | | | |
| Brussels, Belgium | Foreign Relations and Defense Policy Manager. | Career Incumbent | CA | ES | | | |
| | **OFFICE OF THE UNDER SECRETARY OF DEFENSE (COMPTROLLER)** | | | | | | |
| Arlington, VA | Deputy Comptroller for Budget and Appropriations Affairs. | George E Kovatch | NA | ES | | | |
| Do | Deputy Comptroller Program/Budget | Career Incumbent | CA | ES | | | |
| Do | Associate Director for Military Personnel and Health Care. | ......do | CA | ES | | | |
| Do | Associate Director for Air, Space, and Intelligence Programs. | ......do | CA | ES | | | |
| Do | Director for Operations | ......do | CA | ES | | | |
| Do | Director for Investment | ......do | CA | ES | | | |
| Do | Associate Director, External Affairs | ......do | CA | ES | | | |
| Do | Director for Military Personnel and Construction. | ......do | CA | ES | | | |
| Do | Associate Director, Defense-Wide Programs | ......do | CA | ES | | | |
| Do | Associate Director for Military Operations | ......do | CA | ES | | | |
| Do | Associate Director for Military Construction | ......do | CA | ES | | | |
| Do | Under Secretary of Defense (Comptroller) | Vacant | PAS | EX | III | | |
| Do | Director, Resource Issues | Timothy Ryan Jost | NA | ES | | | |
| Do | Director, Financial Improvement and Audit Remediation. | Career Incumbent | CA | ES | | | |
| Do | Deputy Under Secretary of Defense (Comptroller). | Vacant | PAS | EX | IV | | |
| Do | Associate Director, Contingency and International Programs. | Career Incumbent | CA | ES | | | |
| Do | Assistant Deputy Chief Financial Officer | ......do | CA | ES | | | |
| Do | Associate Director Ground Sea and Other Programs. | ......do | CA | ES | | | |
| Do | Special Assistant | Steven Gilleland | SC | GS | 15 | | |
| Do | Director, Financial Management Policy & Reporting. | Career Incumbent | CA | ES | | | |
| Do | Assistant Deputy Comptroller (Program/Budget/Execution). | ......do | CA | ES | | | |
| Do | Director, Chief Financial Officer Data Transformation. | ......do | CA | ES | | | |
| Do | Chief of Staff | Vacant | | ES | | | |
| Do | Deputy Director, Program and Financial Control. | Career Incumbent | CA | ES | | | |
| Do | Director, Program and Financial Control | ......do | CA | ES | | | |
| Do | Director, Human Capital and Resource Management. | ......do | CA | ES | | | |
| | **DEFENSE CONTRACT AUDIT AGENCY** | | | | | | |
| Alexandria, VA | General Counsel | ......do | CA | ES | | | |
| | **DEFENSE FINANCE AND ACCOUNTING SERVICE** | | | | | | |
| Do | Director, Defense Finance and Accounting Service. | ......do | CA | ES | | | |
| Do | Principal Deputy Director, Defense Finance and Accounting Service. | Vacant | | ES | | | |
| Whitehall, OH | Deputy Site Director - Columbus | Career Incumbent | CA | ES | | | |

# DEPARTMENT OF DEFENSE—Continued

## OFFICE OF THE SECRETARY OF DEFENSE—Continued

| Location | Position Title | Name of Incumbent | Type of Appt. | Pay Plan | Level, Grade, or Pay | Tenure | Expires |
|---|---|---|---|---|---|---|---|
| Cleveland, OH ......... | Site Director - Cleveland ............................... | Career Incumbent ................ | CA | ES | ............... | ............... | |
| Whitehall, OH ......... | Director for Enterprise Solutions and Standards. | ......do ...... | CA | ES | ............... | ............... | |
| Fort Ben Harrison, IN. | Site Director - Indianapolis ............... | ......do ...... | CA | ES | ............... | ............... | |
| Whitehall, OH ......... | Site Director - Columbus ............... | ......do ...... | CA | ES | ............... | ............... | |
| Alexandria, VA ....... | Director, Information and Technology ............. | ......do ...... | CA | ES | ............... | ............... | |
| Fort Ben Harrison, IN. | Deputy Site Director, Indianapolis ................... | ......do ...... | CA | ES | ............... | ............... | |
| Alexandria, VA ....... | Deputy Director for Information and Technology. | ......do ...... | CA | ES | ............... | ............... | |
| Whitehall, OH ......... | Deputy Director for Operations ............... | ......do ...... | CA | ES | ............... | ............... | |
| Fort Ben Harrison, IN. | General Counsel ............... | ......do ...... | CA | ES | ............... | ............... | |
| Alexandria, VA ....... | Director for Internal Review ............... | ......do ...... | CA | ES | ............... | ............... | |
| Rome, NY ................ | Site-Director Rome ............... | ......do ...... | CA | ES | ............... | ............... | |
| Whitehall, OH ......... | Deputy Site Director, Cleveland ............... | ......do ...... | CA | ES | ............... | ............... | |
| Fort Ben Harrison, IN. | Chief Financial Officer ............... | ......do ...... | CA | ES | ............... | ............... | |
| Do ...... | Director, Strategy, Policy, and Requirements .... | ......do ...... | CA | ES | ............... | ............... | |
| Indianapolis, IN ..... | Deputy Director, Strategy and Support............. | ......do ...... | CA | ES | ............... | ............... | |
| Do ...... | Director, Enterprise Management Services ....... | ......do ...... | CA | ES | ............... | ............... | |
| Do ...... | Director for Finance Standards & Customer Services. | ......do ...... | CA | ES | ............... | ............... | |
| Cleveland, OH ......... | Director, Enterprise Audit Support ................... | ......do ...... | CA | ES | ............... | ............... | |
| Whitehall, OH ......... | Director, Accounting Standards and Reporting . | ......do ...... | CA | ES | ............... | ............... | |
| Indianapolis, IN ...... | Director, Systems ............... | ......do ...... | CA | ES | ............... | ............... | |
| | **OFFICE OF THE UNDER SECRETARY OF DEFENSE (PERSONNEL AND READINESS)** | | | | | | |
| Arlington, VA ........... | Under Secretary of Defense (Personnel and Readiness). | Matthew P Donovan............ | PAS | EX | III | ............... | |
| Do ...... | Deputy Under Secretary of Defense (Personnel and Readiness). | Vacant ............... | PAS | EX | IV | ............... | |
| Do ...... | Director, Accession Policy ............... | Career Incumbent ................ | CA | ES | ............... | ............... | |
| Do ...... | Director Dept of Defense/Veteran Affairs Collaboration Office. | ......do ...... | CA | ES | ............... | ............... | |
| Do ...... | Deputy Director for Force Resiliency ................ | ......do ...... | CA | ES | ............... | ............... | |
| Do ...... | Special Assistant to the Under Secretary of Defense (Personnel and Readiness). | William Bushman............... | NA | ES | ............... | ............... | |
| Do ...... | Special Assistant............... | Nicole Kirsch ............... | SC | GS | 12 | ............... | |
| Do ...... | Executive Director for Force Resiliency ............ | Career Incumbent ............... | CA | ES | ............... | ............... | |
| Do ...... | Special Assistant............... | Mary Cullinan ............... | SC | GS | 13 | ............... | |
| Do ...... | Deputy Assistant Secretary of Defense for Safety and Occupational Health. | Vacant ............... | ............... | ES | ............... | ............... | |
| Do ...... | Senior Advisor to the Under Secretary of Defense (Personnel and Readiness). | Jane Horton ............... | SC | GS | 14 | ............... | |
| Do ...... | Executive Director ............... | Career Incumbent ............... | CA | ES | ............... | ............... | |
| Do ...... | Special Assistant............... | Dennis Skelton Jr............... | SC | GS | 13 | ............... | |
| | **OFFICE OF THE ASSISTANT SECRETARY OF DEFENSE (HEALTH AFFAIRS)** | | | | | | |
| Do ...... | Principal Deputy Assistant Secretary of Defense (Health Affairs). | Vacant ............... | ............... | ES | ............... | ............... | |
| Do ...... | Deputy Assistant Secretary of Defense (Health Readiness Policy & Oversight). | Career Incumbent ............... | CA | ES | ............... | ............... | |
| Falls Church, VA ..... | Deputy Assistant Secretary of Defense (Health Resources Management and Policy). | ......do ...... | CA | ES | ............... | ............... | |
| Arlington, VA ........... | Deputy Assistant Secretary of Defense (Health Services Policy & Oversight). | Vacant ............... | ............... | ES | ............... | ............... | |
| Do ...... | Assistant Secretary of Defense (Health Affairs). | Thomas Patrick McCaffery .. | PAS | EX | IV | ............... | |
| | **OFFICE OF THE ASSISTANT SECRETARY OF DEFENSE (MANPOWER AND RESERVE AFFAIRS)** | | | | | | |
| Do ...... | Deputy Assistant Secretary of Defense (Civilian Personnel Policy). | Anita K Blair ............... | NA | ES | ............... | ............... | |
| Do ...... | Principal Director (Military Community and Family Policy). | Career Incumbent ............... | CA | ES | ............... | ............... | |
| Do ...... | Director of Military Compensation ................... | ......do ...... | CA | ES | ............... | ............... | |

# DEPARTMENT OF DEFENSE—Continued

## OFFICE OF THE SECRETARY OF DEFENSE—Continued

| Location | Position Title | Name of Incumbent | Type of Appt. | Pay Plan | Level, Grade, or Pay | Tenure | Expires |
|---|---|---|---|---|---|---|---|
| Arlington, VA........... | Principal Deputy Assistant Secretary of Defense for Manpower and Reserve Affairs. | Career Incumbent ............... | CA | ES | ............. | ............. | |
| Do .................... | Principal Director Military Personnel Policy..... | ......do ................. | CA | ES | ............. | ............. | |
| Do .................... | Special Assistant to the Assistant Secretary of Defense (Manpower and Reserve Affairs). | Anthony Lynnwood Cook..... | SC | GS | 14 | ............. | |
| Do .................... | Deputy Assistant Secretary of Defense (Reserve Integration). | Career Incumbent ............... | CA | ES | ............. | ............. | |
| Do .................... | Deputy Assistant Secretary of Defense (Military Personnel Policy). | ......do ................. | CA | ES | ............. | ............. | |
| Do .................... | Director, Total Force, Manpower, and Analysis.. | Vacant ............................. | ............. | ES | ............. | ............. | |
| Do .................... | Assistant Secretary of Defense (Manpower and Reserve Affairs). | ......do ................. | PAS | EX | IV | ............. | |
| Do .................... | Deputy Assitant Secretary of Defense for Military Community and Family Policy. | Anne Kimberley Joiner ........ | NA | ES | ............. | ............. | |
| Do .................... | Principal Director, Civilian Personnel Policy..... | Career Incumbent ............... | CA | ES | ............. | ............. | |
| | **OFFICE OF THE ASSISTANT SECRETARY OF DEFENSE (READINESS)** | | | | | | |
| Do .................... | Deputy Assistant Secretary of Defense (Readiness). | Matthew Shipley ............... | NA | ES | ............. | ............. | |
| Do .................... | Deputy Assistant Secretary of Defense for Force Education and Training. | Charles Frederick Drummond. | NA | ES | ............. | ............. | |
| Do .................... | Assistant Secretary of Defense (Readiness)....... | Vacant ............................. | PAS | EX | ............. | ............. | |
| Do .................... | Principal Deputy Assistant Secretary of Defense (Readiness). | Career Incumbent ............... | CA | ES | ............. | ............. | |
| | **DEFENSE COMMISSARY AGENCY** | | | | | | |
| Do .................... | Deputy Director/Chief Operating Officer ........... | ......do ................. | CA | ES | ............. | ............. | |
| Fort Lee, VA............. | Executive Director, Store Operations ................ | ......do ................. | CA | ES | ............. | ............. | |
| Do .................... | Executive Advisor, Defense Commissary Agency. | Vacant ............................. | ............. | ES | ............. | ............. | |
| Do .................... | Executive Director Information Technology....... | ......do ................. | ............. | ES | ............. | ............. | |
| Do .................... | Executive Director Sales Marketing and Logistics. | Career Incumbent ............... | CA | ES | ............. | ............. | |
| | **DEFENSE HEALTH AGENCY** | | | | | | |
| Falls Church, VA ..... | Deputy Director, Defense Health Agency........... | ......do ................. | CA | ES | ............. | ............. | |
| Do .................... | Deputy Assistant Director for Health Care Operations. | ......do ................. | CA | ES | ............. | ............. | |
| Do .................... | Deputy Assistant Director for Financial Operations. | Vacant ............................. | ............. | ES | ............. | ............. | |
| Do .................... | Assistant Director Health Care Administration. | Career Incumbent ............... | CA | ES | ............. | ............. | |
| Do .................... | Deputy Assistant Director for Acquisitions........ | ......do ................. | CA | ES | ............. | ............. | |
| Do .................... | Program Executive Officer, Defense Healthcare Mgmt Systems. | ......do ................. | CA | ES | ............. | ............. | |
| Rosslyn, VA............. | Director Federal and Commercial Interoperability. | ......do ................. | CA | ES | ............. | ............. | |
| Falls Church, VA ..... | Deputy Assistant Director for Information Operations/Military Health System Chief Information Officer. | ......do ................. | CA | ES | ............. | ............. | |
| Do .................... | Deputy Assistant Director for Medical Affairs .. | ......do ................. | CA | ES | ............. | ............. | |
| Arlington, VA........... | Director, Federal Electronic Health Record Modernization. | Vacant ............................. | ............. | ES | ............. | ............. | |
| Falls Church, VA ..... | Assistant Director for Management / Component Acquisition Executive. | Career Incumbent ............... | CA | ES | ............. | ............. | |
| | **DEFENSE HUMAN RESOURCES ACTIVITY** | | | | | | |
| Arlington, VA........... | Director, Defense Human Resources Activity .... | ......do ................. | CA | ES | ............. | ............. | |
| Seaside, CA............. | Deputy Director, Defense Manpower Data Center. | ......do ................. | CA | ES | ............. | ............. | |
| Arlington, VA........... | Director, Defense Travel Management .............. | ......do ................. | CA | ES | ............. | ............. | |
| Alexandria, VA ....... | Deputy Director, Defense Human Resources Activity. | ......do ................. | CA | ES | ............. | ............. | |
| Do .................... | Deputy Director, Defense Civilian Personnel Advisory Services. | ......do ................. | CA | ES | ............. | ............. | |
| Do .................... | Director, Defense Civilian Personnel Advisory Service. | ......do ................. | CA | ES | ............. | ............. | |
| Do .................... | Director, Office of People Analytics.................. | ......do ................. | CA | ES | ............. | ............. | |
| Do .................... | Director, Defense Personnel and Family Support Center. | Brian Davis.......................... | NA | ES | ............. | ............. | |
| Do .................... | Director, Diversity Management Operations Center. | Career Incumbent ............... | CA | ES | ............. | ............. | |

# DEPARTMENT OF DEFENSE—Continued

## OFFICE OF THE SECRETARY OF DEFENSE—Continued

| Location | Position Title | Name of Incumbent | Type of Appt. | Pay Plan | Level, Grade, or Pay | Tenure | Expires |
|---|---|---|---|---|---|---|---|
| Alexandria, VA ........ | Director, Dhra Enterprise Operations Center ... | Career Incumbent ................ | CA | ES | ............... | ............... | |
| Arlington, VA............ | Director, Defense Manpower Data Center ........ | ......do ................................. | CA | ES | ............... | ............... | |
| Alexandria, VA ........ | Director, Defense Suicide Prevention Office ...... | ......do ................................. | CA | ES | ............... | ............... | |
| | **DEPARTMENT OF DEFENSE EDUCATION ACTIVITY** | | | | | | |
| Okinawa Island, Japan. | Director, Department of Defense Dependents Schools Pacific & Domestic Dependent Elementary and Secondary Schools Guam. | ......do ................................. | CA | ES | ............... | ............... | |
| Wiesbaden, Germany. | Director, Department of Defense Dependents Schools Europe. | ......do ................................. | CA | ES | ............... | ............... | |
| Arlington, VA............ | Director, Department of Defense Education Activity. | ......do ................................. | CA | ES | ............... | ............... | |
| Do ...................... | Associate Director for Financial and Business Operations. | ......do ................................. | CA | ES | ............... | ............... | |
| Alexandria, VA ........ | Chief Academic Officer ................................. | ......do ................................. | CA | ES | ............... | ............... | |
| Do ...................... | Director, Department of Defense Education Activity Americas and Performance and Accountability. | ......do ................................. | CA | ES | ............... | ............... | |
| | **OFFICE OF THE UNDER SECRETARY OF DEFENSE (INTELLIGENCE)** | | | | | | |
| Arlington, VA............ | Under Secretary of Defense (Intelligence) ........ | Joseph Kernan...................... | PAS | EX | III | ............... | |
| Do ...................... | Special Assistant to the Under Secretary of Defense for Intelligence. | Mark G McKinnon .............. | SC | GS | 15 | ............... | |
| Do ...................... | Special Assistant................................. | Nikolas Mikula.................... | SC | GS | 14 | ............... | |
| Do ...................... | Deputy Under Secretary of Defense (Intelligence). | Vacant .................................. | PAS | EX | IV | ............... | |
| | **OFFICE OF THE ASSISTANT SECRETARY OF DEFENSE (LEGISLATIVE AFFAIRS)** | | | | | | |
| Do ...................... | Special Assistant to the Assistant Secretary of Defense for Legislative Affairs, Chief, Policy. | David E. Abner .................... | SC | GS | 14 | ............... | |
| Do ...................... | Principal Deputy Assistant Secretary of Defense Legislative Affairs. | Ann Johnston........................ | NA | ES | ............... | ............... | |
| Do ...................... | Deputy Assistant Secretary of Defense (House Affairs). | William Wolfe ...................... | NA | ES | ............... | ............... | |
| Do ...................... | Special Assistant................................. | Ryan P Shellooe................... | SC | GS | 13 | ............... | |
| Do ...................... | ......do ................................. | Brenton Coy McNeely .......... | SC | GS | 14 | ............... | |
| Do ...................... | ......do ................................. | Victoria Lynn Barton .......... | SC | GS | 14 | ............... | |
| Do ...................... | ......do ................................. | Matthew I Kenney .............. | SC | GS | 15 | ............... | |
| Do ...................... | ......do ................................. | Robert Ganim ...................... | SC | GS | 13 | ............... | |
| Do ...................... | ......do ................................. | Emily Wilson ...................... | SC | GS | 12 | ............... | |
| Do ...................... | Special Assistant to Assistant Secretary of Defense for Legislative Affairs. | Abbey Overland.................... | SC | GS | 14 | ............... | |
| Do ...................... | Deputy Assistant Secretary of Defense for Senate Affairs. | Andrew H Tabler.................. | NA | ES | ............... | ............... | |
| Do ...................... | Special Assistant................................. | David Turkovic .................... | SC | GS | 14 | ............... | |
| Do ...................... | ......do ................................. | Andrew Warren .................... | SC | GS | 15 | ............... | |
| Do ...................... | Assistant Secretary of Defense (Legislative Affairs). | Robert R Hood .................... | PAS | EX | IV | ............... | |
| Do ...................... | Special Assistant................................. | Bobby Cornett...................... | SC | GS | 14 | ............... | |
| | **OFFICE OF THE DIRECTOR, OPERATIONAL TEST AND EVALUATION** | | | | | | |
| Do ...................... | Principal Deputy Director, Operational Test and Evaluation. | Career Incumbent ................ | CA | ES | ............... | ............... | |
| Do ...................... | Deputy Director for Land and Expeditionary Warfare. | ......do ................................. | CA | ES | ............... | ............... | |
| Do ...................... | Deputy Director for Air Warfare .................... | ......do ................................. | CA | ES | ............... | ............... | |
| Do ...................... | Deputy Director, Net-Centric Space and Missile Defense Systems. | ......do ................................. | CA | ES | ............... | ............... | |
| Do ...................... | Director, Operational Test and Evaluation ........ | Robert Behler ...................... | PAS | EX | IV | ............... | |
| | **OFFICE OF THE DIRECTOR (COST ASSESSMENT AND PROGRAM EVALUATION)** | | | | | | |
| Do ...................... | Director, Irregular Warfare Division ................ | Career Incumbent ................ | CA | ES | ............... | ............... | |
| Do ...................... | Director, Intelligence, Surveillance, and Reconnaissance Programs Division. | ......do ................................. | CA | ES | ............... | ............... | |
| Do ...................... | Deputy Director, Analysis and Innovation ........ | ......do ................................. | CA | ES | ............... | ............... | |
| Do ...................... | Director, Tactical Air Forces Division ................ | ......do ................................. | CA | ES | ............... | ............... | |
| Do ...................... | Director, Land Forces Division........................ | ......do ................................. | CA | ES | ............... | ............... | |

## DEPARTMENT OF DEFENSE—Continued

### OFFICE OF THE SECRETARY OF DEFENSE—Continued

| Location | Position Title | Name of Incumbent | Type of Appt. | Pay Plan | Level, Grade, or Pay | Tenure | Expires |
|---|---|---|---|---|---|---|---|
| Arlington, VA........... | Deputy Director, Cost Assessment..................... | Career Incumbent ................ | CA | ES | .............. | .............. | |
| Do ..................... | Director, Advanced Systems Cost Analysis Division. | ......do ...... | CA | ES | .............. | .............. | |
| Do ..................... | Director, Weapon Systems Cost Analysis Division. | ......do ...... | CA | ES | .............. | .............. | |
| Do ..................... | Director, Program Resources and Information Systems Management Division. | ......do ...... | CA | ES | .............. | .............. | |
| Do ..................... | Director, Command, Control, Communications, Computers (C4) and Information Programs Division. | ......do ...... | CA | ES | .............. | .............. | |
| Do ..................... | Deputy Director Capability Enablers................. | ......do ...... | CA | ES | .............. | .............. | |
| Do ..................... | Director, Cost Assessment and Program Evaluation. | Vacant ................ | PAS | EX | IV | .............. | |
| Do ..................... | Director, Operating and Support Cost Analysis Division. | Career Incumbent ................ | CA | ES | .............. | .............. | |
| Do ..................... | Director, Strategic Analysis and Wargaming..... | ......do ...... | CA | ES | .............. | .............. | |
| Do ..................... | Director, Economic & Manpower Analysis ........ | ......do ...... | CA | ES | .............. | .............. | |
| Do ..................... | Deputy Director, Program Evaluation................. | ......do ...... | CA | ES | .............. | .............. | |
| Do ..................... | Principal Deputy Director ..................... | ......do ...... | CA | ES | .............. | .............. | |
| Do ..................... | Special Assistant.................... | Colin Bosse | SC | GS | 13 | .............. | |
| Do ..................... | Director, Force and Infrastructure and Analysis Division. | Career Incumbent ................ | CA | ES | .............. | .............. | |
| Do ..................... | Director, Strategic, Defensive and Space Programs. | ......do ...... | CA | ES | .............. | .............. | |
| Do ..................... | Director, Program Analysis Division ................. | ......do ...... | CA | ES | .............. | .............. | |
| Do ..................... | Director, Naval Forces Division ......................... | ......do ...... | CA | ES | .............. | .............. | |
| | **OFFICE OF THE GENERAL COUNSEL** | | | | | | |
| Do ..................... | Principal Deputy General Counsel..................... | William Sherman Castle...... | NA | ES | .............. | .............. | |
| Do ..................... | Deputy General Counsel (Fiscal)....................... | Career Incumbent ................ | CA | ES | .............. | .............. | |
| Do ..................... | Deputy General Counsel (International Affairs). | ......do ...... | CA | ES | .............. | .............. | |
| Do ..................... | Director, Standards of Conduct Office............... | ......do ...... | CA | ES | .............. | .............. | |
| Do ..................... | Deputy General Counsel Legal Counsel ........... | Platte M Moring III............. | NA | ES | .............. | .............. | |
| Do ..................... | Deputy General Counsel (Environment and Installations). | Harry Kelso ......................... | NA | ES | .............. | .............. | |
| Do ..................... | Special Counsel to the General Counsel ........... | Vacant ......................... | .............. | ES | .............. | .............. | |
| Do ..................... | Deputy General Counsel (Acquisition and Logistics). | Career Incumbent ................ | CA | ES | .............. | .............. | |
| Do ..................... | General Counsel of the Department of Defense. | Paul C Ney Jr. ...................... | PAS | EX | IV | .............. | |
| Do ..................... | Senior Deputy General Counsel & Defense General Counsel (Pers & Health Policy). | Career Incumbent ................ | CA | ES | .............. | .............. | |
| Do ..................... | Deputy General Counsel (Legislation) ............. | Vacant ......................... | .............. | ES | .............. | .............. | |
| | **OFFICE OF INSPECTOR GENERAL** | | | | | | |
| Do ..................... | Strategic Planning Advisor for SWA Affairs...... | ......do ...... | .............. | ES | .............. | .............. | |
| | **OFFICE OF THE DEPARTMENT OF DEFENSE CHIEF INFORMATION OFFICER** | | | | | | |
| Do ..................... | Deputy Chief Information Officer for Resources and Analysis. | Career Incumbent ................ | CA | ES | .............. | .............. | |
| Do ..................... | Director, Spectrum Policy and Programs ........... | Vacant ......................... | .............. | ES | .............. | .............. | |
| Do ..................... | Principal Director to the Deputy Chief Information Officer (Information Enterprise). | Career Incumbent ................ | CA | ES | .............. | .............. | |
| Do ..................... | Deputy Chief Information Officer for Information Enterprise. | Vacant ......................... | .............. | ES | .............. | .............. | |
| Do ..................... | Principal Deputy, Chief Information Officer...... | Career Incumbent ................ | CA | ES | .............. | .............. | |
| Alexandria, VA ....... | Director of Technical Integration....................... | Vacant ......................... | .............. | ES | .............. | .............. | |
| Arlington, VA........... | Special Assistant (Career Broadening) ............. | Career Incumbent ................ | CA | ES | .............. | .............. | |
| Do ..................... | Director, Chief Information Officer Action Group. | Caroline Emily Bledsoe........ | SC | GS | 12 | .............. | |
| Do ..................... | Director, Cybersecurity Capabilities.................. | Career Incumbent ................ | CA | ES | .............. | .............. | |
| Do ..................... | Deputy Chief Information Officer (Cybersecurity). | ......do ...... | CA | ES | .............. | .............. | |
| Do ..................... | Special Assistant for Strategic Programs ......... | Peter J Dickson ..................... | NA | ES | .............. | .............. | |
| Do ..................... | Chief Information Officer of the Department of Defense. | Dana Deasy........................... | PAS | EX | IV | .............. | |
| Do ..................... | Director, Cloud Computing Program Office ....... | Sharon Woods ...................... | TA | ES | .............. | .............. | 06/08/22 |
| Do ..................... | Deputy Chief Information Officer (Command, Control, and Computers). | Career Incumbent ................ | CA | ES | .............. | .............. | |

# DEPARTMENT OF DEFENSE—Continued

## OFFICE OF THE SECRETARY OF DEFENSE—Continued

| Location | Position Title | Name of Incumbent | Type of Appt. | Pay Plan | Level, Grade, or Pay | Tenure | Expires |
|---|---|---|---|---|---|---|---|
| Arlington, VA........... | Principal Director to the Deputy Chief Information Officer for Command Control and Communications. | Career Incumbent ................ | CA | ES | ............... | ............... | |
| Do ................... | Director, C4 and Information Infrastructure..... | Vacant ................................. | ............ | ES | ............... | ............... | |
| Do ................... | Principal Director to the Deputy Chief Information Officer for Resources and Analysis. | ......do ............................. | ............ | ES | ............... | ............... | |
| Do ................... | Chief of Staff, (DOD Chief Information Oñicer). | Blake Moore......................... | NA | ES | ............... | ............... | |
| | **DEFENSE INFORMATION SYSTEMS AGENCY** | | | | | | |
| Do ................... | General Counsel.................................... | Career Incumbent ................ | CA | ES | ............... | ............... | |
| | **OFFICE OF THE ASSISTANT TO THE SECRETARY OF DEFENSE (PUBLIC AFFAIRS)** | | | | | | |
| Do ................... | Principal Deputy Assistant to the Secretary of Defense for Public Affairs. | Charles Summers................ | NA | ES | ............... | ............... | |
| Do ................... | Deputy Assistant to the Secretary of Defense for Strategy and Engagement. | Carmen Michele Covelli-Ingwell. | NA | ES | ............... | ............... | |
| Do ................... | Special Assistant.................................... | Laura A Schlapp.................. | SC | GS | 12 | ............... | |
| Fort Meade, MD ...... | Deputy Director, Defense Media Activity.......... | Vacant ................................. | ............ | ES | ............... | ............... | |
| Arlington, VA........... | Deputy Assistant to the Secretary of Defense for Public Affairs for Media and Press Secretary. | ......do ............................. | ............ | ES | ............... | ............... | |
| Do ................... | Special Assistant.................................... | Lauren Weber ...................... | SC | GS | 12 | ............... | |
| Do ................... | ......do ............................. | Teresa Davis ....................... | SC | GS | 12 | ............... | |
| Do ................... | Assistant to the Secretary of Defense for Public Affairs. | Jonathan R Hoffman............ | NA | ES | ............... | ............... | |
| Do ................... | Special Assistant.................................... | David Vasquez ..................... | SC | GS | 12 | ............... | |
| | **OFFICE OF THE DIRECTOR, NET ASSESSMENT** | | | | | | |
| Do ................... | Director of Net Assessment............................ | Career Incumbent ................ | CA | ES | ............... | ............... | |
| Do ................... | Deputy Director of Net Assessment ................. | ......do ............. | CA | ES | ............... | ............... | |
| Do ................... | Associate Director for Net Assessment ............. | ......do ............. | CA | ES | ............... | ............... | |
| | **UNITED STATES COURT OF APPEALS FOR THE ARMED FORCES** | | | | | | |
| Washington, DC ...... | Associate Judge, United States Court of Appeals for the Armed Forces. | Margaret A Ryan.................. | PAS | OT | ............... | ............... | |
| Do ................... | Chief Judge, United States Court of Appeals for the Armed Forces. | Scott W Stucky ..................... | PAS | OT | ............... | ............... | |
| Do ................... | Associate Judge, United States Court of Appeals for the Armed Forces. | John E Sparks Jr.................. | PAS | OT | ............... | ............... | |
| Do ................... | Clerk of the Court.................................... | Vacant ................................. | ............ | ES | ............... | ............... | |
| Do ................... | Chief Deputy Clerk of the Court........................ | Career Incumbent ................ | CA | ES | ............... | ............... | |
| Do ................... | Associate Judge, United States Court of Appeals for the Armed Forces. | Gregory Maggs ..................... | PAS | OT | ............... | ............... | |
| Do ................... | Clerk of the Court.................................... | Career Incumbent ................ | CA | ES | ............... | ............... | |
| Do ................... | Associate Judge, United States Court of Appeals for the Armed Forces. | Kevin A Ohlson ................... | PAS | OT | ............... | ............... | |

## DEPARTMENT OF EDUCATION

| Location | Position Title | Name of Incumbent | Type of Appt. | Pay Plan | Level, Grade, or Pay | Tenure | Expires |
|---|---|---|---|---|---|---|---|
| | **OFFICE OF THE SECRETARY** | | | | | | |
| Washington, DC ...... | Special Assistant................................................ | Mckenzie Snow...................... | SC | GS | 13 | .............. | |
| Do .................... | Secretary............................................................. | Elisabeth Devos...................... | PAS | EX | I | .............. | |
| Do .................... | Deputy Secretary of Education........................... | Mitchell Zais .......................... | PAS | EX | II | .............. | |
| Do .................... | Chief of Staff....................................................... | Nathan Bailey ........................ | NA | ES | .............. | | |
| Do .................... | Deputy Assistant Secretary for Grants Management. | Career Incumbent ................. | CA | ES | .............. | | |
| Do .................... | Deputy Chief of Staff for Operations................. | Lee-Douglass Simmons........ | NA | ES | .............. | | |
| Do .................... | Director, Executive Management Staff .............. | Vacant .................................. | ............ | ES | .............. | | |
| Do .................... | Director, Executive Secretariat......................... | Career Incumbent ................. | CA | ES | .............. | | |
| Do .................... | Director, Office of Small and Disadvantaged Business Utilization. | ......do ............................... | CA | ES | .............. | | |
| Do .................... | Director, International Affairs and Senior Advisor. | ......do ............................... | CA | ES | .............. | | |
| Do .................... | Director, White House Liaison ........................... | Thomas Andrew Wilson ...... | SC | GS | 14 | .............. | |
| Do .................... | Performance Improvement Officer ..................... | Career Incumbent ................. | CA | ES | .............. | | |
| Do .................... | Senior Advisor.................................................... | Robert Scott Eitel................. | NA | ES | .............. | | |
| Do .................... | ......do ............................................................... | Kent D Talbert....................... | NA | ES | .............. | | |
| Do .................... | Special Assistant (Supervisory) ........................ | Carly Robb ............................ | SC | GS | 15 | .............. | |
| Do .................... | Special Assistant................................................ | Allen Ernst ........................... | SC | GS | 13 | .............. | |
| Do .................... | ......do ............................................................... | Nathaniel Breeding.............. | SC | GS | 14 | .............. | |
| Do .................... | ......do ............................................................... | Sarah Delahunty................... | SC | GS | 13 | .............. | |
| Do .................... | ......do ............................................................... | Jessica Newman .................... | SC | GS | 14 | .............. | |
| Do .................... | ......do ............................................................... | Cecilia Ines Martinez.......... | SC | GS | 15 | .............. | |
| Do .................... | Confidential Assistant for Policy ...................... | Noah Mitchell ....................... | SC | GS | 9 | .............. | |
| Do .................... | Confidential Assistant ....................................... | Kendyl Willox ....................... | SC | GS | 9 | .............. | |
| Do .................... | ......do ............................................................... | Matthew Ide ......................... | SC | GS | 7 | .............. | |
| Do .................... | ......do ............................................................... | Alexandra Pena .................... | SC | GS | 11 | .............. | |
| Do .................... | ......do ............................................................... | Jude Al-Hmoud...................... | SC | GS | 7 | .............. | |
| Do .................... | ......do ............................................................... | Rebekah Clark....................... | SC | GS | 11 | .............. | |
| Do .................... | ......do ............................................................... | James Rogers........................ | SC | GS | 9 | .............. | |
| Do .................... | ......do ............................................................... | Kara Neumann...................... | SC | GS | 9 | .............. | |
| | *Office of the Under Secretary* | | | | | | |
| Do .................... | Under Secretary.................................................. | Vacant .................................. | PAS | EX | III | .............. | |
| Do .................... | Principal Deputy Under Secretary ..................... | Diane Auer Jones ................. | NA | ES | .............. | | |
| Do .................... | Executive Director, White House Initiative on Historically Black Colleges and Universities. | Johnathan Holifield ............ | SC | GS | 15 | .............. | |
| Do .................... | Confidential Assistant ....................................... | Jesse Hokanson .................... | SC | GS | 7 | .............. | |
| Do .................... | Confidential Assistant (Policy)........................... | John Lucas Adair ................. | SC | GS | 12 | .............. | |
| Do .................... | Senior Advisor.................................................... | Michael Brickman ............... | SC | GS | 15 | .............. | |
| | *Office of the Chief Financial Officer* | | | | | | |
| Do .................... | Chief Financial Officer ...................................... | Vacant .................................. | PAS | EX | IV | .............. | |
| Do .................... | Director, Financial Management Operations..... | Career Incumbent ................. | CA | ES | .............. | | |
| | *Office of the Chief Information Officer* | | | | | | |
| Do .................... | Deputy Chief Information Officer....................... | ......do ............................... | CA | ES | .............. | | |
| Do .................... | Director, Information Technology and Program Services. | ......do ............................... | CA | ES | .............. | | |
| Do .................... | Director, Enterprise Technology Services.......... | ......do ............................... | CA | ES | .............. | | |
| Do .................... | Director, Financial Systems Services ................ | ......do ............................... | CA | ES | .............. | | |
| | *Office of Financial Operations* | | | | | | |
| Do .................... | Principal Deputy Assistant Secretary................ | ......do ............................... | CA | ES | .............. | | |
| Do .................... | Director, Hearings and Appeals ........................ | ......do ............................... | CA | ES | .............. | | |
| Do .................... | Director, Cost Estimation and Analysis Division. | ......do ............................... | CA | ES | .............. | | |
| Do .................... | Senior Advisor.................................................... | Wanda Davis.......................... | TA | ES | .............. | .............. | 03/16/22 |
| Do .................... | ......do ............................................................... | Daniel Currell...................... | NA | ES | .............. | | |
| | *Office of the General Counsel* | | | | | | |
| Do .................... | General Counsel.................................................. | Vacant .................................. | PAS | EX | IV | .............. | |
| Do .................... | Deputy General Counsel, Postsecondary Service. | Jedediah Brinton.................. | NA | ES | .............. | | |
| Do .................... | Deputy General Counsel for Program Service... | Career Incumbent ................. | CA | ES | .............. | | |
| Do .................... | Deputy General Counsel ..................................... | Candice Jackson ................... | NA | ES | .............. | | |
| Do .................... | Deputy General Council for Ethics, Regulatory and Legislative Services. | Vacant .................................. | ............ | ES | .............. | | |
| Do .................... | Deputy General Counsel ..................................... | Farnaz Thompson................. | NA | ES | .............. | | |
| Do .................... | Assistant General Counsel for Legislative Counsel Division. | Career Incumbent ................. | CA | ES | .............. | | |
| Do .................... | Assistant General Counsel................................. | ......do ............................... | CA | ES | .............. | | |
| Do .................... | Assistant General Counsel for Regulatory Services. | ......do ............................... | CA | ES | .............. | | |

## DEPARTMENT OF EDUCATION—Continued

| Location | Position Title | Name of Incumbent | Type of Appt. | Pay Plan | Level, Grade, or Pay | Tenure | Expires |
|---|---|---|---|---|---|---|---|
| Washington, DC ...... | Assistant General Counsel Ethics ..................... | Career Incumbent .............. | CA | ES | .............. | .............. | |
| Do .................. | Principal Deputy General Counsel.................... | Reed Rubinstein .................. | NA | ES | .............. | .............. | |
| Do .................. | Attorney Adviser .................................. | Jonathan Helwink.............. | SC | GS | 15 | .............. | |
| Do .................. | ......do ..................................... | Audrey Levorse.................... | SC | GS | 14 | .............. | |
| Do .................. | ......do ..................................... | Martin Menezes.................... | SC | GS | 12 | .............. | |
| Do .................. | ......do ..................................... | Brandon S Sherman............ | SC | GS | 15 | .............. | |
| Do .................. | Attorney Advisor ................................. | Sarah Child.......................... | SC | GS | 12 | .............. | |
| Do .................. | ......do ..................................... | Christopher Brinson............ | SC | GS | 15 | .............. | |
| Do .................. | Attorney Adviser ................................. | Paul Moore.......................... | SC | GS | 15 | .............. | |
| Do .................. | Confidential Assistant ........................... | Thea Dunlevie .................... | SC | GS | 7 | .............. | |
| Do .................. | ......do ..................................... | Patrick Shaheen .................. | SC | GS | 11 | .............. | |
| Do .................. | ......do ..................................... | Catherine Francois.............. | SC | GS | 9 | .............. | |
| Do .................. | ......do ..................................... | Richard El-Rassy.................. | SC | GS | 9 | .............. | |
| | *Office of Legislation and Congressional Affairs* | | | | | | |
| Do .................. | Special Assistant................................. | Jonas Linde.......................... | SC | GS | 13 | .............. | |
| Do .................. | Assistant Secretary for Legislation and Congressional Affairs. | Vacant .................. | PAS | EX | IV | .............. | |
| Do .................. | Principal Deputy Assistant Secretary .............. | Jordan Forbes .................. | NA | ES | .............. | .............. | |
| Do .................. | Director, Office of Legislation and Congressional Affairs. | Anna Bartlett ...................... | SC | GS | 15 | .............. | |
| Do .................. | Special Assistant................................. | Mary Riley .......................... | SC | GS | 13 | .............. | |
| Do .................. | Confidential Assistant ........................... | Sara Ratliff ........................ | SC | GS | 9 | .............. | |
| Do .................. | ......do ..................................... | Drew Baney .......................... | SC | GS | 12 | .............. | |
| | *Office for Civil Rights* | | | | | | |
| Do .................. | Assistant Secretary for Civil Rights................. | Kenneth L Marcus .............. | PAS | EX | IV | .............. | |
| Do .................. | Principal Deputy Assistant Secretary .............. | Kimberly M Richey ............ | NA | ES | .............. | .............. | |
| Do .................. | Deputy Assistant Secretary for Policy and Development. | David Tryon ...................... | SC | SL | $158,500 | .............. | |
| Do .................. | Deputy Assistant Secretary for Management and Planning. | Vacant .................. | | ES | | .............. | |
| Denver, CO ............ | Senior Counsel for Civil Rights ......................... | William Trachman.............. | SC | SL | $170,292 | .............. | |
| Washington, DC ...... | Attorney Advisor ................................. | Patrick Lichtenstein............ | SC | GS | 12 | .............. | |
| Do .................. | Attorney Adviser (Special Counsel).................. | Samantha Christensen ........ | SC | GS | 12 | .............. | |
| Do .................. | Attorney Adviser (Senior Counsel) ................. | Christian Corrigan .............. | SC | GS | 15 | .............. | |
| Do .................. | Confidential Assistant ........................... | Jared Harris Wrede.............. | SC | GS | 9 | .............. | |
| Do .................. | ......do ..................................... | Lauren Roppolo .................. | SC | GS | 7 | .............. | |
| | *Office of Elementary and Secondary Education* | | | | | | |
| Do .................. | Assistant Secretary for Elementary and Secondary Education. | Frank Brogan ...................... | PAS | EX | IV | .............. | |
| Do .................. | Principal Deputy Assistant Secretary .............. | Aimee Viana ...................... | NA | ES | .............. | .............. | |
| Do .................. | Deputy Assistant Secretary for Management and Planning. | Career Incumbent .............. | CA | ES | .............. | .............. | |
| Do .................. | Deputy Assistant Secretary for Evidence Based Research. | Christopher Rinkus.............. | NA | ES | .............. | .............. | |
| Do .................. | Deputy Assistant Secretary for Policy and Programs. | Career Incumbent .............. | CA | ES | .............. | .............. | |
| Do .................. | Confidential Assistant ........................... | Sarah Feldpausch.............. | SC | GS | 9 | .............. | |
| Do .................. | Confidential Assisstant ........................... | Caitlin Condie.................... | SC | GS | 11 | .............. | |
| Do .................. | Confidential Assistant ........................... | Ashley Dalton ...................... | SC | GS | 9 | .............. | |
| | *Office of English Language Acquisition, Language Enhancement, and Academic Achievement for Limited English Proficient Students* | | | | | | |
| Do .................. | Assistant Deputy Secretary and Director .......... | Lorena Orozco McElwain..... | NA | ES | .............. | .............. | |
| | *Office of Postsecondary Education* | | | | | | |
| Do .................. | Assistant Secretary for Postsecondary Education. | Robert King.......................... | PAS | EX | IV | .............. | |
| Do .................. | Deputy Assistant Secretary for Policy Planning and Innovation. | Career Incumbent .............. | CA | ES | .............. | .............. | |
| Do .................. | Deputy Assistant Secretary, Higher Education Programs. | Christopher McCaghren ...... | NA | ES | .............. | .............. | |
| Do .................. | Deputy Assistant Secretary for Management and Planning. | Vacant .................. | | ES | | .............. | |
| Do .................. | Director, Student Services............................ | Career Incumbent .............. | CA | ES | .............. | .............. | |
| Do .................. | Special Assistant................................. | Erin Paige Agostin ............ | SC | GS | 13 | .............. | |
| Do .................. | ......do ..................................... | Johnathon Huston.............. | SC | GS | 14 | .............. | |
| Do .................. | Confidential Assistant ........................... | Shaina Hilsey ...................... | SC | GS | 11 | .............. | |
| Do .................. | ......do ..................................... | Jack Cox.............................. | SC | GS | 7 | .............. | |

## DEPARTMENT OF EDUCATION—Continued

| Location | Position Title | Name of Incumbent | Type of Appt. | Pay Plan | Level, Grade, or Pay | Tenure | Expires |
|---|---|---|---|---|---|---|---|
| | *Office of Special Education and Rehabilitative Services* | | | | | | |
| Washington, DC ...... | Assistant Secretary for Special Education and Rehabilitative Services. | Vacant ...................... | PAS | EX | IV | .............. | |
| Do .................... | Commissioner Rehabilitation Services Administration. | Mark Schultz ...................... | PAS | EX | V | .............. | |
| Do .................... | Director, Office of Special Education Programs. | Laurie Vanderploeg .............. | NA | ES | | .............. | |
| Do .................... | Deputy Director, Special Education Programs .. | Career Incumbent ............... | CA | ES | | .............. | |
| Do .................... | Special Assistant........................................ | Margaret Winkler.............. | SC | GS | 15 | .............. | |
| Do .................... | Confidential Assistant ........................................ | Leslie Sawyer ...................... | SC | GS | 7 | .............. | |
| | *Office of Career Technical and Adult Education* | | | | | | |
| Do .................... | Assistant Secretary for Career, Technical and Adult Education. | Scott Stump .......................... | PAS | EX | IV | .............. | |
| Do .................... | Deputy Assistant Secretary .............................. | Casey Sacks .......................... | NA | ES | | .............. | |
| Do .................... | Deputy Assistant Secretary on Community Colleges. | Vacant ...................... | ............ | ES | | .............. | |
| Do .................... | Deputy Assistant Secretary for Management and Planning. | Career Incumbent ............... | CA | ES | | .............. | |
| Do .................... | Special Assistant........................................ | Richard Pettey ...................... | SC | GS | 13 | .............. | |
| Do .................... | Confidential Assistant ........................................ | Alicia Criscuolo.................... | SC | GS | 11 | .............. | |
| Do .................... | ......do ........................................ | Douglas Burrichter.............. | SC | GS | 9 | .............. | |
| | *Institute of Education Sciences* | | | | | | |
| Do .................... | Director of the Institute of Education Sciences. | Mark Schneider .................... | PAS | EX | II | .............. | |
| Do .................... | Deputy Director for Administration and Policy. | Career Incumbent ............... | CA | ES | | .............. | |
| Do .................... | Commissioner of Education Statistics................ | James Woodworth.............. | PA | EX | IV | .............. | |
| Do .................... | Associate Commissioner, Management Systems. | Career Incumbent ............... | CA | ES | | .............. | |
| Do .................... | Associate Commissioner, Sample Survey ........... | ......do ...................... | CA | ES | | .............. | |
| | *Federal Student Aid* | | | | | | |
| Do .................... | Chief Operating Officer .................................... | Mark Brown.......................... | XS | AD | | .............. | |
| Do .................... | Director, Financial Management Group............. | Vacant ...................... | ............ | ES | | .............. | |
| Do .................... | Director, Budget Group ...................................... | Career Incumbent ............... | CA | ES | | .............. | |
| Do .................... | Director, Financial Management Systems Group. | Vacant ...................... | ............ | ES | | .............. | |
| Do .................... | Director, Systems Operations and Aid Delivery Management Services Group. | Career Incumbent ............... | CA | ES | | .............. | |
| Do .................... | Internal Review Officer Reporting Group.......... | Vacant ...................... | ............ | ES | | .............. | |
| Do .................... | Senior Cybersecurity Risk Advisor.................... | ......do ...................... | ............ | ES | | .............. | |
| Do .................... | Senior Advisor to the Chief Informaion Officer. | ......do ...................... | ............ | ES | | .............. | |
| | *Office of Planning, Evaluation and Policy Development* | | | | | | |
| Do .................... | Assistant Secretary for Planning, Evaluation, and Policy Development. | James Blew.......................... | PAS | EX | IV | .............. | |
| Do .................... | Principal Deputy Assistant Secretary .............. | Vacant ...................... | ............ | ES | | .............. | |
| Do .................... | Director, Elementary, Secondary, and Vocational Analysis Division. | Career Incumbent ............... | CA | ES | | .............. | |
| Do .................... | Director, Budget Execution and Administration Analysis Division. | ......do ...................... | CA | ES | | .............. | |
| Do .................... | Director, Budget Services .................................... | ......do ...................... | CA | ES | | .............. | |
| Do .................... | Director, Budget Policy ...................................... | Emily Slack.......................... | SC | GS | 15 | .............. | |
| Do .................... | Director, Educational Technology ...................... | Adam Safir.......................... | NA | ES | | .............. | |
| Do .................... | Deputy Director Budget Service ...................... | Career Incumbent ............... | CA | ES | | .............. | |
| Do .................... | Deputy Director, Office of Educational Technology. | Jake Steel.......................... | SC | GS | 15 | .............. | |
| Do .................... | Senior Advisor, Policy and Programs................. | Vacant ...................... | ............ | ES | | .............. | |
| Do .................... | Chief Data Officer............................................ | Career Incumbent ............... | CA | ES | | .............. | |
| Do .................... | Senior Advisor for Budget and Financial Management. | Vacant ...................... | ............ | ES | | .............. | |
| Do .................... | Special Assistant........................................ | Jean Morrow.......................... | SC | GS | 12 | .............. | |
| Do .................... | Confidential Assistant ........................................ | Elizabeth Simpson .............. | SC | GS | 7 | .............. | |
| | *Office of Communications and Outreach* | | | | | | |
| Do .................... | Assistant Secretary, Office of Communications and Outreach. | Vacant ...................... | PAS | EX | IV | .............. | |
| Do .................... | Deputy Assistant Secretary for Communications. | Elizabeth Hill ...................... | NA | ES | | .............. | |
| Do .................... | Deputy Assistant Secretary for Outreach .......... | Daniela Garcia.................... | NA | ES | | .............. | |
| Do .................... | Deputy Assistant Secretary for Management and Planning. | Career Incumbent ............... | CA | ES | | .............. | |
| Do .................... | Director, Center for Faith and Opportunity Initiatives. | Marjorie Kilgannon .............. | SC | GS | 15 | .............. | |
| Do .................... | Director of Outreach............................................ | Jacqueline Gonzalez.............. | SC | GS | 15 | .............. | |

## DEPARTMENT OF EDUCATION—Continued

| Location | Position Title | Name of Incumbent | Type of Appt. | Pay Plan | Level, Grade, or Pay | Tenure | Expires |
|---|---|---|---|---|---|---|---|
| Washington, DC ...... | Executive Director, White House Initiative on Educational Excellence for African Americans. | Terris Todd.......................... | SC | GS | 15 | .............. | |
| Do .................... | Senior Advisor.................................................. | Vacant ........................... | .......... | ES | .............. | .............. | |
| Do .................... | Special Assistant.............................................. | Nicholas Hahn................... | SC | GS | 15 | .............. | |
| Do .................... | ......do .......... | Michael Chamberlain........... | SC | GS | 13 | .............. | |
| Do .................... | ......do .......... | Angela Morabito.................. | SC | GS | 14 | .............. | |
| Do .................... | ......do .......... | Susan Falconer................... | SC | GS | 14 | .............. | |
| Do .................... | Confidential Assistant ..................................... | John Mabrey...................... | SC | GS | 11 | .............. | |
| Do .................... | ......do .......... | Mark Mansour II................. | SC | GS | 11 | .............. | |
| Do .................... | ......do .......... | Ryan Strand...................... | SC | GS | 7 | .............. | |
| Do .................... | Confidential Assistant (Digital)........................ | Valeria Tkacik................... | SC | GS | 9 | .............. | |
| Do .................... | Confidential Assistant ..................................... | Nicholas Bell.................... | SC | GS | 12 | .............. | |
| Do .................... | ......do .......... | Teresa Adams ................... | SC | GS | 11 | .............. | |

## DEPARTMENT OF EDUCATION OFFICE OF THE INSPECTOR GENERAL

| Location | Position Title | Name of Incumbent | Type of Appt. | Pay Plan | Level, Grade, or Pay | Tenure | Expires |
|---|---|---|---|---|---|---|---|
| Washington, DC ...... | Inspector General ............................................. | Vacant ........................... | PAS | EX | IV | .............. | |

## DEPARTMENT OF ENERGY

| Location | Position Title | Name of Incumbent | Type of Appt. | Pay Plan | Level, Grade, or Pay | Tenure | Expires |
|---|---|---|---|---|---|---|---|
| | **OFFICE OF THE SECRETARY** | | | | | | |
| Washington, DC ...... | Secretary, Department of Energy ...................... | Danny R Brouillette............ | PAS | EX | I | .............. | |
| Do .................... | Chief of Staff................................................... | James J Colgary................... | NA | ES | .............. | .............. | |
| Do .................... | Senior Advisor.................................................. | Mark R Maddox................... | NA | ES | .............. | .............. | |
| Do .................... | Senior Policy Advisor........................................ | Victoria Coates................... | NA | ES | .............. | .............. | |
| Do .................... | Deputy Chief of Staff........................................ | Alexa Ann Turner................. | SC | GS | 15 | .............. | |
| Do .................... | White House Liaison ........................................ | Jonathan Wetzel................. | SC | GS | 15 | .............. | |
| Do .................... | Director of Operations ..................................... | Matthew Jacob Johnson....... | SC | GS | 15 | .............. | |
| Do .................... | Special Assistant to the White House Liaison ... | Coleman Tolbert.................. | SC | GS | 9 | .............. | |
| | **OFFICE OF THE SECRETARY OF ENERGY ADVISORY BOARD** | | | | | | |
| Do .................... | Director, Office of Secretarial Boards and Councils. | Kurt Lloyd Heckman ........... | SC | GS | 15 | .............. | |
| Do .................... | Deputy Director, Office of Secretarial Boards and Councils. | Allison Mills......................... | SC | GS | 12 | .............. | |
| | **OFFICE OF THE DEPUTY SECRETARY** | | | | | | |
| Do .................... | Deputy Secretary of Energy............................. | Vacant ........................... | PAS | EX | II | .............. | |
| Do .................... | Chief of Staff................................................... | Sophia A Varnasidis ............. | NA | ES | .............. | .............. | |
| Do .................... | Senior Advisor.................................................. | Joshua Campbell.................. | SC | GS | 15 | .............. | |
| Do .................... | Scheduler to the Deputy Secretary.................... | Courtney Mullen ................. | SC | GS | 13 | .............. | |
| | **UNDER SECRETARY OF ENERGY** | | | | | | |
| Do .................... | Under Secretary of Energy ............................... | Mark Wesley Menezes.......... | PAS | EX | III | .............. | |
| Do .................... | Chief Operating Officer for Research Management Operations. | Cathleen Tripodi.................. | NA | ES | .............. | .............. | |
| Do .................... | Director of National Laboratory Operations Board. | Vacant ........................... | .......... | ES | .............. | .............. | |
| Do .................... | Senior Advisor.................................................. | Allan Lee Webster ............... | SC | GS | 15 | .............. | |
| Do .................... | ......do .......... | Carole Mae Plowfield ........... | SC | GS | 14 | .............. | |
| Do .................... | Special Advisor................................................. | Hunter Budd...................... | SC | GS | 13 | .............. | |
| Do .................... | Special Assistant.............................................. | Kristen Walker ................... | SC | GS | 9 | .............. | |
| | **UNDER SECRETARY FOR SCIENCE** | | | | | | |
| Do .................... | Under Secretary for Science.............................. | Paul Michel Dabbar ............. | PAS | EX | III | .............. | |
| Do .................... | Senior Advisor.................................................. | Vacant ........................... | .......... | ES | .............. | .............. | |
| Do .................... | Deputy Under Secretary for Science ................. | Thomas Leon Cubbage III ... | SC | GS | 15 | .............. | |
| Do .................... | Senior Advisor.................................................. | Anthony Vincent Giannetti.. | SC | GS | 13 | .............. | |
| | **NATIONAL NUCLEAR SECURITY ADMINISTRATION** | | | | | | |
| Do .................... | Under Secretary for Nuclear Security/Administrator for Nuclear Security. | Lisa E Gordon-Hagerty........ | PAS | EX | III | .............. | |

## DEPARTMENT OF ENERGY—Continued

| Location | Position Title | Name of Incumbent | Type of Appt. | Pay Plan | Level, Grade, or Pay | Tenure | Expires |
|---|---|---|---|---|---|---|---|
| Washington, DC ...... | Principal Deputy Administrator for National Nuclear Security. | William Alwill Bookless ....... | PAS | EX | IV | .............. | |
| Do .................... | Deputy Administrator for Defense Programs, National Nuclear Security Administration. | Charles Verdon ..................... | PAS | EX | IV | .............. | |
| Do .................... | Deputy Administrator for Defense Nuclear Nonproliferation. | Brent K Park ........................ | PAS | EX | IV | .............. | |
| Do .................... | Associate Administrator for External Affairs .... | Vacant ................................ | ............ | ES | .............. | .............. | |
| Do .................... | Deputy Associate Administrator for Infrastructure. | Career Incumbent ............... | CA | ES | .............. | .............. | |
| Do .................... | Assistant Deputy Administrator for Decision Support. | Vacant ................................ | ............ | ES | .............. | .............. | |
| Do .................... | Chief of Staff .......................................... | Career Incumbent ............... | CA | ES | .............. | .............. | |
| Do .................... | Senior Advisor ....................................... | ...... do ............................... | CA | ES | .............. | .............. | |
| Do .................... | Director, Office of Business Services ................. | ...... do ............................... | CA | ES | .............. | .............. | |
| Do .................... | Director of Congressional Affairs...................... | Donald Mckinnon ............... | SC | GS | 15 | .............. | |
| Do .................... | Senior Advisor ....................................... | Steven Michael Parr............. | SC | GS | 13 | .............. | |
| Do .................... | Program Analyst ..................................... | Matthew Kessler ................. | SC | GS | 12 | .............. | |
| Do .................... | ......do ................................................... | Cassandra E Roper ............. | SC | GS | 12 | .............. | |
| | **DEPUTY ADMINISTRATOR FOR DEFENSE PROGRAMS** | | | | | | |
| Do .................... | Senior Advisor ....................................... | Vacant ................................ | ............ | ES | .............. | .............. | |
| | **ADVANCED RESEARCH PROJECTS AGENCY - ENERGY** | | | | | | |
| Do .................... | Director, Advanced Research Project Agency - Energy. | Siegfried Lane Genatowski.. | PAS | EX | III | .............. | |
| Do .................... | Principal Deputy Director ............................. | Chanette Armstrong............. | NA | ES | .............. | .............. | |
| Do .................... | Chief of Staff .......................................... | Kyle Xavier Nicholas............ | SC | GS | 15 | .............. | |
| Do .................... | Senior Advisor ....................................... | Jennifer R Locetta .............. | SC | GS | 15 | .............. | |
| Do .................... | Special Advisor ...................................... | Hunter Douglas Faseler....... | SC | GS | 13 | .............. | |
| | **OFFICE OF ARTIFICIAL INTELLIGENCE AND TECHNOLOGY** | | | | | | |
| Do .................... | Director Office of Artificial Intelligence and Technology. | Cheryl Ingstad..................... | SC | SL | .............. | .............. | |
| | **ASSISTANT SECRETARY FOR CONGRESSIONAL AND INTERGOVERNMENTAL AFFAIRS** | | | | | | |
| Do .................... | Assistant Secretary for Congressional and Intergovernmental Affairs. | Melissa Figge Burnison ....... | PAS | EX | IV | .............. | |
| Do .................... | Principal Deputy Assistant Secretary............... | Dwayne S Bolton ................. | NA | ES | .............. | .............. | |
| Do .................... | ......do ................................................... | Kathleen Elena Hazlett ....... | NA | ES | .............. | .............. | |
| Do .................... | Deputy Assistant Secretary for Intergovernmental and External Affairs. | Mark David Planning .......... | SC | GS | 15 | .............. | |
| Do .................... | Deputy Assistant Secretary for House Affairs... | Christopher James Morris... | SC | GS | 15 | .............. | |
| Do .................... | Chief of Staff .......................................... | Nicholas J Catroppo............. | SC | GS | 15 | .............. | |
| Do .................... | Deputy Assistant Secretary for Senate Affairs.. | Shawn Dean Affolter............. | SC | GS | 14 | .............. | |
| Do .................... | Associate Deputy Assistant Secretary for Intergovernmental and External Affairs. | Michael Robert Pasko .......... | SC | GS | 14 | .............. | |
| Do .................... | Director of Labor Outreach ............................. | Douglas Matheney................. | SC | GS | 14 | .............. | |
| Do .................... | Associate Deputy Assistant Secrtary for House Affairs. | Conner William Brace.......... | SC | GS | 13 | .............. | |
| Do .................... | Director of Intergovernmental and External Affairs. | Scott Santamaria................. | SC | GS | 13 | .............. | |
| Do .................... | Legislative Affairs Advisor ............................. | Thomas Conner Ingram....... | SC | GS | 13 | .............. | |
| Do .................... | ......do ................................................... | Andrew Preston Mooney...... | SC | GS | 11 | .............. | |
| Do .................... | Special Assistant...................................... | Michael Edward Helmer...... | SC | GS | 9 | .............. | |
| Do .................... | Special Advisor ...................................... | Dillian Knight..................... | SC | GS | 9 | .............. | |
| | **ASSISTANT SECRETARY FOR INTERNATIONAL AFFAIRS** | | | | | | |
| Do .................... | Assistant Secretary for International Affairs .... | Theodore J Garrish .............. | PAS | EX | IV | .............. | |
| Do .................... | Principal Deputy Assistant Secretary for International Affairs. | Matthew Mann Zais............. | NA | ES | .............. | .............. | |
| Do .................... | Senior Advisor ....................................... | Vacant ................................ | ............ | ES | .............. | .............. | |
| Do .................... | Deputy Assistant Secretary for Energy Innovation and Market Development. | Joseph Uddo III ................... | NA | ES | .............. | .............. | |
| Do .................... | Deputy Assistant Secretary for Market Development and Energy Innovation. | Vacant ................................ | ............ | ES | .............. | .............. | |
| Do .................... | Chief of Staff .......................................... | Deidre Ann Almstead.......... | SC | GS | 15 | .............. | |
| Do .................... | Deputy Assistant Secretary for the Office of Global Energy Security and Multilateral Engagement. | William Thomas Joyce ........ | SC | GS | 15 | .............. | |
| Do .................... | Senior Advisor........................................ | Thomas Storch..................... | SC | GS | 15 | .............. | |

## DEPARTMENT OF ENERGY—Continued

| Location | Position Title | Name of Incumbent | Type of Appt. | Pay Plan | Level, Grade, or Pay | Tenure | Expires |
|---|---|---|---|---|---|---|---|
| Washington, DC ...... | Senior Advisor | Vincent Timothy Trovato ..... | SC | GS | 14 | ............... | |
| Do .................... | Deputy Chief of Staff | Thomas Edward Mapes ....... | SC | GS | 12 | ............... | |
| Do .................... | Special Assistant | Erica Tillotson | SC | GS | 9 | ............... | |
| | **LOAN PROGRAMS OFFICE** | | | | | | |
| Do .................... | Executive Director, Loan Program Office and Chairman, Project Management Risk Committee. | Career Incumbent ................ | CA | ES | ............... | ............... | |
| Do .................... | Director, Loan Guarantee Origination Division. | ......do ...................... | CA | ES | ............... | ............... | |
| Do .................... | Chief Operating Officer | ......do ...................... | CA | ES | ............... | ............... | |
| Do .................... | Director, Technical and Project Management Division. | ......do ...................... | CA | ES | ............... | ............... | |
| Do .................... | Senior Advisor | Daniel Nicholas .................. | SC | GS | 15 | ............... | |
| | **OFFICE OF STRATEGIC PLANNING AND POLICY** | | | | | | |
| Do .................... | Executive Director | Benjamin Tyler Reinke ........ | SC | SL | $176,905 | ............... | |
| Do .................... | Deputy Director | Allison Anne Bury .............. | SC | GS | 14 | ............... | |
| | **OFFICE OF POLICY** | | | | | | |
| Do .................... | Special Assistant | Mckenzie Brooke Bobbitt..... | SC | GS | 9 | ............... | |
| | **OFFICE OF CYBERSECURITY, ENERGY SECURITY & EMERGENCY RESPONSE** | | | | | | |
| Do .................... | Assistant Secretary for Cybersecurity, Energy Security & Emergency Response. | Vacant ...................... | PAS | EX | ............... | ............... | |
| Do .................... | Principal Deputy Assistant Secretary | Sean Paul Plankey .............. | NA | ES | ............... | ............... | |
| Do .................... | Deputy Assistant Secretary, Cybersecurity for Energy Delivery Systems. | Vacant ...................... | ............ | ES | ............... | ............... | |
| Do .................... | Deputy Assistant Secretary for Infrastructure Security & Energy Restoration. | Nicholas Maxwell Andersen. | NA | ES | ............... | ............... | |
| Do .................... | Senior Advisor and Director of Strategic Initiatives. | Pedro M Allende .................. | SC | GS | 15 | ............... | |
| Do .................... | Special Advisor | Timothy Kocher .................. | SC | GS | 11 | ............... | |
| Do .................... | Special Assistant for Integration Services | Anthony Rene Travieso........ | SC | GS | 11 | ............... | |
| | **OFFICE OF ENTERPRISE ASSESSMENTS** | | | | | | |
| Do .................... | Director, Office of Enterprise Assessments | Career Incumbent ................ | CA | ES | ............... | ............... | |
| Do .................... | Director, Office of Cyber Assessments | ......do ...................... | CA | ES | ............... | ............... | |
| Do .................... | Director, Office of the National Training Center. | ......do ...................... | CA | ES | ............... | ............... | |
| Germantown, MD.... | Director, Office of Resources, Communications and Analysis. | ......do ...................... | CA | ES | ............... | ............... | |
| Do .................... | Director, Office of Analysis and Evaluation | ......do ...................... | CA | ES | ............... | ............... | |
| Do .................... | Deputy Director, Office of Resources, Communications, and Analysis. | ......do ...................... | CA | ES | ............... | ............... | |
| | **OFFICE OF GENERAL COUNSEL** | | | | | | |
| Washington, DC ...... | General Counsel | William Sherman Cooper III. | PAS | EX | IV | ............... | |
| Do .................... | Deputy General Counsel | Career Incumbent ................ | CA | ES | ............... | ............... | |
| Do .................... | Deputy General Counsel for Litigation | Joseph Desanctis .................. | NA | ES | ............... | ............... | |
| Do .................... | Deputy General Counsel for Energy Policy | Mark Russell Robeck .......... | NA | ES | ............... | ............... | |
| Do .................... | Deputy General Counsel for Compliance | Gary Michael Brown II ........ | NA | ES | ............... | ............... | |
| Do .................... | Assistant General Counsel for Electricity | Career Incumbent ................ | CA | ES | ............... | ............... | |
| Do .................... | Assistant General Counsel for Environment | ......do ...................... | CA | ES | ............... | ............... | |
| Do .................... | Assistant General Counsel, Federal Litigation | ......do ...................... | CA | ES | ............... | ............... | |
| Do .................... | Assistant General Counsel for International and National Security Programs. | ......do ...................... | CA | ES | ............... | ............... | |
| Do .................... | Assistant General Counsel, Civilian Nuclear Programs. | ......do ...................... | CA | ES | ............... | ............... | |
| Do .................... | Assistant General Counsel for Legislation, Regulation and Energy Efficiency. | ......do ...................... | CA | ES | ............... | ............... | |
| Do .................... | Director, Office of Standard Contract Management. | ......do ...................... | CA | ES | ............... | ............... | |
| Do .................... | Counselor to the Secretary | Emily Singer ...................... | SC | GS | 15 | ............... | |
| Do .................... | Attorney-Advisor | William Eugene Cody Esq. .. | SC | GS | 15 | ............... | |
| Do .................... | Attorney-Adviser | Charles Woo Park .............. | SC | GS | 15 | ............... | |
| Do .................... | Attorney-Advisor | Shawn Michael Flynn ......... | SC | GS | 14 | ............... | |
| Do .................... | Senior Oversight Advisor | Alexa Mae Armstrong ......... | SC | GS | 14 | ............... | |
| Do .................... | Senior Advisor | Janet R Naughton ................ | SC | GS | 13 | ............... | |
| | **OFFICE OF PUBLIC AFFAIRS** | | | | | | |
| Do .................... | Director of Strategic Communications and Messaging. | William Joseph Turenne Jr.. | SC | GS | 15 | ............... | |

## DEPARTMENT OF ENERGY—Continued

| Location | Position Title | Name of Incumbent | Type of Appt. | Pay Plan | Level, Grade, or Pay | Tenure | Expires |
|---|---|---|---|---|---|---|---|
| Washington, DC ...... | Writer- Editor (Chief Speechwriter).................... | Paul Howard Liben ............. | SC | GS | 15 | .............. | |
| Do .................. | Director of Communications ............................ | Kelsey Mellar Knight........... | SC | GS | 15 | .............. | |
| Do .................. | Press Secretary .............................................. | Shaylyn Hynes...................... | SC | GS | 15 | .............. | |
| Do .................. | Writer-Editor (Speechwriter) ............................ | Rebecca Starr Brown .......... | SC | GS | 13 | .............. | |
| Do .................. | Deputy Press Secretary ................................... | Jessica Murphy Szymanski . | SC | GS | 12 | .............. | |
| Do .................. | Deputy Creative Director ................................. | Ryan Patrick Flynn ............. | SC | GS | 12 | .............. | |
| Do .................. | Writer-Editor (Speechwriter) ............................ | Gregory Clement Lemon...... | SC | GS | 12 | .............. | |
| Do .................. | Senior Content Creator ................................... | Rachael Jane Oury.............. | SC | GS | 12 | .............. | |
| Do .................. | Deputy Press Secretary ................................... | Miki Allison Carver............. | SC | GS | 11 | .............. | |
| Do .................. | Writer-Editor (Speechwriter) ............................ | Timothy J Meads................. | SC | GS | 11 | .............. | |
| Do .................. | Press Assistant .............................................. | Claire Young Nance............. | SC | GS | 7 | .............. | |
| | **OFFICE OF SMALL AND DISADVANTAGED BUSINESS UTILIZATION** | | | | | | |
| Do .................. | Director Office of Small and Disadvantaged Business Utilization. | Charles Robert Smith .......... | NA | ES | .............. | .............. | |
| Do .................. | Senior Advisor................................................ | Briana Turpin McClain....... | SC | GS | 15 | .............. | |
| Do .................. | ....do .............................................. | Jennifer Katherine Crone.... | SC | GS | 13 | .............. | |
| | **OFFICE OF THE CHIEF FINANCIAL OFFICER** | | | | | | |
| Do .................. | Chief Financial Officer .................................... | Vacant ................................. | PAS | EX | IV | .............. | |
| Do .................. | Chief Performance Officer................................. | James Patrick Herz............. | NA | ES | .............. | .............. | |
| Do .................. | Chief Risk Officer .......................................... | Career Incumbent ............... | CA | ES | .............. | .............. | |
| | **U.S. ENERGY INFORMATION ADMINISTRATION** | | | | | | |
| Do .................. | Administrator-Energy Information Administration. | Linda Ann Capuano ............. | PAS | EX | IV | .............. | |
| Do .................. | Senior Advisor................................................ | Career Incumbent ............... | CA | ES | .............. | .............. | |
| | **ASSISTANT SECRETARY FOR ENVIRONMENTAL MANAGEMENT** | | | | | | |
| Do .................. | Assistant Secretary of Energy (Environmental Management). | Vacant ................................. | PAS | EX | IV | .............. | |
| Do .................. | Principal Deputy Assistant Secretary for Environmental Management. | Career Incumbent ............... | CA | ES | .............. | .............. | |
| Do .................. | Chief of Staff ................................................ | Vacant ................................. | | ES | .............. | .............. | |
| Do .................. | Deputy Assistant Secretary for Acquisition and Project Management. | Career Incumbent ............... | CA | ES | .............. | .............. | |
| Do .................. | Deputy Assistant Secretary for Safety, Security and Quality. | Vacant ................................. | | ES | .............. | .............. | |
| Do .................. | Deputy Assistant Secretary for Waste and Materials Management. | Career Incumbent ............... | CA | ES | .............. | .............. | |
| Do .................. | Deputy Assistant Secretary for Resource Management. | ......do ................... | CA | ES | .............. | .............. | |
| Do .................. | Associate Principal Deputy Assistant Secretary for Corporate Services. | ......do ................... | CA | ES | .............. | .............. | |
| Do .................. | Associate Principal Deputy Assistant Secretary for Regulatory & Policy Affairs. | ......do ................... | CA | ES | .............. | .............. | |
| Do .................. | Assoicate Principal Deputy Assistant Secretary for Field Operations. | Vacant ................................. | | ES | .............. | .............. | |
| Do .................. | Associate Deputy Assistant Secretary for Field Operations Oversight (Chief of Nuclear Safety). | Career Incumbent ............... | CA | ES | .............. | .............. | |
| Do .................. | Director for Budget and Planning ...................... | ......do ................... | CA | ES | .............. | .............. | |
| Los Alamos, NM ...... | Manager, Environmental Management Los Alamos Field Office. | ......do ................... | CA | ES | .............. | .............. | |
| Washington, DC ...... | Director for Information Systems...................... | ......do ................... | CA | ES | .............. | .............. | |
| Do .................. | Chief of Staff ................................................ | Thomas Francis Mooney...... | SC | GS | 15 | .............. | |
| Do .................. | Senior Advisor ............................................... | Gina Miles .......................... | SC | GS | 15 | .............. | |
| Do .................. | ....do .............................................. | Leonard Spearman Jr. ......... | SC | GS | 15 | .............. | |
| Do .................. | Special Assistant............................................ | Daniel S Thayer................... | SC | GS | 7 | .............. | |
| | *Carlsbad Field Office* | | | | | | |
| Carlsbad, NM .......... | Manager, Carlsbad Field Office ........................ | Vacant ................................. | | ES | .............. | .............. | |
| Do .................. | Deputy Manager Carlsbad Field Office............... | ......do ................... | | ES | .............. | .............. | |
| | *Environmental Management Consolidated Business Center* | | | | | | |
| Cincinnati, OH ....... | Director, Consolidated Business Center............. | Career Incumbent ............... | CA | ES | .............. | .............. | |
| Do .................. | Deputy Director, Environmental Management Consolidated Business Center. | ......do ................... | CA | ES | .............. | .............. | |
| | *Portsmouth/Paducah Project Office* | | | | | | |
| Lexington, KY ........ | Manager, Portsmouth and Paducah Sites .......... | ......do ................... | CA | ES | .............. | .............. | |

## DEPARTMENT OF ENERGY—Continued

| Location | Position Title | Name of Incumbent | Type of Appt. | Pay Plan | Level, Grade, or Pay | Tenure | Expires |
|---|---|---|---|---|---|---|---|
| Lexington, KY ......... | Deputy Manager, Portsmouth Paducah Project Office. | Career Incumbent ................ | CA | ES | ................ | ................ | |
| | *Richland Operations Office* | | | | | | |
| Richland, WA........... | Manager, Richland Operations Office............... | Vacant ........................ | ............ | ES | ................ | ................ | |
| Do .................... | Manager Office of River Protection ................... | Brian Vance ................ | TA | ES | ................ | ................ | 11/05/20 |
| Do .................... | Deputy Manager, Richland Operations Office ... | Career Incumbent ........ | CA | ES | ................ | ................ | |
| Do .................... | Deputy Manager, Office of River Protection ..... | ......do ........................ | CA | ES | ................ | ................ | |
| Do .................... | Assistant Manager for Business and Financial Operations (Chief Financial Officer). | ......do ........................ | CA | ES | ................ | ................ | |
| Do .................... | Assistant Manager for Mission Support ........... | ......do ........................ | CA | ES | ................ | ................ | |
| Do .................... | Assistant Manager for River and Plateau ........ | ......do ........................ | CA | ES | ................ | ................ | |
| Do .................... | Assistant Manager for Technical and Regulatory Support. | ......do ........................ | CA | ES | ................ | ................ | |
| Do .................... | Assistant Manager for Waste Treatment Operations. | ......do ........................ | CA | ES | ................ | ................ | |
| Do .................... | Assistant Manager for Waste Treatment and Immobilization Plant Project. | ......do ........................ | CA | ES | ................ | ................ | |
| Do .................... | Assistant Manager for Tank Farms Project ...... | ......do ........................ | CA | ES | ................ | ................ | |
| | *Savannah River Operations Office* | | | | | | |
| Aiken, SC ................ | Manager, Savannah River Operations Office..... | ......do ........................ | CA | ES | ................ | ................ | |
| Do .................... | Deputy Manager ....................... | ......do ........................ | CA | ES | ................ | ................ | |
| Do .................... | Director, Salt Waste Processing Facility Project Office. | ......do ........................ | CA | ES | ................ | ................ | |
| Do .................... | Assistant Manager for Infrastructure and Environmental Stewardship. | ......do ........................ | CA | ES | ................ | ................ | |
| Do .................... | Assistant Manager for Nuclear Material Stabilization Project. | ......do ........................ | CA | ES | ................ | ................ | |
| Do .................... | Assistant Manager for Waste Disposition Project. | ......do ........................ | CA | ES | ................ | ................ | |
| | **ASSOCIATE UNDER SECRETARY FOR ENVIRONMENT, HEALTH, SAFETY AND SECURITY** | | | | | | |
| Washington, DC ...... | Associate Under Secretary for Environment, Health, Safety and Security. | ......do ........................ | CA | ES | ................ | ................ | |
| Do .................... | Deputy Associate Under Secretary for Environment, Health and Safety. | ......do ........................ | CA | ES | ................ | ................ | |
| Germantown, MD.... | Director, Office of Classification ........................ | ......do ........................ | CA | ES | ................ | ................ | |
| Washington, DC ...... | Director, Office of Corporate Security Strategy, Analysis and Special Operations. | ......do ........................ | CA | ES | ................ | ................ | |
| Do .................... | Director Office of the Departmental Representative to the Defense Nuclear Facilities Safety Board. | ......do ........................ | CA | ES | ................ | ................ | |
| Do .................... | Director, Headquarters Security Operations .... | ......do ........................ | CA | ES | ................ | ................ | |
| Do .................... | Director, Office of Health and Safety................ | ......do ........................ | CA | ES | ................ | ................ | |
| Germantown, MD.... | Director, Office of Resource Management.......... | ......do ........................ | CA | ES | ................ | ................ | |
| Do .................... | Director, Office of Security .............................. | ......do ........................ | CA | ES | ................ | ................ | |
| | **OFFICE OF ECONOMIC IMPACT AND DIVERSITY** | | | | | | |
| Washington, DC ...... | Director of the Office of Minority Economic Impact. | James Edward Campos........ | PAS | EX | IV | ................ | |
| Do .................... | Principal Deputy Director............................. | Career Incumbent ................ | CA | ES | ................ | ................ | |
| Do .................... | Senior Advisor .......................... | ......do ........................ | CA | ES | ................ | ................ | |
| Do .................... | Chief, Energy Workforce Division...................... | Huston Tyler Pullen............ | SC | GS | 15 | ................ | |
| Do .................... | Chief of Staff .......................... | Neri Ann Martinez ............... | SC | GS | 13 | ................ | |
| Do .................... | Senior Advisor on Civil Rights, Equal Employment Opportunity and Diversity and Inclusion. | Kelly Yvonne Mitchell.......... | SC | GS | 13 | ................ | |
| Do .................... | Senior Advisor on Minority Education .............. | Janelle N Moore .................. | SC | GS | 12 | ................ | |
| Do .................... | Special Advisor .......................... | Kristin Elizabeth Repass ..... | SC | GS | 11 | ................ | |
| | **OFFICE OF LEGACY MANAGEMENT** | | | | | | |
| Do .................... | Director.......................... | Career Incumbent ................ | CA | ES | ................ | ................ | |
| Do .................... | Deputy Director, Legacy Management ............. | ......do ........................ | CA | ES | ................ | ................ | |
| | **OFFICE OF MANAGEMENT** | | | | | | |
| Do .................... | Director, Office of the Executive Secretariat...... | Rachael J Beitler................ | NA | ES | ................ | ................ | |
| Do .................... | Director, Office of Management ......................... | Career Incumbent ................ | CA | ES | ................ | ................ | |
| Do .................... | Director, Office of Asset Management ............... | ......do ........................ | CA | ES | ................ | ................ | |
| Do .................... | Director, Office of Contract Management........... | ......do ........................ | CA | ES | ................ | ................ | |
| Do .................... | Deputy Director, Office of Acquisition Management. | ......do ........................ | CA | ES | ................ | ................ | |
| Do .................... | Chief Operating Officer for Research Management Operations. | Vacant ........................ | ............ | ES | ................ | ................ | |

## DEPARTMENT OF ENERGY—Continued

| Location | Position Title | Name of Incumbent | Type of Appt. | Pay Plan | Level, Grade, or Pay | Tenure | Expires |
|---|---|---|---|---|---|---|---|
| Washington, DC ...... | Senior Advisor............................................ | Preston Wells Griffith III..... | NA | ES | .............. | .............. | |
| Do ................... | ......do ......................................... | Samuel Buchan ................... | SC | GS | 15 | .............. | |
| Do ................... | ......do ......................................... | Andrew L Horn...................... | SC | GS | 15 | .............. | |
| Do ................... | ......do ......................................... | Robert Charles Greenway.... | SC | GS | 15 | .............. | |
| Do ................... | Senior Advisor to the Staff Secretary............... | Zead Haddad...................... | SC | GS | 15 | .............. | |
| Do ................... | Senior Advisor for Special Projects.................... | Joshua James Jones............ | SC | GS | 15 | .............. | |
| Do ................... | Director of Advance ...................................... | Raymond Anthony Casler.... | SC | GS | 15 | .............. | |
| Do ................... | Advance Lead ............................................. | Auria Mcalicher.................. | SC | GS | 15 | .............. | |
| Do ................... | Senior Advisor............................................ | Sierra Cato......................... | SC | GS | 13 | .............. | |
| Do ................... | Deputy Director of Operations for Scheduling .. | Noelle Madison Spencer ...... | SC | GS | 12 | .............. | |
| Do ................... | Deputy Director of Scheduling...................... | Ashley Ann Hebert.............. | SC | GS | 12 | .............. | |
| Do ................... | Special Assistant to the Staff Secretary........... | Daniel Horning.................... | SC | GS | 12 | .............. | |
| Do ................... | Deputy Director of Operations for Advance....... | Christopher John Kojaian ... | SC | GS | 12 | .............. | |
| Do ................... | Advance Representative................................. | Michael Arthur Watson........ | SC | GS | 11 | .............. | |
| Do ................... | Advance Lead ............................................. | Michael Joseph Ditlevson .... | SC | GS | 11 | .............. | |
| Do ................... | Special Assistant ......................................... | Fiona Gabrielle Obeirne ...... | SC | GS | 11 | .............. | |
| Do ................... | Operations Manager ..................................... | Lucille Powers ................... | SC | GS | 11 | .............. | |
| Do ................... | Trip Coordinator .......................................... | Aliya Ruth Boyer................. | SC | GS | 11 | .............. | |
| Do ................... | Operations Assistant .................................... | James Ronan ...................... | SC | GS | 9 | .............. | |
| | **OFFICE OF THE CHIEF HUMAN CAPITAL OFFICER** | | | | | | |
| Do ................... | Chief Human Capital Officer............................ | Career Incumbent .............. | CA | ES | .............. | .............. | |
| | **OFFICE OF THE CHIEF INFORMATION OFFICER** | | | | | | |
| Do ................... | Chief Information Officer............................... | ......do ........................ | CA | ES | .............. | .............. | |
| Germantown, MD.... | Principal Deputy Chief Information Officer ...... | ......do ........................ | CA | ES | .............. | .............. | |
| Do ................... | Deputy Chief Information Officer for Enterprise Operations and Shared Services. | ......do ........................ | CA | ES | .............. | .............. | |
| Washington, DC ...... | Deputy Chief Information Officer for Architecture, Engineering, Technology and Innovation. | ......do ........................ | CA | ES | .............. | .............. | |
| Do ................... | Deputy Chief Information Officer for Cybersecurity. | ......do ........................ | CA | ES | .............. | .............. | |
| Do ................... | Deputy Chief Information Officer for Resources Management. | ......do ........................ | CA | ES | .............. | .............. | |
| Do ................... | Deputy Chief Information Officer for Enterprise Records Management, Privacy & Compliance. | ......do ........................ | CA | ES | .............. | .............. | |
| | **ASSISTANT SECRETARY FOR ELECTRICITY** | | | | | | |
| Do ................... | Assistant Secretary Office of Electricity ........... | Bruce John Walker.............. | PAS | EX | IV | .............. | |
| Do ................... | Principal Deputy Assistant Secretary ............... | Career Incumbent .............. | CA | ES | .............. | .............. | |
| Do ................... | Deputy Assistant Secretary, Transmission Permitting and Technical Assistance. | ......do ........................ | CA | ES | .............. | .............. | |
| Do ................... | Deputy Assistant Secretary for Advanced Grid Research and Development. | ......do ........................ | CA | ES | .............. | .............. | |
| Phoenix, AZ ........... | Senior Advisor ............................................ | Douglas Blane Little ........... | NA | ES | .............. | .............. | |
| Washington, DC ...... | Special Advisor........................................... | Juan Caro ......................... | SC | GS | 12 | .............. | |
| Do ................... | ......do ......................................... | Emily Brigid Burdick........... | SC | GS | 11 | .............. | |
| Do ................... | ......do ......................................... | Andrew Douglas Farquharson. | SC | GS | 11 | .............. | |
| Do ................... | Special Assistant.......................................... | Evan Paul Echols ................ | SC | GS | 7 | .............. | |
| | *Bonneville Power Administration* | | | | | | |
| Portland, OR........... | Administrator and Chief Executive Officer ....... | Career Incumbent .............. | CA | ES | .............. | .............. | |
| Do ................... | Chief Administrative Officer ........................... | ......do ........................ | CA | ES | .............. | .............. | |
| Do ................... | Executive Vice President, Compliance and Risk Management. | ......do ........................ | CA | ES | .............. | .............. | |
| | *Southeastern Power Administration* | | | | | | |
| Elberton, GA........... | Administrator, Southeastern Power Administration. | Vacant .............................. | .............. | ES | .............. | .............. | |
| | *Southwestern Power Administration* | | | | | | |
| Tulsa, OK................. | Administrator Southwestern Power Administration. | Career Incumbent .............. | CA | ES | .............. | .............. | |
| | *Western Area Power Administration* | | | | | | |
| Lakewood, CO ........ | Administrator, Western Area Power Administration. | ......do ........................ | CA | ES | .............. | .............. | |

## DEPARTMENT OF ENERGY—Continued

| Location | Position Title | Name of Incumbent | Type of Appt. | Pay Plan | Level, Grade, or Pay | Tenure | Expires |
|---|---|---|---|---|---|---|---|
| | **ASSISTANT SECRETARY FOR ENERGY EFFICIENCY AND RENEWABLE ENERGY** | | | | | | |
| Washington, DC ...... | Assistant Secretary (Energy Efficiency and Renewable Energy). | Daniel Simmons ................... | PAS | EX | IV | ............... | |
| Do .................. | Deputy Assistant Secretary for Energy Efficiency. | Alexander Nicholas Fitzsimmons. | NA | ES | ............. | ............. | |
| Do .................. | Deputy Assistant Secretary for Operations ...... | Career Incumbent ............... | CA | ES | ............. | ............. | |
| Do .................. | Deputy Assistant Secretary of Renewable Power. | David F Solan .................. | NA | ES | ............. | ............. | |
| Do .................. | Deputy Assistant Secretary for Transportation. | Vacant .............. | ............. | ES | ............. | ............. | |
| Do .................. | Director, Building Technologies Office............ | Career Incumbent ............... | CA | ES | ............. | ............. | |
| Do .................. | Director, Bioenergy Technology Office............ | ......do | CA | ES | ............. | ............. | |
| Do .................. | Director, Budget Office ........................ | Vacant .............. | ............. | ES | ............. | ............. | |
| Do .................. | Director, Business Services Division ............... | ......do | ............. | ES | ............. | ............. | |
| Do .................. | Director, Federal Energy Management Programs Office. | Career Incumbent ............... | CA | ES | ............. | ............. | |
| Do .................. | Director, Fuel Cell Technologies Office.............. | ......do | CA | ES | ............. | ............. | |
| Do .................. | Director, Geothermal Technologies Office ......... | ......do | CA | ES | ............. | ............. | |
| Do .................. | Director, Solar Energy Technologies Office ...... | ......do | CA | ES | ............. | ............. | |
| Do .................. | Director, Vehicle Technologies Office ............. | ......do | CA | ES | ............. | ............. | |
| Do .................. | Director, Weatherization and Integrovernmental Program Office. | ......do | CA | ES | ............. | ............. | |
| Do .................. | Director, Wind Energy Technologies Office ...... | Vacant .............. | ............. | ES | ............. | ............. | |
| Do .................. | Director, Water Power Technologies Office......... | Career Incumbent ............... | CA | ES | ............. | ............. | |
| Do .................. | Deputy Director, Office of Solar Energy Technology Programs. | ......do | CA | ES | ............. | ............. | |
| Do .................. | Deputy Director, Vehicle Technologies Office..... | ......do | CA | ES | ............. | ............. | |
| Do .................. | Director, Project Management Coordination Office. | Vacant .............. | ............. | ES | ............. | ............. | |
| Golden, CO ............ | Manager, Golden Field Office................ | Career Incumbent ............... | CA | ES | ............. | ............. | |
| Washington, DC ...... | Senior Advisor................ | Justin Bis ............... | SC | GS | 15 | ............. | |
| Do .................. | Chief of Staff................ | Zachery T Michael............... | SC | GS | 15 | ............. | |
| Do .................. | Senior Advisor................ | Kevin Alan Jayne ............... | SC | GS | 13 | ............. | |
| Do .................. | Special Advisor................ | Catherine Beatrice Moeder-Brady. | SC | GS | 13 | ............. | |
| Do .................. | Senior Advisor................ | Reid Evan Dagul ............... | SC | GS | 12 | ............. | |
| Do .................. | Special Assistant................ | Hannah Elizabeth Craig...... | SC | GS | 11 | ............. | |
| Do .................. | ......do | Maria Victoria Pereyra-Vera. | SC | GS | 11 | ............. | |
| | **ASSISTANT SECRETARY FOR FOSSIL ENERGY** | | | | | | |
| Do .................. | Assistant Secretary for Fossil Energy ............ | Steven Eric Winberg ............ | PAS | EX | IV | ............. | |
| Do .................. | Principal Deputy Assistant Secretary ............... | Kenneth King Humphreys Jr.. | NA | ES | ............... | ............. | |
| Do .................. | Deputy Assistant Secretary for Oil and Natural Gas. | Shawn P Bennett ................. | NA | ES | ............. | ............. | |
| Do .................. | Deputy Assistant Secretary for Clean Coal and Carbon Management. | Louis Hrkman Jr. ................. | NA | ES | ............. | ............. | |
| Do .................. | Deputy Assistant Secretary for Petroleum Reserves. | Career Incumbent ............... | CA | ES | ............. | ............. | |
| Bruceton, PA............ | Director National Energy Technology Laboratory. | ......do | CA | ES | ............. | ............. | |
| Washington, DC ...... | Associate Deputy Assistant Secretary for Clean Coal and Carbon Management. | Vacant ................. | ............. | ES | ............. | ............. | |
| Do .................. | Associate Deputy Assistant Secretary for Petroleum Reserves. | Career Incumbent ............... | CA | ES | ............. | ............. | |
| Do .................. | Deputy Assistant Secretary for Operations ...... | ......do | CA | ES | ............. | ............. | |
| Do .................. | Associate Deputy Assistant Secretary for Clean Coal and Carbon Management. | ......do | CA | ES | ............. | ............. | |
| Do .................. | Chief of Staff................ | Michael Tadeo................ | SC | GS | 15 | ............. | |
| Do .................. | Senior Advisor................ | Dane Michael Bahnsen ....... | SC | GS | 15 | ............. | |
| | **ASSISTANT SECRETARY FOR NUCLEAR ENERGY** | | | | | | |
| Do .................. | Assistant Secretary for Energy (Nuclear Energy). | Rita Baranwal ...................... | PAS | EX | IV | ............. | |
| Do .................. | Principal Deputy Assistant Secretary ............... | Vacant ................. | ............. | ES | ............. | ............. | |
| Germantown, MD.... | Deputy Assistant Secretary ................ | Career Incumbent ............... | CA | ES | ............. | ............. | |
| Do .................. | Deputy Assistant Secretary for Nuclear Infrastructure Programs. | ......do | CA | ES | ............. | ............. | |
| Washington, DC ...... | Deputy Assistant Secretary for Reactor Fleet and Advanced Reactor Deployment. | ......do | CA | ES | ............. | ............. | |

## DEPARTMENT OF ENERGY—Continued

| Location | Position Title | Name of Incumbent | Type of Appt. | Pay Plan | Level, Grade, or Pay | Tenure | Expires |
|---|---|---|---|---|---|---|---|
| Washington, DC ...... | Senior Advisor | Suzanne Jaworowski | SC | GS | 15 | | |
| Do | ......do | Madeline K Lefton | SC | GS | 14 | | |
| Do | Special Advisor | Anushya Ramaswamy | SC | GS | 12 | | |
| Do | Special Assistant | Mark Clifford Yale | SC | GS | 9 | | |
| | **OFFICE OF INDIAN ENERGY POLICY AND PROGRAMS** | | | | | | |
| Do | Director Office of Indian Energy Policy and Programs. | Frost Ray Kevin | XS | AD | | | |
| | **OFFICE OF PROJECT MANAGEMENT OVERSIGHT AND ASSESSMENTS** | | | | | | |
| Do | Director, Office of Project Management Oversight and Assessments. | Career Incumbent | CA | ES | | | |
| | **OFFICE OF SCIENCE** | | | | | | |
| Do | Director, Office of Science | Christopher Fall | PAS | EX | IV | | |
| Do | Principal Deputy Director, Office of Science | Career Incumbent | CA | ES | | | |
| Do | Deputy Director for Field Operations | ......do | CA | ES | | | |
| Do | Deputy Director for Resource Management | Vacant | | ES | | | |
| Do | Deputy Director for Science Programs | Career Incumbent | CA | ES | | | |
| Germantown, MD.... | Associate Deputy Director for Field Operations. | ......do | CA | ES | | | |
| Do | Director, Biological Systems Sciences Division.. | ......do | CA | ES | | | |
| Do | Director, Chemical Sciences, Geoscience and Bioscience Division. | ......do | CA | ES | | | |
| Do | Director, Climate and Environmental Sciences Division. | ......do | CA | ES | | | |
| Do | Director, Computational Science Research and Partnership Division. | Vacant | | ES | | | |
| Do | Director, Facilities Division | Career Incumbent | CA | ES | | | |
| Do | Director Facilities Operations and Projects | ......do | CA | ES | | | |
| Do | Director, Facility and Project Management Division. | ......do | CA | ES | | | |
| Do | Director, High Energy Research and Technology Division. | ......do | CA | ES | | | |
| Do | Director Information Technology Services Division. | ......do | CA | ES | | | |
| Do | Director, Material Sciences and Engineering Division. | Vacant | | ES | | | |
| Do | Director, Office of Budget | Career Incumbent | CA | ES | | | |
| Washington, DC ...... | Director, Office of Engineering and Technology. | ......do | CA | ES | | | |
| Germantown, MD.... | Director, Office of Field Operations Safety, Security and Infrastructure. | ......do | CA | ES | | | |
| Do | Director, Office of Project Assessment | ......do | CA | ES | | | |
| Do | Director Research Division | Vacant | | ES | | | |
| Do | Director, Scientific User Facilities | ......do | | ES | | | |
| Do | Associate Director, Office of Advanced Scientific Computing. | Career Incumbent | CA | ES | | | |
| Do | Associate Director, Office of Basic Energy Sciences. | ......do | CA | ES | | | |
| Do | Associate Director, Office of Biological and Environmental Research. | ......do | CA | ES | | | |
| Do | Associate Director, Office of Fusion Energy Sciences. | ......do | CA | ES | | | |
| Do | Associate Director, Office of High Energy Physics. | ......do | CA | ES | | | |
| Do | Associate Director, Office of Nuclear Physics .... | ......do | CA | ES | | | |
| Oak Ridge, TN ........ | Manager, Consolidated Service Center | ......do | CA | ES | | | |
| Do | Deputy Manager, Consolidated Service Center . | ......do | CA | ES | | | |
| Washington, DC ...... | Senior Advisor | ......do | CA | ES | | | |
| Do | ......do | James Clark Akin | SC | GS | 15 | | |
| Do | ......do | Charles Cunningham | SC | GS | 15 | | |
| Do | ......do | Daniel Wilmot | SC | GS | 15 | | |
| Do | ......do | Marilu Andrea Yuzon | SC | GS | 14 | | |
| Do | ......do | Penelope Marie Jones | SC | GS | 13 | | |
| Do | Chief of Staff | Steven Troy Hall | SC | GS | 12 | | |
| Do | Special Advisor | Brandon Zanon | SC | GS | 12 | | |
| | **OFFICE OF TECHNOLOGY TRANSITION** | | | | | | |
| Do | Director and Chief Commercialization Officer .. | Conner Hahn Prochaska | SC | GS | 15 | | |
| Chicago, IL.............. | Regional Engagement Executive | Sarah Habansky | SC | GS | 15 | | |
| Washington, DC ...... | Senior Advisor | Elise Kilpatrick Atkins | SC | GS | 14 | | |
| Do | ......do | Phillip Kyle Wiley | SC | GS | 13 | | |
| Do | Special Advisor | Aaron David Michael | SC | GS | 12 | | |

## DEPARTMENT OF ENERGY OFFICE OF THE INSPECTOR GENERAL

| Location | Position Title | Name of Incumbent | Type of Appt. | Pay Plan | Level, Grade, or Pay | Tenure | Expires |
|---|---|---|---|---|---|---|---|
| Idaho Falls, ID | Senior Advisor | Johnathan Black | | ES | | 2 Years | |
| Washington, DC | Inspector General | Teri L Donaldson | PAS | OT | | | |

## DEPARTMENT OF HEALTH AND HUMAN SERVICES

| Location | Position Title | Name of Incumbent | Type of Appt. | Pay Plan | Level, Grade, or Pay | Tenure | Expires |
|---|---|---|---|---|---|---|---|
| | **OFFICE OF THE SECRETARY** | | | | | | |
| Washington, DC | Secretary, Health and Human Services | Alex M Azar II | PAS | EX | I | | |
| Do | Chief of Staff | Brian Edward Harrison | NA | ES | | | |
| Do | Deputy Chief of Staff for Policy Coordination | Paul David Mango | NA | ES | | | |
| Do | Deputy Chief of Staff for Operations and Strategy. | Judith Hope Mayka Stecker | NA | ES | | | |
| Do | Special Assistant to the Deputy Chief of Staff for Operations and Strategy. | Ashton Elizabeth Pollard | SC | GS | 9 | | |
| Do | Senior Advisor, Immediate Office of the Secretary. | Paula Stannard | NA | ES | | | |
| Do | ......do | Danielle Lee Steele | NA | ES | | | |
| Do | ......do | Charles N Keckler | NA | ES | | | |
| Do | ......do | James Thomas Parker | NA | ES | | | |
| Do | Deputy Director and Advisor, Office of Health Reform. | George Sigounas | NA | ES | | | |
| Do | Senior Advisor to the Secretary | Laura Christine Pence | NA | ES | | | |
| Do | Director of Drug Pricing Reform | Tyler Mcguffee | SC | GS | 15 | | |
| Do | Advisor | Nicholas Young Uehlecke | SC | GS | 15 | | |
| Do | Advisor for Value-Based Transformation | Brendan Patrick Fulmer | SC | GS | 13 | | |
| Do | Special Assistant to the Secretary | Matthew John Apple | SC | GS | 9 | | |
| Do | Executive Secretary to the Department | Ann C Agnew | NA | ES | | | |
| Do | Director, Office of Documents and Regulations Management. | Janice M Cotter | SC | GS | 15 | | |
| Do | Briefing Book Coordinator | Cesar Augusto Puesan Juarez. | SC | GS | 7 | | |
| Do | White House Liaison for Political Personnel, Boards and Commissions. | Emily Newman | NA | ES | | | |
| Do | Advisor | Timothy Patrick Kaiser II | SC | GS | 11 | | |
| Do | Special Assistant | Catherine Rose Granito | SC | GS | 9 | | |
| Do | Director of Advance | Horace M Lukens IV | SC | GS | 15 | | |
| Do | Deputy Director of Advance | Carolyn Faye Olson | SC | GS | 14 | | |
| Do | Director of Scheduling | Beth Bernadette Tignor | SC | GS | 14 | | |
| Do | Deputy Scheduler | Katy Covey Morris | SC | GS | 11 | | |
| Do | Advance Representative | John Parker Davis | SC | GS | 11 | | |
| Do | Deputy Executive Secretary | Career Incumbent | CA | ES | | | |
| Do | Senior Advisor | Vacant | | ES | | | |
| Do | Deputy Chief Technology Officer | ......do | | ES | | | |
| Do | Deputy Executive Secretary for Operations | ......do | | ES | | | |
| Do | Senior Advisor | Carl Sciacchitano | TA | ES | | | 02/02/23 |
| Do | ......do | Sanjay J Koyani | TA | ES | | | 01/31/21 |
| | **OFFICE OF THE DEPUTY SECRETARY** | | | | | | |
| Do | Deputy Secretary, Health and Human Services. | Eric D Hargan | PAS | EX | II | | |
| Do | Senior Advisor and Chief of Staff to the Deputy Secretary. | William Michael Brady | NA | ES | | | |
| Do | Assistant to the Deputy Secretary | Kenneth Robert Callahan III. | SC | GS | 13 | | |
| Do | Chair, Departmental Appeals Board | Career Incumbent | CA | ES | | | |
| Do | Member Departmental Appeals Board | Leslie Sussan | XS | SL | | | |
| | **OFFICE OF INTERGOVERNMENTAL AND EXTERNAL AFFAIRS** | | | | | | |
| Do | Director, Office of Intergovernmental and External Affairs. | Laura Clay Trueman | NA | ES | | | |
| Do | Principal Deputy Director, Office of Intergovernmental and External Affairs. | Laura Christine Keehner Rigas. | NA | ES | | | |
| Do | Director, Center for Faith-Based and Neighborhood Partnerships. | Shannon O'Chester Royce. | NA | ES | | | |
| Boston, MA | Regional Director, Boston, Massachusetts, Region I. | John Glenn Mcgough | SC | GS | 15 | | |
| New York, NY | Regional Director, New York, New York, Region II. | Anthony Christie Ferreri | SC | GS | 15 | | |

## DEPARTMENT OF HEALTH AND HUMAN SERVICES—Continued

| Location | Position Title | Name of Incumbent | Type of Appt. | Pay Plan | Level, Grade, or Pay | Tenure | Expires |
|---|---|---|---|---|---|---|---|
| Philadelphia, PA...... | Regional Director Philadelphia Region III........ | Matthew Edward Baker ...... | SC | GS | 15 | ................ | |
| Atlanta, GA ............ | Regional Director, Atlanta,Georgia, Region IV .. | April Clark Weaver .............. | SC | GS | 15 | ................ | |
| Chicago, IL.............. | Regional Director, Chicago, Illinois-Region V .... | Douglas S O'Brien ................ | SC | GS | 15 | ................ | |
| Kansas City, MO ..... | Regional Director, Kansas City, Missouri, Region VII. | William Jeffrey Kahrs.......... | SC | GS | 15 | ................ | |
| Denver, CO ............. | Regional Director, Denver, Colorado, Region VIII. | Susan Elaine Beckman ........ | SC | GS | 15 | ................ | |
| San Francisco, CA ... | Regional Director, San Francisco, California, Region IX. | Edward George Heidig II..... | SC | GS | 15 | ................ | |
| Seattle, WA ............ | Regional Director Region X Seattle ................... | John Robertson Graham ...... | NA | ES | ................ | ................ | |
| Washington, DC ...... | Director of Intergovernmental Affairs................ | Darcie Lang Johnston .......... | SC | GS | 15 | ................ | |
| Do ................... | Director of External Affairs ............................. | Gary Michael Beck .............. | SC | GS | 13 | ................ | |
| Do ................... | External Affairs Specialist ................................ | Erin Kiernan Reilly.............. | SC | GS | 9 | ................ | |
| Do ................... | Special Assistant................................................ | Allie Michelle Hoover.......... | SC | GS | 9 | ................ | |
| | **OFFICE OF THE ASSISTANT SECRETARY FOR ADMINISTRATION** | | | | | | |
| Do ................... | Assistant Secretary for Administration ............ | Scott W Rowell...................... | NA | ES | | ................ | |
| Do ................... | Principal Deputy Assistant Secretary for Administration and Senior Advisor to the Chief of Staff. | Catherine Elaine Bird.......... | NA | ES | | ................ | |
| Do ................... | Deputy Assistant Secretary, Chief Information Officer. | Career Incumbent ................ | CA | ES | | ................ | |
| Do ................... | Deputy Chief Information Officer...................... | Vacant ................................... | ............ | ES | | ................ | |
| Do ................... | Deputy Assistant Secretary for Human Resources. | Career Incumbent ................ | CA | ES | | ................ | |
| Do ................... | Associate Deputy Assistant Secretary for Human Resources. | ......do ................................. | CA | ES | | ................ | |
| Do ................... | Senior Financial Advisor ................................... | ......do ................................. | CA | ES | | ................ | |
| Do ................... | Deputy Assistant Secretary for Acquisitions ..... | ......do ................................. | CA | ES | | ................ | |
| Bethesda, MD ......... | Director, Federal Occupational Health.............. | ......do ................................. | CA | ES | | ................ | |
| Washington, DC ...... | Senior Advisor, Chief Information Officer.......... | Vacant ................................... | ............ | ES | | ................ | |
| Do ................... | Executive Officer............................................... | ......do ................................. | ............ | ES | | ................ | |
| Do ................... | Senior Advisor.................................................... | Julie A Murphy...................... | TA | ES | | ................ | 01/31/22 |
| Do ................... | ......do ............................................................... | Shalley Kim .......................... | TA | ES | | ................ | 03/13/22 |
| Do ................... | ......do ............................................................... | Perryn B Ashmore................ | TA | ES | | ................ | 01/31/22 |
| Do ................... | ......do ............................................................... | Lori L Ruderman.................. | TA | ES | | ................ | 02/01/23 |
| Do ................... | ......do ............................................................... | Career Incumbent ................ | CA | ES | | ................ | |
| Do ................... | Chief Product Officer ........................................ | Vacant ................................... | ............ | ES | | ................ | |
| Do ................... | Chief Modernization Officer.............................. | Career Incumbent ................ | CA | ES | | ................ | |
| | *Program Support Center* | | | | | | |
| Rockville, MD ......... | Director, Program Support Center..................... | ......do ................................. | CA | ES | | ................ | |
| Bethesda, MD ......... | Director, Facilities and Logistics....................... | Vacant ................................... | ............ | ES | | ................ | |
| | **OFFICE OF THE ASSISTANT SECRETARY FOR FINANCIAL RESOURCES** | | | | | | |
| Washington, DC ...... | Assistant Secretary for Financial Resources ..... | ......do ................................. | PAS | EX | IV | ................ | |
| Do ................... | Principal Deputy Assistant Secretary for Financial Resources and Senior Advisor for Operations. | Jennifer Crowley Moughalian. | NA | ES | | ................ | |
| Do ................... | Senior Advisor.................................................... | James Phillip Appel ............ | SC | GS | 15 | ................ | |
| Do ................... | Chief of Staff, Office of the Assistant Secretary for Financial Resources. | Patricia Taylor Hittle .......... | SC | GS | 13 | ................ | |
| Do ................... | Deputy Assistant Secretary for Operations and Management. | Career Incumbent ................ | CA | ES | | ................ | |
| Do ................... | Deputy Assistant Secretary, Congressional Relations. | Caitrin Mccarron Shuy ........ | SC | GS | 15 | ................ | |
| Do ................... | Associate Deputy Assistant Secretary................ | Alexander Dows Pinson ....... | SC | GS | 15 | ................ | |
| Do ................... | Deputy Assistant Secretary, Office of Grants .... | Career Incumbent ................ | CA | ES | | ................ | |
| Do ................... | Director, Office of Financial Policy and Reporting. | ......do ................................. | CA | ES | | ................ | |
| Do ................... | Division Director................................................ | Vacant ................................... | ............ | ES | | ................ | |
| Do ................... | Executive Director ............................................. | ......do ................................. | ............ | ES | | ................ | |
| Do ................... | Senior Advisor.................................................... | Michael S Peckham.............. | TA | ES | | ................ | 11/22/20 |
| | **OFFICE OF THE DEPUTY ASSISTANT SECRETARY FOR BUDGET** | | | | | | |
| Do ................... | Deputy Assistant Secretary, Budget.................. | Career Incumbent ................ | CA | ES | | ................ | |
| Do ................... | Associate Deputy Assistant Secretary, Budget .. | ......do ................................. | CA | ES | | ................ | |
| Do ................... | Director, Division of Budget Policy, Execution, and Review. | ......do ................................. | CA | ES | | ................ | |
| Do ................... | Director, Division of Discretionary Programs .... | ......do ................................. | CA | ES | | ................ | |
| Do ................... | Director, Division of Health Benefits and Income Security. | ......do ................................. | CA | ES | | ................ | |

## DEPARTMENT OF HEALTH AND HUMAN SERVICES—Continued

| Location | Position Title | Name of Incumbent | Type of Appt. | Pay Plan | Level, Grade, or Pay | Tenure | Expires |
|---|---|---|---|---|---|---|---|
| | **OFFICE OF THE DEPUTY ASSISTANT SECRETARY FOR FINANCE** | | | | | | |
| Washington, DC ...... | Director, Office of Program Management and Systems Policy. | Career Incumbent ............... | CA | ES | ............... | ............... | |
| Do .................... | Deputy Assistant Secretary, Finance.................. | ......do ...................... | CA | ES | ............... | ............... | |
| | **OFFICE OF THE ASSISTANT SECRETARY FOR HEALTH** | | | | | | |
| Do .................... | Assistant Secretary, Health................................ | Brett Paul Giroir M.D. ......... | PAS | EX | IV | ............... | |
| Do .................... | Surgeon General ............................................. | Jerome Michael Adams M.D.. | PAS | EX | IV | ............... | |
| Do .................... | Senior Advisor, Office of the Surgeon General... | Career Incumbent ............... | CA | ES | ............... | ............... | |
| Do .................... | Deputy Assistant Secretary for Policy.............. | Steven Richards Valentine Jr.. | NA | ES | ............... | ............... | |
| Do .................... | Senior Advisor................................................... | Mary Martha Mcgeein ........ | NA | ES | ............... | ............... | |
| Rockville, MD ......... | Deputy Assistant Secretary for Population Affairs. | Deborah Diane Foley............ | NA | ES | ............... | ............... | |
| Washington, DC ...... | Director of Media Affairs.................................. | Jennifer Marie Sherman...... | SC | GS | 14 | ............... | |
| Do .................... | Director of External Affairs .............................. | Mia Palmieri Heck ............. | SC | GS | 15 | ............... | |
| Do .................... | Advisor............................................................... | Jacob James Wainwright ..... | SC | GS | 9 | ............... | |
| Do .................... | Deputy Assistant Secretary for Health (Regional Operations). | Career Incumbent ............... | CA | ES | ............... | ............... | |
| Do .................... | Deputy Assistant Secretary for Health (Healthcare Quality). | Vacant .............................. | | ES | ............... | ............... | |
| Do .................... | Deputy Assistant Secretary for Women's Health and Director. | Career Incumbent ............... | CA | ES | ............... | ............... | |
| Do .................... | Chief Information Officer, Executive Director for Information Technology. | ......do ...................... | CA | ES | ............... | ............... | |
| Do .................... | Director, Office of Research Integrity............... | ......do ...................... | CA | ES | ............... | ............... | |
| Do .................... | Deputy Director, Office of Research Integrity.... | ......do ...................... | CA | ES | ............... | ............... | |
| Do .................... | Director of Office of Adolescent Health ............ | Vacant .............................. | | ES | ............... | ............... | |
| Rockville, MD ......... | Senior Advisor to the Assistant Secretary for Health. | ......do ...................... | | ES | ............... | ............... | |
| Washington, DC ...... | Advisor............................................................... | Dolly (Mari) Moorhead........ | SC | GS | 12 | ............... | |
| Do .................... | ......do ....................................................... | Rachel Elise Kellogg ............ | SC | GS | 9 | ............... | |
| Do .................... | Executive Director, Presidents Council on Sports, Fitness, and Nutrition. | Kristina Lyn Harder ............ | SC | GS | 14 | ............... | |
| | **OFFICE OF THE ASSISTANT SECRETARY FOR LEGISLATION** | | | | | | |
| Do .................... | Assistant Secretary for Legislation ................... | Sarah Cudworth Arbes ........ | PAS | EX | IV | ............... | |
| Do .................... | Principal Deputy Assistant Secretary for Legislation. | Vacant .............................. | | ES | ............... | ............... | |
| Do .................... | Deputy Assistant Secretary for Legislation (Mandatory Health Programs). | Rebekah West Armstrong .... | NA | ES | ............... | ............... | |
| Do .................... | Deputy Assistant Secretary for Legislation (Human Services). | Traci Lynn Vitek ................. | NA | ES | ............... | ............... | |
| Do .................... | Deputy Assistant Secretary for Legislation (Mandatory Health Programs and Congressional Liaison). | Sara Nur Morse................... | NA | ES | ............... | ............... | |
| Do .................... | Deputy Assistant Secretary for Legislation (Public Health and Science). | Vacant .............................. | | ES | ............... | ............... | |
| Do .................... | Senior Counselor............................................... | Anne Catherine Parrette Rohall-Andrade Esq.. | NA | ES | ............... | ............... | |
| Do .................... | Deputy Assistant Secretary for Legislation - Oversight and Investigations. | Vacant .............................. | | ES | ............... | ............... | |
| Do .................... | Chief of Staff .................................................... | John Kirkland Twomey........ | SC | GS | 12 | ............... | |
| Do .................... | Director of Congressional Liaison...................... | Courtney Blair Bradway...... | SC | GS | 13 | ............... | |
| Do .................... | Senior Advisor................................................... | Jordan Paschal Cox.............. | SC | GS | 13 | ............... | |
| Do .................... | Special Assistant............................................... | John Emory Boyd ................ | SC | GS | 7 | ............... | |
| Do .................... | Policy Advisor - Oversight and Investigations... | Esther Yocheved Honig ........ | SC | GS | 9 | ............... | |
| Do .................... | Special Assistant............................................... | Maris Virginia Paden .......... | SC | GS | 7 | ............... | |
| | **OFFICE OF THE ASSISTANT SECRETARY FOR PLANNING AND EVALUATION** | | | | | | |
| Do .................... | Assistant Secretary for Planning and Evaluation. | Vacant .............................. | PAS | EX | IV | ............... | |
| Do .................... | Principal Deputy Assistant Secretary for Planning and Evaluation. | ......do ...................... | | ES | ............... | ............... | |
| Do .................... | Deputy Assistant Secretary for Planning and Evaluation (Human Services Policy). | Brenda C Destro................. | NA | ES | ............... | ............... | |
| Do .................... | Deputy Assistant Secretary for Planning and Evaluation (Disablity, Aging, and Long-Term Care Policy). | Arne W Owens..................... | NA | ES | ............... | ............... | |

## DEPARTMENT OF HEALTH AND HUMAN SERVICES—Continued

| Location | Position Title | Name of Incumbent | Type of Appt. | Pay Plan | Level, Grade, or Pay | Tenure | Expires |
|---|---|---|---|---|---|---|---|
| Washington, DC ...... | Associate Deputy Assistant Secretary for Planning and Evaluation (Disability, Aging, and Long-Term Care Policy). | Career Incumbent ................ | CA | ES | ................ | ................ | |
| Do .................... | Deputy Assistant Secretary Planning and Evaluation (Health Policy). | Matthew John Kiley............. | NA | ES | ................ | ................ | |
| Do .................... | Associate Deputy Assistant Secretary for Planning and Evaluation. | Career Incumbent ................ | CA | ES | ................ | ................ | |
| Do .................... | Associate Deputy Assistant Secretary for Planning and Evaluation (Health Policy). | ......do ................ | CA | ES | ................ | ................ | |
| Do .................... | Deputy Assistant Secretary for Planning and Evaluation (Science and Data Policy). | ......do ................ | CA | ES | ................ | ................ | |
| | **OFFICE OF THE ASSISTANT SECRETARY FOR PREPAREDNESS AND RESPONSE** | | | | | | |
| Do .................... | Assistant Secretary for Preparedness and Response. | Robert Peter Kadlec M.D. ..... | PAS | EX | IV | ................ | |
| Do .................... | Deputy Assistant Secretary and Chief of Staff.. | Bryan Russell Shuy............. | NA | ES | ................ | ................ | |
| Do .................... | Senior Advisor.................................................... | Jonathan Hildreth Hayes .... | NA | ES | ................ | ................ | |
| Do .................... | ......do ................ | Zachary Khan Dareshori ..... | SC | GS | 12 | ................ | |
| Do .................... | Advisor............................................................. | Amanda Christine Anger..... | SC | GS | 13 | ................ | |
| Do .................... | Deputy Assistant Secretary for Incident Command and Control. | Vacant ................ | ............ | ES | ................ | ................ | |
| Do .................... | Office Director/Deputy Assistant Secretary for Management Finance and Human Capital. | ......do ................ | ............ | ES | ................ | ................ | |
| Do .................... | Director, Office of Preparedness & Emergency Operations. | Career Incumbent ................ | CA | ES | ................ | ................ | |
| Do .................... | Director of Resource Planning and Evaluation . | ......do ................ | CA | ES | ................ | ................ | |
| Do .................... | Director of Executive Management ................... | ......do ................ | CA | ES | ................ | ................ | |
| Do .................... | Director, Office of Resource Management .......... | Vacant ................ | ............ | ES | ................ | ................ | |
| Do .................... | ......do ................ | Victor Harper................ | TA | ES | ................ | ................ | 11/11/21 |
| Do .................... | Director, Office of Policy and Strategic Planning. | Vacant ................ | ............ | ES | ................ | ................ | |
| Do .................... | Director, Joint Information Center.................... | ......do ................ | ............ | ES | ................ | ................ | |
| Atlanta, GA ........... | Director, Strategic National Stockpile................ | ......do ................ | ............ | ES | ................ | ................ | |
| Washington, DC ...... | Senior Advisor.................................................... | ......do ................ | ............ | ES | ................ | ................ | |
| | **OFFICE OF THE ASSISTANT SECRETARY FOR PUBLIC AFFAIRS** | | | | | | |
| Do .................... | Assistant Secretary for Public Affairs................ | Michael Raymon Caputo...... | PA | EX | IV | ................ | |
| Do .................... | Principal Deputy Assistant Secretary for Public Affairs and Senior Advisor for Operations. | Patrick Murphy .................... | NA | ES | ................ | ................ | |
| Do .................... | Senior Advisor.................................................... | Scott Bradley Traverse ........ | NA | ES | ................ | ................ | |
| Do .................... | ......do ................ | Gordon H Hensley................ | SC | GS | 15 | ................ | |
| Do .................... | Deputy Assistant Secretary, National Spokesperson. | Caitlin Brooke Oakley.......... | SC | GS | 15 | ................ | |
| Do .................... | Special Assistant............................................... | Natalie Evelina Baldassarre. | SC | GS | 11 | ................ | |
| Do .................... | Director, Speechwriting and Editorial Services. | Patrick Theodore Brennan... | SC | GS | 15 | ................ | |
| Do .................... | Deputy Speechwriter ......................................... | Scott Joseph Blakeman........ | SC | GS | 12 | ................ | |
| Do .................... | Director of Communication Strategy and Campaigns. | Michael Joseph Pratt .......... | SC | GS | 15 | ................ | |
| Do .................... | Advisor - Strategic Communications.................. | Timothy Scott Foster............ | SC | GS | 12 | ................ | |
| Do .................... | Press Secretary ................................................ | Katherine Adele Mckeogh.... | SC | GS | 11 | ................ | |
| Do .................... | Special Assistant............................................... | Madeleine Diane Hubbard... | SC | GS | 7 | ................ | |
| Do .................... | Deputy Assistant Secretary for Public Affairs (Public Health). | Career Incumbent ................ | CA | ES | ................ | ................ | |
| Do .................... | Deputy Assistant Secretary for Human Services. | ......do ................ | CA | ES | ................ | ................ | |
| | **OFFICE FOR CIVIL RIGHTS** | | | | | | |
| Do .................... | Director Office for Civil Rights ......................... | Roger Thomas Severino ....... | NA | ES | ................ | ................ | |
| Do .................... | Principal Advisor to the Director........................ | Matthew Scott Bowman........ | NA | ES | ................ | ................ | |
| Do .................... | Principal Deputy Director.................................. | Career Incumbent ................ | CA | ES | ................ | ................ | |
| Do .................... | Deputy Director for Civil Rights........................ | ......do ................ | CA | ES | ................ | ................ | |
| Do .................... | Chief of Staff and Senior Advisor ..................... | Thomas March Bell.............. | NA | ES | ................ | ................ | |
| Do .................... | Special Advisor for Civil Rights......................... | Luciana Estefania Milano ... | SC | GS | 12 | ................ | |
| Do .................... | Special Advisor.................................................. | Maya Michelle Noronha....... | SC | GS | 15 | ................ | |
| Do .................... | Deputy Director for Conscience ......................... | Career Incumbent ................ | CA | ES | ................ | ................ | |
| Do .................... | Senior Advisor for Conscience and Religious Freedom. | Christine Pratt .................... | SC | GS | 14 | ................ | |
| Do .................... | Deputy Director for Health Information Privacy. | Career Incumbent ................ | CA | ES | ................ | ................ | |

## DEPARTMENT OF HEALTH AND HUMAN SERVICES—Continued

| Location | Position Title | Name of Incumbent | Type of Appt. | Pay Plan | Level, Grade, or Pay | Tenure | Expires |
|---|---|---|---|---|---|---|---|
| Washington, DC ...... | Deputy Director, Planning and Business Administration Management. | Career Incumbent ................ | CA | ES | ................ | ................ | |
| | **OFFICE OF THE GENERAL COUNSEL** | | | | | | |
| Do ................. | General Counsel................................ | Robert P Charrow | PAS | EX | IV | | |
| Do ................... | Principal Deputy General Counsel................... | Brian Richard Stimson ....... | NA | ES | ................ | ................ | |
| White Oak, MD ...... | Deputy General Counsel and Chief Counsel, Food and Drug Administration. | Stacy Cline Amin................. | NA | ES | ................ | ................ | |
| Washington, DC ...... | Deputy General Counsel ...................... | William Shih Wei Chang...... | NA | ES | ................ | ................ | |
| Do ................... | Associate General Counsel...................... | Jonah R. Hecht ................. | NA | ES | ................ | ................ | |
| Do ................... | Senior Counsel ...................... | James Ruffin Lawrence III.. | NA | ES | ................ | ................ | |
| Do ................... | Deputy General Counsel ...................... | Brenna Leider...................... | NA | ES | ................ | ................ | |
| Do ................... | Associate Deputy General Counsel.................... | Kyle Patrick Brosnan .......... | SC | GS | 15 | ................ | |
| Do ................... | .......do | Carrie-Lee Early................. | SC | GS | 15 | ................ | |
| Do ................... | ......do | John Harrison Strom .......... | SC | GS | 15 | ................ | |
| Do ................... | Assistant Deputy General Counsel ................ | Tyler Jonathan Sanderson... | SC | GS | 12 | ................ | |
| Do ................... | Advisor and Legal Counsel ...................... | Allison Morgan Beattie........ | SC | GS | 12 | ................ | |
| Do ................... | Assistant to the General Counsel...................... | Caroline Lee White ............ | SC | GS | 13 | ................ | |
| Do ................... | Deputy General Counsel ...................... | Career Incumbent ................ | CA | ES | ................ | ................ | |
| Do ................... | Director, Office of Legal Resources/Executive Officer. | Vacant ...................... | ............ | ES | ................ | ................ | |
| San Francisco, CA... | Chief Counsel (San Francisco)...................... | Career Incumbent ................ | CA | ES | ................ | ................ | |
| Washington, DC ...... | Deputy Program Integrity...................... | ......do | CA | ES | ................ | ................ | |
| Do ................... | Deputy Associate General Counsel for Public Health (National Institutes of Health). | ......do | CA | ES | ................ | ................ | |
| Do ................... | Senior Advisor...................... | Judith R Haron.................... | TA | ES | ................ | ................ | 04/26/22 |
| Do ................... | Associate General Counsel, Civil Rights Division. | Career Incumbent ................ | CA | ES | ................ | ................ | |
| | *Chief Counsels* | | | | | | |
| Atlanta, GA ............ | Chief Counsel, Region Iv...................... | ......do | CA | ES | ................ | ................ | |
| Chicago, IL.............. | Chief Counsel, Region V...................... | ......do | CA | ES | ................ | ................ | |
| Dallas, TX ............... | Chief Counsel, Region Vi...................... | ......do | CA | ES | ................ | ................ | |
| Seattle, WA ............. | Chief Counsel, Region Vii...................... | ......do | CA | ES | ................ | ................ | |
| Denver, CO ............. | Chief Counsel, Region Viii...................... | Vacant ...................... | ............ | ES | ................ | ................ | |
| | *Associate General Counsel Divisions* | | | | | | |
| Washington, DC ...... | Associate General Counsel, Legislation Division. | Career Incumbent ................ | CA | ES | ................ | ................ | |
| Rockville, MD ......... | Associate General Counsel, Public Health........ | ......do | CA | ES | ................ | ................ | |
| Washington, DC ...... | Associate General Counsel, Centers for Medicaid and Medicare Services. | ......do | CA | ES | ................ | ................ | |
| Do ................... | Associate General Counsel Children, Family and Aging Division. | Vacant ...................... | ............ | ES | ................ | ................ | |
| Rockville, MD ......... | Deputy Associate General Counsel for Public Health and Science. | Career Incumbent ................ | CA | ES | ................ | ................ | |
| Washington, DC ...... | Deputy Associate General Counsel for Procurement, Fiscal, and Information Law. | ......do | CA | ES | ................ | ................ | |
| Do ................... | Deputy Associate General Counsel, Centers for Medicare and Medicaid Services Division. | ......do | CA | ES | ................ | ................ | |
| Woodlawn, MD ........ | Deputy Associate General Counsel for Litigation, Centers for Medicare and Medicaid Services Division. | ......do | CA | ES | ................ | ................ | |
| Washington, DC ...... | Deputy Associate General Counsel for Public Health Division. | ......do | CA | ES | ................ | ................ | |
| Atlanta, GA ............ | Deputy Associate General Counsel............... | Vacant ...................... | ............ | ES | ................ | ................ | |
| Rockville, MD .......... | Associate General Counsel, Food and Drug Division. | ......do | ............ | ES | ................ | ................ | |
| | **OFFICE OF GLOBAL AFFAIRS** | | | | | | |
| Washington, DC ...... | Director of Global Affairs ...................... | Glenn Garrett Grigsby........ | NA | ES | ................ | ................ | |
| Do ................... | Principal Deputy Director of Global Affairs and Senior Advisor for Health Diplomacy. | Thomas B Alexander............ | NA | ES | ................ | ................ | |
| Do ................... | Chief of Staff and Senior Advisor ..................... | Kyle Zebley ......................... | SC | GS | 15 | ................ | |
| Do ................... | Special Representative for Global Women's Health. | Valerie Jean Huber ............ | SC | GS | 15 | ................ | |
| Do ................... | Senior Advisor........................................ | Juliana Kimberly Richardson. | SC | GS | 13 | ................ | |
| Do ................... | Director, Office of Pandemics and Emerging Threats. | Career Incumbent ................ | CA | ES | ................ | ................ | |
| | **OFFICE OF MEDICARE HEARINGS AND APPEALS** | | | | | | |
| Do ................... | Executive Director, Office of Medicare Hearings and Appeals. | ......do | CA | ES | ................ | ................ | |

## DEPARTMENT OF HEALTH AND HUMAN SERVICES—Continued

| Location | Position Title | Name of Incumbent | Type of Appt. | Pay Plan | Level, Grade, or Pay | Tenure | Expires |
|---|---|---|---|---|---|---|---|
| Baltimore, MD......... | Executive Director, Program Integrity and Ethics. | Career Incumbent ................ | CA | ES | ................ | ................ | |
| | **OFFICE OF THE NATIONAL COORDINATOR FOR HEALTH INFORMATION TECHNOLOGY** | | | | | | |
| Washington, DC ...... | National Health Information Technology Coordinator. | Donald Walter Rucker.......... | NA | ES | ................ | ................ | |
| Do .................... | Senior Advisor to the National Coordinator for Health Information Technology. | Mark Basil Vafiades............. | SC | GS | 15 | ................ | |
| Do .................... | Principal Deputy National Coordinator for Health Information Technology. | Vacant .................................. | ............. | ES | ................ | ................ | |
| Do .................... | Deputy National Coordinator ....................... | Career Incumbent ................ | CA | ES | ................ | ................ | |
| Do .................... | Deputy National Coordinator for Operations .... | ......do ............................. | CA | ES | ................ | ................ | |
| Do .................... | Chief of Staff and Senior Advisor ..................... | Vacant .................................. | ............. | ES | ................ | ................ | |
| Do .................... | Executive Director, Office of Policy.................. | Career Incumbent ................ | CA | ES | ................ | ................ | |
| Do .................... | Chief Medical Information Officer................... | ......do ............................. | CA | ES | ................ | ................ | |
| Do .................... | Executive Director ...................................... | Vacant .................................. | ............. | ES | ................ | ................ | |
| | **ADMINISTRATION FOR CHILDREN AND FAMILIES** | | | | | | |
| Do .................... | Assistant Secretary for Children and Families . | Lynn Ann Johnson ............... | PAS | EX | IV | ................ | |
| Do .................... | Principal Deputy Assistant Secretary Administration for Children and Families. | Scott Michael Lekan ............ | NA | ES | ................ | ................ | |
| Do .................... | Senior Advisor to the Assistant Secretary ........ | Anna Pilato.......................... | NA | ES | ................ | ................ | |
| Do .................... | Chief of Staff...................................... | Bradley John Wassink........ | SC | GS | 15 | ................ | |
| Do .................... | Senior Advisor....................................... | Amy Grove Stephens............ | SC | GS | 15 | ................ | |
| Do .................... | Senior Advisor for Communications .................. | Caroline Hope Thorman ...... | SC | GS | 13 | ................ | |
| Do .................... | Communications Advisor................................. | Samantha-Ashley Bagnell Leonardo. | SC | GS | 11 | ................ | |
| Do .................... | Deputy Assistant Secretary for Office of Planning, Research and Evaluation. | Career Incumbent ................ | CA | ES | ................ | ................ | |
| Do .................... | Associate Deputy Assistant Secretary for Grants. | ......do ............................. | CA | ES | ................ | ................ | |
| Do .................... | Associate Deputy Assistant Secretary for Administration. | ......do ............................. | CA | ES | ................ | ................ | |
| Do .................... | Director, Office of Legislative Affairs and Budget. | ......do ............................. | CA | ES | ................ | ................ | |
| Do .................... | Director, National Grants Center of Excellence. | ......do ............................. | CA | ES | ................ | ................ | |
| Do .................... | Director, Office of Child Care............................ | Shannon Christian .............. | NA | ES | ................ | ................ | |
| Do .................... | Director, Office of Regional Operations ............. | Vacant .................................. | ............. | ES | ................ | ................ | |
| Do .................... | Senior Policy Advisor....................................... | Career Incumbent ................ | CA | ES | ................ | ................ | |
| Do .................... | Director, Office of Head Start and Early Childhood Development. | Deborah Lynne Bergeron..... | NA | ES | ................ | ................ | |
| Do .................... | Advisor........................................................ | Pedro Moreno........................ | SC | GS | 15 | ................ | |
| Do .................... | ......do ........................................................ | Warren Anthony Negri......... | SC | GS | 13 | ................ | |
| Do .................... | *Office of Policy and External Affairs* Deputy Assistant Secretary for Children and Families (Policy). | Heidi Hiltgen Stirrup........... | NA | ES | ................ | ................ | |
| Atlanta, GA ........... | *Office of Information Systems Management* Regional Hub Director........................................ | Career Incumbent ................ | CA | ES | ................ | ................ | |
| Chicago, IL.............. | ......do ............................................................. | ......do ............................. | CA | ES | ................ | ................ | |
| Washington, DC ...... | *Administraton for Children, Youth and Families / Office of Commissioner* Commissioner Administration for Children Youth and Families. | Elizabeth Darling................. | PAS | EX | V | ................ | |
| Do .................... | Associate Commissioner, Children's Bureau...... | Jerry Lee Milner................... | NA | ES | ................ | ................ | |
| Do .................... | Associate Commissioner, Family and Youth Services. | Vacant .................................. | ............. | ES | ................ | ................ | |
| Do .................... | *Office of Family Assistance / Office of the Director* Director, Office of Family Assistance................. | Clarence H Carter ............... | NA | ES | ................ | ................ | |
| Do .................... | *Office of Child Support Enforcement / Office of the Director* Deputy Director, Office of Child Support Enforcement, and Director of the Federal Parent Locator Service. | Vacant .................................. | ............. | ES | ................ | ................ | |
| Do .................... | *Office of Refugee Resettlement / Office of the Director* Director, Office of Refugee Resettlement............ | ......do ............................. | ............. | ES | ................ | ................ | |

## DEPARTMENT OF HEALTH AND HUMAN SERVICES—Continued

| Location | Position Title | Name of Incumbent | Type of Appt. | Pay Plan | Level, Grade, or Pay | Tenure | Expires |
|---|---|---|---|---|---|---|---|
| Washington, DC ...... | Chief of Staff .............................. | Kimberley Lorraine Womack. | SC | GS | 15 | ............... | |
| Do ..................... | Senior Advisor ............................. | Nicole Ann Cubbage ............ | SC | GS | 15 | ............... | |
| | *Administration for Native Americans / Office of Commissioner* | | | | | | |
| Do ..................... | Commissioner, Administration for Native Americans. | Jean Hovland ...................... | PAS | EX | V | ............... | |
| | *Administration for Community Living* | | | | | | |
| Do ..................... | Assistant Secretary for Aging and Administrator, Administration for Community Living. | Lance Allen Robertson ......... | PAS | EX | IV | ............... | |
| Do ..................... | Principal Deputy Administrator ...................... | Mary Margaret Lazare ........ | NA | ES | ............... | ............... | |
| Do ..................... | Commissioner of the Administration on Disabilities. | Julie Elizabeth Hocker......... | NA | ES | ............... | ............... | |
| Do ..................... | Deputy Administrator for Regional Operations and Partnership Development. | Thomas Eugene Moran ........ | NA | ES | ............... | ............... | |
| Do ..................... | Advisor.......................................... | Juanita Balenger ................. | SC | GS | 13 | ............... | |
| Do ..................... | Director....................................... | Kristi Hill............................ | TA | ES | ............... | ............... | 05/10/23 |
| Do ..................... | Deputy Assistant Secretary for Policy and Programs. | Career Incumbent ............... | CA | ES | ............... | ............... | |
| Do ..................... | Senior Advisor to the Administrator Chief of Staff. | Vacant ................................. | ............ | ES | ............... | ............... | |
| | **AGENCY FOR HEALTHCARE RESEARCH AND QUALITY** | | | | | | |
| Rockville, MD ......... | Director........................................ | Gopal Khanna...................... | NA | ES | ............... | ............... | |
| Do ..................... | Deputy Director ........................... | Vacant ................................. | ............ | ES | ............... | ............... | |
| Do ..................... | Advisor......................................... | Samuel Woodward Watters.. | SC | GS | 12 | ............... | |
| Do ..................... | Director, Office of Communications ................... | Career Incumbent ............... | CA | ES | ............... | ............... | |
| Do ..................... | Executive Officer .......................... | ......do ................................ | CA | ES | ............... | ............... | |
| | **CENTERS FOR DISEASE CONTROL AND PREVENTION** | | | | | | |
| Atlanta, GA ............ | Director, Center for Disease Control and Prevention Administration. | Robert Ray Redfield M.D. .... | NA | ES | ............... | ............... | |
| Do ..................... | Chief of Staff ............................... | Robert Kyle Mcgowan ......... | NA | ES | ............... | ............... | |
| Do ..................... | Deputy Chief of Staff....................... | Amanda Caroline Campbell. | SC | GS | 15 | ............... | |
| Do ..................... | Senior Advisor for Communications ................... | Nina Bishop ........................ | SC | GS | 15 | ............... | |
| Do ..................... | Senior Advisor............................... | Chester C Moeller III........... | SC | GS | 15 | ............... | |
| Do ..................... | Director of Communications ............................ | Loretta Ann Lepore ............. | SC | GS | 15 | ............... | |
| Do ..................... | Director, Office of Diversity Management and Equal Employment Opportunity. | Career Incumbent ............... | CA | ES | ............... | ............... | |
| Washington, DC ...... | Director, Centers for Disease Control and Prevention, Washington Office. | Vacant ................................. | ............ | ES | ............... | ............... | |
| Atlanta, GA ............ | Director for Strategic Business Management.... | Career Incumbent ............... | CA | ES | ............... | ............... | |
| Do ..................... | Associate Director for Communications ............... | Vacant ................................. | ............ | ES | ............... | ............... | |
| Do ..................... | Associate Deputy Director for Policy, Communications and Strategic Operations. | Career Incumbent ............... | CA | ES | ............... | ............... | |
| Do ..................... | Deputy Director for Management and Operations. | ......do ................................ | CA | ES | ............... | ............... | |
| Do ..................... | Chief, Human Capital and Resources Management Office. | ......do ................................ | CA | ES | ............... | ............... | |
| Do ..................... | Deputy Director National Center for Environmental Health/Agency for Toxic Substances and Disease Registry. | ......do ................................ | CA | ES | ............... | ............... | |
| Do ..................... | Deputy Director for Management and Overseas Operations. | ......do ................................ | CA | ES | ............... | ............... | |
| Do ..................... | Deputy Director, National Center for Chronic Disease Prevention and Health Promotion. | ......do ................................ | CA | ES | ............... | ............... | |
| Do ..................... | Deputy Director for Management and Operations. | ......do ................................ | CA | ES | ............... | ............... | |
| Do ..................... | ......do ....................................... | ......do ................................ | CA | ES | ............... | ............... | |
| Do ..................... | Deputy Director for Management and Overseas Operations. | ......do ................................ | CA | ES | ............... | ............... | |
| Do ..................... | Deputy Director for Management and Operations, National Center for Injury Prevention and Control. | ......do ................................ | CA | ES | ............... | ............... | |
| Do ..................... | Senior Advisor to the Director of the Chief Human Capital and Resources Office. | ......do ................................ | CA | ES | ............... | ............... | |
| Do ..................... | Supervisory Public Health Advisor ................... | ......do ................................ | CA | ES | ............... | ............... | |

## DEPARTMENT OF HEALTH AND HUMAN SERVICES—Continued

| Location | Position Title | Name of Incumbent | Type of Appt. | Pay Plan | Level, Grade, or Pay | Tenure | Expires |
|---|---|---|---|---|---|---|---|
| | **CENTERS FOR MEDICARE AND MEDICAID SERVICES** | | | | | | |
| Washington, DC ...... | Administrator Centers for Medicare and Medicaid Services. | Seema Verma......................... | PAS | EX | IV | .............. | |
| Baltimore, MD......... | Deputy Administrator and Chief of Staff........... | Brady Brookes ..................... | NA | ES | .............. | .............. | |
| Do .................... | Principal Deputy Administrator for Medicare... | Demetrios L Kouzoukas....... | NA | ES | .............. | .............. | |
| Do .................... | Principal Deputy Administrator for Operations. | Kimberly L Brandt.............. | NA | ES | .............. | .............. | |
| Woodlawn, MD ....... | Chief Operating Officer ................................... | Career Incumbent .............. | CA | ES | .............. | .............. | |
| Do .................... | Deputy Chief Operating Officer........................ | ......do ........................... | CA | ES | .............. | .............. | |
| Do .................... | Director, Office of Strategy, Performance and Results. | Vacant ................................ | ............ | ES | .............. | .............. | |
| Do .................... | Director, Emergency Preparedness and Response Operations. | Career Incumbent .............. | CA | ES | .............. | .............. | |
| Baltimore, MD......... | Director of Communications ............................... | Thomas Paul Corry .............. | NA | ES | .............. | .............. | |
| Washington, DC ...... | Senior Advisor...................................................... | Peter James Nelson............... | SC | GS | 15 | .............. | |
| Baltimore, MD......... | Principal Deputy Director ............................... | John Brooks ......................... | NA | ES | .............. | .............. | |
| Do .................... | Director of Strategic Communications .............. | Ninio Joseph H Fetalvo........ | SC | GS | 13 | .............. | |
| Do .................... | Senior Advisor for External Affairs ................... | Benjamin Kenney.................. | SC | GS | 15 | .............. | |
| Do .................... | Senior Advisor....................................................... | Brett Michael Logan ............ | SC | GS | 15 | .............. | |
| Do .................... | Advisor to the Principal Deputy Administrator for Medicare. | Eric Antonio Miranda-Marin. | SC | GS | 12 | .............. | |
| Washington, DC ...... | Senior Advisor....................................................... | Gurjeet Singh Guram .......... | SC | GS | 15 | .............. | |
| | *Office of Human Capital* | | | | | | |
| Woodlawn, MD ........ | Director, Office of Human Capital ..................... | Career Incumbent .............. | CA | ES | .............. | .............. | |
| | *Office of Program Operations and Local Engagement* | | | | | | |
| Boston, MA .............. | Deputy Director for Strategy and Business Operations. | ......do ................................ | CA | ES | .............. | .............. | |
| Seattle, WA .............. | Deputy Director for Local Enaggement and Administration. | ......do ................................ | CA | ES | .............. | .............. | |
| Philadelphia, PA...... | Director, Office of Program Operations and Local Engagement. | ......do ................................ | CA | ES | .............. | .............. | |
| Do .................... | Deputy Director for Drug and Health Plan Operations. | Vacant ................................ | ............ | ES | .............. | .............. | |
| | *Center for Consumer Information and Insurance Oversight* | | | | | | |
| Baltimore, MD......... | Deputy Administrator and Director, Center for Consumer Information and Insurance Oversight. | Randolph W Pate.................. | NA | ES | .............. | .............. | |
| Bethesda, MD.......... | Director, Payment Policy and Financial Management Group. | Career Incumbent .............. | CA | ES | .............. | .............. | |
| Woodlawn, MD ........ | Deputy Director for Policy................................... | ......do ................................ | CA | ES | .............. | .............. | |
| Bethesda, MD.......... | Deputy Director for Operations .......................... | ......do ................................ | CA | ES | .............. | .............. | |
| | **CENTER FOR MEDICARE AND MEDICAID INNOVATION** | | | | | | |
| Baltimore, MD......... | Deputy Administrator and Director, Center for Medicare and Medicaid Innovation and Senior Advisor to the Secretary. | Brad Michael Smith.............. | NA | ES | .............. | .............. | |
| Woodlawn, MD ........ | Director, Center for Medicare and Medicaid Innovation. | Vacant ................................ | ............ | ES | .............. | .............. | |
| Do .................... | Director, Patient Care Models Group ................. | Career Incumbent .............. | CA | ES | .............. | .............. | |
| Baltimore, MD......... | Deputy Director .................................................. | ......do ................................ | CA | ES | .............. | .............. | |
| Woodlawn, MD ........ | ......do .................................................................. | ......do ................................ | CA | ES | .............. | .............. | |
| Baltimore, MD......... | Speechwriter ........................................................ | Damian O'Donnell Bell ........ | SC | GS | 11 | .............. | |
| | *Office of Communications* | | | | | | |
| Washington, DC ...... | Director, Office of Communications, Centers for Medicare and Medicaid Services. | Vacant ................................ | ............ | ES | .............. | .............. | |
| Do .................... | Deputy Director .................................................. | ......do ................................ | ............ | ES | .............. | .............. | |
| Woodlawn, MD ........ | Deputy Director for Operations .......................... | Career Incumbent .............. | CA | ES | .............. | .............. | |
| Do .................... | Director, Web and New Media Group ................. | ......do ................................ | CA | ES | .............. | .............. | |
| | *Office of Legislation* | | | | | | |
| Washington, DC ...... | Director, Office of Legislation............................. | Alexander Fraser Aramanda. | NA | ES | .............. | .............. | |
| Do .................... | Deputy Director, Office of Legislation ............... | Career Incumbent .............. | CA | ES | .............. | .............. | |
| | *Office of Strategic Operations and Regulatory Affairs* | | | | | | |
| Do .................... | Director, Office of Strategic Operations and Regulatory Affairs. | ......do ................................ | CA | ES | .............. | .............. | |

## DEPARTMENT OF HEALTH AND HUMAN SERVICES—Continued

| Location | Position Title | Name of Incumbent | Type of Appt. | Pay Plan | Level, Grade, or Pay | Tenure | Expires |
|---|---|---|---|---|---|---|---|
| | *Center for Clinical Standards and Quality* | | | | | | |
| Woodlawn, MD ........ | Director, Quality, Safety, and Oversight Group . | Career Incumbent ................ | CA | ES | .............. | .............. | |
| Do .................... | Director, Survey and Operations Group............ | Vacant ............................. | | ES | .............. | .............. | |
| Do .................... | Director, Information Systems Group ............... | Career Incumbent ................ | CA | ES | .............. | .............. | |
| Do .................... | Director, Quality Improvement and Innovation Group. | Vacant ............................. | | ES | .............. | .............. | |
| Do .................... | Deputy Center Director..................................... | Career Incumbent ................ | CA | ES | .............. | .............. | |
| Do .................... | ......do | ......do | CA | ES | .............. | .............. | |
| | *Federal Coordinated Health Care Office* | | | | | | |
| Do .................... | Director, Federal Coordinated Health Care Office. | ......do | CA | ES | .............. | .............. | |
| | *Center for Medicare* | | | | | | |
| Do .................... | Deputy Center Director, Center for Medicare.... | ......do | CA | ES | .............. | .............. | |
| Do .................... | ......do | ......do | CA | ES | .............. | .............. | |
| Do .................... | Director, Chronic Care Policy Group ................ | ......do | CA | ES | .............. | .............. | |
| Do .................... | Director Provider Billing Group ...................... | ......do | CA | ES | .............. | .............. | |
| Baltimore, MD........ | Director, Hospital and Ambulatory Policy Group. | ......do | CA | ES | .............. | .............. | |
| Woodlawn, MD ....... | Director, Medicare Drug and Health Plan Contract Administration Group. | ......do | CA | ES | .............. | .............. | |
| Do .................... | Director, Medicare Drug Benefit and C and D Data Group. | ......do | CA | ES | .............. | .............. | |
| Do .................... | Director, Medicare Enrollment and Appeals Group. | ......do | CA | ES | .............. | .............. | |
| Do .................... | Director, Medicare Plan Payment Group .......... | ......do | CA | ES | .............. | .............. | |
| Do .................... | Director, Medicare Parts C and D Oversight and Enforcement Group. | ......do | CA | ES | .............. | .............. | |
| Do .................... | Director, Performance Based Payment Policy Group. | ......do | CA | ES | .............. | .............. | |
| Do .................... | Director, Technology, Coding and Pricing Group. | Vacant ............................. | | ES | .............. | .............. | |
| Do .................... | Director, Coverage and Analysis ...................... | ......do | | ES | .............. | .............. | |
| | *Center for Program Integrity* | | | | | | |
| Baltimore, MD........ | Deputy Administrator and Director, Center for Program Integrity, Centers for Medicare and Medicaid Services. | Albert George Alexander Jr.. | NA | ES | .............. | .............. | |
| Woodlawn, MD ....... | Director, Provider Enrollment and Oversight Group. | Career Incumbent ................ | CA | ES | .............. | .............. | |
| Do .................... | Director, Data Analytics and Systems Group .... | ......do | CA | ES | .............. | .............. | |
| | *Center for Medicaid and Chip Services* | | | | | | |
| Baltimore, MD........ | Deputy Administrator and Director, Center for Medicaid and Chip Services. | Calder Addison Lynch.......... | NA | ES | .............. | .............. | |
| Woodlawn, MD ....... | Deputy Center Director..................................... | Career Incumbent ................ | CA | ES | .............. | .............. | |
| Do .................... | ......do | ......do | CA | ES | .............. | .............. | |
| Do .................... | Director, Children and Adults Health Programs Group. | Vacant ............................. | | ES | .............. | .............. | |
| Do .................... | Director, Disabled and Elderly Health Programs Group. | Career Incumbent ................ | CA | ES | .............. | .............. | |
| Do .................... | Director, Data and Systems Group.................... | ......do | CA | ES | .............. | .............. | |
| Do .................... | Director, Financial Management Group............. | ......do | CA | ES | .............. | .............. | |
| Do .................... | Director, State Demonstrations Group.............. | ......do | CA | ES | .............. | .............. | |
| Baltimore, MD........ | Director, Medicaid and Chip Operations Group. | ......do | CA | ES | .............. | .............. | |
| | *Office of Enterprise Data and Analytics* | | | | | | |
| Woodlawn, MD ....... | Director, Office of Enterprise Data and Analytics/Chief Data Offcer. | ......do | CA | ES | .............. | .............. | |
| | *Office of Security, Facilities and Logistics Operations* | | | | | | |
| Do .................... | Director, Office of Security, Facilities and Logistics Operations. | ......do | CA | ES | .............. | .............. | |
| | *Office of Information Technology* | | | | | | |
| Do .................... | Director, Enterprise Architecture and Data Group. | ......do | CA | ES | .............. | .............. | |
| Do .................... | Director, Applications Management Group........ | ......do | CA | ES | .............. | .............. | |
| Do .................... | Director, Enterprise Systems Solutions Group.. | ......do | CA | ES | .............. | .............. | |
| Do .................... | Director, Infrastructure and User Services Group. | ......do | CA | ES | .............. | .............. | |
| | *Office of Financial Management* | | | | | | |
| Do .................... | Director, Budget and Analysis Group................ | ......do | CA | ES | .............. | .............. | |

## DEPARTMENT OF HEALTH AND HUMAN SERVICES—Continued

| Location | Position Title | Name of Incumbent | Type of Appt. | Pay Plan | Level, Grade, or Pay | Tenure | Expires |
|---|---|---|---|---|---|---|---|
| Woodlawn, MD ........ | Director, Financial Management Systems Group. | Career Incumbent ................ | CA | ES | ............... | ............... | |
| | *Consortium for Medicare Health Plans Operations* | | | | | | |
| New York New York, NY. | Consortium Administrator ................................... | Vacant ................................... | ............. | ES | ............... | ............... | |
| | **FOOD AND DRUG ADMINISTRATION** | | | | | | |
| Rockville, MD ......... | Commissioner of Food and Drugs ...................... | Stephen Michael Hahn M.D.. | PAS | EX | IV | ............... | |
| Silver Spring, MD ... | Senior Advisor to the Commissioner ................. | Lowell Matthew Zeta .......... | NA | ES | ............... | ............... | |
| Do ................... | Senior Advisor ............................................... | David Seth Gortler ............... | NA | ES | ............... | ............... | |
| Rockville, MD ......... | Chief of Staff ................................................ | Keagan Resler Lenihan ....... | NA | ES | ............... | ............... | |
| Silver Spring, MD ... | Counselor to the Commissioner ........................ | Carlyle Seward Mcwilliams. | SC | GS | 15 | ............... | |
| Do ................... | Deputy Commissioner for Policy ..... | Anna Abram........................ | NA | ES | ............... | ............... | |
| Do ................... | Principal Associate Commissioner for Policy .... | Lowell Jacob Schiller .......... | NA | ES | ............... | ............... | |
| Rockville, MD ......... | Associate Commissioner for Policy .................... | Career Incumbent ................ | CA | ES | ............... | ............... | |
| Do ................... | Advisor.......................................................... | Colin Frederick Rom .......... | SC | GS | 12 | ............... | |
| Silver Spring, MD ... | Associate Commissioner for Legislative Affairs. | Karas Arlie Pattison Gross.. | NA | ES | ............... | ............... | |
| White Oak, MD ....... | Associate Commissioner for External Affairs .... | Laura M Caliguiri ................ | NA | ES | ............... | ............... | |
| Silver Spring, MD ... | Deputy Commissioner for Medical and Scientific Affairs. | Anand Shah.......................... | TA | ES | ............... | ............... | 01/31/21 |
| Do ................... | Associate Commissioner for Diplomacy and Partnerships. | Vacant ................................... | ............. | ES | ............... | ............... | |
| Do ................... | Associate Commissioner for Global Policy and Strategy. | Career Incumbent ................ | CA | ES | ............... | ............... | |
| Do ................... | Assistant Commissioner for Partnerships and Policy. | ......do ............................... | CA | ES | ............... | ............... | |
| Do ................... | Assistant Commissioner for Human and Animal Food Operations. | ......do ............................... | CA | ES | ............... | ............... | |
| Rockville, MD ......... | Deputy Director, Center for Veterinary Medicine. | ......do ............................... | CA | ES | ............... | ............... | |
| Do ................... | Deputy Director, Office of Partnerships and Operational Policy. | ......do ............................... | CA | ES | ............... | ............... | |
| Bethesda, MD.......... | Associate Director for Policy ............................. | Vacant ................................... | ............. | ES | ............... | ............... | |
| Rockville, MD ......... | Associate Director for Management ................... | Career Incumbent ................ | CA | ES | ............... | ............... | |
| Washington, DC ...... | Deputy Associate General Counsel for Program Review. | ......do ............................... | CA | ES | ............... | ............... | |
| Rockville, MD ......... | Associate Director for Management ................... | ......do ............................... | CA | ES | ............... | ............... | |
| Do ................... | ......do ................. | ......do ............................... | CA | ES | ............... | ............... | |
| Silver Spring, MD ... | Deputy Associate General Counsel for Litigation Food and Drug Division. | ......do ............................... | CA | ES | ............... | ............... | |
| Jefferson, AR ........... | Associate Director for Management (Executive Officer). | ......do ............................... | CA | ES | ............... | ............... | |
| Rockville, MD ......... | Director, Office of Communications, Education and Radiation Programs. | Vacant ................................... | ............. | ES | ............... | ............... | |
| Do ................... | Associate Director for Management ................... | Career Incumbent ................ | CA | ES | ............... | ............... | |
| Silver Spring, MD ... | ......do ................. | Vacant ................................... | ............. | ES | ............... | ............... | |
| Do ................... | Deputy Associate General Counsel.................... | Career Incumbent ................ | CA | ES | ............... | ............... | |
| Do ................... | ......do ................. | ......do ............................... | CA | ES | ............... | ............... | |
| Washington, DC ...... | Deputy General Counsel for Program Review... | ......do ............................... | CA | ES | ............... | ............... | |
| Silver Spring, MD ... | Principal Deputy Associate General Counsel, Food and Drug Division. | ......do ............................... | CA | ES | ............... | ............... | |
| College Park, MD .... | Director Office of Regulations and Policy ......... | ......do ............................... | CA | ES | ............... | ............... | |
| Rockville, MD ......... | Associate Commissioner for Legislation ............ | ......do ............................... | CA | ES | ............... | ............... | |
| Do ................... | Assistant Commissioner for Regulatory Management Operations. | ......do ............................... | CA | ES | ............... | ............... | |
| Do ................... | Director, Office of Regulations ........................ | ......do ............................... | CA | ES | ............... | ............... | |
| Do ................... | Associate Director for Management ................... | ......do ............................... | CA | ES | ............... | ............... | |
| White Oak, MD ....... | Director, Office of Health Communication and Education. | ......do ............................... | CA | ES | ............... | ............... | |
| Silver Spring, MD ... | Director, Office of Facilities Engineering and Mission Support Services. | ......do ............................... | CA | ES | ............... | ............... | |
| Rockville, MD ......... | Deputy Director, Center for Tobacco Products... | ......do ............................... | CA | ES | ............... | ............... | |
| Silver Spring, MD ... | Director, Office of Compliance............................ | ......do ............................... | CA | ES | ............... | ............... | |
| Rockville, MD ......... | Director, Office of Communications Quality and Program Management. | ......do ............................... | CA | ES | ............... | ............... | |
| Silver Spring, MD ... | Program Director, Office of Medical Device and Radiological Health Operations. | Vacant ................................... | ............. | ES | ............... | ............... | |
| Do ................... | Program Director, Office of Human and Animal Food Operations-West. | Career Incumbent ................ | CA | ES | ............... | ............... | |
| Rockville, MD ......... | Director, Office of Partnerships......................... | ......do ............................... | CA | ES | ............... | ............... | |

## DEPARTMENT OF HEALTH AND HUMAN SERVICES—Continued

| Location | Position Title | Name of Incumbent | Type of Appt. | Pay Plan | Level, Grade, or Pay | Tenure | Expires |
|---|---|---|---|---|---|---|---|
| Silver Spring, MD ... | Program Director, Office of Human and Animal Food Operations-East. | Career Incumbent ................ | CA | ES | ............... | ............... | |
| College Park, MD .... | Deputy Director for Regulatory Affairs.............. | ......do ...................... | CA | ES | ............... | ............... | |
| Rockville, MD ......... | Chief Information Security Officer..................... | ......do ...................... | CA | ES | ............... | ............... | |
| Silver Spring, MD ... | Deputy Center Director for Regulatory Policy and Nutrition Engagement. | ......do ...................... | CA | ES | ............... | ............... | |
| Do .................... | Director of Stakeholder Engagement ................ | Vacant ...................... | ............ | ES | ............... | ............... | |
| Do .................... | Director, Office of Enterprise Management Services. | Career Incumbent ................ | CA | ES | ............... | ............... | |
| Do .................... | Deputy Director, Office of Laboratory Science and Safety. | ......do ...................... | CA | ES | ............... | ............... | |
| Do .................... | Deputy Director, Office of Regulatory Policy, Cder. | Vacant ...................... | ............ | ES | ............... | ............... | |
| Rockville, MD ......... | Deputy Director for Import Operations Enforcement. | ......do ...................... | ............ | ES | ............... | ............... | |
| College Park, MD .... | Director, Office of Dietary Supplement Programs. | Career Incumbent ................ | CA | ES | ............... | ............... | |
| Silver Spring, MD ... | Senior Deputy Associate General Counsel........ | ......do ...................... | CA | ES | ............... | ............... | |
| | *Office of Operations* | | | | | | |
| Do .................... | Director, Office of Equal Employment Opportunity. | Vacant ...................... | ............ | ES | ............... | ............... | |
| | *Office of External Relations* | | | | | | |
| Do .................... | Assistant Commissioner for Media Affairs ........ | ......do ...................... | ............ | ES | ............... | ............... | |
| | *Office of Policy and Planning* | | | | | | |
| Rockville, MD ......... | Associate Commissioner for Planning................. | ......do ...................... | ............ | ES | ............... | ............... | |
| | *Office of External Affairs* | | | | | | |
| Do .................... | Deputy Associate Commissioner for External Affairs. | ......do ...................... | ............ | ES | ............... | ............... | |
| | *Office of Regulatory Affairs* | | | | | | |
| Silver Spring, MD ... | Director, Office of Strategic Planning and Operational Policy. | ......do ...................... | ............ | ES | ............... | ............... | |
| Do .................... | Program Director, Office of Pharmaceutical Quality Operations. | ......do ...................... | ............ | ES | ............... | ............... | |
| | **HEALTH RESOURCES AND SERVICES ADMINISTRATION** | | | | | | |
| Rockville, MD ......... | Administrator, Health Resources and Services Administration. | Thomas James Engels.......... | NA | ES | ............... | ............... | |
| Do .................... | Deputy Administrator ....................................... | Brian Jesse Leclair.............. | NA | ES | ............... | ............... | |
| Do .................... | Senior Director, Communications ...................... | Brian T Marriott.................... | SC | GS | 15 | ............... | |
| Do .................... | Deputy Administrator, Health Resources and Services Administration. | Career Incumbent ................ | CA | ES | ............... | ............... | |
| Do .................... | Director, Office of Communications ................... | ......do ...................... | CA | ES | ............... | ............... | |
| Do .................... | Associate Administrator, Office of Federal Assistance Management. | ......do ...................... | CA | ES | ............... | ............... | |
| Do .................... | Deputy Associate Administrator, Office of Federal Assistance Management. | Vacant ...................... | ............ | ES | ............... | ............... | |
| Do .................... | Director, Office of Legislation........................... | Career Incumbent ................ | CA | ES | ............... | ............... | |
| Do .................... | Associate Administrator for Operations............. | ......do ...................... | CA | ES | ............... | ............... | |
| Do .................... | Director, Office of Planning, Analysis and Evaluation. | ......do ...................... | CA | ES | ............... | ............... | |
| Do .................... | Associate Administrator, Office of Regional Operations. | ......do ...................... | CA | ES | ............... | ............... | |
| Do .................... | Associate Administrator, Bureau of Health Workforce. | ......do ...................... | CA | ES | ............... | ............... | |
| Do .................... | Associate Administrator for Bureau of Primary Health Care. | ......do ...................... | CA | ES | ............... | ............... | |
| Do .................... | Associate Administrator, Office of Federal Rural Health Policy. | ......do ...................... | CA | ES | ............... | ............... | |
| Do .................... | Associate Administrator, Healthcare Systems Bureau. | ......do ...................... | CA | ES | ............... | ............... | |
| Do .................... | Associate Administrator, Hiv/Aids Bureau ........ | ......do ...................... | CA | ES | ............... | ............... | |
| Do .................... | Deputy Associate Administrator, Hiv/Aids Bureau. | ......do ...................... | CA | ES | ............... | ............... | |
| Do .................... | Associate Administrator, Maternal and Child Health Bureau. | ......do ...................... | CA | ES | ............... | ............... | |
| Do .................... | Deputy Associate Administrator, Maternal and Child Health Bureau. | ......do ...................... | CA | ES | ............... | ............... | |
| Do .................... | Deputy Associate Administrator, Healthcare Systems Bureau. | ......do ...................... | CA | ES | ............... | ............... | |
| Do .................... | Director, Office of Information Technology and Chief Information Officer. | ......do ...................... | CA | ES | ............... | ............... | |

## DEPARTMENT OF HEALTH AND HUMAN SERVICES—Continued

| Location | Position Title | Name of Incumbent | Type of Appt. | Pay Plan | Level, Grade, or Pay | Tenure | Expires |
|---|---|---|---|---|---|---|---|
| Rockville, MD ......... | Director, Office of Acquisitions Management and Policy. | Career Incumbent ................ | CA | ES | ............... | ............... | |
| Do .................... | Deputy Associate Administrator, Office of Operations. | ......do .................... | CA | ES | ............... | ............... | |
| Do .................... | Deputy Associate Administrator, Bureau of Primary Health Care. | ......do .................... | CA | ES | ............... | ............... | |
| Do .................... | Director, Office of Human Resources................ | ......do .................... | CA | ES | ............... | ............... | |
| Do .................... | Director, Office of Budget ........................... | ......do .................... | CA | ES | ............... | ............... | |
| Do .................... | Deputy Associate Administrator, Bureau of Health Workforce. | ......do .................... | CA | ES | ............... | ............... | |
| Do .................... | Associate Administrator, Office of Provider Support. | Vacant ................ | ............ | ES | ............... | ............... | |
| Do .................... | Deputy Associate Administrator, Office of Provider Support. | ......do .................... | ............ | ES | ............... | ............... | |
| | **INDIAN HEALTH SERVICE** | | | | | | |
| Do .................... | Director, Indian Health Service ........................ | Michael Dean Weahkee........ | PAS | EX | V | ............... | |
| Do .................... | Principal Deputy Director of the Indian Health Service. | Vacant ................ | ............ | ES | ............... | ............... | |
| Do .................... | Deputy Director for Management Operations ... | Career Incumbent ................ | CA | ES | ............... | ............... | |
| Do .................... | Deputy Director for Quality Health Care .......... | ......do .................... | CA | ES | ............... | ............... | |
| Do .................... | Deputy Director for Intergovernmental Affairs. | ......do .................... | CA | ES | ............... | ............... | |
| Anchorage, AK........ | Deputy Director for Field Operations................ | ......do .................... | CA | ES | ............... | ............... | |
| Rockville, MD .......... | Director, Office of Clinical and Preventive Services. | ......do .................... | CA | ES | ............... | ............... | |
| Do .................... | Director, Office of Direct Service and Contracting Tribes. | ......do .................... | CA | ES | ............... | ............... | |
| Do .................... | Director, Office of Environmental Health and Engineering. | ......do .................... | CA | ES | ............... | ............... | |
| Do .................... | Director, Office of Human Resources................ | ......do .................... | CA | ES | ............... | ............... | |
| Do .................... | Director, Office of Information Technology........ | ......do .................... | CA | ES | ............... | ............... | |
| Do .................... | Director, Office of Tribal Self-Governance........ | ......do .................... | CA | ES | ............... | ............... | |
| Do .................... | Director, Office of Finanace and Accounting...... | ......do .................... | CA | ES | ............... | ............... | |
| Do .................... | Director, Office of Urban Indian Health Programs. | Vacant ................ | ............ | ES | ............... | ............... | |
| Anchorage, AK........ | Director, Alaska Area................................... | Career Incumbent ................ | CA | ES | ............... | ............... | |
| Billings, MT ........... | Director, Billings Area ................................ | ......do .................... | CA | ES | ............... | ............... | |
| Sacramento, CA...... | Director, California Area ............................. | ......do .................... | CA | ES | ............... | ............... | |
| Aberdeen, SD.......... | Director, Great Plains Area Indian Health Service. | ......do .................... | CA | ES | ............... | ............... | |
| Nashville, TN .......... | Director, Nashville Area .............................. | ......do .................... | CA | ES | ............... | ............... | |
| Window Rock, AZ .... | Director, Navajo Area.................................. | ......do .................... | CA | ES | ............... | ............... | |
| Portland, OR........... | Director, Portland Area................................ | ......do .................... | CA | ES | ............... | ............... | |
| Tucson, AZ .............. | Director, Tucson Area ................................. | ......do .................... | CA | ES | ............... | ............... | |
| Bemidji, MN ........... | Director, Bemidji Area ................................ | ......do .................... | CA | ES | ............... | ............... | |
| Gallup, NM .............. | Chief Executive Officer, Gallup Indian Medical Center. | ......do .................... | CA | ES | ............... | ............... | |
| Rockville, MD ......... | Director, Diversity Management and Eeo.......... | ......do .................... | CA | ES | ............... | ............... | |
| Do .................... | Director, Office of Management Services ........... | ......do .................... | CA | ES | ............... | ............... | |
| | **NATIONAL INSTITUTES OF HEALTH** | | | | | | |
| Bethesda, MD.......... | Director, National Institutes of Health ............ | Francis S Collins M.D......... | PAS | EX | IV | ............... | |
| Do .................... | Associate Director for Communications and Public Liaison. | Career Incumbent ................ | CA | ES | ............... | ............... | |
| Do .................... | Associate Director for Budget ........................ | ......do .................... | CA | ES | ............... | ............... | |
| Do .................... | Associate Director for Financial Management and Legislation. | ......do .................... | CA | ES | ............... | ............... | |
| Do .................... | Associate Director for Legislative Policy Analysis. | ......do .................... | CA | ES | ............... | ............... | |
| Do .................... | Director, Office of Research Services................ | ......do .................... | CA | ES | ............... | ............... | |
| Do .................... | Director, Office of Equity, Diversity, and Inclusion. | ......do .................... | CA | ES | ............... | ............... | |
| Do .................... | Director, Office of Human Resources................ | ......do .................... | CA | ES | ............... | ............... | |
| Do .................... | Director, Office of Communications and Government Relations. | ......do .................... | CA | ES | ............... | ............... | |
| Do .................... | Director, Office of Health Education, Communications, and Science Policy. | ......do .................... | CA | ES | ............... | ............... | |
| Do .................... | Chief Information Officer................................ | ......do .................... | CA | ES | ............... | ............... | |
| | *National Cancer Institute* | | | | | | |
| Rockville, MD .......... | Director, National Cancer Institute.................... | Norman Edward Sharpless M.D.. | PA | EX | ............... | ............... | |

## DEPARTMENT OF HEALTH AND HUMAN SERVICES—Continued

| Location | Position Title | Name of Incumbent | Type of Appt. | Pay Plan | Level, Grade, or Pay | Tenure | Expires |
|---|---|---|---|---|---|---|---|
| | **SUBSTANCE ABUSE AND MENTAL HEALTH SERVICES ADMINISTRATION** | | | | | | |
| Rockville, MD .......... | Assistant Secretary for Mental Health and Substance Use. | Elinore Frances Mccance-Katz M.D.. | PAS | EX | IV | ............... | |
| Do .................... | Deputy Assistant Secretary ................................ | Roberto Coquis ...................... | NA | ES | ............... | ............... | |
| Do .................... | Senior Advisor (Substance Abuse)...................... | Arthur George Kleinschmidt. | SC | GS | 15 | ............... | |
| Do .................... | Chief of Staff.................................................... | Career Incumbent ................ | CA | ES | ............... | ............... | |
| Do .................... | Director, Center for Substance Abuse Prevention. | Vacant .................................. | ............... | ES | ............... | ............... | |
| Do .................... | Director, Center for Behavioral Health Statistics and Quality. | Career Incumbent ................ | CA | ES | ............... | ............... | |
| Do .................... | Director, Office of Communications .................... | ......do ........ | CA | ES | ............... | ............... | |
| Do .................... | Executive Officer.............................................. | ......do ........ | CA | ES | ............... | ............... | |
| Do .................... | Director, Center for Substance Abuse Treatment. | Vacant .................................. | ............... | ES | ............... | ............... | |
| | *Office of the Administrator* | | | | | | |
| Do .................... | Director, Center for Behavioral Health Statistics and Quality. | ......do ........ | ............... | ES | ............... | ............... | |
| | *Center for Mental Health Services* | | | | | | |
| Do .................... | Deputy Director, Center for Mental Health Services. | ......do ........ | ............... | ES | ............... | ............... | |

## DEPARTMENT OF HEALTH AND HUMAN SERVICES OFFICE OF THE INSPECTOR GENERAL

| Location | Position Title | Name of Incumbent | Type of Appt. | Pay Plan | Level, Grade, or Pay | Tenure | Expires |
|---|---|---|---|---|---|---|---|
| Washington, DC ...... | Inspector General ............................................. | Vacant .................................. | PAS | IG | ............... | ............... | |

## DEPARTMENT OF HOMELAND SECURITY

| Location | Position Title | Name of Incumbent | Type of Appt. | Pay Plan | Level, Grade, or Pay | Tenure | Expires |
|---|---|---|---|---|---|---|---|
| | **OFFICE OF THE SECRETARY** | | | | | | |
| Washington, DC ...... | Secretary of the Department of Homeland Security. | Vacant .................................. | PAS | EX | I | ............... | |
| Do .................... | Senior Counselor................................................ | Adrienne F Spero ................ | NA | ES | ............... | ............... | |
| Do .................... | Chief of Staff..................................................... | Chad Robert Mizelle ............ | NA | ES | ............... | ............... | |
| Do .................... | Deputy Chief of Staff......................................... | Vacant .................................. | ............... | ES | ............... | ............... | |
| Do .................... | Chief of Staff..................................................... | ......do ........ | ............... | ES | ............... | ............... | |
| Do .................... | Deputy Chief of Staff......................................... | Scott Gerald Erickson .......... | NA | ES | ............... | ............... | |
| Do .................... | Assistant Secretary for International Engagement. | Vacant .................................. | ............... | ES | ............... | ............... | |
| Do .................... | Advance Representative...................................... | Savannah Morgan Holsten .. | SC | GS | 9 | ............... | |
| Do .................... | Senior White House Advisor ............................. | Vacant .................................. | ............... | ES | ............... | ............... | |
| Do .................... | White House Liaison ......................................... | Michael Quentin Wheatley Holley. | SC | GS | 13 | ............... | |
| Do .................... | Special Assistant to the Executive Secretary .... | Jennifer Lee...................... | SC | GS | 9 | ............... | |
| Do .................... | White House Liaison ......................................... | Joshua Daniel Whitehouse .. | SC | GS | 14 | ............... | |
| Do .................... | Deputy Chief of Staff......................................... | Tyler Houlton ...................... | NA | ES | ............... | ............... | |
| Do .................... | Director, Joint Requirements Council ............... | Career Incumbent ................ | CA | ES | ............... | ............... | |
| | *Office of the General Counsel* | | | | | | |
| Do .................... | Principal Deputy General Counsel...................... | ......do ........ | CA | ES | ............... | ............... | |
| Do .................... | Associate General Counsel for Legal Counsel ... | Vacant .................................. | ............... | ES | ............... | ............... | |
| Do .................... | Associate General Counsel for General Law ..... | Career Incumbent ................ | CA | ES | ............... | ............... | |
| Do .................... | Associate General Counsel for Operations and Enforcement. | ......do ........ | CA | ES | ............... | ............... | |
| Do .................... | Associate General Counsel for Immigration ...... | ......do ........ | CA | ES | ............... | ............... | |
| Do .................... | Associate General Counsel for Regulatory Affairs. | ......do ........ | CA | ES | ............... | ............... | |
| Do .................... | Associate General Counsel for Technology Programs. | ......do ........ | CA | ES | ............... | ............... | |
| Do .................... | Associate General Counsel for Intelligence ...... | ......do ........ | CA | ES | ............... | ............... | |
| Do .................... | Deputy General Counsel .................................... | Riddhi Dasgupta.................. | SC | GS | 15 | ............... | |

## DEPARTMENT OF HOMELAND SECURITY—Continued

| Location | Position Title | Name of Incumbent | Type of Appt. | Pay Plan | Level, Grade, or Pay | Tenure | Expires |
|---|---|---|---|---|---|---|---|
| Washington, DC ...... | Special Assistant to the General Counsel .......... | Christine Lee Kortokrax...... | SC | GS | 12 | .............. | |
| Do .................... | Deputy General Counsel ..................................... | Ian Joseph Brekke .............. | NA | ES | .............. | .............. | |
| Do .................... | ......do ................................................ | George Maurice Fishman .... | NA | ES | .............. | .............. | |
| Do .................... | ......do ................................................ | Ketan Bhirud...................... | NA | ES | .............. | .............. | |
| Do .................... | General Counsel................................................... | Vacant .................................. | PAS | EX | IV | .............. | |
| | *Countering Weapons of Mass Destruction Office* | | | | | | |
| Do .................... | Program Analyst.................................................. | William Patrick Sheehan..... | SC | GS | 9 | .............. | |
| Do .................... | Director of Requirements, Countering Weapons of Mass Destruction. | Jeffrey Marquez.................... | TA | ES | .............. | 3 Years | 02/03/21 |
| Do .................... | Deputy Assistant Secretary for Enterprise Serivces. | Vacant .................................. | ............ | ES | .............. | .............. | |
| | **OFFICE OF STRATEGY, POLICY, AND PLANS** | | | | | | |
| Do .................... | Deputy Under Secretary for Strategy, Policy, and Plans. | Career Incumbent ................ | CA | ES | .............. | .............. | |
| Do .................... | Director, Plans Division........................................ | ......do ................................. | CA | ES | .............. | .............. | |
| Do .................... | Senior Advisor, National and Transnational Threats. | Vacant .................................. | ............ | ES | .............. | .............. | |
| Do .................... | Deputy Assistant Secretary for International Affairs (Eastern Hemisphere). | Career Incumbent ................ | CA | ES | .............. | .............. | |
| Do .................... | Deputy Assistant Secretary for Screening Coordination. | Alex Zemek ........................... | ............ | ES | .............. | .............. | |
| Do .................... | Chief of Staff........................................................ | David Richard Dorey............ | NA | ES | .............. | .............. | |
| Do .................... | Deputy Director, Targeted Violence and Terrorism Prevention. | Career Incumbent ................ | CA | ES | .............. | .............. | |
| Do .................... | Director, Targeted Violence and Terrorism Prevention. | Vacant .................................. | ............ | ES | .............. | .............. | |
| Do .................... | Assistant Secretary for Cyber, Infrastructure, Risk, and Resilience. | ......do ................................. | ............ | ES | .............. | .............. | |
| Do .................... | Assistant Secretary for Counterterrorism and Threat Prevention. | ......do ................................. | ............ | ES | .............. | .............. | |
| Do .................... | Policy Analyst...................................................... | Ian Smith ............................. | SC | GS | 12 | .............. | |
| Do .................... | Assistant Secretary for Border Security and Immigration. | Vacant .................................. | ............ | ES | .............. | .............. | |
| Do .................... | Advisor................................................................... | Adam Parker Stahl .............. | SC | GS | 12 | .............. | |
| Do .................... | Policy Advisor....................................................... | Elizabeth Deane Bettis........ | SC | GS | 13 | .............. | |
| Do .................... | Confidential Assistant to the Assistant Secretary, Border, Immigration and Trade Policy. | Gerard Khatchadourian....... | SC | GS | 7 | .............. | |
| Do .................... | Special Assistant.................................................. | Alex Mcquade ....................... | SC | GS | 9 | .............. | |
| Do .................... | Strategic Advisor ................................................. | Colton Reid Overcash........... | SC | GS | 12 | .............. | |
| Do .................... | Senior Advsor ....................................................... | Scott David Friedman .......... | SC | GS | 15 | .............. | |
| Do .................... | Confidential Assistant ......................................... | Alexis Marie Dromgoole....... | SC | GS | 7 | .............. | |
| Do .................... | Special Assistant.................................................. | Regan Williams .................... | SC | GS | 9 | .............. | |
| Do .................... | Assistant Secretary for International Affairs .... | Valerie Smith Boyd .............. | NA | ES | .............. | .............. | |
| Do .................... | Special Assistant.................................................. | Andrew Whitaker.................. | SC | GS | 9 | .............. | |
| Do .................... | Confidential Assistant ......................................... | Joshua Bradley...................... | SC | GS | 9 | .............. | |
| Do .................... | Special Assistant.................................................. | Emily Massey Scala ............. | SC | GS | 12 | .............. | |
| Do .................... | Senior Advisor ..................................................... | Jonathan Fahey .................... | SC | GS | 15 | .............. | |
| Do .................... | Advisor to the Chief of Staff............................... | Jeffrey Orzechowski ............. | SC | GS | 13 | .............. | |
| Do .................... | Senior Policy Advisor ........................................... | Trevor Whetstone.................. | SC | GS | 15 | .............. | |
| Do .................... | Policy Advisor....................................................... | Cooper James Smith ............ | SC | GS | 14 | .............. | |
| Do .................... | Senior Advisor, Immigration ............................... | Career Incumbent ................ | CA | ES | .............. | .............. | |
| Do .................... | Special Advisor..................................................... | Emma Ashooh........................ | SC | GS | 11 | .............. | |
| Do .................... | Assistant Secretary for Trade and Economic Security. | Scott L Glabe ....................... | NA | ES | .............. | .............. | |
| Do .................... | Deputy Assistant Secretary for Trade Policy, Foreign Investment, and Transport Security. | Career Incumbent ................ | CA | ES | .............. | .............. | |
| Do .................... | Deputy Assistant Secretary for Strategy and Analysis. | Vacant .................................. | ............ | ES | .............. | .............. | |
| London, United Kingdom. | Department of Homeland Security Attache to European Union. | ......do ................................. | ............ | ES | .............. | .............. | |
| Washington, DC ...... | Under Secretary for Strategy, Policy, and Plans. | Chad F Wolf ......................... | PAS | EX | IV | .............. | |
| Do .................... | Policy Advisor....................................................... | Kristine E Adams ................. | SC | GS | 11 | .............. | |
| | **OFFICE OF INTELLIGENCE AND ANALYSIS** | | | | | | |
| Do .................... | Deputy Under Secretary for Intelligence Enterprise Operations. | Vacant .................................. | ............ | ES | .............. | .............. | |
| Do .................... | Director, Counterintelligence Mission Center.... | Career Incumbent ................ | CA | ES | .............. | .............. | |
| Do .................... | Senior Homeland Representative to the Office of the Director of National Intelligence. | ......do ................................. | CA | ES | .............. | .............. | |

## DEPARTMENT OF HOMELAND SECURITY—Continued

| Location | Position Title | Name of Incumbent | Type of Appt. | Pay Plan | Level, Grade, or Pay | Tenure | Expires |
|---|---|---|---|---|---|---|---|
| Washington, DC ...... | Director, Counterterrorism Mission Center ....... | Career Incumbent ................. | CA | ES | .............. | .............. | |
| Do ..................... | Chief Information Officer and Information Sharing. | Vacant ..................... | | ES | .............. | .............. | |
| Do ..................... | Director, Field Operations Division .................... | Career Incumbent ................. | CA | ES | .............. | .............. | |
| Do ..................... | Under Secretary for Intelligence and Analysis.. | Vacant .................... | PAS | EX | III | .............. | |
| | **CYBERSECURITY AND INFRASTRUCTURE SECURITY AGENCY** | | | | | | |
| Do ..................... | Deputy Director, Cybersecurity and Infrastructure Security Agency. | Matthew Kenneth Travis..... | NA | ES | .............. | .............. | |
| Do ..................... | | Vacant .................... | | ES | .............. | .............. | |
| Do ..................... | Deputy Associate General Counsel for Cybersecurity and Infrastructure Security Agency. | Career Incumbent ................. | CA | ES | .............. | .............. | |
| Do ..................... | Assistant Director for Infrastructure Security .. | Vacant .................... | | ES | .............. | .............. | |
| Do ..................... | Director, Office of Biometric Identity Management. | Career Incumbent ................. | CA | ES | .............. | .............. | |
| Do ..................... | Associate General Counsel for Cybersecurity and Infrastructure Security Agency. | ......do ............ | CA | ES | .............. | .............. | |
| Do ..................... | Senior Advisor ....................................... | William Matthew Hayden.... | NA | ES | .............. | .............. | |
| Do ..................... | Chief of Staff ...................................... | Emily Early.................... | NA | ES | .............. | .............. | |
| Do ..................... | Confidential Assistant ...................... | Ronald Connor Gauvin ........ | SC | GS | 7 | .............. | |
| Do ..................... | Director of External Affairs ........................ | Kevin William Benacci........ | NA | ES | .............. | .............. | |
| Do ..................... | Director of Public Affairs............................ | Sara Elizabeth Sendek........ | SC | GS | 14 | .............. | |
| Do ..................... | Director of Legislative Affairs...................... | Vacant .................... | | ES | .............. | .............. | |
| Do ..................... | Senior Advisor ....................................... | Daniel Gregory Kroese........ | NA | ES | .............. | .............. | |
| Do ..................... | .......do ............ | Matthew V Masterson.......... | NA | ES | .............. | .............. | |
| Do ..................... | Policy Advisor ....................................... | John Kyle Costello................. | SC | GS | 15 | .............. | |
| Do ..................... | Senior Advisor ....................................... | Dimple R Shah .................. | NA | ES | .............. | .............. | |
| Do ..................... | Director, Strategy, Policy and Plans ................. | Career Incumbent ................. | CA | ES | .............. | .............. | |
| Do ..................... | Director, Cybersecurity and Infrastructure Security Agency. | Christopher Cox Krebs ........ | PAS | EX | III | .............. | |
| | **MANAGEMENT DIRECTORATE** | | | | | | |
| Do ..................... | Chief of Staff ...................................... | Vacant .................... | | ES | .............. | .............. | |
| Do ..................... | Deputy Under Secretary for Mangement.......... | Career Incumbent ................. | CA | ES | .............. | .............. | |
| Do ..................... | Associate Deputy Under Secretary for Management. | Bradley F Hayes................. | NA | ES | .............. | .............. | |
| Do ..................... | Director, Portfolio and Planning, National Capital Region (Ncr). | Career Incumbent ................. | CA | ES | .............. | .............. | |
| Do ..................... | Chief Financial Officer Advisor, Budgets and Legislative Coordination. | Christine M Ciccone............ | NA | ES | .............. | .............. | |
| Do ..................... | Director, Field Efficiency Program Management Office. | Mark E Butt ........................ | TA | ES | .............. | 3 Years | 11/11/20 |
| Do ..................... | Under Secretary for Management .................... | Vacant .................... | PAS | EX | II | .............. | |
| | **SCIENCE AND TECHNOLOGY DIRECTORATE** | | | | | | |
| Do ..................... | Deputy Under Secretary for Science and Technology. | Career Incumbent ................. | CA | ES | .............. | .............. | |
| Do ..................... | Chief of Staff ...................................... | ......do ............ | CA | ES | .............. | .............. | |
| Do ..................... | Director, Plum Island Animal Disease Center... | ......do ............ | CA | ES | .............. | .............. | |
| Do ..................... | Principal Director, Office of Mission and Capability Support. | ......do ............ | CA | ES | .............. | .............. | |
| Do ..................... | Executive Director, Office of Innovation & Collaboration. | ......do ............ | CA | ES | .............. | .............. | |
| Do ..................... | Executive Director, Office of Mission and Capability Support. | ......do ............ | CA | ES | .............. | .............. | |
| Do ..................... | Director, Compliance............................. | ......do ............ | CA | ES | .............. | .............. | |
| Do ..................... | Executive Director for Management ................ | Glenn Podonsky.................... | TA | ES | .............. | .............. | 08/30/21 |
| Do ..................... | Executive Director, Office of Science and Engineering. | Career Incumbent ................. | CA | ES | .............. | .............. | |
| Do ..................... | Director, Office of National Laboratories .......... | ......do ............ | CA | ES | .............. | .............. | |
| Do ..................... | Under Secretary for Science and Technology..... | Vacant .................... | PAS | EX | III | .............. | |
| | **U.S. CUSTOMS AND BORDER PROTECTION** | | | | | | |
| Do ..................... | Assistant Commissioner for Congressional Affairs. | ......do ............ | | ES | .............. | .............. | |
| Do ..................... | Chief Counsel ....................................... | Career Incumbent ................. | CA | ES | .............. | .............. | |
| Do ..................... | Assistant Commissioner, Office of Public Affairs. | Cory J Custer ...................... | NA | ES | .............. | .............. | |
| Do ..................... | Press Secretary ..................................... | Corry Schiermeyer ............ | SC | GS | 15 | .............. | |
| Do ..................... | Chief Operating Officer .............................. | Mark Morgan...................... | NA | ES | .............. | .............. | |
| Do ..................... | Staff Assistant...................................... | Matthew Daniel Boggs......... | SC | GS | 7 | .............. | |
| Do ..................... | Executive Director, Office Trade Relations ....... | Vacant .................... | | ES | .............. | .............. | |

## DEPARTMENT OF HOMELAND SECURITY—Continued

| Location | Position Title | Name of Incumbent | Type of Appt. | Pay Plan | Level, Grade, or Pay | Tenure | Expires |
|---|---|---|---|---|---|---|---|
| Washington, DC ...... | Chief of Staff ................................................ | Meghann Peterlin................ | NA | ES | .............. | .............. | |
| Do ................... | Confidential Assistant ................................... | Joshua Keith Herman.......... | SC | GS | 7 | .............. | |
| Do ................... | Senior Policy Advisor.................................... | Jason Abend......................... | SC | GS | 15 | .............. | |
| Do ................... | Executive Director of Policy and Planning ....... | Surya Gunasekara ............. | NA | ES | .............. | .............. | |
| Do ................... | Director, National Vetting Center................... | Monte Hawkins ................... | TA | ES | .............. | 3 Years | 03/31/21 |
| Do ................... | Commissioner, United States Customs and Border Protection. | Vacant ................................. | PAS | EX | III | .............. | |
| | **U.S. IMMIGRATION AND CUSTOMS ENFORCEMENT** | | | | | | |
| Do ................... | Chief of Staff ................................................ | ......do ................................. | .............. | ES | .............. | .............. | |
| Do ................... | Assistant Director, Office of Policy and Planning. | ......do ................................. | .............. | ES | .............. | .............. | |
| Do ................... | Principal Legal Advisor ................................. | Tony Pham.......................... | NA | ES | .............. | .............. | |
| Do ................... | Special Assistant........................................... | Andrew John Healey........... | SC | GS | 9 | .............. | |
| Do ................... | Congressional Relations Director .................... | Raymond Kovacic ............... | NA | ES | .............. | .............. | |
| Do ................... | Press Assistant............................................. | Rachel Lauren Walker ........ | SC | GS | 7 | .............. | |
| Do ................... | Assistant Director, Opa ................................. | Vacant ................................. | .............. | ES | .............. | .............. | |
| Do ................... | Senior Advisor, Oversight.............................. | Tamas Simon ...................... | SC | GS | 15 | .............. | |
| Do ................... | Senior Advisor............................................... | Jon David Feere................... | NA | ES | .............. | .............. | |
| Do ................... | Assistant Director, Office of Public Affairs ....... | Stacey Marie Daniels .......... | NA | ES | .............. | .............. | |
| Do ................... | Assistant Secretary, Immigration and Customs Enforcement. | Vacant ................................. | PAS | EX | IV | .............. | |
| | **U.S. CITIZENSHIP AND IMMIGRATION SERVICES** | | | | | | |
| Do ................... | Deputy Director, Operations, Citizenship and Immigration Services. | Career Incumbent ............... | CA | ES | .............. | .............. | |
| Do ................... | Chief Counsel ............................................... | Vacant ................................. | .............. | ES | .............. | .............. | |
| Do ................... | Chief of Staff ................................................ | Kathy Nuebel-Kovarik........ | NA | ES | .............. | .............. | |
| Do ................... | Senior Advisor to the Principal Deputy Director. | Diana Louise Banister ......... | NA | ES | .............. | .............. | |
| Do ................... | Deputy Chief, Office of Policy and Strategy...... | Career Incumbent ............... | CA | ES | .............. | .............. | |
| Do ................... | Chief, Office of Legislative Affairs .................. | Steven Koncar .................... | NA | ES | .............. | .............. | |
| Do ................... | Special Assistant........................................... | Mary Warren Mcdaniel Sheets. | SC | GS | 9 | .............. | |
| Do ................... | Senior Advisor to the Chief Counsel................. | Elizabeth Ann Jacobs........... | SC | GS | 13 | .............. | |
| Do ................... | Chief, Office of Policy and Strategy ................ | Robert Thomas Law ............ | NA | ES | .............. | .............. | |
| Do ................... | Senior Advisor............................................... | Troy Finnegan .................... | SC | GS | 15 | .............. | |
| Do ................... | Principal Deputy Chief Counsel ...................... | Vacant ................................. | .............. | ES | .............. | .............. | |
| Do ................... | Senior Advisor............................................... | John Paul Junge II.............. | SC | GS | 15 | .............. | |
| Do ................... | Deputy Director ............................................ | Joseph Benjamin Edlow....... | NA | ES | .............. | .............. | |
| Do ................... | Associate Director, External Affairs ................ | Kathryn Rexrode ................. | NA | ES | .............. | .............. | |
| Do ................... | Principal Deputy Director .............................. | Kenneth Thomas Cuccinelli. | NA | ES | .............. | .............. | |
| Do ................... | Chief, Office of Public Affairs ........................ | Vacant ................................. | .............. | ES | .............. | .............. | |
| Do ................... | Director, United States Citizenship and Immigration Services. | ......do ................................. | PAS | EX | III | .............. | |
| Do ................... | Chief, Citizenship and Applicant Information Services. | Career Incumbent ............... | CA | ES | .............. | .............. | |
| | **UNITED STATES COAST GUARD** | | | | | | |
| Do ................... | Director for Civil Rights................................ | ......do ................................. | CA | ES | .............. | .............. | |
| Do ................... | Deputy Judge Advocate General and Deputy Chief Counsel. | ......do ................................. | CA | ES | .............. | .............. | |
| Do ................... | Director of Commercial Regulations and Standards. | ......do ................................. | CA | ES | .............. | .............. | |
| Do ................... | Director, International Affairs and Foreign Policy Advisor. | ......do ................................. | CA | ES | .............. | .............. | |
| Do ................... | Director, Civilian Human Resources, Diversity and Leadership. | ......do ................................. | CA | ES | .............. | .............. | |
| Norfolk, VA .............. | Director, Hurricane Reconstitution Program..... | James M Heinz...................... | TA | ES | .............. | .............. | 12/01/21 |
| Do ................... | Deputy, Force Readiness Command ................... | Career Incumbent ............... | CA | ES | .............. | .............. | |
| Washington, DC ...... | Deputy Assistant Commandant for Engineering and Logistics. | ......do ................................. | CA | ES | .............. | .............. | |
| | **FEDERAL EMERGENCY MANAGEMENT AGENCY** | | | | | | |
| Do ................... | Assistant Administrator, Logistics.................... | ......do ................................. | CA | ES | .............. | .............. | |
| Do ................... | Chief Counsel ............................................... | ......do ................................. | CA | ES | .............. | .............. | |
| Do ................... | Chief Component Human Capital Officer.......... | ......do ................................. | CA | ES | .............. | .............. | |
| Do ................... | Deputy Assistant Administrator, Logistics ....... | ......do ................................. | CA | ES | .............. | .............. | |
| Do ................... | Deputy Assistant Administrator, National Continuity Programs. | ......do ................................. | CA | ES | .............. | .............. | |
| New York New York, NY. | Regional Administrator, Region Ii .................... | Thomas Joseph Von Essen... | NA | ES | .............. | .............. | |

## DEPARTMENT OF HOMELAND SECURITY—Continued

| Location | Position Title | Name of Incumbent | Type of Appt. | Pay Plan | Level, Grade, or Pay | Tenure | Expires |
|---|---|---|---|---|---|---|---|
| Emmitsburg, MD..... | Deputy Assistant Administrator, U.S. Fire Administration. | Career Incumbent ................ | CA | ES | ................ | ............ | |
| Washington, DC ...... | Assistant Administrator for Response................ | ......do ...................... | CA | ES | ................ | ............ | |
| Do .................... | Chief Information Officer........................... | ......do ...................... | CA | ES | ................ | ............ | |
| Do .................... | Deputy Assistant Administrator for Recovery... | ......do ...................... | CA | ES | ................ | ............ | |
| Emmitsburg, MD..... | Superintendent, National Fire Academy........... | Vacant ...................... | ............ | ES | ................ | ............ | |
| Philadelphia, PA..... | Regional Administrator, Region Iii .................... | Career Incumbent ................ | CA | ES | ................ | ............ | |
| Washington, DC ...... | Director, Law Enforcement Engagement and Integration. | ......do ...................... | CA | ES | ................ | ............ | |
| Atlanta, GA ............ | Regional Administrator, Region Iv .................... | ......do ...................... | CA | ES | ................ | ............ | |
| Chicago, IL............. | Regional Administrator, Region V ..................... | James K. Joseph ................. | NA | ES | ................ | ............ | |
| Herndon, VA ........... | National Incident Management Assistant Team Leader, East. | Career Incumbent ................ | CA | ES | ................ | ............ | |
| Denton, TX............... | Regional Administrator, Region Vi .................... | ......do ...................... | CA | ES | ................ | ............ | |
| Sacramento, CA....... | National Incident Management Assistance Team Leader, West. | Vacant ...................... | ............ | ES | ................ | ............ | |
| Kansas City, MO ..... | Regional Administrator, Region Vii ................... | Paul Joseph Taylor ............. | NA | ES | ................ | ............ | |
| Denver, CO ............. | Regional Administrator, Region Viii ................. | Lee Kevin Depalo ............... | NA | ES | ................ | ............ | |
| San Francisco, CA... | Regional Administrator, Region Ix .................... | Career Incumbent ................ | CA | ES | ................ | ............ | |
| Seattle, WA ............. | Regional Administrator, Region X ...................... | Michael Francis O'Hare ....... | NA | ES | ................ | ............ | |
| Washington, DC ...... | Director, Individual and Community Preparedness. | Natalie Enclade .................... | SC | GS | 15 | ............ | |
| Do .................... | Assistant Press Secretary ............................... | Abigail Paige Dennis ............ | SC | GS | 9 | ............ | |
| Do .................... | Director, Legislative Affairs ............................ | Robert Wehagen ................... | SC | GS | 15 | ............ | |
| Do .................... | Director of Legislative Affairs.......................... | Jessica Nalepa ................... | SC | GS | 15 | ............ | |
| Do .................... | Assistant Administrator for National Continuity Programs. | William Zito ...................... | NA | ES | ................ | ............ | |
| San Juan, Puerto Rico. | Federal Disaster Recovery Coordinator, San Juan, Pr. | Vacant ...................... | ............ | ES | ................ | ............ | |
| Washington, DC ...... | Deputy Administrator for Resilience................ | ......do ...................... | PAS | EX | III | ............ | |
| Do .................... | Confidential Assistant .................................... | Genaralene Lorenz ............. | SC | GS | 7 | ............ | |
| Boston, MA ............. | Regional Administrator, Region I ...................... | William R Webster ............. | NA | ES | ................ | ............ | |
| Washington, DC ...... | Director of External Affairs and Communications. | Vacant ...................... | ............ | ES | ................ | ............ | |
| Do .................... | Deputy Chief of Staff........................... | ......do ...................... | ............ | ES | ................ | ............ | |
| Do .................... | Associate Administrator for Resilience ............ | Carlos Jesus Castillo........... | NA | ES | ................ | ............ | |
| Do .................... | Assistant Administrator, Grants Programs ...... | Bridget E Bean ................... | PA | EX | IV | ............ | |
| Do .................... | Associate Administrator for Policy, Program Analysis, and International Affairs. | Career Incumbent ................ | CA | ES | ................ | ............ | |
| Do .................... | Deputy Associate Administrator for Response and Recovery. | ......do ...................... | CA | ES | ................ | ............ | |
| Do .................... | Associate Administrator for Response and Recovery. | Vacant ...................... | ............ | ES | ................ | ............ | |
| Do .................... | National Incident Management Assistance Team Leader Ii, East. | Career Incumbent ................ | CA | ES | ................ | ............ | |
| Bluemont, VA .......... | Executive Administrator, Mount Weather Emergency Operations Center. | ......do ...................... | CA | ES | ................ | ............ | |
| Washington, DC ...... | Chief of Staff.................................................. | Eric B Heighberger .............. | NA | ES | ................ | ............ | |
| Do .................... | Deputy Administrator for Federal Emergency Management Agency. | Vacant ...................... | PAS | EX | III | ............ | |
| Do .................... | Administrator for Federal Emergency Management Agency. | Peter Gaynor........................ | PAS | EX | II | ............ | |
| Do .................... | Administrator, United States Fire Administration. | Gerald Keith Bryant ............ | PAS | EX | IV | ............ | |
| Do .................... | Assistant Administrator for Recovery .............. | Career Incumbent ................ | CA | ES | ................ | ............ | |
| | **TRANSPORTATION SECURITY ADMINISTRATION** | | | | | | |
| Arlington, VA........... | Assistant Administrator of Legislative Affairs .. | Wilbur Clinton Fisher III .... | XS | OT | ................ | ............ | |
| Do .................... | Executive Director, Test and Evaluation........... | Vacant ...................... | XS | OT | ................ | ............ | |
| Do .................... | Assistant Administrator for Acquisitions Program Management. | Mario Wilson........................ | XS | OT | ................ | ............ | |
| Do .................... | Assistant Administrator, Enterprise Support Management Coordination. | Karen R Shelton-Waters ...... | XS | OT | ................ | ............ | |
| Do .................... | Deputy Assistant Administrator for Intelligence and Analysis. | Vacant ...................... | XS | OT | ................ | ............ | |
| Do .................... | Chief, Marketing Officer.................................. | John Sammon ...................... | XS | OT | ................ | ............ | |
| Do .................... | Supervisory Air Marshal in Charge, Washington Field Office. | Dwain G Troutt ................... | XS | OT | ................ | ............ | |
| San Diego, CA ......... | Federal Security Director; San Diego International Airport; San Diego, California. | Kathleen A Connon ............. | XS | OT | ................ | ............ | |
| Honolulu, HI............ | Federal Security Director, Honolulu International Airport, Honolulu, Hawaii. | Jenel L Cline...................... | XS | OT | ................ | ............ | |
| Arlington, VA........... | Director, Financial Management ...................... | Hee Kwon Song ................... | XS | OT | ................ | ............ | |

## DEPARTMENT OF HOMELAND SECURITY—Continued

| Location | Position Title | Name of Incumbent | Type of Appt. | Pay Plan | Level, Grade, or Pay | Tenure | Expires |
|---|---|---|---|---|---|---|---|
| Arlington, VA............ | Deputy Chief Counsel for Regulations and Security Standards. | Susan M Prosnitz ................. | XS | OT | ................ | ................ | |
| Do ..................... | Federal Security Director, Nashville International Airport, Nashville, Tennessee. | Stephen Wood ...................... | XS | OT | ................ | ................ | |
| Houston, TX............. | Federal Security Director, George Bush International Airport; Houston, Texas. | Juan Sanchez Jr. ................. | XS | OT | ................ | ................ | |
| Arlington, VA........... | Deputy Chief Counsel for Procurement ............ | Ross W Dembling ................ | XS | OT | ................ | ................ | |
| Do ..................... | Deputy Assistant Administrator for Acquisitions Program Management. | Vacant .................................. | XS | OT | ................ | ................ | |
| Los Angeles, CA....... | Federal Security Director, Los Angeles International Airport; Los Angeles, California. | Boyd Keith Jeffries............... | XS | OT | ................ | ................ | |
| Newark, NJ ............. | Director, Training Centers Division.................... | Barbara Schukraft ............ | XS | OT | ................ | ................ | |
| Denver, CO .............. | Federal Security Director, Denver International Airport; Aurora, Colorado. | Lawrence Nau ...................... | XS | OT | ................ | ................ | |
| Phoenix, AZ ............. | Federal Security Director, Phoenix International Airport; Phoenix, Arizona. | Jerry W Agnew ................... | XS | OT | ................ | ................ | |
| Atlanta, GA ............. | Deputy Federal Security Director, Atlanta International Airport; Atlanta, Georgia. | Ronald Edge......................... | XS | OT | ................ | ................ | |
| Seattle, WA .............. | Federal Security Director, Seattle-Tacoma International Airport; Seattle, Washington. | Jeffrey Holmgren................... | XS | OT | ................ | ................ | |
| Salt Lake City, UT .. | Assistant Administrator, Aviation Operations... | Gary O Renfrow..................... | XS | OT | ................ | ................ | |
| Arlington, VA........... | Executive Director, Small Hubs.......................... | Carolyn Dorgham .............. | XS | OT | ................ | ................ | |
| Do ..................... | Executive Director, Surface Policy..................... | Scott Gorton........................ | XS | OT | ................ | ................ | |
| Miami, FL................ | Federal Security Director, Miami International Airport; Miami, Florida. | Daniel Ronan........................ | XS | OT | ................ | ................ | |
| Arlington, VA........... | Executive Director, Information Assurance and Cyber Security Division. | Vacant .................................. | XS | OT | ................ | ................ | |
| Los Angeles, CA....... | Deputy Federal Security Director (Security), Los Angeles International Airport; Los Angeles, California. | Martin R Elam ..................... | XS | OT | ................ | ................ | |
| Chicago, IL............... | Deputy Federal Security Director, O'Hare International Airport; Chicago, Illinois. | Louis A Traverzo ................. | XS | OT | ................ | ................ | |
| Arlington, VA........... | Executive Director, Large Hubs.......................... | Paul John Leyh..................... | XS | OT | ................ | ................ | |
| Las Vegas, NV ........ | Federal Security Director, Mccarrin International Airport; Las Vegas, Nevada. | Karen Burke ........................ | XS | OT | ................ | ................ | |
| Philadelphia, PA...... | Federal Security Director, Philadelphia International Airport; Philadelphia, Pa. | Gerardo J Spero ................. | XS | OT | ................ | ................ | |
| San Francisco, CA... | Federal Security Director, San Francisco International Airport; San Francisco, California. | Fred H Lau .......................... | XS | OT | ................ | ................ | |
| Fort Lauderdale, FL. | Federal Security Director, Fort Lauderdale-Hollywood International Airport; Fort Lauderdale, Florida. | Jason Martin ....................... | XS | OT | ................ | ................ | |
| Newark, NJ ............. | Federal Security Director, Newark International Airport; Newark, New Jersey. | Thomas J Carter ................. | XS | OT | ................ | ................ | |
| San Antonio, TX ...... | Federal Security Director, San Antonio International Airport; San Antonio, Texas. | Jesus S Presas ..................... | XS | OT | ................ | ................ | |
| Newark, NJ ............. | Deputy Federal Security Director (Security), Newark Liberty International Airport; Newark, New Jersey. | Christopher Murgia ............ | XS | OT | ................ | ................ | |
| San Juan, Puerto Rico. | Federal Security Director, Luis Munoz Marin International Airport; San Juan, Puerto Rico. | Vacant .................................. | XS | OT | ................ | ................ | |
| Arlington, VA........... | Executive Director, Coordination & Analysis Division. | ......do ................................. | XS | OT | ................ | ................ | |
| Boston, MA .............. | Deputy Federal Security Director, Boston Logan International Airport; Boston, Massachusetts. | Marcy Donnelly ................... | XS | OT | ................ | ................ | |
| Arlington, VA........... | Supervisory Federal Air Marshal (Executive Director, Flight Operations). | Vacant .................................. | XS | OT | ................ | ................ | |
| New York, NY ......... | Federal Security Director, John F Kennedy Airport; New York. | John Bambury ..................... | XS | OT | ................ | ................ | |
| Orlando, FL ............. | Federal Security Director; Orlando International Airport; Orlando, Florida. | Pete R Garcia....................... | XS | OT | ................ | ................ | |
| Dallas, TX ............... | Federal Security Director, Dallas/Fort Worth International Airport; Dallas, Texas. | Kriste M Jordan ................... | XS | OT | ................ | ................ | |
| Arlington, VA........... | Federal Security Director, Reagan National Airport; Washington, Dc. | Kerwin Phillip Wilson.......... | XS | OT | ................ | ................ | |
| Baltimore, MD......... | Federal Security Director, Baltimore-Washington International Airport; Baltimore, Maryland. | Andrea R Mishoe................. | XS | OT | ................ | ................ | |
| Arlington, VA........... | Assistant Administrator for Inspections ............ | Scott Mulligan ...................... | XS | OT | ................ | ................ | |

## DEPARTMENT OF HOMELAND SECURITY—Continued

| Location | Position Title | Name of Incumbent | Type of Appt. | Pay Plan | Level, Grade, or Pay | Tenure | Expires |
|---|---|---|---|---|---|---|---|
| Arlington, VA............ | Assistant Administrator, Office of Civil Rights and Ombudsman/Traveler Engagement. | Christine Griggs.................. | XS | OT | .............. | .............. | |
| Miami, FL................ | Deputy Federal Security Director, Miami International Airport; Miami, Florida. | John T Lewis ........................ | XS | OT | .............. | .............. | |
| Boston, MA.............. | Federal Security Director, Boston Logan International Airport; Boston, Massachusetts. | Robert P Allison.................. | XS | OT | .............. | .............. | |
| Atlanta, GA ............ | Federal Security Director, Atlanta International Airport; Atlanta, Georgia. | Mary Leftridge-Byrd ........... | XS | OT | .............. | .............. | |
| Arlington, VA........... | Chief Counsel ..................................... | Francine J Kerner ............... | XS | OT | .............. | .............. | |
| Do ................... | Assistant Administrator for Human Capital ..... | Patricia Bradshaw............... | XS | OT | .............. | .............. | |
| Do ................... | Deputy Assistant Administrator, Office of Civil Rights and Ombudsman/Traveler Engagement. | Seena Foster ........................ | XS | OT | .............. | .............. | |
| Do ................... | Deputy Assistant Administrator, Office of Contracting and Procurement. | Dina Thompson .................... | XS | OT | .............. | .............. | |
| Do ................... | Executive Director for Realignment and Government. | Vacant ................................ | XS | OT | .............. | .............. | |
| Do ................... | Director, Budget and Performance Division...... | Annemarie Juhlin ............... | XS | OT | .............. | .............. | |
| Do ................... | Federal Security Director, Minneapolis/St Paul International Airport; Minneapolis, Minnesota. | Clifford Charles Van Leuven. | XS | OT | .............. | .............. | |
| Do ................... | Deputy Chief Counsel for Litigation ................. | Gillian Flory ....................... | XS | OT | .............. | .............. | |
| Do ................... | Assistant Administrator, Operations Management. | Julie A Scanlon.................... | XS | OT | .............. | .............. | |
| Do ................... | Deputy Chief Counsel (Enforcement)................. | Kelly D Wheaton .................. | XS | OT | .............. | .............. | |
| Do ................... | Director, Air Cargo Division........................... | John Beckius........................ | XS | OT | .............. | .............. | |
| Chicago, IL.............. | Federal Security Director, O'Hare International Airport; Chicago, Illinois. | Dereck Starks ...................... | XS | OT | .............. | .............. | |
| Arlington, VA........... | Assistant Administrator for Finance and Administration/Chief Financial Officer. | Pat A Rose Jr. ..................... | XS | OT | .............. | .............. | |
| Do ................... | Assistant Administrator, Office of International Operations. | Paul Fujimura ..................... | XS | OT | .............. | .............. | |
| Detroit, MI.............. | Federal Security Director, Detroit Airport; Detroit, Michigan. | Steve C Lorincz ................... | XS | OT | .............. | .............. | |
| Dulles Airport, VA... | Federal Security Director, Washington-Dulles International Airport; Fairfax, Virginia. | Scott T Johnson ................... | XS | OT | .............. | .............. | |
| Orlando, FL ............ | Deputy Federal Security Director; Orlando International Airport; Orlando, Florida. | Gregory Hawko..................... | XS | OT | .............. | .............. | |
| Arlington, VA........... | Administrator, Transportation Security Administration. | David P Pekoske.................. | PAS | EX | IV | .............. | |
| Do ................... | Deputy Assistant Administrator, Office of Training and Development. | Vacant ................................ | XS | OT | .............. | .............. | |
| Do ................... | Executive Director, Vetting ............................... | Hao Y Froemling .................. | XS | OT | .............. | .............. | |
| New York New York, NY. | Deputy Federal Security Director, John F Kennedy Airport; New York. | John Essig............................ | XS | OT | .............. | .............. | |
| Arlington, VA........... | Executive Director, Screening Systems .............. | Kenneth Lee ........................ | XS | OT | .............. | .............. | |
| Do ................... | Deputy Administrator for Transportation Security Administration. | Patricia Cogswell................ | XS | OT | .............. | .............. | |
| Do ................... | Executive Assistant Administrator for Security Operations. | Darby R Lajoye..................... | XS | OT | .............. | .............. | |
| Do ................... | Deputy Assistant Administrator for Policy, Plans and Engagement. | Victoria E Newhouse............ | XS | OT | .............. | .............. | |
| Do ................... | Deputy Assistant Administrator for Human Capital. | Roger E Brown ..................... | XS | OT | .............. | .............. | |
| Do ................... | Deputy Executive Director, Compliance............. | Demetrios Lambropoulos..... | XS | OT | .............. | .............. | |
| Do ................... | Executive Director, Medium Hubs ..................... | Susan M Tashiro ................. | XS | OT | .............. | .............. | |
| Do ................... | Deputy Chief Counsel (Operations)................... | Mary Kate Whalen ............... | XS | OT | .............. | .............. | |
| Baltimore, MD........ | Deputy Federal Security Director, Baltimore-Washington International Airport; Baltimore, Maryland. | Ronald J Juhl ...................... | XS | OT | .............. | .............. | |
| Arlington, VA........... | Assistant Administrator for Information Technology/Chief Information Officer. | Russell A Roberts ................. | XS | OT | .............. | .............. | |
| Portland, OR........... | Executive Director, Analysis and Engineering .. | Erick J Rekstad.................... | XS | OT | .............. | .............. | |
| Arlington, VA........... | Assistant Administrator, Surface Operations .... | Sonya T Proctor ................... | XS | OT | .............. | .............. | |
| Do ................... | Assistant Administrator, Enrollment Services and Vetting Programs. | Kelli Ann Burriesci .............. | XS | OT | .............. | .............. | |
| Miami, FL................ | Regional Director (Western Hemisphere/Miami). | Mariely Loperena ................. | XS | OT | .............. | .............. | |
| Arlington, VA........... | Senior Advisor........................................ | Vacant ................................ | XS | OT | .............. | .............. | |
| Do ................... | Assistant Administrator, Security and Administrative Services. | Larry Smith ......................... | XS | OT | .............. | .............. | |
| Do ................... | Assistant Administrator, Investigations............. | John Busch .......................... | XS | OT | .............. | .............. | |

## DEPARTMENT OF HOMELAND SECURITY—Continued

| Location | Position Title | Name of Incumbent | Type of Appt. | Pay Plan | Level, Grade, or Pay | Tenure | Expires |
|---|---|---|---|---|---|---|---|
| Arlington, VA............ | Regional Director (Central Region), Office of Field Operations. | Richard H Stein.................... | XS | OT | ............... | ............... | |
| Do ..................... | Director, International Policies and Programs .. | Peter Hearding ..................... | XS | OT | ............... | ............... | |
| Chicago, IL............... | Supervisory Air Marshal in Charge, Chicago Field Office. | Ronald Phifer....................... | XS | OT | ............... | ............... | |
| New York New York, NY. | Federal Security Director, La Guardia International Airport; New York. | Robert A Duffy..................... | XS | OT | ............... | ............... | |
| Philadelphia, PA...... | Supervisory Air Marshal in Charge, Philadelphia Field Office. | John J Schaal ...................... | XS | OT | ............... | ............... | |
| Arlington, VA........... | Assistant Administrator for Policy, Plans and Engagement. | Eddie D Mayenschein .......... | XS | OT | ............... | ............... | |
| Los Angeles, CA....... | Supervisory Air Marshal in Charge, Los Angeles Field Office. | Daniel Babor........................ | XS | OT | ............... | ............... | |
| Newark, NJ ............. | Supervisory Air Marshal in Charge, Newark Field Office. | Joseph Koury ....................... | XS | OT | ............... | ............... | |
| Seattle, WA.............. | Deputy Federal Security Director, Honolulu International Airport, Honolulu, Hawaii. | Jimmie Jaye Wells............... | XS | OT | ............... | ............... | |
| Queens, NY.............. | Regional Director, Region 1 (Northeast Region). | Marisa M Maola ................... | XS | OT | ............... | ............... | |
| Chicago, IL............... | Regional Security Director, Chicago, Illinois..... | James M Spriggs ................. | XS | OT | ............... | ............... | |
| Arlington, VA........... | Executive Director, Capability Management & Innovation. | Vacant ................................ | XS | OT | ............... | ............... | |
| Seattle, WA ............. | Regional Director, Region 5 (Northwest Region). | ......do  ............................... | XS | OT | ............... | ............... | |
| Phoenix, AZ ............. | Deputy Federal Security Director, Phoenix International Airport; Phoenix, Arizona. | John Scot Thaxton............... | XS | OT | ............... | ............... | |
| New York New York, NY. | Deputy Federal Security Director; La Guardia International Airport; New York. | Matthew McKeon ................. | XS | OT | ............... | ............... | |
| Boston, MA .............. | Supervisory Air Marshal in Charge, Boston Field Office. | David F Bassett ................... | XS | OT | ............... | ............... | |
| Arlington, VA........... | Deputy Federal Security Director; Washington-Dulles International Airport; Fairfax, Virginia. | Eric A Beane ........................ | XS | OT | ............... | ............... | |
| Los Angeles, CA....... | Deputy Assistant Administrator/Chief Security Officer. | Vacant ................................ | XS | OT | ............... | ............... | |
| Salt Lake City, UT .. | Federal Security Director, Salt Lake City International Airport; Salt Lake City, Utah. | Mark Lewis.......................... | XS | OT | ............... | ............... | |
| Arlington, VA........... | Deputy Executive Assistant Administrator for Security Operations. | Vacant ................................ | XS | OT | ............... | ............... | |
| Do ..................... | Director, Aviation Division ............................. | Vera Adams......................... | XS | OT | ............... | ............... | |
| Do ..................... | Executive Director, Information Technology (It) Operations. | Robert Vojtik....................... | XS | OT | ............... | ............... | |
| Washington, DC ...... | Deputy Federal Security Director, Reagan National Airport; Washington, Dc. | Ron Mildiner....................... | XS | OT | ............... | ............... | |
| Arlington, VA........... | Executive Assistant Administrator for Operations Support. | Stacey Fitzmaurice............... | XS | OT | ............... | ............... | |
| Do ..................... | Assistant Administrator, Office of Requirements and Capabilities Analysis. | Austin Gould........................ | XS | OT | ............... | ............... | |
| Do ..................... | Deputy Assistant Administrator, Office of International Operations. | Melanie Harvey ................... | XS | OT | ............... | ............... | |
| Dallas, TX ............... | Regional Director, Region 4 (South Central Region). | Melvin J Carraway.............. | XS | OT | ............... | ............... | |
| Charlotte, NC .......... | Federal Security Director, Charlotte-Douglas International Airport; Charlotte, North Carolina. | Kevin Frederick................... | XS | OT | ............... | ............... | |
| Arlington, VA........... | Executive Assistant Administrator for Law Enforcement/Federal Air Marshals. | Michael A Ondocin ............... | XS | OT | ............... | ............... | |
| Do ..................... | Deputy Chief Counsel (General Law)................ | Vacant ................................ | XS | OT | ............... | ............... | |
| Do ..................... | Assistant Administrator, Flight Operations Division. | Richard S Mcshaffrey........... | XS | OT | ............... | ............... | |
| Do ..................... | Executive Director, Human Capital Operations. | Vacant ................................ | XS | OT | ............... | ............... | |
| Do ..................... | Deputy Assistant Administrator for Information Technology/Deputy Chief Information Officer. | Robert Fortner..................... | XS | OT | ............... | ............... | |
| Do ..................... | Assistant Administrator, Office of Contracting and Procurement. | Henrietta K Brisbon............. | XS | OT | ............... | ............... | |
| Atlanta, GA ............. | Regional Security Director, Atlanta, Georgia..... | Vacant ................................ | XS | OT | ............... | ............... | |
| Arlington, VA........... | | ......do  ............................... | XS | OT | ............... | ............... | |
| Dallas, TX ............... | Deputy Federal Security Director, Dallas-Fort Worth International Airport; Dallas, Texas. | Jose Baquero....................... | XS | OT | ............... | ............... | |
| Arlington, VA........... | Executive Advisor ........................................ | Jerry G Henderson............... | XS | OT | ............... | ............... | |
| Do ..................... | Regional Director (Western Region), Office of Field Operations. | Sterling Keys ....................... | XS | OT | ............... | ............... | |

## DEPARTMENT OF HOMELAND SECURITY—Continued

| Location | Position Title | Name of Incumbent | Type of Appt. | Pay Plan | Level, Grade, or Pay | Tenure | Expires |
|---|---|---|---|---|---|---|---|
| Arlington, VA........... | Deputy Assistant Administrator, Office of Requirements and Capabilities Analysis. | Keith E Goll............................ | XS | OT | ............... | ............... | |
| Do .................... | Deputy Assistant Administrator for Finance and Administration/Deputy Chief Financial Officer. | John David Barth................ | XS | OT | ............... | ............... | |
| Do .................... | Deputy Executive Assistant Administrator/Deputy Director, Office of Law Enforcement/Federal Air Marshal Service. | Vacant ................................ | XS | OT | ............... | ............... | |
| Singapore, Singapore. | ................................................. | Eric Sarandrea ..................... | XS | OT | ............... | ............... | |
| New York New York, NY. | Supervisory Air Marshal in Charge, New York Field Office. | William R Hall..................... | XS | OT | ............... | ............... | |
| Arlington, VA........... | Assistant Administrator, Office of Intelligence and Analysis. | Vacant ................................ | XS | OT | ............... | ............... | |
| Philadelphia, PA...... | Director, Traveler Engagement Division............ | Jose Bonilla........................ | XS | OT | ............... | ............... | |
| Arlington, VA........... | Deputy Chief Counsel (Legislation and Authorities). | John A Wasowicz ................ | XS | OT | ............... | ............... | |
| Do .................... | Deputy Chief Counsel for Field Operations...... | Bryan Bonner ..................... | XS | OT | ............... | ............... | |
| Orlando, FL ............. | Supervisory Air Marshal in Charge, Orlando Field Office. | Gary V Milano ..................... | XS | OT | ............... | ............... | |
| Arlington, VA........... | Deputy Executive Assistant Administrator for Enterprise Support. | Brett A Gunter ................... | XS | OT | ............... | ............... | |
| Do .................... | Assistant Administrator, Field Operations Division. | Norman D Robinson............ | XS | OT | ............... | ............... | |
| Do .................... | Regional Director (Eastern Region), Office of Field Operations. | Brian C Belcher................... | XS | OT | ............... | ............... | |
| Germany, Germany . | Regional Director (Europe) ................................. | Robert P Vente..................... | XS | OT | ............... | ............... | |
| Arlington, VA........... | Assistant Administrator, Office of Training and Development. | Kimberly Hutchinson........... | XS | OT | ............... | ............... | |
| Do .................... | Deputy Executive Assistant Administrator for Operations Support. | Thomas L Bush ................... | XS | OT | ............... | ............... | |
| Miami, FL................ | Supervisory Air Marshal in Charge, Miami Field Office. | Adam Nikaj.......................... | XS | OT | ............... | ............... | |
| Houston, TX............. | Supervisory Air Marshal in Charge, Houston Field Office. | William R Aupperlee............ | XS | OT | ............... | ............... | |
| Dallas, TX ............... | Supervisory Air Marshal in Charge, Dallas Field Office. | Byron J Irby......................... | XS | OT | ............... | ............... | |
| Atlanta, GA ............. | Supervisory Air Marshal in Charge, Atlanta Field Office. | Tirrell D Stevenson .............. | XS | OT | ............... | ............... | |
| Washington, DC ...... | Executive Director, Compliance ......................... | Craig M Lynes ..................... | XS | OT | ............... | ............... | |
| Arlington, VA........... | Executive Director, Intelligence ......................... | John H Beattie ................... | XS | OT | ............... | ............... | |
| Anchorage, AK......... | Assistant Administrator, Operations Management. | Rana Khan.......................... | XS | OT | ............... | ............... | |
| Newark, NJ .............. | Deputy Federal Security Director (Operations), Newark Liberty International Airport; Newark, New Jersey. | Alicia R Elsetinow .............. | XS | OT | ............... | ............... | |
| Arlington, VA........... | Executive Director, Mission Operations ............. | Vacant ................................ | XS | OT | ............... | ............... | |
| Ethiopia, Ethiopia ... | Regional Director (Middle East/Africa).............. | Jason E Schwabel................ | XS | OT | ............... | ............... | |
| Arlington, VA........... | Director, Security Operations Training Directorate. | Vacant ................................ | XS | OT | ............... | ............... | |
| Las Vegas, NV ......... | Deputy Federal Security Director, Mccarran International Airport; Las Vegas, Nevada. | Daniel Wyllie ....................... | XS | OT | ............... | ............... | |
| Washington, DC ...... | Chief of Staff ...................................................... | Ryan Jeffrey Propis.............. | XS | OT | ............... | ............... | |
| Arlington, VA........... | Senior Counselor to the Administrator .............. | Vacant ................................ | XS | OT | ............... | ............... | |
| Washington, DC ...... | Assistant Administrator for Public Relations and External Communications. | ......do ................................. | XS | OT | ............... | ............... | |
| Do .................... | ......do ..................................................... | ......do ................................. | ............... | ES | ............... | ............... | |
| Arlington, VA........... | Executive Assistant Administrator for Enterprise Support. | Kimberly Walton................... | XS | OT | ............... | ............... | |
| Washington, DC ...... | Chief of Staff ...................................................... | Vacant ................................ | ............... | ES | ............... | ............... | |
| Do .................... | Senior Counselor to the Administrator .............. | Samuel Wisch ..................... | SC | OT | $118,041 | ............... | |
| Do .................... | ......do ..................................................... | ......do ................................. | SC | OT | $114,000 | ............... | |
| Do .................... | Executive Director for Strategy, Policy Coordination, and Innovation. | Christina Nelson ................. | XS | OT | ............... | ............... | |
| Do .................... | Program Manager (Deputy Director, Analysis Division). | Domenic A Bianchini............ | XS | OT | ............... | ............... | |
| Arlington, VA........... | Chief Innovation Officer........................................ | Daniel J Mccoy .................... | XS | OT | ............... | ............... | |
| Do .................... | Assistant Administrator, Strategic Communications and Public Affairs, Transportation Security Administration. | Andrew Post......................... | NA | OT | ............... | ............... | |

## DEPARTMENT OF HOMELAND SECURITY—Continued

| Location | Position Title | Name of Incumbent | Type of Appt. | Pay Plan | Level, Grade, or Pay | Tenure | Expires |
|---|---|---|---|---|---|---|---|
| | **OFFICE OF THE SECRETARY** | | | | | | |
| Washington, DC ...... | Deputy Secretary of the Department of Homeland Security. | Vacant .................................. | PAS | EX | II | .............. | |
| Do .................... | Special Assistant............................ | Patrick Reed Weaver ........... | SC | GS | 9 | .............. | |
| Do .................... | Director of Advance and Scheduling & Chief of Protocol. | Edward Miyagishima........... | SC | GS | 15 | .............. | |
| Do .................... | Special Assistant............................ | Carolyn Prill....................... | SC | GS | 9 | .............. | |
| Do .................... | Special Assistant to the Deputy Chief of Staff .. | Evan R Hughes................... | SC | GS | 9 | .............. | |
| Do .................... | Advance Representative...................... | Allison Bimber.................... | SC | GS | 7 | .............. | |
| Do .................... | Advisor...................................... | Eliza Thurston..................... | SC | GS | 13 | .............. | |
| Do .................... | Special Assistant............................ | Mallory Rascher ................. | SC | GS | 11 | .............. | |
| Do .................... | Special Assistant to the Deputy Chief of Staff .. | Julia Bristol....................... | SC | GS | 7 | .............. | |
| Do .................... | Executive Secretary......................... | William Clark Barrow.......... | NA | ES | .............. | .............. | |
| Do .................... | Senior Advisor............................... | Meredith Williams............... | SC | GS | 13 | .............. | |
| Do .................... | Brieging Book Coordinator................... | Quinn M Jones O'Brien ....... | SC | GS | 7 | .............. | |
| Do .................... | Advisor to the Executive Secretary ........... | Drew Bailey ........................ | SC | GS | 11 | .............. | |
| | **PRIVACY OFFICE** | | | | | | |
| Do .................... | Chief Privacy Officer and Chief Freedom of Information Act Officer. | Constantina Kozanas........... | NA | ES | .............. | .............. | |
| Do .................... | Deputy Chief Freedom of Information Act Officer. | Career Incumbent ................. | CA | ES | .............. | .............. | |
| Do .................... | Senior Advisor, Chief Privacy Officer and Chief Foia Officer. | Roman Jankowski ................ | SC | GS | 15 | .............. | |
| Do .................... | Deputy Chief Privacy Officer .................. | Career Incumbent ................. | CA | ES | .............. | .............. | |
| | **OFFICE FOR CIVIL RIGHTS AND CIVIL LIBERTIES** | | | | | | |
| Do .................... | Senior Advisor.............................. | Bennett Matthew Miller ...... | SC | GS | 14 | .............. | |
| Do .................... | Officer for Civil Rights and Civil Liberties........ | Cameron P Quinn................. | NA | ES | .............. | .............. | |
| | **OFFICE OF CITIZENSHIP AND IMMIGRATION SERVICES OMBUDSMAN** | | | | | | |
| Do .................... | Citizenship and Immigration Services Ombudsman. | Vacant .................................. | .............. | ES | .............. | .............. | |
| Do .................... | Senior Advisor, Office of the Ombudsman for Immigration Detention. | ......do ................................ | .............. | ES | .............. | .............. | |
| Do .................... | Deputy Director, Office of Citizenship and Immigration Services Ombudsman. | Career Incumbent ................. | CA | ES | .............. | .............. | |
| | **OFFICE OF OPERATIONS COORDINATION** | | | | | | |
| Do .................... | Director, Office of Operations Coordination and Planning. | ......do ................................ | CA | ES | .............. | .............. | |
| Do .................... | Deputy Director, Office of Operations Coordination and Planning. | ......do ................................ | CA | ES | .............. | .............. | |
| Do .................... | Chief of Staff .............................. | ......do ................................ | CA | ES | .............. | .............. | |
| Do .................... | Director, Operations Coordination Division........ | Vacant .................................. | .............. | ES | .............. | .............. | |
| Do .................... | Director, National Operations Center ............. | Career Incumbent ................. | CA | ES | .............. | .............. | |
| Do .................... | Director, Resources Division .................... | ......do ................................ | CA | ES | .............. | .............. | |
| Do .................... | Director, Continuity Division ................... | Vacant .................................. | .............. | ES | .............. | .............. | |
| | **OFFICE OF LEGISLATIVE AFFAIRS** | | | | | | |
| Do .................... | Deputy Assistant Secretary (Senate), Office of Legislative Affairs. | Joseph R Kasper................... | NA | ES | .............. | .............. | |
| Do .................... | Assistant Secretary for Legislative Affairs ........ | Elizabeth Spivey................... | PA | EX | IV | .............. | |
| Do .................... | Confidential Assistant ........................ | Laura Ann Licata ............... | SC | GS | 9 | .............. | |
| Do .................... | Legislative Manager .......................... | Andrew Rocca ..................... | SC | GS | 11 | .............. | |
| Do .................... | Associate Director, Office of Legislative Affairs. | Laura Simmons ................... | SC | GS | 13 | .............. | |
| Do .................... | Senior Advisor .............................. | Robert Goad ........................ | NA | ES | .............. | .............. | |
| Do .................... | Deputy Assistant Secretary (House), Office of Legislative Affairs. | Aaron Lee Calkins............... | NA | ES | .............. | .............. | |
| | **OFFICE OF PUBLIC AFFAIRS** | | | | | | |
| Do .................... | Chief of Staff .............................. | Career Incumbent ................. | CA | ES | .............. | .............. | |
| Do .................... | Assistant Secretary for Public Affairs............ | Dirk John Vande Beek ........ | PA | EX | IV | .............. | |
| Do .................... | Deputy Assistant Secretary for Strategic Communications. | Vacant .................................. | .............. | ES | .............. | .............. | |
| Do .................... | Principal Deputy Assistant Secretary for Public Affairs. | Daniel Woltornist ................ | NA | ES | .............. | .............. | |
| Do .................... | Speechwriter ................................ | Emily P Costanzo ............... | SC | GS | 11 | .............. | |
| Do .................... | Assistant Press Secretary ..................... | Mclaurine Elizabeth Klingler. | SC | GS | 12 | .............. | |
| | **MANAGEMENT DIRECTORATE** | | | | | | |
| Do .................... | Chief Readiness Support Officer................. | Career Incumbent ................. | CA | ES | .............. | .............. | |
| Do .................... | Executive Director, Digital Transformation....... | James Punteney ................... | TA | ES | .............. | .............. | 10/26/21 |

## DEPARTMENT OF HOMELAND SECURITY—Continued

| Location | Position Title | Name of Incumbent | Type of Appt. | Pay Plan | Level, Grade, or Pay | Tenure | Expires |
|---|---|---|---|---|---|---|---|
| Washington, DC ...... | Chief Information Officer | Karen Evans | PA | EX | IV | | |
| Do ................... | Executive Director, Office of Small and Disadvantaged Business Utilization. | Career Incumbent | CA | ES | | | |
| Do ................... | Deputy Director, Program Accountability & Risk Mgmt. | John A Wells | TA | ES | | | 09/20/21 |
| Do ................... | Director, Office of Selective Acquisitions | Career Incumbent | CA | ES | | | |
| Do ................... | Deputy Chief Financial Officer | ......do | CA | ES | | | |
| Do ................... | Director, Financial Operations | ......do | CA | ES | | | |
| Do ................... | Deputy Director, Office of Program Analysis and Evaluation. | Vacant | | ES | | | |
| Do ................... | Director, Financial Systems Modernization | ......do | | ES | | | |
| Do ................... | Senior Advisor to the Director, Financial Management. | Michael Horton | TA | ES | | | 08/17/22 |
| Do ................... | Chief Financial Officer | Troy Edgar | PAS | EX | IV | | |
| Do ................... | Director, Program Analysis and Evaluation | Career Incumbent | CA | ES | | | |
| Do ................... | Chief Learning and Engagement Officer | ......do | CA | ES | | | |
| Do ................... | Director, Cyber Statutory Authority Program | Vacant | | ES | | | |
| Do ................... | Executive Director, Cybersecurity and Intelligence Talent Experience. | Career Incumbent | CA | ES | | | |
| Do ................... | Chief Human Capital Officer | ......do | CA | ES | | | |
| | **COUNTERING WEAPONS OF MASS DESTRUCTION OFFICE** | | | | | | |
| Do ................... | Deputy Assistant Secretary for Policy, Plans and Requirements. | William Alfred Clift | NA | ES | | | |
| Do ................... | Assistant Secretary of Countering Weapons of Mass Destruction. | Vacant | | ES | | | |
| Do ................... | Deputy Assistant Secretary for Systems Support. | Scott Jansson | TA | ES | | 3 Years | 07/08/21 |
| Do ................... | Special Advisor | Duncan Braid | SC | GS | 13 | | |
| Do ................... | Senior Medical Advisor | Duane Carl Caneva | NA | ES | | | |
| | **OFFICE OF PARTNERSHIP AND ENGAGEMENT** | | | | | | |
| Do ................... | Assistant Secretary for Office of Partnership and Engagement. | John H Hill | NA | ES | | | |
| Do ................... | Special Assistant | Susanne Kelly Cassil | SC | GS | 11 | | |
| Do ................... | ......do | Katherine Mary Telford | SC | GS | 11 | | |
| Do ................... | Executive Director, Academic Engagement | Career Incumbent | CA | ES | | | |
| Do ................... | Special Assistant | Silver Joy Prout | SC | GS | 9 | | |
| Do ................... | Associate Director, Office of Partnership and Engagement. | Kelbi Culwell | SC | GS | 9 | | |
| Do ................... | Engagement Manger | Nicholas Barbknecht | SC | GS | 13 | | |
| Do ................... | Deputy Assistant Secretary for Intergovernmental Affairs. | Cherie Short | NA | ES | | | |
| Do ................... | Special Assstant | Kelsey Elizabeth Edwards | SC | GS | 9 | | |
| Do ................... | Special Assistant | Andrew Joseph Pavoncello | SC | GS | 9 | | |
| Do ................... | Deputy Assistant Secretary for State and Local Law Enforcement. | Vacant | | ES | | | |
| Do ................... | Deputy Assistant Secretary for Private Sector Office. | Andrew Teitelbaum | NA | ES | | | |

## DEPARTMENT OF HOMELAND SECURITY OFFICE OF THE INSPECTOR GENERAL

| Location | Position Title | Name of Incumbent | Type of Appt. | Pay Plan | Level, Grade, or Pay | Tenure | Expires |
|---|---|---|---|---|---|---|---|
| Washington, DC ...... | Inspector General | Joseph Cuffari | PAS | EX | II | | |
| Do ................... | Assistant Inspector General for External Affairs. | Career Incumbent | CA | ES | | | |

## DEPARTMENT OF HOUSING AND URBAN DEVELOPMENT

| Location | Position Title | Name of Incumbent | Type of Appt. | Pay Plan | Level, Grade, or Pay | Tenure | Expires |
|---|---|---|---|---|---|---|---|
| | **OFFICE OF THE SECRETARY** | | | | | | |
| Washington, DC ...... | Chief Operations Officer | Vacant | | ES | | | |
| Do ................... | Chief of Staff | Andrew D. Hughes | NA | ES | | | |

## DEPARTMENT OF HOUSING AND URBAN DEVELOPMENT—Continued

| Location | Position Title | Name of Incumbent | Type of Appt. | Pay Plan | Level, Grade, or Pay | Tenure | Expires |
|---|---|---|---|---|---|---|---|
| Washington, DC ...... | Deputy Chief of Staff.................................. | Vacant .......................... | ............ | ES | .............. | .............. | |
| Do ................... | Senior Advisor .................................. | John Laird Ligon................. | SC | GS | 15 | .............. | |
| Do ................... | ......do ............................................ | Vacant .......................... | ............ | ES | .............. | .............. | |
| Do ................... | Chief of Staff ..................................... | ......do .......................... | ............ | ES | .............. | .............. | |
| Do ................... | White House Liaison ............................ | Todd Matthew Thurman...... | SC | GS | 15 | .............. | |
| Do ................... | Deputy Chief of Staff.......................... | John Coalter Baker Jr......... | NA | ES | .............. | .............. | |
| Do ................... | Senior Advisor, Executive Director of Strategic Initiatives. | Vacant .......................... | ............ | ES | .............. | .............. | |
| Do ................... | Deputy Chief of Staff.......................... | Jonathan McCall ............... | NA | ES | .............. | .............. | |
| Do ................... | Executive Operations Officer ............... | Vacant .......................... | ............ | ES | .............. | .............. | |
| Do ................... | Deputy Chief of Staff for Policy and Programs.. | ......do .......................... | ............ | ES | .............. | .............. | |
| Do ................... | Senior Advisor for Infrastructure Resilience .... | ......do .......................... | ............ | ES | .............. | .............. | |
| Do ................... | Special Assistant.................................. | Grant A Cooper................... | SC | GS | 11 | .............. | |
| Do ................... | Deputy Chief of Staff.......................... | Alfonso Costa Jr................. | SC | GS | 15 | .............. | |
| Do ................... | Executive Assistant ............................ | Sarah June Garza ............. | SC | GS | 12 | .............. | |
| Do ................... | Senior Advisor .................................. | Vacant .......................... | ............ | ES | .............. | .............. | |
| Do ................... | ......do ............................................ | John Gibbs ...................... | SC | GS | 15 | .............. | |
| Do ................... | Deputy Chief of Staff.......................... | Vacant .......................... | ............ | ES | .............. | .............. | |
| Do ................... | Senior Advisor .................................. | ......do .......................... | ............ | ES | .............. | .............. | |
| Do ................... | ......do ............................................ | ......do .......................... | ............ | ES | .............. | .............. | |
| Do ................... | ......do ............................................ | ......do .......................... | ............ | ES | .............. | .............. | |
| Do ................... | Senior White House Advisor ................ | ......do .......................... | ............ | ES | .............. | .............. | |
| Do ................... | Executive Assistant ............................ | Dragana Bozic .................. | SC | GS | 9 | .............. | |
| Do ................... | Senior White House Advisor ................ | Vacant .......................... | ............ | ES | .............. | .............. | |
| Do ................... | Senior Advisor .................................. | Michael Norman Burley ...... | NA | ES | .............. | .............. | |
| Do ................... | ......do ............................................ | Vacant .......................... | ............ | ES | .............. | .............. | |
| Do ................... | ......do ............................................ | ......do .......................... | ............ | ES | .............. | .............. | |
| Do ................... | ......do ............................................ | ......do .......................... | ............ | ES | .............. | .............. | |
| Do ................... | ......do ............................................ | Dana Wade....................... | NA | ES | .............. | .............. | |
| Do ................... | ......do ............................................ | Vacant .......................... | ............ | ES | .............. | .............. | |
| Do ................... | ......do ............................................ | Elie Greenbaum.................. | SC | GS | 15 | .............. | |
| Do ................... | Secretary, Housing and Urban Development..... | Benjamin Carson................. | PAS | EX | I | .............. | |
| | *Office of the Deputy Secretary* | | | | | | |
| Do ................... | Chief of Staff ..................................... | Vacant .......................... | ............ | ES | .............. | .............. | |
| Do ................... | Associate Deputy Secretary ............... | David Woll, Jr ................... | NA | ES | .............. | .............. | |
| Do ................... | Chief of Staff to the Deputy Secretary ..... | Vacant .......................... | ............ | ES | .............. | .............. | |
| Do ................... | ......do ............................................ | ......do .......................... | ............ | ES | .............. | .............. | |
| Do ................... | Scheduler........................................... | Jacklyn Ward ................... | SC | GS | 9 | .............. | |
| Do ................... | Senior Advisor .................................. | Vacant .......................... | ............ | ES | .............. | .............. | |
| Do ................... | Chief of Staff ..................................... | Michael Welch Dendas ........ | NA | ES | .............. | .............. | |
| Do ................... | Deputy Secretary, Housing and Urban Development. | Brian Montgomery .............. | PAS | EX | II | .............. | |
| | *Office of the Administration* | | | | | | |
| Do ................... | Director, Executive Secretariat ............ | Career Incumbent ............... | CA | ES | .............. | .............. | |
| Do ................... | Senior Advisor for Special Projects..... | Vacant .......................... | ............ | ES | .............. | .............. | |
| Do ................... | Senior Advisor.................................. | Richard A Youngblood ......... | SC | GS | 15 | .............. | |
| Do ................... | Briefing Book Coordinator ................. | Garrison Grisedale.............. | SC | GS | 7 | .............. | |
| Do ................... | Advance Coordinator ......................... | Leonel Cantillo ................. | SC | GS | 11 | .............. | |
| Do ................... | Program Specialist ............................ | Kelsey Holt ...................... | SC | GS | 9 | .............. | |
| Do ................... | Special Assistant............................... | Albert Bullock................... | SC | GS | 9 | .............. | |
| Do ................... | Director of Scheduling....................... | Jennifer Naaden ................ | SC | GS | 12 | .............. | |
| Do ................... | Chief Administrative Officer............... | Vacant .......................... | ............ | ES | .............. | .............. | |
| Do ................... | Advance Coordinator ......................... | Richard Everett Jr.............. | SC | GS | 11 | .............. | |
| Do ................... | Director of Executive Scheduling and Advance . | Abigail Delahoyde ............. | SC | GS | 14 | .............. | |
| Do ................... | General Deputy Assistant Secretary for Administration. | Vacant .......................... | ............ | ES | .............. | .............. | |
| Do ................... | Senior Advisor for Transformation ...... | ......do .......................... | ............ | ES | .............. | 36 Months | |
| Do ................... | Assistant Secretary for Administration ............ | John N Bobbitt ................. | PAS | EX | IV | .............. | |
| Do ................... | Principal Deputy Assistant Secretary for Administration. | Vacant .......................... | ............ | ES | .............. | .............. | |
| Do ................... | Deputy Chief Administrative Officer............... | ......do .......................... | ............ | ES | .............. | .............. | |
| Do ................... | Chief Administrative Officer.................... | ......do .......................... | ............ | ES | .............. | .............. | |
| Do ................... | Deputy Chief Administrative Officer................. | ......do .......................... | ............ | ES | .............. | .............. | |
| | *Office of the Chief Financial Officer* | | | | | | |
| Do ................... | Deputy Assistant Chief Financial Officer for Budget. | Career Incumbent ............... | CA | ES | .............. | .............. | |
| Do ................... | Senior Advisor.................................. | Vacant .......................... | ............ | ES | .............. | .............. | |
| Do ................... | Senior Advisor to Chief Financial Officer ........ | ......do .......................... | ............ | ES | .............. | .............. | |
| Do ................... | Senior Advisor.................................. | Demetrios Logothetis .......... | SC | GS | 15 | .............. | |
| Do ................... | Chief Financial Officer ...................... | Irving Dennis.................... | PAS | EX | IV | .............. | |

## DEPARTMENT OF HOUSING AND URBAN DEVELOPMENT—Continued

| Location | Position Title | Name of Incumbent | Type of Appt. | Pay Plan | Level, Grade, or Pay | Tenure | Expires |
|---|---|---|---|---|---|---|---|
| | *Office of the Chief Human Capital Officer* | | | | | | |
| Washington, DC ...... | Chief Performance Officer............................ | Vacant ............................. | ............ | ES | ............... | ............... | |
| Do ..................... | Associate, General Deputy Assistant Secretary/Deputy Chief Human Capital Officer. | ......do ....................... | ............ | ES | | | |
| Do ..................... | Dep Assistant Sec for Business Management and Admin/Chief Management Officer. | ......do ....................... | ............ | ES | ............... | | |
| Do ..................... | Deputy Chief Human Capital Officer................. | Career Incumbent ................. | CA | ES | | | |
| Do ..................... | Chief Management Officer............................ | ......do ....................... | CA | ES | ............... | | |
| | *Office of the Chief Information Officer* | | | | | | |
| Do ..................... | Chief Information Officer............................. | Vacant ............................. | ............ | ES | ............... | | |
| Do ..................... | Management Analyst................................... | Stacy Dawn......................... | SC | GS | 15 | | |
| Do ..................... | Business Change and Integration Officer.......... | Career Incumbent ................. | CA | ES | | | |
| Do ..................... | Chief, Business and Information Technology Resource Management. | Vacant ............................. | ............ | ES | | | |
| Do ..................... | Senior Advisor (Cyber Security and Risk Management). | James Buntyn....................... | NA | ES | ............... | | |
| Do ..................... | Deputy Chief Information Officer, Office of Customer Relationship and Performance Management. | Vacant ............................. | ............ | ES | | | |
| Do ..................... | Senior Advisor...................................... | Michael T Allen ................... | SC | GS | 15 | ............... | |
| Do ..................... | Chief Information Officer............................. | David C Chow....................... | NA | ES | | | |
| | *Office of the Chief Procurement Officer* | | | | | | |
| Do ..................... | Chief Procurement Officer............................ | Career Incumbent ................. | CA | ES | ............... | | |
| Do ..................... | Deputy Chief Procurement Officer ................... | Vacant ............................. | ............ | ES | ............... | | |
| Do ..................... | ......do ................................................ | Career Incumbent ................. | CA | ES | ............... | | |
| | *Office of Community Planning and Development* | | | | | | |
| Do ..................... | Deputy Assistant Secretary for Operations ...... | ......do ....................... | CA | ES | ............... | | |
| Do ..................... | Senior Advisor...................................... | Maribel Gatica..................... | SC | GS | 14 | | |
| Do ..................... | Special Assistant................................... | Matthew Mangiaracina........ | SC | GS | 11 | | |
| Do ..................... | Director, Office of Technical Assistance and Management. | Vacant ............................. | ............ | ES | ............... | | |
| Do ..................... | Senior Advisor...................................... | Mark A Sanborn.................... | SC | GS | 15 | ............... | |
| Do ..................... | Associate Deputy Assistant Secretary for Grant Programs. | Steven Wayne Rawlinson..... | SC | GS | 15 | | |
| Los Angeles, CA...... | Senior Advisor...................................... | Paul Webster........................ | SC | GS | 15 | | |
| Washington, DC ...... | General Deputy Assistant Secretary for Community Planning and Development. | Vacant ............................. | ............ | ES | ............... | | |
| Do ..................... | Deputy Assistant Secretary for Economic Development. | ......do ....................... | ............ | ES | ............... | | |
| Do ..................... | Director, Office of Sustainable Housing and Communities. | ......do ....................... | ............ | ES | ............... | | |
| Do ..................... | Senior Advisor the The Assistant Secretary for Community Planning and Development. | ......do ....................... | ............ | ES | | | |
| Do ..................... | Senior Advisor...................................... | Peter Coffin........................ | SC | GS | 15 | ............... | |
| Do ..................... | Principal Deputy Planning and Development ... | Vacant ............................. | ............ | ES | | | |
| Birmingham, AL...... | Director of Financial Monitoring....................... | Robert M Couch.................... | TA | ES | ............... | 3 Years | 01/07/23 |
| Washington, DC ...... | Director, Disaster Recovery and Special Issues Division. | Career Incumbent ................. | CA | ES | ............... | | |
| Do ..................... | Principal Deputy Assistant Secretary ............. | Vacant ............................. | ............ | ES | ............... | | |
| San Juan, Puerto Rico. | Director, Community Engagement ................... | Career Incumbent ................. | CA | ES | ............... | | |
| San Antonio, TX ...... | Special Assistant.................................... | Melanie Deon Palmas ......... | SC | GS | 13 | | |
| Washington, DC ...... | Senior Advisor...................................... | Reese Cody Inman................ | SC | GS | 14 | | |
| Do ..................... | Director, Office of Block Grant Assistance ........ | Career Incumbent ................. | CA | ES | ............... | | |
| Do ..................... | Special Assistant.................................... | Christopher Yablonski.......... | SC | GS | 13 | | |
| Los Angeles, CA...... | Deputy Assistant Secretary for Field Operations. | Vacant ............................. | ............ | ES | ............... | | |
| Washington, DC ...... | Assistant Secretary for Community Planning and Development. | ......do ....................... | PAS | EX | IV | ............... | |
| Do ..................... | Director Office of Affordable Housing Programs. | Career Incumbent ................. | CA | ES | ............... | ............... | |
| | *Office of Congressional and Intergovernmental Relations* | | | | | | |
| Do ..................... | General Deputy Assistant Secretary for Congressional and Intergovernmental Relations. | Michael Kelley..................... | NA | ES | ............... | ............... | |
| Do ..................... | Congressional Relations Specialist.................... | Zachary Charles Barnes ...... | SC | GS | 11 | ............... | |
| Do ..................... | ......do ................................................ | Elizabeth Hancock ............... | SC | GS | 12 | ............... | |

## DEPARTMENT OF HOUSING AND URBAN DEVELOPMENT—Continued

| Location | Position Title | Name of Incumbent | Type of Appt. | Pay Plan | Level, Grade, or Pay | Tenure | Expires |
|---|---|---|---|---|---|---|---|
| Washington, DC ...... | Deputy Assistant Secretary for Congressional Relations. | Abigail Gunderson-Schwarz. | SC | GS | 15 | .............. | |
| Do .................... | Deputy Assistant Secretary for Intergovernmental Relations. | Stephanie Fila ..................... | SC | GS | 15 | .............. | |
| Do .................... | Assistant Secretary for Congressional and Intergovernmental Relations. | Leonard Wolfson ................... | PAS | EX | IV | .............. | |
| Do .................... | Senior Advisor................................................ | Vacant ............................... | .............. | ES | | .............. | |
| Do .................... | General Deputy Assistant Secretary for Congressional and Relations. | ......do ................................ | .............. | ES | | .............. | |
| | *Office of Fair Housing and Equal Opportunity* | | | | | | |
| Do .................... | General Deputy Assistant Secretary for Fair Housing and Equal Opportunity. | Daniel Huff .......................... | NA | ES | | .............. | |
| Do .................... | Deputy Assistant Secretary, Office of Policy, Legislative Initiatives and Outreach. | Career Incumbent ................ | CA | ES | | .............. | |
| Do .................... | Deputy Assistant Secretary for Enforcement and Program. | ......do ................................ | CA | ES | | .............. | |
| Do .................... | Deputy Assistant Secretary for Operations and Management. | ......do ................................ | CA | ES | | .............. | |
| Do .................... | ......do | Vacant ............................... | .............. | ES | | .............. | |
| Do .................... | Deputy Assistant Secretary for Operations ...... | ......do ................................ | .............. | ES | | .............. | |
| Do .................... | Senior Advisor to the Assistant Secretary for Fair Housing and Equal Opportunity. | John G Bravacos.................. | NA | ES | | .............. | |
| Do .................... | Assistant Secretary for Fair Housing and Equal Opportunity. | Anna Farias ......................... | PAS | EX | IV | .............. | |
| Do .................... | Deputy Assistant Secretary for Operations and Managment. | Career Incumbent ................ | CA | ES | | .............. | |
| Do .................... | Special Policy Advisor.................................... | Angela L Beckles.................. | SC | GS | 12 | .............. | |
| | *Office of Faith-Based and Community Initiatives* | | | | | | |
| Do .................... | Director, Center for Faith Based and Community Initiatives. | Vacant ............................... | .............. | ES | | .............. | |
| Do .................... | Senior Advisor................................................ | Julia Haller.......................... | SC | GS | 15 | .............. | |
| Do .................... | Special Advisor............................................... | Chelsea Barnett.................... | SC | GS | 12 | .............. | |
| | *Office of the General Counsel* | | | | | | |
| Do .................... | Associate General Counsel for Fair Housing ..... | Career Incumbent ................ | CA | ES | | .............. | |
| Do .................... | General Counsel.............................................. | Paul Compton ...................... | PAS | EX | IV | .............. | |
| Do .................... | Principal Deputy General Counsel.................... | Vacant ............................... | .............. | ES | | .............. | |
| Do .................... | Associate General Counsel Legislation and Regulations. | Career Incumbent ................ | CA | ES | | .............. | |
| Do .................... | Associate General Counsel, Office of Ethics, Appeals and Personnel Law. | ......do ................................ | CA | ES | | .............. | |
| Do .................... | Associate General Counsel for Assistant Housing and Community Development. | ......do ................................ | CA | ES | | .............. | |
| Do .................... | | Vacant ............................... | .............. | ES | | .............. | |
| Do .................... | Deputy General Counsel (Operations) .............. | Career Incumbent ................ | CA | ES | | .............. | |
| Do .................... | Associate General Counsel for Litigation........... | Vacant ............................... | .............. | ES | | .............. | |
| Do .................... | Senior Counsel............................................... | Nichole Wilson ..................... | SC | GS | 15 | .............. | |
| Do .................... | Deputy General Counsel for Housing Programs. | Vacant ............................... | .............. | ES | | .............. | |
| Do .................... | Deputy General Counsel for Enforcement ......... | ......do ................................ | .............. | ES | | .............. | |
| Do .................... | Principal Deputy General Counsel.................... | ......do ................................ | .............. | ES | | .............. | |
| Do .................... | Director of Regulatory Reform......................... | Christina Brown................... | NA | ES | | .............. | |
| Do .................... | Deputy General Counsel for Enforcement ......... | Vacant ............................... | .............. | ES | | .............. | |
| Do .................... | General Deputy G Counsel ............................... | ......do ................................ | .............. | ES | | .............. | |
| Do .................... | Senior Counsel............................................... | ......do ................................ | .............. | ES | | .............. | |
| Do .................... | ......do | Jeremy Lippert ..................... | SC | GS | 14 | .............. | |
| Do .................... | Special Counsel.............................................. | Scott A Knittle...................... | SC | GS | 14 | .............. | |
| Do .................... | Paralegal Specialist ....................................... | John L Sullivan .................... | SC | GS | 9 | .............. | |
| Do .................... | Deputy General Counsel for Enforcement and Fair Housing. | Timothy James Petty ........... | NA | ES | | .............. | |
| Do .................... | Deputy General Counsel for Civil Rights and Fair Housing. | Vacant ............................... | .............. | ES | | .............. | |
| Do .................... | Deputy General Counsel ................................. | ......do ................................ | .............. | ES | | .............. | |
| | *Government National Mortgage Association* | | | | | | |
| Do .................... | Executive Vice President and Chief Operating Officer. | Eric Blankenstein................. | NA | ES | | .............. | |
| Do .................... | ......do | Vacant ............................... | .............. | ES | | .............. | |
| Do .................... | Executive Vice President (Policy) ..................... | ......do ................................ | .............. | ES | | .............. | |
| Do .................... | President, Government National Mortgage Association. | ......do ................................ | PAS | EX | IV | .............. | |
| Do .................... | Senior Vice President, Office of Program Operations. | ......do ................................ | .............. | ES | | .............. | |

## DEPARTMENT OF HOUSING AND URBAN DEVELOPMENT—Continued

| Location | Position Title | Name of Incumbent | Type of Appt. | Pay Plan | Level, Grade, or Pay | Tenure | Expires |
|---|---|---|---|---|---|---|---|
| Washington, DC | Executive Vice President | Vacant | | ES | | | |
| Do | Senior Vice President of Administration and Senior Advisor to the Office of the President. | Career Incumbent | CA | ES | | | |
| Do | Senior Vice President of Strategic Planning and Policy. | ......do | CA | ES | | | |
| Do | Executive Vice President | Vacant | | ES | | | |
| Do | Senior Advisor to the President, Government National Mortgage Association. | Career Incumbent | CA | ES | | | |
| | *Office of Healthy Homes Initiatives and Lead Hazard Control* | | | | | | |
| Do | Director, Healthy Homes and Lead Hazard Control. | Vacant | | ES | | | |
| Do | ......do | Career Incumbent | CA | ES | | | |
| | *Office of Housing* | | | | | | |
| Do | Deputy Assistant Secretary for Single Family Housing. | Vacant | | ES | | | |
| Do | Deputy Assistant Secretary for Multifamily Housing. | ......do | | ES | | | |
| Do | Assistant Secretary for Housing, Federal Housing Commissioner. | ......do | PAS | EX | IV | | |
| Do | Deputy Assistant Secretary for Mulitfamily Housing. | ......do | | ES | | | |
| Do | Senior Advisor | ......do | | ES | | | |
| Do | ......do | Michael Marshall | SC | GS | 15 | | |
| Do | Senior Advisor (Safe Act) | Vacant | | ES | | | |
| Do | Associate General Deputy Assistant Secretary for Housing. | Career Incumbent | CA | ES | | | |
| Do | Special Advisor for Project Management | Vacant | | ES | | | |
| Do | Deputy Assistant Secretary for Risk Management and Regulatory Affairs. | Keith Becker | NA | ES | | | |
| Do | Deputy Assistant Secretary for Operations | Vacant | | ES | | | |
| Do | Senior Advisor | ......do | | ES | | | |
| Do | Director, Office of Asset Management and Portfolio Oversight. | Career Incumbent | CA | ES | | | |
| Do | Associate Deputy Assistant Secretary for Risk Management and Regulatory Affairs. | Vacant | | ES | | | |
| Do | Chief Risk Officer | ......do | | ES | | | |
| Do | Director, Office of Multifamily Production | Career Incumbent | CA | ES | | | |
| Do | Deputy Assistant Secretary for Office of Housing Counseling. | Vacant | | ES | | | |
| Do | Associate Deputy Assistant Secretary for Single Family Housing. | ......do | | ES | | | |
| Do | Associate Deputy Assistant Secretary Multifamily Housing Programs. | Career Incumbent | CA | ES | | | |
| Do | Senior Advisor to the Assistant Secretary | Vacant | | ES | | | |
| Do | Associate Deputy Assistant Secretary for Risk Managment and Regulatory Affairs. | Eileen Frances Lyons | SC | GS | 15 | | |
| Do | Deputy Assistant Secretary for Healthcare Programs. | Career Incumbent | CA | ES | | | |
| Do | Chief of Staff | Vacant | | ES | | | |
| Do | Director, Office of Recapitalization | Career Incumbent | CA | ES | | | |
| Do | Director, Office of Single Family Program Development. | ......do | CA | ES | | | |
| Do | Director, Office of Lender Activities and Program Compliance. | ......do | CA | ES | | | |
| Do | Director, Office of Single Family Asset Management. | Vacant | | ES | | | |
| Do | Senior Advisor | William Beckmann | SC | GS | 15 | | |
| Do | Deputy Assistant Secretary for Single Family | Joseph Gormley | NA | ES | | | |
| Do | Special Assistant | Joseph Fichthorn | SC | GS | 11 | | |
| Do | Senior Advisor to the Deputy Assistant Secretary for Risk Managment and Regulatory Affairs. | Vacant | | ES | | | |
| Do | Senior Advisor for Organization Transformation and Modernization. | John L Garvin | TA | ES | | | 02/13/22 |
| Do | Senior Advisor | Martin Dannenfelser | NA | ES | | | |
| Do | Associate Deputy Assistant Secretary for Healthcare Programs. | Vacant | | ES | | | |
| Do | Senior Advisor | Career Incumbent | CA | ES | | | |
| Do | Senior Advisor for Resource Management | Dror Oppenheimer | TA | ES | | | 12/09/21 |
| Do | Gen Deputy Assistant Secretary for Housing | Vacant | | ES | | | |
| Do | Senior Advisor to the Assistant Secretary | Robert B Bowes | NA | ES | | | |

## DEPARTMENT OF HOUSING AND URBAN DEVELOPMENT—Continued

| Location | Position Title | Name of Incumbent | Type of Appt. | Pay Plan | Level, Grade, or Pay | Tenure | Expires |
|---|---|---|---|---|---|---|---|
| | *Office of Policy Development and Research* | | | | | | |
| Washington, DC ...... | Deputy Assistant Secretary for Economic Affairs. | Career Incumbent ............... | CA | ES | .............. | .............. | |
| Do .................... | General Deputy Assistant Secretary for Policy Development Research. | ......do ................. | CA | ES | .............. | .............. | |
| Do .................... | Policy Advisor ................................. | Casey Charles Cheap ........... | SC | GS | 11 | .............. | |
| Do .................... | Associate Deputy Assistant Secretary for Economic Affairs. | Vacant .................................. | ............ | ES | .............. | .............. | |
| Do .................... | Executive Director for Strong Cities and Strong Communities. | ......do ................. | ............ | ES | .............. | .............. | |
| Do .................... | Deputy Assistant Secretary for Research, Evaluation and Monitoring. | Career Incumbent ............... | CA | ES | .............. | .............. | |
| Do .................... | Deputy Assistant Secretary for Innovation ....... | Christopher Bourne............. | SC | GS | 15 | .............. | |
| Do .................... | Special Advisor to the Assistant Secretary ........ | James Earl Redfield III ....... | SC | GS | 13 | .............. | |
| Do .................... | Deputy Assistant Secretary for Policy Development. | Paige Jessica Esterkin ......... | SC | GS | 15 | .............. | |
| Do .................... | Associate Deputy Assistant Secetary for Policy Development and Research. | Vacant .................................. | ............ | ES | .............. | .............. | |
| Do .................... | Assistant Secretary for Policy Development and Research. | Seth Appleton ...................... | PAS | EX | IV | .............. | |
| | *Office of Public Affairs* | | | | | | |
| Do .................... | Deputy Assistant Secretary for Public Affairs... | Vacant .................................. | ............ | ES | .............. | .............. | |
| Do .................... | Special Assistant................................ | Evonne Georgiana Heredia . | SC | GS | 9 | .............. | |
| Do .................... | Deputy Assistant Secretary for Media Relations. | Caitlin Thompson ............... | SC | GS | 14 | .............. | |
| Do .................... | Das for Strategic Communication ..................... | Bradley Bishop .................... | SC | GS | 14 | .............. | |
| Do .................... | Director of Strategic Communications .............. | Matthew Schuck................... | SC | GS | 14 | .............. | |
| Do .................... | Assistant Press Secretary ................................ | Sadie Thorman .................... | SC | GS | 11 | .............. | |
| Do .................... | Digital Strategist ........................................... | Robert Vernon Myers III...... | SC | GS | 14 | .............. | |
| Do .................... | Director of Speechwriting................................. | John Shosky.......................... | SC | GS | 15 | .............. | |
| Do .................... | Press Secretary .............................................. | Kasey Lovett......................... | SC | GS | 12 | .............. | |
| Do .................... | Deputy Director of Speechwriting ................... | Michael Adam Benz ............. | SC | GS | 13 | .............. | |
| Do .................... | Assistant Secretary for Public Affairs .............. | Caroline Grace Vanvick ...... | PA | EX | IV | .............. | |
| | *Office of Public and Indian Housing* | | | | | | |
| Do .................... | Deputy Assistant Secretary for Public Housing and Voucher Programs. | Vacant .................................. | ............ | ES | .............. | .............. | |
| Do .................... | Deputy Assistant Secretary for Native American Programs. | Career Incumbent ............... | CA | ES | .............. | .............. | |
| Do .................... | Senior Advisor ............................................... | Vacant .................................. | ............ | ES | .............. | .............. | |
| Do .................... | Special Assistant............................................ | Brendan John Quinn............ | SC | GS | 7 | .............. | |
| Do .................... | Special Policy Advisor.................................... | Mary Croghan....................... | SC | GS | | .............. | |
| Do .................... | Deputy Assistant Secretary for Field Operations. | Career Incumbent ............... | CA | ES | .............. | .............. | |
| Do .................... | Principal Deputy Assistant Secretary ................ | Vacant .................................. | ............ | ES | .............. | .............. | |
| Do .................... | Policy Advisor................................................ | Alexander Coffey ................. | SC | GS | 12 | .............. | |
| Fort Worth, TX........ | Senior Advisor .............................................. | Eric Turner .......................... | SC | GS | 15 | .............. | |
| Washington, DC ...... | General Deputy Assistant Secretary for Public and Indian Housing. | Career Incumbent ............... | CA | ES | .............. | .............. | |
| Do .................... | Policy Advisor................................................ | Mary Margaret Jenkins ....... | SC | GS | 12 | .............. | |
| Do .................... | Senior Advisor ............................................... | Vacant .................................. | ............ | ES | .............. | .............. | |
| Do .................... | ......do ........................................................ | ......do ................................. | ............ | ES | .............. | .............. | |
| Do .................... | Assistant Secretary for Public and Indian Housing. | Robert H Kurtz.................... | PAS | EX | IV | .............. | |
| | *Office of Small and Disadvantaged Business Utilization* | | | | | | |
| Do .................... | Director, Office of Small and Disadvantage Business Utilization. | Career Incumbent ............... | CA | ES | .............. | .............. | |
| | *Office of Field Policy and Management* | | | | | | |
| Las Vegas, NV ........ | Regional Administrator .................................. | Vacant .................................. | ............ | ES | .............. | .............. | |
| Washington, DC ...... | Special Assistant............................................ | Coleman James Hopkins ..... | SC | GS | 7 | .............. | |
| San Francisco, CA ... | Regional Administrator .................................. | Christopher Michael Patterson. | SC | GS | 15 | .............. | |
| Kansas City, MO ..... | ......do ........................................................ | Jason Michael Mohr............. | SC | GS | 15 | .............. | |
| Denver, CO ............. | ......do ........................................................ | Marie E Lim ........................ | SC | GS | 15 | .............. | |
| Philadelphia, PA...... | Special Assistant............................................ | Phillip Trometter................. | SC | GS | 9 | .............. | |
| Washington, DC ...... | Associate Assistant Deputy Secretary for Field Policy and Management. | Vacant .................................. | ............ | ES | .............. | .............. | |
| New York, NY ......... | Senior Advisor to the Regional Administrator... | Ashley Ludlow ...................... | SC | GS | 15 | .............. | |
| Washington, DC ...... | Senior Advisor ............................................... | Vacant .................................. | ............ | ES | .............. | .............. | |
| Do .................... | Deputy Director, Office of Field Policy and Management. | Career Incumbent ............... | CA | ES | .............. | .............. | |

## DEPARTMENT OF HOUSING AND URBAN DEVELOPMENT—Continued

| Location | Position Title | Name of Incumbent | Type of Appt. | Pay Plan | Level, Grade, or Pay | Tenure | Expires |
|---|---|---|---|---|---|---|---|
| Boston, MA .............. | Regional Administrator-Region 1 ..................... | David Tille ........................... | SC | GS | 15 | .............. | |
| Washington, DC ...... | Assistant Deputy Secretary for Field Policy and Management. | Benjamin Demarzo............... | NA | ES | .............. | .............. | |
| Denver, CO ............. | Special Assistant................................... | Dylan Mitchell..................... | SC | GS | 7 | .............. | |
| Do ..................... | Regional Administrator-Region 8 ................... | Vacant ................................. | .............. | ES | .............. | .............. | |
| Philadelphia, PA...... | Regional Administrator -Region Iii ................... | Joseph Defelice ................... | NA | ES | .............. | .............. | |
| Seattle, WA .............. | Regional Administrator-Region 10 ................... | Vacant ................................. | .............. | ES | .............. | .............. | |
| Kansas City, KS ...... | Regional Administrator-Region 7 ................... | ......do ................................ | .............. | ES | .............. | .............. | |
| Fort Worth, TX........ | Advisor to Regional Administrator.................... | Eric Davis Mahroum............ | SC | GS | 14 | .............. | |
| San Francisco, CA ... | Senior Advisor to the Regional Administrator... | James Stracner II................ | SC | GS | 15 | .............. | |
| Los Angeles, CA....... | Senior Advisor for Region Ix ........................... | Michael Nason ..................... | SC | GS | 15 | .............. | |
| Atlanta, GA ............. | Senior Advisor.................................... | Mason O'Alexander ............. | SC | GS | 15 | .............. | |
| Columbus, OH ........ | Assistant Advisor................................. | Colleen M Okane.................. | SC | GS | 12 | .............. | |
| Seattle, WA .............. | Regional Administrator-Region 10 ................... | Vacant ................................. | .............. | ES | .............. | .............. | |
| Boston, MA .............. | Regional Administrator - Region 1 ................... | ......do ................................ | .............. | ES | .............. | .............. | |
| Washington, DC ...... | Director, Field Policy and Management ........... | Career Incumbent ............... | CA | ES | .............. | .............. | |
| Do ..................... | Deputy Director for Disaster Initiatives ......... | ......do ................................ | CA | ES | .............. | .............. | |
| New York, NY......... | Advisor to the Regional Adminstrator ............. | Barbara R Gruson ............... | SC | GS | 14 | .............. | |
| Columbus, OH ........ | Senior Advisor................................... | Rosa Maria Ailabouni ......... | SC | GS | 15 | .............. | |
| Washington, DC ...... | ......do ................................... | Vacant ................................. | .............. | ES | .............. | .............. | |
| Chicago, IL.............. | Regional Administrator.......................... | Joseph P Galvan .................. | SC | GS | 15 | .............. | |
| Seattle, WA .............. | ......do ................................... | Jeffrey Wayne Mcmorris ...... | SC | GS | 15 | .............. | |
| Washington, DC ...... | Advisor to the Assistant Deputy Secretary....... | Alexander David Stowe........ | SC | GS | 12 | .............. | |
| Fort Worth, TX........ | Regional Administrator, Region Vi; Ft. Worth, Tx. | Vacant ................................. | .............. | ES | .............. | .............. | |
| Washington, DC ...... | Senior Advisor .................................... | Elvis Solivan ....................... | SC | GS | 14 | .............. | |
| | *New York / New Jersey (New York)* | | | | | | |
| New York New York, NY. | Regional Administrator (New York/New Jersey). | Lynne M Patton.................... | NA | ES | .............. | .............. | |
| | *Southeast (Atlanta)* | | | | | | |
| Atlanta, GA ............. | Regional Administrator ................................ | Denise Cleveland-Leggett.... | NA | ES | .............. | .............. | |
| | *Midwest (Chicago)* | | | | | | |
| Chicago, IL.............. | ......do ................................... | Vacant ................................. | .............. | ES | .............. | .............. | |
| Do ..................... | Deputy Regional Director.......................... | ......do ................................ | .............. | ES | .............. | .............. | |
| | *Southwest (Fort Worth)* | | | | | | |
| Fort Worth, TX........ | Regional Administrator ................................ | ......do ................................ | .............. | ES | .............. | .............. | |
| | *Pacific / Hawaii (San Francisco)* | | | | | | |
| San Francisco, CA ... | Regional Administrator-Region 9 ..................... | ......do ................................ | .............. | ES | .............. | .............. | |

## DEPARTMENT OF HOUSING AND URBAN DEVELOPMENT OFFICE OF THE INSPECTOR GENERAL

| Location | Position Title | Name of Incumbent | Type of Appt. | Pay Plan | Level, Grade, or Pay | Tenure | Expires |
|---|---|---|---|---|---|---|---|
| Washington, DC ...... | Inspector General ............................................. | Valeria Davis ....................... | PAS | EX | III | .............. | |
| Do ..................... | Chief of Staff ............................................ | Stephen M Begg ................... | TA | ES | .............. | .............. | 07/06/20 |

## DEPARTMENT OF JUSTICE

| Location | Position Title | Name of Incumbent | Type of Appt. | Pay Plan | Level, Grade, or Pay | Tenure | Expires |
|---|---|---|---|---|---|---|---|
| | **OFFICE OF THE ATTORNEY GENERAL** | | | | | | |
| Washington, DC ...... | Attorney General ............................................. | William P Barr ..................... | PAS | EX | I | .............. | |
| Do ..................... | Chief of Staff and Senior Counselor to the Attorney General. | William Ranney Levi .......... | NA | ES | .............. | .............. | |
| Do ..................... | Deputy Chief of Staff and Counselor to the Attorney General. | Rachel P Bissex ................... | NA | ES | .............. | .............. | |
| Do ..................... | Counselor to the Attorney General.................... | Gene P Hamilton.................. | NA | ES | .............. | .............. | |
| Do ..................... | ......do ............................... | Vacant ................................. | .............. | ES | .............. | .............. | |
| Do ..................... | ......do ............................... | Ryan Newman ..................... | NA | ES | .............. | .............. | |
| Do ..................... | ......do ............................... | Vacant ................................. | .............. | ES | .............. | .............. | |
| Do ..................... | Counsel................................................ | ......do ................................ | .............. | ES | .............. | .............. | |

## DEPARTMENT OF JUSTICE—Continued

| Location | Position Title | Name of Incumbent | Type of Appt. | Pay Plan | Level, Grade, or Pay | Tenure | Expires |
|---|---|---|---|---|---|---|---|
| Washington, DC ...... | White House Liaison Officer and Special Assistant to the Attorney General. | Camellia A. Delaplane ......... | SC | GS | 12 | ............... | |
| Do .................... | Special Assistant.................................... | Hannah G. Kunasek............. | SC | GS | 9 | ............... | |
| | **OFFICE OF THE DEPUTY ATTORNEY GENERAL** | | | | | | |
| Do .................... | Deputy Attorney General ........................ | Jeffrey A Rosen..................... | PAS | EX | II | ............... | |
| Do .................... | Principal Associate Deputy Attorney General ... | Vacant .................................. | ............. | ES | ............... | ............... | |
| Do .................... | Deputy Chief of Staff and Counselor to the Attorney General. | John Savage Moran............. | NA | ES | ............... | ............... | |
| Do .................... | Chief of Staff, Director of Counter-Transnational Organized Crime and Associate Deputy Attorney General. | Patrick Hovakimian ............. | TA | ES | ............... | ............... | 03/02/22 |
| Do .................... | Deputy Chief of Staff and Associate Deputy Attorney General. | Vacant .................................. | ............. | ES | ............... | ............... | |
| Do .................... | Associate Deputy Attorney General ................... | Career Incumbent ................ | CA | ES | ............... | ............... | |
| Do .................... | ......do ............................... | Jennifer Lee Mascott............ | NA | ES | ............... | ............... | |
| Do .................... | ......do ............................... | Ryan Ashby Shores .............. | NA | ES | ............... | ............... | |
| Do .................... | ......do ............................... | Erin Creegan ....................... | NA | ES | ............... | ............... | |
| Do .................... | ......do ............................... | Career Incumbent ................ | CA | ES | ............... | ............... | |
| Do .................... | ......do ............................... | William Compton Hughes.... | NA | ES | ............... | ............... | |
| Do .................... | National Criminal Discovery Coordinator ......... | Career Incumbent ................ | CA | ES | ............... | ............... | |
| Do .................... | Director, Office of Small and Disadvantaged Business Utilization. | ......do ............................... | CA | ES | ............... | ............... | |
| Do .................... | Chief Privacy and Civil Liberties Officer ........... | Vacant .................................. | ............. | ES | ............... | ............... | |
| Do .................... | Senior Counsel........................................................ | Daniel J Feith....................... | SC | GS | 15 | ............... | |
| Do .................... | ......do ............................... | Christopher Koehler Grieco. | SC | GS | 15 | ............... | |
| Do .................... | Counsel.................................................................... | Laura Jenkins Plack ............ | SC | GS | 15 | ............... | |
| | *Criminal Division* | | | | | | |
| Do .................... | Assistant Attorney General Criminal Division.. | Brian A Benczkowski............ | PAS | EX | IV | ............... | |
| Do .................... | Principal Deputy Assistant Attorney General ... | Brian Rabbitt....................... | NA | ES | ............... | ............... | |
| Do .................... | Deputy Assistant Attorney General ................... | John P Cronan...................... | NA | ES | ............... | ............... | |
| Do .................... | ......do ............................... | Vacant .................................. | ............. | ES | ............... | ............... | |
| Do .................... | ......do ............................... | Career Incumbent ................ | CA | ES | ............... | ............... | |
| Do .................... | ......do ............................... | ......do ............................... | CA | ES | ............... | ............... | |
| Do .................... | ......do ............................... | ......do ............................... | CA | ES | ............... | ............... | |
| Do .................... | ......do ............................... | Vacant .................................. | ............. | ES | ............... | ............... | |
| Do .................... | Senior Counsel........................................................ | Sam G Nazzaro...................... | NA | ES | ............... | ............... | |
| Do .................... | Director, Office of Policy and Legislation .......... | Career Incumbent ................ | CA | ES | ............... | ............... | |
| Do .................... | Director, Office of International Affairs ............. | ......do ............................... | CA | ES | ............... | ............... | |
| Do .................... | Deputy Director, Office of International Affairs. | ......do ............................... | CA | ES | ............... | ............... | |
| Do .................... | Chief, Capital Case Unit ....................................... | ......do ............................... | CA | ES | ............... | ............... | |
| Do .................... | Deputy Director, Office of Enforcement Operations. | Vacant .................................. | ............. | ES | ............... | ............... | |
| Do .................... | Deputy Chief, Human Rights Enforcement Strategy and Policy. | Career Incumbent ................ | CA | ES | ............... | ............... | |
| Do .................... | Director Office of Enforcement Operations........ | ......do ............................... | CA | ES | ............... | ............... | |
| Do .................... | Deputy Director, Office of International Affairs. | ......do ............................... | CA | ES | ............... | ............... | |
| Do .................... | Senior Counsel for International Affairs............. | ......do ............................... | CA | ES | ............... | ............... | |
| Do .................... | Chief of Staff and Counselor ............................... | James Mandolfo.................... | SC | GS | 15 | ............... | |
| | *National Security Division* | | | | | | |
| Do .................... | Assistant Attorney General.................................. | John C Demers ..................... | PAS | EX | IV | ............... | |
| Do .................... | Principal Deputy Assistant Attorney General ... | David Penn Burns ................ | NA | ES | ............... | ............... | |
| Do .................... | Chief of Staff and Counselor ............................... | Kelli Andrews ...................... | NA | ES | ............... | ............... | |
| Do .................... | Deputy Assistant Attorney General ................... | Vacant .................................. | ............. | ES | ............... | ............... | |
| Do .................... | ......do ............................... | Career Incumbent ................ | CA | ES | ............... | ............... | |
| Do .................... | ......do ............................... | ......do ............................... | CA | ES | ............... | ............... | |
| Do .................... | Senior Counselor to the Assistant Attorney General. | David Palmer....................... | TA | ES | ............... | ............... | 09/01/21 |
| Do .................... | Senior Counsel to the Assistant Attorney General. | Vacant .................................. | ............. | ES | ............... | ............... | |
| Do .................... | Chief, Counterintelligence, Export Control, and Economic Espionage. | Career Incumbent ................ | CA | ES | ............... | ............... | |
| Do .................... | Chief, Counterterrorism Section ......................... | ......do ............................... | CA | ES | ............... | ............... | |
| Do .................... | Chief, Policy, Office of Law and Policy............... | ......do ............................... | CA | ES | ............... | ............... | |
| | *Office of Legislative Affairs* | | | | | | |
| Do .................... | Assistant Attorney General (Legislative Affairs). | Stephen Elliott Boyd............ | PAS | EX | IV | ............... | |
| Do .................... | Principal Deputy Assistant Attorney General ... | Elizabeth Prim Escalona ..... | NA | ES | ............... | ............... | |
| Do .................... | Deputy Assistant Attorney General ................... | Vacant .................................. | ............. | ES | ............... | ............... | |

## DEPARTMENT OF JUSTICE—Continued

| Location | Position Title | Name of Incumbent | Type of Appt. | Pay Plan | Level, Grade, or Pay | Tenure | Expires |
|---|---|---|---|---|---|---|---|
| Washington, DC ...... | Deputy Assistant Attorney General ................... | Mary Blanche Hankey ......... | NA | ES | ............. | ............. | |
| Do .................... | ......do .................... | Vacant .................... | | ES | ............. | ............. | |
| Do .................... | Special Counsel.................... | ......do .................... | | ES | ............. | ............. | |
| Do .................... | Law Enforcement Liaison .............................. | Theophani Stamos............... | TA | ES | ............. | ............. | 03/30/23 |
| Do .................... | Senior Counsel .................... | Megan Louise Greer............ | SC | GS | 15 | ............. | |
| Do .................... | Attorney Advisor .................... | Danielle Elysees Douglas...... | SC | GS | 12 | ............. | |
| Do .................... | Legislative Advisor .................... | Alexis M Reuss .................... | SC | GS | 12 | ............. | |
| Do .................... | ......do .................... | Brittany Alexandra Psyhogios-Smith. | SC | GS | 14 | ............. | |
| Do .................... | Attorney Advisor .................... | Lauren Goldschmidt............ | SC | GS | 14 | ............. | |
| Do .................... | Confidential Assistant .................... | Alexa Meade Vance ........... | SC | GS | 9 | ............. | |
| | *Office of the Legal Counsel* | | | | | | |
| Do .................... | Assistant Attorney General.................... | Steven A Engel .................... | PAS | EX | IV | ............. | |
| Do .................... | Principal Deputy Assistant Attorney General... | Curtis Gannon .................... | NA | ES | ............. | ............. | |
| Do .................... | Deputy Assistant Attorney General ............... | Henry Whitaker.................... | NA | ES | ............. | ............. | |
| Do .................... | ......do .................... | Vacant .................... | | ES | ............. | ............. | |
| Do .................... | ......do .................... | Liam Hardy .................... | NA | ES | ............. | ............. | |
| Do .................... | ......do .................... | Career Incumbent .................... | CA | ES | ............. | ............. | |
| Do .................... | Special Counsel.................... | Vacant .................... | | ES | ............. | ............. | |
| | *Office of Legal Policy* | | | | | | |
| Do .................... | Assistant Attorney General, Office of Legal Policy. | Beth Ann Williams .............. | PAS | EX | IV | ............. | |
| Do .................... | Principal Deputy Assistant Attorney General... | Mark Eugene Champoux ..... | NA | ES | ............. | ............. | |
| Do .................... | Deputy Assistant Attorney General ............... | Career Incumbent .................... | CA | ES | ............. | ............. | |
| Do .................... | ......do .................... | ......do .................... | CA | ES | ............. | ............. | |
| Do .................... | ......do .................... | Benjamin Wilson .................... | NA | ES | ............. | ............. | |
| Do .................... | ......do .................... | Christian Eric Ford ............ | NA | ES | ............. | ............. | |
| Do .................... | Senior Counselor .................... | Uttam Dhillon .................... | NA | ES | ............. | ............. | |
| Do .................... | ......do .................... | Timothy J Shea .................... | NA | ES | ............. | ............. | |
| Do .................... | ......do .................... | Vacant .................... | | ES | ............. | ............. | |
| Do .................... | Senior Counsel .................... | Jordan E. Pratt.................... | SC | GS | 15 | ............. | |
| Do .................... | Chief of Staff and Counsel .................... | Lindsey A. Freeman ............ | SC | GS | 15 | ............. | |
| Do .................... | Senior Counsel .................... | Matthew Downer.................... | SC | GS | 15 | ............. | |
| Do .................... | ......do .................... | Austin Lipari .................... | SC | GS | 15 | ............. | |
| Do .................... | ......do .................... | Katherine Crytzer ............ | SC | GS | 15 | ............. | |
| Do .................... | Counsel .................... | Jessica Helmers.................... | SC | GS | 14 | ............. | |
| Do .................... | ......do .................... | Mary Doocy .................... | SC | GS | 13 | ............. | |
| Do .................... | Senior Counselor.................... | Vacant .................... | | ES | ............. | ............. | |
| | *United States Parole Commission* | | | | | | |
| Do .................... | Chairman .................... | ......do .................... | PAS | EX | IV | ............. | |
| Do .................... | Parole Commissioner .................... | ......do .................... | PAS | EX | IV | ............. | |
| Do .................... | ......do .................... | ......do .................... | PAS | EX | V | ............. | |
| Do .................... | ......do .................... | Patricia K Cushwa .............. | PAS | EX | V | ............. | |
| Do .................... | ......do .................... | Charles Thomas Massarone. | PAS | EX | V | ............. | |
| | *Executive Office for United States Attorneys* | | | | | | |
| Do .................... | Director .................... | Vacant .................... | | ES | ............. | ............. | |
| Do .................... | Principal Deputy Director .................... | Career Incumbent .................... | CA | ES | ............. | ............. | |
| Grand Rapids, MI.... | United States Attorney, Michigan, Western District. | Vacant .................... | PAS | AD | ............. | ............. | |
| Minneapolis, MN .... | United States Attorney, Minnesota .................. | Erica H Macdonald ............ | PAS | AD | ............. | ............. | |
| Oxford, MS.............. | United States Attorney, Mississippi, Northern District. | William C Lamar.................... | PAS | AD | ............. | ............. | |
| Jackson, MS............ | United States Attorney, Mississippi, Southern District. | David Michael Hurst Jr. ...... | PAS | AD | ............. | ............. | |
| St. Louis, MO.......... | United States Attorney, Missouri, Eastern District. | Jeffrey B Jensen .................. | PAS | AD | ............. | ............. | |
| Chattanooga, TN .... | United States Attorney, Tennessee, Eastern District. | James Douglas Overbey....... | PAS | AD | ............. | ............. | |
| San Antonio, TX ...... | United States Attorney, Texas, Western District. | John F Bash.......................... | PAS | AD | ............. | ............. | |
| Philadelphia, PA...... | United States Attorney, Pennsylvania, Eastern District. | William Miller Mcswain....... | PAS | AD | ............. | ............. | |
| Oklahoma City, OK . | United States Attorney, Oklahoma, Western District. | Kevin M Downing................. | PAS | AD | ............. | ............. | |
| Boston, MA ............ | United States Attorney, Massachusetts ............ | Andrew Everett Lelling ...... | PAS | AD | ............. | ............. | |
| Mobile, AL.............. | United States Attorney, Alabama, Southern District. | Richard W Moore .................. | PAS | AD | ............. | ............. | |
| Concord, NH .......... | United States Attorney, New Hampshire.......... | Scott Walter Murray .......... | PAS | AD | ............. | ............. | |
| Cheyenne, WY ........ | United States Attorney, Wyoming...................... | Mark A Klaassen.................. | PAS | AD | ............. | ............. | |

## DEPARTMENT OF JUSTICE—Continued

| Location | Position Title | Name of Incumbent | Type of Appt. | Pay Plan | Level, Grade, or Pay | Tenure | Expires |
|---|---|---|---|---|---|---|---|
| Detroit, MI | United States Attorney, Michigan, Eastern District. | Matthew Schneider | PAS | AD | | | |
| Kansas City, KS | United States Attorney, Kansas | Stephen Mcallister | PAS | AD | | | |
| Sioux Falls, SD | United States Attorney, South Dakota | Ronald A Parsons Jr | PAS | AD | | | |
| Little Rock, AR | United States Attorney, Arkansas, Eastern District. | James Cody Hiland | PAS | AD | | | |
| Tulsa, OK | United States Attorney, Oklahoma, Northern District. | Robert Trent Shores | PAS | AD | | | |
| Buffalo, NY | United States Attorney, New York, Western District. | Vacant | PAS | AD | | | |
| Omaha, NE | United States Attorney, Nebraska | Joseph P Kelly | PAS | AD | | | |
| Albuquerque, NM | United States Attorney, New Mexico | John C Anderson | PAS | AD | | | |
| Wilmington, DE | United States Attorney, Delaware | David Charles Weiss | PAS | AD | | | |
| Fort Smith, AR | United States Attorney, Arkansas, Western District. | Vacant | PAS | AD | | | |
| Wheeling, WV | United States Attorney, West Virginia, Northern District. | William J Powell | PAS | AD | | | |
| Montgomery, AL | United States Attorney, Alabama, Middle District. | Louis V. Franklin | PAS | AD | | | |
| Huntsville, AL | United States Attorney, Alabama, Northern District. | John E. Town | PAS | AD | | | |
| Anchorage, AK | United States Attorney, Alaska | Bryan D Schroder | PAS | AD | | | |
| Phoenix, AZ | United States Attorney, Arizona | Michael G Bailey | PAS | AD | | | |
| Los Angeles, CA | United States Attorney, California, Central District. | Nicola T Hanna | PAS | AD | | | |
| San Francisco, CA | United States Attorney, California, Northern District. | David Lloyd Anderson | PAS | AD | | | |
| San Diego, CA | United States Attorney, California, Southern District. | Robert Selden Brewer Jr | PAS | AD | | | |
| Denver, CO | United States Attorney, Colorado | Jason Robert Dunn | PAS | AD | | | |
| New Haven, CT | United States Attorney, Connecticut | John H Durham | PAS | AD | | | |
| Washington, DC | United States Attorney, District of Columbia | Vacant | PAS | AD | | | |
| Tampa, FL | United States Attorney, Florida, Middle District. | Maria Chapa Lopez | PAS | AD | | | |
| Tallahassee, FL | United States Attorney, Florida, Northern District. | Lawrence Keefe | PAS | AD | | | |
| Miami, FL | United States Attorney, Florida, Southern District. | Ariana Fajardo Orshan | PAS | AD | | | |
| Macon, GA | United States Attorney, Georgia, Middle District. | Charles Edward Peeler | PAS | AD | | | |
| Atlanta, GA | United States Attorney, Georgia, Northern District. | Byung J Pak | PAS | AD | | | |
| Savannah, GA | United States Attorney, Georgia, Southern District. | Bobby Lee Christine | PAS | AD | | | |
| Agana, Guam | United States Attorney, Guam | Vacant | PAS | AD | | | |
| Honolulu, HI | United States Attorney, Hawaii | Kenji Marcel Price | PAS | AD | | | |
| Boise, ID | United States Attorney, Idaho | Bart Mckay Davis | PAS | AD | | | |
| Springfield, IL | United States Attorney, Illinois, Central District. | John C Milhiser | PAS | AD | | | |
| Chicago, IL | United States Attorney, Illinois, Northern District. | John R Lausch Jr | PAS | AD | | | |
| Fairview Heights, IL. | United States Attorney, Southern District, Illinois. | Vacant | PAS | AD | | | |
| Hammond, IN | United States Attorney, Indiana, Northern District. | Thomas L Kirsch II | PAS | AD | | | |
| Baltimore, MD | United States Attorney, Maryland | Robert Hur | PAS | AD | | | |
| Indianapolis, IN | United States Attorney, Indiana, Southern District. | Joshua J Minkler | PAS | AD | | | |
| Cedar Rapids, IA | United States Attorney, Iowa, Northern District. | Peter E. Deegan Jr. | PAS | AD | | | |
| Des Moines, IA | United States Attorney, Iowa, Southern District. | Marc L Krickbaum | PAS | AD | | | |
| Lexington, KY | United States Attorney, Kentucky, Eastern District. | Robert M Duncan Jr | PAS | AD | | | |
| Louisville, KY | United States Attorney, Kentucky, Western District. | Russell M Coleman | PAS | AD | | | |
| New Orleans, LA | United States Attorney, Louisiana, Eastern District. | Peter G Strasser | PAS | AD | | | |
| Baton Rouge, LA | United States Attorney, Louisiana, Middle District. | Brandon Joseph Fremin | PAS | AD | | | |
| Portland, ME | United States Attorney, Maine | Halsey B Frank | PAS | AD | | | |
| Kansas City, MO | United States Attorney, Missouri, Western District. | Timothy Allen Garrison | PAS | AD | | | |

## DEPARTMENT OF JUSTICE—Continued

| Location | Position Title | Name of Incumbent | Type of Appt. | Pay Plan | Level, Grade, or Pay | Tenure | Expires |
|---|---|---|---|---|---|---|---|
| Billings, MT | United States Attorney, Montana | Kurt G Alme | PAS | AD | | | |
| Las Vegas, NV | United States Attorney, Nevada | Nicholas Andrew Trutanich. | PAS | AD | | | |
| Newark, NJ | United States Attorney, New Jersey | Vacant | PAS | AD | | | |
| New York-Kings, NY. | United States Attorney, New York, Eastern District. | ......do | PAS | AD | | | |
| Syracuse, NY | United States Attorney, New York, Northern District. | ......do | PAS | AD | | | |
| New York New York, NY. | United States Attorney, New York, Southern District. | ......do | PAS | AD | | | |
| Raleigh, NC | United States Attorney, North Carolina, Eastern District. | Robert J Higdon Jr. | PAS | AD | | | |
| Greensboro, NC | United States Attorney, North Carolina, Middle District. | Matthew Grady Martin | PAS | AD | | | |
| Charlotte, NC | United States Attorney, North Carolina, Western District. | Raymond Andrew Murray ... | PAS | AD | | | |
| Fargo, ND | United States Attorney, North Dakota | Drew H Wrigley | PAS | AD | | | |
| Cleveland, OH | United States Attorney, Ohio, Northern District. | Justin E Herdman | PAS | AD | | | |
| Columbus, OH | United States Attorney, Ohio, Southern District. | David M Devillers | PAS | AD | | | |
| Muskogee, OK | United States Attorney, Oklahoma, Eastern District. | Brian John Kuester | PAS | AD | | | |
| Portland, OR | United States Attorney, Oregon | Billy J Williams | PAS | AD | | | |
| Harrisburg, PA | United States Attorney, Pennsylvania, Middle District. | David James Freed | PAS | AD | | | |
| Pittsburgh, PA | United States Attorney, Pennsylvania, Western District. | Scott W Brady | PAS | AD | | | |
| Hato Rey, Puerto Rico. | United States Attorney, Puerto Rico | William S Muldrow | PAS | AD | | | |
| Providence, RI | United States Attorney, Rhode Island | Aaron Louis Weisman | PAS | AD | | | |
| Columbia, SC | United States Attorney, South Carolina | Vacant | PAS | AD | | | |
| Nashville, TN | United States Attorney, Tennessee, Middle District. | Donald Q Cochran | PAS | AD | | | |
| Memphis, TN | United States Attorney, Western District, Tennessee. | David Michael Dunavant | PAS | AD | | | |
| Beaumont, TX | United States Attorney, Texas, Eastern District. | Vacant | PAS | AD | | | |
| Dallas, TX | United States Attorney, Texas, Northern District. | Erin A Nealy Cox | PAS | AD | | | |
| Houston, TX | United States Attorney, Texas, Southern District. | Ryan Kelley Patrick | PAS | AD | | | |
| Salt Lake City, UT .. | United States Attorney, Utah | John W Huber | PAS | AD | | | |
| Burlington, VT | United States Attorney, Vermont | Christina E Nolan | PAS | AD | | | |
| St. Croix, Virgin Islands. | United States Attorney, Virgin Islands | Vacant | PAS | AD | | | |
| Alexandria, VA | United States Attorney, Virginia, Eastern District. | George Zachary Terwilliger . | PAS | AD | | | |
| Roanoke, VA | United States Attorney, Virginia, Western District. | Thomas Tullidge Cullen | PAS | AD | | | |
| Milwaukee, WI | United States Attorney, Wisconsin, Eastern District. | Matthew Dean Krueger | PAS | AD | | | |
| Madison, WI | United States Attorney, Wisconsin, Western District. | Scott Chester Blader | PAS | AD | | | |
| Sacramento, CA | United States Attorney, California, Eastern District. | Mcgregor W Scott | PAS | AD | | | |
| Seattle, WA | United States Attorney, Washington, Western District. | Brian T Moran | PAS | AD | | | |
| Spokane, WA | United States Attorney, Washington, Eastern District. | William Douglas Hyslop | PAS | AD | | | |
| Charleston, WV | United States Attorney, West Virginia, Southern District. | Michael Bryan Stuart | PAS | AD | | | |
| Shreveport, LA | United States Attorney, Louisiana, Western District. | David C Joseph | PAS | AD | | | |
| Miami, FL | Secretary | Bernice Diaz | SC | GS | 10 | | |
| Tulsa, OK | Program Support Specialist | Payton Bullard | SC | GS | 7 | | |
| Atlanta, GA | Secretary | Sandra Olson Connelly | SC | GS | 10 | | |
| Phoenix, AZ | ......do | Valerie Neumann | SC | GS | 10 | | |
| Springfield, IL | ......do | Tamara Richmond | SC | GS | 9 | | |
| Dallas, TX | ......do | Suzanne Martin | SC | GS | 10 | | |
| Savannah, GA | ......do | Angela Oldfield | SC | GS | 9 | | |
| | *Executive Office for Immigration Review* | | | | | | |
| Falls Church, VA | Director | Career Incumbent | CA | ES | | | |
| Do | Deputy Director | Vacant | | ES | | | |

## DEPARTMENT OF JUSTICE—Continued

| Location | Position Title | Name of Incumbent | Type of Appt. | Pay Plan | Level, Grade, or Pay | Tenure | Expires |
|---|---|---|---|---|---|---|---|
| Falls Church, VA ..... | Chief Management Officer ................................ | Career Incumbent ............... | CA | ES | ............. | ............. | |
| Do ..................... | Chief Information Officer ................................ | ......do ................................ | CA | ES | ............. | ............. | |
| | *Office of the Pardon Attorney* | | | | | | |
| Washington, DC ...... | Pardon Attorney................................ | Vacant ............................ | ............. | ES | ............. | ............. | |
| | *Office of Public Affairs* | | | | | | |
| Do ..................... | Director of Communications and Public Affairs. | Kerri Ann Kupec ............... | NA | ES | ............. | ............. | |
| Do ..................... | Principal Deputy Director ................................ | Matthew Lloyd ................... | NA | ES | ............. | ............. | |
| Do ..................... | Director of Press Advance and Public Affairs Officer. | Brianna Herlihy ................... | SC | GS | 12 | ............. | |
| Do ..................... | Public Affairs Specialist ................................ | Alison Kjergaard ............... | SC | GS | 9 | ............. | |
| Do ..................... | Special Assistant and Press Assistant .............. | Mollie Rose Timmons........... | SC | GS | 9 | ............. | |
| Do ..................... | Press Assistant................................ | Melissa D. Clark................... | SC | GS | 7 | ............. | |
| Do ..................... | ......do ...... | Jeffery Charles Cardwell ..... | SC | GS | 7 | ............. | |
| | *Office of Professional Responsibility* | | | | | | |
| Do ..................... | Senior Counselor................................ | Career Incumbent ............... | CA | ES | ............. | ............. | |
| | *Rule of Law Office* | | | | | | |
| Kabul, Afghanistan . | Justice Attaché Afghanistan ............................. | Vacant ............................ | ............. | ES | ............. | ............. | |
| Baghdad, Iraq......... | Justice Attache, Iraq................................ | Spencer Bassett................... | TA | ES | ............. | ............. | 08/04/21 |
| Do ..................... | ......do ................................ | James Joyner................... | TA | ES | ............. | ............. | 11/23/22 |
| | **EXECUTIVE OFFICE FOR ORGANIZED CRIME DRUG ENFORCEMENT TASK FORCES** | | | | | | |
| Washington, DC ...... | Director, Organized Crime Drug Enforcement Task Forces, Fusion Center. | Career Incumbent ............... | CA | ES | ............. | ............. | |
| Do ..................... | Deputy Director, Organized Crime Drug Enforcement Task Forces. | ......do ................................ | CA | ES | ............. | ............. | |
| | *Federal Bureau of Investigation* | | | | | | |
| Do ..................... | Director, Federal Bureau of Investigation.......... | Christopher A Wray ............. | PAS | EX | II | ............. | |
| Do ..................... | Senior Intelligence Officer ................................ | Walter A Levin....................... | XS | SL | ............. | ............. | |
| | *Drug Enforcement Administration* | | | | | | |
| Do ..................... | Administrator, Drug Enforcement Administration. | Vacant ............................ | PAS | EX | III | ............. | |
| Do ..................... | Deputy Administrator, Drug Enforcement Administration. | ......do ................................ | PAS | EX | V | ............. | |
| | *Bureau of Alcohol, Tobacco, Firearms and Explosives* | | | | | | |
| Do ..................... | Director, Bureau of Alcohol, Tobacco, Firearms, and Explosives. | ......do ................................ | PAS | EX | III | ............. | |
| Do ..................... | Chief Counsel ................................ | Career Incumbent ............... | CA | ES | ............. | ............. | |
| Do ..................... | Deputy Chief Counsel ................................ | ......do ................................ | CA | ES | ............. | ............. | |
| | *United States Marshals Service* | | | | | | |
| Arlington, VA.......... | Director................................ | Donald W Washington.......... | PAS | EX | IV | ............. | |
| Do ..................... | General Counsel................................ | Career Incumbent ............... | CA | ES | ............. | ............. | |
| Do ..................... | Director, Business Strategy and Integration ..... | Vacant ............................ | ............. | ES | ............. | ............. | |
| Do ..................... | Capture Program Manager ................................ | Career Incumbent ............... | CA | ES | ............. | ............. | |
| New York-Kings, NY. | United States Marshal Eastern District of New York (Kings). | Vacant ............................ | PAS | SL | ............. | ............. | |
| San Antonio, TX ...... | United States Marshal, Western District of Texas(San Antonio). | Susan L Pamerleau .............. | PAS | SL | ............. | ............. | |
| Chicago, IL............... | United States Marshal, Northern District of Illinois (Chicago). | Vacant ............................ | PAS | SL | ............. | ............. | |
| Los Angeles, CA....... | United States Marshal, Central District of California (Los Angeles). | David Singer ........................ | PAS | SL | ............. | ............. | |
| Alexandria, VA ........ | United States Marshal, Eastern District of Virginia (Alexandria). | Nick E. Proffitt .................... | PAS | SL | ............. | ............. | |
| Washington, DC ...... | United States Marshal, District of Columbia (Washington, District of Columbia). | Vacant ............................ | PAS | SL | ............. | ............. | |
| Phoenix, AZ ............ | United States Marshal, District of Arizona (Phoenix). | David P Gonzales ................. | PAS | SL | ............. | ............. | |
| Philadelphia, PA...... | United States Marshal, Eastern District of Pennsylvania (Philadelphia). | Eric S Gartner ..................... | PAS | SL | ............. | ............. | |
| San Juan, Puerto Rico. | United States Marshal, Puerto Rico................... | Wilmer Ocasio ..................... | PAS | SL | ............. | ............. | |
| Washington, DC ...... | United States Marshal, Superior Court (Washington District of Columbia). | Robert A Dixon ..................... | PAS | SL | ............. | ............. | |
| Newark, NJ ............ | United States Marshal, District of New Jersey (Newark). | Juan Mattos Jr. ................... | PAS | SL | ............. | ............. | |
| San Francisco, CA... | United States Marshal, Northern District of California (San Francisco). | Donald M Okeefe................... | PAS | SL | ............. | ............. | |

## DEPARTMENT OF JUSTICE—Continued

| Location | Position Title | Name of Incumbent | Type of Appt. | Pay Plan | Level, Grade, or Pay | Tenure | Expires |
|---|---|---|---|---|---|---|---|
| San Diego, CA ......... | United States Marshal, Southern District of California (San Diego). | Steven C Stafford ................. | PAS | SL | .............. | .............. | |
| Tampa, FL ............... | United States Marshal, Middle District of Florida (Tampa). | William B Berger Sr. ............. | PAS | SL | .............. | .............. | |
| Houston, TX............. | United States Marshal, Southern District of Texas (Houston). | Thomas M O'Connor ............ | PAS | SL | .............. | .............. | |
| Atlanta, GA ............. | United States Marshal, Northern District of Georgia (Atlanta). | Michael S Yeager ................. | PAS | SL | .............. | .............. | |
| Detroit, MI............... | United States Marshal, Eastern District of Michigan (Detroit). | Vacant ................................ | PAS | SL | .............. | .............. | |
| Baltimore, MD......... | United States Marshal District of Maryland (Baltimore). | Johnny L Hughes ................. | PAS | SL | .............. | .............. | |
| Sacramento, CA....... | United States Marshal, Eastern District of California (Sacramento). | Vacant ................................ | PAS | SL | .............. | .............. | |
| Tallahassee, FL ....... | United States Marshal, Northern District of Florida (Tallahassee). | Robert Don Ladner Jr. ......... | PAS | SL | .............. | .............. | |
| Minneapolis, MN ..... | United States Marshal, District of Minnesota (Minneapolis). | Ramona L Dohman ............. | PAS | SL | .............. | .............. | |
| Cleveland, OH ......... | United States Marshal, Northern District of Ohio (Cleveland). | Peter J Elliott ..................... | PAS | SL | .............. | .............. | |
| Dallas, TX ................ | United States Marshal, Northern District of Texas (Dallas). | Richard E Taylor Jr. ............ | PAS | SL | .............. | .............. | |
| Columbia, SC........... | United States Marshal, District of South Carolina (Columbia). | Thomas Griffin Jr................ | PAS | SL | .............. | .............. | |
| Miami, FL................. | United States Marshal, Southern District of Florida (Miami). | Gadyaces S Serralta............ | PAS | SL | .............. | .............. | |
| New York New York, NY. | United States Marshal, Southern District of New York (New York). | Ralph Sozio ........................ | PAS | SL | .............. | .............. | |
| Birmingham, AL...... | United States Marshal, Northern District, Alabama. | Chester M Keely.................. | PAS | GS | .............. | .............. | |
| Montgomery, AL ...... | United States Marshall, Middle District, Alabama. | Jesse Seroyer Jr.................. | PAS | GS | .............. | .............. | |
| Mobile, AL............... | United States Marshal, Southern District, Alabama. | Mark F Sloke ...................... | PAS | GS | .............. | .............. | |
| Anchorage, AK........ | United States Marshal, Alaska......................... | Robert W Heun .................... | PAS | GS | .............. | .............. | |
| Little Rock, AR ....... | United States Marshal, Eastern District, Arkansas. | Vacant ................................ | PAS | GS | .............. | .............. | |
| Fort Smith, AR ........ | United States Marshal, Western District, Arkansas. | ......do | PAS | GS | .............. | .............. | |
| New Haven, CT ....... | United States Marshal, Connecticut ................. | ......do | PAS | GS | .............. | .............. | |
| Wilmington, DE....... | United States Marshal, Delaware ..................... | Michael C McGowan ............ | PAS | GS | .............. | .............. | |
| Macon, GA ............... | United States Marshal, Middle District, Georgia. | John C Bittick..................... | PAS | GS | .............. | .............. | |
| Savannah, GA ......... | United States Marshal, Southern District, Georgia. | David L Lyons ..................... | PAS | GS | .............. | .............. | |
| Agana, Guam........... | United States Marshal, Guam/Northern Mariana Islands. | Fernando Lg Sablan ............ | PAS | GS | .............. | .............. | |
| Honolulu, HI............ | United States Marshal, Hawaii ......................... | Charles Lockridge Goodwin. | PAS | GS | .............. | .............. | |
| Boise, ID ................. | United States Marshal, Idaho......................... | Brent R Bunn ...................... | PAS | GS | .............. | .............. | |
| Springfield, IL ......... | United States Marshal, Central District, Illinois. | Brendan O Heffner.............. | PAS | GS | .............. | .............. | |
| East St Louis, IL ..... | United States Marshal, Southern District, Illinois. | Bradley A Maxwell.............. | PAS | GS | .............. | .............. | |
| Hammond, IN.......... | United States Marshal, Northern District, Indiana. | Todd L Nukes ...................... | PAS | GS | .............. | .............. | |
| Indianapolis, IN ...... | United States Marshal, Southern District, Indiana. | Joseph D Mcclain ................ | PAS | GS | .............. | .............. | |
| Kansas City, KS ...... | United States Marshal, Kansas......................... | Ronald Miller...................... | PAS | GS | .............. | .............. | |
| Lexington, KY ......... | United States Marshal, Eastern District, Kentucky. | Norman Euell Arflack.......... | PAS | GS | .............. | .............. | |
| Des Moines, IA ........ | United States Marshal, Southern District, Iowa. | Theoharris G Kamatchus .... | PAS | GS | .............. | .............. | |
| Louisville, KY ......... | United States Marshal, Western District, Kentucky. | Gary B Burman.................... | PAS | GS | .............. | .............. | |
| New Orleans, LA..... | United States Marshal, Eastern District, Louisiana. | Scott P Illing........................ | PAS | GS | .............. | .............. | |
| Baton Rouge, LA ..... | United States Marshal, Middle District, Louisiana. | William T Brown ................. | PAS | GS | .............. | .............. | |
| Shreveport, LA ........ | United States Marshal, Western District, Louisiana. | Vacant ................................ | PAS | GS | .............. | .............. | |
| Portland, ME ........... | United States Marshal, Maine......................... | Theodor G Short.................. | PAS | GS | .............. | .............. | |
| Grand Rapids, MI.... | United States Marshal, Western District, Michigan. | Vacant ................................ | PAS | GS | .............. | .............. | |

## DEPARTMENT OF JUSTICE—Continued

| Location | Position Title | Name of Incumbent | Type of Appt. | Pay Plan | Level, Grade, or Pay | Tenure | Expires |
|---|---|---|---|---|---|---|---|
| Oxford, MS............. | United States Marshal, Northern District, Mississippi. | Daniel R Mckittrick............. | PAS | GS | ................ | ............... | |
| Jackson, MS............ | United States Marshal, Southern District, Mississippi. | Mark B Shepherd................. | PAS | GS | ................ | ............... | |
| Kansas City, MO ..... | United States Marshal, Western District, Missouri. | Mark S James....................... | PAS | GS | ................ | ............... | |
| Billings, MT............ | United States Marshal, Montana ...................... | Rodney D Ostermiller ......... | PAS | GS | ................ | ............... | |
| Omaha, NE.............. | United States Marshal, Nebraska ...................... | Scott E Kracl ....................... | PAS | GS | ................ | ............... | |
| Concord, NH ........... | United States Marshal, New Hampshire.......... | Enoch F Willard .................. | PAS | GS | ................ | ............... | |
| Syracuse, NY ........... | United States Marshal, Northern District, New York. | David L McNulty ................. | PAS | GS | ................ | ............... | |
| Buffalo, NY ............. | United States Marshal, Western District, New York. | Vacant ................................. | PAS | GS | ................ | ............... | |
| Raleigh, NC ............. | United States Marshal, Eastern District, North Carolina. | Michael B East .................... | PAS | GS | ................ | ............... | |
| Greensboro, NC ....... | United States Marshal, Middle District, North Carolina. | Steven L Gladden................. | PAS | GS | ................ | ............... | |
| Fargo, ND ............... | United States Marshal, North Dakota.............. | Dallas L Carlson.................. | PAS | GS | ................ | ............... | |
| Tulsa, OK................. | United States Marshal, Northern District, Oklahoma. | Clayton D Johnson .............. | PAS | GS | ................ | ............... | |
| Muskogee, OK ......... | United States Marshal, Eastern District, Oklahoma. | Kerry L Pettingill ............... | PAS | GS | ................ | ............... | |
| Oklahoma City, OK. | United States Marshal, Western District, Oklahoma. | Johnny Lee Kuhlman........... | PAS | GS | ................ | ............... | |
| Pittsburgh, PA......... | United States Marshal, Western District, Pennsylvania. | Michael D Baughman ......... | PAS | GS | ................ | ............... | |
| Providence, RI ........ | United States Marshal, Rhode Island ............... | Wing Chau ........................... | PAS | GS | ................ | ............... | |
| Sioux Falls, SD ....... | United States Marshal, South Dakota .............. | Daniel C Mosteller .............. | PAS | GS | ................ | ............... | |
| Knoxville, TN........... | United States Marshal, Eastern District, Tennessee. | David G Jolley ..................... | PAS | GS | ................ | ............... | |
| Nashville, TN........... | United States Marshal, Middle District, Tennessee. | Denny W King ..................... | PAS | GS | ................ | ............... | |
| Memphis, TN .......... | United States Marshal, Western District, Tennessee. | Jeffrey T Holt...................... | PAS | GS | ................ | ............... | |
| Salt Lake City, UT .. | United States Marshal, Utah............................ | Matthew D Harris ............... | PAS | GS | ................ | ............... | |
| Burlington, VT........ | United States Marshal, Vermont ....................... | Bradley Jay Larose ............. | PAS | GS | ................ | ............... | |
| St. Thomas, Virgin Islands. | United States Marshal, Virgin Islands ............. | James E Clark ..................... | PAS | GS | ................ | ............... | |
| Roanoke, VA............. | United States Marshal, Western District, Virginia. | Vacant ................................. | PAS | GS | ................ | ............... | |
| Spokane, WA............ | United States Marshal, Eastern District, Washington. | Craig E Thayer .................... | PAS | GS | ................ | ............... | |
| Charleston, WV ....... | United States Marshal, Southern District, West Virginia. | Michael T Baylous ............... | PAS | GS | ................ | ............... | |
| Milwaukee, WI ........ | United States Marshal, Eastern District, Wisconsin. | Vacant ................................. | PAS | GS | ................ | ............... | |
| Madison, WI ........... | United States Marshal, Western District, Wisconsin. | Kim V Gaffney..................... | PAS | GS | ................ | ............... | |
| Cheyenne, WY ........ | United States Marshal, Wyoming...................... | Randall P Huff..................... | PAS | GS | ................ | ............... | |
| Charlotte, NC .......... | United States Marshal, Western District, North Carolina. | Gregory Forest..................... | PAS | GS | ................ | ............... | |
| Albuquerque, NM.... | United States Marshal District New Mexico (Albuquerque). | Sonya K Chavez ................... | PAS | SL | ................ | ............... | |
| St. Louis, MO........... | United States Marshal, Eastern District, Missouri (St. Louis). | Jonathan D Jordan.............. | PAS | SL | ................ | ............... | |
| Portland, OR............ | United States Marshal, Oregon (Portland) ....... | Russel E Burger ................... | PAS | SL | ................ | ............... | |
| Seattle, WA .............. | United States Marshal, Western District, Washington (Seattle). | Vacant ................................. | PA | SL | ................ | ............... | |
| Cincinnati, OH ........ | United States Marshal, Southern District, Ohio (Cincinnati). | Peter Tobin.......................... | PAS | SL | ................ | ............... | |
| Denver, CO ............. | United States Marshal, Colorado (Denver)....... | David A Weaver ................... | PAS | SL | ................ | ............... | |
| Tyler, TX ................. | United States Marshal, Eastern District, Texas (Tyler). | John W Garrison ................. | PA | SL | ................ | ............... | |
| Las Vegas, NV ........ | United States Marshal, Nevada (Las Vegas) ..... | Gary G Schofield ................. | PAS | SL | ................ | ............... | |
| Scranton, PA............ | United States Marshal, Middle District, Pennsylvania. | Martin J Pane...................... | PAS | SL | ................ | ............... | |
| Arlington, VA............ | Special Assistant for Financial Systems ........... | Vacant ................................. | ............ | ES | ................ | ............... | |
| Boston, MA .............. | United States Marshal, Massachusetts............ | John Gibbons ...................... | PAS | SL | ................ | ............... | |
| Cedar Rapids, IA..... | United States Marshal, Northern District, Iowa. | Douglas J Strike.................. | PAS | GS | ................ | ............... | |
| Clarksburg, WV ....... | United States Marshal, Northern District, West Virginia. | J C Raffety.......................... | PAS | GS | ................ | ............... | |
| Buffalo, NY ............. | United States Marshal, Western District, New York. | Charles F Salina.................. | PAS | GS | ................ | ............... | |

## DEPARTMENT OF JUSTICE—Continued

| Location | Position Title | Name of Incumbent | Type of Appt. | Pay Plan | Level, Grade, or Pay | Tenure | Expires |
|---|---|---|---|---|---|---|---|
| | *Federal Bureau of Prisons* | | | | | | |
| Washington, DC ...... | Director.................................................. | Career Incumbent ................ | CA | ES | .............. | .............. | |
| Do ..................... | Director National Institute of Corrections........ | Vacant ................................ | ............. | ES | | | |
| | OFFICE OF THE ASSOCIATE ATTORNEY GENERAL | | | | | | |
| Do ..................... | Associate Attorney General.......................... | ......do .............................. | PAS | EX | III | .............. | |
| Do ..................... | Principal Deputy Associate Attorney General ... | Claire Mccusker Murray...... | NA | ES | .............. | .............. | |
| Do ..................... | Deputy Associate Attorney General ................ | Patrick D. Davis.................. | NA | ES | .............. | .............. | |
| Do ..................... | ......do .............................................. | Vacant ................................ | ............. | ES | .............. | .............. | |
| Do ..................... | ......do .............................................. | ......do .............................. | | ES | .............. | .............. | |
| Do ..................... | ......do .............................................. | Jennifer Dickey.................... | NA | ES | .............. | .............. | |
| Do ..................... | ......do .............................................. | Brian H Pandya.................... | NA | ES | .............. | .............. | |
| Do ..................... | ......do .............................................. | Gerald Brinton Lucas IV ..... | NA | ES | .............. | .............. | |
| | *Antitrust Division* | | | | | | |
| Do ..................... | Assistant Attorney General.......................... | Makan Delrahim ................ | PAS | EX | IV | .............. | |
| Do ..................... | Principal Deputy Assistant Attorney General ... | Bernard Angelo Nigro Jr...... | NA | ES | .............. | .............. | |
| Do ..................... | Deputy Assistant Attorney General ................ | Michael Murray.................... | NA | ES | .............. | .............. | |
| Do ..................... | ......do .............................................. | Vacant ................................ | ............. | ES | .............. | .............. | |
| Do ..................... | ......do .............................................. | Career Incumbent ................ | CA | ES | .............. | .............. | |
| Do ..................... | ......do .............................................. | Rene Irene Augustine ......... | NA | ES | .............. | .............. | |
| Do ..................... | ......do .............................................. | Alexander Paul Okuliar....... | NA | ES | .............. | .............. | |
| Do ..................... | Senior Counsel and Director of Risk Management. | Career Incumbent ................ | CA | ES | .............. | .............. | |
| New York New York, NY. | Chief, New York Field Office........................ | ......do .............................. | CA | ES | .............. | .............. | |
| Chicago, IL............. | Chief, Chicago Field Office.......................... | ......do .............................. | CA | ES | .............. | .............. | |
| Washington, DC ...... | Chief Competition Policy Section.................... | ......do .............................. | CA | ES | .............. | .............. | |
| San Francisco, CA... | Chief, San Francisco Field Office.................. | ......do .............................. | CA | ES | .............. | .............. | |
| Washington, DC ...... | Chief, Foreign Commerce Section.................. | ......do .............................. | CA | ES | .............. | .............. | |
| Do ..................... | Chief, National Criminal Enforcement Section . | ......do .............................. | CA | ES | .............. | .............. | |
| Do ..................... | Director, Criminal Enforcement.................... | ......do .............................. | CA | ES | .............. | .............. | |
| Do ..................... | Chief, Healthcare and Consumer Products....... | Vacant ................................ | ............. | ES | .............. | .............. | |
| Do ..................... | Chief, Defense, Industrial and Aerospace ........ | Career Incumbent ................ | CA | ES | .............. | .............. | |
| Do ..................... | Chief, Media and Entertainment.................... | ......do .............................. | CA | ES | .............. | .............. | |
| Do ..................... | Chief Economic Litigation Section.................. | ......do .............................. | CA | ES | .............. | .............. | |
| Do ..................... | Chief, Competition Policy and Advocacy Section. | ......do .............................. | CA | ES | .............. | .............. | |
| Do ..................... | Chief, Appellate Section .............................. | ......do .............................. | CA | ES | .............. | .............. | |
| Do ..................... | Chief, Networks and Technology Enforcement Section. | ......do .............................. | CA | ES | .............. | .............. | |
| Do ..................... | Chief, Washington Criminal Ii Section............. | ......do .............................. | CA | ES | .............. | .............. | |
| Do ..................... | Director of Civil Enforcement...................... | Vacant ................................ | ............. | ES | .............. | .............. | |
| Do ..................... | Senior Director of Investigation and Litigation. | Career Incumbent ................ | CA | ES | .............. | .............. | |
| Do ..................... | Counsel.................................................. | Julia A Schiller .................. | SC | GS | 15 | .............. | |
| Do ..................... | ......do .............................................. | Elyse Dorsey ...................... | SC | GS | 15 | .............. | |
| Do ..................... | ......do .............................................. | Taylor Mayly Owings ........... | SC | GS | 15 | .............. | |
| Do ..................... | Chief of Staff and Senior Counsel ................ | William Joseph Rinner ........ | SC | GS | 15 | .............. | |
| Do ..................... | Chief, Economic Regulatory Section................ | Career Incumbent ................ | CA | ES | .............. | .............. | |
| Do ..................... | Senior Counsel ........................................ | Vacant ................................ | ............. | ES | .............. | .............. | |
| Do ..................... | Director of Professional Development and Counsel to the Assistant Attorney General. | Career Incumbent ................ | CA | ES | .............. | .............. | |
| Do ..................... | Chief, Transportation/Energy/Agriculture Section. | ......do .............................. | CA | ES | .............. | .............. | |
| | *Civil Division* | | | | | | |
| Do ..................... | Assistant Attorney General Civil Division........ | Joseph H Hunt .................... | PAS | EX | IV | .............. | |
| Do ..................... | Principal Deputy Assistant Attorney General ... | Ethan Price Davis ................ | NA | ES | .............. | .............. | |
| Do ..................... | Deputy Assistant Attorney General ................ | Vacant ................................ | ............. | ES | .............. | .............. | |
| Do ..................... | ......do .............................................. | Scott Stewart...................... | NA | ES | .............. | .............. | |
| Do ..................... | ......do .............................................. | Vacant ................................ | ............. | ES | .............. | .............. | |
| Do ..................... | ......do .............................................. | Hashim Mandayappurath Mooppan. | NA | ES | .............. | .............. | |
| Do ..................... | ......do .............................................. | Career Incumbent ................ | CA | ES | .............. | .............. | |
| Do ..................... | ......do .............................................. | David Michael Morrell......... | NA | ES | .............. | .............. | |
| Do ..................... | Director, Appellate Staff.............................. | Career Incumbent ................ | CA | ES | .............. | .............. | |
| Do ..................... | Director, Appellate Section.......................... | ......do .............................. | CA | ES | .............. | .............. | |
| Do ..................... | Appellate Litigation Counsel ........................ | ......do .............................. | CA | ES | .............. | .............. | |
| Do ..................... | Director, Commercial Litigation Branch, Corporate/Financial Section. | ......do .............................. | CA | ES | .............. | .............. | |
| Do ..................... | Director, Commercial Litigation Branch, Civil Fraud Section. | ......do .............................. | CA | ES | .............. | .............. | |

## DEPARTMENT OF JUSTICE—Continued

| Location | Position Title | Name of Incumbent | Type of Appt. | Pay Plan | Level, Grade, or Pay | Tenure | Expires |
|---|---|---|---|---|---|---|---|
| Washington, DC ...... | Director, Commercial Litigation Branch, Intellectual Property Section. | Career Incumbent ............... | CA | ES | ............... | ............... | |
| Do ................... | Director, Commercial Litigation Branch, National Courts Section. | ......do ............... | CA | ES | ............... | ............... | |
| Do ................... | Deputy Director, National Courts Section.......... | ......do ............... | CA | ES | ............... | ............... | |
| Do ................... | Branch Director, Federal Programs.................. | ......do ............... | CA | ES | ............... | ............... | |
| Do ................... | Special Litigation Counsel, Federal Programs .. | ......do ............... | CA | ES | ............... | ............... | |
| Do ................... | Branch Director, Federal Programs.................. | ......do ............... | CA | ES | ............... | ............... | |
| Do ................... | ......do ............... | ......do ............... | CA | ES | ............... | ............... | |
| Do ................... | Director, Aviation and Admiralty Section ......... | ......do ............... | CA | ES | ............... | ............... | |
| Do ................... | Director, Constitutional and Specialized Tort Litigation Section. | ......do ............... | CA | ES | ............... | ............... | |
| Do ................... | Director, Environmental Tort Litigation Section. | ......do ............... | CA | ES | ............... | ............... | |
| Do ................... | Director, Office of Immigration Litigation (Denaturalization Section). | Vacant ............... | ............ | ES | ............... | ............... | |
| Do ................... | Director, Federal Tort Claims Act Section.......... | Career Incumbent ............... | CA | ES | ............... | ............... | |
| Do ................... | Director, Office of Immigration Litigation (District Court Section). | ......do ............... | CA | ES | ............... | ............... | |
| Do ................... | Deputy Director for International Policy .......... | ......do ............... | CA | ES | ............... | ............... | |
| Do ................... | Deputy Director, Constitutional and Specialized Torts Litigation-Bivens. | ......do ............... | CA | ES | ............... | ............... | |
| Do ................... | Senior Counsel ............... | Christopher Bates ............... | SC | GS | 15 | ............... | |
| Do ................... | Counsel ............... | Matthew Glover................... | SC | GS | 15 | ............... | |
| Do ................... | ......do ............... | William Lane III................... | SC | GS | 15 | ............... | |
| Do ................... | ......do ............... | Lindsay Ann Pickell ............ | SC | GS | 14 | ............... | |
| | *Civil Rights Division* | | | | | | |
| Do ................... | Assistant Attorney General............... | Eric S Dreiband ............... | PAS | EX | IV | | |
| Do ................... | Principal Deputy Assistant Attorney General ... | John B. Daukas ............... | NA | ES | ............... | ............... | |
| Do ................... | Deputy Assistant Attorney General ................. | Alexander V Maugeri ........... | NA | ES | ............... | ............... | |
| Do ................... | ......do ............... | Cynthia M Mcknight........... | NA | ES | ............... | ............... | |
| Do ................... | Director of Operational Management................ | Career Incumbent ............... | CA | ES | ............... | ............... | |
| Do ................... | Chief of Staff and Counsel ............... | Omeed Assefi ............... | SC | GS | 13 | ............... | |
| Do ................... | Special Counsel for Immigration-Related Unfair Employment Practices. | Vacant ............... | PAS | SL | ............... | ............... | |
| Do ................... | Special Assistant to the Assistant Attorney General. | Cassandra Collins ............... | SC | GS | 11 | ............... | |
| Do ................... | Counsel ............... | Bethany Rose Pickett........ | SC | GS | 13 | ............... | |
| Do ................... | ......do ............... | Alexander Kazam ............... | SC | GS | 14 | ............... | |
| | *Environment and Natural Resources Division* | | | | | | |
| Do ................... | Assistant Attorney General Environment and Natural Resources. | Jeffrey B Clark ............... | PAS | EX | IV | | |
| Do ................... | Principal Deputy Assistant Attorney General ... | Jonathan Daniel Brightbill... | NA | ES | ............... | ............... | |
| Do ................... | Deputy Assistant Attorney General ................. | Career Incumbent ............... | CA | ES | ............... | ............... | |
| Do ................... | ......do ............... | Prerak Ghanshyam Shah .... | NA | ES | ............... | ............... | |
| Do ................... | ......do ............... | Eric Grant................... | NA | ES | ............... | ............... | |
| Do ................... | ......do ............... | Career Incumbent ............... | CA | ES | ............... | ............... | |
| Do ................... | Chief, Law and Policy Section....................... | Vacant ............... | ............ | ES | ............... | ............... | |
| Do ................... | Senior Counsel ............... | Paul Emmanuel Salamanca. | SC | GS | 15 | ............... | |
| Do ................... | Counsel ............... | Stephanie Ann Maloney....... | SC | GS | 15 | ............... | |
| Do ................... | ......do ............... | Michael Blandford Buschbacher. | SC | GS | 15 | ............... | |
| | *Tax Division* | | | | | | |
| Do ................... | Assistant Attorney General Tax Division.......... | Vacant ............... | PAS | EX | IV | | |
| Do ................... | Deputy Assistant Attorney General ................. | Theodore Joshua Wu ........... | NA | ES | ............... | ............... | |
| Do ................... | ......do ............... | Vacant ............... | ............ | ES | ............... | ............... | |
| Do ................... | ......do ............... | Richard Engle Zuckerman ... | NA | ES | ............... | ............... | |
| Do ................... | Senior Counselor to the Assistant Attorney General. | Career Incumbent ............... | CA | ES | ............... | ............... | |
| | **OFFICE OF JUSTICE PROGRAMS** | | | | | | |
| Do ................... | Assistant Attorney General, Office of Justice Programs. | Vacant ............... | PAS | EX | IV | | |
| Do ................... | Principal Deputy Assistant Attorney General ... | Katharine Taylor Sullivan ... | NA | ES | ............... | ............... | |
| Do ................... | Deputy Assistant Attorney General, Operations and Management. | Career Incumbent ............... | CA | ES | ............... | ............... | |
| Do ................... | General Counsel............... | ......do ............... | CA | ES | ............... | ............... | |
| Do ................... | Chief Information Officer............... | ......do ............... | CA | ES | ............... | ............... | |
| Do ................... | Deputy Director, Policy and Management.......... | ......do ............... | CA | ES | ............... | ............... | |
| Do ................... | Deputy Director for Programs, Bureau of Justice Assistance. | ......do ............... | CA | ES | ............... | ............... | |

## DEPARTMENT OF JUSTICE—Continued

| Location | Position Title | Name of Incumbent | Type of Appt. | Pay Plan | Level, Grade, or Pay | Tenure | Expires |
|---|---|---|---|---|---|---|---|
| Washington, DC | Chief of Staff | Michael J Costigan | NA | ES | | | |
| Do | Human Trafficking Program Director | William C. Woolf III | TA | ES | | | 12/15/22 |
| Do | Senior Counselor | Brady C Toensing | NA | ES | | | |
| Do | .....do | Matt M Dummermuth | NA | ES | | | |
| Do | Senior Advisor | Cheryl L Nolan | NA | ES | | | |
| Do | Senior Counselor | Gary Evan Barnett | NA | ES | | | |
| Do | Executive Director, Federal Interagency Council on Crime Prevention and Improving Reentry. | John Anthony Lowden | NA | ES | | | |
| Do | Special Advisor for Policy and Communications. | Clare Murphy Morell | SC | GS | 12 | | |
| Do | Chief of Staff | James Russell Sapp | SC | GS | 15 | | |
| Do | Policy Advisor | Mark Alden Morgan | SC | GS | 12 | | |
| Do | Senior Advisor | Edward James Puccerella | SC | GS | 15 | | |
| Do | .....do | Guy F Burnett | SC | GS | 14 | | |
| Do | .....do | Darlene L Hutchinson | SC | GS | 15 | | |
| Do | .....do | Patricia M Nation | SC | GS | 15 | | |
| Do | Legislative Assistant | Taylor Beth Stephens | SC | GS | 11 | | |
| Do | Outreach Coordinator | Rebecca Sears Holdenried | SC | GS | 13 | | |
| Do | Staff Assistant | Mary Ellen Flynn | SC | GS | 5 | | |
| Do | Director Office for Victims of Crime | Jessica Elizabeth Hart | PA | EX | IV | | |
| Do | Director, Smart Office | Kendel Sibiski Ehrlich | PA | EX | IV | | |
| Do | Director, Bureau of Justice Assistance | Vacant | PA | EX | IV | | |
| Do | Deputy Director for Planning, Bureau of Justice Assistance. | .....do | | ES | | | |
| | *Bureau of Justice Statistics* | | | | | | |
| Do | Deputy Director | .....do | | ES | | | |
| Do | Director, Bureau of Justice Statistics | Jeffrey Hagen Anderson | PA | EX | IV | | |
| | *National Institute of Justice* | | | | | | |
| Do | Executive Science Advisor | Vacant | | ES | | | |
| Do | Deputy Director, National Institute of Justice | .....do | | ES | | | |
| Do | Director, National Institute of Justice | David Muhlhausen | PA | EX | IV | | |
| | *Office of Juvenile Justice and Delinquency Prevention* | | | | | | |
| Do | Deputy Administrator for Policy | Career Incumbent | CA | ES | | | |
| Do | Deputy Administrator | .....do | CA | ES | | | |
| Do | Administrator, Office of Juvenile Justice and Delinquency Prevention. | Caren Lee Harp | PA | EX | IV | | |
| Do | Principal Deputy Administrator | Vacant | | ES | | | |
| | *Community Relations Service* | | | | | | |
| Do | Director, Community Relations Service | .....do | PAS | EX | IV | | |
| Do | Deputy Director | Career Incumbent | CA | ES | | | |
| | *Foreign Claims Settlement Commission* | | | | | | |
| Do | Chairman | Vacant | PAS | EX | V | | |
| Do | Member | Patrick Hovakimian | PAS | EX | V | | |
| Do | .....do | Sylvia Becker | PAS | EX | V | | |
| | *Office on Violence Against Women* | | | | | | |
| Do | Director, Office on Violence Against Women | Vacant | PAS | EX | V | | |
| Do | Principal Deputy Director | Laura Rogers | NA | ES | | | |
| Do | Deputy Director for Policy | Mary Elizabeth Powers | SC | GS | 14 | | |
| Do | Special Advisor | Heather Courtney Fischer | SC | GS | 12 | | |
| Do | Advisor | Errical Bryant | SC | GS | 14 | | |
| | *Executive Office for United States Trustees* | | | | | | |
| Do | Director | Career Incumbent | CA | ES | | | |
| Do | Deputy Director (General Counsel) | .....do | CA | ES | | | |
| Do | Deputy Director (Management) | .....do | CA | ES | | | |
| Do | Deputy Director (Field Operations) | Vacant | | ES | | | |
| | *Community Oriented Policing Services* | | | | | | |
| Do | Director | Phillip Edward Keith | NA | ES | | | |
| Do | Principal Deputy Director | Vacant | | ES | | | |
| Do | Senior Advisor | Career Incumbent | CA | ES | | | |
| Do | .....do | Joseph David Brown | SC | GS | 15 | | |
| | *Office of Information Policy* | | | | | | |
| Do | Director, Office of Information Policy | Career Incumbent | CA | ES | | | |
| | *Office of the Solicitor General* | | | | | | |
| Do | Solicitor General | Noel Francisco | PAS | EX | III | | |
| Do | Principal Deputy Solicitor General | Jeffrey Bryan Wall | NA | ES | | | |
| Do | Deputy Solicitor General | Career Incumbent | CA | ES | | | |
| Do | .....do | .....do | CA | ES | | | |

## DEPARTMENT OF JUSTICE—Continued

| Location | Position Title | Name of Incumbent | Type of Appt. | Pay Plan | Level, Grade, or Pay | Tenure | Expires |
|---|---|---|---|---|---|---|---|
| Washington, DC ...... | Deputy Solicitor General................................... | Career Incumbent ................ | CA | ES | .............. | .............. | |
| Do ..................... | ......do ......................................... | Vacant ................................... | .............. | ES | .............. | .............. | |
| | *Department of Justice* | | | | | | |
| Do ..................... | Director, Office of Privacy and Civil Liberties ... | Career Incumbent ................ | CA | ES | .............. | .............. | |
| Do ..................... | Inspector General .......................................... | Michael Horowitz ................ | PAS | EX | IV | .............. | |

## DEPARTMENT OF JUSTICE OFFICE OF THE INSPECTOR GENERAL

| Location | Position Title | Name of Incumbent | Type of Appt. | Pay Plan | Level, Grade, or Pay | Tenure | Expires |
|---|---|---|---|---|---|---|---|
| Washington, DC ...... | **FRONT OFFICE**<br>Inspector General .......................................... | Michael E Horowitz.............. | PAS | EX | II | .............. | |

## DEPARTMENT OF LABOR

| Location | Position Title | Name of Incumbent | Type of Appt. | Pay Plan | Level, Grade, or Pay | Tenure | Expires |
|---|---|---|---|---|---|---|---|
| Washington, DC ...... | **OFFICE OF THE SECRETARY**<br>Secretary of Labor ............................................. | Eugene Scalia ...................... | PAS | EX | I | .............. | |
| Do ..................... | Executive Assistant ........................................ | Brenda Russell ..................... | SC | GS | 14 | .............. | |
| Do ..................... | Chief of Staff ................................................. | Rachel Mondl....................... | NA | ES | .............. | .............. | |
| Do ..................... | Deputy Chief of Staff.............................. | Catherine Bartley.............. | SC | GS | 14 | .............. | |
| Do ..................... | Special Assistant to the Chief of Staff............ | Jordan Goldstein ................. | SC | GS | 7 | .............. | |
| Do ..................... | Special Assistant to the Deputy Chief of Staff .. | Allison Dunn........................ | SC | GS | 7 | .............. | |
| Do ..................... | Counselor to the Secretary............................... | Andrew Kilberg ................... | NA | ES | .............. | .............. | |
| Do ..................... | Senior Policy Advisor ...................................... | Morgan Bowles ..................... | SC | GS | 14 | .............. | |
| Do ..................... | Executive Secretary ........................................ | Caroline Robinson .............. | SC | GS | 14 | .............. | |
| Do ..................... | Senior Advisor ................................................ | Beverly Mckittrick .............. | SC | GS | 15 | .............. | |
| Do ..................... | Special Assistant............................................. | Vanessa Barnes .................... | SC | GS | 7 | .............. | |
| Do ..................... | Director of Scheduling and Operations ............. | Abbie Sumbrum.................... | SC | GS | 11 | .............. | |
| Do ..................... | Advance Lead.................................................. | Stephanie Laudner............... | SC | GS | 13 | .............. | |
| Do ..................... | Advance Representative ................................... | Eric Evans ........................... | SC | GS | 15 | .............. | |
| Do ..................... | ......do ......................................... | Andrew Nixon ...................... | SC | GS | 7 | .............. | |
| Do ..................... | Director, Office of the White House Liaison....... | Colton Meehan ..................... | SC | GS | 12 | .............. | |
| Do ..................... | Deputy White House Liaison ............................ | Mitchell Brown .................... | SC | GS | 11 | .............. | |
| Do ..................... | Director, Office of Faith-Based and Community Initiatives. | Mark Zelden ........................ | SC | GS | 15 | .............. | |
| Do ..................... | Deputy Director, Office of Faith-Based and Community Initiatives. | Nicole Hudgens.................... | SC | GS | 13 | .............. | |
| Do ..................... | Chief of Staff................................................. | David Thomas....................... | SC | GS | 15 | .............. | |
| Do ..................... | Special Assistant............................................ | Andrew Schwarz.................. | SC | GS | 7 | .............. | |
| Do ..................... | ......do ......................................... | Daniel Sinton....................... | SC | GS | 11 | .............. | |
| Do ..................... | Speechwriter.................................................. | Kyle Huwa ........................... | SC | GS | 14 | .............. | |
| Do ..................... | Special Assistant............................................ | Blake Lanning ..................... | SC | GS | 13 | .............. | |
| Do ..................... | ......do ......................................... | Chad Squitieri ..................... | SC | GS | 15 | .............. | |
| Do ..................... | Principal Travel Aide....................................... | Fernando Espinoza.............. | SC | GS | 9 | .............. | |
| Do ..................... | Special Assistant............................................ | Sophia Cabana...................... | SC | GS | 7 | .............. | |
| Do ..................... | Director, Office of Public Liaison ...................... | Dean Heyl ............................ | NA | ES | .............. | .............. | |
| Do ..................... | Deputy Director .............................................. | Sylvester Giustino............... | SC | GS | 14 | .............. | |
| Do ..................... | Special Assistant............................................ | Amanda Bryson ................... | SC | GS | 11 | .............. | |
| Do ..................... | Senior Advisor................................................ | Rodolph Olivo ...................... | SC | GS | 14 | .............. | |
| Do ..................... | *Office of the Deputy Secretary*<br>Deputy Secretary of Labor ............................... | Patrick Pizzella.................... | PAS | EX | II | .............. | |
| Do ..................... | Associate Deputy Secretary .............................. | Nathan Paul Mehrens.......... | NA | ES | .............. | .............. | |
| Do ..................... | Counselor to the Deputy Secretary ................... | Brett Swearingen ................ | SC | GS | 15 | .............. | |
| Do ..................... | Special Assistant and Policy Advisor................. | Robert Minchin III .............. | SC | GS | 14 | .............. | |
| Do ..................... | Confidential Assistant ..................................... | Heather Wadyka.................. | SC | GS | 9 | .............. | |
| Do ..................... | **OFFICE OF THE SOLICITOR**<br>Solicitor of Labor............................................. | Kate Siobhan Oscannlain .... | PAS | EX | IV | .............. | |
| Do ..................... | Deputy Solicitor ............................................. | Timothy Taylor .................... | NA | ES | .............. | .............. | |
| Do ..................... | Senior Counsel ............................................... | Sharon Rose ......................... | SC | GS | 15 | .............. | |
| Do ..................... | ......do ......................................... | Robbie J Norton.................... | SC | GS | 15 | .............. | |
| Do ..................... | ......do ......................................... | Courtney Walter .................. | SC | GS | 15 | .............. | |
| Do ..................... | Counsel........................................................ | Rebecca Furdek ................... | SC | GS | 15 | .............. | |

## DEPARTMENT OF LABOR—Continued

| Location | Position Title | Name of Incumbent | Type of Appt. | Pay Plan | Level, Grade, or Pay | Tenure | Expires |
|---|---|---|---|---|---|---|---|
| Washington, DC ...... | Associate Solicitor for Employment and Training Legal Services. | Career Incumbent ................. | CA | ES | ............... | ............... | |
| Do .................... | Associate Solicitor for Legislation and Legal Counsel. | ......do ........................... | CA | ES | ............... | ............... | |
| | **OFFICE OF THE ASSISTANT SECRETARY FOR ADMINISTRATION AND MANAGEMENT** | | | | | | |
| Do .................... | Assistant Secretary for Administration and Management. | George B Slater .................... | PAS | EX | IV | ............... | |
| Do .................... | Deputy Assistant Secretary for Policy.............. | David Langhaim.................... | NA | ES | ............... | ............... | |
| Do .................... | Senior Advisor.......................................... | Mark Baker........................ | SC | GS | 15 | ............... | |
| Do .................... | Special Assistant....................................... | Edward Wilkinson ................ | SC | GS | 15 | ............... | |
| Do .................... | ......do ..................................................... | Lisa S. Freeman ................. | SC | GS | 14 | ............... | |
| Do .................... | Chief Information Officer............................ | Career Incumbent ................. | CA | ES | ............... | ............... | |
| Do .................... | Deputy Chief Information Officer.................. | ......do ........................... | CA | ES | ............... | ............... | |
| | **OFFICE OF THE ASSISTANT SECRETARY FOR POLICY** | | | | | | |
| Do .................... | Assistant Secretary for Policy...................... | Vacant ............................ | PAS | EX | IV | ............... | |
| Do .................... | Principal Deputy Assistant Secretary ............. | ......do ........................... | | ES | ............... | ............... | |
| Do .................... | Deputy Assistant Secretary ........................ | Alison Kilmartin.................. | NA | ES | ............... | ............... | |
| Do .................... | ......do ..................................................... | Jonathan Wolfson ................ | NA | ES | ............... | ............... | |
| Do .................... | Senior Counselor for Compliance Initiatives ..... | Nicole Brightbill ................. | SC | GS | 15 | ............... | |
| Do .................... | Senior Counsel and Policy Advisor ................ | Wilson Freeman ................... | SC | GS | 15 | ............... | |
| Do .................... | Senior Policy Advisor for Workforce Health Initiatives. | Meghan Stringer ................. | SC | GS | 13 | ............... | |
| Do .................... | Deputy Chief Economist.............................. | Feliks Pleszczynski.............. | SC | GS | 14 | ............... | |
| Do .................... | Policy Advisor.......................................... | Jared Meyer........................ | SC | GS | 14 | ............... | |
| Do .................... | Special Assistant....................................... | Jay Sirot ........................... | SC | GS | 9 | ............... | |
| | **MINE SAFETY AND HEALTH ADMINISTRATION** | | | | | | |
| Do .................... | Assistant Secretary for Mine Safety and Health. | David George Zatezalo ......... | PAS | EX | IV | ............... | |
| Do .................... | Deputy Assistant Secretary for Mine Safety and Health. | Wayne Palmer...................... | NA | ES | ............... | ............... | |
| Do .................... | Senior Policy Advisor ................................ | Paul Krivokuca ................... | SC | GS | 15 | ............... | |
| Do .................... | ......do ..................................................... | James Vicini....................... | SC | GS | 15 | ............... | |
| Arlington, VA........... | Deputy Administrator for Metal and Nonmetal. | Vacant ............................ | | ES | ............... | ............... | |
| Washington, DC ...... | Administrator, Mine Safety Health Enforcement. | Career Incumbent ................. | CA | ES | ............... | ............... | |
| Arlington, VA........... | Director, Office of Standards, Regulation and Variances. | Vacant ............................ | | ES | ............... | ............... | |
| | **OFFICE OF PUBLIC AFFAIRS** | | | | | | |
| Washington, DC ...... | Assistant Secretary for Public Affairs.............. | Robert Bozzuto III ............... | PA | EX | IV | ............... | |
| Do .................... | Deputy Assistant Secretary for Opa................. | Eric W Holland .................... | NA | ES | ............... | ............... | |
| Do .................... | Chief of Staff.......................................... | John Ross Stewart................ | SC | GS | 12 | ............... | |
| Do .................... | Senior Advisor for Policy and Media .............. | Erica Clayton Wright .......... | SC | GS | 15 | ............... | |
| Do .................... | Senior Advisor for Communications ................ | Megan P Sweeney ................ | SC | GS | 15 | ............... | |
| Do .................... | Senior Advisor for Digital Strategy and Creative Services. | Stan Olshefski...................... | SC | GS | 15 | ............... | |
| Do .................... | Press Secretary........................................ | Emily Weeks ....................... | SC | GS | 11 | ............... | |
| Do .................... | Special Assistant....................................... | Mattie Nicholson ................ | SC | GS | 11 | ............... | |
| Do .................... | Deputy Assistant Secretary for Public Affairs... | Career Incumbent ................. | CA | ES | ............... | ............... | |
| | **OFFICE OF THE CHIEF FINANCIAL OFFICER** | | | | | | |
| Do .................... | Chief Financial Officer .............................. | James Williams ................... | PAS | EX | IV | ............... | |
| Do .................... | Chief of Staff.......................................... | James Hudgens ................... | SC | GS | 13 | ............... | |
| Do .................... | Associate Deputy Chief Financial Officer for Fiscal Integrity. | Career Incumbent ................. | CA | ES | ............... | ............... | |
| | **WAGE AND HOUR DIVISION** | | | | | | |
| Do .................... | Wage and Hour Administrator........................... | Cheryl Stanton ................... | PAS | EX | V | ............... | |
| Do .................... | Counselor to the Administrator ..................... | Sheng Li ........................... | SC | GS | 15 | ............... | |
| Do .................... | Senior Policy Advisor ................................ | Sarah Martin ...................... | SC | GS | 13 | ............... | |
| Do .................... | ......do ..................................................... | Andrew Rogers .................... | SC | GS | 15 | ............... | |
| Do .................... | Deputy Administrator ................................ | Susan Boone ...................... | NA | ES | ............... | ............... | |
| Do .................... | ......do ..................................................... | Keith E Sonderling.............. | NA | ES | ............... | ............... | |
| Do .................... | Chief of Staff.......................................... | Michael Stojsavljevich........... | SC | GS | 15 | ............... | |
| Do .................... | Senior Policy Advisor ................................ | Bradford Kelley ................... | SC | GS | 15 | ............... | |
| Do .................... | ......do ..................................................... | Leif Olson.......................... | SC | GS | 14 | ............... | |
| Do .................... | Policy Advisor.......................................... | Mateo Forero...................... | SC | GS | 13 | ............... | |
| Philadelphia, PA...... | Regional Administrator for Wage and Hour ...... | Career Incumbent ................. | CA | ES | ............... | ............... | |

## DEPARTMENT OF LABOR—Continued

| Location | Position Title | Name of Incumbent | Type of Appt. | Pay Plan | Level, Grade, or Pay | Tenure | Expires |
|---|---|---|---|---|---|---|---|
| Chicago, IL............ | Regional Administrator for Wage and Hour ...... | Career Incumbent ................ | CA | ES | .............. | .............. | |
| Atlanta, GA ........... | ......do ........... | ......do ........... | CA | ES | .............. | .............. | |
| Dallas, TX ............... | ......do ........... | ......do ........... | CA | ES | .............. | .............. | |
| San Francisco, CA... | ......do ........... | ......do ........... | CA | ES | .............. | .............. | |
| Washington, DC ...... | Assistant Administrator for Policy .................... | Vacant ..................... | ............ | ES | .............. | .............. | |
| Do ..................... | Assistant Administrator for Planning, Performance Evaluation and Training. | Career Incumbent ................ | CA | ES | .............. | .............. | |
| | **VETERANS EMPLOYMENT AND TRAINING SERVICE** | | | | | | |
| Do ..................... | Assistant Secretary for Veterans Employment and Training. | John Lowry ........................... | PAS | EX | IV | .............. | |
| Do ..................... | Chief of Staff and Policy Advisor ....................... | Jonathan Vanderplas ........... | SC | GS | 14 | .............. | |
| Do ..................... | Senior Policy Advisor ...................................... | Daniel Greenberg ................ | SC | GS | 15 | .............. | |
| Do ..................... | Special Assistant............................................... | Rieder Grunseth.................... | SC | GS | 7 | .............. | |
| Do ..................... | Deputy Assistant Secretary for Veterans Employment and Training Services (Policy). | Vacant ...................... | ............ | ES | .............. | .............. | |
| | **OFFICE OF CONGRESSIONAL AND INTERGOVERNMENTAL AFFAIRS** | | | | | | |
| Do ..................... | Assistant Secretary for Congressional and Intergovernmental Affairs. | ......do ........... | PAS | EX | IV | .............. | |
| Do ..................... | Deputy Assistant Secretary ............................. | James J Wheeler .................. | NA | ES | .............. | .............. | |
| Do ..................... | ......do ........... | Michael R Downing.............. | NA | ES | .............. | .............. | |
| Do ..................... | Chief of Staff for Operations ........................... | John Patrick Walsh ............. | SC | GS | 13 | .............. | |
| Do ..................... | Senior Advisor ................................................ | James Blazer ........................ | SC | GS | 15 | .............. | |
| Do ..................... | Senior Legislative Officer................................. | Robert Rische........................ | SC | GS | 14 | .............. | |
| Do ..................... | ......do ........... | Sharon Utz............................ | SC | GS | 13 | .............. | |
| Do ..................... | ......do ........... | David McFadden.................... | SC | GS | 15 | .............. | |
| Do ..................... | ......do ........... | Adam Turner ........................ | SC | GS | 13 | .............. | |
| Do ..................... | ......do ........... | Brian Maves ......................... | SC | GS | 14 | .............. | |
| Do ..................... | ......do ........... | Aaron Krejci......................... | SC | GS | 13 | .............. | |
| Do ..................... | Legislative Officer............................................ | Bradley Thomas..................... | SC | GS | 11 | .............. | |
| Chicago, IL............ | Regional Representative.................................... | Christopher Eric Hagerup ... | SC | GS | 15 | .............. | |
| Denver, CO ........... | ......do ........... | Jonathan Kent Finer............. | SC | GS | 13 | .............. | |
| San Francisco, CA... | ......do ........... | Jeffrey Earle Stone............... | SC | GS | 15 | .............. | |
| Atlanta, GA ........... | ......do ........... | Ruth Sherlock ....................... | SC | GS | 15 | .............. | |
| New York, NY......... | ......do ........... | Allie Schroeder ..................... | SC | GS | 14 | .............. | |
| Kansas City, MO ..... | ......do ........... | Kevin Corlew ........................ | SC | GS | 15 | .............. | |
| Boston, MA ............. | ......do ........... | Peter Steele........................... | SC | GS | 15 | .............. | |
| Washington, DC ...... | Case Officer...................................................... | Jacob Smith .......................... | SC | GS | 7 | .............. | |
| Do ..................... | ......do ........... | Joseph Gollinger.................... | SC | GS | 7 | .............. | |
| Do ..................... | Senior Legislative Officer................................. | Margarita A Almanza .......... | SC | GS | 14 | .............. | |
| | **EMPLOYMENT AND TRAINING ADMINISTRATION** | | | | | | |
| Do ..................... | Assistant Secretary for Employment and Training. | John P Pallasch .................... | PAS | EX | IV | .............. | |
| Do ..................... | Deputy Assistant Secretary ............................. | Matthew F Hunter .............. | NA | ES | .............. | .............. | |
| Do ..................... | Senior Advisor ................................................ | Jonathan J Blyth.................. | NA | ES | .............. | .............. | |
| Do ..................... | Deputy Assistant Secretary and Chief of Staff.. | Amy Simon ........................... | NA | ES | .............. | .............. | |
| Do ..................... | Deputy Chief of Staff........................................ | Bronte Wigen ........................ | SC | GS | 12 | .............. | |
| Do ..................... | Senior Counsel ................................................ | Shawn Michael Packer........ | SC | GS | 15 | .............. | |
| Do ..................... | Senior Policy Advisor ...................................... | Robert Jordan Richardson ... | SC | GS | 12 | .............. | |
| Do ..................... | ......do ........... | Charles Drummond............... | SC | GS | 14 | .............. | |
| Do ..................... | Special Assistant............................................... | John Kashuba........................ | SC | GS | 13 | .............. | |
| Do ..................... | Special Assistant (Events and Operations)........ | Katie Renee Lagomarsino.... | SC | GS | 12 | .............. | |
| Do ..................... | Special Assistant............................................... | James Blohm ........................ | SC | GS | 9 | .............. | |
| Do ..................... | Administrator, Office of Management and Administrative Services. | Career Incumbent ................ | CA | ES | .............. | .............. | |
| Do ..................... | Administrator, Office of Workforce Investment . | Vacant ..................... | ............ | ES | .............. | .............. | |
| Do ..................... | Deputy Assistant Secretary ............................. | ......do ........... | ............ | ES | .............. | .............. | |
| | **EMPLOYEE BENEFITS SECURITY ADMINISTRATION** | | | | | | |
| Do ..................... | Assistant Secretary for Employee Benefits Security. | ......do ........... | PAS | EX | IV | .............. | |
| Do ..................... | Principal Deputy Assistant Secretary ............... | Jeanne Wilson...................... | NA | ES | .............. | .............. | |
| Do ..................... | Chief of Staff.................................................... | Timothy Cummings.............. | SC | GS | 13 | .............. | |
| Do ..................... | Senior Policy Advisor ...................................... | Monica Mcguire .................... | SC | GS | 14 | .............. | |
| Do ..................... | ......do ........... | Rebecca Cole ........................ | SC | GS | 15 | .............. | |
| Do ..................... | Policy Advisor.................................................. | Trevor Carlsen ..................... | SC | GS | 12 | .............. | |
| Do ..................... | Special Assistant............................................... | Matthew Mullins .................. | SC | GS | 7 | .............. | |
| Do ..................... | Administrative Officer....................................... | Career Incumbent ................ | CA | ES | .............. | .............. | |

## DEPARTMENT OF LABOR—Continued

| Location | Position Title | Name of Incumbent | Type of Appt. | Pay Plan | Level, Grade, or Pay | Tenure | Expires |
|---|---|---|---|---|---|---|---|
| | **OCCUPATIONAL SAFETY AND HEALTH ADMINISTRATION** | | | | | | |
| Washington, DC ...... | Assistant Secretary for Occupational Safety and Health. | Vacant ...................... | PAS | EX | IV | ............... | |
| Do .................... | Principal Deputy Assistant Secertary ............... | Loren E Sweatt...................... | NA | ES | ............... | ............... | |
| Do .................... | Chief of Staff........................................ | Krisann Pearce ...................... | SC | GS | 15 | ............... | |
| Do .................... | Special Assistant ........................ | Brian Walsh ...................... | SC | GS | 11 | ............... | |
| Kansas City, MO ..... | Safety and Health Administrator - Kansas City. | Career Incumbent ............... | CA | ES | ............... | ............... | |
| Washington, DC ...... | Deputy Assistant Secretary ...................... | ......do ...................... | CA | ES | ............... | ............... | |
| Boston, MA ............ | Regional Administrator - Boston ...................... | ......do ...................... | CA | ES | ............... | ............... | |
| Washington, DC ...... | Director, Office of Whistleblower Protection Program. | Vacant ...................... | ............ | ES | ............... | ............... | |
| San Francisco, CA... | Regional Administrator - San Francisco ............ | Career Incumbent ............... | CA | ES | ............... | ............... | |
| Dallas, TX .............. | Regional Administrator ...................... | ......do ...................... | CA | ES | ............... | ............... | |
| New York New York, NY. | Regional Administrator - New York .................. | ......do ...................... | CA | ES | ............... | ............... | |
| Atlanta, GA ........... | Regional Administrator - Atlanta ...................... | ......do ...................... | CA | ES | ............... | ............... | |
| Philadelphia, PA..... | Regional Administrator - Philadelphia ............. | ......do ...................... | CA | ES | ............... | ............... | |
| Washington, DC ...... | Director, Directorate of Enforcement Programs. | Vacant ...................... | ............ | ES | ............... | ............... | |
| Chicago, IL............. | Regional Administrator - Chicago ...................... | ......do ...................... | | ES | ............... | ............... | |
| Denver, CO ............ | Regional Administrator - Denver...................... | ......do ...................... | | ES | ............... | ............... | |
| Washington, DC ...... | Director, Directorate of Standards and Guidance. | ......do ...................... | | ES | ............... | ............... | |
| Do .................... | Director of Technical Support and Emergency Management. | ......do ...................... | | ES | ............... | ............... | |
| Do .................... | Director, Directorate of Cooperative and State Programs. | Career Incumbent ............... | CA | ES | ............... | ............... | |
| | **OFFICE OF DISABILITY EMPLOYMENT POLICY** | | | | | | |
| Do .................... | Assistant Secretary for Disability Employment Policy. | Vacant ...................... | PAS | EX | IV | ............... | |
| Do .................... | Chief of Staff.......................................... | Patrick Mannix...................... | SC | GS | 14 | ............... | |
| | **BUREAU OF LABOR STATISTICS** | | | | | | |
| Do .................... | Commissioner of Labor Statistics...................... | William Warren Beach ........ | PAS | EX | IV | 4 Years | |
| Do .................... | Economic Advisor to the Commissioner ............ | Career Incumbent ............... | CA | ES | ............... | ............... | |
| | **BUREAU OF INTERNATIONAL LABOR AFFAIRS** | | | | | | |
| Do .................... | Deputy Undersecretary for International Affairs. | Martha E Newton................ | NA | ES | ............... | ............... | |
| Do .................... | Chief of Staff........................................ | Grant B Lebens .................... | SC | GS | 15 | ............... | |
| Do .................... | Director, Office of Child Labor, Forced Labor Human Trafficking. | Career Incumbent ............... | CA | ES | ............... | ............... | |
| Do .................... | Associate Deputy Undersecretary for International Affairs (Policy and Management). | ......do ...................... | CA | ES | ............... | ............... | |
| Do .................... | Director, Office of Trade and Labor Affairs........ | ......do ...................... | CA | ES | ............... | ............... | |
| | **OFFICE OF FEDERAL CONTRACT COMPLIANCE PROGRAMS** | | | | | | |
| Do .................... | Director, Office of Federal Contract Compliance Programs. | Craig Leen ........................... | NA | ES | ............... | ............... | |
| Do .................... | Deputy Director Office of Federal Contract Compliance Programs. | Robert Gaglione.................... | NA | ES | ............... | ............... | |
| Do .................... | Senior Policy Advisor........................................ | Matthew Mimnaugh............ | SC | GS | 14 | ............... | |
| Do .................... | ......do ........................................ | Valerie Maloney...................... | SC | GS | 13 | ............... | |
| Do .................... | Deputy Director, Office of Federal Contract Compliance Program. | Career Incumbent ............... | CA | ES | ............... | ............... | |
| Do .................... | Director, Division of Program Operations.......... | ......do ...................... | CA | ES | ............... | ............... | |
| Do .................... | Director of Enforcement ...................... | ......do ...................... | CA | ES | ............... | ............... | |
| | **OFFICE OF LABOR-MANAGEMENT STANDARDS** | | | | | | |
| Do .................... | Director, Office of Labor-Management Standards. | Vacant ...................... | ............ | ES | ............... | ............... | |
| Do .................... | Senior Policy Advisor........................................ | Geoffrey Macleay...................... | SC | GS | 14 | ............... | |
| Do .................... | Policy Advisor........................................ | Russell Brown...................... | SC | GS | 14 | ............... | |
| Do .................... | Special Assistant........................................ | William Kovacs...................... | SC | GS | 12 | ............... | |
| Do .................... | ......do ........................................ | Edward Valentine................ | SC | GS | 11 | ............... | |

## DEPARTMENT OF LABOR—Continued

| Location | Position Title | Name of Incumbent | Type of Appt. | Pay Plan | Level, Grade, or Pay | Tenure | Expires |
|---|---|---|---|---|---|---|---|
| | **OFFICE OF WORKERS COMPENSATION PROGRAMS** | | | | | | |
| Washington, DC ...... | Director, Office of Workers Compensation Programs. | Julia K Hearthway .............. | NA | ES | .............. | .............. | |
| Do .................... | Senior Policy Advisor.................................... | Michael Vovakes .................. | SC | GS | 15 | .............. | |
| Do .................... | Policy Advisor................................................ | Christopher Mcguinn .......... | SC | GS | 12 | .............. | |
| Dallas, TX .............. | National Admin of Field Operations, Division of Coal Mine Workers Compensation. | Career Incumbent .............. | CA | ES | .............. | .............. | |
| Washington, DC ...... | Director, Longshore and Harbor Workers' Compensation. | Vacant .................................... | .............. | ES | .............. | .............. | |
| | **WOMEN'S BUREAU** | | | | | | |
| Do .................... | Director of the Women's Bureau........................ | Laurie Todd Smith .............. | PA | SL | .............. | .............. | |
| Do .................... | Senior Advisor.................................... | Erica Nurnberg.................... | SC | GS | 14 | .............. | |
| Do .................... | Chief of Staff.................................... | Jillian Rogers...................... | SC | GS | 15 | .............. | |
| Do .................... | Special Assistant............................ | Hannah Fritz...................... | SC | GS | 9 | .............. | |

## DEPARTMENT OF LABOR OFFICE OF INSPECTOR GENERAL

| Location | Position Title | Name of Incumbent | Type of Appt. | Pay Plan | Level, Grade, or Pay | Tenure | Expires |
|---|---|---|---|---|---|---|---|
| Washington, DC ...... | Inspector General ................................................. | Vacant .................................... | PAS | IG | .............. | .............. | |

## DEPARTMENT OF STATE

| Location | Position Title | Name of Incumbent | Type of Appt. | Pay Plan | Level, Grade, or Pay | Tenure | Expires |
|---|---|---|---|---|---|---|---|
| | **OFFICE OF THE SECRETARY** | | | | | | |
| Washington, DC ...... | Secretary of State ................................................. | Michael Pompeo.................... | PAS | EX | I | .............. | |
| Do .................... | Counselor........................................................ | Thomas-Ulrich Brechbuhl ... | NA | ES | .............. | .............. | |
| Do .................... | Senior Advisor to the Secretary ........................ | Mary Kissel.......................... | NA | ES | .............. | .............. | |
| Do .................... | Advisor to the Secretary.................................... | Toni Porter.......................... | SC | GS | 15 | .............. | |
| Do .................... | Special Assistant............................................. | Kathryn Donnell.................. | SC | GS | 13 | .............. | |
| Do .................... | ......do ........................................ | Victoria Lynn Ellington ...... | SC | GS | 12 | .............. | |
| Do .................... | Staff Assistant (Scheduler)................................ | Christine Ruth Fisher.......... | SC | GS | 11 | .............. | |
| Do .................... | Special Representative for Iran ........................ | Brian Hook.......................... | NA | ES | .............. | .............. | |
| Do .................... | Special Representative for Venezuela .............. | Elliott Abrams ...................... | TA | ES | .............. | .............. | 05/25/22 |
| Do .................... | Special Presidential Envoy for Arms Control.... | Marshall S Billingslea ......... | TA | ES | .............. | .............. | 10/31/20 |
| Do .................... | Special Presidential Envoy for Hostage Affairs. | Roger Carstens ...................... | PA | EX | .............. | .............. | |
| Do .................... | Deputy Special Presidential Envoy for Hostage Affairs. | Christopher C Pratt .............. | NA | ES | .............. | .............. | |
| Do .................... | White House Liaison ............................................ | Nilda Pedrosa ...................... | NA | ES | .............. | .............. | |
| Do .................... | Senior Advisor.................................... | Nicholas Stewart .................. | SC | GS | 15 | .............. | |
| Do .................... | ......do ........................................ | John McInnis........................ | SC | GS | 15 | .............. | |
| Do .................... | Deputy White House Liaison ............................ | Brittney May ........................ | SC | GS | 12 | .............. | |
| Do .................... | Special Assistant............................................. | Gabriel Luke Noronha.......... | SC | GS | 12 | .............. | |
| Do .................... | ......do ........................................ | Danielle M Stoebe ................ | SC | GS | 12 | .............. | |
| Do .................... | ......do ........................................ | Sara Elizabeth Grove.......... | SC | GS | 11 | .............. | |
| | *Office of the Deputy Secretary* | | | | | | |
| Do .................... | Deputy Secretary of State............................ | Stephen Biegun .................. | PAS | EX | II | .............. | |
| Do .................... | Special Advisor.................................... | Jennifer Ehlinger ................ | SC | GS | 14 | .............. | |
| | *Office of the Deputy Secretary for Management and Resources* | | | | | | |
| Do .................... | Deputy Secretary of State for Management and Resources. | Vacant .................................... | PAS | EX | II | .............. | |
| | *Office of U.S. Foreign Assistance* | | | | | | |
| Do .................... | Director.............................................. | James L Richardson.............. | NA | ES | .............. | .............. | |
| Do .................... | Special Advisor.................................... | Martha Van Lieshout .......... | SC | GS | 13 | .............. | |
| | *Office of the Counselor* | | | | | | |
| Do .................... | Senior Advisor.................................... | Clara Kyim .......................... | SC | GS | 15 | .............. | |
| Do .................... | Staff Assistant................................. | Rebecca Colehower.............. | SC | GS | 7 | .............. | |
| | *Office of Policy Planning* | | | | | | |
| Do .................... | Senior Advisor.................................... | Charles J. Mclaughlin IV ..... | NA | ES | .............. | .............. | |
| Do .................... | ......do ........................................ | Andrew Doran ...................... | SC | GS | 15 | .............. | |

## DEPARTMENT OF STATE—Continued

| Location | Position Title | Name of Incumbent | Type of Appt. | Pay Plan | Level, Grade, or Pay | Tenure | Expires |
|---|---|---|---|---|---|---|---|
| Washington, DC ...... | Senior Advisor................................ | David C Wilezol.................. | SC | GS | 15 | ............... | |
| Do ............... | .....do .................. | Amanda Rothschild............ | SC | GS | 15 | ............... | |
| Do ............... | .....do .................. | Robert Zarate..................... | SC | GS | 15 | ............... | |
| Do ............... | .....do .................. | Cartwright Weiland | SC | GS | 15 | ............... | |
| Do ............... | Special Advisor....................... | Martha Simms..................... | SC | GS | 14 | ............... | |
| Do ............... | Writer-Editor (Speechwriter) ....... | Michaela Joi Bortle ............. | SC | GS | 13 | ............... | |
| Do ............... | .....do .................. | Wilson Shirley ..................... | SC | GS | 12 | ............... | |
| Do ............... | Special Assistant........................ | Alexandra Jameson............. | SC | GS | 11 | ............... | |
| Do ............... | Staff Assistant.......................... | Madison Sparber ................. | SC | GS | 11 | ............... | |
| Do ............... | .....do .................. | Morgan Augustus Howard Dively. | SC | GS | 9 | ............... | |
| | *United States Mission to United Nations* | | | | | | |
| Do ................... | Representative of the USA to the United Nations, With the Rank and Status of Ambassador Extraordinary and Plenipotentiary, and the Representative of the USA to the Security Council of the United Nations. | Kelly Craft ...................... | PAS | EX | III | ............... | |
| New York New York, NY. | Deputy Representative of the USA to the United Nations, With the Rank and Status of Ambassador Extraordinary and Plenipotentiary and the Deputy Representative of the USA in the Security Council of the United Nations. | Vacant ................................. | PAS | EX | IV | ............... | |
| Do ................... | Representative of the USA on the Economic and Social Council of the Un, With the Rank of Ambassador. | ......do ................................ | PAS | EX | IV | ............... | |
| Do ................... | Representative of the USA to the United Nations for Un Management and Reform, With the Rank of Ambassador. | Cherith Norman Chalet....... | PAS | EX | IV | ............... | |
| Do ................... | Alternate Representative of the USA for Special Political Affairs in the United Nations, With the Rank of Ambassador. | Vacant ................................. | PAS | EX | IV | ............... | |
| Washington, DC ...... | Counselor, International Legal Affairs .............. | Career Incumbent ................ | CA | ES | | ............... | |
| | *Office of the Chief of Protocol* | | | | | | |
| Do ............... | Chief of Protocol........................ | Katherine Henderson........... | NA | ES | | ............... | |
| Do ............... | Deputy Chief of Protocol ................ | Mary-Kate Fisher ................ | NA | ES | | ............... | |
| Do ............... | Assistant Chief of Protocol for Ceremonials ..... | Catherine Fenton ................ | SC | GS | 15 | ............... | |
| Do ............... | Assistant Chief of Protocol (Visits).................... | Daniel Fisher ...................... | SC | GS | 15 | ............... | |
| Do ............... | Senior Protocol Officer.................... | Zoe Louise Jackman............. | SC | GS | 15 | ............... | |
| Do ............... | .....do .................. | Tracy A Rich ...................... | SC | GS | 14 | ............... | |
| Do ............... | Assistant Manager.................... | Jennifer Watson.................. | SC | GS | 14 | ............... | |
| Do ............... | Protocol Officer (Visits) ............... | Kyle Maxwell ...................... | SC | GS | 13 | ............... | |
| Do ............... | Protocol Officer ....................... | Jaclyn Schwinghamer .......... | SC | GS | 13 | ............... | |
| Do ............... | Protocol Officer (Ceremonials)............ | Ericka Jordan Morris........... | SC | GS | 13 | ............... | |
| Do ............... | Protocol Officer (Visits) ............... | Estephania Gongora............ | SC | GS | 12 | ............... | |
| Do ............... | Protocol Officer (Gifts) ................ | Jenna Semsar ...................... | SC | GS | 12 | ............... | |
| Do ............... | Protocol Officer (Visits) ............... | Michael Mahfouz ................ | SC | GS | 12 | ............... | |
| | *Office of the U.S. Global Aids Coordinator* | | | | | | |
| Do ............... | Ambassador At Large and Coordinator of United States Government Activities to Combat Hiv/Aids Globally. | Deborah Leah Birx.............. | PAS | EX | IV | ............... | |
| Do ............... | Principal Deputy Coordinator.................... | Vacant ................................. | .......... | ES | | ............... | |
| Do ............... | Deputy Coordinator ...................... | Career Incumbent ................ | CA | ES | | ............... | |
| Do ............... | Senior Advisor for Strategy.................... | Matthew Mcmanus Barnes.. | SC | GS | 15 | ............... | |
| | *Office of Global Womens Issues* | | | | | | |
| Do ............... | Ambassador At Large for Global Womens Issues. | Kelley Eckels-Currie ............ | PAS | EX | IV | ............... | |
| Do ............... | Senior Advisor............................ | Amy Mitchell ...................... | NA | ES | | ............... | |
| Do ............... | Special Advisor........................... | Hannah Anona Duke .......... | SC | GS | 13 | ............... | |
| | *Office of Civil Rights* | | | | | | |
| Do ............... | Director (Assistant Secretary Equivalent)......... | Career Incumbent ................ | CA | ES | | ............... | |
| | *Office of the Legal Adviser* | | | | | | |
| Do ............... | Legal Adviser of the Department of State ........ | Vacant ................................. | PAS | EX | IV | ............... | |
| Do ............... | Principal Deputy Legal Adviser........................ | Career Incumbent ................ | CA | ES | | ............... | |
| Do ............... | Deputy Legal Adviser ....................... | ......do ................................ | CA | ES | | ............... | |
| Do ............... | .....do .................. | ......do ................................ | CA | ES | | ............... | |
| Do ............... | .....do .................. | ......do ................................ | CA | ES | | ............... | |
| Do ............... | Assistant Legal Adviser......................... | ......do ................................ | CA | ES | | ............... | |
| Do ............... | .....do .................. | ......do ................................ | CA | ES | | ............... | |
| Do ............... | .....do .................. | ......do ................................ | CA | ES | | ............... | |

## DEPARTMENT OF STATE—Continued

| Location | Position Title | Name of Incumbent | Type of Appt. | Pay Plan | Level, Grade, or Pay | Tenure | Expires |
|---|---|---|---|---|---|---|---|
| Washington, DC ...... | Assistant Legal Adviser.................................. | Career Incumbent ................. | CA | ES | .............. | .............. | |
| Do ................... | ......do ....................................................... | ......do ...................... | CA | ES | .............. | .............. | |
| Do ................... | ......do ....................................................... | ......do ...................... | CA | ES | .............. | .............. | |
| Do ................... | ......do ....................................................... | ......do ...................... | CA | ES | .............. | .............. | |
| Do ................... | ......do ....................................................... | ......do ...................... | CA | ES | .............. | .............. | |
| Do ................... | ......do ....................................................... | ......do ...................... | CA | ES | .............. | .............. | |
| Do ................... | ......do ....................................................... | ......do ...................... | CA | ES | .............. | .............. | |
| Do ................... | ......do ....................................................... | ......do ...................... | CA | ES | .............. | .............. | |
| Do ................... | ......do ....................................................... | ......do ...................... | CA | ES | .............. | .............. | |
| Do ................... | ......do ....................................................... | ......do ...................... | CA | ES | .............. | .............. | |
| Do ................... | ......do ....................................................... | ......do ...................... | CA | ES | .............. | .............. | |
| Do ................... | ......do ....................................................... | ......do ...................... | CA | ES | .............. | .............. | |
| Do ................... | ......do ....................................................... | ......do ...................... | CA | ES | .............. | .............. | |
| Do ................... | ......do ....................................................... | ......do ...................... | CA | ES | .............. | .............. | |
| Do ................... | Deputy Assistant Legal Adviser .............. | ......do ...................... | CA | ES | .............. | .............. | |
| Do ................... | Executive Director ...................................... | ......do ...................... | CA | ES | .............. | .............. | |
| Do ................... | Assistant Legal Adviser.................................. | ......do ...................... | CA | ES | .............. | .............. | |
| Do ................... | ......do ....................................................... | ......do ...................... | CA | ES | .............. | .............. | |
| Do ................... | Senior Advisor............................................ | Joshua Bradford Simmons... | SC | GS | 15 | .............. | |
| | *Bureau of Legislative Affairs* | | | | | | |
| Do ................... | Assistant Secretary of State (Legislative Affairs). | Mary Elizabeth Taylor ......... | PAS | EX | IV | .............. | |
| Do ................... | Principal Deputy Assistant Secretary .............. | Ryan Kaldahl...................... | NA | ES | .............. | .............. | |
| Do ................... | Deputy Assistant Secretary for House Affairs... | Jessica Moore...................... | SC | GS | 15 | .............. | |
| Do ................... | Special Advisor............................................ | William K Killion .............. | SC | GS | 14 | .............. | |
| Do ................... | Supervisory Legislative Management Officer.... | Adam Farris...................... | SC | GS | 14 | .............. | |
| Do ................... | Legislative Management Officer...................... | Giulia Roesch Giannangeli.. | SC | GS | 13 | .............. | |
| Do ................... | Special Advisor............................................ | Chloe Barz ...................... | SC | GS | 12 | .............. | |
| | *Bureau of Intelligence and Research* | | | | | | |
| Do ................... | Assistant Secretary of State (Intelligence and Research). | Ellen McCarthy ................... | PAS | EX | IV | .............. | |
| Do ................... | Deputy Assistant Secretary .............................. | Career Incumbent ................. | CA | ES | .............. | .............. | |
| Do ................... | ......do ....................................................... | ......do ...................... | CA | ES | .............. | .............. | |
| Do ................... | ......do ....................................................... | ......do ...................... | CA | ES | .............. | .............. | |
| Do ................... | Executive Director ...................................... | ......do ...................... | CA | ES | .............. | .............. | |
| Do ................... | Office Director ........................................... | ......do ...................... | CA | ES | .............. | .............. | |
| Do ................... | ......do ....................................................... | ......do ...................... | CA | ES | .............. | .............. | |
| Do ................... | ......do ....................................................... | ......do ...................... | CA | ES | .............. | .............. | |
| Do ................... | ......do ....................................................... | ......do ...................... | CA | ES | .............. | .............. | |
| Do ................... | ......do ....................................................... | ......do ...................... | CA | ES | .............. | .............. | |
| Do ................... | ......do ....................................................... | ......do ...................... | CA | ES | .............. | .............. | |
| Do ................... | Geographer ................................................ | ......do ...................... | CA | ES | .............. | .............. | |
| | *Office of the Under Secretary for Political Affairs* | | | | | | |
| Do ................... | Under Secretary of State (Political Affairs) ....... | David M Hale ...................... | PAS | EX | III | .............. | |
| Do ................... | Permanent Representative of the USA to the Organization of American States, With the Rank of Ambassador. | Carlos Trujillo................... | PAS | FA | .............. | .............. | |
| Madrid, Spain.......... | Ambassador to the Principality of Andorra ....... | Richard Duke Buchan III .... | PAS | FA | .............. | .............. | |
| Buenos Aires, Argentina. | Ambassador to the Argentine Republic............ | Edward Charles Prado........ | PAS | FA | .............. | .............. | |
| Brussels, Belgium ... | Ambassador to the Kingdom of Belgium............ | Ronald Gidwitz.................... | PAS | FA | .............. | .............. | |
| Bujumbura, Burundi. | Ambassador to the Republic of Burundi ............ | Vacant ................................. | PAS | FA | .............. | .............. | |
| Chad, Chad............ | Ambassador to the Republic of Chad ............... | ......do ...................... | PAS | FA | .............. | .............. | |
| Mbabane, Swaziland. | Ambassador to the Kingdom of Eswatini.......... | Lisa J. Peterson ................. | PAS | FA | .............. | .............. | |
| Helsinki, Finland .... | Ambassador to the Republic of Finland ............ | Robert Frank Pence.............. | PAS | FA | .............. | .............. | |
| Paris, France .......... | Ambassador to the French Republic.................. | Jamie McCourt ................... | PAS | FA | .............. | .............. | |
| Berlin, Germany...... | Ambassador to the Federal Republic of Germany. | Vacant ................................. | PAS | FA | .............. | .............. | |
| Athens, Greece ........ | Ambassador to Greece (Hellenic Republic) ........ | Geoffrey R. Pyatt .............. | PAS | FA | .............. | .............. | |
| Georgetown, Guyana. | Ambassador to the Co-Operative Republic of Guyana. | Sarah-Ann Lynch ................. | PAS | FA | .............. | .............. | |
| Reykjavik, Iceland... | Ambassador to the Republic of Iceland ............ | Jeffrey Ross Gunter.............. | PAS | FA | .............. | .............. | |
| Bishkek, Kyrgyzstan. | Ambassador to the Kyrgyz Republic ................. | Donald Lu .......................... | PAS | FA | .............. | .............. | |
| Bern, Switzerland ... | Ambassador to the Principality of Liechtenstein. | Edward T. McMullen Jr........ | PAS | FA | .............. | .............. | |

## DEPARTMENT OF STATE—Continued

| Location | Position Title | Name of Incumbent | Type of Appt. | Pay Plan | Level, Grade, or Pay | Tenure | Expires |
|---|---|---|---|---|---|---|---|
| Algiers, Algeria........ | Ambassador to the Peoples Democratic Republic of Algeria. | John P Desrocher ................ | PAS | FA | ............... | ............... | |
| Santiago, Chile ........ | Ambassador to the Republic of Chile ................ | Vacant .................................. | PAS | FA | ............... | ............... | |
| Kinshasa, Congo, Democratic Republic of the. | Ambassador to the Democratic Republic of the Congo. | Michael A. Hammer ............ | PAS | FA | ............... | ............... | |
| Zagreb, Croatia........ | Ambassador to the Republic of Croatia............ | W. Robert Kohorst ................ | PAS | FA | ............... | ............... | |
| Havana, Cuba.......... | Ambassador to the Republic of Cuba ................ | Vacant .................................. | PAS | FA | ............... | ............... | |
| Nicosia, Cyprus ....... | Ambassador to the Republic of Cyprus ............ | Judith Gail Garber ............... | PAS | FA | ............... | ............... | |
| Tegucigalpa, Honduras. | Ambassador to the Republic of Honduras.......... | Vacant .................................. | PAS | FA | ............... | ............... | |
| Amman, Jordan....... | Ambassador to the Hashemite Kingdom of Jordan. | ......do ............................... | PAS | FA | ............... | ............... | |
| Kazakhstan, Kazakhstan. | Ambassador to the Republic of Kazakhstan ...... | William H. Moser ................ | PAS | FA | ............... | ............... | |
| Vientiane, Laos........ | Ambassador to the Lao People's Democratic Republic. | Peter M. Haymond .............. | PAS | FA | ............... | ............... | |
| Lilongwe, Malawi .... | Ambassador to the Republic of Malawi............ | Robert K. Scott .................... | PAS | FA | ............... | ............... | |
| Kuala Lumpur, Malaysia. | Ambassador to Malaysia .................................. | Kamala Shirin Lakhdhir ..... | PAS | FA | ............... | ............... | |
| Colombo, Sri Lanka. | Ambassador to the Republic of Maldives .......... | Alaina B. Teplitz ................. | PAS | FA | ............... | ............... | |
| Bratislava, Slovakia. | Ambassador to the Slovak Republic .................. | Bridget A. Brink ................. | PAS | FA | ............... | ............... | |
| Ljubljana, Slovenia . | Ambassador to the Republic of Slovenia ........... | Lynda Blanchard ................. | PAS | FA | ............... | ............... | |
| Lome, Togo.............. | Ambassador to the Togolese Republic ............... | Eric William Stromayer ....... | PAS | FA | ............... | ............... | |
| Kabul, Afghanistan . | Ambassador to the Islamic Republic of Afghanistan. | Vacant .................................. | PAS | FA | ............... | ............... | |
| Yerevan, Armenia.... | Ambassador to the Republic of Armenia........... | Lynne M Tracy .................... | PAS | FA | ............... | ............... | |
| Minsk, Belarus ........ | Ambassador to the Republic of Belarus ............ | Vacant .................................. | PAS | FA | ............... | ............... | |
| Bogota, Colombia .... | Ambassador to the Republic of Colombia........... | Philip S. Goldberg ............... | PAS | FA | ............... | ............... | |
| Bridgetown, Barbados. | Ambassador to Grenada ................................... | Linda Swartz Taglialatela ... | PAS | FA | ............... | ............... | |
| Suva, Viti Levu, Fiji. | Ambassador to the Republic of Kiribati ............ | Joseph Cella........................ | PAS | FA | ............... | ............... | |
| Beirut, Lebanon ...... | Ambassador to the Lebanese Republic............... | Dorothy Shea ...................... | PAS | FA | ............... | ............... | |
| Maputo, Mozambique. | Ambassador to the Republic of Mozambique..... | Dennis Walter Hearne ......... | PAS | FA | ............... | ............... | |
| The Hague, Netherlands. | Ambassador to the Kingdom of the Netherlands. | Peter Hoekstra...................... | PAS | FA | ............... | ............... | |
| Niamey, Niger.......... | Ambassador to the Republic of Niger............... | Eric P. Whitaker ................. | PAS | FA | ............... | ............... | |
| Port Moresby, Papua New Guinea. | Ambassador to the Solomon Islands ................. | Erin Elizabeth McKee.......... | PAS | FA | ............... | ............... | |
| Tunis, Tunisia ......... | Ambassador to the Republic of Tunisia............ | Donald Armin Blome............ | PAS | FA | ............... | ............... | |
| Kyiv, Ukraine........... | Ambassador to Ukraine.................................... | Vacant .................................. | PAS | FA | ............... | ............... | |
| Abu Dhabi, United Arab Emirates. | Ambassador to the United Arab Emirates.......... | John Rakolta Jr. .................. | PAS | FA | ............... | ............... | |
| London, United Kingdom. | Ambassador to the United Kingdom of Great Britain and Northern Ireland. | Robert Wood Johnson IV...... | PAS | FA | ............... | ............... | |
| Tashkent, Uzbekistan. | Ambassador to the Republic of Uzbekistan ....... | Daniel N. Rosenblum .......... | PAS | FA | ............... | ............... | |
| Port Moresby, Papua New Guinea. | Ambassador to the Republic of Vanuatu ........... | Erin Elizabeth McKee.......... | PAS | FA | ............... | ............... | |
| Paris, France .......... | U.S. Representative to the United Nations Educational, Scientific and Cultural Organization, With the Rank of Ambassador. | Vacant .................................. | PAS | FA | ............... | ............... | |
| Rome, Italy ............. | U.S. Representative to the United Nations Agencies for Food and Agriculture, With the Rank of Ambassador. | Kip Tom .............................. | PAS | FA | ............... | ............... | |
| Geneva, Switzerland. | Representative of the United States to the Office of the United Nations and Other International Organizations in Geneva, With the Rank of Ambassador. | Andrew P. Bremberg ............ | PAS | FA | ............... | ............... | |
| Do ..................... | U.S. Representative to the Un Human Rights Council, With the Rank of Ambassador. | Vacant .................................. | PAS | FA | ............... | ............... | |
| Vienna, Austria ....... | U.S. Representative to the Organization for Security & Cooperation in Europe, With the Rank of Ambassador. | James S. Gilmore................. | PAS | FA | ............... | ............... | |
| Do ..................... | Representative of the U.S. to the Vienna Office of the United Nations and Representative of the U.S. to the International Atomic Energy Agency, With the Rank of Ambassador. | Jackie Wolcott...................... | PAS | FA | ............... | ............... | |

## DEPARTMENT OF STATE—Continued

| Location | Position Title | Name of Incumbent | Type of Appt. | Pay Plan | Level, Grade, or Pay | Tenure | Expires |
|---|---|---|---|---|---|---|---|
| Bridgetown, Barbados. | Ambassador to Antigua and Barbuda ................ | Linda Swartz Taglialatela ... | PAS | FA | ................ | ................ | |
| Baku, Azerbaijan..... | Ambassador to the Republic of Azerbaijan ....... | Earle D. Litzenberger.......... | PAS | FA | ................ | ................ | |
| Nassau, Bahamasthe. | Ambassador to the Commonwealth of the Bahamas. | Vacant ................................. | PAS | FA | ................ | ................ | |
| Dhaka, Bangladesh . | Ambassador to the People's Republic of Bangladesh. | Earl Robert Miller ............... | PAS | FA | ................ | ................ | |
| Bridgetown, Barbados. | Ambassador to Barbados.................................... | Linda Swartz Taglialatela ... | PAS | FA | ................ | ................ | |
| Ouagadougou, Burkina Faso. | Ambassador to Burkina Faso............................ | Vacant ................................. | PAS | FA | ................ | ................ | |
| Rangoon, Burma ..... | Ambassador to the Union of Burma.................. | ......do  ................ | PAS | FA | ................ | ................ | |
| Bangui, Central African Republic. | Ambassador to the Central African Republic .... | Lucy Tamlyn ........................ | PAS | FA | ................ | ................ | |
| Beijing, China.......... | Ambassador to the People's Republic of China.. | Terry Edward Branstad ....... | PAS | FA | ................ | ................ | |
| Malabo, Equatorial Guinea. | Ambassador to the Republic of Equatorial Guinea. | Susan N. Stevenson.............. | PAS | FA | ................ | ................ | |
| Asmara, Eritrea ...... | Ambassador to the State of Eritrea................... | Vacant ................................. | PAS | FA | ................ | ................ | |
| Jakarta, Java, Indonesia. | Ambassador to the Republic of Indonesia.......... | ......do  ................ | PAS | FA | ................ | ................ | |
| Baghdad, Iraq......... | Ambassador to the Republic of Iraq .................. | Matthew H. Tueller ............. | PAS | FA | ................ | ................ | |
| Rome, Italy .............. | Ambassador to the Republic of San Marino....... | Lewis M. Eisenberg.............. | PAS | FA | ................ | ................ | |
| Riyadh, Saudi Arabia. | Ambassador to the Kingdom of Saudi Arabia.... | John P. Abizaid ................... | PAS | FA | ................ | ................ | |
| Dakar, Senegal ........ | Ambassador to the Republic of Senegal ............ | Tulinabo Salama Mushingi . | PAS | FA | ................ | ................ | |
| Port Louis, Mauritius. | Ambassador to the Republic of Seychelles ......... | David Dale Reimer .............. | PAS | FA | ................ | ................ | |
| Somalia, Somalia..... | Ambassador to the Federal Republic of Somalia. | Donald Y. Yamamoto ............ | PAS | FA | ................ | ................ | |
| Pretoria, South Africa. | Ambassador to the Republic of South Africa ..... | Lana J. Marks........................ | PAS | FA | ................ | ................ | |
| Juba, South Sudan.. | Ambassador to the Republic of South Sudan..... | Thomas J. Hushek................ | PAS | FA | ................ | ................ | |
| Port of Spain, Trinidad and Tobago. | Ambassador to the Republic of Trinidad and Tobago. | Joseph N. Mondello .............. | PAS | FA | ................ | ................ | |
| Hanoi, Vietnam ....... | Ambassador to the Socialist Republic of Vietnam. | Daniel J Kritenbrink............ | PAS | FA | ................ | ................ | |
| Brussels, Belgium ... | Representative of the U.S. to the European Union, With the Rank and Status of Ambassador Extraordinary and Plenipotentiary. | Kay Bailey Hutchinson ........ | PAS | FA | ................ | ................ | |
| Montreal, Quebec, Canada. | Representative of the U.S. on the Council of the International Civil Aviation Organization. | Sean Doocey.......................... | PAS | FA | ................ | ................ | |
| Brussels, Belgium ... | U. S. Permanent Representative on the Council of the North Atlantic Treaty Organization, With the Rank and Status of Ambassador Extraordinary and Plenipotentiary. | Vacant ................................. | PAS | FA | ................ | ................ | |
| The Hague, Netherlands. | U.S. Representative to the Organization for the Prohibition of Chemical Weapons, With the Rank of Ambassador. | Kenneth Damian Ward ........ | PAS | FA | ................ | ................ | |
| Paris, France ........... | Representative of the U.S. to the Organization for Economic Cooperation and Development, With the Rank of Ambassador. | Vacant ................................. | PAS | FA | ................ | ................ | |
| Nouakchott, Mauritania. | Ambassador to the Islamic Republic of Mauritania. | Michael James Dodman....... | PAS | FA | ................ | ................ | |
| Suva, Viti Levu, Fiji. | Ambassador to the Republic of Nauru .............. | Joseph Cella.......................... | PAS | FA | ................ | ................ | |
| Nepal, Nepal............ | Ambassador to the Federal Democratic Republic of Nepal. | Randy W. Berry..................... | PAS | FA | ................ | ................ | |
| Vienna, Austria ....... | Ambassador to the Republic of Austria............. | Trevor D. Traina.................. | PAS | FA | ................ | ................ | |
| Pristina, Kosovo ...... | Ambassador to the Republic of Kosovo ............. | Philip S. Kosnett ................. | PAS | FA | ................ | ................ | |
| Windhoek, Namibia. | Ambassador to the Republic of Namibia............ | Lisa A. Johnson ................... | PAS | FA | ................ | ................ | |
| Kuwait, Kuwait ....... | Ambassador to the State of Kuwait................... | Alina L. Romanowski........... | PAS | FA | ................ | ................ | |
| Nairobi, Kenya ........ | Ambassador to the Republic of Kenya .............. | Kyle McCarter ...................... | PAS | FA | ................ | ................ | |
| Oslo, Norway ........... | Ambassador to the Kingdom of Norway............. | Vacant ................................. | PAS | FA | ................ | ................ | |
| Muscat, Oman ........ | Ambassador to the Sultanate of Oman ............. | Leslie Meredith Tsou .......... | PAS | FA | ................ | ................ | |
| Canberra, Australia. | Ambassador to the Commonwealth of Australia. | Arthur B Culvahouse Jr....... | PAS | FA | ................ | ................ | |
| Maseru, Lesotho...... | Ambassador to the Kingdom of Lesotho............ | Rebecca Eliza Gonzales........ | PAS | FA | ................ | ................ | |
| Bamako, Mali .......... | Ambassador to the Republic of Mali................. | Dennis B. Hankins ............... | PAS | FA | ................ | ................ | |
| Tirana, Albania ....... | Ambassador to the Republic of Albania ............ | Yuri Kim ............................... | PAS | FA | ................ | ................ | |

## DEPARTMENT OF STATE—Continued

| Location | Position Title | Name of Incumbent | Type of Appt. | Pay Plan | Level, Grade, or Pay | Tenure | Expires |
|---|---|---|---|---|---|---|---|
| Sarajevo, Bosnia and Herzegovina. | Ambassador to Bosnia and Herzegovina........... | Eric George Nelson .............. | PAS | FA | ................ | ................ | |
| Port-Au-Prince, Haiti. | Ambassador to the Republic of Haiti................. | Michele Jeanne Sison........... | PAS | FA | ................ | ................ | |
| Seoul, Korea, Republic of. | Ambassador to the Republic of Korea .............. | Harry B. Harris, Jr. .............. | PAS | FA | ................ | ................ | |
| Monrovia, Liberia.... | Ambassador to the Republic of Liberia ............. | Vacant ........................ | PAS | FA | ................ | ................ | |
| Rabat, Morocco........ | Ambassador to the Kingdom of Morocco ........... | David T. Fischer.................... | PAS | FA | ................ | ................ | |
| Praia, Cape Verde ... | Ambassador to the Republic of Cabo Verde ...... | John Jefferson Daigle........... | PAS | FA | ................ | ................ | |
| Santo Domingo, Dominican Republic. | Ambassador to the Dominican Republic ........... | Robin S. Bernstein................ | PAS | FA | ................ | ................ | |
| Cairo, Egypt............. | Ambassador to the Arab Republic of Egypt ...... | Jonathan R. Cohen .............. | PAS | FA | ................ | ................ | |
| San Salvador, El Salvador. | Ambassador to the Republic of El Salvador....... | Ronald Douglas Johnson...... | PAS | FA | ................ | ................ | |
| Skopje, Macedonia... | Ambassador to the Republic of North Macedonia. | Kate Marie Byrnes .............. | PAS | FA | ................ | ................ | |
| Kolonia, Micronesia, Federated States of. | Ambassador to the Federated States of Micronesia. | Carmen G. Cantor ............. | PAS | FA | ................ | ................ | |
| Chisinau, Moldova .. | Ambassador to the Republic of Moldova ........... | Dereck J. Hogan ................... | PAS | FA | ................ | ................ | |
| Podgorica, Montenegro. | Ambassador to Montenegro ........................... | Judy Rising Reinke .............. | PAS | FA | ................ | ................ | |
| Asuncion, Paraguay. | Ambassador to the Republic of Paraguay ......... | M. Lee McClenny.................. | PAS | FA | ................ | ................ | |
| Moscow, Russia........ | Ambassador to the Russian Federation ............ | John Joseph Sullivan .......... | PAS | FA | ................ | ................ | |
| Kigali, Rwanda........ | Ambassador to the Republic of Rwanda........... | Peter Hendrick Vrooman ..... | PAS | FA | ................ | ................ | |
| Bridgetown, Barbados. | Ambassador to the Federation of Saint Kitts and Nevis. | Linda Swartz Taglialatela ... | PAS | FA | ................ | ................ | |
| Do ..................... | Ambassador to Saint Lucia ............................ | ......do ......... | PAS | FA | ................ | ................ | |
| Stockholm, Sweden . | Ambassador to the Kingdom of Sweden............. | Kenneth A. Howery.............. | PAS | FA | ................ | ................ | |
| Bern, Switzerland ... | Ambassador to the Swiss Confederation........... | Edward T. McMullen Jr........ | PAS | FA | ................ | ................ | |
| Damascus, Syria...... | Ambassador to the Syrian Arab Republic ......... | Vacant ........................ | PAS | FA | ................ | ................ | |
| Dushanbe, Tajikistan. | Ambassador to the Republic of Tajikistan ........ | John Mark Pommersheim.... | PAS | FA | ................ | ................ | |
| Dar es Salaam, Tanzania. | Ambassador to the United Republic of Tanzania. | Donald Wright .................... | PAS | FA | ................ | ................ | |
| Luanda, Angola ....... | Ambassador to the Republic of Angola............. | Nina Maria Fite................... | PAS | FA | ................ | ................ | |
| Phnom Penh, Cambodia. | Ambassador to the Kingdom of Cambodia........ | W. Patrick Murphy .............. | PAS | FA | ................ | ................ | |
| Yaounde, Cameroon. | Ambassador to the Republic of Cameroon ........ | Peter Henry Barlerin .......... | PAS | FA | ................ | ................ | |
| Ottawa, Ontario, Canada. | Ambassador to Canada................................. | Vacant ........................ | PAS | FA | ................ | ................ | |
| Prague, Czech Republic. | Ambassador to the Czech Republic ................... | Stephen B. King................... | PAS | FA | ................ | ................ | |
| Addis Ababa, Ethiopia. | Ambassador to the Federal Democratic Republic of Ethiopia. | Michael Arthur Raynor........ | PAS | FA | ................ | ................ | |
| Suva, Viti Levu, Fiji. | Ambassador to the Republic of Fiji ................... | Joseph Cella......................... | PAS | FA | ................ | ................ | |
| Libreville, Gabon..... | Ambassador to the Gabonese Republic ............. | Vacant ........................ | PAS | FA | ................ | ................ | |
| Banjul, Gambia The. | Ambassador to the Republic of the Gambia....... | Richard Carlton Paschall III. | PAS | FA | ................ | ................ | |
| Tbilisi, Georgia........ | Ambassador to Georgia ................................. | Kelly C. Degnan................... | PAS | FA | ................ | ................ | |
| Accra, Ghana........... | Ambassador to the Republic of Ghana .............. | Stephanie Sanders Sullivan. | PAS | FA | ................ | ................ | |
| Guatemala, Guatemala. | Ambassador to the Republic of Guatemala........ | Luis E. Arreaga ................... | PAS | FA | ................ | ................ | |
| Conakry, Guinea...... | Ambassador to the Republic of Guinea ............. | Vacant ........................ | PAS | FA | ................ | ................ | |
| Dakar, Senegal ........ | Ambassador to the Republic of Guinea-Bissau.. | Tulinabo Salama Mushingi . | PAS | FA | ................ | ................ | |
| Bogota, Colombia .... | Ambassador to the Bolivarian Republic of Venezuela. | Vacant ........................ | PAS | FA | ................ | ................ | |
| Riyadh, Saudi Arabia. | Ambassador to the Republic of Yemen .............. | Christopher Paul Henzel ..... | PAS | FA | ................ | ................ | |
| Lusaka, Zambia........ | Ambassador to the Republic of Zambia............. | Vacant ........................ | PAS | FA | ................ | ................ | |
| La Paz, Bolivia ........ | Ambassador to the Plurinational State of Bolivia. | ......do ......... | PAS | FA | ................ | ................ | |
| Brasilia, Brazil ........ | Ambassador to the Federative Republic of Brazil. | Todd C. Chapman.............. | PAS | FA | ................ | ................ | |
| Bandar Seri Begawan, Brunei Darussalam. | Ambassador to Brunei Darussalam.................. | Vacant ........................ | PAS | FA | ................ | ................ | |
| Sofia, Bulgaria......... | Ambassador to the Republic of Bulgaria........... | Herro Mustafa ..................... | PAS | FA | ................ | ................ | |

| Location | Position Title | Name of Incumbent | Type of Appt. | Pay Plan | Level, Grade, or Pay | Tenure | Expires |
|---|---|---|---|---|---|---|---|
| Antananarivo, Madagascar. | Ambassador to the Union of the Comoros | Michael Peter Pelletier | PAS | FA | | | |
| Brazzaville, Congo... | Ambassador to the Republic of the Congo | Todd Philip Haskell | PAS | FA | | | |
| San Jose, Costa Rica. | Ambassador to the Republic of Costa Rica | Sharon Day | PAS | FA | | | |
| Abidjan, Cote D'Ivoire. | Ambassador to the Republic of Cote D'Ivoire | Richard K. Bell | PAS | FA | | | |
| Quito, Ecuador | Ambassador to the Republic of Ecuador | Michael J. Fitzpatrick | PAS | FA | | | |
| Tallinn, Estonia | Ambassador to the Republic of Estonia | Vacant | PAS | FA | | | |
| Vatican City, Vatican City. | Ambassador to the Holy See | Callista L. Gingrich | PAS | FA | | | |
| Rome, Italy | Ambassador to the Italian Republic | Lewis M. Eisenberg | PAS | FA | | | |
| Tokyo, Japan | Ambassador to Japan | Vacant | PAS | FA | | | |
| Luxembourg, Luxembourg. | Ambassador to the Grand Duchy of Luxembourg. | James Randolph Evans | PAS | FA | | | |
| Wellington, New Zealand. | Ambassador to New Zealand | Scott P. Brown | PAS | FA | | | |
| Managua, Nicaragua. | Ambassador to the Republic of Nicaragua | Kevin K. Sullivan | PAS | FA | | | |
| Lima, Peru | Ambassador to the Republic of Peru | Krishna R. Urs | PAS | FA | | | |
| Manila, Philippines. | Ambassador to the Republic of the Philippines. | Sung Y. Kim | PAS | FA | | | |
| Warsaw, Poland | Ambassador to the Republic of Poland | Georgette Mosbacher | PAS | FA | | | |
| Lisbon, Portugal | Ambassador to the Portugese Republic | George Edward Glass | PAS | FA | | | |
| Doha, Qatar | Ambassador to the State of Qatar | Vacant | PAS | FA | | | |
| Bucharest, Romania. | Ambassador to Romania | Adrian Zuckerman | PAS | FA | | | |
| Libreville, Gabon | Ambassador to the Democratic Republic of Sao Tome and Principe. | Vacant | PAS | FA | | | |
| Belgrade, Serbia | Ambassador to the Republic of Serbia | Anthony F. Godfrey | PAS | FA | | | |
| Freetown, Sierra Leone. | Ambassador to the Republic of Sierra Leone | Maria E. Brewer | PAS | FA | | | |
| Singapore, Singapore. | Ambassador to the Republic of Singapore | Vacant | PAS | FA | | | |
| Colombo, Sri Lanka. | Ambassador to the Democratic Socialist Republic of Sri Lanka. | Alaina B. Teplitz | PAS | FA | | | |
| Khartoum, Sudan | Ambassador to the Republic of the Sudan | Vacant | PAS | FA | | | |
| Paramaribo, Suriname. | Ambassador to the Republic of Suriname | Karen L. Williams | PAS | FA | | | |
| Bangkok, Thailand.. | Ambassador to the Kingdom of Thailand | Michael George DeSombre | PAS | FA | | | |
| Ankara, Turkey | Ambassador to the Republic of Turkey | David Michael Satterfield | PAS | FA | | | |
| Ashkhabad, Turkmenistan. | Ambassador to Turkmenistan | Matthew S. Kilmow | PAS | FA | | | |
| Suva, Viti Levu, Fiji. | Ambassador to Tuvalu | Joseph Cella | PAS | FA | | | |
| Kampala, Uganda | Ambassador to the Republic of Uganda | Vacant | PAS | FA | | | |
| Montevideo, Uruguay. | Ambassador to the Oriental Republic of Uruguay. | Kenneth S. George | PAS | FA | | | |
| Harare, Zimbabwe | Ambassador to the Republic of Zimbabwe | Brian A. Nichols | PAS | FA | | | |
| Manama, Bahrain | Ambassador to the Kingdom of Bahrain | Justin Siberell | PAS | FA | | | |
| Cotonou, Benin | Ambassador to the Republic of Benin | Patricia Mahoney | PAS | FA | | | |
| Sarajevo, Bosnia and Herzegovina. | Ambassador to Bosnia and Herzegovina | Eric George Nelson | PAS | FA | | | |
| Gaberone, Botswana. | Ambassador to the Republic of Botswana | Craig Lewis Cloud | PAS | FA | | | |
| Copenhagen, Denmark. | Ambassador to the Kingdom of Denmark | Carla Sands | PAS | FA | | | |
| Djibouti, Djibouti | Ambassador to the Republic of Djibouti | Larry Edward Andre, Jr. | PAS | FA | | | |
| Bridgetown, Barbados. | Ambassador to the Commonwealth of Dominica. | Linda Swartz Taglialatela | PAS | FA | | | |
| Budapest, Hungary. | Ambassador to Hungary | David B. Cornstein | PAS | FA | | | |
| New Delhi, India | Ambassador to the Republic of India | Kenneth Ian Juster | PAS | FA | | | |
| Dublin, Ireland | Ambassador to Ireland | Edward F. Crawford | PAS | FA | | | |
| Jerusalem, Israel | Ambassador to the State of Israel | David Friedman | PAS | FA | | | |
| Kingston, Jamaica | Ambassador to Jamaica | Donald R. Tapia | PAS | FA | | | |
| Valletta, Malta | Ambassador to the Republic of Malta | Vacant | PAS | FA | | | |
| Majuro Atoll, Marshall Islands. | Ambassador to the Republic of the Marshall Islands. | Roxanne Cabral | PAS | FA | | | |
| Mexico City, Mexico. | Ambassador to the United Mexican States | Christopher Landau | PAS | FA | | | |
| Paris, France | Ambassador to the Principality of Monaco | Jamie McCourt | PAS | FA | | | |
| Ulaanbaatar, Mongolia. | Ambassador to Mongolia | Michael S. Klecheski | PAS | FA | | | |
| Oslo, Norway | Ambassador to the Federal Republic of Nigeria. | Mary Beth Leonard | PAS | FA | | | |

## DEPARTMENT OF STATE—Continued

| Location | Position Title | Name of Incumbent | Type of Appt. | Pay Plan | Level, Grade, or Pay | Tenure | Expires |
|---|---|---|---|---|---|---|---|
| Islamabad, Pakistan. | Ambassador to the Islamic Republic of Pakistan. | Vacant ................................ | PAS | FA | ............... | ............... | |
| Koror, Palau............ | Ambassador to the Republic of Palau................ | John Hennessey-Niland ....... | PAS | FA | ............... | ............... | |
| Panama, Panama .... | Ambassador to the Republic of Panama............ | Vacant ................................ | PAS | FA | ............... | ............... | |
| Port Moresby, Papua New Guinea. | Ambassador to the Independent State of Papua New Guinea. | Erin Elizabeth McKee.......... | PAS | FA | ............... | ............... | |
| Bridgetown, Barbados. | Ambassador to Saint Vincent and the Grenadines. | Linda Swartz Taglialatela ... | PAS | FA | ............... | ............... | |
| Wellington, New Zealand. | Ambassador to the Independent State of Samoa. | Scott P. Brown ...................... | PAS | FA | ............... | ............... | |
| Madrid, Spain.......... | Ambassador to the Kingdom of Spain ................ | Richard Duke Buchan III .... | PAS | FA | ............... | ............... | |
| Dili, East Timor....... | Ambassador to the Democratic Republic of Timor-Leste. | Kathleen M. Fitzpatrick....... | PAS | FA | ............... | ............... | |
| Riga, Latvia ............ | Ambassador to the Republic of Latvia .............. | John Leslie Carwile............. | PAS | FA | ............... | ............... | |
| Vilnius, Lithuania ... | Ambassador to the Republic of Lithuania.......... | Robert S. Gilchrist................ | PAS | FA | ............... | ............... | |
| Antananarivo, Madagascar. | Ambassador to the Republic of Madagascar...... | Michael Peter Pelletier ........ | PAS | FA | ............... | ............... | |
| Port Louis, Mauritius. | Ambassador to the Republic of Mauritius ......... | David Dale Reimer.............. | PAS | FA | ............... | ............... | |
| Addis Ababa, Ethiopia. | Representative of the U.S. to the African Union, With the Rank and Status of Ambassador Extraordinary and Plenipotentiary. | Jessica E Lapenn ................. | PAS | FA | ............... | ............... | |
| Jakarta, Java, Indonesia. | Representative of the U.S. to the Association of the Southeast Asian Nations, With the Rank and Status of Ambassador Extraordinary and Plenipotentiary. | Vacant ................................ | PAS | FA | ............... | ............... | |
| Geneva, Switzerland. | U.S. Representative to the Conference on Disarmament, With the Rank of Ambassador. | Robert A Wood ...................... | PAS | FA | ............... | ............... | |
| Suva, Fiji ................. | Ambassador to the Kingdom of Tonga................ | Joseph Cella.......................... | PAS | FA | ............... | ............... | |
| | *Bureau of African Affairs* | | | | | | |
| Washington, DC ...... | Assistant Secretary of State (African Affairs) ... | Tibor Nagy ............................ | PAS | EX | IV | ............... | |
| Do ..................... | Special Envoy for the Sahel Region of Africa .... | John Peter Pham.................. | SC | GS | 15 | ............... | |
| | *Bureau of East Asian and Pacific Affairs* | | | | | | |
| Do ..................... | Senior Advisor........................................................ | David Feith ............................ | SC | GS | 15 | ............... | |
| Do ..................... | Assistant Secretary of State (East Asian and Pacific Affairs). | David Stilwell ...................... | PAS | EX | IV | ............... | |
| Do ..................... | Special Representative and Policy Coordinator for Burma, With the Rank of Ambassador. | Vacant ................................ | PAS | EX | IV | ............... | |
| Do ..................... | Special Envoy on North Korean Human Rights Issues, With the Rank of Ambassador. | ......do | PAS | EX | IV | ............... | |
| Do ..................... | Deputy Assistant Secretary ................................ | Alex Wong ............................ | NA | ES | | ............... | |
| Do ..................... | Senior Advisor........................................................ | Vacant ................................ | | ES | | ............... | |
| | *Bureau of European and Eurasian Affairs* | | | | | | |
| Do ..................... | Assistant Secretary of State (European and Eurasian Affairs). | ......do | PAS | EX | IV | ............... | |
| Do ..................... | Deputy Assistant Secretary ................................ | Alexander T Alden............... | NA | ES | | ............... | |
| Do ..................... | Office Director........................................................ | Career Incumbent ................ | CA | ES | | ............... | |
| Do ..................... | Strategic Advisor .................................................. | Tyler Brace .......................... | SC | GS | 13 | ............... | |
| | *Bureau of Near Eastern Affairs* | | | | | | |
| Do ..................... | Assistant Secretary of State (Near Eastern Affairs). | David Schenker ...................... | PAS | EX | IV | ............... | |
| Do ..................... | Deputy Assistant Secretary & Special Envoy for Syria. | Joel Rayburn........................ | NA | ES | | ............... | |
| Do ..................... | Deputy Assistant Secretary ................................ | Career Incumbent ................ | CA | ES | | ............... | |
| Do ..................... | Office Director........................................................ | Vacant ................................ | | ES | | ............... | |
| Do ..................... | Deputy Assistant Secretary ................................ | David J Copley ...................... | SC | GS | 15 | ............... | |
| | *Bureau of South and Central Asian Affairs* | | | | | | |
| Do ..................... | Assistant Secretary of State for South Asian Affairs. | Vacant ................................ | PAS | EX | IV | ............... | |
| Do ..................... | Deputy Assistant Secretary ................................ | Career Incumbent ................ | CA | ES | | ............... | |
| | *Bureau of Western Hemisphere Affairs* | | | | | | |
| Do ..................... | Assistant Secretary of State (Western Hemisphere Affairs). | Vacant ................................ | PAS | EX | IV | ............... | |
| Do ..................... | Office Director........................................................ | ......do | | ES | | ............... | |
| Do ..................... | ......do | Career Incumbent ................ | CA | ES | | ............... | |
| Do ..................... | Deputy Assistant Secretary ................................ | Carrie Filipetti .................... | SC | GS | 15 | ............... | |
| Do ..................... | Senior Advisor........................................................ | Carlos Suarez ...................... | SC | GS | 15 | ............... | |
| Do ..................... | Special Assistant................................................... | Federico G Klein.................. | SC | GS | 12 | ............... | |

## DEPARTMENT OF STATE—Continued

| Location | Position Title | Name of Incumbent | Type of Appt. | Pay Plan | Level, Grade, or Pay | Tenure | Expires |
|---|---|---|---|---|---|---|---|
| | *Bureau of International Organizational Affairs* | | | | | | |
| Washington, DC ...... | Assistant Secretary of State (International Organization Affairs). | Vacant .................................. | PAS | EX | IV | .............. | |
| Do .................... | Deputy Assistant Secretary ............................... | Career Incumbent ............... | CA | ES | .............. | .............. | |
| Do .................... | ......do ....................................... | ......do ...................... | CA | ES | .............. | .............. | |
| Do .................... | ......do | Katherine Wright .............. | NA | ES | .............. | .............. | |
| Do .................... | Senior Advisor.......................................... | Eric Ueland...................... | NA | ES | .............. | .............. | |
| Do .................... | Office Director........................................ | Career Incumbent ............... | CA | ES | .............. | .............. | |
| Do .................... | Special Assistant........................... | Robby Smith ...................... | SC | GS | 12 | .............. | |
| | *Office of the Under Secretary for Management* | | | | | | |
| Do .................... | Under Secretary of State (Management) .......... | Brian J Bulatao.................. | PAS | EX | III | .............. | |
| Do .................... | Deputy Under Secretary for Management........ | Career Incumbent ............... | CA | ES | .............. | .............. | |
| Do .................... | Advisor....................................... | John W Hutchison .............. | SC | GS | 15 | .............. | |
| Do .................... | Managing Director......................... | Career Incumbent ............... | CA | ES | .............. | .............. | |
| Do .................... | Principal Deputy Director ....................... | ......do ...................... | CA | ES | .............. | .............. | |
| | *Office of Management Policy, Rightsizing and Innovation* | | | | | | |
| Do .................... | Director....................................... | James Schwab .................... | NA | ES | .............. | .............. | |
| | *Bureau of Administration* | | | | | | |
| Do .................... | Assistant Secretary of State (Administration)... | Carrie Cabelka .................. | PA | EX | IV | .............. | |
| Do .................... | Office Director........................................ | Career Incumbent ............... | CA | ES | .............. | .............. | |
| Do .................... | Director........................................ | ......do ...................... | CA | ES | .............. | .............. | |
| Do .................... | Director, Small and Disadvantaged Business Utilization. | ......do ...................... | CA | ES | .............. | .............. | |
| Do .................... | Office Director, Office of Program Management and Policy. | ......do ...................... | CA | ES | .............. | .............. | |
| Do .................... | Director, Office of Acquisitions Management..... | Vacant ...................... | .............. | ES | .............. | .............. | |
| Do .................... | Special Assistant........................... | Shannon Bell ...................... | SC | GS | 11 | .............. | |
| | *Bureau of Budget and Planning* | | | | | | |
| Do .................... | Director....................................... | Career Incumbent ............... | CA | ES | .............. | .............. | |
| Do .................... | Deputy Director ....................... | Career Incumbent ............... | CA | ES | .............. | .............. | |
| Do .................... | Deputy Director, Resource Planning and Budget Information. | ......do ...................... | CA | ES | .............. | .............. | |
| | *Bureau of the Comptroller and Global Financial Services* | | | | | | |
| Do .................... | Chief Financial Officer ............................. | Vacant ...................... | PAS | EX | IV | .............. | |
| Charleston, SC ........ | Comptroller ............................. | Career Incumbent ............... | CA | ES | .............. | .............. | |
| Do .................... | Deputy Comptroller.......................... | ......do ...................... | CA | ES | .............. | .............. | |
| Washington, DC ...... | Executive Director ............................. | ......do ...................... | CA | ES | .............. | .............. | |
| Do .................... | Managing Director, Global Compensation ........ | Vacant ...................... | .............. | ES | .............. | .............. | |
| Charleston, SC ........ | Managing Director........................... | Career Incumbent ............... | CA | ES | .............. | .............. | |
| Washington, DC ...... | ......do ...................... | ......do ...................... | CA | ES | .............. | .............. | |
| | *Bureau of Consular Affairs* | | | | | | |
| Do .................... | Assistant Secretary of State (Consular Affairs). | Carl Risch ...................... | PAS | EX | IV | .............. | |
| Do .................... | Deputy Assistant Secretary ....................... | Career Incumbent ............... | CA | ES | .............. | .............. | |
| Do .................... | Managing Director Passport Services ............. | ......do ...................... | CA | ES | .............. | .............. | |
| Do .................... | Office Director........................................ | ......do ...................... | CA | ES | .............. | .............. | |
| Do .................... | Managing Director, Passport Support Services . | ......do ...................... | CA | ES | .............. | .............. | |
| Do .................... | Managing Director.......................... | ......do ...................... | CA | ES | .............. | .............. | |
| Do .................... | Director for Consular Systems and Technology. | ......do ...................... | CA | ES | .............. | .............. | |
| Do .................... | Senior Advisor.......................................... | Kaitlin Vogt Stoddard ........ | SC | GS | 14 | .............. | |
| | *Bureau of Diplomatic Security* | | | | | | |
| Do .................... | Assistant Secretary of State (Diplomatic Security). | Michael Evanoff.................. | PAS | EX | IV | .............. | |
| Do .................... | Executive Director ............................. | Career Incumbent ............... | CA | ES | .............. | .............. | |
| Do .................... | Comptroller ............................. | ......do ...................... | CA | ES | .............. | .............. | |
| | *Office of Foreign Missions* | | | | | | |
| Do .................... | Director of the Office of Foreign Missions.......... | Stephen J Akard.............. | PAS | EX | IV | .............. | |
| Do .................... | Deputy Director ............................. | Career Incumbent ............... | CA | ES | .............. | .............. | |
| | *Foreign Service Institute* | | | | | | |
| Do .................... | Executive Director ............................. | ......do ...................... | CA | ES | .............. | .............. | |
| Do .................... | Associate Dean............................. | ......do ...................... | CA | ES | .............. | .............. | |
| Do .................... | Office Director, Education Programs................. | ......do ...................... | CA | ES | .............. | .............. | |
| | *Bureau of Global Talent Management* | | | | | | |
| Do .................... | Director General of the Foreign Service............ | Carol Z Perez ...................... | PAS | EX | IV | .............. | |
| Do .................... | Senior Advisor.......................................... | Career Incumbent ............... | CA | ES | .............. | .............. | |

## DEPARTMENT OF STATE—Continued

| Location | Position Title | Name of Incumbent | Type of Appt. | Pay Plan | Level, Grade, or Pay | Tenure | Expires |
|---|---|---|---|---|---|---|---|
| Washington, DC ...... | Director, Resource Management and Organization Analysis. | Career Incumbent ................ | CA | ES | ................ | ................ | |
| Do .................... | Office Director.................... | ......do ................ | CA | ES | ................ | ................ | |
| Do .................... | ......do .................... | ......do ................ | CA | ES | ................ | ................ | |
| Do .................... | ......do .................... | ......do ................ | CA | ES | ................ | ................ | |
| Do .................... | ......do .................... | ......do ................ | CA | ES | ................ | ................ | |
| | *Bureau of Information Resources Management* | | | | | | |
| Do .................... | Chief Information Officer.................... | Stuart Mcguigan.................... | NA | ES | ................ | ................ | |
| Do .................... | Deputy Chief Information Officer.................... | Career Incumbent ................ | CA | ES | ................ | ................ | |
| Do .................... | Office Director, Enterprise Network Management. | ......do ................ | CA | ES | ................ | ................ | |
| Do .................... | Office Director, Strategic Planning Office.......... | ......do ................ | CA | ES | ................ | ................ | |
| Do .................... | Office Director.................... | ......do ................ | CA | ES | ................ | ................ | |
| Do .................... | ......do .................... | ......do ................ | CA | ES | ................ | ................ | |
| Do .................... | Managing Director.................... | ......do ................ | CA | ES | ................ | ................ | |
| | *Bureau of Overseas Buildings Operations* | | | | | | |
| Do .................... | Senior Advisor.................... | Ranjit Gill .................... | SC | GS | 14 | ................ | |
| Do .................... | Director.................... | Addison Davis.................... | NA | ES | ................ | ................ | |
| Do .................... | Deputy Director, Overseas Buildings Operations. | Career Incumbent ................ | CA | ES | ................ | ................ | |
| Do .................... | Managing Director.................... | ......do ................ | CA | ES | ................ | ................ | |
| Do .................... | Office Director.................... | ......do ................ | CA | ES | ................ | ................ | |
| Do .................... | Supervisory General Engineer.................... | ......do ................ | CA | ES | ................ | ................ | |
| Do .................... | Office Director.................... | ......do ................ | CA | ES | ................ | ................ | |
| Do .................... | ......do .................... | ......do ................ | CA | ES | ................ | ................ | |
| Do .................... | Managing Director.................... | ......do ................ | CA | ES | ................ | ................ | |
| Do .................... | Senior Advisor.................... | Kimberly Badenhop ............ | SC | GS | 15 | ................ | |
| Do .................... | Senior Strategic Advisor.................... | Marc Moyer.................... | SC | GS | 15 | ................ | |
| | *Office of the Under Secretary for Economic Growth, Energy, and the Environment* | | | | | | |
| Do .................... | Under Secretary of State (Economic Growth, Energy, and the Environment). | Keith Joseph Krach.......... | PAS | EX | III | ................ | |
| Do .................... | Senior Advisor for Energy Economic Security ... | Career Incumbent ................ | CA | ES | ................ | ................ | |
| Do .................... | Senior Advisor.................... | Hiroaki Rodriguez ............ | SC | GS | 15 | ................ | |
| | *Bureau of Economic and Business Affairs* | | | | | | |
| Do .................... | Assistant Secretary of State (Economic and Business Affairs). | Manisha Singh .................... | PAS | EX | IV | ................ | |
| Do .................... | Deputy Assistant Secretary .................... | Career Incumbent ................ | CA | ES | ................ | ................ | |
| Do .................... | ......do .................... | Robert Strayer .................... | NA | ES | ................ | ................ | |
| Do .................... | ......do .................... | David Peyman .................... | NA | ES | ................ | ................ | |
| Do .................... | ......do .................... | Vacant ................ | ............ | ES | ................ | ................ | |
| Do .................... | Office Director.................... | Career Incumbent ................ | CA | ES | ................ | ................ | |
| Do .................... | ......do .................... | ......do ................ | CA | ES | ................ | ................ | |
| Do .................... | Special Representative .................... | Dan Negrea.................... | SC | GS | 15 | ................ | |
| Do .................... | Special Advisor.................... | Taylor M Bush .................... | SC | GS | 14 | ................ | |
| Do .................... | Special Assistant.................... | Kristine Bucci .................... | SC | GS | 12 | ................ | |
| | *Bureau of Energy Resources* | | | | | | |
| Do .................... | Assistant Secretary of State (Energy Resources). | Francis Fannon.................... | PAS | EX | IV | ................ | |
| Do .................... | Deputy Assistant Secretary .................... | Career Incumbent ................ | CA | ES | ................ | ................ | |
| Do .................... | ......do .................... | Melissa M Simpson ............ | NA | ES | ................ | ................ | |
| Do .................... | Senior Advisor.................... | Aaron Ringel.................... | SC | GS | 15 | ................ | |
| | *Bureau of Oceans and International Environmental and Scientific Affairs* | | | | | | |
| Do .................... | Assistant Secretary of State for Oceans and International Environmental and Scientific Affairs. | Vacant ................ | PAS | EX | IV | ................ | |
| Do .................... | Deputy Assistant Secretary .................... | Career Incumbent ................ | CA | ES | ................ | ................ | |
| Do .................... | Senior Advisor.................... | ......do ................ | CA | ES | ................ | ................ | |
| Do .................... | Executive Director.................... | ......do ................ | CA | ES | ................ | ................ | |
| Do .................... | Office Director.................... | ......do ................ | CA | ES | ................ | ................ | |
| Do .................... | ......do .................... | ......do ................ | CA | ES | ................ | ................ | |
| Do .................... | Director.................... | ......do ................ | CA | ES | ................ | ................ | |
| Do .................... | Office Director.................... | ......do ................ | CA | ES | ................ | ................ | |
| | *Office of Chief Economist* | | | | | | |
| Do .................... | Chief Economist.................... | Sharon J Brown-Hruska...... | NA | ES | ................ | ................ | |
| Do .................... | Deputy Chief Economist.................... | Trevor Wagener .................... | SC | GS | 15 | ................ | |

## DEPARTMENT OF STATE—Continued

| Location | Position Title | Name of Incumbent | Type of Appt. | Pay Plan | Level, Grade, or Pay | Tenure | Expires |
|---|---|---|---|---|---|---|---|
| | *Office of the Under Secretary for Arms Control and International Security Affairs* | | | | | | |
| Washington, DC ...... | Under Secretary of State for Arms Control and International Security. | Vacant ..................... | PAS | EX | III | ............... | |
| Do ................... | Senior Advisor...................................................... | Ryan Tully .......................... | SC | GS | 15 | ............... | |
| Do ................... | Special Advisor..................................................... | Isaac J Fong........................ | SC | GS | 15 | ............... | |
| | *Bureau of Arms Control, Verification, and Compliance* | | | | | | |
| Do ................... | Assistant Secretary of State (Verification and Compliance). | Vacant ..................... | PAS | EX | IV | ............... | |
| Do ................... | Deputy Assistant Secretary ............................... | Thomas G Dinanno .............. | NA | ES | ............... | ............... | |
| Do ................... | Senior Advisor...................................................... | Michael A Westphal.............. | NA | ES | ............... | ............... | |
| Do ................... | Office Director ...................................................... | Career Incumbent ................ | CA | ES | ............... | ............... | |
| Do ................... | ......do ................................................................... | ......do ................................ | CA | ES | ............... | ............... | |
| Do ................... | ......do ................................................................... | ......do ................................ | CA | ES | ............... | ............... | |
| Do ................... | Senior Advisor...................................................... | Golan Rodgers ...................... | SC | GS | 15 | ............... | |
| | *Bureau of International Security and Nonproliferation* | | | | | | |
| Do ................... | Assistant Secretary of State (International Security and Non-Proliferation). | Christopher A Ford .............. | PAS | EX | IV | ............... | |
| Do ................... | Special Representative of the President for Nuclear Nonproliferation, With the Rank of Ambassador. | Jeffrey L Eberhardt.............. | PAS | EX | IV | ............... | |
| Do ................... | Deputy Assistant Secretary ............................... | Benjamin Swift Purser III ... | NA | ES | ............... | ............... | |
| Do ................... | ......do ................................................................... | Career Incumbent ................ | CA | ES | ............... | ............... | |
| Do ................... | Executive Director ............................................... | ......do ................................ | CA | ES | ............... | ............... | |
| Do ................... | Office Director ...................................................... | Vacant ..................... | ............. | ES | ............... | ............... | |
| Do ................... | ......do ................................................................... | Career Incumbent ................ | CA | ES | ............... | ............... | |
| Do ................... | ......do ................................................................... | ......do ................................ | CA | ES | ............... | ............... | |
| Do ................... | Senior Advisor...................................................... | Thomas Grant...................... | SC | GS | 15 | ............... | |
| | *Bureau of Political-Military Affairs* | | | | | | |
| Do ................... | Assistant Secretary of State (Political-Military Affairs). | Rene Clarke Cooper .............. | PAS | EX | V | ............... | |
| Do ................... | Deputy Assistant Secretary ............................... | Marik String........................ | NA | ES | ............... | ............... | |
| Do ................... | ......do ................................................................... | Joel E Starr......................... | SC | GS | 15 | ............... | |
| Do ................... | Senior Advisor...................................................... | William H Buckey ................ | SC | GS | 15 | ............... | |
| Do ................... | Office Director ...................................................... | Career Incumbent ................ | CA | ES | ............... | ............... | |
| Do ................... | ......do ................................................................... | ......do ................................ | CA | ES | ............... | ............... | |
| | *Office of the Under Secretary for Public Diplomacy and Public Affairs* | | | | | | |
| Do ................... | Under Secretary of State for Public Diplomacy. | Vacant ..................... | PAS | EX | III | ............... | |
| Do ................... | Special Envoy and Coordinator ......................... | Lea Potts............................ | NA | ES | ............... | ............... | |
| Do ................... | Director, U.S. Diplomacy Center ....................... | Mary Deely Kane .............. | NA | ES | ............... | ............... | |
| | *Bureau of Global Public Affairs* | | | | | | |
| Do ................... | Assistant Secretary of State (Public Affairs) ..... | Vacant ..................... | PA | EX | IV | ............... | |
| Do ................... | Deputy Assistant Secretary for Media Strategy / Press Secretary. | Kathryn Martin.................... | NA | ES | ............... | ............... | |
| Do ................... | Deputy Assistant Secretary for Digital Strategy. | Benjamin Lewis Friedmann. | NA | ES | ............... | ............... | |
| Do ................... | Spokesperson........................................................ | Morgan Ortagus .................. | NA | ES | ............... | ............... | |
| Do ................... | Deputy Spokesperson .......................................... | John Cale Brown .................. | SC | GS | 15 | ............... | |
| Do ................... | Senior Advisor...................................................... | Elizabeth Robbins ................ | SC | GS | 15 | ............... | |
| Do ................... | ......do ................................................................... | Morvared Namdarkhan ....... | SC | GS | 15 | ............... | |
| Do ................... | Special Advisor..................................................... | Michael Abboud .................. | SC | GS | 14 | ............... | |
| | *Bureau of Educational and Cultural Affairs* | | | | | | |
| Do ................... | Assistant Secretary of State (Educational and Cultural Affairs). | Marie Royce ........................ | PAS | EX | IV | ............... | |
| Do ................... | Deputy Assistant Secretary ............................... | Caroline Casagrande............ | SC | GS | 15 | ............... | |
| Do ................... | Senior Advisor...................................................... | Michelle Cangelosi .............. | SC | GS | 15 | ............... | |
| Do ................... | Communications Director ................................... | Matthew Bartlett ................ | SC | GS | 14 | ............... | |
| Do ................... | Special Advisor..................................................... | Bari Rogoff.......................... | SC | GS | 14 | ............... | |
| Do ................... | Special Assistant................................................. | Emily Sissell........................ | SC | GS | 13 | ............... | |
| | *Office of the Under Secretary for Civilian Security, Democracy, and Human Rights* | | | | | | |
| Do ................... | Under Secretary of State (Civilian Security, Democracy, and Human Rights). | Vacant ..................... | PAS | EX | III | ............... | |
| Do ................... | Senior Advisor...................................................... | Pamela D Pryor ................... | NA | ES | ............... | ............... | |
| Do ................... | Special Envoy to Monitor & Combat Anti-Semitism. | Elan Carr............................ | NA | ES | ............... | ............... | |

## DEPARTMENT OF STATE—Continued

| Location | Position Title | Name of Incumbent | Type of Appt. | Pay Plan | Level, Grade, or Pay | Tenure | Expires |
|---|---|---|---|---|---|---|---|
| Washington, DC ...... | Deputy Special Envoy to Monitor & Combat Anti-Semitism. | Elham Cohanim.................... | SC | GS | 15 | .............. | |
| Do .................. | Senior Advisor........................................ | Chadwick Gore .................... | SC | GS | 15 | .............. | |
| Do .................. | Special Assistant.................................... | Catharine P O'Neill............. | SC | GS | 11 | .............. | |
| Do .................. | ......do ................................................ | Peter Isaiah Burns .............. | SC | GS | 9 | .............. | |
| Do .................. | Senior Advisor........................................ | Vacant .............................. | ............ | ES | .............. | .............. | |
| | *Bureau of Conflict and Stabilization Operations* | | | | | | |
| Do .................. | Assistant Secretary of State (Conflict and Stabilization Operations). | Denise Natali...................... | PAS | EX | IV | .............. | |
| | *Bureau of Counterterrorism* | | | | | | |
| Do .................. | Coordinator for Counterterrorism, With the Rank and Status of Ambassador At Large. | Nathan A Sales.................... | PAS | EX | IV | .............. | |
| Do .................. | Principal Deputy Coord........................... | Career Incumbent .............. | CA | ES | | .............. | |
| Do .................. | Deputy Coordinator ............................... | Christopher Harnisch .......... | NA | ES | | .............. | |
| Do .................. | ......do ................................................ | Career Incumbent .............. | CA | ES | | .............. | |
| Do .................. | Office Director ...................................... | ......do ................................ | CA | ES | | .............. | |
| | *Bureau of Democracy, Human Rights and Labor* | | | | | | |
| Do .................. | Assistant Secretary of State for Democracy, Human Rights, and Labor. | Robert A Destro.................... | PAS | EX | IV | .............. | |
| Do .................. | Ambassador At Large for International Religious Freedom. | Samuel Dale Brownback...... | PAS | EX | IV | .............. | |
| Do .................. | Deputy Assistant Secretary ................... | Career Incumbent .............. | CA | ES | | .............. | |
| Do .................. | Senior Advisor........................................ | ......do ................................ | CA | ES | | .............. | |
| Do .................. | ......do ................................................ | Riley Barnes ...................... | SC | GS | 15 | .............. | |
| Do .................. | Special Assistant.................................... | Evan Berlanti ...................... | SC | GS | 11 | .............. | |
| | *Office of Global Criminal Justice* | | | | | | |
| Do .................. | Ambassador At Large for Global Criminal Justice. | Morse Tan ........................... | PAS | EX | IV | .............. | |
| | *Bureau of International Narcotics and Law Enforcement Affairs* | | | | | | |
| Do .................. | Assistant Secretary of State (International Narcotics and Law Enforcement Affairs). | Kirsten Madison .................. | PAS | EX | IV | .............. | |
| Do .................. | Principal Deputy Assistant Secretary ............... | Career Incumbent .............. | CA | ES | | .............. | |
| Do .................. | Controller/Executive Director ................. | ......do ................................ | CA | ES | | .............. | |
| Patrick Air Force Base, FL. | Office Director ...................................... | ......do ................................ | CA | ES | | .............. | |
| Washington, DC ...... | ......do ................................................ | ......do ................................ | CA | ES | | .............. | |
| | *Office to Monitor and Combat Trafficking In Persons* | | | | | | |
| Do .................. | Director of the Office to Monitor and Combat Trafficking, With Rank of Ambassador At Large. | John Richmond.................... | PAS | EX | IV | .............. | |
| Do .................. | Principal Deputy Director........................ | Career Incumbent .............. | CA | ES | | .............. | |
| Do .................. | Senior Advisor........................................ | Christine Buchholz.............. | SC | GS | 15 | .............. | |
| | *Bureau of Population, Refugees and Migration* | | | | | | |
| Do .................. | Assistant Secretary of State (Population, Refugees, and Migration). | Vacant ................................ | PAS | EX | IV | .............. | |
| Do .................. | Principal Deputy Assistant Secretary ............... | Carol Oconnell.................... | NA | ES | | .............. | |
| Do .................. | Deputy Assistant Secretary ................... | Career Incumbent .............. | CA | ES | | .............. | |
| Do .................. | Comptroller ........................................... | ......do ................................ | CA | ES | | .............. | |
| Do .................. | Office Director ...................................... | ......do ................................ | CA | ES | | .............. | |
| Do .................. | ......do ................................................ | ......do ................................ | CA | ES | | .............. | |
| Do .................. | ......do ................................................ | ......do ................................ | CA | ES | | .............. | |
| Do .................. | ......do ................................................ | ......do ................................ | CA | ES | | .............. | |
| | *Office of Religion and Global Affairs* | | | | | | |
| Tunisia, Tunisia ...... | Ambassador to Libya............................. | Richard B. Norland ............. | PAS | FA | .............. | .............. | |

## DEPARTMENT OF STATE OFFICE OF THE INSPECTOR GENERAL

| Location | Position Title | Name of Incumbent | Type of Appt. | Pay Plan | Level, Grade, or Pay | Tenure | Expires |
|---|---|---|---|---|---|---|---|
| Washington, DC ...... | **OFFICE OF INSPECTOR GENERAL** Attorney Adviser.................................... | Jill Baisinger ...................... | XS | SL | .............. | .............. | |

## DEPARTMENT OF STATE OFFICE OF THE INSPECTOR GENERAL—Continued

| Location | Position Title | Name of Incumbent | Type of Appt. | Pay Plan | Level, Grade, or Pay | Tenure | Expires |
|---|---|---|---|---|---|---|---|
| Washington, DC ...... | Assistant Inspector General for Overseas Contingency Operations (Oco). | David C Stewart.................. | XS | SL | .............. | .............. | |
| | **DEPARTMENT OF STATE OFFICE OF THE INSPECTOR GENERAL** | | | | | | |
| Do .................. | Inspector General ............................... | Vacant ............................... | PAS | EX | III | .............. | |
| Do .................. | Deputy Inspector General ..................... | ......do ............................... | .............. | ES | .............. | .............. | |

## DEPARTMENT OF THE INTERIOR

| Location | Position Title | Name of Incumbent | Type of Appt. | Pay Plan | Level, Grade, or Pay | Tenure | Expires |
|---|---|---|---|---|---|---|---|
| Washington, DC ...... | Secretary ............................................. | David L Bernhardt............. | PAS | EX | I | .............. | |
| | **SECRETARYS IMMEDIATE OFFICE** | | | | | | |
| Do .................. | Chief of Staff ...................................... | Todd D Willens ................. | NA | ES | .............. | .............. | |
| Do .................. | Deputy Chief of Staff........................... | Jeffrey Dwayne Small.......... | NA | ES | .............. | .............. | |
| Do .................. | Counselor to the Secretary.................... | Vacant ............................... | .............. | ES | .............. | .............. | |
| Do .................. | ......do ............................................... | Gary Michael Lawkowski .... | NA | ES | .............. | .............. | |
| Do .................. | Senior Counselor to the Secretary........ | Vacant ............................... | .............. | ES | .............. | .............. | |
| Do .................. | ......do ............................................... | Gregg Dale Renkes.............. | NA | ES | .............. | .............. | |
| Do .................. | Counselor for Energy Policy................... | Vacant ............................... | .............. | ES | .............. | .............. | |
| Do .................. | Senior Advisor to the Secretary............ | Rick May .......................... | NA | ES | .............. | .............. | |
| Do .................. | ......do ............................................... | Vacant ............................... | .............. | ES | .............. | .............. | |
| Do .................. | Senior Advisor .................................... | Carol L Danko ................... | NA | ES | .............. | .............. | |
| Do .................. | Senior Advisor to the Secretary............ | John Bockmier.................... | NA | ES | .............. | .............. | |
| San Diego, CA ........ | ......do ............................................... | Vacant ............................... | .............. | ES | .............. | .............. | |
| Denver, CO ............. | Senior Advisor for Water and Western Issues ... | Alan Wayne Mikkelsen ....... | NA | ES | .............. | .............. | |
| Missoula, MT........... | ......do ............................................... | Vacant ............................... | .............. | ES | .............. | .............. | |
| Washington, DC ...... | Senior Advisor to the Secretary............ | Lori K Mashburn................. | NA | ES | .............. | .............. | |
| Anchorage, AK........ | Senior Advisor for Alaskan Affairs........ | Stephen M Wackowski ........ | SC | GS | 15 | .............. | |
| Washington, DC ...... | Advisor to the Secretary....................... | Natalie D Davis.................. | SC | GS | 14 | .............. | |
| Do .................. | Deputy White House Liaison.................. | Elinor Werner .................... | SC | GS | 12 | .............. | |
| Do .................. | Advisor to the Secretary....................... | Matthew Dermody............... | SC | GS | 12 | .............. | |
| Do .................. | Special Assistant to the Secretary......... | Hannah Cooke .................... | SC | GS | 11 | .............. | |
| Do .................. | Special Assistant................................. | Lacey Smethers .................. | SC | GS | 9 | .............. | |
| Do .................. | Assistant............................................. | Ileana Beatriz Kennedy....... | SC | GS | 7 | .............. | |
| Do .................. | Special Assistant................................. | Skyler Thomas Zunk........... | SC | GS | 7 | .............. | |
| Do .................. | Chief Information Officer...................... | Career Incumbent .............. | CA | ES | .............. | .............. | |
| Do .................. | Director of Executive Secretariat and Office of Regulatory Affairs. | ......do ............................... | CA | ES | .............. | .............. | |
| Do .................. | Communications Director ...................... | Nicholas Robbins Goodwin .. | NA | ES | .............. | .............. | |
| Do .................. | Press Secretary ................................... | Benjamin Hughes Goldey .... | SC | GS | 14 | .............. | |
| Do .................. | Deputy Press Secretary ........................ | Melissa Lafferty Brown ....... | SC | GS | 12 | .............. | |
| Do .................. | ......do ............................................... | Conner David Swanson........ | SC | GS | 11 | .............. | |
| Do .................. | Writer ................................................ | Maximos Nicholas Nikitas... | SC | GS | 9 | .............. | |
| Do .................. | Director, Office of Intergovernmental and External Affairs. | Vacant ............................... | .............. | ES | .............. | .............. | |
| Do .................. | Principal Deputy Director Intergovernmental and External Affairs. | Timothy G Williams Jr......... | SC | GS | 15 | .............. | |
| Do .................. | Deputy Director, Office of Intergovernmental and External Affairs. | Marshall T Critchfield ........ | SC | GS | 15 | .............. | |
| Do .................. | Special Assistant................................. | Sarah Elizabeth Spaulding.. | SC | GS | 11 | .............. | |
| Do .................. | Director, Office of Scheduling and Advance and Operations. | Vacant ............................... | .............. | ES | .............. | .............. | |
| Do .................. | Director of Scheduling and Advance ................. | Samantha Hebert................. | SC | GS | 15 | .............. | |
| Do .................. | Deputy Director, Office of Scheduling and Advance. | Leila Getto ........................ | SC | GS | 14 | .............. | |
| Do .................. | Deputy Director, Office of Advance...................... | Andrew Patterson................ | SC | GS | 14 | .............. | |
| Do .................. | Special Assistant (Scheduling and Advance) ..... | Caroline H Boulton ............. | SC | GS | 11 | .............. | |
| Do .................. | Advance Representative........................ | Isaac Hunter William Piller. | SC | GS | 11 | .............. | |
| | **OFFICE OF THE DEPUTY SECRETARY** | | | | | | |
| Do .................. | Deputy Secretary of the Interior ........................ | Katharine M.F. MacGregor.. | PAS | EX | II | .............. | |
| Do .................. | Associate Deputy Secretary ................. | James E Cason ................... | NA | ES | .............. | .............. | |
| Do .................. | ......do ............................................... | Vacant ............................... | .............. | ES | .............. | .............. | |
| Do .................. | Assistant Deputy Secretary ................. | ......do ............................... | .............. | ES | .............. | .............. | |
| Do .................. | Senior Science Advisor ........................ | Career Incumbent .............. | CA | ES | .............. | .............. | |
| Do .................. | Director, Office of Small and Disadvantaged Business Utilization. | Vacant ............................... | .............. | ES | .............. | .............. | |

## DEPARTMENT OF THE INTERIOR—Continued

| Location | Position Title | Name of Incumbent | Type of Appt. | Pay Plan | Level, Grade, or Pay | Tenure | Expires |
|---|---|---|---|---|---|---|---|
| | **OFFICE OF CONGRESSIONAL AND LEGISLATIVE AFFAIRS** | | | | | | |
| Washington, DC ...... | Director, Office of Congressional and Legislative Affairs. | Cole Jonathan Rojewski....... | NA | ES | .............. | .............. | |
| Do .................... | Senior Counselor to the Office of Congressional and Legislative Affairs. | Vacant ...................... | ............ | ES | .............. | .............. | |
| Do .................... | Legislative Counsel...................... | Career Incumbent ............... | CA | ES | .............. | .............. | |
| Do .................... | Deputy Director, Office of Congressional and Legislative Affairs. | Faith Cchristine Vander Voort. | SC | GS | 15 | .............. | |
| Do .................... | Senior Advisor.......................... | Taylor Playforth .................. | SC | GS | 14 | .............. | |
| Do .................... | Advisor.................................. | Aaron Joseph Thiele............ | SC | GS | 12 | .............. | |
| Do .................... | ......do | Amanda Loy Hall ............... | SC | GS | 11 | .............. | |
| | **OFFICE OF SPECIAL TRUSTEE FOR AMERICAN INDIANS** | | | | | | |
| Do .................... | Special Trustee for American Indians ............... | Vacant ...................... | PAS | EX | II | .............. | |
| Do .................... | Principal Deputy Special Trustee.................... | Career Incumbent ............... | CA | ES | .............. | .............. | |
| Albuquerque, NM.... | Deputy Special Trustee - Program Management. | Vacant ...................... | ............ | ES | .............. | .............. | |
| Do .................... | Deputy Special Trustee - Trust Services........... | ......do | ............ | ES | .............. | .............. | |
| Do .................... | Deputy Special Trustee - Field Operations....... | Career Incumbent ............... | CA | ES | .............. | .............. | |
| Do .................... | Regional Fiduciary Trust Administrator........... | ......do | CA | ES | .............. | .............. | |
| Do .................... | ......do | ......do | CA | ES | .............. | .............. | |
| Do .................... | ......do | ......do | CA | ES | .............. | .............. | |
| Arlee, MT............. | ......do | ......do | CA | ES | .............. | .............. | |
| Albuquerque, NM.... | Senior Advisor.......................... | ......do | CA | ES | .............. | .............. | |
| Do .................... | ......do | ......do | CA | ES | .............. | .............. | |
| | **NATIONAL INDIAN GAMING COMMISSION** | | | | | | |
| Washington, DC ...... | Chairman, National Indian Gaming Commission. | Edward Sequoyah Simermeyer. | PAS | EX | IV | .............. | |
| Do .................... | Associate Member, National Indian Gaming Commission. | Kathryn C Isom-Clause ....... | XS | AD | .............. | .............. | |
| Do .................... | ......do | Vacant ...................... | XS | AD | .............. | .............. | |
| | **OFFICE OF THE SOLICITOR** | | | | | | |
| Do .................... | Solicitor.................................. | Daniel Jorjani .................... | PAS | EX | IV | .............. | |
| Do .................... | Counselor to the Solicitor............... | Kevin O'Scannlain............... | NA | ES | .............. | .............. | |
| Do .................... | Principal Deputy Solicitor............... | Gregory P Zerzan ............... | NA | ES | .............. | .............. | |
| Lakewood, CO ........ | Counselor to the Principal Deputy Solicitor ...... | Career Incumbent ............... | CA | ES | .............. | .............. | |
| Washington, DC ...... | Deputy Solicitor for Land Resources ................. | Vacant ...................... | ............ | ES | .............. | .............. | |
| Do .................... | Deputy Solicitor for Water Resources.............. | Brandon Middleton ............ | NA | ES | .............. | .............. | |
| Do .................... | Deputy Solicitor for Indian Affairs ................. | Kyle Scherer .................... | NA | ES | .............. | .............. | |
| Do .................... | Deputy Solicitor for Parks and Wildlife ............ | Karen Jean Budd-Falen ....... | NA | ES | .............. | .............. | |
| Do .................... | Deputy Solicitor for Energy and Mineral Resources. | Vacant ...................... | ............ | ES | .............. | .............. | |
| Do .................... | Deputy Solicitor - General Law ...................... | Hubbel Relat...................... | NA | ES | .............. | .............. | |
| Do .................... | Associate Solicitor - Indian Affairs ................. | Career Incumbent ............... | CA | ES | .............. | .............. | |
| Do .................... | Associate Solicitor - Land Resources................ | ......do | CA | ES | .............. | .............. | |
| Do .................... | Associate Solicitor - Parks and Wildlife ........... | ......do | CA | ES | .............. | .............. | |
| Do .................... | Associate Solicitor - Mineral Resources ............ | ......do | CA | ES | .............. | .............. | |
| Do .................... | Associate Solicitor - Water Resources................ | ......do | CA | ES | .............. | .............. | |
| Do .................... | Associate Solicitor - General Law.................... | ......do | CA | ES | .............. | .............. | |
| Do .................... | Deputy Associate Solicitor for General Law ..... | ......do | CA | ES | .............. | .............. | |
| Do .................... | Senior Counselor for Environmental Policy...... | ......do | CA | ES | .............. | .............. | |
| Do .................... | Counselor.............................. | Marc Marie .......................... | SC | GS | 15 | .............. | |
| Do .................... | Senior Ethics Advisor .................... | Heather Gottry .................. | XS | SL | .............. | .............. | |
| Do .................... | ......do | Edward McDonnell............ | XS | SL | .............. | .............. | |
| | *Field Offices - SOL* | | | | | | |
| Bloomington, MN .... | Regional Solicitor, Interior Unified Regions 1 & 3. | Career Incumbent ............... | CA | ES | .............. | .............. | |
| Atlanta, GA ........... | Regional Solicitor, Interior Unified Regions 2 & 4. | ......do | CA | ES | .............. | .............. | |
| Portland, OR........... | Regional Solicitor, Interior Unified Regions 5 & 9. | ......do | CA | ES | .............. | .............. | |
| Lakewood, CO ........ | Regional Solicitor, Interior Unified Regions 6 & 7. | Vacant ...................... | ............ | ES | .............. | .............. | |
| Sacramento, CA....... | Regional Solicitor, Interior Unified Regions 8 & 10. | Career Incumbent ............... | CA | ES | .............. | .............. | |
| Anchorage, AK........ | Regional Solicitor, Interior Unified Region 11 ... | Vacant ...................... | ............ | ES | .............. | .............. | |
| Albuquerque, NM.... | Regional Solicitor, Southwest Region ................. | Career Incumbent ............... | CA | ES | .............. | .............. | |
| Salt Lake City, UT .. | Regional Solicitor, Intermountain Region .......... | ......do | CA | ES | .............. | .............. | |

# DEPARTMENT OF THE INTERIOR—Continued

| Location | Position Title | Name of Incumbent | Type of Appt. | Pay Plan | Level, Grade, or Pay | Tenure | Expires |
|---|---|---|---|---|---|---|---|
| | **ASSISTANT SECRETARY - POLICY, MANAGEMENT AND BUDGET** | | | | | | |
| Washington, DC ...... | Assistant Secretary - Policy Management and Budget. | Vacant ...................... | PAS | EX | IV | .............. | |
| Do .................. | Principal Deputy Assistant Secretary ............... | Scott J Cameron .................. | NA | ES | .............. | .............. | |
| Do .................. | Chief of Staff to the Assistant Secretary - Policy, Management and Budget. | Career Incumbent ............... | CA | ES | .............. | .............. | |
| Do .................. | Deputy Assistant Secretary for Policy............... | Michael Thomas Freeman ... | NA | ES | .............. | .............. | |
| Do .................. | Deputy Assistant Secretary - Administrative Services. | Career Incumbent ............... | CA | ES | .............. | .............. | |
| Do .................. | Director, Gulf of Mexico Restoration .................. | ......do ...................... | CA | ES | .............. | .............. | |
| Do .................. | Director, Office of Environmental Policy and Compliance. | Vacant ...................... | | ES | .............. | .............. | |
| Do .................. | Deputy Director, Office of Environmental Policy and Compliance. | Career Incumbent ............... | CA | ES | .............. | .............. | |
| Do .................. | Director, Office of Restoration and Damage Assessment. | ......do ...................... | CA | ES | .............. | .............. | |
| Do .................. | Director, Office of Policy Analysis ............... | ......do ...................... | CA | ES | .............. | .............. | |
| Do .................. | Senior Advisor ...................... | ......do ...................... | CA | ES | .............. | .............. | |
| Do .................. | Director, Office of Budget ...................... | ......do ...................... | CA | ES | .............. | .............. | |
| Do .................. | Deputy Director, Office of Budget ............... | ......do ...................... | CA | ES | .............. | .............. | |
| Do .................. | Director, Office of Acquisition and Property Management. | ......do ...................... | CA | ES | .............. | .............. | |
| Do .................. | Associate Director for Acquisition and Financial Assistance. | ......do ...................... | CA | ES | .............. | .............. | |
| Do .................. | Associate Director - Asset Management............ | Vacant ...................... | | ES | .............. | .............. | |
| Do .................. | Director, Office of Planning and Performance Management. | Career Incumbent ............... | CA | ES | .............. | .............. | |
| Lakewood, CO ........ | Director, Business Integration Office ............... | ......do ...................... | CA | ES | .............. | .............. | |
| Washington, DC ...... | Deputy Director, Business Integration Office .... | Vacant ...................... | | ES | .............. | .............. | |
| Do .................. | Chief Learning Officer/Director, Office of Strategic Employee and Organizational Development. | Career Incumbent ............... | CA | ES | .............. | .............. | |
| Do .................. | Director, Office of Wildland Fire ...................... | ......do ...................... | CA | ES | .............. | .............. | |
| Boise, ID ............... | Director, Office of Aviation Services .................. | ......do ...................... | CA | ES | .............. | .............. | |
| Washington, DC ...... | Deputy Chief Information Officer...................... | ......do ...................... | CA | ES | .............. | .............. | |
| Lakewood, CO ........ | Deputy Chief Information Officer - Bureau/Office Support. | ......do ...................... | CA | ES | .............. | .............. | |
| Washington, DC ...... | Deputy Chief Information Officer - Enterprise Services. | ......do ...................... | CA | ES | .............. | .............. | |
| Do .................. | Deputy Chief Information Officer - Program Management. | ......do ...................... | CA | ES | .............. | .............. | |
| Do .................. | Deputy Chief Information Officer - Resource Management. | ......do ...................... | CA | ES | .............. | .............. | |
| Do .................. | Chief Information Security Officer...................... | ......do ...................... | CA | ES | .............. | .............. | |
| Lakewood, CO ........ | Director, Office of Appraisal and Valuation Services. | ......do ...................... | CA | ES | .............. | .............. | |
| Washington, DC ...... | Director, Office of Facilities and Administrative Services. | ......do ...................... | CA | ES | .............. | .............. | |
| Do .................. | Senior Advisor...................... | Steven Howke...................... | SC | GS | 15 | .............. | |
| Do .................. | Special Assistant...................... | Eva Amelia Vrana Cline ...... | SC | GS | 11 | .............. | |
| | *Interior Business Center* | | | | | | |
| Do .................. | Director, Interior Business Center...................... | Vacant ...................... | | ES | .............. | .............. | |
| Do .................. | Deputy Director, Interior Business Center ........ | Career Incumbent ............... | CA | ES | .............. | .............. | |
| Lakewood, CO ........ | Associate Director, Human Resources Directorate. | ......do ...................... | CA | ES | .............. | .............. | |
| Herndon, VA ............ | Associate Director, Acquisition Services Directorate. | ......do ...................... | CA | ES | .............. | .............. | |
| Do .................. | Associate Director, Financial Management Directorate. | ......do ...................... | CA | ES | .............. | .............. | |
| Washington, DC ...... | Associate Director, Enterprise Management ..... | ......do ...................... | CA | ES | .............. | .............. | |
| | *Office of Natural Resources Revenue Management* | | | | | | |
| Lakewood, CO ......... | Director, Office of Natural Resources Revenue Management. | ......do ...................... | CA | ES | .............. | .............. | |
| | **ASSISTANT SECRETARY - INSULAR AREAS** | | | | | | |
| Washington, DC ...... | Assistant Secretary - Insular Areas .................. | Douglas Domenech............ | PAS | EX | IV | .............. | |
| Do .................. | Deputy Assistant Secretary- Insular and International Affairs. | Sarah Jorgenson .................. | NA | ES | .............. | .............. | |
| Do .................. | Director, Office of Insular Affairs...................... | Career Incumbent ............... | CA | ES | .............. | .............. | |

## DEPARTMENT OF THE INTERIOR—Continued

| Location | Position Title | Name of Incumbent | Type of Appt. | Pay Plan | Level, Grade, or Pay | Tenure | Expires |
|---|---|---|---|---|---|---|---|
| | **ASSISTANT SECRETARY - FISH AND WILDLIFE AND PARKS** | | | | | | |
| Washington, DC ...... | Assistant Secretary - Fish and Wildlife and Parks. | George R Wallace.................. | PAS | EX | IV | .............. | |
| Do .................... | Principal Deputy Assistant Secretary for Fish and Wildlife and Parks. | John Richard Tanner............. | NA | ES | .............. | .............. | |
| Do .................... | Deputy Assistant Secretary - Fish and Wildlife and Parks. | Ryan Hambleton.................. | NA | ES | .............. | .............. | |
| Do .................... | ......do | Vacant ........................... | ............ | ES | .............. | .............. | |
| Do .................... | ......do | ......do ........................... | ............ | ES | .............. | .............. | |
| Miami, FL.............. | Director Everglades Restoration Initiatives/Executive Director South Florida Ecosystem Restoration Task Force. | Career Incumbent ............. | CA | ES | .............. | .............. | |
| Washington, DC ...... | Counselor to the Assistant Secretary-Fish and Wildlife and Parks. | Katie Mills ........................... | SC | GS | 14 | .............. | |
| | *United States Fish and Wildlife Service* | | | | | | |
| Do .................... | Director, United States Fish and Wildlife Service. | Aurelia Nmn Skipwith......... | PAS | EX | V | .............. | |
| Do .................... | Principal Deputy Director, Us Fish and Wildlife Service. | Margaret Emma Everson .... | NA | ES | .............. | .............. | |
| Do .................... | Deputy Director - Operations............................. | Career Incumbent ............. | CA | ES | .............. | .............. | |
| Do .................... | Deputy Director - Program Management and Policy. | ......do | CA | ES | .............. | .............. | |
| Do .................... | Assistant Director - Fisheries and Aquatic Conservation. | ......do | CA | ES | .............. | .............. | |
| Do .................... | Assistant Director - International Affairs.......... | ......do | CA | ES | .............. | .............. | |
| Do .................... | Assistant Director - External Affairs ............ | ......do | CA | ES | .............. | .............. | |
| Baileys Crossroads, VA. | Assistant Director - Migratory Bird Programs.. | ......do | CA | ES | .............. | .............. | |
| Washington, DC ...... | Assistant Director - Ecological Services............. | ......do | CA | ES | .............. | .............. | |
| Do .................... | Assistant Director - Wildlife and Sportfish Restoration Programs. | ......do | CA | ES | .............. | .............. | |
| Falls Church, VA ..... | Assistant Director - Science Application............ | ......do | CA | ES | .............. | .............. | |
| Washington, DC ...... | Assistant Director - Management and Administration. | ......do | CA | ES | .............. | .............. | |
| Shepherdstown, WV. | Director, National Conservation Training Center. | ......do | CA | ES | .............. | .............. | |
| Washington, DC ...... | Chief, National Wildlife Refuge System ............. | ......do | CA | ES | .............. | .............. | |
| Do .................... | Senior Advisor - Energy Policy ............................ | ......do | CA | ES | .............. | .............. | |
| Baileys Crossroads, VA. | Associate Chief Information Officer .................. | ......do | CA | ES | .............. | .............. | |
| Denver, CO ............. | Advisor.................................................... | Zachariah James Gambill.... | SC | GS | 12 | .............. | |
| | *Field Offices - Fws* | | | | | | |
| Hadley, MA ............ | Regional Director - Interior Unified Region 1 ... | Career Incumbent ............. | CA | ES | .............. | .............. | |
| Atlanta, GA ............ | Regional Director - Interior Unified Regions 2 & 4. | ......do | CA | ES | .............. | .............. | |
| Minneapolis, MN ..... | Regional Director - Interior Unified Region 3 ... | ......do | CA | ES | .............. | .............. | |
| Lakewood, CO ......... | Regional Director - Interior Unified Region 5 ... | ......do | CA | ES | .............. | .............. | |
| Albuquerque, NM.... | Regional Director - Interior Unified Regions 6 & 8. | ......do | CA | ES | .............. | .............. | |
| Portland, OR........... | Regional Director - Interior Unified Regions 9 & 12. | ......do | CA | ES | .............. | .............. | |
| Sacramento, CA...... | Regional Director - Interior Unified Region 10 . | ......do | CA | ES | .............. | .............. | |
| Anchorage, AK........ | Regional Director - Interior Unified Region 11 . | ......do | CA | ES | .............. | .............. | |
| | *National Park Service* | | | | | | |
| Washington, DC ...... | Director, National Park Service .......................... | Vacant ........................... | PAS | EX | V | .............. | |
| Do .................... | Deputy Director, Operations ............................. | Career Incumbent ............. | CA | ES | .............. | .............. | |
| Do .................... | Deputy Director for Congressional and External Relations. | Vacant ........................... | ............ | ES | .............. | .............. | |
| Do .................... | Associate Director, Parks Planning, Facilities and Lands. | Career Incumbent ............. | CA | ES | .............. | .............. | |
| Do .................... | Associate Director, Workforce Management....... | Vacant ........................... | ............ | ES | .............. | .............. | |
| Do .................... | Associate Director, Visitor Resource and Protection. | Career Incumbent ............. | CA | ES | .............. | .............. | |
| Do .................... | Associate Director, Business Services ............... | Vacant ........................... | ............ | ES | .............. | .............. | |
| Do .................... | Associate Director, Cultural Resources ............ | ......do | ............ | ES | .............. | .............. | |
| Do .................... | Associate Director, Natural Resource Stewardship and Science. | Career Incumbent ............. | CA | ES | .............. | .............. | |
| Do .................... | Associate Chief Information Officer .................. | ......do | CA | ES | .............. | .............. | |
| Do .................... | Assistant Director for Congressional Relations. | Charles Laudner.................. | SC | GS | 15 | .............. | |
| Do .................... | Special Assistant.................................... | Nicholas Erick Davis............ | SC | GS | 9 | .............. | |

# DEPARTMENT OF THE INTERIOR—Continued

| Location | Position Title | Name of Incumbent | Type of Appt. | Pay Plan | Level, Grade, or Pay | Tenure | Expires |
|---|---|---|---|---|---|---|---|
| | *Field Offices - NPS* | | | | | | |
| Lakewood, CO ......... | Director, Denver Service Center ................. | Career Incumbent ................ | CA | ES | ............... | ................ | |
| Washington, DC ...... | National Capital Area Director.......................... | Vacant ............................ | ............. | ES | ............... | ................ | |
| Philadelphia, PA..... | Regional Director, Interior Unified Region 1 .... | Career Incumbent ................ | CA | ES | ............... | ................ | |
| Atlanta, GA ............ | Regional Director, Interior Unified Region 2 ..... | ......do ........ | CA | ES | ............... | ................ | |
| Omaha, NE.............. | Regional Director, Interior Unified Regions 3, 4 & 5. | ......do ........ | CA | ES | ............... | ................ | |
| Oakland, CA ............ | Regional Director, Interior Unified Regions 9, 10 & 12. | Vacant ............................ | ............. | ES | ............... | ................ | |
| Lakewood, CO ......... | Regional Director, Interior Unified Regions 6, 7 & 8. | Career Incumbent ................ | CA | ES | ............... | ................ | |
| Anchorage, AK........ | Regional Director, Interior Unified Region 11 ... | Vacant ............................ | ............. | ES | ............... | ................ | |
| Yosemite Natl Park, CA. | Park Manager, Yosemite National Park ............ | ......do ........ | ............. | ES | ............... | ................ | |
| Gatlinburg, TN ........ | Park Manager, Great Smoky Mountains National Park. | Career Incumbent ................ | CA | ES | ............... | ................ | |
| San Francisco, CA ... | Park Manager, Golden Gate National Recreation Area. | ......do ........ | CA | ES | ............... | ................ | |
| Boulder City, NV ..... | Park Manager, Lake Mead National Recreation Area. | ......do ........ | CA | ES | ............... | ................ | |
| Miami, FL.............. | Park Manager, Everglades National Park ........ | ......do ........ | CA | ES | ............... | ................ | |
| Washington, DC ...... | Park Manager, National Mall and Memorial Parks. | ......do ........ | CA | ES | ............... | ................ | |
| Moose, WY .............. | Park Manager, Grand Teton National Park ...... | Vacant ............................ | ............. | ES | ............... | ................ | |
| New York New York, NY. | Executive Director, National Parks of New York Harbor. | ......do ........ | ............. | ES | ............... | ................ | |
| | **ASSISTANT SECRETARY - WATER AND SCIENCE** | | | | | | |
| Washington, DC ...... | Assistant Secretary - Water and Science .......... | Tim R Petty.......................... | PAS | EX | IV | ................ | |
| Do ..................... | Principal Deputy Assistant Secretary- Water and Science. | Kiel Paul Weaver ................. | NA | ES | ............... | ................ | |
| Do ..................... | Principal Deputy Assistant Secretary - Water and Science. | Vacant ............................ | ............. | ES | ............... | ................ | |
| Do ..................... | Deputy Assistant Secretary- Water and Science. | Aubrey Bettencourt.............. | NA | ES | ............... | ................ | |
| Do ..................... | Deputy Assistant Secretary - Water and Science. | Vacant ............................ | ............. | ES | ............... | ................ | |
| Do ..................... | Senior Advisor to the Assistant Secretary for Water and Science. | Ryan C Nichols .................... | SC | GS | 14 | ................ | |
| | *Bureau of Reclamation* | | | | | | |
| Do ..................... | Commissioner Bureau of Reclamation .............. | Brenda W Burman .............. | PAS | EX | V | ................ | |
| Do ..................... | Deputy Commissioner ................................. | Shelby Lynne Hagenauer .... | NA | ES | ............... | ................ | |
| Do ..................... | Deputy Commissioner - Operations .................. | Career Incumbent ................ | CA | ES | ............... | ................ | |
| Do ..................... | Director, Program and Budget ........................ | ......do ........ | CA | ES | ............... | ................ | |
| Do ..................... | Deputy Commissioner, Program, Administration and Budget. | ......do ........ | CA | ES | ............... | ................ | |
| Lakewood, CO ......... | Director, Policy and Programs......................... | ......do ........ | CA | ES | ............... | ................ | |
| Do ..................... | Director, Technical Service Center.................... | Vacant ............................ | ............. | ES | ............... | ................ | |
| Do ..................... | Associate Chief Infomation Officer.................... | Career Incumbent ................ | CA | ES | ............... | ................ | |
| Do ..................... | Senior Advisor ........................................ | ......do ........ | CA | ES | ............... | ................ | |
| Do ..................... | Chief Engineer ........................................ | ......do ........ | CA | ES | ............... | ................ | |
| Washington, DC ...... | Advisor........................................... | James William Young.......... | SC | GS | 11 | ................ | |
| Lakewood, CO ......... | ......do ........ | Alexander Sterhan .............. | SC | GS | 11 | ................ | |
| | *Field Offices - BOR* | | | | | | |
| Boulder City, NV ..... | Regional Director, Interior Unified Region 8 .... | Career Incumbent ................ | CA | ES | ............... | ................ | |
| Sacramento, CA....... | ......do ........ | ......do ........ | CA | ES | ............... | ................ | |
| Salt Lake City, UT .. | Regional Director, Upper Colorado Basin Region. | Vacant ............................ | ............. | ES | ............... | ................ | |
| Billings, MT ............ | Regional Director, Interior Unified Region 5 & 6. | Career Incumbent ................ | CA | ES | ............... | ................ | |
| Boise, ID .................. | Regional Director, Interior Unified Region 9 .... | ......do ........ | CA | ES | ............... | ................ | |
| | *United States Geological Survey* | | | | | | |
| Reston, VA .............. | Director, U.S. Geological Survey ........................ | James Reilly ........................ | PAS | EX | V | ................ | |
| Washington, DC ...... | Senior Advisor to the Director ........................... | Robert Earl Gordon Jr.......... | NA | ES | ............... | ................ | |
| | **ASSISTANT SECRETARY - LAND AND MINERALS MANAGEMENT** | | | | | | |
| Do ..................... | Assistant Secretary-Land and Minerals Management. | Vacant ............................ | PAS | EX | IV | ................ | |
| Do ..................... | Principal Deputy Assistant Secretary - Land and Minerals Management. | Casey B Hammond.............. | NA | ES | ............... | ................ | |

## DEPARTMENT OF THE INTERIOR—Continued

| Location | Position Title | Name of Incumbent | Type of Appt. | Pay Plan | Level, Grade, or Pay | Tenure | Expires |
|---|---|---|---|---|---|---|---|
| Washington, DC | Deputy Assistant Secretary - Land and Minerals Management. | Vacant | | ES | | | |
| Do | .....do | .....do | | ES | | | |
| Do | Counselor to the Assistant Secretary Land and Minerals Management. | Matthew J Flynn | GG | GG | 15 | | |
| Do | Advisor | Thomas P Baptiste | SC | GS | 13 | | |
| Do | .....do | William Thomas Dove | SC | GS | 13 | | |
| | *Bureau of Land Management* | | | | | | |
| Do | Director Bureau of Land Management | Vacant | PAS | EX | V | | |
| Grand Junction, CO. | Deputy Director - Operations | Career Incumbent | CA | ES | | | |
| Washington, DC | Deputy Director, Programs and Policy | William P Pendley | NA | ES | | | |
| Do | Senior Advisor | Kathleen M. F. Benedetto | NA | ES | | | |
| Grand Junction, CO. | Assistant Director, Resources and Planning | Vacant | | ES | | | |
| Do | Assistant Director, Energy, Minerals and Realty Management. | Career Incumbent | CA | ES | | | |
| Do | Assistant Director, Business and Fiscal Resources Management. | .....do | CA | ES | | | |
| Do | Assistant Director, Communications and Public Relations. | Vacant | | ES | | | |
| Boise, ID | Assistant Director, Fire and Aviation | Career Incumbent | CA | ES | | | |
| Grand Junction, CO. | Assistant Director, National Conservation Lands and Community Partnerships. | Vacant | | ES | | | |
| Washington, DC | Senior Advisor | Amanda E Kaster | SC | GS | 14 | | |
| Do | Special Assistant | William Henry King | SC | GS | 9 | | |
| | *Field Offices - BLM* | | | | | | |
| Falls Church, VA | State Director, Eastern States | Vacant | | ES | | | |
| Salt Lake City, UT | State Director, Utah | .....do | | ES | | | |
| Cheyenne, WY | State Director, Wyoming | .....do | | ES | | | |
| Billings, MT | State Director, Montana | Career Incumbent | CA | ES | | | |
| Sacramento, CA | State Director, California | .....do | CA | ES | | | |
| Anchorage, AK | State Director, Alaska | .....do | CA | ES | | | |
| Portland, OR | State Director, Oregon | .....do | CA | ES | | | |
| Phoenix, AZ | State Director, Arizona | .....do | CA | ES | | | |
| Santa Fe, NM | State Director, New Mexico | .....do | CA | ES | | | |
| Boise, ID | State Director, Idaho | .....do | CA | ES | | | |
| Reno, NV | State Director, Nevada | .....do | CA | ES | | | |
| Denver, CO | State Director, Colorado | .....do | CA | ES | | | |
| | *Office of Surface Mining* | | | | | | |
| Washington, DC | Director Office of Surface Mining Reclamation and Enforcement. | Vacant | PAS | EX | V | | |
| Do | Principal Deputy Director, Osmre | Lanny Erdos | NA | ES | | | |
| Do | Deputy Director | Career Incumbent | CA | ES | | | |
| Do | Assistant Director, Program Support | .....do | CA | ES | | | |
| Do | Assistant Director, Finance and Administration. | .....do | CA | ES | | | |
| Do | Senior Advisor | Christian Robert Palich | SC | GS | 15 | | |
| | *Field Offices - OSM* | | | | | | |
| Denver, CO | Regional Director, Interior Unified Region 7 | Career Incumbent | CA | ES | | | |
| | *Bureau of Safety and Environmental Enforcement* | | | | | | |
| Washington, DC | Director, Bureau of Safety and Environmental Enforcement. | Scott Anthony Angelle | NA | ES | | | |
| Do | Deputy Director | Vacant | | ES | | | |
| Sterling, VA | Associate Director for Administration | Career Incumbent | CA | ES | | | |
| Washington, DC | Regulatory Programs Chief | Vacant | | ES | | | |
| Do | Senior Advisor to the Director - Bureau of Environmental Enforcement. | Preston Richard Beard | SC | GS | 14 | | |
| | *Field Offices - BSEE* | | | | | | |
| Jefferson, LA | Regional Director, Interior Unified Region 2 & 6. | Career Incumbent | CA | ES | | | |
| | *Bureau of Ocean Energy Management* | | | | | | |
| Washington, DC | Director, Bureau of Ocean Energy Management. | Vacant | | ES | | | |
| Do | Deputy Director | Career Incumbent | CA | ES | | | |
| Do | Chief Environmental Officer | .....do | CA | ES | | | |
| Do | Program Manager, Office of Budget and Program Coordination. | .....do | CA | ES | | | |

## DEPARTMENT OF THE INTERIOR—Continued

| Location | Position Title | Name of Incumbent | Type of Appt. | Pay Plan | Level, Grade, or Pay | Tenure | Expires |
|---|---|---|---|---|---|---|---|
| Washington, DC ...... | Senior Advisor to the Director -Bureau of Ocean Energy Management. | James R Schindler............... | SC | GS | 14 | .............. | |
| | *Field Offices - BOEM* | | | | | | |
| Jefferson, LA .......... | Regional Director, Interior Unified Regions 1, 2, 4 & 6. | Career Incumbent ................ | CA | ES | .............. | .............. | |
| Anchorage, AK......... | Regional Director, Interior Unified Region 11 ... | ......do ................... | CA | ES | .............. | .............. | |
| | **ASSISTANT SECRETARY - INDIAN AFFAIRS** | | | | | | |
| Washington, DC ...... | Assistant Secretary - Indian Affairs.................. | Tara Mac Lean Sweeney...... | PAS | EX | IV | .............. | |
| Do ................... | Principal Deputy Assistant Secretary - Indian Affairs. | John Tahsuda III.................. | NA | ES | | .............. | |
| Do ................... | Deputy Assistant Secretary - Policy and Economic Development. | Mark Antonio Cruz .............. | NA | ES | | .............. | |
| Do ................... | Chief of Staff to the Assistant Secretary - Indian Affairs. | Career Incumbent ................ | CA | ES | | .............. | |
| Do ................... | Deputy Assistant Secretary - Indian Affairs (Management). | ......do ................... | CA | ES | | .............. | |
| Reston, VA .............. | Chief Financial Officer ....................... | ......do ................... | CA | ES | | .............. | |
| Washington, DC ...... | Director, Office of Indian Gaming Management. | ......do ................... | CA | ES | | .............. | |
| Do ................... | Budget Officer............................. | ......do ................... | CA | ES | | .............. | |
| Reston, VA .............. | Director, Facilities, Property and Safety Management. | ......do ................... | CA | ES | | .............. | |
| Washington, DC ...... | Director, Indian Energy and Economic Development. | Vacant ........................ | | ES | | .............. | |
| Do ................... | Director, Office of Self-Governance.................... | Career Incumbent ................ | CA | ES | | .............. | |
| | *Bureau of Indian Affairs* | | | | | | |
| Do ................... | Director, Bureau of Indian Affairs .......... | ......do ................... | CA | ES | | .............. | |
| Albuquerque, NM.... | Deputy Director, Field Operations.................... | ......do ................... | CA | ES | | .............. | |
| Washington, DC ...... | Deputy Director, Indian Services ................ | ......do ................... | CA | ES | | .............. | |
| Do ................... | Deputy Director, Justice Services ................ | ......do ................... | CA | ES | | .............. | |
| Do ................... | Deputy Director, Trust Services................... | ......do ................... | CA | ES | | .............. | |
| | *Field Offices - BIA* | | | | | | |
| Muskogee, OK ......... | Regional Director - Eastern Oklahoma Region . | ......do ................... | CA | ES | | .............. | |
| Anadarko, OK......... | Regional Director - Southern Plains Region ...... | ......do ................... | CA | ES | | .............. | |
| Anchorage, AK......... | Regional Director - Alaska Region.................... | ......do ................... | CA | ES | | .............. | |
| Sacramento, CA...... | Regional Director - Pacific Region .............. | ......do ................... | CA | ES | | .............. | |
| Bloomington, MN .... | Regional Director - Midwest Region.................... | ......do ................... | CA | ES | | .............. | |
| Nashville, TN.......... | Regional Director - Eastern Region................... | Vacant ........................ | | ES | | .............. | |
| Aberdeen, SD......... | Regional Director - Great Plains Region........... | Career Incumbent ................ | CA | ES | | .............. | |
| Billings, MT............ | Regional Director - Rocky Mountain Region...... | ......do ................... | CA | ES | | .............. | |
| Gallup, NM .............. | Regional Director - Navajo Region .................... | ......do ................... | CA | ES | | .............. | |
| Albuquerque, NM.... | Regional Director - Southwest .................... | ......do ................... | CA | ES | | .............. | |
| Portland, OR............ | Regional Director - Northwest .................... | ......do ................... | CA | ES | | .............. | |
| Phoenix, AZ ............. | Regional Director - Western Region .................... | ......do ................... | CA | ES | | .............. | |
| | *Bureau of Indian Education* | | | | | | |
| Washington, DC ...... | Director - Bureau of Indian Education.............. | ......do ................... | CA | ES | | .............. | |
| Albuquerque, NM.... | Deputy Director - School Operations................... | ......do ................... | CA | ES | | .............. | |
| Bloomington, MN .... | Associate Deputy Director - Tribally Controlled Schools. | Vacant ........................ | | ES | | .............. | |
| Window Rock, AZ .... | Associate Deputy Director - Navajo................... | ......do ................... | | ES | | .............. | |
| Washington, DC ...... | Associate Deputy Director - Performance and Accountability. | ......do ................... | | ES | | .............. | |
| Albuquerque, NM.... | Associate Deputy Director - Bie Operated Schools. | Career Incumbent ................ | CA | ES | | .............. | |
| Do ................... | Chief Academic Officer................................. | ......do ................... | CA | ES | | .............. | |

## DEPARTMENT OF THE INTERIOR OFFICE OF THE INSPECTOR GENERAL

| Location | Position Title | Name of Incumbent | Type of Appt. | Pay Plan | Level, Grade, or Pay | Tenure | Expires |
|---|---|---|---|---|---|---|---|
| Washington, DC ...... | **OFFICE OF THE INSPECTOR GENERAL** <br> Inspector General ................................................ | Mark Lee Greenblatt ........... | PAS | EX | III | .............. | |

# DEPARTMENT OF THE TREASURY

| Location | Position Title | Name of Incumbent | Type of Appt. | Pay Plan | Level, Grade, or Pay | Tenure | Expires |
|---|---|---|---|---|---|---|---|
| | **SECRETARY OF THE TREASURY** | | | | | | |
| Washington, DC ...... | Secretary .......................................................... | Steven Terner Mnuchin ....... | PAS | EX | I | .............. | |
| Do .................... | Deputy Secretary of the Treasury ..................... | Justin George Muzinich ....... | PAS | EX | II | .............. | |
| Do .................... | Chief of Staff ................................................. | Vacant ............................. | | ES | | .............. | |
| Do .................... | Deputy Chief of Staff......................................... | John Baylor Myers .............. | SC | GS | 15 | .............. | |
| Do .................... | ......do ....................................................... | Zachary Lawrence Mcentee . | SC | GS | 14 | .............. | |
| Do .................... | Counselor to the Secretary................................ | Daniel Joseph Kowalski....... | NA | ES | | .............. | |
| Do .................... | ......do ....................................................... | Carter Hamilton Burwell..... | NA | ES | | .............. | |
| Do .................... | ......do ....................................................... | Adam Lerrick...................... | NA | ES | | .............. | |
| Do .................... | Executive Secretary ........................................ | Vacant ............................. | | ES | | .............. | |
| Do .................... | Deputy Executive Secretary.............................. | Alexandra Harrison Gaiser . | NA | ES | | .............. | |
| Do .................... | White House Liaison ...................................... | Alex Hinson ...................... | SC | GS | 14 | .............. | |
| Do .................... | Associate Director of Scheduling and Advance.. | Caleb Patrick Baca .............. | SC | GS | 9 | .............. | |
| Do .................... | Dir, Scheduling and Advance ............................ | William Joseph Mitchelson.. | SC | GS | 12 | .............. | |
| Do .................... | Advance Representative.................................... | Shane Robert Hofer.............. | SC | GS | 9 | .............. | |
| Do .................... | Senior Advisor to the Deputy Secretary and Counselor to the General Counsel. | Joseph Roger Clark .............. | NA | ES | | .............. | |
| Do .................... | Special Advisor............................................... | Robert Michael Baldwin ...... | SC | GS | 13 | .............. | |
| Do .................... | Special Assistant............................................. | Muhammad Usman Rahim . | SC | GS | 9 | .............. | |
| Do .................... | ......do ....................................................... | Jackson Brooks Miles.......... | SC | GS | 7 | .............. | |
| Do .................... | Special Assistant to the Executive Secretary .... | Ariana Michelle Woodson .... | SC | GS | 9 | .............. | |
| Do .................... | ......do ....................................................... | Elizabeth Anne Navin.......... | SC | GS | 7 | .............. | |
| Do .................... | ......do ....................................................... | Katya Natalia Welch ............ | SC | GS | 7 | .............. | |
| Do .................... | Special Inspector General for Pandemic Recovery. | Brian D Miller ...................... | PAS | EX | | 5 Years | |
| | **GENERAL COUNSEL** | | | | | | |
| Do .................... | General Counsel................................................ | Brian Callanan .................... | PAS | EX | IV | .............. | |
| Do .................... | Deputy General Counsel ................................... | Vacant ............................. | | ES | | .............. | |
| Do .................... | ......do ....................................................... | Brian Paul Morrissey Jr....... | NA | ES | | .............. | |
| Do .................... | ......do ....................................................... | James Yarbrough Stern ....... | NA | ES | | .............. | |
| Do .................... | Assistant General Counsel (General Law, Ethics and Regulations). | Career Incumbent ................ | CA | ES | | .............. | |
| Do .................... | Assistant General Counsel (International Affairs). | Vacant ............................. | | ES | | .............. | |
| Do .................... | Assistant General Counsel (Banking and Finance). | Career Incumbent ................ | CA | ES | | .............. | |
| Do .................... | Assistant General Counsel (Enforcement and Intelligence). | ......do ......... | CA | ES | | .............. | |
| Do .................... | Deputy Assistant General Counsel (General Law and Regulation). | ......do ......... | CA | ES | | .............. | |
| Do .................... | Deputy Assistant General Counsel (Ethics)...... | ......do ......... | CA | ES | | .............. | |
| Do .................... | Deputy Assistant General Counsel (International Affairs). | ......do ......... | CA | ES | | .............. | |
| Do .................... | Principal Dep Asst Gen Csl Banking and Finance. | ......do ......... | CA | ES | | .............. | |
| Do .................... | Deputy Assistant General Counsel (Banking and Finance). | ......do ......... | CA | ES | | .............. | |
| Do .................... | Deputy Assistant General Counsel (Enforcement and Intelligence). | Vacant ............................. | | ES | | .............. | |
| Do .................... | Deputy Assistant General Counsel for Oversight and Litigation. | Career Incumbent ................ | CA | ES | | .............. | |
| Do .................... | Tax Legislative Counsel .................................... | ......do ......... | CA | ES | | .............. | |
| Do .................... | International Tax Counsel ................................. | ......do ......... | CA | ES | | .............. | |
| Do .................... | Benefits Tax Counsel ....................................... | Vacant ............................. | | ES | | .............. | |
| Do .................... | Deputy International Tax Counsel ..................... | Career Incumbent ................ | CA | ES | | .............. | |
| Do .................... | Deputy Benefits Tax Counsel............................. | ......do ......... | CA | ES | | .............. | |
| Do .................... | Deputy Tax Legislative Counsel ........................ | ......do ......... | CA | ES | | .............. | |
| Do .................... | Chief Counsel, Office of Foreign Assets Control. | Vacant ............................. | | ES | | .............. | |
| Do .................... | Chief Counsel, (Alcohol and Tobacco, Tax and Trade Bureau). | Career Incumbent ................ | CA | ES | | .............. | |
| Do .................... | Chief Counsel, United States Mint.................... | Vacant ............................. | | ES | | .............. | |
| Do .................... | Chief Counsel, Bureau of Engraving and Printing. | ......do ......... | | ES | | .............. | |
| Do .................... | Chief Counsel, Bureau of the Fiscal Service..... | ......do ......... | | ES | | .............. | |
| Do .................... | Special Assistant to the General Counsel.......... | Arianne Claire Minks .......... | SC | GS | 9 | .............. | |
| | **UNDER SECRETARY FOR INTERNATIONAL AFFAIRS** | | | | | | |
| Do .................... | Under Secretary for International Affairs ........ | Brent J Mcintosh................ | PAS | EX | III | .............. | |
| Do .................... | Counselor to the Under Secretary for International Affairs. | Vacant ............................. | | ES | | .............. | |

## DEPARTMENT OF THE TREASURY—Continued

| Location | Position Title | Name of Incumbent | Type of Appt. | Pay Plan | Level, Grade, or Pay | Tenure | Expires |
|---|---|---|---|---|---|---|---|
| Washington, DC ...... | Counselor to the Under Secretary for International Affairs .................................... | Thomas Emanuel Dans........ | NA | ES | ............... | ............... | |
| Do .................... | Senior Advisor.................................... | Dan Patrick Debono ............. | NA | ES | ............... | ............... | |
| Do .................... | Director, Office of Development Results and Accountability. | Vacant ................................... | ............... | ES | ............... | ............... | |
| Do .................... | Director, Markets Room........................ | ......do .................................. | ............... | ES | ............... | ............... | |
| Do .................... | Senior Advisor.................................... | Daniel Scott Katz ............. | SC | GS | 15 | ............... | |
| Do .................... | Special Assistant to the U/S for International Affairs. | John Archer Poulson III....... | SC | GS | 9 | ............... | |
| Do .................... | Special Assistant................................ | Samantha Morgan Heyrich . | SC | GS | 7 | ............... | |
| | *Assistant Secretary Investment Security* | | | | | | |
| Do .................... | Assistant Secretary Investment Security ......... | Thomas P Feddo ..................... | PAS | EX | | ............... | |
| Do .................... | Deputy Assistant Secretary (Investment Security). | Jon Tyler McGaughey .......... | NA | ES | ............... | ............... | |
| Do .................... | Director, Investment Security Office ................. | Vacant ................................... | ............... | ES | ............... | ............... | |
| | *Assistant Secretary for International Finance* | | | | | | |
| Do .................... | Deputy Under Secretary/Designated Assistant Secretary for International Finance. | ......do .................................. | PAS | EX | IV | ............... | |
| Do .................... | Principal Deputy Assistant Secretary International Monetary Policy. | Career Incumbent ............. | CA | ES | | ............... | |
| Do .................... | Deputy Assistant Secretary (International Monetary and Financial Policy). | Vacant ................................... | ............... | ES | | ............... | |
| Do .................... | Deputy Assistant Secretary (South and East Asia). | Career Incumbent ................ | CA | ES | | ............... | |
| Do .................... | Deputy Assistant Secretary (Western Hemisphere & South Asia. | ......do .................................. | CA | ES | | ............... | |
| Do .................... | Deputy Assistant Secretary (Europe and Eurasia). | Vacant ................................... | ............... | ES | | ............... | |
| Do .................... | Deputy Assistant Secretary International Development Finance and Policy. | Career Incumbent ................ | CA | ES | | ............... | |
| Do .................... | Director Office of International Monetary Policy. | ......do .................................. | CA | ES | | ............... | |
| Do .................... | Director, Office of Europe and Eurasia ............. | Vacant ................................... | ............... | ES | | ............... | |
| | *Assistant Secretary for International Markets and Development* | | | | | | |
| Do .................... | Assistant Secretary for International Markets and Development. | Mitchell Allen Silk ............... | PAS | EX | IV | ............... | |
| Do .................... | Deputy Assistant Secretary, Africa and Middle East. | Career Incumbent ................ | CA | ES | | ............... | |
| Do .................... | Deputy Assistant Secretary (Trade Policy)........ | ......do .................................. | CA | ES | | ............... | |
| Do .................... | Deputy Assistant Secretary, International Financial Markets. | ......do .................................. | CA | ES | | ............... | |
| Do .................... | Deputy Assistant Secretary (Environment and Energy). | Vacant ................................... | ............... | ES | | ............... | |
| Do .................... | Deputy Assistant Secretary (Technical Assistance Policy). | Career Incumbent ................ | CA | ES | | ............... | |
| Do .................... | Director, Office of Investment, Energy and Infrastructure. | Vacant ................................... | ............... | ES | | ............... | |
| Do .................... | Director, Office of Trade Finance ........................ | Career Incumbent ................ | CA | ES | | ............... | |
| Do .................... | Director, International Financial Markets........ | Vacant ................................... | ............... | ES | | ............... | |
| Do .................... | Deputy Assistant Secretary, Investment, Energy and Infrastructure. | Devesh Bharat Ashra.......... | NA | ES | | ............... | |
| Do .................... | Director, Office of Technical Assistance............ | Career Incumbent ................ | CA | ES | | ............... | |
| | **UNDER SECRETARY FOR DOMESTIC FINANCE** | | | | | | |
| Do .................... | Under Secretary for Domestic Finance ............. | Vacant ................................... | PAS | EX | III | ............... | |
| Do .................... | Director, Office of Financial Research ............... | Dino Dominic Falaschetti .... | PAS | EX | III | 6 Years | |
| Do .................... | Member, Financial Stability Oversight Council. | Thomas Eldon Workman ........ | PAS | EX | III | 6 Years | |
| Do .................... | Deputy Assistant Secretary for Financial Institutions Policy. | Jonathan Shulman Greenstein. | NA | ES | | ............... | |
| Do .................... | Deputy Assistant Secretary, Financial Stability Oversight Council. | Howard Bruce Adler............. | NA | ES | | ............... | |
| Do .................... | Deputy Assistant Secretary, Capital Markets ... | Peter Michael Phelan.......... | NA | ES | | ............... | |
| Do .................... | Director of Analysis ............................. | Vacant ................................... | ............... | ES | | ............... | |
| Do .................... | Director of Policy.................................... | Career Incumbent ................ | CA | ES | | ............... | |
| Do .................... | Director Community Development Financial Institutions Fund. | ......do .................................. | CA | ES | | ............... | |
| Do .................... | Deputy Director for Policy and Programs .......... | ......do .................................. | CA | ES | | ............... | |
| Do .................... | Deputy Director for Finance and Operations .... | ......do .................................. | CA | ES | | ............... | |

## DEPARTMENT OF THE TREASURY—Continued

| Location | Position Title | Name of Incumbent | Type of Appt. | Pay Plan | Level, Grade, or Pay | Tenure | Expires |
|---|---|---|---|---|---|---|---|
| | *Fiscal Assistant Secretary* | | | | | | |
| Washington, DC ...... | Director, Office of Grants and Asset Management. | Career Incumbent ................ | CA | ES | .............. | .............. | |
| Do .................... | Director, Office of Fiscal Projections................... | ......do ...... | CA | ES | .............. | .............. | |
| | *Bureau of the Fiscal Service* | | | | | | |
| Do .................... | Executive Architect................ | ......do ...... | CA | ES | .............. | .............. | |
| Do .................... | Director, Office of Financial Innovation and Transformation. | ......do ...... | CA | ES | .............. | .............. | |
| | *Assistant Secretary for Financial Markets* | | | | | | |
| Do .................... | Assistant Secretary for Financial Markets ...... | Vacant ..................... | PAS | EX | IV | .............. | |
| Do .................... | Principal Deputy Assistant Secretary, Financial Markets. | Michael Kipp Kranbuhl ...... | NA | ES | .............. | .............. | |
| Do .................... | Deputy Assistant Secretary (Government Financial Policy). | Career Incumbent ................ | CA | ES | .............. | .............. | |
| Do .................... | Deputy Assistant Secretary (Federal Finance).. | ......do ...... | CA | ES | .............. | .............. | |
| Do .................... | Director, Capital Markets........................ | Vacant ..................... | | ES | .............. | .............. | |
| Do .................... | Director, Office of State and Local Finance ...... | Career Incumbent ................ | CA | ES | .............. | .............. | |
| Do .................... | Director, Office of Debt Management ................. | ......do ...... | CA | ES | .............. | .............. | |
| Do .................... | Director of Federal Program Finance................. | ......do ...... | CA | ES | .............. | .............. | |
| Do .................... | Special Advisor to the Assistant Secretary for Financial Markets. | Alexander Joseph Redle....... | SC | GS | 13 | .............. | |
| | *Assistant Secretary for Financial Institutions* | | | | | | |
| Do .................... | Assistant Secretary (Financial Institutions)...... | Bimal Patel ......................... | PAS | EX | IV | .............. | |
| Do .................... | Principal Deputy Assistant Secretary Financial Institutions. | Vacant ..................... | | ES | .............. | .............. | |
| Do .................... | Deputy Assistant Secretary, Cybersecurity and Critical Infrastructure Protection. | David Brand Lacquement.... | NA | ES | .............. | .............. | |
| Do .................... | Deputy Assistant Secretary for Community and Economic Development. | Gavin Andrew Beske........... | NA | ES | .............. | .............. | |
| Do .................... | Director of Cyber Policy, Preparedness and Response. | Vacant ..................... | | ES | .............. | .............. | |
| Do .................... | Director of International Coordination and Mission Support. | Career Incumbent ................ | CA | ES | .............. | .............. | |
| Do .................... | Director, Small Business Community Development and Affordable Housing Policy. | Vacant ..................... | | ES | .............. | .............. | |
| Do .................... | Director, Office of Financial Institutions Policy. | Career Incumbent ................ | CA | ES | .............. | .............. | |
| Do .................... | Senior Advisor to the Assistant Secretary for Financial Institutions. | Robert William Greene ........ | SC | GS | 15 | .............. | |
| | **UNDER SECRETARY FOR TERRORISM AND FINANCIAL INTELLIGENCE** | | | | | | |
| Do .................... | Under Secretary for Terrorism and Financial Intelligence. | Vacant ..................... | PAS | EX | III | .............. | |
| Do .................... | Director, Foreign Assets Control........................ | Career Incumbent ................ | CA | ES | .............. | .............. | |
| Do .................... | Deputy Director, Office of Foreign Assets Control. | ......do ...... | CA | ES | .............. | .............. | |
| Do .................... | Associate Director, Office of Global Targeting ... | ......do ...... | CA | ES | .............. | .............. | |
| Do .................... | Deputy Associate Director, Office of Global Targeting. | ......do ...... | CA | ES | .............. | .............. | |
| Do .................... | Associate Director, Program Policy and Implementation. | ......do ...... | CA | ES | .............. | .............. | |
| Do .................... | Associate Director, Resource Management ........ | ......do ...... | CA | ES | .............. | .............. | |
| Do .................... | Deputy Director, Treasury Executive Office for Asset Forfeiture. | ......do ...... | CA | ES | .............. | .............. | |
| Do .................... | Associate Director, Office of Compliance and Enforcement. | ......do ...... | CA | ES | .............. | .............. | |
| | **ASSISTANT SECRETARY FOR TERRORIST FINANCING** | | | | | | |
| Do .................... | Senior Counselor........................ | Jessica Renier...................... | SC | GS | 15 | .............. | |
| Do .................... | Assistant Secretary (Terrorist Financing) ........ | Vacant ..................... | PAS | EX | IV | .............. | |
| Do .................... | Principal Deputy Assistant Secretary (Terrorism and Financial Intelligence). | Career Incumbent ................ | CA | ES | .............. | .............. | |
| Do .................... | Deputy Assistant Secretary, Office of Strategic Policy. | ......do ...... | CA | ES | .............. | .............. | |
| Do .................... | Deputy Assistant Secretary, Office of Global Affairs. | Vacant ..................... | | ES | .............. | .............. | |
| | **ASSISTANT SECRETARY FOR INTELLIGENCE AND ANALYSIS** | | | | | | |
| Do .................... | Assistant Secretary (Intelligence and Analysis). | Isabel Marie Patelunas........ | PAS | EX | IV | .............. | |
| Do .................... | Deputy Assistant Secretary for Analysis and Production. | Career Incumbent ................ | CA | ES | .............. | .............. | |

## DEPARTMENT OF THE TREASURY—Continued

| Location | Position Title | Name of Incumbent | Type of Appt. | Pay Plan | Level, Grade, or Pay | Tenure | Expires |
|---|---|---|---|---|---|---|---|
| Washington, DC ...... | Deputy Assistant Secretary Cyber Intelligence. | Vacant ...................... | ........... | ES | ............... | ............... | |
| Do .................... | Deputy Assistant Secretary (Intelligence Community Integration). | Career Incumbent ................ | CA | ES | ............... | ............... | |
| Do .................... | Director, Office of Transnational Issues ............ | ...... do ......... | CA | ES | ............... | ............... | |
| Do .................... | Director, Office of Economics and Finance........ | ...... do ......... | CA | ES | ............... | ............... | |
| | **FINANCIAL CRIMES ENFORCEMENT NETWORK** | | | | | | |
| Do .................... | Associate Director, Liaison Division ................... | Annalou T Tirol ................ | TA | ES | ............... | ............... | 11/13/24 |
| Do .................... | Associate Director, Global Investigations Division. | Career Incumbent ................ | CA | ES | ............... | ............... | |
| Vienna, VA .............. | Deputy Associate Director, Chief Technology Officer. | Vacant ...................... | ........... | ES | ............... | ............... | |
| | **ASSISTANT SECRETARY (LEGISLATIVE AFFAIRS)** | | | | | | |
| Washington, DC ...... | Assistant Secretary (Deputy Under Secretary) for Legislative Affairs. | ...... do ......... | PAS | EX | IV | ............... | |
| Do .................... | Principal Deputy Assistant Secretary for Legislative Affairs. | Frederick W Vaughan .......... | NA | ES | ............... | ............... | |
| Do .................... | Deputy Assistant Secretary for Legislative Affairs (Appropriations and Management). | Vacant ...................... | ........... | ES | ............... | ............... | |
| Do .................... | Deputy Assistant Secretary for Legislative Affairs (Banking and Finance, and Terrorism and Financial Intelligence). | Jonathan Maxwell Blum...... | NA | ES | ............... | ............... | |
| Do .................... | Deputy Assistant Secretary, Legislative Affairs (Terrorism and Financial Intelligence). | Andrew Quinn Eck.............. | NA | ES | ............... | ............... | |
| Do .................... | Deputy Assistant Secretary for Legislative Affairs (International Affairs). | Michael Diroma .................... | NA | ES | ............... | ............... | |
| Do .................... | Deputy Assistant Secretary for Legislative Affairs (Tax and Budget). | Kimberly Jane Pinter........... | NA | ES | ............... | ............... | |
| Do .................... | Senior Advisor............................................... | Joseph Brady Howell .......... | SC | GS | 15 | ............... | |
| Do .................... | Special Advisor.............................................. | William Benson Dargusch ... | SC | GS | 11 | ............... | |
| Do .................... | ......do ......................... | Julia Anne Prus.................... | SC | GS | 11 | ............... | |
| Do .................... | Special Assistant............................................ | Kelsey Susan Hayes............. | SC | GS | 7 | ............... | |
| | **ASSISTANT SECRETARY (PUBLIC AFFAIRS)** | | | | | | |
| Do .................... | Assistant Secretary (Public Affairs) ................... | Monica Elizabeth Crowley ... | PA | EX | IV | ............... | |
| Do .................... | Principal Deputy Assistant Secretary for Public Affairs. | Vacant ...................... | ........... | ES | ............... | ............... | |
| Do .................... | Deputy Assistant Secretary ............................ | Brian Robert Morgenstern... | NA | ES | ............... | ............... | |
| Do .................... | ......do ......................... | Rebecca Miller ...................... | NA | ES | ............... | ............... | |
| Do .................... | Deputy Assistant Secretary, Public Affairs (Terrorism and Financial Intelligence). | Vacant ...................... | ........... | ES | ............... | ............... | |
| Do .................... | Senior Advisor............................................... | Kaelan Kirk Dorr ................ | SC | GS | 14 | ............... | |
| Do .................... | Director, Public Affairs ................................... | Patricia Mclaughlin.............. | SC | GS | 12 | ............... | |
| Do .................... | Public Affairs Specialist ................................. | William Jordan Upton ......... | SC | GS | 12 | ............... | |
| Do .................... | Director, Public Affairs (Terrorism and Financial Intelligence). | Zachary Noah Isakowitz ...... | SC | GS | 11 | ............... | |
| Do .................... | Special Assistant to the Assistant Secretary for Public Affairs. | Katherine Elizabeth McCarthy. | SC | GS | 7 | ............... | |
| Do .................... | Confidential Assistant ....................................... | Hunter Huang Dai Ihrman . | SC | GS | 7 | ............... | |
| Do .................... | Senior Advisor............................................... | Vacant ...................... | ........... | ES | ............... | ............... | |
| | **ASSISTANT SECRETARY (ECONOMIC POLICY)** | | | | | | |
| Do .................... | Assistant Secretary (Economic Policy).............. | Michael William Faulkender. | PAS | EX | IV | ............... | |
| Do .................... | Principal Deputy Assistant Secretary for Economic Policy. | Vacant ...................... | ........... | ES | ............... | ............... | |
| Do .................... | Deputy Assistant Secretary for Financial Economics. | ...... do ......... | ........... | ES | ............... | ............... | |
| Do .................... | Deputy Assistant Secretary (Macroeconomic Analysis). | ...... do ......... | ........... | ES | ............... | ............... | |
| Do .................... | Director, Office of Macroeconomic Analysis ....... | ...... do ......... | ........... | ES | ............... | ............... | |
| Do .................... | Director, Office of Microeconomic Analysis ........ | Career Incumbent ................ | CA | ES | ............... | ............... | |
| Do .................... | Senior Advisor............................................... | Stephen Ira Miran.............. | SC | GS | 15 | ............... | |
| Do .................... | Special Advisor.............................................. | Waelston Tanner Black ........ | SC | GS | 12 | ............... | |
| | **ASSISTANT SECRETARY (TAX POLICY)** | | | | | | |
| Do .................... | Assistant Secretary (Tax Policy)........................ | David John Kautter ............ | PAS | EX | IV | ............... | |
| Do .................... | Deputy Assistant Secretary (Tax Policy)............ | Vacant ...................... | ........... | ES | ............... | ............... | |
| Do .................... | Deputy Assistant Secretary (International Tax Affairs). | Lafayette George Harter III. | NA | ES | ............... | ............... | |
| Do .................... | Deputy Assistant Secretary (Tax Analysis) ....... | Vacant ...................... | ........... | ES | ............... | ............... | |

## DEPARTMENT OF THE TREASURY—Continued

| Location | Position Title | Name of Incumbent | Type of Appt. | Pay Plan | Level, Grade, or Pay | Tenure | Expires |
|---|---|---|---|---|---|---|---|
| Washington, DC ...... | Deputy Assistant Secretary (Tax, Trade, and Tariff Policy). | Career Incumbent ................ | CA | ES | ................ | ................ | |
| Do .................... | Director, Office of Tax Analysis........................... | Vacant ................................ | ............ | ES | ................ | ................ | |
| Do .................... | Director for Individual Taxation ....................... | Career Incumbent ................ | CA | ES | ................ | ................ | |
| Do .................... | Director for Business Revenue ........................ | ......do ................................ | CA | ES | ................ | ................ | |
| Do .................... | Director for Receipts Forecasting ..................... | ......do ................................ | CA | ES | ................ | ................ | |
| Do .................... | Director for Business and International Taxation. | ......do ................................ | CA | ES | ................ | ................ | |
| Do .................... | Senior Advisor for Tax Policy ........................... | Jeffery Van Hove ................ | TA | ES | ................ | ................ | 05/27/23 |
| Do .................... | Senior Advisor to the Assistant Secretary for Tax Policy. | Jeffrey Eric Friedman......... | SC | GS | 15 | ................ | |
| | **ASSISTANT SECRETARY FOR MANAGEMENT** | | | | | | |
| Do .................... | Assistant Secretary (Management) ................... | David Farrell Eisner ........... | PA | EX | IV | ................ | |
| Do .................... | Deputy Assistant Secretary for Management and Budget. | Career Incumbent ................ | CA | ES | ................ | ................ | |
| Do .................... | Deputy Assistant Secretary, Information Systems and Chief Information Officer. | ......do ................................ | CA | ES | ................ | ................ | |
| Do .................... | Associate Chief Information Officer for Cyber Security. | Vacant ................................ | ............ | ES | ................ | ................ | |
| Do .................... | Associate Chief Information Officer for Enterprise Infrastructure Operations Services. | Career Incumbent ................ | CA | ES | ................ | ................ | |
| Do .................... | Associate Chief Information Officer for Enterprise Application Services. | ......do ................................ | CA | ES | ................ | ................ | |
| Do .................... | Associate Chief Information Officer for Information Technology Strategy and Technology Management and Chief Technology Officer. | ......do ................................ | CA | ES | ................ | ................ | |
| Do .................... | Deputy Assistant Secretary (Human Resources) and Chief Human Capital Officer. | ......do ................................ | CA | ES | ................ | ................ | |
| Do .................... | Human Resources Officer, Treasury Departmental Offices. | ......do ................................ | CA | ES | ................ | ................ | |
| Do .................... | Director, Integrated Talent Management Implementation. | David M Aten ...................... | TA | ES | ................ | ................ | 09/28/22 |
| Do .................... | Deputy Assistant Secretary for Privacy, Transparency, and Records. | Career Incumbent ................ | CA | ES | ................ | ................ | |
| Do .................... | Director, Office of District of Columbia Pensions. | ......do ................................ | CA | ES | ................ | ................ | |
| Do .................... | Director, Office of Financial Management ........ | ......do ................................ | CA | ES | ................ | ................ | |
| Do .................... | Director, Office of Special Entity Accounting..... | ......do ................................ | CA | ES | ................ | ................ | |
| Do .................... | Director, Office of Accounting and Internal Control. | Vacant ................................ | ............ | ES | ................ | ................ | |
| Do .................... | Deputy Assistant Secretary for Treasury Operations. | Career Incumbent ................ | CA | ES | ................ | ................ | |
| Do .................... | Director, Civil Rights and Diversity ................. | ......do ................................ | CA | ES | ................ | ................ | |
| Do .................... | Director of Strategic Planning and Performance Improvement. | ......do ................................ | CA | ES | ................ | ................ | |
| Do .................... | Departmental Budget Director ........................ | ......do ................................ | CA | ES | ................ | ................ | |
| Do .................... | Chief Data Officer............................................. | Vacant ................................ | ............ | ES | ................ | ................ | |
| | **TREASURER OF THE UNITED STATES** | | | | | | |
| Do .................... | Treasurer of the United States........................... | ......do ................................ | PA | SL | ................ | ................ | |
| Do .................... | Director, Office of Consumer Policy .................. | Career Incumbent ................ | CA | ES | ................ | ................ | |
| Do .................... | Senior Advisor ................................................... | Kelsey Kats......................... | SC | GS | 15 | ................ | |
| | *United States Mint* | | | | | | |
| Do .................... | Director of the Mint........................................... | David J Ryder ...................... | PAS | SL | ................ | ................ | |
| Do .................... | Deputy Director of the Mint.............................. | Career Incumbent ................ | CA | ES | ................ | ................ | |
| Do .................... | Senior Advisor ................................................... | ......do ................................ | CA | ES | ................ | ................ | |
| Do .................... | ......do ............................................................... | ......do ................................ | CA | ES | ................ | ................ | |
| | *Bureau of Engraving and Printing* | | | | | | |
| Do .................... | Director, Bureau of Engraving and Printing...... | ......do ................................ | CA | ES | ................ | ................ | |
| Do .................... | Deputy Director, Chief Administrative Officer .. | ......do ................................ | CA | ES | ................ | ................ | |
| Do .................... | Deputy Director, Chief Operating Officer .......... | ......do ................................ | CA | ES | ................ | ................ | |
| Do .................... | Associate Director (Management) ..................... | ......do ................................ | CA | ES | ................ | ................ | |
| Do .................... | Associate Director, Quality............................... | ......do ................................ | CA | ES | ................ | ................ | |
| Do .................... | Associate Director (Chief Financial Officer) ...... | ......do ................................ | CA | ES | ................ | ................ | |
| Do .................... | Associate Director (Chief Information Officer).. | ......do ................................ | CA | ES | ................ | ................ | |
| Do .................... | Associate Director (Product Design and Development). | ......do ................................ | CA | ES | ................ | ................ | |
| Do .................... | Senior Advisor ................................................... | ......do ................................ | CA | ES | ................ | ................ | |

## DEPARTMENT OF THE TREASURY—Continued

| Location | Position Title | Name of Incumbent | Type of Appt. | Pay Plan | Level, Grade, or Pay | Tenure | Expires |
|---|---|---|---|---|---|---|---|
| | **COMPTROLLER OF THE CURRENCY** | | | | | | |
| Washington, DC ...... | Comptroller of the Currency ............................... | Vacant ................................... | PAS | EX | III | 5 Years | |
| | **INTERNAL REVENUE SERVICE** | | | | | | |
| Do ..................... | Commissioner of Internal Revenue ................... | Charles Paul Rettig............. | PAS | EX | III | 5 Years | |
| Do ..................... | Chairperson, Internal Revenue Service Oversight Board. | Vacant ................................... | PAS | AD | ................ | 5 Years | |
| Do ..................... | Member, Internal Revenue Service Oversight Board. | ......do ................................... | PAS | AD | .............. | 5 Years | |
| Do ..................... | ......do ................................................. | ......do ................................... | PAS | AD | .............. | 5 Years | |
| Do ..................... | ......do ................................................. | Robert Tobias...................... | PAS | AD | .............. | 5 Years | |
| Do ..................... | ......do ................................................. | Vacant ................................... | PAS | AD | .............. | 5 Years | |
| Do ..................... | ......do ................................................. | ......do ................................... | PAS | AD | .............. | 5 Years | |
| Do ..................... | ......do ................................................. | ......do ................................... | PAS | AD | .............. | 5 Years | |
| Do ..................... | ......do ................................................. | ......do ................................... | PAS | AD | .............. | 5 Years | |
| | **INTERNAL REVENUE SERVICE CHIEF COUNSEL** | | | | | | |
| Do ..................... | Chief Counsel, Internal Revenue Service........... | Michael J Desmond............. | PAS | EX | V | ................ | |
| | **SPECIAL INSPECTOR GENERAL FOR THE TROUBLED ASSET RELIEF PROGRAM** | | | | | | |
| Do ..................... | Special Inspector General for the Troubled Asset Relief Program. | Vacant ................................... | PAS | EX | IV | ................ | |

## DEPARTMENT OF THE TREASURY OFFICE OF THE INSPECTOR GENERAL

| Location | Position Title | Name of Incumbent | Type of Appt. | Pay Plan | Level, Grade, or Pay | Tenure | Expires |
|---|---|---|---|---|---|---|---|
| Washington, DC ...... | Inspector General .................................................. | Vacant ................................... | PAS | EX | IV | ................ | |
| | **OFFICE OF INVESTIGATIONS** | | | | | | |
| Do ..................... | Assistant Inspector General for Investigations . | Career Incumbent ................ | CA | ES | ................ | ................ | |

## DEPARTMENT OF THE TREASURY SPECIAL INSPECTOR GENERAL FOR THE TROUBLED ASSET RELIEF PROGRAM

| Location | Position Title | Name of Incumbent | Type of Appt. | Pay Plan | Level, Grade, or Pay | Tenure | Expires |
|---|---|---|---|---|---|---|---|
| Washington, DC ...... | Special Inspector General for the Troubled Asset Relief Program. | Christy Lynne Goldsmith Romero. | PAS | IG | ................ | ................ | |
| Do ..................... | Deputy Special Inspector General...................... | Career Incumbent ................ | CA | ES | ................ | ................ | |
| Do ..................... | Senior Policy Advisor............................................ | Vacant ................................... | ............ | ES | ................ | ................ | |
| Do ..................... | Deputy Chief of Staff............................................ | ......do ................................... | ............ | ES | ................ | ................ | |
| Do ..................... | ......do ................................................. | ......do ................................... | ............ | ES | ................ | ................ | |
| Do ..................... | Chief of Staff for Sigtarp ................................... | ......do ................................... | ............ | ES | ................ | ................ | |

## DEPARTMENT OF THE TREASURY TAX ADMINISTRATION OFFICE OF THE INSPECTOR GENERAL

| Location | Position Title | Name of Incumbent | Type of Appt. | Pay Plan | Level, Grade, or Pay | Tenure | Expires |
|---|---|---|---|---|---|---|---|
| Washington, DC ...... | Inspector General .................................................. | J Russell George................... | PAS | IG | ................ | ................ | |

# DEPARTMENT OF TRANSPORTATION

| Location | Position Title | Name of Incumbent | Type of Appt. | Pay Plan | Level, Grade, or Pay | Tenure | Expires |
|---|---|---|---|---|---|---|---|
| | **OFFICE OF THE SECRETARY** | | | | | | |
| Washington, DC | Secretary | Elaine L Chao | PAS | EX | I | | |
| Do | Chief of Staff | James Todd Inman | NA | ES | | | |
| Do | Deputy Chief of Staff | Sean Mcmaster | NA | ES | | | |
| Do | Associate Deputy Secretary | Laura Genero | NA | ES | | | |
| Do | Senior Advisor | Tamara Somerville | NA | ES | | | |
| Do | ......do | Cathy Foster Gautreaux | NA | ES | | | |
| | *Secretary* | | | | | | |
| Do | White House Liaison | Douglas Simon | SC | GS | 15 | | |
| Do | Deputy White House Liaison | Joyce Myung-Hwah Yoon | SC | GS | 11 | | |
| Do | Special Assistant for Scheduling and Advance Operations. | Amanda Gray Bailey | SC | GS | 12 | | |
| Do | Special Assistant for Scheduling and Advance.. | Kathy Vences | SC | GS | 13 | | |
| Do | Senior Advisor for Advance | Geoffrey Clark Smith | SC | GS | 15 | | |
| Do | Senior Assistant for Scheduling and Advance ... | Cameron Senft Morabito | SC | GS | 13 | | |
| Do | Special Assistant for Advance Operations | Peter Francis Murray | SC | GS | 15 | | |
| Do | Special Assistant for Advance | Guy Alexander Foster | SC | GS | 11 | | |
| Do | ......do | Jordan Lee Cooper | SC | GS | 11 | | |
| | *Office of the Deputy Secretary* | | | | | | |
| Do | Deputy Secretary | Vacant | PAS | EX | II | | |
| Do | Special Assistant | Jenny Xia Gao | SC | GS | 14 | | |
| Do | Executive Assistant | Kayla Kathleen Mykeloff | SC | GS | 7 | | |
| Do | Special Assistant | Mackenzie Baker | SC | GS | 7 | | |
| | *Office of the Under Secretary of Transportation For Policy* | | | | | | |
| Do | Under Secretary of Transportation for Policy | Vacant | PAS | EX | II | | |
| Do | Director, Office of Credit Programs | Career Incumbent | CA | ES | | | |
| | *Executive Secretariat* | | | | | | |
| Do | Director, Executive Secretariat and Senior Advisor to the Secretary. | Ruth D Knouse | NA | ES | | | |
| Do | Deputy Director | Michael Anthony Curto Jr. | SC | GS | 13 | | |
| Do | Special Assistant | Sean Michael Kelly | SC | GS | 11 | | |
| Do | ......do | Samuel Duane Richardson | SC | GS | 7 | | |
| Do | ......do | Samuel Josef Zelden | SC | GS | 7 | | |
| | *Office of Civil Rights* | | | | | | |
| Do | Director, Office of Civil Rights | Charles James | NA | ES | | | |
| Do | Deputy Director, Office of Civil Rights | Vacant | | ES | | | |
| Do | Senior Advisor | Emily Mee Sam Wong | NA | ES | | | |
| | *Small and Disadvantaged Business Utilization* | | | | | | |
| Do | Director, Office of Small and Disadvantaged Business Utilization and Senior Advisor to the Secretary. | Willis A Morris | NA | ES | | | |
| Do | Senior Advisor | Barry F. Plans | SC | GS | 15 | | |
| Do | Public Liaison Officer | Sharon Worthy | SC | GS | 15 | | |
| | *Office of the Chief Information Officer* | | | | | | |
| Do | Chief Information Officer | Ryan Ernest Cote II | NA | ES | | | |
| Do | Associate Chief Information Officer for It Policy Oversight. | Career Incumbent | CA | ES | | | |
| Do | Associate Chief Information Officer for Information Technology Shared Services. | ......do | CA | ES | | | |
| Do | Associate Director for Strategic It Initiatives | Megan Jo Bowser | SC | GS | 15 | | |
| Do | Associate Director for Technology and Information Services. | Scott Sechser | SC | GS | 14 | | |
| | *Office of Public Affairs* | | | | | | |
| Do | Assistant to the Secretary and Director of Public Affairs. | Vacant | | ES | | | |
| Do | Deputy Director for Public Affairs | Katherine Knight Patterson. | SC | GS | 15 | | |
| Do | Press Secretary | Mckenzie Christine Barbknecht. | SC | GS | 12 | | |
| Do | Senior Deputy Press Secretary | George Francis O'Connor | SC | GS | 12 | | |
| Do | Press Advance | Otto Heck | SC | GS | 15 | | |
| Do | Senior Media Affairs Coordinator | Nickolaus Julian-Clark Minock. | SC | GS | 13 | | |
| Do | Digital Communications Manager | Alexander Michael Koehlke. | SC | GS | 12 | | |
| Do | Speechwriter | Douglas Graham | SC | GS | 15 | | |
| Do | Special Assistant | Kyle Michael Mimbs | SC | GS | 9 | | |
| | *Office of the General Counsel* | | | | | | |
| Do | General Counsel | Steven Bradbury | PAS | EX | IV | | |

## DEPARTMENT OF TRANSPORTATION—Continued

| Location | Position Title | Name of Incumbent | Type of Appt. | Pay Plan | Level, Grade, or Pay | Tenure | Expires |
|---|---|---|---|---|---|---|---|
| Washington, DC | Deputy General Counsel | Christina G Aizcorbe | NA | ES | | | |
| Do | .....do | Career Incumbent | CA | ES | | | |
| Do | Associate General Counsel | Gregory Dakent Cote | NA | ES | | | |
| Do | ......do | William Mckenna | NA | ES | | | |
| Do | Senior Counsel | Jessica Marie Conrad | TA | ES | | | 02/03/21 |
| Do | Special Counsel | Parker Andrew Reid | NA | ES | | | |
| | *Office of General Law* | | | | | | |
| Do | Assistant General Counsel for General Law | Career Incumbent | CA | ES | | | |
| | *Office of Legislation* | | | | | | |
| Do | Assistant General Counsel for Legislation | ......do | CA | ES | | | |
| | *Office of Regulation and Enforcement* | | | | | | |
| Do | Assistant General Counsel for Regulation and Enforcement. | ......do | CA | ES | | | |
| | *Office of Litigation* | | | | | | |
| Do | Assistant General Counsel for Litigation | ......do | CA | ES | | | |
| | *Office of Aviation Enforcement and Proceedings* | | | | | | |
| Do | Assistant General Counsel for Aviation Enforcement and Proceedings. | ......do | CA | ES | | | |
| | *Office of Operations* | | | | | | |
| Do | Assistant General Counsel for Operations | ......do | CA | ES | | | |
| | *Office of International Law* | | | | | | |
| Do | Assistant General Counsel for International Law. | ......do | CA | ES | | | |
| | *Assistant Secretary for Budget and Programs* | | | | | | |
| Do | Assistant Secretary for Budget and Programs and Chief Financial Officer. | John Edmund Kramer | PAS | EX | IV | | |
| Do | Special Assistant for Budget and Programs | David Nicholas Yonkovich | SC | GS | 13 | | |
| | *Office of Financial Management* | | | | | | |
| Do | Director, Office of Financial Management | Career Incumbent | CA | ES | | | |
| | *Office of Budget and Program Performance* | | | | | | |
| Do | Deputy Director, Office of Budget and Program Performance. | ......do | CA | ES | | | |
| | *Assistant Secretary for Administration* | | | | | | |
| Do | Assistant Secretary for Administration | Vacant | | ES | | | |
| Do | Director of Management Services | Career Incumbent | CA | ES | | | |
| Do | Special Assistant | Connie Zhu | SC | GS | 11 | | |
| | *Departmental Office of Human Resource Management* | | | | | | |
| Do | Director, Departmental Office of Human Resource Management. | Career Incumbent | CA | ES | | | |
| Do | Deputy Director, Departmental Office of Human Resource Management. | ......do | CA | ES | | | |
| | *Office of Security* | | | | | | |
| Do | Director, Office of Security | ......do | CA | ES | | | |
| | *Office of Financial Management* | | | | | | |
| Do | Director, Office of Financial Management and Transit Benefits Programs. | ......do | CA | ES | | | |
| Do | Deputy Director, Office of Financial Management and Transit Benefit Programs. | ......do | CA | ES | | | |
| | *Office of Facilities, Information and Asset Management* | | | | | | |
| Do | Director, Office of Facilities, Information and Asset Management. | Vacant | | ES | | | |
| | *Assistant Secretary for Transportation Policy* | | | | | | |
| Do | Assistant Secretary for Transportation Policy | ......do | PAS | EX | IV | | |
| Do | Deputy Assistant Secretary for Transportation Policy. | Thomas Finch Fulton | NA | ES | | | |
| Do | ......do | Vacant | | ES | | | |
| Do | ......do | David Glenn Wonnenberg | NA | ES | | | |
| Do | Senior Director of Public Liaison | Caryn Grace Moore | SC | GS | 15 | | |
| Do | Special Assistant for Public Engagement and External Outreach. | Dominic Bonaduce | SC | GS | 15 | | |
| Do | Public Liaison and Engagement Advisor | Laura Janae Hudson | SC | GS | 14 | | |
| Do | Public Liaison Officer | Carolyn Joy O'Malley | SC | GS | 15 | | |
| Do | Special Assistant | Sofia Gallo | SC | GS | 11 | | |

## DEPARTMENT OF TRANSPORTATION—Continued

| Location | Position Title | Name of Incumbent | Type of Appt. | Pay Plan | Level, Grade, or Pay | Tenure | Expires |
|---|---|---|---|---|---|---|---|
| | *Office of the Chief Economist* | | | | | | |
| Washington, DC ...... | Chief Economist ................ | Career Incumbent ............... | CA | ES | ............. | ............. | |
| | *Office of Infrastructure Finance and Innovation* | | | | | | |
| Do .................... | Director, Office of Infrastructure Finance and Innovation. | ......do ................... | CA | ES | ............. | ............. | |
| | *Assistant Secretary for Aviation and International Affairs* | | | | | | |
| Do .................... | Assistant Secretary for Aviation and International Affairs. | Joel M Szabat ...................... | PAS | EX | IV | | |
| Do .................... | Deputy Assistant Secretary for Aviation and International Affairs. | David E Short ...................... | NA | ES | ............. | ............. | |
| Do .................... | ......do | Jared L Smith............... | NA | ES | ............. | ............. | |
| Do .................... | Strategic Advisor for Aviation Policy................ | Luke Peter Bellocchi ........... | NA | ES | ............. | ............. | |
| | *Office of Aviation Analysis* | | | | | | |
| Do .................... | Director, Office of Aviation Analysis ................ | Career Incumbent ............... | CA | ES | ............. | ............. | |
| Do .................... | Deputy Director, Office of Aviation Analysis...... | ......do ................ | CA | ES | ............. | ............. | |
| | *Office of International Aviation* | | | | | | |
| Do .................... | Director, Office of International Aviation.......... | Vacant ................ | ............. | ES | ............. | ............. | |
| | *Office of International Transportation and Trade* | | | | | | |
| Do .................... | Director, Office of International Transportation and Trade. | Career Incumbent ............... | CA | ES | ............. | ............. | |
| | *Assistant Secretary for Governmental Affairs* | | | | | | |
| Do .................... | Assistant Secretary for Governmental Affairs... | Adam J Sullivan................... | PAS | EX | IV | ............. | |
| Do .................... | Deputy Assistant Secretary for Congressional Affairs. | Anne Chettle Reinke........... | NA | ES | ............. | ............. | |
| Do .................... | Senior Governmental Affairs Officer................ | Mira Lindsey Lezell ............ | SC | GS | 15 | ............. | |
| Do .................... | ......do | Brett Michael Scott ............. | SC | GS | 15 | ............. | |
| Do .................... | ......do | Nathan Daniel Pick.............. | SC | GS | 14 | ............. | |
| Do .................... | Special Assistant................ | Mindy Shaw ...................... | SC | GS | 9 | ............. | |
| Do .................... | ......do | David L Karol ...................... | SC | GS | 7 | ............. | |
| | *Assistant Secretary for Research and Technology* | | | | | | |
| Do .................... | Assistant Secretary for Research and Technology. | Vacant ................ | PAS | EX | IV | ............. | |
| Do .................... | Deputy Assistant Secretary for Research and Technology. | Diana Elizabeth Furchtgott-Roth. | NA | ES | ............. | ............. | |
| Do .................... | Senior Advisor for Facility Acquisition and Management, Volpe Center. | Raymond Martinez.............. | NA | ES | ............. | ............. | |
| Do .................... | Director for Strategic Initiatives ..................... | Tim Wang........................ | NA | ES | ............. | ............. | |
| Do .................... | Senior Advisor for Economic Policy ................ | Theodore Boll...................... | SC | GS | 15 | ............. | |
| Do .................... | Senior Advisor for Research and Technology..... | Steven Polzin ...................... | SC | GS | 15 | ............. | |
| Do .................... | Senior Advisor................ | Aaron Max Wolff.................. | SC | GS | 15 | ............. | |
| Do .................... | Special Assistant................ | Eric William Ragan ............ | SC | GS | 9 | ............. | |
| | *Office of Research, Development and Technology* | | | | | | |
| Do .................... | Director, Office of Research Development and Technology. | Vacant ................ | ............. | ES | ............. | ............. | |
| Do .................... | Director, National Space-Based Positioning, Navigation, and Timing Coordination Office. | Career Incumbent ............... | CA | ES | ............. | ............. | |
| | *Bureau of Transportation Statistics* | | | | | | |
| Do .................... | Director, Bureau of Transportation Statistics.... | ......do ................ | CA | ES | ............. | ............. | |
| Do .................... | Deputy Director, Bureau of Transportation Statistics. | ......do ................ | CA | ES | ............. | ............. | |
| | *Volpe National Transportation Systems Center* | | | | | | |
| Cambridge, MA ...... | Director, Volpe National Transportation Systems Center. | ......do ................ | CA | ES | ............. | ............. | |
| | *Office of the Deputy Associate Administrator For Operations* | | | | | | |
| Do .................... | Deputy Director for Operations ......................... | ......do ................ | CA | ES | ............. | ............. | |
| | *Office of the Deputy Associate Administrator For Research and Innovative Technology* | | | | | | |
| Do .................... | Deputy Director for Research and Innovative Technology. | ......do ................ | CA | ES | ............. | ............. | |
| Do .................... | Center Director for Policy, Planning and Environment. | ......do ................ | CA | ES | ............. | ............. | |

## DEPARTMENT OF TRANSPORTATION—Continued

| Location | Position Title | Name of Incumbent | Type of Appt. | Pay Plan | Level, Grade, or Pay | Tenure | Expires |
|---|---|---|---|---|---|---|---|
| Cambridge, MA | Center Director for Infrastructure Systems and Technology. | Career Incumbent | CA | ES | | | |
| Do | Center Director for Air Traffic Systems and Operations. | Vacant | | ES | | | |
| Do | Center Director for Safety Management and Human Factors. | ......do | | ES | | | |
| | *Immediate Office of the Administrator* | | | | | | |
| Washington, DC | Administrator | Stephen Marshall Dickson | PAS | EX | II | | |
| Do | Deputy Administrator | Daniel K Elwell | PA | EX | IV | | |
| | *Office of the Chief Counsel* | | | | | | |
| Do | Chief Counsel | Arjun Garg | XS | OT | | | |
| | *Assistant Administrator for Communications* | | | | | | |
| Do | Assistant Administrator for Communications | Brianna Manzelli | XS | OT | | | |
| | *Assistant Administrator for Aviation Policy, International Affairs, and Environment* | | | | | | |
| Do | Assistant Administrator for Aviation Policy, Planning and Environment. | Benjamin Bailey Edwards | XS | OT | | | |
| | *Associate Administrator for Airports* | | | | | | |
| Do | Associate Administrator for Airports | D Kirk Shaffer | XS | OT | | | |
| | *Office of Government and Industry* | | | | | | |
| Do | Governmental Affairs and External Outreach Advisor. | Andrew F Giacini | SC | GS | 13 | | |
| | *Immediate Office of the Administrator* | | | | | | |
| Do | Administrator | Nicole R Nason | PAS | EX | II | | |
| Do | Deputy Administrator | Mala Krishnamoorti | NA | ES | | | |
| Do | Program Manager for the Intelligent Transportation Systems Joint Programs Office. | Career Incumbent | CA | ES | | | |
| Do | Special Assistant for Policy, Governmental and Public Affairs. | Lauren Michele Baker | SC | GS | 15 | | |
| | *Office of the Chief Counsel* | | | | | | |
| Do | Chief Counsel | Adrienne Elizabeth Camire | NA | ES | | | |
| Do | Deputy Chief Counsel | Career Incumbent | CA | ES | | | |
| Do | Assistant Chief Counsel for Legislation and Regulations and General Law Division. | Vacant | | ES | | | |
| | *Office of Public Affairs* | | | | | | |
| Do | Director of Public Affairs | Michael H Reynard | SC | GS | 15 | | |
| | *Associate Administrator for Administration* | | | | | | |
| Do | Associate Administrator for Administration | Career Incumbent | CA | ES | | | |
| Do | Director, Office of Human Resources | ......do | CA | ES | | | |
| Lakewood, CO | Associate Administrator for Infrastructure | ......do | CA | ES | | | |
| Washington, DC | Director, Office of Stewardship, Oversight, and Management. | ......do | CA | ES | | | |
| Do | Director, Office of Bridges and Structures | ......do | CA | ES | | | |
| Do | Director, Office of Preconstruction, Construction and Pavements. | ......do | CA | ES | | | |
| | *Office of Stewardship, Oversight, & Management* | | | | | | |
| Do | Director, Office of Program Administration | Vacant | | ES | | | |
| | *Associate Administrator for Operations* | | | | | | |
| Do | Associate Administrator for Operations | Career Incumbent | CA | ES | | | |
| Do | Director, Office of Freight Management and Operations. | ......do | CA | ES | | | |
| Do | Director, Office of Transportation Management. | ......do | CA | ES | | | |
| Do | Director, Office of Transportation Operations | ......do | CA | ES | | | |
| | *Associate Administrator for Planning, Environment and Realty* | | | | | | |
| Do | Associate Administrator for Planning, Environment, and Realty. | ......do | CA | ES | | | |
| Do | Director, Office of Human Environment | ......do | CA | ES | | | |
| Do | Director, Office of Project Development and Environmental Review. | ......do | CA | ES | | | |
| Do | Director, Office of Natural Environment | ......do | CA | ES | | | |
| Do | Director, Office of Planning | ......do | CA | ES | | | |
| | *Associate Administrator for Safety* | | | | | | |
| Do | Director, Office of Safety Integration | ......do | CA | ES | | | |
| Do | Director, Office of Safety Programs | ......do | CA | ES | | | |

## DEPARTMENT OF TRANSPORTATION—Continued

| Location | Position Title | Name of Incumbent | Type of Appt. | Pay Plan | Level, Grade, or Pay | Tenure | Expires |
|---|---|---|---|---|---|---|---|
| | *Associate Administrator for Research, Development and Technology* | | | | | | |
| Washington, DC ...... | Associate Administrator for Research, Development and Technology. | Career Incumbent ................ | CA | ES | ............... | ............... | |
| McLean, VA ............ | Director, Office of Corporate Research, Technology and Innovation Management. | ......do ................. | CA | ES | ............... | ............... | |
| Washington, DC ...... | Director, Office of Infrastructure Research, and Development. | ......do ................. | CA | ES | ............... | ............... | |
| Do .................... | Director, Office of Safety and Operations Research, Development and Technology. | ......do ................. | CA | ES | ............... | ............... | |
| | *Office of Operations Research and Development* | | | | | | |
| McLean, VA ............ | Director, Office of Operations Research, Development and Technology. | Vacant .................... | ............ | ES | ............... | ............... | |
| | *Associate Administrator for Federal Lands Highway Programs* | | | | | | |
| Washington, DC ...... | Associate Administrator for Federal Lands Highway Programs. | Career Incumbent ................ | CA | ES | ............... | ............... | |
| Sterling, VA ............ | Federal Lands Highway Division Engineer, Eastern. | ......do ................. | CA | ES | ............... | ............... | |
| Lakewood, CO ........ | Federal Lands Highway Division Engineer, Central. | ......do ................. | CA | ES | ............... | ............... | |
| Vancouver, WA........ | Federal Lands Highway Division Engineer, Western. | Vacant .................... | ............ | ES | ............... | ............... | |
| | *Associate Administrator for Highway Policy and External Affairs* | | | | | | |
| Washington, DC ...... | Associate Administrator for Highway Policy and External Affairs. | Alexander Joel Etchen ......... | NA | ES | ............... | ............... | |
| Do .................... | Director, Office of International Programs........ | Career Incumbent ................ | CA | ES | ............... | ............... | |
| Do .................... | Director, Office of Highway Policy Information . | ......do ................. | CA | ES | ............... | ............... | |
| Do .................... | Director, Office of Transportation Policy Studies. | ......do ................. | CA | ES | ............... | ............... | |
| Do .................... | Director, Office of Legislative Affairs and Policy Communications. | ......do ................. | CA | ES | ............... | ............... | |
| | *Associate Administrator for Civil Rights* | | | | | | |
| Do .................... | Associate Administrator for Civil Rights .......... | ......do ................. | CA | ES | ............... | ............... | |
| | *Field Services* | | | | | | |
| Lakewood, CO ........ | Chief Technical Services Officer .................... | ......do ................. | CA | ES | ............... | ............... | |
| Denver, CO ............ | Resource Center Director (Austin, Tx) ............. | ......do ................. | CA | ES | ............... | ............... | |
| Atlanta, GA ............ | Director of Field Services - South.................... | ......do ................. | CA | ES | ............... | ............... | |
| Salt Lake City, UT .. | Director of Field Services - West.................... | ......do ................. | CA | ES | ............... | ............... | |
| Matteson, IL ............ | Director of Field Services - Mid-America .......... | Vacant .................... | ............ | ES | ............... | ............... | |
| Baltimore, MD........ | Director of Field Services - North.................... | ......do ................. | ............ | ES | ............... | ............... | |
| Sacramento, CA...... | Division Administrator, California .................... | Career Incumbent ................ | CA | ES | ............... | ............... | |
| Washington, DC ...... | Division Administrator, Florida .................... | ......do ................. | CA | ES | ............... | ............... | |
| Albany, NY............ | Division Administrator, New York .................... | ......do ................. | CA | ES | ............... | ............... | |
| Austin, TX.............. | Division Administrator, Austin, Texas.............. | ......do ................. | CA | ES | ............... | ............... | |
| | *Immediate Office of the Administrator* | | | | | | |
| Washington, DC ...... | Administrator.................................... | Vacant .................... | PAS | EX | III | ............... | |
| Do .................... | Deputy Administrator .................................... | James A Mullen.................... | NA | ES | ............... | ............... | |
| Do .................... | Chief Technology Officer .................................... | Vacant .................... | ............ | ES | ............... | ............... | |
| Do .................... | Senior Governmental Affairs Officer .................... | Sean D Poole.................... | SC | GS | 13 | ............... | |
| Do .................... | Director of Communications .................................... | Kyle S Bonini...................... | SC | GS | 15 | ............... | |
| Do .................... | Senior Policy Advisor .................................... | James Wiley Deck ............... | NA | ES | ............... | ............... | |
| | *Office of the Chief Counsel* | | | | | | |
| Do .................... | Chief Counsel .................................... | Heather Eilers-Bowser........ | NA | ES | ............... | ............... | |
| Do .................... | Deputy Chief Counsel .................................... | Career Incumbent ................ | CA | ES | ............... | ............... | |
| | *Associate Administrator for Administration* | | | | | | |
| Do .................... | Associate Administrator for Administration...... | ......do ................. | CA | ES | ............... | ............... | |
| | *Associate Administrator for Policy and Program Development* | | | | | | |
| Do .................... | Associate Administrator for Policy and Program Development. | ......do ................. | CA | ES | ............... | ............... | |
| | *Office of Policy, Plans and Regulations* | | | | | | |
| Do .................... | Director, Office of Policy, Plans and Regulations. | ......do ................. | CA | ES | ............... | ............... | |
| | *Associate Administrator for Research and Registration* | | | | | | |
| Do .................... | Associate Administrator for Research and Registration. | Vacant .................... | ............ | ES | ............... | ............... | |

# DEPARTMENT OF TRANSPORTATION—Continued

| Location | Position Title | Name of Incumbent | Type of Appt. | Pay Plan | Level, Grade, or Pay | Tenure | Expires |
|---|---|---|---|---|---|---|---|
| | *Office of Analysis, Research and Technology* | | | | | | |
| Washington, DC ...... | Director, Office of Analysis Research and Technology. | Vacant ................................. | ............ | ES | ............... | ............... | |
| | *Associate Administrator for Field Operations* | | | | | | |
| Do .................... | Associate Administrator for Field Operations ... | ......do ................................. | ............ | ES | ............... | ............... | |
| Lakewood, CO ........ | Regional Field Administrator, Western Region.. | Career Incumbent ................ | CA | ES | ............... | ............... | |
| Baltimore, MD......... | Regional Field Administrator, Eastern Region .. | ......do ................................. | CA | ES | ............... | ............... | |
| | *Associate Administrator for Enforcement and Program Delivery* | | | | | | |
| Washington, DC ...... | Associate Administrator for Enforcement and Program Delivery. | Vacant ................................. | ............ | ES | ............... | ............... | |
| | *Office of Motor Carrier Safety Programs* | | | | | | |
| Do .................... | Director, Office of Motor Carrier Safety Programs. | Career Incumbent ................ | CA | ES | ............... | ............... | |
| | *Immediate Office of the Administrator* | | | | | | |
| Do .................... | Administrator........................................... | Ronald Louis Batory ............ | PAS | EX | III | ............... | |
| Do .................... | Deputy Administrator .......................... | Quintin Kendall............... | NA | ES | ............... | ............... | |
| Do .................... | Director of Public Affairs.......................... | David William James ........... | NA | ES | ............... | ............... | |
| Do .................... | Senior Advisor for Policy and Infrastructure..... | Peter E Cipriano.................. | SC | GS | 15 | ............... | |
| Do .................... | Senior Policy Advisor.............................. | George Beck Riccardo .......... | SC | GS | 15 | ............... | |
| Do .................... | Senior Policy Advisor for Infrastructure ........... | Vacant ................................. | ............ | ES | ............... | ............... | |
| | *Office of the Chief Counsel* | | | | | | |
| Do .................... | Chief Counsel........................................ | Gerald A Reynolds............... | NA | ES | ............... | ............... | |
| Do .................... | Deputy Chief Counsel.............................. | Career Incumbent ................ | CA | ES | ............... | ............... | |
| | *Associate Administrator for Administration* | | | | | | |
| Do .................... | Associate Administrator for Administration...... | ......do ................................. | CA | ES | ............... | ............... | |
| | *Office of the Chief Financial Officer* | | | | | | |
| Do .................... | Associate Administrator for Budget and Programs/Chief Financial Officer. | ......do ................................. | CA | ES | ............... | ............... | |
| | *Associate Administrator for Railroad Safety* | | | | | | |
| Do .................... | Director, Office Railroad Infrastructure and Mechanical. | Vacant ................................. | ............ | ES | ............... | ............... | |
| Do .................... | Director, Office of Railroad Systems, Technology and Innovation. | Career Incumbent ................ | CA | ES | ............... | ............... | |
| Do .................... | Director, Office of Regional Operations and Outreach. | ......do ................................. | CA | ES | ............... | ............... | |
| Do .................... | Director, Office of Data Analysis and Program Support. | ......do ................................. | CA | ES | ............... | ............... | |
| | *Associate Administrator for Railroad Policy and Development* | | | | | | |
| Do .................... | Associate Administrator for Railroad Policy and Development. | ......do ................................. | CA | ES | ............... | ............... | |
| Do .................... | Director, Office of Research, Development and Technology. | ......do ................................. | CA | ES | ............... | ............... | |
| Do .................... | Director, Office of Program Delivery ................. | ......do ................................. | CA | ES | ............... | ............... | |
| Do .................... | Director, Office of Planning and Policy Analysis. | ......do ................................. | CA | ES | ............... | ............... | |
| | *Immediate Office of the Administrator* | | | | | | |
| Do .................... | Administrator........................................... | Vacant ................................. | PAS | EX | II | ............... | |
| Do .................... | Deputy Administrator and Senior Advisor to the Secretary. | Kimberly Jane Williams ...... | NA | ES | ............... | ............... | |
| Do .................... | Executive Director ...................................... | Career Incumbent ................ | CA | ES | ............... | ............... | |
| Do .................... | Director of Communications ...................... | Alan Bailey Wood ................. | SC | GS | 15 | ............... | |
| Do .................... | Director of Governmental and Legislative Affairs. | Alexander Joseph Poirot ...... | SC | GS | 15 | ............... | |
| | *Office of the Chief Counsel* | | | | | | |
| Do .................... | Chief Counsel........................................ | John Joseph Brennan III ...... | NA | ES | ............... | ............... | |
| Do .................... | Deputy Chief Counsel.............................. | Career Incumbent ................ | CA | ES | ............... | ............... | |
| Do .................... | Attorney Advisor (Special Counsel).................... | ......do ................................. | CA | ES | ............... | ............... | |
| | *Associate Administrator for Administration* | | | | | | |
| Do .................... | Associate Administrator for Administration...... | ......do ................................. | CA | ES | ............... | ............... | |
| | *Associate Administrator for Safety and Oversight* | | | | | | |
| Do .................... | Associate Administrator for Safety and Oversight. | ......do ................................. | CA | ES | ............... | ............... | |
| | *Associate Administrator for Budget and Policy* | | | | | | |
| Do .................... | Associate Administrator for Budget and Policy. | ......do ................................. | CA | ES | ............... | ............... | |

## DEPARTMENT OF TRANSPORTATION—Continued

| Location | Position Title | Name of Incumbent | Type of Appt. | Pay Plan | Level, Grade, or Pay | Tenure | Expires |
|---|---|---|---|---|---|---|---|
| | *Associate Administrator for Program Management* | | | | | | |
| Washington, DC ...... | Associate Administrator for Program Management. | Career Incumbent .............. | CA | ES | .............. | .............. | |
| | *Associate Administrator for Planning and Environment* | | | | | | |
| Do .................... | Associate Administrator for Planning and Environment. | ......do ..................... | CA | ES | .............. | .............. | |
| | *Associate Administrator for Research, Demonstration and Innovation* | | | | | | |
| Do .................... | Associate Administrator for Research, Demonstration and Innovation. | Vacant ..................... | | ES | .............. | .............. | |
| | *Associate Administrator for Civil Rights* | | | | | | |
| Do .................... | Associate Administrator for Civil Rights .......... | Career Incumbent .............. | CA | ES | .............. | .............. | |
| | *Regional Administrator* | | | | | | |
| Cambridge, MA ...... | Regional Administrator, Region 1 ...................... | ......do .................... | CA | ES | .............. | .............. | |
| New York, NY ......... | Regional Administrator, Region 2 .................... | ......do .................... | CA | ES | .............. | .............. | |
| Philadelphia, PA...... | Regional Administrator, Region 3 .................... | ......do .................... | CA | ES | .............. | .............. | |
| Atlanta, GA ............ | Regional Administrator, Region 4 .................... | ......do .................... | CA | ES | .............. | .............. | |
| Chicago, IL.............. | Regional Administrator, Region 5 .................... | ......do .................... | CA | ES | .............. | .............. | |
| Fort Worth, TX......... | Regional Administrator, Region 6 .................... | ......do .................... | CA | ES | .............. | .............. | |
| Kansas City, MO ..... | Regional Administrator, Region 7 .................... | ......do .................... | CA | ES | .............. | .............. | |
| Denver, CO ............. | Regional Administrator, Region 8 .................... | ......do .................... | CA | ES | .............. | .............. | |
| San Francisco, CA ... | Regional Administrator, Region 9 .................... | ......do .................... | CA | ES | .............. | .............. | |
| Seattle, WA ............. | Regional Administrator, Region 10 .................. | ......do .................... | CA | ES | .............. | .............. | |
| | *Immediate Office of the Administrator* | | | | | | |
| Washington, DC ...... | Administrator.................................................. | Mark H Buzby ..................... | PAS | EX | III | .............. | |
| Do .................... | Deputy Administrator .................................... | Richard Anthony Balzano..... | NA | ES | | .............. | |
| Do .................... | Special Assistant............................................ | James B Wilkinson.............. | SC | GS | 15 | .............. | |
| Do .................... | Governmental and Legislative Affairs Officer ... | Cameron Michael Humphrey. | SC | GS | 11 | .............. | |
| | *Office of the Chief Counsel* | | | | | | |
| Do .................... | Chief Counsel ................................................. | Douglas R Burnett .............. | NA | ES | .............. | .............. | |
| | *Associate Administrator for Administration* | | | | | | |
| Do .................... | Associate Administrator for Administration...... | Career Incumbent .............. | CA | ES | .............. | .............. | |
| | *Associate Administrator for Strategic Sealift* | | | | | | |
| Do .................... | Associate Administrator for Strategic Sealift .... | ......do .................... | CA | ES | .............. | .............. | |
| Do .................... | Deputy Associate Administrator for Commercial Sealift. | ......do .................... | CA | ES | .............. | .............. | |
| | *Associate Administrator for Ports and Inland Waterways* | | | | | | |
| Do .................... | Associate Administrator for Ports and Inland Waterways. | ......do ..................... | CA | ES | .............. | .............. | |
| | *Associate Administrator for Business and Finance Development* | | | | | | |
| Do .................... | Associate Administrator for Business and Finance Development. | Vacant ..................... | | ES | .............. | .............. | |
| | *Merchant Marine Academy* | | | | | | |
| Kings Point, NY....... | Superintendent ................................................. | Career Incumbent .............. | CA | ES | .............. | .............. | |
| Do .................... | Deputy Superintendent ................................... | ......do .................... | CA | ES | .............. | .............. | |
| Do .................... | Academic Dean/Provost ................................... | ......do .................... | CA | ES | .............. | .............. | |
| | *Immediate Office of the Administrator* | | | | | | |
| Washington, DC ...... | Administrator.................................................. | Vacant ..................... | PAS | EX | III | .............. | |
| Do .................... | Deputy Administrator .................................... | James C Owens Jr. .............. | NA | ES | | .............. | |
| Do .................... | Director of Communications ............................ | Sean Rushton ..................... | NA | ES | | .............. | |
| Do .................... | Director of Governmental Affairs ..................... | Steven H Bayless.................. | SC | GS | 15 | .............. | |
| Do .................... | Special Assistant for Policy, Governmental and Public Affairs. | Mitchell Scott Kominsky...... | SC | GS | 15 | .............. | |
| Do .................... | Special Assistant............................................ | Caitlin Mary Murray .......... | SC | GS | 14 | .............. | |
| Do .................... | Chief Safety Scientist ..................................... | Career Incumbent .............. | CA | ES | .............. | .............. | |
| Do .................... | Senior Advisor ................................................ | ......do .................... | CA | ES | .............. | .............. | |
| | *Office of the Chief Counsel* | | | | | | |
| Do .................... | Chief Counsel ................................................. | Jonathan C Morrison .......... | NA | ES | | .............. | |
| Do .................... | Assistant Chief Counsel (Vehicle Safety Standards & Harmonization). | Vacant ..................... | | ES | .............. | .............. | |
| Do .................... | Assistant Chief Counsel (Litigation and Enforcement). | Career Incumbent .............. | CA | ES | .............. | .............. | |

## DEPARTMENT OF TRANSPORTATION—Continued

| Location | Position Title | Name of Incumbent | Type of Appt. | Pay Plan | Level, Grade, or Pay | Tenure | Expires |
|---|---|---|---|---|---|---|---|
| Washington, DC ...... | Assistant Chief Counsel (Legislation and General Law). | Vacant ..................... | ............ | ES | ................ | ................ | |
| | *Associate Administrator for Administration* | | | | | | |
| Do .................... | Associate Administrator for Administration...... | ......do ..................... | ............ | ES | ................ | ................ | |
| | *Office of the Chief Financial Officer* | | | | | | |
| Do .................... | Chief Financial Officer ................................. | Career Incumbent ................ | CA | ES | ................ | ................ | |
| | *Associate Administrator for Vechicle Safety Research* | | | | | | |
| Do .................... | Associate Administrator for Vehicle Safety Research. | ......do ..................... | CA | ES | ................ | ................ | |
| Ohio, OH ................ | Director, Vehicle Research and Test Center (Ohio). | ......do ..................... | CA | ES | ................ | ................ | |
| Washington, DC ...... | Director, Office of Crash Avoidance and Electronic Controls Research. | ......do ..................... | CA | ES | ................ | ................ | |
| | *Associate Administrator for Rulemaking* | | | | | | |
| Do .................... | Associate Administrator for Rulemaking........... | ......do ..................... | CA | ES | ................ | ................ | |
| Do .................... | Director, Office of Crash Avoidance Standards.. | ......do ..................... | CA | ES | ................ | ................ | |
| Do .................... | Director, Office of International Policy, Fuel, Economy and Consumer Programs. | ......do ..................... | CA | ES | ................ | ................ | |
| | *Associate Administrator for the National Center for Statistics and Analysis* | | | | | | |
| Do .................... | Associate Administrator for the National Center for Statistics and Analysis. | ......do ..................... | CA | ES | ................ | ................ | |
| Do .................... | Director, Office of Regulatory Analysis and Evaluation. | ......do ..................... | CA | ES | ................ | ................ | |
| | *Associate Administrator for Communications and Consumer Information* | | | | | | |
| Do .................... | Associate Administrator for Communications and Consumer Information. | ......do ..................... | CA | ES | ................ | ................ | |
| | *Associate Administrator for Research and Program Development* | | | | | | |
| Do .................... | Associate Administrator for Research and Program Development. | ......do ..................... | CA | ES | ................ | ................ | |
| Do .................... | Director, Office of Impaired Driving and Occupant Protection. | ......do ..................... | CA | ES | ................ | ................ | |
| Do .................... | Director, Office of Safety Programs ................... | ......do ..................... | CA | ES | ................ | ................ | |
| | *Office of the Chief Technology Officer* | | | | | | |
| Do .................... | Chief Technology Officer ............................. | Vacant ..................... | ............ | ES | ................ | ................ | |
| | **PIPELINE AND HAZARDOUS MATERIALS SAFETY ADMINISTRATION** | | | | | | |
| Do .................... | Administrator.............................. | Howard R Elliott ................ | PAS | EX | III | ................ | |
| Do .................... | Deputy Administrator ......................... | Drue Pearce ......................... | NA | ES | ................ | ................ | |
| Do .................... | Senior Policy Advisor.......................... | Robert Joel Fraser.............. | SC | GS | 15 | ................ | |
| | *Immediate Office of the Administrator* | | | | | | |
| Do .................... | Director of Governmental, International and Public Affairs. | Benjamin David Kochman... | SC | GS | 14 | ................ | |
| Do .................... | Special Assistant for Strategic Communications. | Randon Kory Lane .............. | SC | GS | 15 | ................ | |
| | *Office of the Chief Counsel* | | | | | | |
| Do .................... | Chief Counsel......................................... | Paul J Roberti........................ | NA | ES | ................ | ................ | |
| Do .................... | Deputy Chief Counsel.............................. | Career Incumbent ................ | CA | ES | ................ | ................ | |
| | *Associate Administrator Administration* | | | | | | |
| Do .................... | Associate Administrator for Administration...... | ......do ..................... | CA | ES | ................ | ................ | |
| | *Office of Hazardous Materials Safety* | | | | | | |
| Do .................... | Deputy Associate Administrator for Field Operations. | ......do ..................... | CA | ES | ................ | ................ | |
| Do .................... | Deputy Associate Administrator for Policy and Programs. | ......do ..................... | CA | ES | ................ | ................ | |
| | *Associate Administrator for Planning and Analytics* | | | | | | |
| Do .................... | Associate Administrator for Planning and Analytics. | ......do ..................... | CA | ES | ................ | ................ | |
| | *Immediate Office of the Administrator* | | | | | | |
| Do .................... | Administrator............................ | Vacant ..................... | PA | EX | IV | ................ | |
| Do .................... | Deputy Administrator ......................... | Career Incumbent ................ | CA | ES | ................ | ................ | |
| Massena, NY ........ | Associate Administrator/Resident Manager ...... | Vacant ..................... | ............ | ES | ................ | ................ | |
| Washington, DC ...... | Senior Policy Advisor.................................... | ......do ..................... | ............ | ES | ................ | ................ | |

## DEPARTMENT OF TRANSPORTATION OFFICE OF THE INSPECTOR GENERAL

| Location | Position Title | Name of Incumbent | Type of Appt. | Pay Plan | Level, Grade, or Pay | Tenure | Expires |
|---|---|---|---|---|---|---|---|
| | **OFFICE OF INSPECTOR GENERAL IMMEDIATE OFFICE** | | | | | | |
| Washington, DC ...... | Inspector General ............................................. | Vacant ...................................... | PAS | EX | IV | ............... | |

## DEPARTMENT OF VETERANS AFFAIRS

| Location | Position Title | Name of Incumbent | Type of Appt. | Pay Plan | Level, Grade, or Pay | Tenure | Expires |
|---|---|---|---|---|---|---|---|
| Washington, DC ...... | Associate Deputy Assistant Secretary for Planning and Performance Management. | Vacant ...................................... | ............ | ES | ............... | ............... | |
| | **OFFICE OF THE SECRETARY AND DEPUTY** | | | | | | |
| Do .................... | Secretary of Veterans Affairs ............................. | Robert L Wilkie ................... | PAS | EX | I | ............... | |
| Do .................... | Deputy Secretary of Veterans Affairs ............... | Vacant ...................................... | PAS | EX | II | ............... | |
| Do .................... | Chief of Staff ................................................... | Pamela Powers .................... | NA | ES | | ............... | |
| Do .................... | Deputy Chief of Staff ...................................... | Christopher D Syrek ........... | NA | ES | | ............... | |
| Do .................... | Senior Advisor to the Secretary ....................... | John Mashburn .................... | NA | ES | | ............... | |
| Do .................... | Senior Advisor ................................................. | Vacant ...................................... | ............ | ES | | ............... | |
| Do .................... | ......do .............................................................. | ......do ...................................... | ............ | ES | | ............... | |
| Do .................... | White House Liaison ......................................... | Darren John Bossie ............. | SC | GS | 15 | ............... | |
| Do .................... | Executive Secretary to the Department............. | Career Incumbent ............... | CA | ES | ............... | ............... | |
| Do .................... | Director, Office of Support and Mission Operations. | Katherine Childress ............ | SC | GS | 14 | ............... | |
| Do .................... | Senior Advisor and Veterans Service Organization Liaison. | Jason Roberts Beardsley...... | SC | GS | 15 | ............... | |
| Do .................... | Senior Advisor for Strategic Communications... | Traci A Scott ........................ | SC | GS | 15 | ............... | |
| Do .................... | Director, Center for Minority Veterans............... | Stephen Bryant Dillard ....... | NA | ES | | ............... | |
| Do .................... | Director, Center for Women Veterans ............... | Jacquelyn Hayes-Byrd ......... | NA | ES | | ............... | |
| Do .................... | Senior Advisor for Appeals Modernization........ | Vacant ...................................... | ............ | ES | | ............... | |
| New York New York, NY. | District Veterans Experience Officer................. | Career Incumbent ............... | CA | ES | | ............... | |
| Washington, DC ...... | Executive Director, Office of Electronic Health Record Modernization. | Vacant ...................................... | ............ | ES | | ............... | |
| Do .................... | Deputy Executive Director, Office of Electronic Health Record Modernization. | ......do ...................................... | ............ | ES | | ............... | |
| Do .................... | Executive Director/Chief of Staff...................... | ......do ...................................... | ............ | ES | ............... | ............... | |
| Do .................... | Chief Technology Officer .................................. | ......do ...................................... | ............ | ES | ............... | ............... | |
| Do .................... | Executive Director, Prevents Program Office .... | Barbara Van Dahlen ............ | TA | ES | ............... | ............... | 07/21/22 |
| Do .................... | Executive Advisor (Strategic Partnerships)....... | Deborah Lafer Scher ........... | TA | ES | ............... | 36 Months | 01/14/21 |
| Do .................... | Executive Director ............................................ | Ashleigh Barry .................... | TA | ES | ............... | ............... | 03/03/22 |
| Do .................... | Senior Advisor (Veteran Experience)................. | Vacant ...................................... | ............ | ES | | ............... | |
| Do .................... | Senior Advisor (Policy & Planning) .................... | ......do ...................................... | ............ | ES | | ............... | |
| Do .................... | Senior White House Advisor .............................. | ......do ...................................... | ............ | ES | | ............... | |
| Do .................... | Senior White House Advisor (Va Transition Team). | ......do ...................................... | ............ | ES | | ............... | |
| | **OFFICE OF THE ASSISTANT SECRETARY FOR ACCOUNTABILITY AND WHISTLEBLOWER PROTECTION** | | | | | | |
| Do .................... | Assistant Secretary for Accountability and Whistleblower Protection. | Tamara Bonzanto................. | PAS | EX | IV | ............... | |
| Do .................... | Deputy Executive Director, Office of Accountability and Whistleblower Protection. | Vacant ...................................... | ............ | ES | ............... | ............... | |
| | **OFFICE OF THE GENERAL COUNSEL** | | | | | | |
| Do .................... | General Counsel................................................ | ......do ...................................... | PAS | EX | IV | ............... | |
| Do .................... | Principal Deputy General Counsel..................... | William A Hudson Jr............ | NA | ES | ............... | ............... | |
| Do .................... | Special Counsel................................................. | Vacant ...................................... | ............ | ES | ............... | ............... | |
| Do .................... | Counselor (Healthcare)...................................... | Caitlin Lisa Vannoy.............. | SC | GS | 14 | ............... | |
| Do .................... | Special Assistant (Attorney Advisor)................. | Benjamin Riggs ................... | SC | GS | 11 | ............... | |
| Do .................... | Associate Chief Counsel ................................... | Vacant ...................................... | XS | SL | ............... | ............... | |
| | **OFFICE OF THE ASSISTANT SECRETARY FOR HUMAN RESOURCES AND ADMINISTRATION/OPERATIONS, SECURITY, AND PREPAREDNESS** | | | | | | |
| Do .................... | Asst Secretary Human Resources and Administration/Operations, Security and Preparedness. | Daniel R Sitterly ................. | PA | EX | IV | ............... | |

## DEPARTMENT OF VETERANS AFFAIRS—Continued

| Location | Position Title | Name of Incumbent | Type of Appt. | Pay Plan | Level, Grade, or Pay | Tenure | Expires |
|---|---|---|---|---|---|---|---|
| Washington, DC ...... | Principal Deputy Assistant Secretary for Human Resources and Administration. | Career Incumbent ................ | CA | ES | ................ | ................ | |
| Do .................... | Chief of Staff.................................................... | ......do ................................. | CA | ES | ................ | ................ | |
| Do .................... | Associate Deputy Assistant Secretary for Human Resources, Information Technology Systems and Analytics. | ......do ................................. | CA | ES | ................ | ................ | |
| Do .................... | Chief Learning Officer/ Executive Director, Human Resource Enterprise Center. | ......do ................................. | CA | ES | ................ | ................ | |
| | **OFFICE OF ADMINISTRATION** | | | | | | |
| Do .................... | Deputy Assistant Secretary ............................ | ......do ................................. | CA | ES | ................ | ................ | |
| Do .................... | Associate Deputy Assistant Secretary for Administration. | ......do ................................. | CA | ES | ................ | ................ | |
| | **OFFICE OF HUMAN RESOURCES MANAGEMENT** | | | | | | |
| Do .................... | Chief Human Capitol Officer........................... | ......do ................................. | CA | ES | ................ | ................ | |
| Do .................... | Senior Advisor, Human Capital Services Center. | Vacant ................................. | ............ | ES | ................ | ................ | |
| Do .................... | Executive Director, Management, Planning, and Analysis. | Career Incumbent ................ | CA | ES | ................ | ................ | |
| | **OFFICE OF OPERATIONS, SECURITY AND PREPAREDNESS** | | | | | | |
| Do .................... | Associate Deputy Assistant Secretary, Emergency Management and Resilience. | ......do ................................. | CA | ES | ................ | ................ | |
| | **OFFICE OF THE ASSISTANT SECRETARY FOR MANAGEMENT** | | | | | | |
| Do .................... | Assistant Secretary for Management................. | Jon J Rychalski .................... | PA | EX | IV | ................ | |
| Do .................... | Executive Director, Financial Planning and Analysis. | Vacant ................................. | ............ | ES | ................ | ................ | |
| Do .................... | Executive Director, Programming Analysis and Evaluation. | Career Incumbent ................ | CA | ES | ................ | ................ | |
| | **OFFICE OF FINANCE** | | | | | | |
| Do .................... | Deputy Executive Director, Financial Services Center. | ......do ................................. | CA | ES | ................ | ................ | |
| | **OFFICE OF ACQUISITION, LOGISITICS AND CONSTRUCTION** | | | | | | |
| Do .................... | Principal Executive Director............................. | Karen Luann Brazell ............ | NA | ES | ................ | ................ | |
| Do .................... | Deputy Executive Director, Office of Acquisitions, Logistics and Construction. | Career Incumbent ................ | CA | ES | ................ | ................ | |
| Do .................... | Deputy Executive Director, Office of Construction and Facilities Management. | ......do ................................. | CA | ES | ................ | ................ | |
| Do .................... | Executive Director, Business Operations Center. | ......do ................................. | CA | ES | ................ | ................ | |
| Frederick, MD ......... | Chancellor, Veterans Affairs Acquisition Academy. | ......do ................................. | CA | ES | ................ | ................ | |
| | **OFFICE OF ACQUISITION AND MATERIEL MANAGEMENT** | | | | | | |
| Washington, DC ...... | Associate Executive Director, Logistics and Supply Management. | ......do ................................. | CA | ES | ................ | ................ | |
| | **OFFICE OF THE ASSISTANT SECRETARY FOR ENTERPRISE INTEGRATION** | | | | | | |
| Do .................... | Assistant Secretary for Enterprise Integration. | Vacant ................................. | PAS | EX | IV | ................ | |
| Do .................... | Principal Deputy Assistant Secretary ............... | Career Incumbent ................ | CA | ES | ................ | ................ | |
| Do .................... | Executive Director of the Veterans Affairs/Department of Defense Collaboration Service. | Vacant ................................. | ............ | ES | ................ | ................ | |
| Do .................... | Executive Director, National Center for Veterans Analysis and Statistics. | Career Incumbent ................ | CA | ES | ................ | ................ | |
| Do .................... | Executive Director, Data Governance and Analysis. | ......do ................................. | CA | ES | ................ | ................ | |
| Do .................... | Executive Director, Office of Performance Management. | ......do ................................. | CA | ES | ................ | ................ | |
| Do .................... | Senior Call Center Advisor, Architecture and Design. | Vacant ................................. | ............ | ES | ................ | ................ | |
| Do .................... | Executive Director, Office of Revolving Fund .... | ......do ................................. | ............ | ES | ................ | ................ | |
| Do .................... | Senior Advisor................................................. | Debra S Del Mar .................. | NA | ES | ................ | ................ | |
| Do .................... | Director, Enterprise Access and Integration...... | Vacant ................................. | ............ | ES | ................ | ................ | |
| Do .................... | Senior Advisor/Chief Veteran Experience Officer. | Lynda C Davis ..................... | NA | ES | ................ | ................ | |
| Do .................... | Deputy Chief Veterans Experience Officer ........ | Career Incumbent ................ | CA | ES | ................ | ................ | |

## DEPARTMENT OF VETERANS AFFAIRS—Continued

| Location | Position Title | Name of Incumbent | Type of Appt. | Pay Plan | Level, Grade, or Pay | Tenure | Expires |
|---|---|---|---|---|---|---|---|
| Chicago, IL............ | District Veterans Experience Officer (Midwest). | Career Incumbent ............... | CA | ES | ............... | ............... | |
| Los Angeles, CA...... | District Veterans Experience Officer (Pacific) ... | ......do .................... | CA | ES | ............... | ............... | |
| Dallas, TX | Executive Director, Patient Experience | ......do .................... | CA | ES | ............... | ............... | |
| Washington, DC ..... | Senior Advisor, Veterans Affairs Innovation Center, Care and Innovation. | Vacant .................... | ............ | ES | ............... | ............... | |
| Do .................... | Deputy Executive Director, Data Governance and Analytics, Office of Enterprise Integration. | ......do .................... | ............ | ES | ............... | ............... | |
| | **OFFICE OF POLICY** | | | | | | |
| Do .................... | Deputy Assistant Secretary for Policy................ | Career Incumbent ............... | CA | ES | ............... | ............... | |
| Do .................... | Executive Director ................................ | ......do .................... | CA | ES | ............... | ............... | |
| Do .................... | ......do .................... | ......do .................... | CA | ES | ............... | ............... | |
| | **OFFICE OF THE ASSISTANT SECRETARY FOR PUBLIC AND INTERGOVERNMENTAL AFFAIRS** | | | | | | |
| Do .................... | Assistant Secretary for Public and Intergovernmental Affairs. | James Eric Hutton .............. | PA | EX | IV | ............... | |
| Do .................... | Principal Deputy Assistant Secretary ............... | John E. Wagner .................... | NA | ES | ............... | ............... | |
| Do .................... | Senior Advisor ................................. | Lawrence J Purpuro............ | NA | ES | ............... | ............... | |
| Do .................... | Director of Media Affairs........................ | William Jordan Eason......... | SC | GS | 13 | ............... | |
| Do .................... | Speechwriter ................................. | Peter Ilych Kasperowicz...... | SC | GS | 15 | ............... | |
| | **OFFICE OF PUBLIC AFFAIRS** | | | | | | |
| Do .................... | Deputy Assistant Secretary, Office of Public Affairs. | Curtis E. Cashour................ | NA | ES | ............... | ............... | |
| Do .................... | Executive Director, Strategic Planning and Veterans Outreach. | Career Incumbent ............... | CA | ES | ............... | ............... | |
| Do .................... | Press Secretary ................................. | Christina Noel .................... | SC | GS | 13 | ............... | |
| | **OFFICE OF INTERGOVERNMENTAL AFFAIRS** | | | | | | |
| Do .................... | Deputy Assistant Secretary for Intergovernmental Affairs. | Thayer Lamont Verschoor.... | NA | ES | ............... | ............... | |
| Do .................... | Director, Office of Tribal Government Relations. | Career Incumbent ............... | CA | ES | ............... | ............... | |
| Do .................... | Director State and Local Government Relations. | John Nicholas Fish.............. | SC | GS | 15 | ............... | |
| | **OFFICE OF THE ASSISTANT SECRETARY FOR CONGRESSIONAL AND LEGISLATIVE AFFAIRS** | | | | | | |
| Do .................... | Assistant Secretary for Congressional and Legislative Affairs. | Brooks D Tucker.................. | PAS | EX | IV | ............... | |
| Do .................... | Principal Deputy Assistant Secretary for Congressional and Legislative Affairs. | Career Incumbent ............... | CA | ES | ............... | ............... | |
| Do .................... | Deputy Assistant Secretary for Congressional Affairs. | David J Balland.................. | NA | ES | ............... | ............... | |
| Do .................... | Special Assistant................................. | Christopher J Anderson....... | SC | GS | 14 | ............... | |
| | **OFFICE OF CONGRESSIONAL AFFAIRS** | | | | | | |
| Do .................... | Senior Advisor................................. | Cathleen A Haverstock ........ | NA | ES | ............... | ............... | |
| | **OFFICE OF THE ASSISTANT SECRETARY FOR INFORMATION AND TECHNOLOGY** | | | | | | |
| Do .................... | Assistant Secretary for Information and Technology. | James Paul Gfrerer ............. | PAS | EX | IV | ............... | |
| Do .................... | Principal Deputy Assistant Secretary for Information and Technology. | Career Incumbent ............... | CA | ES | ............... | ............... | |
| Do .................... | Deputy Chief Information Security Officer........ | Vacant .................... | ............ | ES | ............... | ............... | |
| Do .................... | Deputy Chief Information Officer.................. | Career Incumbent ............... | CA | ES | ............... | ............... | |
| Do .................... | Deputy Chief Information Officer, Account Management Office. | ......do .................... | CA | ES | ............... | ............... | |
| Do .................... | Deputy Chief Information Officer, Account Manager. | Vacant .................... | ............ | ES | ............... | ............... | |
| Do .................... | Deputy Chief Information Officer for Benefits, Account Management Office. | Career Incumbent ............... | CA | ES | ............... | ............... | |
| Do .................... | Deputy Chief Information Officer for Corporate, Account Management Office. | ......do .................... | CA | ES | ............... | ............... | |
| Do .................... | Deputy Chief Information Officer, Information Technology Resource Management. | ......do .................... | CA | ES | ............... | ............... | |
| Vancouver, WA........ | Executive Director, End User Operations .......... | ......do .................... | CA | ES | ............... | ............... | |
| Washington, DC ...... | Executive Director, Enterprise Portfolio Management Division. | ......do .................... | CA | ES | ............... | ............... | |
| Do .................... | Executive Director, It Systems Modernization .. | John A Short...................... | TA | ES | ............... | 3 Years | 09/01/20 |

## DEPARTMENT OF VETERANS AFFAIRS—Continued

| Location | Position Title | Name of Incumbent | Type of Appt. | Pay Plan | Level, Grade, or Pay | Tenure | Expires |
|---|---|---|---|---|---|---|---|
| Washington, DC ...... | Executive Director for Quality and Risk............ | Vacant ................................. | ............. | ES | ............... | ............... | |
| Do .................... | Executive Director, Office of Technical Integration. | Career Incumbent ................ | CA | ES | ............... | ............... | |
| Do .................... | Executive Director, Information Security Policy and Strategy. | ......do .................... | CA | ES | ............... | ............... | |
| Austin, TX............... | Executive Director, Enterprise Command Operations. | ......do .................... | CA | ES | ............... | ............... | |
| Washington, DC ...... | Executive Director, Demand Management ........ | ......do .................... | CA | ES | ............... | ............... | |
| Austin, TX............... | Executive Director, Solution Delivery ............. | ......do .................... | CA | ES | ............... | ............... | |
| Washington, DC ...... | Executive Director, Information Technology Program Integration/Chief of Staff. | ......do .................... | CA | ES | ............... | ............... | |
| Lafayette, LA........... | Executive Director, Acquisition Strategy and Category Management. | ......do .................... | CA | ES | ............... | ............... | |
| Washington, DC ...... | Chief Talent Management Officer ..................... | ......do .................... | CA | ES | ............... | ............... | |
| Do .................... | Deputy Assistant Secretary, Information Technology Development and Operations. | Vacant ................................. | ............. | ES | ............... | ............... | |
| Do .................... | Associate Deputy Assistant Secretary, Development, Security, and Operations. | Career Incumbent ................ | CA | ES | ............... | ............... | |
| Do .................... | Chief Technology Officer ................................. | ......do .................... | CA | ES | ............... | ............... | |
| Do .................... | Chief Data Technology Officer ......................... | Vacant ................................. | ............. | ES | ............... | ............... | |
| Do .................... | Chief Interoperability and Veteran Access Officer. | Career Incumbent ................ | CA | ES | ............... | ............... | |
| Do .................... | Senior Advisor, Health Data Management ........ | Vacant ................................. | ............. | ES | ............... | ............... | |
| Do .................... | Senior Advisor, Strategic Sourcing Transformation Management. | ......do .................... | ............. | ES | ............... | ............... | |
| Do .................... | Executive Director, Application Programming Interface (Api) Mgmt Platform. | ......do .................... | ............. | ES | ............... | ............... | |
| | **BOARD OF VETERANS' APPEALS** | | | | | | |
| Do .................... | Chairman, Board of Veterans Appeals ............. | Cheryl Mason ...................... | PAS | EX | IV | ............... | |
| Do .................... | Senior Advisor ................................................. | Elizabeth Anne Murphy....... | SC | GS | 13 | ............... | |
| | **NATIONAL CEMETERY ADMINISTRATION** | | | | | | |
| Do .................... | Under Secretary for Memorial Affairs ............. | Randy Clay Reeves............... | PAS | EX | III | ............... | |
| Do .................... | Principal Deputy Under Secretary for Memorial Affairs. | Career Incumbent ................ | CA | ES | ............... | ............... | |
| Do .................... | Chief of Staff ................................................... | ......do .................... | CA | ES | ............... | ............... | |
| Do .................... | Deputy Under Secretary for Field Programs and Cemetery. | ......do .................... | CA | ES | ............... | ............... | |
| Do .................... | Deputy Under Secretary for Management........ | ......do .................... | CA | ES | ............... | ............... | |
| Do .................... | Associate Director, Office of Field Programs...... | ......do .................... | CA | ES | ............... | ............... | |
| Philadelphia, PA...... | Executive Director, North Atlantic District ....... | ......do .................... | CA | ES | ............... | ............... | |
| Oakland, CA ........... | Executive Director, Pacific District.................... | ......do .................... | CA | ES | ............... | ............... | |
| Decatur, GA ............ | Executive Director, Southeast District.............. | ......do .................... | CA | ES | ............... | ............... | |
| Indianapolis, IN ...... | Executive Director, Midwest District ................ | ......do .................... | CA | ES | ............... | ............... | |
| Washington, DC ...... | Executive Director, Cemetery Operations.......... | ......do .................... | CA | ES | ............... | ............... | |
| Do .................... | Executive Director, Human Capital Management. | ......do .................... | CA | ES | ............... | ............... | |
| Do .................... | Executive Director, Strategy and Analysis........ | ......do .................... | CA | ES | ............... | ............... | |
| Riverside, CA........... | Executive Director, Riverside National Cemetery. | ......do .................... | CA | ES | ............... | ............... | |
| Calverton, NY.......... | Executive Director, Calverton National Cemetery. | ......do .................... | CA | ES | ............... | ............... | |
| St. Louis, MO........... | Executive Director, Jefferson Barrack National Cemetery. | ......do .................... | CA | ES | ............... | ............... | |
| Minneapolis, MN ..... | Executive Director, Ft. Snelling National Cemetery. | ......do .................... | CA | ES | ............... | ............... | |
| Florida, FL............... | Executive Director, Florida National Cemetery. | ......do .................... | CA | ES | ............... | ............... | |
| Washington, DC ...... | Senior Advisor................................................. | Melissa Sue Decker.............. | TA | ES | ............... | ............... | 07/20/21 |
| Do .................... | Executive Director, Office of Public Engagement. | Vacant ................................. | ............. | ES | ............... | ............... | |
| Do .................... | Executive Director, Engagement and Memorial Innovations. | Career Incumbent ................ | CA | ES | ............... | ............... | |
| Denver, CO ............. | Executive Director, Continental District........... | ......do .................... | CA | ES | ............... | ............... | |
| | **VETERANS BENEFITS ADMINISTRATION** | | | | | | |
| Washington, DC ...... | Under Secretary for Benefits ........................... | Paul Reynold Lawrence ....... | PAS | EX | III | ............... | |
| Do .................... | Principal Deputy Under Secretary for Benefits. | Career Incumbent ................ | CA | ES | ............... | ............... | |
| Do .................... | Chief of Staff ................................................... | ......do .................... | CA | ES | ............... | ............... | |
| Do .................... | Deputy Chief of Staff........................................ | ......do .................... | CA | ES | ............... | ............... | |
| Do .................... | Deputy Under Secretary for Field Operations... | ......do .................... | CA | ES | ............... | ............... | |
| Do .................... | Director, Office of Management ........................ | Vacant ................................. | ............. | ES | ............... | ............... | |

## DEPARTMENT OF VETERANS AFFAIRS—Continued

| Location | Position Title | Name of Incumbent | Type of Appt. | Pay Plan | Level, Grade, or Pay | Tenure | Expires |
|---|---|---|---|---|---|---|---|
| Nashville, TN | Chief Production Officer | Career Incumbent | CA | ES | | | |
| Denver, CO | District Executive Director, Continental District. | ......do | CA | ES | | | |
| St. Louis, MO | District Executive Director, Midwest District | ......do | CA | ES | | | |
| Phoenix, AZ | District Executive Director Pacific District | ......do | CA | ES | | | |
| Nashville, TN | District Executive Director, Southeast District | Vacant | | ES | | | |
| Washington, DC | Executive Director, Administration and Facilities. | Career Incumbent | CA | ES | | | |
| Do | Executive Director Appeals Management Center. | ......do | CA | ES | | | |
| Austin, TX | Executive Director, Business Process Integration. | Vacant | | ES | | | |
| Washington, DC | Executive Director, Compensation Service | Career Incumbent | CA | ES | | | |
| Do | Executive Director Education Service | ......do | CA | ES | | | |
| Philadelphia, PA | Executive Director Insurance Service | ......do | CA | ES | | | |
| Washington, DC | Executive Director Office of Talent Management. | Vacant | | ES | | | |
| Do | Executive Director, Office of Transition & Economic Development. | Career Incumbent | CA | ES | | | |
| Do | Executive Director, Pension and Fiduciary Service. | ......do | CA | ES | | | |
| Salt Lake City, UT | Executive Director, Salt Lake City Regional Office. | ......do | CA | ES | | | |
| Washington, DC | Executive Director, Strategic Initiatives & Collaboration. | ......do | CA | ES | | | |
| Do | Executive Director Vocational Rehabilitation and Employment. | ......do | CA | ES | | | |
| Do | Deputy Executive Director, Appeals Management Center. | ......do | CA | ES | | | |
| Do | Deputy Executive Director, Contract Medical Disability Examinations. | ......do | CA | ES | | | |
| Do | Assistant Deputy Under Secretary for Field Operations-National Work Queue. | ......do | CA | ES | | | |
| Do | Assistant Deputy Under Secretary for Field Operations, Outreach and Stakeholder Engagement. | ......do | CA | ES | | | |
| Do | Assistant Deputy Under Secretary for Field Operations National Contact Centers. | Vacant | | ES | | | |
| Do | Senior Advisor, Process Integration and Acceleration. | ......do | | ES | | | |
| Do | Senior Advisor, Strategic Change Management. | Crystal Myung | TA | ES | | | 09/28/21 |
| Do | ......do | Andrea Lee | TA | ES | | | 09/14/21 |
| | *Regional Office Directors* | | | | | | |
| Atlanta, GA | Executive Director, Atlanta Regional Office | Career Incumbent | CA | ES | | | |
| Baltimore, MD | Executive Director, Baltimore Regional Office | ......do | CA | ES | | | |
| Buffalo, NY | Executive Director, Buffalo Regional Office | ......do | CA | ES | | | |
| Chicago, IL | Executive Director, Chicago Regional Office | Vacant | | ES | | | |
| Cleveland, OH | Executive Director, Cleveland Regional Office | Career Incumbent | CA | ES | | | |
| Columbia, SC | Executive Director, Columbus Regional Office | ......do | CA | ES | | | |
| Lakewood, CO | Executive Director, Denver Regional Office | ......do | CA | ES | | | |
| Detroit, MI | Executive Director, Detroit Regional Office | ......do | CA | ES | | | |
| Houston, TX | Executive Director, Houston Regional Office | ......do | CA | ES | | | |
| Indianapolis, IN | Executive Director, Indianapolis Regional Office. | ......do | CA | ES | | | |
| Jackson, MS | Executive Director, Jackson Regional Office | ......do | CA | ES | | | |
| Lincoln, NE | Executive Director, Lincoln Regional Office | ......do | CA | ES | | | |
| Little Rock, AR | Executive Director, Little Rock Regional Office. | Vacant | | ES | | | |
| Los Angeles, CA | Executive Director, Los Angeles Regional Office. | Career Incumbent | CA | ES | | | |
| Louisville, KY | Executive Director, Louisville Regional Office | ......do | CA | ES | | | |
| Manila, Philippines | Executive Director, Manila Regional Office | ......do | CA | ES | | | |
| Milwaukee, WI | Executive Director, Milwaukee Regional Office | ......do | CA | ES | | | |
| Montgomery, AL | Executive Director, Montgomery Regional Office. | ......do | CA | ES | | | |
| Muskogee, OK | Executive Director, Muskogee Regional Office | ......do | CA | ES | | | |
| Nashville, TN | Executive Director, Nashville Regional Office | ......do | CA | ES | | | |
| New Orleans, LA | Executive Director, New Orleans Regional Office. | ......do | CA | ES | | | |
| New York New York, NY. | Executive Director, New York Regional Office | ......do | CA | ES | | | |
| Oakland, CA | Executive Director, Oakland Regional Office | ......do | CA | ES | | | |

## DEPARTMENT OF VETERANS AFFAIRS—Continued

| Location | Position Title | Name of Incumbent | Type of Appt. | Pay Plan | Level, Grade, or Pay | Tenure | Expires |
|---|---|---|---|---|---|---|---|
| Philadelphia, PA...... | Executive Director, Philadelphia Regional Office. | Career Incumbent ............... | CA | ES | ............... | ............... | |
| Phoenix, AZ ............ | Executive Director, Phoenix Regional Office...... | ......do ...................... | CA | ES | ............... | ............... | |
| Pittsburgh, PA........ | Executive Director, Pittsburgh Regional Office . | ......do ...................... | CA | ES | ............... | ............... | |
| Portland, OR.......... | Executive Director, Portland Regional Office..... | Vacant ...................... | ............. | ES | ............... | ............... | |
| Providence, RI ........ | Executive Director Providence Regional Office . | ......do ...................... | ............. | ES | ............... | ............... | |
| Roanoke, VA............ | Executive Director, Roanoke Regional Office..... | Career Incumbent ............... | CA | ES | ............... | ............... | |
| San Diego, CA ........ | Executive Director San Diego Regional Office... | ......do ...................... | CA | ES | ............... | ............... | |
| San Juan, Puerto Rico. | Executive Director, San Juan Regional Office ... | ......do ...................... | CA | ES | ............... | ............... | |
| Seattle, WA ............ | Executive Director, Seattle Regional Office ...... | ......do ...................... | CA | ES | ............... | ............... | |
| St. Louis, MO.......... | Executive Director, St. Louis Regional Office .... | ......do ...................... | CA | ES | ............... | ............... | |
| St. Paul, MN ........... | Executive Director, Saint Paul Regional Office . | ......do ...................... | CA | ES | ............... | ............... | |
| St. Petersburg, FL ... | Executive Director, St. Petersburg Regional Office. | ......do ...................... | CA | ES | ............... | ............... | |
| Winston Salem, NC. | Executive Director, Winston-Salem Regional Office. | ......do ...................... | CA | ES | ............... | ............... | |
| Waco, TX ................ | Executive Director, Waco Regional Office........... | ......do ...................... | CA | ES | ............... | ............... | |
| | *Veterans Health Administration* | | | | | | |
| Washington, DC ...... | Under Secretary for Health ....................... | Vacant ...................... | PAS | EX | III | ............... | |
| Do .................... | Assistant Under Secretary for Health for Operations. | Career Incumbent ............... | CA | ES | ............... | ............... | |
| Do .................... | Deputy to the Assistant Under Secretary for Health for Operations. | ......do ...................... | CA | ES | ............... | ............... | |
| Do .................... | Chief of Staff ............................... | ......do ...................... | CA | ES | ............... | ............... | |
| Do .................... | Deputy Chief of Staff Veterans Health Administration. | Vacant ...................... | ............. | ES | ............... | ............... | |
| Do .................... | Senior Advisor ............................... | ......do ...................... | ............. | ES | ............... | ............... | |
| Do .................... | Executive Director Office of Communication..... | Career Incumbent ............... | CA | ES | ............... | ............... | |
| Do .................... | Chief Officer Workforce Management and Consulting. | Vacant ...................... | ............. | ES | ............... | ............... | |
| Do .................... | Deputy Chief Officer, Workforce Management and Consulting. | Career Incumbent ............... | CA | ES | ............... | ............... | |
| Do .................... | Associate Chief Financial Officer for Resource Management. | ......do ...................... | CA | ES | ............... | ............... | |
| Do .................... | Executive Director Strategic Planning and Analysis. | ......do ...................... | CA | ES | ............... | ............... | |
| Do .................... | Chief Officer Readjustment Counseling Service. | ......do ...................... | CA | ES | ............... | ............... | |
| Do .................... | Deputy Chief Strategy Officer ........................... | ......do ...................... | CA | ES | ............... | ............... | |
| Bay Pines, FL .......... | Executive Director Health Informatics ............. | Vacant ...................... | XS | OT | ............... | ............... | |
| Washington, DC ...... | Deputy Chief Learning Officer, Employee Education System. | Career Incumbent ............... | CA | ES | ............... | ............... | |
| Do .................... | Executive Director, Rural Health ...................... | ......do ...................... | CA | ES | ............... | ............... | |
| Do .................... | Chief Learning Officer, Employee Education System. | ......do ...................... | CA | ES | ............... | ............... | |
| Do .................... | Executive Director, Homeless Program.............. | ......do ...................... | CA | ES | ............... | ............... | |
| Cincinnati, OH ........ | Executive Director, National Center for Organizational Development. | ......do ...................... | CA | ES | ............... | ............... | |
| Do .................... | Deputy Executive Director, National Center for Organizational Development. | Vacant ...................... | ............. | ES | ............... | ............... | |
| Washington, DC ...... | Executive Director, Revenue Operations........... | ......do ...................... | ............. | ES | ............... | ............... | |
| Do .................... | Senior Health Technology Officer ...................... | Career Incumbent ............... | CA | ES | ............... | ............... | |
| Do .................... | Executive Director, Healthcare Leadership Talent Institute. | Vacant ...................... | ............. | ES | ............... | ............... | |
| Do .................... | Executive Director, Administration and Support Services. | Career Incumbent ............... | CA | ES | ............... | ............... | |
| Do .................... | Deputy Executive Director, Clinical Integration. | Clinton Greenstone .............. | XS | OT | ............... | ............... | |
| Do .................... | Executive Director for Electronic Health Records Modernization. | John H Windom ................... | TA | ES | ............... | ............... | 12/07/20 |
| Do .................... | Executive Director Care Management and Social Work Services. | Career Incumbent ............... | CA | ES | ............... | ............... | |
| Do .................... | Chief Officer, Disability and Medical Assessment. | ......do ...................... | CA | ES | ............... | ............... | |
| Do .................... | Deputy Chief Logistics Officer, Veterans Health Administration. | Vacant ...................... | ............. | ES | ............... | ............... | |
| Do .................... | Executive Director, Human Resources Operations. | Career Incumbent ............... | CA | ES | ............... | ............... | |
| Do .................... | Chief Officer, Modernization of Veterans Administration Central Office. | Vacant ...................... | ............. | ES | ............... | ............... | |
| Do .................... | Chief Officer, Modernization of Va Central Office. | Lucille B Beck...................... | TA | ES | ............... | ............... | 04/12/23 |

## DEPARTMENT OF VETERANS AFFAIRS—Continued

| Location | Position Title | Name of Incumbent | Type of Appt. | Pay Plan | Level, Grade, or Pay | Tenure | Expires |
|---|---|---|---|---|---|---|---|
| Washington, DC ...... | Senior Advisor............................................. | Christine Elizabeth Bader ... | NA | ES | ............... | ............... | |
| Do ................... | Chief Audit Executive................................. | Vacant | ............ | ES | ............... | ............... | |
| Do ................... | Deputy Executive Director, Performance Improvement and Reporting. | Career Incumbent ............... | CA | ES | ............... | ............... | |
| Do ................... | Associate Executive Director, Geriatrics and Extended Care. | ......do ...... | CA | ES | ............... | ............... | |
| Do ................... | Executive Director, Member Services................. | ......do ...... | CA | ES | ............... | ............... | |
| Do ................... | Deputy Executive Director, Human Resources Operations. | ......do ...... | CA | ES | ............... | ............... | |
| Superior, WI............ | Executive Director, Revenue Operations............ | ......do ...... | CA | ES | ............... | ............... | |
| Washington, DC ...... | Executive Director, Office of Healthcare Transformation. | ......do ...... | CA | ES | ............... | ............... | |
| Do ................... | National Director Suicide Prevention ............... | Matthew Alan Miller............ | XS | OT | ............... | ............... | |
| Do ................... | Chief Consultant to the Principal Deputy Under Secretary for Health. | Jennifer Macdonald ............ | XS | OT | ............... | ............... | |
| Do ................... | Chief Strategy Officer................................ | Career Incumbent ............... | CA | ES | ............... | ............... | |
| Do ................... | Executive Director, Human Capital Management. | ......do ...... | CA | ES | ............... | ............... | |
| Do ................... | Deputy to the Executive Director for Access to Care. | Susan Riga Kirsh ................ | XS | OT | ............... | ............... | |
| Do ................... | Deputy Executive Director Member Services .... | Career Incumbent ............... | CA | ES | ............... | ............... | |
| Do ................... | Executive Director, Delivery Operations............ | ......do ...... | CA | ES | ............... | ............... | |
| Manchester, NH ...... | Executive Director, Policy and Strategic Planning. | ......do ...... | CA | ES | ............... | ............... | |
| Washington, DC ...... | Senior Advisor............................................. | Vacant ................ | ............ | ES | ............... | ............... | |
| Do ................... | Executive Director, Veterans Affairs Logistics Redesign Program Office. | ......do ...... | ............ | ES | ............... | ............... | |
| Do ................... | Deputy Executive Director of Human Capital Management. | ......do ...... | ............ | ES | ............... | ............... | |
| Cincinnati, OH ........ | Deputy Director, National Center for Organization Development. | ......do ...... | ............ | ES | ............... | ............... | |
| Washington, DC ...... | Chief Human Capital Management ................... | Career Incumbent ............... | CA | ES | ............... | ............... | |
| Do ................... | Senior Advisor............................................. | Vacant ................ | XS | SL | ............... | ............... | |
| Los Angeles, CA....... | Executive Director, Community Engagement and Reintegration Service (Visn 22). | Career Incumbent ............... | CA | ES | ............... | ............... | |
| Nashville, TN.......... | Chief Medical Officer Visn 9 ...................... | Vacant ................ | XS | OT | ............... | ............... | |
| Memphis, TX .......... | Health System Administrator (Memphis, Tn) ... | Career Incumbent ............... | CA | ES | ............... | ............... | |
| Los Angeles, CA....... | Executive Director of Clinical Care (Visn 22).... | Vacant ................ | ............ | ES | ............... | ............... | |
| | *Title 38 Positions* | | | | | | |
| Washington, DC ...... | Chief Consultant, Pharmacy Benefits Management Services. | Michael A Valentino ............ | XS | OT | ............... | ............... | |
| Do ................... | Deputy Chief Officer Office of Research Oversight. | Peter N Poon...................... | XS | OT | ............... | ............... | |
| Do ................... | Director, Continuum of Care and General Mental Health. | Marsden H Mcguire ............. | XS | OT | ............... | ............... | |
| Do ................... | Director, Nutrition and Food Service, Specialty Care Services. | Anne Utech...................... | XS | OT | ............... | ............... | |
| Do ................... | Chief Nursing Officer ........................ | Beth Taylor ...................... | XS | OT | ............... | ............... | |
| Fort Howard, MD .... | Director Optometry Service ........................ | John C Townsend ................ | XS | AD | ............... | ............... | |
| Detroit, MI............. | Executive Director, Medical Center (Detroit)...... | Pamela J Reeves................. | XS | OT | ............... | ............... | |
| Cleveland, OH ........ | Director Podiatry Service ........................ | Jeffrey M Robbins ............. | XS | AD | ............... | ............... | |
| Washington, DC ...... | National Director of Medicine........................ | Vacant ................ | XS | OT | ............... | ............... | |
| Honolulu, HI........... | Director Veterans Affairs Pacific Islands Healthcare System. | ......do ...... | XS | OT | ............... | ............... | |
| San Diego, CA ........ | Executive Director, Medical Center (San Diego). | Robert Smith ...................... | XS | OT | ............... | ............... | |
| Pittsburgh, PA........ | Director Veterans Integrated Service Network . | Vacant ................ | XS | OT | ............... | ............... | |
| Bay Pines, FL ......... | ......do ...... | Miguel H Lapuz M.D............. | XS | OT | ............... | ............... | |
| Portland, OR........... | ......do ...... | Vacant ................ | XS | OT | ............... | ............... | |
| Hampton, VA .......... | Director, Chaplain Service ........................ | Juliana Lesher ................ | XS | OT | ............... | ............... | |
| Washington, DC ...... | Deputy Chief Patient Care Services Officer ...... | Vacant ................ | XS | OT | ............... | ............... | |
| Do ................... | Chief Consultant to the Principal Deputy Under Secretary for Health. | ......do ...... | XS | OT | ............... | ............... | |
| Pittsburgh, PA........ | Chief Medical Officer Visn 4 ........................ | Timothy R Burke M.D........ | XS | OT | ............... | ............... | |
| Washington, DC ...... | Deputy to the Assistant Under Secretary for Health for Support Services. | Edward Litvin ...................... | XS | OT | ............... | ............... | |
| Linthicum Hghts, MD. | Chief Medical Officer Visn 5 ........................ | Raymond Chung.................... | XS | OT | ............... | ............... | |
| Washington, DC ...... | Deputy Chief Research and Development Officer (Field Operations). | Vacant ................ | XS | OT | ............... | ............... | |
| Ann Arbor, MI.......... | National Program Director, Nuclear Medicine and Radiation Safety Service. | David Bushnell...................... | XS | OT | ............... | ............... | |
| Washington, DC ...... | National Director, Anesthesia Services ............. | Vacant ................ | XS | OT | ............... | ............... | |

## DEPARTMENT OF VETERANS AFFAIRS—Continued

| Location | Position Title | Name of Incumbent | Type of Appt. | Pay Plan | Level, Grade, or Pay | Tenure | Expires |
|---|---|---|---|---|---|---|---|
| Washington, DC ...... | Chief Officer, Womens Health Services .............. | Patricia M Hayes................... | XS | OT | .............. | ............... | |
| Ann Arbor, MI......... | Chief Officer, Policy and Services ....................... | Vacant .............................. | XS | OT | .............. | ............... | |
| Seattle, WA .............. | Executive Director, Spinal Cord Injury and Disorders Services. | Itala Wickremasinghe .......... | XS | OT | .............. | ............... | |
| Washington, DC ...... | Deputy Under Secretary for Health for Discovery, Education, Affiliates and Network (Dean). | Carolyn M Clancy................ | XS | OT | .............. | ............... | |
| Hines, IL ................. | Chief Medical Officer Visn 12 ........................... | Praveen Mehta ...................... | XS | OT | .............. | ............... | |
| Washington, DC ...... | Director, Rehabilitation Research and Development Service. | Patricia Dorn ....................... | XS | OT | .............. | ............... | |
| Ann Arbor, MI......... | Executive Director, Clinical Network Manager . | Vacant .............................. | XS | OT | .............. | ............... | |
| Bedford, MA ........... | Chief Medical Officer Visn 1 ............................. | Lisa S Lehmann .................... | XS | OT | .............. | ............... | |
| Washington, DC ...... | Assistant Deputy Chief Patient Care Services .. | Vacant .............................. | XS | OT | .............. | ............... | |
| Do .................... | Executive Director for Health Information Governance. | Marcia Insley....................... | XS | OT | .............. | ............... | |
| Do .................... | Chief Improvement and Analytics Officer.......... | Joseph Francis M.D............. | XS | OT | .............. | ............... | |
| Do .................... | Chief Health Informatics Officer ...................... | Vacant .............................. | XS | OT | .............. | ............... | |
| Do .................... | Executive Director, Geriatrics and Extended Care Services. | Scotte Hartronft ................... | XS | OT | .............. | ............... | |
| Do .................... | Deputy Chief Academics Officer ........................ | Karen Sanders...................... | XS | OT | .............. | ............... | |
| Do .................... | Executive Director, Office of Emergency Management. | Paul Kim ............................. | XS | OT | .............. | ............... | |
| Kansas City, MO ..... | Veterans Integrated Service Network Director-Kansas City, Mo. | William Patterson ............... | XS | OT | .............. | ............... | |
| Washington, DC ...... | Chief Officer, Office of Research Oversight........ | Douglas Bannerman .............. | XS | OT | .............. | ............... | |
| Silver Spring, MD ... | Assistant Deputy Under Secretary for Health for Health Informatics. | Charles C Hume.................... | XS | OT | .............. | ............... | |
| Ann Arbor, MI......... | Executive Director National Center for Patient Safety. | William P Gunnar ................. | XS | OT | .............. | ............... | |
| Washington, DC ...... | Chief Medical Officer for Electronic Health Record Modernization. | Laura Kroupa ....................... | XS | OT | .............. | ............... | |
| Do .................... | Director, Organizational Integrity and Information Synchronization. | Caitlin A O'Brien................ | XS | OT | .............. | ............... | |
| Do .................... | Chief Medical Officer, Visn 06........................... | Vacant .............................. | XS | OT | .............. | ............... | |
| Do .................... | Executive Director Procurement and Logistics Officer. | Andrew Centineo.................. | XS | OT | .............. | ............... | |
| Do .................... | Assistant Under Secretary for Health for Dentistry. | Patricia E Arola.................... | XS | OT | .............. | ............... | |
| Do .................... | Deputy Director, Office of Patient Care Services and Cultural Transformation. | Vacant .............................. | XS | OT | .............. | ............... | |
| Durham, NC ........... | Executive Director, Diagnostic Services............. | Robert H Sherrier ............... | XS | OT | .............. | ............... | |
| Washington, DC ...... | Deputy to the Deputy Under Secretary for Health for Policy and Services. | Vacant .............................. | XS | OT | .............. | ............... | |
| Do .................... | Deputy Chief Patient Care Services Office for Public Health. | ......do ............................... | XS | OT | .............. | ............... | |
| Do .................... | Director, Health Services Research and Development Service. | David Atkins........................ | XS | OT | .............. | ............... | |
| Do .................... | Associate Chief Officer for Assistant Deputy Under Secretary for Health Operations. | Vacant .............................. | XS | OT | .............. | ............... | |
| Palo Alto, CA .......... | Chief Consultant, Population Health ................ | Larry A Mole....................... | XS | OT | .............. | ............... | |
| Washington, DC ...... | Executive Director for Office of Mental Health & Suicide Prevention. | J. David Carroll ................... | XS | OT | .............. | ............... | |
| Do .................... | Senior Medical Advisor....................................... | Thomas Otoole...................... | XS | OT | .............. | ............... | |
| Do .................... | National Director of Surgery ............................ | Vacant .............................. | XS | OT | .............. | ............... | |
| Do .................... | Chief Consultant, Primary Care........................ | ......do ............................... | XS | OT | .............. | ............... | |
| Do .................... | Deputy Chief Nursing Officer ............................ | B. Alan Bernstein ............... | XS | OT | .............. | ............... | |
| Atlanta, GA ............ | Chief Medical Officer Visn 7 ............................. | Ajay K Dhawan M.D. ......... | XS | OT | .............. | ............... | |
| Iowa City, IA............ | National Director, Pathology and Laboratory Medicine Service. | Michael S Icardi .................. | XS | OT | .............. | ............... | |
| Richmond, VA.......... | National Director, Radiation Oncology Program (Physician). | Michael P Hagan.................. | XS | OT | .............. | ............... | |
| Washington, DC ...... | Medical Inspector.............................................. | Erica Scavella ...................... | XS | OT | .............. | ............... | |
| Do .................... | Chief Consultant Occupational Health .............. | Vacant .............................. | XS | OT | .............. | ............... | |
| Do .................... | Executive Director, National Center for Ethics in Health Care. | ......do ............................... | XS | OT | .............. | ............... | |
| Do .................... | Deputy Chief Readjustment Counselor.............. | Alfred Ozanian ..................... | XS | OT | .............. | ............... | |
| Do .................... | Executive Director for Connected Care.............. | Kathleen L Frisbee............... | XS | OT | .............. | ............... | |
| Durham, NC ........... | Chief Consultant for Preventive Medicine........ | Jane Kim............................. | XS | OT | .............. | ............... | |
| Washington, DC ...... | Executive Director, Office of Veterans Affairs/Department of Defense Health Affairs. | Vacant .............................. | XS | OT | .............. | ............... | |
| Do .................... | Assistant Deputy Under Secretary for Health for Quality, Safety, and Value. | Joel Roos ............................. | XS | OT | .............. | ............... | |

## DEPARTMENT OF VETERANS AFFAIRS—Continued

| Location | Position Title | Name of Incumbent | Type of Appt. | Pay Plan | Level, Grade, or Pay | Tenure | Expires |
|---|---|---|---|---|---|---|---|
| Washington, DC ...... | National Director, Prosthetic and Sensory Aids Service, Rehabilitation and Prosthetic Services. | Penny L Nechanicky ............ | XS | OT | ............... | ............... | |
| Do .................... | Chief Consultant, Post Deployment Health...... | Vacant ...................... | XS | OT | ............... | ............... | |
| Do .................... | Deputy Chief, Research and Development Officer. | Wendy N Tenhula................ | XS | OT | ............... | ............... | |
| Do .................... | Deputy Director, Office of Mental Health Operations. | Clifford Smith..................... | XS | OT | ............... | ............... | |
| Do .................... | Executive Director, Rehabilitation and Prosthetic. | Vacant ...................... | XS | OT | ............... | ............... | |
| North Chicago, IL.... | Executive Director, Medical Center (North Chicago). | Robert Buckley ..................... | XS | OT | ............... | ............... | |
| Kansas City, MO ..... | Chief Medical Officer, Visn 15............................ | Kanan Chatterjee................ | XS | OT | ............... | ............... | |
| Washington, DC ...... | Deputy Executive Director, National Center for Patient Safety. | Vacant ...................... | XS | OT | ............... | ............... | |
| Do .................... | National Program Director, Ophthalmology ...... | Glenn Cockerham................ | XS | OT | ............... | ............... | |
| Do .................... | National Director, Physical Medicine and Rehabilitation Services. | Joel Scholten........................ | XS | OT | ............... | ............... | |
| Baltimore, MD........ | Director, Biomedical Research and Development Service. | Christopher T Bever Jr. ....... | XS | OT | ............... | ............... | |
| Washington, DC ...... | Deputy Under Secretary for Health .................. | Richard Stone ..................... | XS | OT | ............... | ............... | |
| Do .................... | Executive Director, Office of Patient Advocacy.. | Ann E Doran........................ | XS | OT | ............... | ............... | |
| Do .................... | Deputy Under Secretary for Health for Organizational Excellence. | Gerard R Cox ...................... | XS | OT | ............... | ............... | |
| Vancouver, WA........ | Chief Medical Officer, Visn 20......................... | Chris Curry......................... | XS | OT | ............... | ............... | |
| Albany, NY.............. | Director Veterans Integrated Service Network . | Joan McInerney ................... | XS | AD | ............... | ............... | |
| Washington, DC ...... | Deputy Principal Deputy Under Secretary for Health. | Vacant ...................... | XS | OT | ............... | ............... | |
| Orlando, FL ........... | Deputy Chief Learning Officer ......................... | ......do ...................... | XS | OT | ............... | ............... | |
| Washington, DC ...... | Executive Director, Office of Health Equity...... | Ernest Moy ......................... | XS | OT | ............... | ............... | |
| Do .................... | Deputy to the Assistant Under Secretary for Health for Community Care. | Mark Upton ........................ | XS | OT | ............... | ............... | |
| Do .................... | Assistant Deputy Under Secretary for Health for Integrity. | David Chiesa ...................... | XS | OT | ............... | ............... | |
| Do .................... | Assistant Deputy Under Secretary for Clinical Operations. | Teresa D Boyd ..................... | XS | OT | ............... | ............... | |
| Do .................... | Deputy Assistant Deputy Under Secretary for Health for Clinical Operations. | Vacant ...................... | XS | OT | ............... | ............... | |
| Do .................... | Director, Office of Patient Centered Care and Cultural Transformation. | ......do ...................... | XS | OT | ............... | ............... | |
| Do .................... | Deputy Under Secretary for Health for Policy and Services. | ......do ...................... | XS | OT | ............... | ............... | |
| Do .................... | Executive Director, Office of Strategic Integration. | ......do ...................... | XS | OT | ............... | ............... | |
| Do .................... | Director, Human Immunodeficiency Virus/Hepatitis C Virus and Public Health Pathogens Program. | David B Ross ....................... | XS | OT | ............... | ............... | |
| Do .................... | Deputy to the Assistant Under Secretary for Health for Patient Care Service. | Maria Llorente...................... | XS | OT | ............... | ............... | |
| Do .................... | Director of Physician Assistant Services............ | Scot Burroughs ..................... | XS | OT | ............... | ............... | |
| Do .................... | Chief Officer, Office of Connected Care.............. | Neil Evans ......................... | XS | OT | ............... | ............... | |
| Do .................... | Director, Bioinformatics............................ | James L Breeling ............. | XS | OT | ............... | ............... | |
| Bay Pines, FL ......... | Chief Medical Officer Visn 8........................ | Edward Cutolo..................... | XS | OT | ............... | ............... | |
| Washington, DC ...... | Chief Officer for Specialty Care Services .......... | Vacant ...................... | XS | OT | ............... | ............... | |
| Minneapolis, MN..... | Chief Medical Officer Visn 23 ......................... | John Smyrski....................... | XS | OT | ............... | ............... | |
| Washington, DC ...... | Chief Research and Development Officer .......... | Rachel B Ramoni................. | XS | OT | ............... | ............... | |
| Do .................... | Chief Academic Affiliations Officer.................... | Marjorie Bowman............... | XS | OT | ............... | ............... | |
| Mare Island(Nav Shipyd), CA. | Chief Medical Officer Visn 21 ......................... | Vacant ...................... | XS | OT | ............... | ............... | |
| Anchorage, AK........ | Executive Director, Medical Center (Anchorage). | Timothy Ballard .................. | XS | OT | ............... | ............... | |
| Washington, DC ...... | Executive Director, Primary Care..................... | Angela Denietolis ............... | XS | OT | ............... | ............... | |
| Do .................... | Chief Officer for Policy and Services .................. | Cassandra Law.................... | XS | OT | ............... | ............... | |
| Arlington, TX.......... | Chief Medical Officer Visn 17 ......................... | Wendell Jones ..................... | XS | OT | ............... | ............... | |
| Long Beach, CA....... | Chief Medical Officer Visn 22 ......................... | Araceli Revote..................... | XS | OT | ............... | ............... | |
| Washington, DC ...... | Director, Program Research Integrity Development and Education. | Mary Klote ......................... | XS | OT | ............... | ............... | |
| Do .................... | Director, Veterans Crisis Line.......................... | Vacant ...................... | XS | OT | ............... | ............... | |
| Do .................... | Deputy Chief Medical Officer........................... | Kevin Kearns ...................... | XS | OT | ............... | ............... | |
| Do .................... | Director Clinical Science Research and Development Service. | Theresa C Gleason ............. | XS | OT | ............... | ............... | |
| Glendale, CO .......... | Chief Medical Officer Visn 19 ......................... | Leigh Anderson.................... | XS | OT | ............... | ............... | |
| Washington, DC ...... | Executive Director for Access............................. | Steven Lieberman ................ | XS | OT | ............... | ............... | |

## DEPARTMENT OF VETERANS AFFAIRS—Continued

| Location | Position Title | Name of Incumbent | Type of Appt. | Pay Plan | Level, Grade, or Pay | Tenure | Expires |
|---|---|---|---|---|---|---|---|
| Washington, DC ...... | Executive Director, Telehealth Services ............. | Kevin Galpin.................... | XS | OT | ............. | ............. | |
| Brecksville, OH ....... | Chief Nursing Informatics Officer.................... | Sheila Ochylski.................... | XS | OT | ............. | ............. | |
| Washington, DC ...... | Deputy Assistant Deputy Under Secretary for Health for Quality, Safety, and Value. | Saurabha Bhatnagar............ | XS | OT | ............. | ............. | |
| Do .................... | Assistant Under Secretary for Health for Community Care. | Kameron Matthews.............. | XS | OT | ............. | ............. | |
| Do .................... | Executive Director, Performance Improvement and Reporting. | Vacant ............ | XS | OT | ............. | ............. | |
| Bronx, NY ............. | Chief Medical Officer Visn 2 ............................. | ......do ........... | XS | OT | ............. | ............. | |
| Cincinnati, OH ........ | Chief Medical Officer Visn 10 ........................... | ......do ........... | XS | OT | ............. | ............. | |
| Ann Arbor, MI.......... | Deputy Executive Director, National Center for Patient Safety. | Edward Yackel.................... | XS | OT | ............. | ............. | |
| Washington, DC ...... | Assistant Under Secretary for Health for Support Services. | Vacant .................... | XS | OT | ............. | ............. | |
| | *Veterans Integrated Service Network Directors* | | | | | | |
| Bedford, MA ........... | Executive Director, Veterans Integrated Systems Network (Visn1). | Career Incumbent ............... | CA | ES | ............. | ............. | |
| Albany, NY.............. | Executive Director, Veterans Integrated Service Network (Visn 2). | Vacant .................... | ............. | ES | ............. | ............. | |
| Pittsburgh, PA........ | Executive Director, Veterans Integrated Service Network (Visn 4). | ......do .......... | ............. | ES | ............. | ............. | |
| Do .................... | ......do ........... | Career Incumbent ............... | CA | ES | ............. | ............. | |
| Linthicum Hghts, MD. | Executive Director, Veterans Integrated Service Network (Visn 5). | ......do .......... | CA | ES | ............. | ............. | |
| Washington, DC ...... | Deputy Executive Director, Veterans Integrated Systems Network (Visn 5). | Vacant .................... | ............. | ES | ............. | ............. | |
| Durham, NC ........... | Executive Director, Veterans Integrated Service Network (Visn 6). | Career Incumbent ............... | CA | ES | ............. | ............. | |
| Atlanta, GA ............ | Executive Director, Veterans Integrated Service Network (Visn 7). | Vacant .................... | ............. | ES | ............. | ............. | |
| Bay Pines, FL .......... | Deputy Executive Director, Veterans Integrated Systems Network (Visn 8). | Career Incumbent ............... | CA | ES | ............. | ............. | |
| Nashville, TN.......... | Executive Director, Veterans Integrated Service Network (Visn 9). | ......do .......... | CA | ES | ............. | ............. | |
| Cincinnati, OH ....... | Executive Director, Veterans Integrated Systems Network (Visn 10). | ......do .......... | CA | ES | ............. | ............. | |
| Hines, IL ................. | Executive Director, Veterans Integrated Service Network (Visn 12). | ......do .......... | CA | ES | ............. | ............. | |
| Jackson, MS............. | Executive Director, Veterans Integrated Service Network (Visn 16). | ......do .......... | CA | ES | ............. | ............. | |
| Dallas, TX .............. | Executive Director, Veterans Integrated Service Network (Visn 17). | ......do .......... | CA | ES | ............. | ............. | |
| Denver, CO ............. | Executive Director, Veterans Integrated Service Network, Visn 19. | ......do .......... | CA | ES | ............. | ............. | |
| Portland, OR........... | Executive Director, Veterans Integrated Service Network (Visn 20). | ......do .......... | CA | ES | ............. | ............. | |
| San Francisco, CA ... | Executive Director, Veterans Integrated Service Network (Visn 21). | ......do .......... | CA | ES | ............. | ............. | |
| Long Beach, CA....... | Executive Director, Veterans Integrated Service Network (Visn 22). | ......do .......... | CA | ES | ............. | ............. | |
| Minneapolis, MN ..... | Executive Director, Veterans Integrated Systems Network (Visn 23). | ......do .......... | CA | ES | ............. | ............. | |
| | *Medical Center Directors* | | | | | | |
| West Haven, CT ...... | Executive Director, Medical Center (Visn 1)..... | ......do .......... | CA | ES | ............. | ............. | |
| White River Junction, VT. | ......do ........ | Vacant .................... | ............. | ES | ............. | ............. | |
| Boston, MA ............. | Executive Director, Medical Center (Visn I) ...... | Career Incumbent ............... | CA | ES | ............. | ............. | |
| Manchester, NH ...... | Executive Director, Medical Center (Visn 1)...... | ......do .......... | CA | ES | ............. | ............. | |
| Providence, RI ........ | ......do ......... | ......do .......... | CA | ES | ............. | ............. | |
| Northampton, MA ... | ......do ......... | ......do .......... | CA | ES | ............. | ............. | |
| Togus, ME.............. | ......do ......... | ......do .......... | CA | ES | ............. | ............. | |
| Canandaigua, NY .... | Executive Director, Medical Center (Visn 2)...... | ......do .......... | CA | ES | ............. | ............. | |
| Bronx, NY ............. | ......do ......... | ......do .......... | CA | ES | ............. | ............. | |
| Buffalo, NY ............ | ......do ......... | ......do .......... | CA | ES | ............. | ............. | |
| Syracuse, NY .......... | ......do ......... | Vacant .................... | ............. | ES | ............. | ............. | |
| East Orange, NJ...... | ......do ......... | Career Incumbent ............... | CA | ES | ............. | ............. | |
| Albany, NY.............. | ......do ......... | ......do .......... | CA | ES | ............. | ............. | |
| Montrose, NY........... | Executive Director, Medical Center (Visn 4)...... | ......do .......... | CA | ES | ............. | ............. | |
| Erie, PA.................. | ......do ......... | ......do .......... | CA | ES | ............. | ............. | |
| Pittsburgh, PA........ | ......do ......... | ......do .......... | CA | ES | ............. | ............. | |
| Philadelphia, PA..... | ......do ......... | ......do .......... | CA | ES | ............. | ............. | |
| Coatesville, PA ........ | ......do ......... | Vacant .................... | ............. | ES | ............. | ............. | |

## DEPARTMENT OF VETERANS AFFAIRS—Continued

| Location | Position Title | Name of Incumbent | Type of Appt. | Pay Plan | Level, Grade, or Pay | Tenure | Expires |
|---|---|---|---|---|---|---|---|
| Lebanon, PA | Executive Director, Medical Center (Visn 4) | Career Incumbent | CA | ES | | | |
| Butler, PA | ......do | ......do | CA | ES | | | |
| New York New York, NY. | ......do | ......do | CA | ES | | | |
| Wilkes Barre, PA | ......do | ......do | CA | ES | | | |
| Wilmington, DE | ......do | ......do | CA | ES | | | |
| Altoona, PA | ......do | ......do | CA | ES | | | |
| Washington, DC | Executive Director, Medical Center (Visn 5) | ......do | CA | ES | | | |
| Beckley, WV | ......do | ......do | CA | ES | | | |
| Martinsburg, WV | ......do | Vacant | | ES | | | |
| Huntington, WV | ......do | Career Incumbent | CA | ES | | | |
| Asheville, NC | Executive Director, Medical Center (Visn 6) | ......do | CA | ES | | | |
| Hampton, VA | ......do | ......do | CA | ES | | | |
| Fayetteville, NC | ......do | ......do | CA | ES | | | |
| Richmond, VA | ......do | ......do | CA | ES | | | |
| Salisbury, NC | ......do | ......do | CA | ES | | | |
| Salem, VA | ......do | ......do | CA | ES | | | |
| Durham, NC | ......do | ......do | CA | ES | | | |
| Charleston, SC | Executive Director, Medical Center (Visn 7) | ......do | CA | ES | | | |
| Tuscaloosa, AL | ......do | ......do | CA | ES | | | |
| Dublin, GA | ......do | ......do | CA | ES | | | |
| Atlanta, GA | ......do | ......do | CA | ES | | | |
| Augusta, GA | ......do | ......do | CA | ES | | | |
| Birmingham, AL | ......do | ......do | CA | | | | |
| Tuskegee, AL | ......do | Vacant | | ES | | | |
| Columbia, SC | ......do | Career Incumbent | CA | ES | | | |
| Orlando, FL | Executive Director, Medical Center (Visn 8) | ......do | CA | ES | | | |
| West Palm Beach, FL. | ......do | Vacant | | ES | | | |
| Tampa, FL | ......do | Career Incumbent | CA | ES | | | |
| San Juan, Puerto Rico. | ......do | ......do | CA | ES | | | |
| Bay Pines, FL | ......do | ......do | CA | ES | | | |
| Gainesville, FL | ......do | ......do | CA | ES | | | |
| Miami, FL | ......do | ......do | CA | ES | | | |
| Nashville, TN | Executive Director, Medical Center (Visn 9) | ......do | CA | ES | | | |
| Johnson City, TN | ......do | ......do | CA | ES | | | |
| Lexington, KY | ......do | ......do | CA | ES | | | |
| Memphis, TN | ......do | Vacant | | ES | | | |
| Louisville, KY | ......do | Career Incumbent | CA | ES | | | |
| Ann Arbor, MI | Executive Director, Medical Center (Visn 10) | ......do | CA | ES | | | |
| Columbus, OH | ......do | ......do | CA | ES | | | |
| Chillicothe, OH | ......do | ......do | CA | ES | | | |
| Indianapolis, IN | ......do | ......do | CA | ES | | | |
| Fort Wayne, IN | ......do | ......do | CA | ES | | | |
| Battle Creek, MI | ......do | Vacant | | ES | | | |
| Cincinnati, OH | ......do | ......do | | ES | | | |
| Dayton, OH | ......do | Career Incumbent | CA | ES | | | |
| Cleveland, OH | ......do | ......do | CA | ES | | | |
| North Chicago, IL | Executive Director, Medical Center (Visn 12) | Vacant | | ES | | | |
| Chicago, IL | ......do | Career Incumbent | CA | ES | | | |
| Milwaukee, WI | ......do | ......do | CA | ES | | | |
| Chicago, IL | ......do | ......do | CA | ES | | | |
| Madison, WI | ......do | ......do | CA | ES | | | |
| Iron Mountain, MI | ......do | ......do | CA | ES | | | |
| Hines, IL | ......do | ......do | CA | ES | | | |
| Tomah, WI | ......do | Vacant | | ES | | | |
| Kansas City, MO | Executive Director, Medical Center (Visn 15) | Career Incumbent | CA | ES | | | |
| Columbia, MO | ......do | ......do | CA | ES | | | |
| Topeka, KS | ......do | ......do | CA | ES | | | |
| St. Louis, MO | ......do | ......do | CA | ES | | | |
| Poplar Bluff, MO | ......do | Vacant | | ES | | | |
| Wichita, KS | ......do | ......do | | ES | | | |
| Marion, IL | ......do | Career Incumbent | CA | ES | | | |
| Jackson, MS | Executive Director, Medical Center (Visn 16) | Vacant | | ES | | | |
| New Orleans, LA | ......do | Career Incumbent | CA | ES | | | |
| Alexandria, LA | ......do | ......do | CA | ES | | | |
| Houston, TX | ......do | ......do | CA | ES | | | |
| Biloxi, MS | ......do | ......do | CA | ES | | | |
| Fayetteville, AR | ......do | ......do | CA | ES | | | |
| Minneapolis, MN | Executive Director, Medical Center, Visn 23 | ......do | CA | ES | | | |
| Big Spring, TX | Executive Director, Medical Center (Visn 17) | ......do | CA | ES | | | |

## DEPARTMENT OF VETERANS AFFAIRS—Continued

| Location | Position Title | Name of Incumbent | Type of Appt. | Pay Plan | Level, Grade, or Pay | Tenure | Expires |
|---|---|---|---|---|---|---|---|
| El Paso, TX | Executive Director, Medical Center (Visn 17) | Career Incumbent | CA | ES | | | |
| Harlingen, TX | ......do | ......do | CA | ES | | | |
| Amarillo, TX | ......do | Rodney Gonzalez | XS | OT | | | |
| San Antonio, TX | ......do | Career Incumbent | CA | ES | | | |
| Temple, TX | ......do | ......do | CA | ES | | | |
| Denver, CO | Executive Director, Medical Center (Visn 19) | ......do | CA | ES | | | |
| Salt Lake City, UT | ......do | ......do | CA | ES | | | |
| Sheridan, WY | ......do | ......do | CA | ES | | | |
| Muskogee, OK | ......do | ......do | CA | ES | | | |
| Fort Harrison, MT | ......do | ......do | CA | ES | | | |
| Cheyenne, WY | ......do | ......do | CA | ES | | | |
| Grand Junction, CO. | ......do | ......do | CA | ES | | | |
| Oklahoma City, OK | ......do | ......do | CA | ES | | | |
| Boise, ID | Executive Director, Medical Center (Visn 20) | ......do | CA | ES | | | |
| Walla Walla, WA | ......do | ......do | CA | ES | | | |
| Portland, OR | ......do | ......do | CA | ES | | | |
| Seattle, WA | ......do | ......do | CA | ES | | | |
| White City, OR | ......do | ......do | CA | ES | | | |
| Roseburg, OR | ......do | ......do | CA | ES | | | |
| Fresno, CA | Executive Director, Medical Center (Visn 21) | ......do | CA | ES | | | |
| Martinez, CA | ......do | ......do | CA | ES | | | |
| San Francisco, CA | ......do | ......do | CA | ES | | | |
| Palo Alto, CA | ......do | ......do | CA | ES | | | |
| Reno, NV | ......do | ......do | CA | ES | | | |
| Honolulu, HI | ......do | ......do | CA | ES | | | |
| Las Vegas, NV | ......do | ......do | CA | ES | | | |
| Albuquerque, NM | Executive Director, Medical Center (Visn 22) | ......do | CA | ES | | | |
| Los Angeles, CA | ......do | Vacant | | ES | | | |
| Loma Linda, CA | ......do | Career Incumbent | CA | ES | | | |
| Prescott, AZ | ......do | Vacant | | ES | | | |
| Phoenix, AZ | ......do | Career Incumbent | CA | ES | | | |
| Long Beach, CA | ......do | ......do | CA | ES | | | |
| Tucson, AZ | ......do | Vacant | | ES | | | |
| Des Moines, IA | Executive Director, Medical Center (Visn 23) | Career Incumbent | CA | ES | | | |
| St. Cloud, MN | ......do | ......do | CA | ES | | | |
| Fort Meade, SD | ......do | ......do | CA | ES | | | |
| Iowa City, IA | ......do | ......do | CA | ES | | | |
| Omaha, NE | ......do | ......do | CA | ES | | | |
| Sioux Falls, SD | ......do | ......do | CA | ES | | | |
| Washington, DC | Executive Director, Medical Center (Advisory) | Vacant | | ES | | | |
| Saginaw, MI | Executive Director , Medical Center (Visn 10) | Barbara Bates | XS | OT | | | |
| Shreveport, LA | Executive Director, Medical Center (Visn 16) | Richard Crockett | XS | OT | | | |
| Spokane, WA | Executive Director, Medical Center (Visn 20) | Robert Fischer | XS | OT | | | |
| Baltimore, MD | Executive Director, Medical Center (Visn 5) | Adam M Robinson M.D. | XS | OT | | | |
| Indianapolis, IN | Executive Director, Medical Center (Visn 10) | James Brian Hancock | XS | OT | | | |
| Jackson, MS | Executive Director, Medical Center (Visn 16) | David Walker | XS | OT | | | |
| Little Rock, AR | ......do | Margie A Scott | XS | OT | | | |
| Clarksburg, WV | Executive Director, Medical Center (Visn 5) | Glenn R Snider Jr | XS | OT | | | |
| Dallas, TX | Executive Director, Medical Center (Visn 17) | Stephen R Holt | XS | OT | | | |
| Hines, IL | Executive Director, Medical Center (Visn 12) | Vacant | XS | OT | | | |
| Los Angeles, CA | Executive Director, Medical Center (Visn 21) | Steven Braverman | XS | OT | | | |

## DEPARTMENT OF VETERANS AFFAIRS OFFICE OF THE INSPECTOR GENERAL

| Location | Position Title | Name of Incumbent | Type of Appt. | Pay Plan | Level, Grade, or Pay | Tenure | Expires |
|---|---|---|---|---|---|---|---|
| | **IMMEDIATE OFFICE OF THE INSPECTOR GENERAL** | | | | | | |
| Washington, DC | Inspector General | Michael Joseph Missal | PAS | EX | III | | |

# INDEPENDENT AGENCIES AND GOVERNMENT CORPORATIONS

## ADVISORY COUNCIL ON HISTORIC PRESERVATION

| Location | Position Title | Name of Incumbent | Type of Appt. | Pay Plan | Level, Grade, or Pay | Tenure | Expires |
|---|---|---|---|---|---|---|---|
| Washington, DC | Chairman | Aimee Jorjani | PAS | EX | ............... | 4 Years | |
| West Palm Beach, FL. | Vice Chairman | Rick Gonzalez | PA | EX | ............... | ............... | |
| Ridgefield, CT | Council Member (General Public) | John H Frey | PA | EX | ............... | ............... | |
| Fairfax, VA | ......do | Jordan E Tannenbaum | PA | EX | ............... | ............... | |
| Evanston, IL | ......do | Bradford J White | PA | EX | ............... | ............... | |
| Fairfax Station, VA | Council Member (Expert) | Robert G Stanton | PA | EX | ............... | ............... | |
| Charleston, SC | ......do | Kristopher B King | PA | EX | ............... | ............... | |
| Pierre, SD | ......do | Jay D Vogt | PA | EX | ............... | ............... | |
| Santa Rosa, CA | Council Member (Indian Tribe Member) | Reno Keoni Franklin | PA | EX | ............... | ............... | |
| Washington, DC | Council Member (Governor) | Vacant | PA | EX | ............... | ............... | |
| Meridian, ID | Council Member (Mayor) | Robert Simison | PA | EX | ............... | ............... | |

## AFRICAN DEVELOPMENT FOUNDATION

| Location | Position Title | Name of Incumbent | Type of Appt. | Pay Plan | Level, Grade, or Pay | Tenure | Expires |
|---|---|---|---|---|---|---|---|
| Greenwich, CT | Board of Directors, Private Member, Chair | John W Leslie | PAS | EX | ............... | ............... | |
| Jacksonville, FL | Board of Directors, Private Member, Vice Chair. | John Agwumobi | PAS | EX | ............... | ............... | |
| Minneapolis, MN | Board of Directors, Private Member | Edward W Brehm | PAS | EX | ............... | ............... | |
| Los Angeles, CA | ......do | Morgan M Davis | PAS | EX | ............... | ............... | |
| Jacksonville, FL | ......do | Iqbal Paroo | PAS | EX | ............... | ............... | |

## AMERICAN BATTLE MONUMENTS COMMISSION

| Location | Position Title | Name of Incumbent | Type of Appt. | Pay Plan | Level, Grade, or Pay | Tenure | Expires |
|---|---|---|---|---|---|---|---|
| Arlington, VA | The Secretary | William Mcdowell Matz Jr. | PA | AD | ............... | 0 Years | |

## APPALACHIAN REGIONAL COMMISSION

| Location | Position Title | Name of Incumbent | Type of Appt. | Pay Plan | Level, Grade, or Pay | Tenure | Expires |
|---|---|---|---|---|---|---|---|
| Washington, DC | Federal Co-Chairman | Tim Thomas | PAS | EX | III | ............... | |
| Do | Alternate Federal Co-Chairman | Vacant | PAS | EX | V | ............... | |
| Do | Speechwriter | Benjamin Jarrett | SC | GS | 11 | ............... | |
| Do | Senior Policy Advisor | Andrew Howard | SC | GS | 15 | ............... | |

## ARCTIC RESEARCH COMMISSION

| Location | Position Title | Name of Incumbent | Type of Appt. | Pay Plan | Level, Grade, or Pay | Tenure | Expires |
|---|---|---|---|---|---|---|---|
| Washington, DC | Chairman | Frances Ulmer | PA | EX | ............... | ............... | |
| Do | Member | Jon Ross Peters Harrison | PA | EX | ............... | ............... | |
| Do | ......do | Marie N. Kasannaaluk Greene. | PA | EX | ............... | ............... | |
| Do | ......do | Larry Mayer | PA | EX | ............... | ............... | |
| Do | ......do | James J. Mccarthy | PA | EX | ............... | ............... | |
| Do | ......do | Mary C. Pete | PA | EX | ............... | ............... | |
| Do | ......do | Michael A. Newton | PA | EX | ............... | ............... | |

## ARCTIC RESEARCH COMMISSION—Continued

| Location | Position Title | Name of Incumbent | Type of Appt. | Pay Plan | Level, Grade, or Pay | Tenure | Expires |
|---|---|---|---|---|---|---|---|
| Washington, DC ...... | Ex Officio Commission Member (Non-Voting) ... | Sethuraman Panchanathan. | PAS | EX | ............... | ............... | |
| Do ................... | Executive Director ................................................ | Career Incumbent ................ | CA | ES | ............... | ............... | |

## ARMED FORCES RETIREMENT HOME

| Location | Position Title | Name of Incumbent | Type of Appt. | Pay Plan | Level, Grade, or Pay | Tenure | Expires |
|---|---|---|---|---|---|---|---|
| Washington, DC ...... | Chief Operating Officer ....................................... | James M. Branham.............. | PA | EX | ............... | ............... | |
| Do ................... | Deputy Chief Operating Officer......................... | John Spencer Riscassi.......... | PA | EX | ............... | ............... | |

## BARRY GOLDWATER SCHOLARSHIP AND EXCELLENCE IN EDUCATION FOUNDATION

| Location | Position Title | Name of Incumbent | Type of Appt. | Pay Plan | Level, Grade, or Pay | Tenure | Expires |
|---|---|---|---|---|---|---|---|
| Alexandria, VA ........ | Executive Secretary............................................. | John F Mateja ..................... | NA | ES | ............... | ............... | |
| Do ................... | Member.................................................................. | Peggy Goldwater-Clay.......... | PAS | WC | ............... | 6 Years | |

## CENTRAL INTELLIGENCE AGENCY

| Location | Position Title | Name of Incumbent | Type of Appt. | Pay Plan | Level, Grade, or Pay | Tenure | Expires |
|---|---|---|---|---|---|---|---|
| | **OFFICE OF THE DIRECTOR** | | | | | | |
| Washington, DC ...... | Director, Central Intelligence Agency................ | Vacant ................................. | PAS | EX | II | ............... | |
| Do ................... | Deputy Director, Central Intelligence Agency ... | ......do ................................. | PAS | EX | III | ............... | |
| Do ................... | Statutory Inspector General .............................. | ......do ................................. | PAS | EX | IV | ............... | |

## CHEMICAL SAFETY AND HAZARD INVESTIGATION BOARD

| Location | Position Title | Name of Incumbent | Type of Appt. | Pay Plan | Level, Grade, or Pay | Tenure | Expires |
|---|---|---|---|---|---|---|---|
| Washington, DC ...... | Senior Advisor..................................................... | Vacant ................................. | ............. | ES | ............... | ............... | |
| Do ................... | Board Chairperson............................................... | Katherine Andrea Lemos...... | PAS | EX | IV | ............... | |
| Do ................... | Board Member...................................................... | Vacant ................................. | PAS | EX | IV | ............... | |
| Do ................... | ......do ................................................................. | ......do ................................. | PAS | EX | IV | ............... | |
| Do ................... | ......do ................................................................. | ......do ................................. | PAS | EX | IV | ............... | |
| Do ................... | General Counsel................................................... | Career Incumbent ................ | CA | ES | ............... | ............... | |
| Do ................... | Chief Operating Officer ...................................... | Vacant ................................. | ............. | ES | ............... | ............... | |
| Do ................... | Executive Director, Office of Investigations and Recommendations. | Career Incumbent ................ | CA | ES | ............... | ............... | |
| Do ................... | Special Assistant - Deepwater Horizon.............. | Vacant ................................. | ............. | ES | ............... | ............... | |

## CHRISTOPHER COLUMBUS FELLOWSHIP FOUNDATION

| Location | Position Title | Name of Incumbent | Type of Appt. | Pay Plan | Level, Grade, or Pay | Tenure | Expires |
|---|---|---|---|---|---|---|---|
| Newton, MA............ | Chairman ............................................................. | Maria Lombardo-Trifiletti ... | PA | AD | ............... | 6 Years | |
| Canton, MS............. | Vice Chairman ..................................................... | James H Herring Esq. ......... | PA | AD | ............... | ............... | |
| New Orleans, LA..... | Member, Board of Trustees ................................. | Cynthia Butler-Mcintyre ..... | PA | AD | ............... | ............... | |
| Las Vegas, NV ........ | ......do ................................................................. | Warren G Hioki ................... | PA | AD | ............... | ............... | |
| Phoenix, AZ ............ | ......do ................................................................. | Kimberly A Owens ............... | PA | AD | ............... | ............... | |
| Williamsburg, VA ... | ......do ................................................................. | Ronald B Rapoport .............. | PA | AD | ............... | ............... | |
| Seattle, WA............. | ......do ................................................................. | Sima Sarrafan Esq............... | PA | AD | ............... | ............... | |
| Washington, DC ...... | ......do ................................................................. | Peter C Schaumber ............. | PA | AD | ............... | ............... | |
| Woodstock, MD........ | ......do ................................................................. | Anthony C Wisniewski Esq.. | PA | AD | ............... | ............... | |

## CHRISTOPHER COLUMBUS FELLOWSHIP FOUNDATION—Continued

| Location | Position Title | Name of Incumbent | Type of Appt. | Pay Plan | Level, Grade, or Pay | Tenure | Expires |
|---|---|---|---|---|---|---|---|
| Auburn, NY ............ | Member, Board of Trustees ............................... | Vacant ................................. | PA | AD | ................ | ................ | |
| Do .................... | ......do ..................................................... | ......do ................................. | PA | AD | ................ | ................ | |
| Do .................... | ......do ..................................................... | ......do ................................. | PA | AD | ................ | ................ | |
| Do .................... | ......do ..................................................... | ......do ................................. | PA | AD | ................ | ................ | |

## COMMISSION OF FINE ARTS

| Location | Position Title | Name of Incumbent | Type of Appt. | Pay Plan | Level, Grade, or Pay | Tenure | Expires |
|---|---|---|---|---|---|---|---|
| Washington, DC ...... | Chairman ................................................ | Earl A. Powell...................... | PA | EX | ................ | ................ | |
| Do .................... | Vice Chairman ........................................ | Elizabeth K. Meyer ............. | PA | EX | ................ | ................ | |
| Do .................... | Member...................................................... | Alex M. Krieger .................... | PA | EX | ................ | ................ | |
| Do .................... | ......do ..................................................... | Toni L. Griffin...................... | PA | EX | ................ | ................ | |
| Do .................... | ......do ..................................................... | Justin B. Shubow................. | PA | EX | ................ | ................ | |
| Do .................... | ......do ..................................................... | James C. Mccrery ................ | PA | EX | ................ | ................ | |
| Do .................... | ......do ..................................................... | Duncan G. Stroik................. | PA | EX | ................ | ................ | |
| | **OFFICE OF THE SECRETARY** | | | | | | |
| Do .................... | Secretary of the Commission ............................ | Career Incumbent ............... | CA | ES | ................ | ................ | |

## COMMISSION ON CIVIL RIGHTS

| Location | Position Title | Name of Incumbent | Type of Appt. | Pay Plan | Level, Grade, or Pay | Tenure | Expires |
|---|---|---|---|---|---|---|---|
| Washington, DC ...... | Special Assistant to the Commissioner ............. | Carissa Beth Mulder........... | SC | GS | 14 | ................ | |
| | **COMMISSIONERS** | | | | | | |
| Takoma Park, MD ... | Chairman ................................................ | Catherine Lhamon ............... | PA | EX | IV | ................ | |
| Concord, MA............ | Vice Chairman ........................................ | Vacant ................................. | PA | EX | IV | ................ | |
| Los Angeles, CA...... | Vice-Chair................................................ | ......do ................................. | XS | EX | IV | ................ | |
| Washington, DC ...... | Vice Chairman ........................................ | ......do ................................. | PA | EX | IV | ................ | |
| Fayetteville, NC....... | Commissioner (Vice Chair) ........................ | ......do ................................. | PA | EX | IV | ................ | |
| San Francisco, CA ... | Commissioner............................................ | Michael Yaki ...................... | XS | EX | IV | ................ | |
| Las Vegas, NV ........ | ......do ..................................................... | David Kladney...................... | XS | EX | IV | ................ | |
| San Diego, CA ........ | ......do ..................................................... | Gail Heriot.......................... | XS | EX | IV | ................ | |
| Cleveland, OH ........ | ......do ..................................................... | Peter N Kirsanow............... | PA | EX | IV | ................ | |
| New York New York, NY. | ......do ..................................................... | Debo P Adegbile.................. | PA | EX | IV | ................ | |
| Washington, DC ...... | ......do ..................................................... | Stephen L Gilchrist............. | PA | EX | IV | ................ | |
| North Tonawanda, NY. | Special Assistant to the Commissioner ............. | Rukku Singla...................... | SC | GS | 14 | ................ | |
| Washington, DC ...... | ......do ..................................................... | Amelia Royce ........................ | SC | GS | 12 | ................ | |
| Herndon, VA............ | ......do ..................................................... | Alec Haniford Deull ............. | SC | GS | 14 | ................ | |
| Washington, DC ...... | Special Assistant...................................... | Irena Vidulovic ................... | SC | GS | 14 | ................ | |
| | **STAFF MEMBERS** | | | | | | |
| Do .................... | Associate Deputy Staff Director ........................ | Vacant ................................. | ............ | ES | | ................ | |
| Do .................... | Assistant Staff Director for Civil Rights Evaluation. | ......do ................................. | ............ | ES | | ................ | |
| Do .................... | Acting Staff Director.................................. | ......do ................................. | ............ | ES | | ................ | |
| Do .................... | General Counsel........................................ | ......do ................................. | ............ | ES | | ................ | |
| Do .................... | Assistant Staff Director for Congressional Affairs. | ......do ................................. | ............ | ES | | ................ | |
| Do .................... | Staff Director .......................................... | Mauro Albert Morales.......... | NA | ES | | ................ | |
| Do .................... | Principal Advisor to the Commission ................. | Vacant ................................. | ............ | ES | | ................ | |

## COMMITTEE FOR PURCHASE FROM PEOPLE WHO ARE BLIND OR SEVERELY DISABLED

| Location | Position Title | Name of Incumbent | Type of Appt. | Pay Plan | Level, Grade, or Pay | Tenure | Expires |
|---|---|---|---|---|---|---|---|
| Winter Haven, FL ... | Member................................................... | Robert T Kelly Jr. ................ | PA | PD | ................ | 5 Years | |
| Arlington, VA........... | ......do ..................................................... | James M Kesteloot............... | PA | PD | ................ | 5 Years | |

## COMMODITY FUTURES TRADING COMMISSION

| Location | Position Title | Name of Incumbent | Type of Appt. | Pay Plan | Level, Grade, or Pay | Tenure | Expires |
|---|---|---|---|---|---|---|---|
| Washington, DC | Legislative & Policy Analyst | Darryl Blakey | SC | OT | $115,000 | | |
| | *Office of the Chairperson* | | | | | | |
| Do | Chairperson | Heath Price Tarbert | PAS | EX | III | 5 Years | |
| Do | Commissioner | Dan M Berkovitz | PAS | EX | IV | 5 Years | |
| Do | ......do | Rostin Behnam | PAS | EX | IV | 5 Years | |
| Do | ......do | Brian Quintenz | PAS | EX | IV | 5 Years | |
| Do | ......do | Dawn Deberry Stump | PAS | EX | IV | | |
| Do | Director of Legislative and Intergovernmental Affairs. | Summer Mersinger | SC | OT | $200,000 | | |
| New York, NY | Senior Advisor | Thomas Benison | SC | OT | $220,816 | | |
| Washington, DC | Executive Assistant | Melissa Benedict | SC | OT | $105,248 | | |
| | *Office of the Chief Economist* | | | | | | |
| Do | Chief Economist | Bruce Tuckman | SC | OT | $234,383 | | |
| | **DIVISION OF CLEARING AND RISK** | | | | | | |
| Do | Director | Clark Hutchison | SC | OT | $230,013 | | |
| | **OFFICE OF PUBLIC AFFAIRS** | | | | | | |
| Do | ......do | Michael Short | SC | OT | $198,802 | | |
| Do | Deputy Director | Rachel Millard | SC | OT | $180,000 | | |
| Do | Public Affairs & Digital Engagement Strategist. | Mollie Wilken | SC | OT | $147,896 | | |

## CONSUMER FINANCIAL PROTECTION BUREAU

| Location | Position Title | Name of Incumbent | Type of Appt. | Pay Plan | Level, Grade, or Pay | Tenure | Expires |
|---|---|---|---|---|---|---|---|
| Washington, DC | Director | Kathleen Kraninger | PAS | EX | II | | |

## CONSUMER PRODUCT SAFETY COMMISSION

| Location | Position Title | Name of Incumbent | Type of Appt. | Pay Plan | Level, Grade, or Pay | Tenure | Expires |
|---|---|---|---|---|---|---|---|
| | **OFFICE OF COMPLIANCE** | | | | | | |
| Bethesda, MD | Deputy Director, Office of Compliance | Career Incumbent | CA | ES | | | |
| | **OFFICE OF COMMISSIONERS** | | | | | | |
| Do | Executive Assistant | Katelyn M Costello | SC | GS | 12 | | |
| Do | Commissioner | Peter Feldman | PAS | EX | IV | 7 Years | |
| Do | ......do | Elliot Franklin Kaye | PAS | EX | IV | 7 Years | |
| Do | ......do | Dana Baiocco | PAS | EX | IV | 7 Years | |
| Do | ......do | Robert Sanford Adler | PAS | EX | IV | | |
| Do | General Counsel | Vacant | | ES | | | |
| Do | Special Assistant (Legal) | Sarah A Klein | SC | GS | 15 | | |
| Do | ......do | Jennifer W Feinberg | SC | GS | 15 | | |
| Do | Special Assistant | Dorothy S Yahr | SC | GS | 14 | | |
| Do | Special Assistant (Legal) | Jana L Fong-Swamidoss | SC | GS | 15 | | |
| Do | Director, Office of Legislative Affairs | Christopher B Hudgins | SC | GS | 15 | | |
| Do | Special Assistant (Legal) | Allison T Steinle | SC | GS | 15 | | |
| Do | ......do | John Gibson Mullan | SC | GS | 15 | | |
| Do | Commissioner | Vacant | PAS | EX | IV | | |
| | **CONSUMER PRODUCT SAFETY COMMISSION** | | | | | | |
| Do | Chairman, Consumer Product Safety Commission. | ......do | PAS | EX | III | 7 Years | |
| | **OFFICE OF EXECUTIVE DIRECTOR** | | | | | | |
| Do | Deputy Executive Director for Safety Operations. | Career Incumbent | CA | ES | | | |
| Do | Chief Financial Officer | Vacant | | ES | | | |
| Do | Deputy Executive Director for Operations Support. | ......do | | ES | | | |
| Do | Executive Director | Career Incumbent | CA | ES | | | |
| | *Office of Hazard Identification and Reduction* | | | | | | |
| Do | Associate Executive Director for Health Sciences. | Vacant | | ES | | | |

## CONSUMER PRODUCT SAFETY COMMISSION—Continued

| Location | Position Title | Name of Incumbent | Type of Appt. | Pay Plan | Level, Grade, or Pay | Tenure | Expires |
|---|---|---|---|---|---|---|---|
| Bethesda, MD.......... | Deputy Associate Executive Director for Executive Resources. | Career Incumbent ................ | CA | ES | .............. | .............. | |
| | *Office of Communications* | | | | | | |
| Do .................... | Supervisory Public Affairs Specialist ................ | Joseph J Martyak................ | SC | GS | 15 | .............. | |

## CORPORATION FOR NATIONAL AND COMMUNITY SERVICE

| Location | Position Title | Name of Incumbent | Type of Appt. | Pay Plan | Level, Grade, or Pay | Tenure | Expires |
|---|---|---|---|---|---|---|---|
| | **DEPARTMENT OF THE CHIEF EXECUTIVE OFFICER** | | | | | | |
| Washington, DC ...... | Chief Executive Officer.............. | Barbara L Stewart ............... | PAS | EX | III | .............. | |
| Do | Policy Advisor.......................... | Vacant ......................... | XS | OT | .............. | .............. | |
| Do | Executive Assistant and Scheduler ................. | Jennifer Wagner .................. | XS | OT | .............. | .............. | |
| Do | Chief of Staff to the Chief Executive Officer .... | Vacant ......................... | XS | OT | .............. | .............. | |
| | **OFFICE GENERAL COUNSEL** | | | | | | |
| Do | General Counsel.......................... | ......do ...... | XS | OT | .............. | .............. | |
| Do | Executive Assistant ....................... | ......do ...... | XS | OT | .............. | .............. | |
| | **OFFICE OF GOVERNMENT RELATIONS AND STRATEGIC ENGAGEMENT** | | | | | | |
| Do | Director, Government Relations.......................... | Chester Bryant...................... | XS | OT | .............. | .............. | |
| Do | Deputy Director ......................... | Vacant | XS | OT | .............. | .............. | |
| Do | Deputy Director, Intergovernmental Relations . | ......do ...... | XS | OT | .............. | .............. | |
| Do | Legislative Assistant ..................... | Latanya Peterson ............... | XS | OT | .............. | .............. | |
| Do | Chief of External Affairs ................. | Chester Bryant...................... | XS | OT | .............. | .............. | |
| Do | Press Secretary .......................... | Vacant ......................... | XS | OT | .............. | .............. | |
| Do | Speech Writer ............................ | ......do ...... | XS | OT | .............. | .............. | |
| | **DEPARTMENT OF PROGRAM OPERATIONS** | | | | | | |
| Do | Senior Advisor for Wounded Warrior, Veteran and Military Family Initiatives. | Earl Gay................................ | XS | OT | .............. | .............. | |
| | **OFFICE OF AMERICORPS VISTA** | | | | | | |
| Do | Director, Americorps Vista ................ | Desiree Tucker-Sorini .......... | XS | OT | .............. | .............. | |
| | **OFFICE OF AMERICORPS STATE AND NATIONAL** | | | | | | |
| Do | Director, Americorps ...................... | Chester Spellman................ | XS | OT | .............. | .............. | |
| | **OFFICE OF SENIOR CORPS** | | | | | | |
| Do | Director, Office of Senior Corps.......................... | Deborah Cox-Roush.............. | XS | OT | .............. | .............. | |
| | **NATIONAL CIVILIAN COMMUNITY CORPS** | | | | | | |
| Do | Director, National Civilian Community Corps... | Vacant ......................... | XS | OT | .............. | .............. | |
| Do | Supervisory Program Outreach Specialist........ | Elliott Stewart...................... | XS | OT | .............. | .............. | |
| | **BOARD OF DIRECTORS** | | | | | | |
| Do | Member.......................... | Vacant ......................... | PAS | WC | .............. | .............. | |
| Do | ......do ...... | ......do ...... | PAS | WC | .............. | .............. | |
| Do | ......do ...... | ......do ...... | PAS | WC | .............. | .............. | |
| Do | ......do ...... | ......do ...... | PAS | WC | .............. | .............. | |
| Do | ......do ...... | ......do ...... | PAS | WC | .............. | .............. | |
| Do | ......do ...... | ......do ...... | PAS | WC | .............. | .............. | |
| Do | ......do ...... | ......do ...... | PAS | WC | .............. | .............. | |
| Do | ......do ...... | ......do ...... | PAS | WC | .............. | .............. | |
| Do | ......do ...... | ......do ...... | PAS | WC | .............. | .............. | |
| Do | ......do ...... | ......do ...... | PAS | WC | .............. | .............. | |
| Do | ......do ...... | ......do ...... | PAS | WC | .............. | .............. | |
| Do | ......do ...... | ......do ...... | PAS | WC | .............. | .............. | |
| Do | ......do ...... | ......do ...... | PAS | WC | .............. | .............. | |
| Do | ......do ...... | ......do ...... | PAS | WC | .............. | .............. | |
| Do | ......do ...... | ......do ...... | PAS | WC | .............. | .............. | |
| | **OFFICE OF THE INSPECTOR GENERAL** | | | | | | |
| Do | Inspector General ........................ | Deborah J Jeffrey ................ | PAS | EX | IV | .............. | |

## COUNCIL OF INSPECTORS GENERAL ON INTEGRITY AND EFFICIENCY

| Location | Position Title | Name of Incumbent | Type of Appt. | Pay Plan | Level, Grade, or Pay | Tenure | Expires |
|---|---|---|---|---|---|---|---|
| Washington, DC ...... | Executive Director................................................ | Career Incumbent ................ | CA | ES | ............... | ............... | |
| Do ..................... | Executive Director for the Inspector General Training Institute. | ......do .................................. | CA | ES | ............... | ............... | |

## COURT SERVICES AND OFFENDER SUPERVISION AGENCY FOR THE DISTRICT OF COLUMBIA

| Location | Position Title | Name of Incumbent | Type of Appt. | Pay Plan | Level, Grade, or Pay | Tenure | Expires |
|---|---|---|---|---|---|---|---|
| Washington, DC ...... | Director................................................................ | Richard S Tischner................ | PAS | EX | IV | ............... | |
| Do ..................... | Attorney (General Counsel) ................................ | Career Incumbent ................ | CA | ES | ............... | ............... | |

## DEFENSE NUCLEAR FACILITIES SAFETY BOARD

| Location | Position Title | Name of Incumbent | Type of Appt. | Pay Plan | Level, Grade, or Pay | Tenure | Expires |
|---|---|---|---|---|---|---|---|
| Washington, DC ...... | General Counsel................................................ | Career Incumbent ................ | CA | ES | ............... | ............... | |
| Do ..................... | General Manager ............................................... | ......do .................................. | CA | ES | ............... | ............... | |
| Do ..................... | Senior Counsel for Nuclear Safety Engineering. | Vacant .................................. | XS | SL | ............... | | |
| Do ..................... | Vice Chairman .................................................. | ......do .................................. | PAS | EX | III | ............... | |
| Do ..................... | Member.............................................................. | Joyce Louise Connery........... | PAS | EX | III | ............... | |
| Do ..................... | ......do .............................................................. | Jessie M Roberson................ | PAS | EX | III | ............... | |
| Do ..................... | ......do .............................................................. | Vacant .................................. | PAS | EX | III | ............... | |
| Do ..................... | Chairman .......................................................... | Joseph Bruce Hamilton........ | PAS | EX | III | ............... | |

## DELAWARE RIVER BASIN COMMISSION

| Location | Position Title | Name of Incumbent | Type of Appt. | Pay Plan | Level, Grade, or Pay | Tenure | Expires |
|---|---|---|---|---|---|---|---|
| Dover, DE................. | U S Commr (Alternate Fed Member) ................ | Vacant .................................. | PA | OT | ............... | ............... | |

## DELTA REGIONAL AUTHORITY

| Location | Position Title | Name of Incumbent | Type of Appt. | Pay Plan | Level, Grade, or Pay | Tenure | Expires |
|---|---|---|---|---|---|---|---|
| Clarksdale, MS........ | Federal Co-Chairman ......................................... | Christopher Caldwell........... | PAS | EX | III | ............... | |
| Do ..................... | Alternate Federal Co-Chairman ......................... | Vacant .................................. | PA | EX | V | ............... | |

## DENALI COMMISSION

| Location | Position Title | Name of Incumbent | Type of Appt. | Pay Plan | Level, Grade, or Pay | Tenure | Expires |
|---|---|---|---|---|---|---|---|
| Anchorage, AK......... | Federal Co-Chair................................................ | John Torgerson .................... | XS | OT | ............... | ............... | |

## DWIGHT D EISENHOWER MEMORIAL COMMISSION

| Location | Position Title | Name of Incumbent | Type of Appt. | Pay Plan | Level, Grade, or Pay | Tenure | Expires |
|---|---|---|---|---|---|---|---|
| Washington, DC ...... | Executive Director ............................................ | Carl W Reddel ..................... | XS | AD | ............... | ............... | |

## ENVIRONMENTAL PROTECTION AGENCY

| Location | Position Title | Name of Incumbent | Type of Appt. | Pay Plan | Level, Grade, or Pay | Tenure | Expires |
|---|---|---|---|---|---|---|---|
| | **OFFICE OF THE ADMINISTRATOR** | | | | | | |
| Washington, DC ...... | Administrator................................... | Andrew Wheeler................... | PAS | EX | II | .............. | |
| Do .................. | Deputy Administrator ....................... | Vacant ................................ | PAS | EX | III | .............. | |
| Do .................. | Associate Deputy Administrator...................... | Douglas Benevento.............. | NA | ES | | .............. | |
| Phoenix, AZ ............ | Assistant Deputy Administrator...................... | Henry Darwin..................... | NA | ES | | .............. | |
| Washington, DC ...... | Chief of Staff .................................. | Amanda Gunasekara .......... | NA | ES | | .............. | |
| Do .................. | Deputy Chief of Staff........................ | Vacant ................................ | | ES | | .............. | |
| Do .................. | Principal Deputy Chief of Staff........................ | Michael Molina.................... | SC | GS | 15 | .............. | |
| Do .................. | Special Advisor to the Administrator ............... | Amanda Kasper.................... | SC | GS | 15 | .............. | |
| Do .................. | Senior Advisor for Strategic Initiatives.............. | Taylor Hoverman Meredith . | SC | GS | 15 | .............. | |
| Denver, CO ............ | Senior Advisor for Oil and Gas, Regional Management and State Affairs. | Megan Garvey ..................... | SC | GS | 15 | .............. | |
| Washington, DC ...... | Director of Advance ........................... | Holly Lane .......................... | SC | GS | 14 | .............. | |
| Do .................. | Deputy Director for Advance................ | Tyler Teresa ....................... | SC | GS | 13 | .............. | |
| Do .................. | Special Advisor to the Deputy Chief of Staff for Operations. | Sean Donahue...................... | SC | GS | 13 | .............. | |
| Do .................. | White House Liaison ........................... | Kaitlyn Shimmin.................. | SC | GS | 15 | .............. | |
| Do .................. | Senior Deputy White House Liaison ................ | Brock Terwilleger ................ | SC | GS | 13 | .............. | |
| Do .................. | Special Assistant to the Deputy Administrator. | Carrie Coxen........................ | SC | GS | 12 | .............. | |
| | **OFFICE OF THE EXECUTIVE SECRETARIAT** | | | | | | |
| Do .................. | Special Advisor................................... | Alexander Heideman .......... | SC | GS | 12 | .............. | |
| Do .................. | Director, Office of the Executive Secretariat...... | Vacant ................................ | ............ | ES | .............. | | |
| Do .................. | Attorney-Adviser............................... | Anna Dziadosz..................... | SC | GS | 15 | .............. | |
| Do .................. | Special Advisor................................... | Paige Gilliard...................... | SC | GS | 12 | .............. | |
| | **Office of Children's Health Protection** | | | | | | |
| Do .................. | Director, Office of Children's Health Protection. | Career Incumbent ................ | CA | ES | .............. | | |
| | **Office of Civil Rights** | | | | | | |
| Do .................. | Director, Office of Civil Rights ............... | ......do ................................ | CA | ES | .............. | | |
| Do .................. | Deputy Director, Office of Civil Rights.............. | Vacant ................................ | ............ | ES | .............. | | |
| | **Office of Homeland Security** | | | | | | |
| Do .................. | Associate Administrator for Homeland Security. | Career Incumbent ................ | CA | ES | .............. | .............. | |
| | **Office of Small Business Programs** | | | | | | |
| Do .................. | Director, Office of Small Business Programs ..... | ......do ................................ | CA | ES | .............. | .............. | |
| | **Office of the Associate Administrator For Congressional and Intergovernmental Relations** | | | | | | |
| Do .................. | Associate Administrator for Congressional and Intergovernmental Relations. | Joseph Brazauskas............... | NA | ES | .............. | .............. | |
| Do .................. | Deputy Associate Administrator, Office of Congressional and Intergovernmental Relations. | Career Incumbent ................ | CA | ES | .............. | .............. | |
| Do .................. | Principal Deputy Associate Administrator for the Office of Congressional and Intergovernmental Relations. | Travis Voyles...................... | SC | GS | 15 | .............. | |
| Do .................. | Attorney-Adviser (General)................................ | Katherine English.............. | SC | GS | 15 | .............. | |
| Do .................. | Director of House Relations ................... | Todd Washam ...................... | SC | GS | 15 | .............. | |
| Do .................. | Assistant Deputy Associate Administrator for Intergovernmental Affairs. | Brittany Carter.................... | SC | GS | 14 | .............. | |
| Do .................. | Senate Affairs Specialist ..................... | Robert Frye.......................... | SC | GS | 12 | .............. | |
| Do .................. | Special Advisor for Oversight ................... | Garrett Kral........................ | SC | GS | 12 | .............. | |
| Do .................. | Special Advisor for Intergovernmental Relations. | Jordan Pic .......................... | SC | GS | 12 | .............. | |
| Do .................. | Special Assistant to the Office of Congressional and Intergovernmental Relations. | John Edwards....................... | SC | GS | 11 | .............. | |
| Do .................. | Special Advisor for House Relations.................. | John Kolb............................ | SC | GS | 11 | .............. | |
| Do .................. | Special Assistant to the Office of Congressional and Intergovernmental Relations. | Kirby Struhar ...................... | SC | GS | 9 | .............. | |
| | **Science Advisory Board** | | | | | | |
| Do .................. | Director, Science Advisory Board...................... | Career Incumbent ................ | CA | ES | .............. | .............. | |
| | **Office of Public Affairs** | | | | | | |
| Do .................. | Associate Administrator for Public Affairs ....... | James Hewitt........................ | NA | ES | .............. | .............. | |
| Do .................. | Principal Deputy Associate Administrator for Public Affairs. | Career Incumbent ................ | CA | ES | .............. | .............. | |

## ENVIRONMENTAL PROTECTION AGENCY—Continued

| Location | Position Title | Name of Incumbent | Type of Appt. | Pay Plan | Level, Grade, or Pay | Tenure | Expires |
|---|---|---|---|---|---|---|---|
| Washington, DC ...... | Assistant Deputy Associate Administrator for Policy. | Molly Block ........................... | SC | GS | 15 | ............... | |
| Do .................... | Senior Advisor for Strategic and Regional Communications. | Jessica Mcfaul ..................... | SC | GS | 15 | ............... | |
| Do .................... | Special Assistant for Digital Media.................. | Taylor Greenberg................. | SC | GS | 9 | ............... | |
| Do .................... | Special Advisor to the Associate Administrator. | Andrea Woods ...................... | SC | GS | 11 | ............... | |
| Do .................... | Special Assistant for Video and Media.............. | Jacob Allen........................... | SC | GS | 9 | ............... | |
| | **Office of Public Engagement and Environmental Education** | | | | | | |
| Do .................... | Associate Administrator for the Office of Public Engagement and Environmental Education. | Brett Doyle ........................... | SC | GS | 15 | ............... | |
| Do .................... | Associate Administrator for the Office of Public Engagement and Environmental Education and Senior Advisor for Agricultural Affairs. | Elizabeth Bennett ............... | NA | ES | | ............... | |
| Do .................... | Special Advisor.................................................. | George Etheridge................. | SC | GS | 12 | ............... | |
| Do .................... | Special Assistant to the Associate Administrator. | Megan Striegel .................... | SC | GS | 7 | ............... | |
| | **Office of the Associate Administrator For Policy** | | | | | | |
| Do .................... | Deputy Associate Administrator for Strategic Planning. | Andrew R Kloster ................ | SC | GS | 15 | ............... | |
| Do .................... | Associate Administrator for the Office of Policy and Senior Counsel to the Administrator. | Brittany Bolen ...................... | NA | ES | | ............... | |
| Do .................... | Principal Deputy Associate Administrator for the Office of Policy. | Kevin Wheeler ...................... | NA | ES | | ............... | |
| Do .................... | Deputy Associate Administrator........................ | Career Incumbent ............... | CA | ES | | ............... | |
| Do .................... | Director, Office of Regulatory Policy and Management. | ......do ................................. | CA | ES | | ............... | |
| Do .................... | Director, Office of Sustainable Communities..... | ......do ................................. | CA | ES | | ............... | |
| Do .................... | Director, National Center for Environmental Economics. | ......do ................................. | CA | ES | | ............... | |
| Do .................... | Senior Advisor to the Associate Administrator for Policy. | Julie Axelrod......................... | SC | GS | 15 | ............... | |
| Do .................... | Policy Assistant.................................................. | Patricia Dziadosz................. | SC | GS | 12 | ............... | |
| Do .................... | ......do ............................................................... | John Yarbrough .................... | SC | GS | 9 | ............... | |
| | **OFFICE OF FEDERAL ACTIVITIES** | | | | | | |
| Do .................... | Director, Office of Federal Activities................... | Career Incumbent ............... | CA | ES | | ............... | |
| | **OFFICE OF THE ASSISTANT ADMINISTRATOR FOR ENFORCEMENT AND COMPLIANCE ASSURANCE** | | | | | | |
| Do .................... | Deputy Assistant Administrator for Enforcement and Compliance Assurance. | John S Irving IV................... | NA | ES | | ............... | |
| Do .................... | Director, Office of Administration and Policy .... | Career Incumbent ............... | CA | ES | | ............... | |
| Do .................... | Principal Deputy Assistant Administrator for Enforcement and Compliance Assurance. | ......do ................................. | CA | ES | | ............... | |
| Do .................... | Policy Advisor..................................................... | Victoria Tran ....................... | SC | GS | 13 | ............... | |
| Do .................... | Assistant Administrator for Enforcement and Compliance Assurance. | Susan Parker Bodine ........... | PAS | EX | IV | ............... | |
| | **OFFICE OF THE GENERAL COUNSEL** | | | | | | |
| Do .................... | General Counsel................................................. | Matthew Leopold................. | PAS | EX | IV | ............... | |
| Do .................... | Principal Deputy General Counsel..................... | David Fotouhi ...................... | NA | ES | | ............... | |
| Do .................... | Deputy General Counsel .................................... | Adam Gustafson .................. | NA | ES | | ............... | |
| Do .................... | ......do ............................................................... | Kamila Lis-Coghlan ............. | NA | ES | | ............... | |
| Do .................... | Deputy General Counsel for Environmental Media and Regional Law Offices. | Career Incumbent ............... | CA | ES | | ............... | |
| Do .................... | Deputy General Counsel for Operations............ | ......do ................................. | CA | ES | | ............... | |
| Do .................... | Principal Associate General Counsel................. | ......do ................................. | CA | ES | | ............... | |
| Do .................... | Associate General Counsel (Cross-Cutting Issues). | Vacant .................................. | | ES | | ............... | |
| Do .................... | Associate General Counsel (Pesticides and Toxic Substances). | Career Incumbent ............... | CA | ES | | ............... | |
| Do .................... | Associate General Counsel (General Law)......... | ......do ................................. | CA | ES | | ............... | |
| Do .................... | Associate General Counsel (Air and Radiation Law Office). | ......do ................................. | CA | ES | | ............... | |
| Do .................... | Associate General Counsel (Water) .................... | ......do ................................. | CA | ES | | ............... | |
| Do .................... | Associate General Counsel (Solid Waste and Emergency Response). | ......do ................................. | CA | ES | | ............... | |
| Do .................... | Associate General Counsel (Civil Rights and Finance Law Office). | ......do ................................. | CA | ES | | ............... | |

## ENVIRONMENTAL PROTECTION AGENCY—Continued

| Location | Position Title | Name of Incumbent | Type of Appt. | Pay Plan | Level, Grade, or Pay | Tenure | Expires |
|---|---|---|---|---|---|---|---|
| Washington, DC ...... | Associate General Counsel (National Freedom of Information Act Office). | Career Incumbent ................ | CA | ES | ............... | ............... | |
| Do .................... | Director, Office of External Compliance............ | ......do ...................... | CA | ES | ............... | ............... | |
| Do .................... | Attorney-Adviser (General)........................ | Katharine Willey ................ | SC | GS | 15 | ............... | |
| Do .................... | ......do ......... | Meredith Cody.................. | SC | GS | 14 | ............... | |
| Do .................... | Special Assistant for the Office of General Counsel. | John Mutz............................ | SC | GS | 9 | ............... | |
| | **OFFICE OF THE ASSISTANT ADMINISTRATOR FOR INTERNATIONAL AND TRIBAL AFFAIRS** | | | | | | |
| Do .................... | Assistant Administrator for International and Tribal Affairs. | William Mcintosh ................ | PAS | EX | IV | ............... | |
| Do .................... | Principal Deputy Assistant Administrator for International and Tribal Affairs. | Career Incumbent ................ | CA | ES | ............... | ............... | |
| Do .................... | Director, Office of Management and International Services. | ......do ...................... | CA | ES | ............... | ............... | |
| Do .................... | Director, Office of Regional and Bilateral Affairs. | ......do ...................... | CA | ES | ............... | ............... | |
| Do .................... | Director, Office of Global Affairs and Policy...... | ......do ...................... | CA | ES | ............... | ............... | |
| Dallas, TX ............... | Director, American Indian Environmental Office. | Walter Mason...................... | SC | GS | 15 | ............... | |
| Washington, DC ...... | Senior Advisor for the Office of International and Tribal Affairs. | Diana K Leo ...................... | SC | GS | 15 | ............... | |
| Do .................... | Senior Advisor for Policy and Management....... | Nathaniel Zimmer ................ | SC | GS | 13 | ............... | |
| | **OFFICE OF THE CHIEF FINANCIAL OFFICER** | | | | | | |
| Do .................... | Chief Financial Officer ............................ | Vacant ............................ | PAS | EX | IV | ............... | |
| Do .................... | Senior Advisor to the Chief Financial Officer.... | Career Incumbent ................ | CA | ES | ............... | ............... | |
| Do .................... | Director, E-Enterprise for the Environment Program. | ......do ...................... | CA | ES | ............... | ............... | |
| Do .................... | Associate Chief Financial Officer for Policy....... | Catherine Hanson ................ | SC | GS | 15 | ............... | |
| Do .................... | Senior Advisor for Budget and Accountability... | Charles Dankert.................. | SC | GS | 13 | ............... | |
| | **OFFICE OF THE ASSISTANT ADMINISTRATOR FOR MISSION SUPPORT** | | | | | | |
| Do .................... | Assistant Administrator for Mission Support.... | Vacant ............................ | PAS | EX | IV | ............... | |
| Do .................... | Principal Deputy Assistant Administrator for Mission Support. | Career Incumbent ................ | CA | ES | ............... | ............... | |
| Do .................... | Deputy Assistant Administrator for Administration and Resources Management. | ......do ...................... | CA | ES | ............... | ............... | |
| Do .................... | Deputy Assistant Administrator for Environmental Information. | ......do ...................... | CA | ES | ............... | ............... | |
| Do .................... | Director, Office of Enterprise Information Programs. | ......do ...................... | CA | ES | ............... | ............... | |
| Do .................... | Director, Office of Information Technology and Operations. | ......do ...................... | CA | ES | ............... | ............... | |
| Do .................... | Deputy Director, Office of Information Technology and Operations. | ......do ...................... | CA | ES | ............... | ............... | |
| Do .................... | Director, Office of Information Management ..... | Vacant ............................ | ............ | ES | ............... | ............... | |
| Do .................... | Director, Office of Information Security and Privacy. | Career Incumbent ................ | CA | ES | ............... | ............... | |
| Do .................... | Director, Office of Customer Advocacy, Policy and Portfolio Management. | Vacant ............................ | ............ | ES | ............... | ............... | |
| Do .................... | Chief Sustainability Officer ............................ | Charlotte Skidmore.............. | SC | GS | 15 | ............... | |
| Do .................... | Associate Deputy Assistant Administrator for the Office of Mission Support. | David Zeckman.................... | SC | GS | 15 | ............... | |
| | **OFFICE OF THE ASSISTANT ADMINISTRATOR FOR WATER** | | | | | | |
| Do .................... | Assistant Administrator for Water ...................... | David Ross ...................... | PAS | EX | IV | ............... | |
| Do .................... | Deputy Assistant Administrator for Management. | Career Incumbent ................ | CA | ES | ............... | ............... | |
| Do .................... | Deputy Assistant Administrator for Policy....... | ......do ...................... | CA | ES | ............... | ............... | |
| Do .................... | Deputy Assistant Administrator for Water ........ | Dennis Forsgren ................ | NA | ES | ............... | ............... | |
| Do .................... | Director, Office of Wastewater Management...... | Career Incumbent ................ | CA | ES | ............... | ............... | |
| Do .................... | Deputy Director, Office of Wastewater Management. | ......do ...................... | CA | ES | ............... | ............... | |
| Do .................... | Director, Office of Science and Technology........ | ......do ...................... | CA | ES | ............... | ............... | |
| Do .................... | Deputy Director, Office of Science and Technology. | ......do ...................... | CA | ES | ............... | ............... | |
| Do .................... | Director, Office of Wetlands, Oceans and Watersheds. | ......do ...................... | CA | ES | ............... | ............... | |

## ENVIRONMENTAL PROTECTION AGENCY—Continued

| Location | Position Title | Name of Incumbent | Type of Appt. | Pay Plan | Level, Grade, or Pay | Tenure | Expires |
|---|---|---|---|---|---|---|---|
| Washington, DC ...... | Deputy Director, Office of Wetlands, Oceans and Watersheds. | Career Incumbent ................ | CA | ES | .............. | .............. | |
| Do .................... | Director, Office of Ground Water and Drinking Water. | ......do ................. | CA | ES | .............. | .............. | |
| Do .................... | Deputy Director, Office of Ground Water and Drinking Water. | ......do ................. | CA | ES | .............. | .............. | |
| Do .................... | Attorney-Adviser (General)................................ | Jessica Kramer .................... | SC | GS | 14 | .............. | |
| Do .................... | Special Assistant................................ | Melissa Mejias .................... | SC | GS | 13 | .............. | |
| | **OFFICE OF THE ASSISTANT ADMINISTRATOR FOR LAND AND EMERGENCY MANAGEMENT** | | | | | | |
| Do .................... | Assistant Administrator, Office of Solid Waste.. | Peter Wright ........................ | PAS | EX | IV | .............. | |
| Do .................... | Principal Deputy Assistant Administrator for Solid Waste and Emergency Response. | Career Incumbent ................ | CA | ES | .............. | .............. | |
| Do .................... | Deputy Assistant Administrator for Land and Emergency Management. | Steven Cook ......................... | NA | ES | .............. | .............. | |
| Do .................... | Director, Office of Program Management........... | Career Incumbent ................ | CA | ES | .............. | .............. | |
| Arlington, VA........... | Director, Office of Superfund Remediation and Technology Innovation. | Vacant ................................ | ............ | ES | .............. | .............. | |
| Do .................... | Deputy Director, Office of Superfund Remediation and Technology Innovation. | Career Incumbent ................ | CA | ES | .............. | .............. | |
| Do .................... | Director, Office of Resource Conservation and Recovery. | Vacant ................................ | ............ | ES | .............. | .............. | |
| Do .................... | Deputy Director, Office of Resource Conservation and Recovery. | Career Incumbent ................ | CA | ES | .............. | .............. | |
| Washington, DC ...... | Director, Office of Underground Storage Tanks. | ......do ................. | CA | ES | .............. | .............. | |
| Do .................... | Director, Office of Brownfields Cleanup and Redevelopment. | ......do ................. | CA | ES | .............. | .............. | |
| Do .................... | Director, Office of Emergency Management ...... | ......do ................. | CA | ES | .............. | .............. | |
| Do .................... | Deputy Director, Office of Emergency Management. | ......do ................. | CA | ES | .............. | .............. | |
| Do .................... | Senior Advisor for Workforce Development ....... | ......do ................. | CA | ES | .............. | .............. | |
| | **OFFICE OF THE ASSISTANT ADMINISTRATOR FOR AIR AND RADIATION** | | | | | | |
| Do .................... | Assistant Administrator for Air and Radiation . | Vacant ................................ | PAS | EX | IV | .............. | |
| Do .................... | Principal Deputy Assistant Administrator ........ | Anne Austin ......................... | NA | ES | .............. | .............. | |
| Do .................... | Deputy Assistant Administrator for Air and Radiation. | Career Incumbent ................ | CA | ES | .............. | .............. | |
| Do .................... | Deputy Assistant Administrator for Policy ....... | Karl Moor............................ | NA | ES | .............. | .............. | |
| Do .................... | Senior Counsel to the Assistant Administrator for Air and Radiation. | David Harlow........................ | NA | ES | .............. | .............. | |
| Do .................... | Director, Office of Atmospheric Programs.......... | Career Incumbent ................ | CA | ES | .............. | .............. | |
| Durham, NC ........... | Director, Office of Air Quality Planning and Standards. | ......do ................. | CA | ES | .............. | .............. | |
| Do .................... | Deputy Director, Office of Air Quality Planning and Standards. | ......do ................. | CA | ES | .............. | .............. | |
| Washington, DC ...... | Director, Office of Transportation and Air Quality. | ......do ................. | CA | ES | .............. | .............. | |
| Ann Arbor, MI........ | Deputy Director, Office of Transportation and Air Quality. | Vacant ................................ | ............ | ES | .............. | .............. | |
| Arlington, VA........... | Director, Office of Radiation and Indoor Air ...... | Career Incumbent ................ | CA | ES | .............. | .............. | |
| Washington, DC ...... | Policy and Communications Advisor for the Office of Air and Radiation. | Katherine Cory..................... | SC | GS | 12 | .............. | |
| Do .................... | Senior Policy Advisor to the Assistant Administrator for the Office of Air and Radiation. | Alexander Dominguez.......... | SC | GS | 12 | .............. | |
| Do .................... | Executive Assistant for the Office of Air and Radiation. | Sarah Landeene ................... | SC | GS | 12 | .............. | |
| Do .................... | Special Assistant for the Office of Air and Radiation. | Abigale Tardif...................... | SC | GS | 11 | .............. | |
| | **OFFICE OF THE ASSISTANT ADMINISTRATOR FOR CHEMICAL SAFETY AND POLLUTION PREVENTION** | | | | | | |
| Do .................... | Assistant Administrator for Toxic Substances... | Alexandra Dunn .................... | PAS | EX | IV | .............. | |
| Do .................... | Principal Deputy Assistant Administrator for Chemical Safety and Pollution Prevention. | Vacant ................................ | ............ | ES | .............. | .............. | |
| Do .................... | Deputy Assistant Administrator for the Office of Chemical Safety and Pollution Prevention. | David Fischer........................ | NA | ES | .............. | .............. | |
| Do .................... | Deputy Assistant Administrator for Chemical Safety and Pollution Prevention (Management). | Vacant ................................ | ............ | ES | .............. | .............. | |

## ENVIRONMENTAL PROTECTION AGENCY—Continued

| Location | Position Title | Name of Incumbent | Type of Appt. | Pay Plan | Level, Grade, or Pay | Tenure | Expires |
|---|---|---|---|---|---|---|---|
| Washington, DC ...... | Deputy Assistant Administrator for Programs.. | Vacant ...................... | ............ | ES | ............... | ............... | |
| Do .................... | Associate Deputy Assistant Administrator for New Chemicals. | Lynn Dekleva........................ | NA | ES | ............... | ............... | |
| Do .................... | Senior Counsel to the Assistant Administrator for the Office of Chemical Safety and Pollution Prevention. | Vacant ...................... | ............ | ES | ............... | ............... | |
| Do .................... | Senior Advisor.................................... | Career Incumbent ............... | CA | ES | ............... | ............... | |
| Do .................... | Director, Office of Science Coordination and Policy. | ......do ........ | CA | ES | ............... | ............... | |
| Do .................... | Director, Office of Pollution Prevention and Toxics. | ......do ........ | CA | ES | ............... | ............... | |
| Do .................... | Deputy Director for Management, Office of Pollution Prevention and Toxics. | ......do ........ | CA | ES | ............... | ............... | |
| Do .................... | Deputy Director (Programs), Office of Pollution Prevention and Toxics. | ......do ........ | CA | ES | ............... | ............... | |
| Arlington, VA.......... | Director, Office of Pesticides Programs ............. | ......do ........ | CA | ES | ............... | ............... | |
| Do .................... | Deputy Director, Office of Pesticides Programs (Management). | ......do ........ | CA | ES | ............... | ............... | |
| Do .................... | Deputy Director (Programs), Office of Pesticides Programs. | ......do ........ | CA | ES | ............... | ............... | |
| Washington, DC ...... | Special Advisor.................................... | Derrick Bolen........................ | SC | GS | 9 | ............... | |
| | **OFFICE OF THE ASSISTANT ADMINISTRATOR FOR RESEARCH AND DEVELOPMENT** | | | | | | |
| Do .................... | Assistant Administrator for Research and Development. | Vacant ................................. | PAS | EX | IV | ............... | |
| Do .................... | Deputy Assistant Administrator for Research and Development (Science). | Career Incumbent ............... | CA | ES | ............... | ............... | |
| Do .................... | Deputy Assistant Administrator for Management. | ......do ........ | CA | ES | ............... | ............... | |
| Do .................... | Deputy Assistant Administrator for Science Policy. | David Dunlap ........................ | NA | ES | ............... | ............... | |
| Do .................... | Environmental Protection Agency Laboratory Enterprise National Program Manager. | Career Incumbent ............... | CA | ES | ............... | ............... | |
| Durham, NC ........... | Director for Sustainable and Healthy Communities. | ......do ........ | CA | ES | ............... | ............... | |
| Washington, DC ...... | Director, Science Policy Division........................ | ......do ........ | CA | ES | ............... | ............... | |
| Do .................... | Senior Science Advisor for the Office of Research and Development. | Lindsey Jones ...................... | SC | GS | 15 | ............... | |
| Do .................... | Special Advisor.................................... | Amanda Fitzmorris ............... | SC | GS | 12 | ............... | |
| | **REGIONAL OFFICES** | | | | | | |
| | *Region 1- Boston, Massachusetts* | | | | | | |
| Boston, MA ............. | Regional Administrator ............................... | Dennis R Deziel.................... | NA | ES | ............... | ............... | |
| Do .................... | Deputy Regional Administrator........................ | Career Incumbent ............... | CA | ES | ............... | ............... | |
| | *Region 2 - New York, New York* | | | | | | |
| New York New York, NY. | Regional Administrator .................................... | Peter Lopez ........................... | NA | ES | ............... | ............... | |
| Do .................... | Deputy Regional Administrator........................ | Career Incumbent ............... | CA | ES | ............... | ............... | |
| New York, NY ......... | Special Advisor to the Regional Administrator . | Slawomir Kopec.................... | SC | GS | 11 | ............... | |
| | *Region 3 - Philadelphia, Pennsylvania* | | | | | | |
| Philadelphia, PA...... | Regional Administrator ............................... | Cosmo Servidio .................... | NA | ES | ............... | ............... | |
| Do .................... | Deputy Regional Administrator........................ | Career Incumbent ............... | CA | ES | ............... | ............... | |
| | *Region 4 - Atlanta, Georgia* | | | | | | |
| Atlanta, GA ............. | Regional Administrator ............................... | Mary Walker ........................ | NA | ES | ............... | ............... | |
| Do .................... | Deputy Regional Administrator........................ | Career Incumbent ............... | CA | ES | ............... | ............... | |
| | *Region 5 - Chicago, Illinois* | | | | | | |
| Chicago, IL.............. | Regional Administrator ............................... | Kurt Thiede ........................ | NA | ES | ............... | ............... | |
| Do .................... | Deputy Regional Administrator........................ | Career Incumbent ............... | CA | ES | ............... | ............... | |
| Do .................... | Senior Advisor to the Deputy Regional Administrator. | ......do ........ | CA | ES | ............... | ............... | |
| Do .................... | Senior Advisor for Water ................................. | Russell Rasmussen............... | SC | GS | 14 | ............... | |
| | *Region 6 - Dallas, Texas* | | | | | | |
| Dallas, TX ............... | Regional Administrator ............................... | Kenley Mcqueen .................... | NA | ES | ............... | ............... | |
| Do .................... | Deputy Regional Administrator........................ | Career Incumbent ............... | CA | ES | ............... | ............... | |
| Do .................... | Chief of Staff for Region 6 ............................. | Stephen Tatum Jr................ | SC | GS | 15 | ............... | |
| Do .................... | Associate Deputy Regional Administrator ........ | Corry Schiermeyer ............... | NA | ES | ............... | ............... | |
| | *Region 7 - Lenexa, Kansas* | | | | | | |
| Lenexa, KS ............. | Regional Administrator ............................... | James B Gulliford ............. | NA | ES | ............... | ............... | |
| Kansas City, KS ...... | Deputy Regional Administrator........................ | Career Incumbent ............... | CA | ES | ............... | ............... | |

## ENVIRONMENTAL PROTECTION AGENCY—Continued

| Location | Position Title | Name of Incumbent | Type of Appt. | Pay Plan | Level, Grade, or Pay | Tenure | Expires |
|---|---|---|---|---|---|---|---|
| Lenexa, KS ............. | Senior Advisor to the Deputy Regional Administrator. | Career Incumbent ................ | CA | ES | ................ | ................ | |
| Do ..................... | Renewable Fuels Advisor ................................... | Jonathan Hackett................ | SC | GS | 15 | ................ | |
| | *Region 8 - Denver, Colorado* | | | | | | |
| Denver, CO ............. | Regional Administrator....................................... | Gregory Sopkin.................... | NA | ES | ................ | ................ | |
| Do ..................... | Deputy Regional Administrator........................ | Career Incumbent ................ | CA | ES | ................ | ................ | |
| Do ..................... | Chief of Staff for Region 8 ............................... | Jagadeesan Sethuraman...... | SC | GS | 15 | ................ | |
| | *Region 9 - San Francisco, California* | | | | | | |
| San Francisco, CA ... | Regional Administrator....................................... | Vacant .................................. | ............. | ES | ................ | ................ | |
| Do ..................... | Deputy Regional Administrator........................ | Career Incumbent ................ | CA | ES | ................ | ................ | |
| Las Vegas, NV ........ | Senior Advisor to the Regional Administrator... | Charles Munoz ..................... | SC | GS | 15 | ................ | |
| San Francisco, CA ... | Senior Advisor for Policy and Congressional Affairs. | Christopher Hage ................. | SC | GS | 15 | ................ | |
| | *Region 10 - Seattle, Washington* | | | | | | |
| Seattle, WA ............. | Regional Administrator....................................... | Christopher Hladick............. | NA | ES | ................ | ................ | |
| Do ..................... | Deputy Regional Administrator........................ | Career Incumbent ................ | CA | ES | ................ | ................ | |

## ENVIRONMENTAL PROTECTION AGENCY OFFICE OF THE INSPECTOR GENERAL

| Location | Position Title | Name of Incumbent | Type of Appt. | Pay Plan | Level, Grade, or Pay | Tenure | Expires |
|---|---|---|---|---|---|---|---|
| Washington, DC ...... | Inspector General ............................................... | Sean William O'Donnell....... | PAS | EX | III | ................ | |

## EQUAL EMPLOYMENT OPPORTUNITY COMMISSION

| Location | Position Title | Name of Incumbent | Type of Appt. | Pay Plan | Level, Grade, or Pay | Tenure | Expires |
|---|---|---|---|---|---|---|---|
| | **OFFICE OF THE CHAIR** | | | | | | |
| Washington, DC ...... | Chair, Equal Employment Opportunity Commission. | Janet Dhillon ........................ | PAS | EX | III | ................ | |
| Do ..................... | Member, Equal Employment Opportunity Commission. | Vacant .................................. | PAS | EX | IV | ................ | |
| Do ..................... | ......do ................................ | Victoria A Lipnic .................. | PAS | EX | IV | ................ | |
| Do ..................... | ......do ................................ | Vacant .................................. | PAS | EX | IV | ................ | |
| Do ..................... | Member Equal Employment Opportunity Commission. | Charlotte A Burrows............. | PAS | EX | IV | ................ | |
| Do ..................... | Chief Operating Officer ..................................... | Career Incumbent ................ | CA | ES | ................ | ................ | |
| Do ..................... | Deputy Chief Operating Officer........................ | ......do .................................. | CA | ES | ................ | ................ | |
| Do ..................... | Senior Attorney-Advisor..................................... | Tabitha R Jenkins ................ | NA | ES | ................ | ................ | |
| Do ..................... | Program Manager ............................................... | Vacant .................................. | ............. | ES | ................ | ................ | |
| Do ..................... | ......do ................................ | ......do .................................. | ............. | ES | ................ | ................ | |
| Do ..................... | ......do ................................ | ......do .................................. | ............. | ES | ................ | ................ | |
| Do ..................... | ......do ................................ | ......do .................................. | ............. | ES | ................ | ................ | |
| | **OFFICE OF GENERAL COUNSEL** | | | | | | |
| Do ..................... | Deputy General Counsel ..................................... | ......do .................................. | ............. | ES | ................ | ................ | |
| Do ..................... | Associate General Counsel for Litigation Management Services. | Career Incumbent ................ | CA | ES | ................ | ................ | |
| Do ..................... | Associate General Counsel for Appellate Services. | ......do .................................. | CA | ES | ................ | ................ | |
| Do ..................... | General Counsel.................................................. | Sharon Fast Gustafson ........ | PAS | EX | V | ................ | |
| Do ..................... | Executive Staff Assistant ................................... | Elizabeth Wilson Malavathu. | SC | GS | 9 | ................ | |
| | **OFFICE OF THE CHIEF FINANCIAL OFFICER** | | | | | | |
| Do ..................... | Chief Financial Officer ...................................... | Career Incumbent ................ | CA | ES | ................ | ................ | |
| | **OFFICE OF CONGRESSIONAL AND LEGISLATIVE AFFAIRS** | | | | | | |
| Do ..................... | Director, Office of Congressional and Legislative Affairs. | Vacant .................................. | ............. | ES | ................ | ................ | |
| | **OFFICE OF FEDERAL OPERATIONS** | | | | | | |
| Do ..................... | Director, Office of Federal Operations................ | Career Incumbent ................ | CA | ES | ................ | ................ | |
| Do ..................... | Director, Appelate Review Programs.................. | ......do .................................. | CA | ES | ................ | ................ | |
| Do ..................... | Director, Federal Sector Programs..................... | ......do .................................. | CA | ES | ................ | ................ | |

## EQUAL EMPLOYMENT OPPORTUNITY COMMISSION—Continued

| Location | Position Title | Name of Incumbent | Type of Appt. | Pay Plan | Level, Grade, or Pay | Tenure | Expires |
|---|---|---|---|---|---|---|---|
| | **OFFICE OF FIELD PROGRAMS** | | | | | | |
| Washington, DC | Director, Office of Field Programs | Career Incumbent | CA | ES | | | |
| Do | Director, State, Local and Tribal Programs | Vacant | | ES | | | |
| Do | Chief Administrative Judge | ......do | | ES | | | |
| | **OFFICE OF THE CHIEF HUMAN CAPITAL OFFICER** | | | | | | |
| Do | Chief Human Capital Officer | Career Incumbent | CA | ES | | | |
| | **OFFICE OF INFORMATION TECHNOLOGY** | | | | | | |
| Do | Chief Information Officer | ......do | CA | ES | | | |
| | **OFFICE OF ENTERPRISE DATA AND ANALYTICS** | | | | | | |
| Do | Director, Office of Enterprise Data and Analytics. | ......do | CA | ES | | | |
| | **OFFICE OF LEGAL COUNSEL** | | | | | | |
| Do | Legal Counsel | Andrew Maunz | NA | ES | | | |
| Do | Associate Legal Counsel | Career Incumbent | CA | ES | | | |

## EXPORT-IMPORT BANK

| Location | Position Title | Name of Incumbent | Type of Appt. | Pay Plan | Level, Grade, or Pay | Tenure | Expires |
|---|---|---|---|---|---|---|---|
| | **BOARD OF DIRECTORS** | | | | | | |
| Washington, DC | First Vice President and Vice Chairman | Vacant | PAS | EX | IV | | |
| Do | Member of the Board of Directors | Spencer Bachus III | PAS | EX | IV | | |
| Do | ......do | Judith Pryor | PAS | EX | IV | | |
| Do | Member Board of Directors | Vacant | PAS | EX | IV | | |
| | **OFFICE OF THE CHAIRMAN** | | | | | | |
| Do | President and Chairman | Kimberly A Reed | PAS | EX | III | | |
| Do | Executive Secretary and Special Advisor | Richard Kisielowski | SC | GS | 12 | | |
| Do | Special Advisor and Deputy Scheduler | Edward Newburn | SC | GS | 15 | | |
| Do | Senior Advisor to the President and Chairman. | Lauren Fuller | SC | SL | $192,300 | | |
| Do | Special Advisor and Deputy Scheduler | Bailee Jones | SC | GS | 12 | | |
| | *Office of the General Counsel* | | | | | | |
| Do | Senior Vice President and General Counsel | David Slade | SC | SL | $192,300 | | |
| Do | Special Advisor | Jennifer M Porter | SC | GS | 11 | | |
| Do | Deputy General Counsel | Molly Conway | SC | SL | $183,100 | | |
| | *Office of the Chief Banking Officer* | | | | | | |
| Do | Chief Banking Officer | Stephen Renna | SC | SL | $188,400 | | |
| Do | Senior Advisor to the Chief Banking Officer | Cameron Dorsey | SC | GS | 14 | | |
| | *Office of the Chief of Staff* | | | | | | |
| Do | Deputy Chief of Staff | Ryan Mccormack | SC | GS | 15 | | |
| Do | Senior Advisor to the Chief of Staff and White House Liaison. | Basel N Alloush | SC | GS | 15 | | |
| Do | Senior Vice President and Chief of Staff | David Fogel | SC | SL | $192,300 | | |
| Do | Senior Advisor, National Security | Jamal Ware | SC | GS | 15 | | |
| Do | ......do | ......do | SC | GS | 15 | | |
| | *Office of Congressional & Intergovernmental Affairs* | | | | | | |
| Do | Congressional Liaison | Kimberly M Manecke | SC | GS | 14 | | |
| Do | Senior Vice President, Congressional & Intergovernmental Affairs. | Ross W Branson | SC | GS | 15 | | |
| Do | Congressional Relations Officer | Sierra Robinson | SC | GS | 14 | | |
| | *Office of External Engagement* | | | | | | |
| Do | Deputy to the Senior Vice President for External Engagement. | Brittany Jaye Walker | SC | GS | 14 | | |
| Do | Senior Vice President for External Engagement. | Luke Lindberg | SC | GS | 15 | | |
| Do | Principal Deputy to the Senior Vice President of External Engagement. | Christine Diane Harbin | SC | GS | 15 | | |
| | *Office of Communications* | | | | | | |
| Do | Speechwriter | Thomas Mcardle | SC | GS | 15 | | |
| Do | Senior Vice President of Communications | Kevin L Schweers | SC | SL | $183,100 | | |
| Do | Press Secretarty | Kelsey Koberg | SC | GS | 12 | | |

## EXPORT-IMPORT BANK OFFICE OF THE INSPECTOR GENERAL

| Location | Position Title | Name of Incumbent | Type of Appt. | Pay Plan | Level, Grade, or Pay | Tenure | Expires |
|---|---|---|---|---|---|---|---|
| Washington, DC ...... | Inspector General ................................................. | Vacant ................................... | PAS | EX | III | ................ | |

## FARM CREDIT ADMINISTRATION

| Location | Position Title | Name of Incumbent | Type of Appt. | Pay Plan | Level, Grade, or Pay | Tenure | Expires |
|---|---|---|---|---|---|---|---|
| | **OFFICE OF THE BOARD** | | | | | | |
| McLean, VA ............. | Chairman, Farm Credit Administration Board . | Glen Smith.................... | PAS | EX | III | 6 Years | |
| Do ................... | Member, Farm Credit Administration Board..... | Jeffery Hall ......................... | PAS | EX | IV | 1 Years | |
| Do ................... | ......do .............................. | Vacant ................................... | PAS | EX | IV | 6 Years | |
| Do ................... | Executive Assistant to Member ....................... | James Russell Middleton..... | SC | VH | $42 | ................ | |
| | **OFFICE OF CONGRESSIONAL AND PUBLIC AFFAIRS** | | | | | | |
| Do ................... | Director.................................................... | Michael Alan Stokke ............ | SC | VH | $44 | ................ | |
| Do ................... | Associate Director of Congressional Affairs....... | William A Meaux................. | SC | VH | $41 | ................ | |

## FEDERAL COMMUNICATIONS COMMISSION

| Location | Position Title | Name of Incumbent | Type of Appt. | Pay Plan | Level, Grade, or Pay | Tenure | Expires |
|---|---|---|---|---|---|---|---|
| | **OFFICE OF THE CHAIRMAN** | | | | | | |
| Washington, DC ...... | Chairman ................................................... | Ajit V Pai.......................... | PAS | EX | III | ................ | |
| Do ................... | Commissioner.............................................. | Michael O'Rielly ................. | PAS | EX | IV | ................ | |
| Do ................... | ......do ............................. | Brendan T Carr .................. | PAS | EX | IV | ................ | |
| Do ................... | ......do ............................. | Jessica Rosenworcel ............ | PAS | EX | IV | ................ | |
| Do ................... | ......do ............................. | Geoffrey Starks................... | PAS | EX | IV | ................ | |
| Do ................... | Chief of Staff .............................. | Matthew B Berry.............. | XS | SL | ................ | | |
| Do ................... | Senior Legal Advisor ............................. | Vacant ................................ | XS | SL | ................ | | |
| Do ................... | Senior Advisor to the Commissioner ................. | ......do ............. | XS | SL | ................ | | |
| Do ................... | ......do ............................. | ......do ............. | XS | SL | ................ | | |
| Do ................... | ......do ............................. | ......do ............. | XS | SL | ................ | | |
| Do ................... | ......do ............................. | ......do ............. | XS | SL | ................ | | |
| | **CONSUMER AND GOVERNMENTAL AFFAIRS BUREAU** | | | | | | |
| Do ................... | Bureau Chief.............................. | Career Incumbent ............... | CA | ES | ................ | | |
| Do ................... | Deputy Bureau Chief.............................. | ......do ............. | CA | ES | ................ | | |
| Do ................... | ......do ............................. | ......do ............. | CA | ES | ................ | | |
| Do ................... | ......do ............................. | ......do ............. | CA | ES | ................ | | |
| Do ................... | ......do ............................. | Vacant ................................ | | ES | ................ | | |
| | **ENFORCEMENT BUREAU** | | | | | | |
| Do ................... | Bureau Chief.............................. | Career Incumbent ............... | CA | ES | ................ | | |
| Do ................... | Deputy Bureau Chief.............................. | ......do ............. | CA | ES | ................ | | |
| | **INTERNATIONAL BUREAU** | | | | | | |
| Do ................... | Bureau Chief.............................. | ......do ............. | CA | ES | ................ | | |
| Do ................... | Deputy Bureau Chief.............................. | ......do ............. | CA | ES | ................ | | |
| Do ................... | ......do ............................. | ......do ............. | CA | ES | ................ | | |
| Do ................... | ......do ............................. | ......do ............. | CA | ES | ................ | | |
| | **MEDIA BUREAU** | | | | | | |
| Do ................... | Bureau Chief.............................. | ......do ............. | CA | ES | ................ | | |
| Do ................... | Deputy Bureau Chief.............................. | ......do ............. | CA | ES | ................ | | |
| Do ................... | ......do ............................. | ......do ............. | CA | ES | ................ | | |
| Do ................... | ......do ............................. | ......do ............. | CA | ES | ................ | | |
| | **OFFICE OF ECONOMICS AND ANALYTICS** | | | | | | |
| Do ................... | Chief ............................. | ......do ............. | CA | ES | ................ | | |
| Do ................... | Deputy Chief............................. | ......do ............. | CA | ES | ................ | | |
| Do ................... | ......do ............................. | ......do ............. | CA | ES | ................ | | |
| | **OFFICE OF ENGINEERING AND TECHNOLOGY** | | | | | | |
| Do ................... | Chief ............................. | Vacant ................................ | | ES | ................ | | |
| Do ................... | Deputy Chief............................. | Career Incumbent ............... | CA | ES | ................ | | |

## FEDERAL COMMUNICATIONS COMMISSION—Continued

| Location | Position Title | Name of Incumbent | Type of Appt. | Pay Plan | Level, Grade, or Pay | Tenure | Expires |
|---|---|---|---|---|---|---|---|
| | **OFFICE OF GENERAL COUNSEL** | | | | | | |
| Washington, DC ...... | General Counsel.................................. | Career Incumbent ................ | CA | ES | .............. | .............. | |
| Do .................... | Deputy General Counsel ...................... | ......do ................................ | CA | ES | .............. | .............. | |
| Do .................... | ......do .................................... | ......do ................................ | CA | ES | .............. | .............. | |
| Do .................... | ......do .................................... | Vacant ................................ | ............. | ES | .............. | .............. | |
| Do .................... | Associate General Counsel for Litigation.......... | Career Incumbent ................ | CA | ES | .............. | .............. | |
| Do .................... | Associate General Counsel.................... | ......do ................................ | CA | ES | .............. | .............. | |
| | **OFFICE OF INSPECTOR GENERAL** | | | | | | |
| Do .................... | Assistant Inspector General for Investigations . | ......do ................................ | CA | ES | .............. | .............. | |
| | **OFFICE OF MEDIA RELATIONS** | | | | | | |
| Do .................... | Director.......................................... | Brian C Hart...................... | NA | ES | .............. | .............. | |
| | **OFFICE OF THE MANAGING DIRECTOR** | | | | | | |
| Do .................... | Managing Director.............................. | Career Incumbent ................ | CA | ES | .............. | .............. | |
| Do .................... | Deputy Managing Director .................... | ......do ................................ | CA | ES | .............. | .............. | |
| Do .................... | ......do .................................... | ......do ................................ | CA | ES | .............. | .............. | |
| Do .................... | Chief Financial Officer ........................ | ......do ................................ | CA | ES | .............. | .............. | |
| Do .................... | Chief Human Capital Officer .................. | ......do ................................ | CA | ES | .............. | .............. | |
| Do .................... | Chief Administrative Officer.................. | ......do ................................ | CA | ES | .............. | .............. | |
| Do .................... | Chief Information Officer...................... | ......do ................................ | CA | ES | .............. | .............. | |
| Do .................... | Senior Procurement Executive ................ | Vacant ................................ | ............. | ES | .............. | .............. | |
| | **PUBLIC SAFETY AND HOMELAND SECURITY BUREAU** | | | | | | |
| Do .................... | Bureau Chief.................................... | Career Incumbent ................ | CA | ES | .............. | .............. | |
| Do .................... | Deputy Bureau Chief............................ | ......do ................................ | CA | ES | .............. | .............. | |
| Do .................... | ......do .................................... | ......do ................................ | CA | ES | .............. | .............. | |
| Do .................... | ......do .................................... | ......do ................................ | CA | ES | .............. | .............. | |
| | **WIRELINE COMPETITION BUREAU** | | | | | | |
| Do .................... | Bureau Chief.................................... | ......do ................................ | CA | ES | .............. | .............. | |
| Do .................... | Deputy Bureau Chief............................ | ......do ................................ | CA | ES | .............. | .............. | |
| Do .................... | ......do .................................... | ......do ................................ | CA | ES | .............. | .............. | |
| | **WIRELESS TELECOMMUNICATIONS BUREAU** | | | | | | |
| Do .................... | Bureau Chief.................................... | ......do ................................ | CA | ES | .............. | .............. | |
| Do .................... | Deputy Bureau Chief............................ | ......do ................................ | CA | ES | .............. | .............. | |
| Do .................... | ......do .................................... | ......do ................................ | CA | ES | .............. | .............. | |
| Do .................... | ......do .................................... | ......do ................................ | CA | ES | .............. | .............. | |
| Do .................... | ......do .................................... | Vacant ................................ | ............. | ES | .............. | .............. | |

## FEDERAL DEPOSIT INSURANCE CORPORATION

| Location | Position Title | Name of Incumbent | Type of Appt. | Pay Plan | Level, Grade, or Pay | Tenure | Expires |
|---|---|---|---|---|---|---|---|
| Washington, DC ...... | Chairman of the Board of Directors (Director).. | Jelena Mcwilliams................ | PAS | EX | III | .............. | |
| Do .................... | Vice Chairman .................................. | Vacant .................................... | PAS | EX | IV | .............. | |
| Do .................... | Member of the Board of Directors .............. | Martin J Gruenberg............. | PAS | EX | IV | .............. | |
| Do .................... | Inspector General ............................... | Vacant .................................... | PAS | EX | IV | .............. | |
| Do .................... | Chief of Staff ................................... | Brandon Lee Milhorn.......... | SC | OT | $283,700 | .............. | |
| Do .................... | Deputy to the Chairman for External Affairs.... | Chad R Davis...................... | SC | OT | $244,560 | .............. | |

## FEDERAL ELECTION COMMISSION

| Location | Position Title | Name of Incumbent | Type of Appt. | Pay Plan | Level, Grade, or Pay | Tenure | Expires |
|---|---|---|---|---|---|---|---|
| Washington, DC ...... | Member.......................................... | James Edwin Trainor III ..... | PAS | EX | IV | 6 Years | |
| Do .................... | ......do .................................... | Steven T Walther................ | PAS | EX | IV | 6 Years | |
| Do .................... | ......do .................................... | Caroline C Hunter.............. | PAS | EX | IV | 6 Years | |
| Do .................... | ......do .................................... | Ellen L Weintraub.............. | PAS | EX | IV | 6 Years | |
| Do .................... | ......do .................................... | Vacant .................................... | PAS | EX | IV | 6 Years | |
| Do .................... | ......do .................................... | .............................................. | PAS | EX | IV | 6 Years | |
| Do .................... | Executive Assistant ............................ | Ashley Stow ...................... | XS | GS | .............. | .............. | |
| Do .................... | ......do .................................... | Joseph Nixon ...................... | XS | GS | .............. | .............. | |
| Do .................... | ......do .................................... | Thomas Moore ...................... | XS | GS | .............. | .............. | |
| Do .................... | ......do .................................... | Dania Korkor...................... | XS | GS | .............. | .............. | |

## FEDERAL ELECTION COMMISSION—Continued

| Location | Position Title | Name of Incumbent | Type of Appt. | Pay Plan | Level, Grade, or Pay | Tenure | Expires |
|---|---|---|---|---|---|---|---|
| Washington, DC ...... | Executive Assistant ........................................... | Vacant ...................................... | XS | GS | .............. | .............. | |
| Do .................... | ......do ..................................................... | ......do ...................................... | XS | GS | .............. | .............. | |
| Do .................... | ......do ..................................................... | ......do ...................................... | XS | GS | .............. | .............. | |
| Do .................... | ......do ..................................................... | ......do ...................................... | XS | GS | .............. | .............. | |
| Do .................... | ......do ..................................................... | ......do ...................................... | XS | GS | .............. | .............. | |
| Do .................... | ......do ..................................................... | ......do ...................................... | XS | GS | .............. | .............. | |
| Do .................... | ......do ..................................................... | ......do ...................................... | XS | GS | .............. | .............. | |
| Do .................... | ......do ..................................................... | ......do ...................................... | XS | GS | .............. | .............. | |
| Do .................... | Executive Assistant (Chair/Vice Chair)............. | ......do ...................................... | XS | GS | .............. | .............. | |
| Do .................... | Executive Assistant (Floater)............................ | ......do ...................................... | XS | GS | .............. | .............. | |
| Do .................... | Executive Assistant (Chair/Vice Chair)............. | ......do ...................................... | XS | GS | .............. | .............. | |
| Do .................... | Executive Assistant (Floater)............................ | ......do ...................................... | XS | GS | .............. | .............. | |
| Do .................... | General Counsel................................................. | ......do ...................................... | XS | EX | V | .............. | |
| Do .................... | Staff Director ................................................... | David A Palmer .................... | XS | EX | IV | .............. | |

## FEDERAL ELECTION COMMISSION OFFICE OF THE INSPECTOR GENERAL

| Location | Position Title | Name of Incumbent | Type of Appt. | Pay Plan | Level, Grade, or Pay | Tenure | Expires |
|---|---|---|---|---|---|---|---|
| Washington, DC ...... | Inspector General ........................................... | Lynne A McFarland.............. | XS | SL | .............. | .............. | |

## FEDERAL ENERGY REGULATORY COMMISSION

| Location | Position Title | Name of Incumbent | Type of Appt. | Pay Plan | Level, Grade, or Pay | Tenure | Expires |
|---|---|---|---|---|---|---|---|
| | **OFFICE OF THE CHAIRMAN** | | | | | | |
| Washington, DC ...... | Chairman-Federal Energy Regulatory Commission. | Neil Chatterjee ..................... | PAS | EX | III | .............. | |
| Do .................... | Program and Policy Advisor.............................. | Michael Smith ...................... | SC | GS | 12 | .............. | |
| Do .................... | Confidential Assistant ...................................... | Jennifer Mellon ................... | SC | GS | 12 | .............. | |
| Do .................... | Administrative Officer....................................... | John Umberger...................... | SC | GS | 13 | .............. | |
| | *Office of the Commissioner* | | | | | | |
| Do .................... | Member-Federal Energy Regulatory Commission. | Bernard McNamee .............. | PAS | EX | IV | .............. | |
| Do .................... | ......do ..................................................... | Richard Glick........................ | PAS | EX | IV | .............. | |
| Do .................... | Confidential Assistant ...................................... | Hannah Dirks........................ | SC | GS | 11 | .............. | |
| Do .................... | Member-Federal Energy Regulatory Commission. | Vacant ..................................... | PAS | EX | IV | .............. | |
| Do .................... | ......do ..................................................... | James Danly ......................... | PAS | EX | IV | .............. | |
| | *Office of Energy Infrastructure Security* | | | | | | |
| Do .................... | Director, Office of Energy Infrastructure Security. | Career Incumbent ............... | CA | ES | .............. | .............. | |
| Do .................... | Deputy Director ................................................ | ......do ...................................... | CA | ES | .............. | .............. | |
| | *Office of Electric Reliability* | | | | | | |
| Do .................... | Director, Office of Electric Reliability............... | ......do ...................................... | CA | ES | .............. | .............. | |
| Do .................... | Deputy Director, Office of Electric Reliability ... | ......do ...................................... | CA | ES | .............. | .............. | |
| Do .................... | Director, Division of Compliance....................... | ......do ...................................... | CA | ES | .............. | .............. | |
| Do .................... | Director, Division of Reliabilty Standards ........ | ......do ...................................... | CA | ES | .............. | .............. | |
| Do .................... | Director, Division of Engineering and Logistics. | ......do ...................................... | CA | ES | .............. | .............. | |
| | *Office of the Secretary* | | | | | | |
| Do .................... | Secretary of the Commission ............................ | ......do ...................................... | CA | ES | .............. | .............. | |
| | *Office of External Affairs* | | | | | | |
| Do .................... | Director, Office of External Affairs.................... | Lindsee Gentry..................... | NA | ES | .............. | .............. | |
| | *Office of General Counsel* | | | | | | |
| Do .................... | General Counsel................................................. | Vacant ..................................... | ............ | ES | .............. | .............. | |
| Do .................... | Deputy General Counsel ................................... | Career Incumbent ............... | CA | ES | .............. | .............. | |
| Do .................... | Associate General Counsel, General and Administrative Law. | ......do ...................................... | CA | ES | .............. | .............. | |
| Do .................... | Associate General Counsel, Energy Projects ..... | ......do ...................................... | CA | ES | .............. | .............. | |
| Do .................... | Deputy Associate General Counsel, Energy Projects. | ......do ...................................... | CA | ES | .............. | .............. | |
| Do .................... | Associate General Counsel................................. | ......do ...................................... | CA | ES | .............. | .............. | |

## FEDERAL ENERGY REGULATORY COMMISSION—Continued

| Location | Position Title | Name of Incumbent | Type of Appt. | Pay Plan | Level, Grade, or Pay | Tenure | Expires |
|---|---|---|---|---|---|---|---|
| Washington, DC ...... | Associate General Counsel.................................. | Career Incumbent ............... | CA | ES | ............... | ............... | |
| Do .................... | Solicitor............................................... | ......do ........................... | CA | ES | ............... | ............... | |
| | *Office of the Executive Director* | | | | | | |
| Do .................... | Executive Director ................................. | ......do ........................... | CA | ES | ............... | ............... | |
| Do .................... | Chief Human Capital Officer........................ | ......do ........................... | CA | ES | ............... | ............... | |
| Do .................... | Chief Information Officer ............................. | ......do ........................... | CA | ES | ............... | ............... | |
| Do .................... | Chief Financial Officer ............................... | ......do ........................... | CA | ES | ............... | ............... | |
| Do .................... | Chief Security Officer ................................ | ......do ........................... | CA | ES | ............... | ............... | |
| | *Office of Energy Market Regulation* | | | | | | |
| Do .................... | Director, Office of Energy Market Regulation ... | ......do ........................... | CA | ES | ............... | ............... | |
| Do .................... | Deputy Director, Office of Energy Market Regulation. | ......do ........................... | CA | ES | ............... | ............... | |
| Do .................... | Director, Division of Electric Power Regulation- Central. | ......do ........................... | CA | ES | ............... | ............... | |
| Do .................... | Director, Division of Electric Power Regulation- West. | ......do ........................... | CA | ES | ............... | ............... | |
| Do .................... | Director, Division of Electric Power Regulation - East. | ......do ........................... | CA | ES | ............... | ............... | |
| Do .................... | Director, Division of Pipeline Regulation ........... | ......do ........................... | CA | ES | ............... | ............... | |
| | *Office of Energy Projects* | | | | | | |
| Do .................... | Director, Office of Energy Projects.................. | ......do ........................... | CA | ES | ............... | ............... | |
| Do .................... | Deputy Director, Office of Energy Projects ........ | ......do ........................... | CA | ES | ............... | ............... | |
| Do .................... | Director, Hydropower Licensing .................... | ......do ........................... | CA | ES | ............... | ............... | |
| Do .................... | Director, Hydropower Administration and Compliance. | ......do ........................... | CA | ES | ............... | ............... | |
| Do .................... | Director, Gas Environment and Engineering .... | ......do ........................... | CA | ES | ............... | ............... | |
| Do .................... | Director, Division of Lng Facility Review & Inspections. | ......do ........................... | CA | ES | ............... | ............... | |
| Do .................... | Director, Division of Pipeline Certificates .......... | ......do ........................... | CA | ES | ............... | ............... | |
| | *Office of Enforcement* | | | | | | |
| Do .................... | Director, Office of Enforcement.................... | ......do ........................... | CA | ES | ............... | ............... | |
| Do .................... | Deputy Director, Office of Enforcement ............ | ......do ........................... | CA | ES | ............... | ............... | |
| Do .................... | Director, Investigations ............................. | ......do ........................... | CA | ES | ............... | ............... | |
| Do .................... | Director and Chief Accountant, Audits Division. | Vacant ............................ | ............... | ES | ............... | ............... | |
| Do .................... | Director, Division of Analytics and Surveillance. | Career Incumbent ............... | CA | ES | ............... | ............... | |
| | *Office of Administrative Litigation* | | | | | | |
| Do .................... | Director, Office of Administrative Litigation .... | ......do ........................... | CA | ES | ............... | ............... | |
| Do .................... | Director, Technical Division ........................ | ......do ........................... | CA | ES | ............... | ............... | |
| Do .................... | Director, Legal Division............................. | Vacant ............................ | ............... | ES | ............... | ............... | |
| | *Office of Energy Policy and Innovation* | | | | | | |
| Do .................... | Director Office of Energy Policy and Innovation. | Career Incumbent ............... | CA | ES | ............... | ............... | |
| Do .................... | Deputy Director, Office of Energy Policy and Innovation. | ......do ........................... | CA | ES | ............... | ............... | |
| Do .................... | Director, Division of Energy Market Assessments. | ......do ........................... | CA | ES | ............... | ............... | |
| Do .................... | Director, Policy Development ....................... | ......do ........................... | CA | ES | ............... | ............... | |
| Do .................... | Director, Economic and Technical Analysis........ | ......do ........................... | CA | ES | ............... | ............... | |

## FEDERAL HOUSING FINANCE AGENCY

| Location | Position Title | Name of Incumbent | Type of Appt. | Pay Plan | Level, Grade, or Pay | Tenure | Expires |
|---|---|---|---|---|---|---|---|
| Washington, DC ...... | **OFFICE OF DIRECTOR**<br>Director of Legislative Affairs............................ | Sarah D Merchak ............... | SC | OT | ............... | 5 Years | |
| Do .................... | **FEDERAL HOUSING FINANCE AGENCY**<br>Director, Federal Housing Finance Agency........ | Melvin L Watt...................... | PAS | SL | ............... | ............... | |

# FEDERAL HOUSING FINANCE BOARD

| Location | Position Title | Name of Incumbent | Type of Appt. | Pay Plan | Level, Grade, or Pay | Tenure | Expires |
|---|---|---|---|---|---|---|---|
| | **OFFICE OF THE BOARD OF DIRECTORS** | | | | | | |
| Washington, DC ...... | Counsel to the Chairman .................... | Daris D Meeks Esq............. | SC | OT | $184,213 | .............. | |
| Do .................... | Special Assistant to the Board Director............. | Jonathan Lindley ................. | SC | TM | $165,672 | .............. | |
| Do .................... | Staff Assistant.................... | John Paul Green.................... | SC | OT | $92,522 | .............. | |

# FEDERAL LABOR RELATIONS AUTHORITY

| Location | Position Title | Name of Incumbent | Type of Appt. | Pay Plan | Level, Grade, or Pay | Tenure | Expires |
|---|---|---|---|---|---|---|---|
| | **OFFICE OF THE CHAIRMAN** | | | | | | |
| Washington, DC ...... | Chairman ............................... | Vacant ................................ | PAS | EX | IV | 5 Years | |
| | **OFFICE OF MEMBER** | | | | | | |
| Do .................... | Member........................ | ......do ................... | PAS | EX | V | .............. | |
| Do .................... | ......do ......................... | ......do ................... | PAS | EX | V | 5 Years | |
| | **OFFICE OF THE GENERAL COUNSEL** | | | | | | |
| Do .................... | General Counsel........................ | ......do ................... | PAS | EX | V | .............. | |
| | **FEDERAL SERVICE IMPASSES PANEL** | | | | | | |
| Do .................... | Chair, Federal Service Impasses Panel ............. | ......do ................... | PA | SL | .............. | .............. | |
| Do .................... | Member, Federal Service Impasses Panel ......... | Marvin E Johnson ................. | PA | SL | .............. | .............. | |
| Do .................... | ......do .......................... | Vacant ................... | PA | SL | .............. | .............. | |
| Do .................... | ......do .......................... | ......do ................... | PA | SL | .............. | .............. | |
| Do .................... | ......do .......................... | ......do ................... | PA | SL | .............. | .............. | |
| Do .................... | ......do .......................... | ......do ................... | PA | SL | .............. | .............. | |
| Do .................... | ......do .......................... | ......do ................... | PA | SL | .............. | .............. | |
| | *Foreign Services Labor Relations Board* | | | | | | |
| Do .................... | Member, Foreign Service Labor Relations Board. | ......do ................... | XS | SL | .............. | .............. | |
| Do .................... | ......do .......................... | ......do ................... | XS | SL | .............. | .............. | |

# FEDERAL MARITIME COMMISSION

| Location | Position Title | Name of Incumbent | Type of Appt. | Pay Plan | Level, Grade, or Pay | Tenure | Expires |
|---|---|---|---|---|---|---|---|
| | **OFFICE OF THE MEMBERS** | | | | | | |
| Washington, DC ...... | Chairman .................................... | Michael A Khouri ................. | PAS | EX | III | 5 Years | |
| Do .................... | Member........................................ | Louis Sola ............................ | PAS | EX | IV | 5 Years | |
| Do .................... | ......do .................................. | Daniel Benjamin Maffei....... | PAS | EX | IV | 5 Years | |
| Do .................... | ......do .................................. | Carl Bentzel......................... | PAS | EX | IV | 5 Years | |
| Do .................... | ......do .................................. | Rebecca F Dye ..................... | PAS | EX | IV | 5 Years | |
| Do .................... | Chief of Staff ................................ | Career Incumbent ............... | CA | ES | .............. | .............. | |
| Do .................... | Counsel to Commissioner.................... | John N Young ...................... | SC | GS | 15 | .............. | |
| Do .................... | Senior Legislative and Public Affairs Specialist. | John Kenneth Decrosta ....... | SC | GS | 15 | .............. | |
| | *Office of the General Counsel* | | | | | | |
| Do .................... | General Counsel........................ | Vacant ................................ | | ES | .............. | .............. | |
| | **OFFICE OF THE MANAGING DIRECTOR** | | | | | | |
| Do .................... | Managing Director............................. | Career Incumbent ............... | CA | ES | .............. | .............. | |

# FEDERAL MEDIATION AND CONCILIATION SERVICE

| Location | Position Title | Name of Incumbent | Type of Appt. | Pay Plan | Level, Grade, or Pay | Tenure | Expires |
|---|---|---|---|---|---|---|---|
| Washington, DC ...... | Agency Principal Deputy Director....................... | Vacant ................................ | | ES | .............. | .............. | |
| Do ................. | Chief Operating Officer.......................... | Career Incumbent ............... | CA | ES | .............. | .............. | |
| | **OFFICE OF THE DIRECTOR** | | | | | | |
| Philadelphia, PA...... | Deputy Director (Field Operations).................... | ......do ................... | CA | ES | .............. | .............. | |
| Seattle, WA.............. | Deputy Director ....................... | Gary Richard Hattal ........... | XS | SL | .............. | .............. | |

## FEDERAL MEDIATION AND CONCILIATION SERVICE—Continued

| Location | Position Title | Name of Incumbent | Type of Appt. | Pay Plan | Level, Grade, or Pay | Tenure | Expires |
|---|---|---|---|---|---|---|---|
| Kansas City, MO ..... | National Representative.................................. | Career Incumbent ................ | CA | ES | .............. | ............. | |

## FEDERAL MINE SAFETY AND HEALTH REVIEW COMMISSION

| Location | Position Title | Name of Incumbent | Type of Appt. | Pay Plan | Level, Grade, or Pay | Tenure | Expires |
|---|---|---|---|---|---|---|---|
| Washington, DC ...... | Confidential Assistant ................................. | Kimberly Burch................... | SC | GS | 11 | .............. | |
| | **OFFICE OF THE CHAIRMAN** | | | | | | |
| Do .................. | ......do ...................................................... | Elizabeth Alicia Smith......... | SC | GS | 9 | .............. | |
| Do .................. | Senior Policy Advisor.................................. | Vacant ................................. | ............ | ES | .............. | .............. | |
| | **OFFICE OF THE COMMISSIONERS** | | | | | | |
| Do .................. | Attorney Advisor (General)......................... | Elizabeth Sarah Symonds ... | SC | GS | 15 | .............. | |
| Do .................. | Commissioner............................................... | William Ira Althen .............. | PAS | EX | IV | .............. | |
| Do .................. | ......do ...................................................... | Vacant ................................. | PAS | EX | IV | .............. | |
| Do .................. | Senior Policy Advisor.................................. | ......do .................................. | ............ | ES | .............. | .............. | |
| Do .................. | Commissioner............................................... | Arthur G Traynor................. | PAS | EX | IV | .............. | |
| Do .................. | ......do ...................................................... | Michael G Young.................. | PAS | EX | IV | 6 Years | |
| Do .................. | Chairman...................................................... | Marco M Rajkovich Jr. ........ | PAS | EX | III | .............. | |
| Do .................. | ......do ...................................................... | Mary L Jordan...................... | PAS | EX | III | .............. | |
| | **OFFICE OF THE GENERAL COUNSEL** | | | | | | |
| Do .................. | General Counsel........................................... | Career Incumbent ................ | CA | ES | .............. | .............. | |
| Do .................. | ......do ...................................................... | Vacant ................................. | ............ | ES | .............. | .............. | |

## FEDERAL PERMITTING IMPROVEMENT STEERING COUNCIL

| Location | Position Title | Name of Incumbent | Type of Appt. | Pay Plan | Level, Grade, or Pay | Tenure | Expires |
|---|---|---|---|---|---|---|---|
| Washington, DC ...... | Executive Director ....................................... | Alexander Harrison Herrgott. | NA | ES | .............. | .............. | |
| Do .................. | Chief of Staff............................................... | Katherine Rose Smith.......... | SC | GS | 15 | .............. | |
| Do .................. | Associate Director of Congressional and Intergovernmental Affairs. | Charles Anthony Castagna.. | SC | GS | 14 | .............. | |

## FEDERAL RESERVE SYSTEM

| Location | Position Title | Name of Incumbent | Type of Appt. | Pay Plan | Level, Grade, or Pay | Tenure | Expires |
|---|---|---|---|---|---|---|---|
| Washington, DC ...... | Chairman ...................................................... | Jerome H. Powell.................. | PAS | EX | II | 14 Years | |
| Do .................. | Vice Chairman ............................................. | Richard H. Clarida ............... | PAS | EX | III | 14 Years | |
| Do .................. | Vice Chair of Supervision........................... | Randal K. Quarles................ | PAS | EX | .............. | .............. | |
| Do .................. | Governor....................................................... | Michelle W. Bowman ............ | PAS | EX | III | 14 Years | |
| Do .................. | ......do ...................................................... | Lael Brainard ....................... | PAS | EX | III | 14 Years | |
| Do .................. | ......do ...................................................... | Vacant ................................. | PAS | EX | III | 14 Years | |
| Do .................. | ......do ...................................................... | ......do .................................. | PAS | EX | III | 14 Years | |

## FEDERAL RETIREMENT THRIFT INVESTMENT BOARD

| Location | Position Title | Name of Incumbent | Type of Appt. | Pay Plan | Level, Grade, or Pay | Tenure | Expires |
|---|---|---|---|---|---|---|---|
| Washington, DC ...... | Chairman of the Board.................................. | Michael Kennedy................... | PAS | OT | .............. | .............. | |
| Do .................. | Board Member .............................................. | Dana Bilyeu ........................ | PAS | OT | .............. | .............. | |
| Do .................. | ......do ...................................................... | Ronald Mccray ..................... | PAS | OT | .............. | .............. | |
| Do .................. | ......do ...................................................... | William S Jasien ................. | PAS | OT | .............. | .............. | |
| Do .................. | ......do ...................................................... | David Jones ......................... | PAS | OT | .............. | .............. | |
| Do .................. | Executive Director ....................................... | Ravindra Deo ....................... | XS | EX | III | .............. | |
| Do .................. | Director of External Affairs ........................ | Career Incumbent ................ | CA | ES | .............. | .............. | |
| Do .................. | General Counsel........................................... | ......do .................................. | CA | ES | .............. | .............. | |
| Do .................. | Director, Office of Enterprise Planning.............. | ......do .................................. | CA | ES | .............. | .............. | |

## FEDERAL RETIREMENT THRIFT INVESTMENT BOARD—Continued

| Location | Position Title | Name of Incumbent | Type of Appt. | Pay Plan | Level, Grade, or Pay | Tenure | Expires |
|---|---|---|---|---|---|---|---|
| Washington, DC ...... | Chief Investment Officer .................................... | Career Incumbent ................ | CA | ES | ................ | ............... | |

## FEDERAL TRADE COMMISSION

| Location | Position Title | Name of Incumbent | Type of Appt. | Pay Plan | Level, Grade, or Pay | Tenure | Expires |
|---|---|---|---|---|---|---|---|
| | **OFFICE OF THE CHAIRMAN** | | | | | | |
| Washington, DC ...... | Chairman ....................................................... | Joseph J Simons ................... | PAS | EX | III | 7 Years | |
| Do .................... | Commissioner................................................ | Christine C Wilson .............. | PAS | EX | IV | 7 Years | |
| Do .................... | ......do ..... | Rohit Chopra ....................... | PAS | EX | IV | 7 Years | |
| Do .................... | ......do ..... | Noah J Phillips .................... | PAS | EX | IV | 7 Years | |
| Do .................... | ......do ..... | Rebecca J Slaughter............. | PAS | EX | IV | 7 Years | |
| Do .................... | Special Advisor to the Chairman...................... | Tara I Koslov ....................... | TA | ES | ............... | ............... | 06/24/21 |
| Do .................... | Confidential Assistant ................................... | Edith Parker ........................ | SC | GS | 12 | ............... | |
| Do .................... | Technology Advisor ....................................... | Erie K Meyer ....................... | SC | GS | 15 | ............... | |
| Do .................... | Secretary ....................................................... | Vacant ................................ | ............. | ES | ............... | ............... | |
| Do .................... | Director, Office of Policy Planning ................... | ......do ..... | ............. | ES | ............... | ............... | |
| Do .................... | ......do ..... | Bilal Konen Sayyed .............. | SC | GS | 15 | ............... | |
| Do .................... | Director, Office of Public Affairs ...................... | Vacant ................................ | ............. | ES | ............... | ............... | |
| Do .................... | ......do ..... | Cathy Macfarlane................. | SC | GS | 15 | ............... | |
| | **OFFICE OF THE GENERAL COUNSEL** | | | | | | |
| Do .................... | General Counsel............................................. | Alden F Abbott ..................... | NA | ES | ............... | ............... | |
| Do .................... | Deputy General Counsel for Legal Counsel....... | Vacant ................................ | ............. | ES | ............... | ............... | |
| Do .................... | Deputy General Counsel for Litigation .............. | Career Incumbent ................ | CA | ES | ............... | ............... | |
| | **OFFICE OF EXECUTIVE DIRECTOR** | | | | | | |
| Do .................... | Executive Director ......................................... | ......do ..... | CA | ES | ............... | ............... | |
| Do .................... | Deputy Executive Director............................... | Vacant ................................ | ............. | ES | ............... | ............... | |
| Do .................... | Chief Administrative Services Officer............... | Career Incumbent ................ | CA | ES | ............... | ............... | |
| Do .................... | Chief Financial Officer .................................... | ......do ..... | CA | ES | ............... | ............... | |
| Do .................... | Chief Human Capital Officer ........................... | ......do ..... | CA | ES | ............... | ............... | |
| Do .................... | Deputy Chief Information Officer...................... | ......do ..... | CA | ES | ............... | ............... | |
| | **OFFICE OF INTERNATIONAL AFFAIRS** | | | | | | |
| Do .................... | Director, Office of International Affairs ............. | ......do ..... | CA | ES | ............... | ............... | |
| Do .................... | Deputy Director for International Consumer Protection. | ......do ..... | CA | ES | ............... | ............... | |
| | **BUREAU OF COMPETITION** | | | | | | |
| Do .................... | Director, Bureau of Competition ...................... | Ian R Conner ....................... | NA | ES | ............... | ............... | |
| Do .................... | Deputy Director, Bureau of Competition............ | Daniel S Francis................... | NA | ES | ............... | ............... | |
| Do .................... | ......do ..... | Gail Levine .......................... | NA | ES | ............... | ............... | |
| Do .................... | Assistant Director for Anticompetitive Practices. | Career Incumbent ................ | CA | ES | ............... | ............... | |
| Do .................... | Assistant Director for Compliance.................... | ......do ..... | CA | ES | ............... | ............... | |
| Do .................... | Assistant Director for Health Care ................... | ......do ..... | CA | ES | ............... | ............... | |
| Do .................... | Assistant Director for Mergers I...................... | Vacant ................................ | ............. | ES | ............... | ............... | |
| Do .................... | Assistant Director for Mergers II ..................... | Career Incumbent ................ | CA | ES | ............... | ............... | |
| Do .................... | Assistant Director for Mergers III..................... | ......do ..... | CA | ES | ............... | ............... | |
| Do .................... | Assistant Director for Mergers IV ..................... | Vacant ................................ | ............. | ES | ............... | ............... | |
| Do .................... | Assistant Director for Technology Enforcement. | ......do ..... | ............. | ES | ............... | ............... | |
| | **BUREAU OF CONSUMER PROTECTION** | | | | | | |
| Do .................... | Director, Bureau of Consumer Protection ......... | Andrew Smith....................... | NA | ES | ............... | ............... | |
| Do .................... | Deputy Director, Bureau of Consumer Protection. | Vacant ................................ | ............. | ES | ............... | ............... | |
| Do .................... | Associate Director for Advertising Practices...... | ......do ..... | ............. | ES | ............... | ............... | |
| Do .................... | Associate Director for Consumer and Business Education. | Career Incumbent ................ | CA | ES | ............... | ............... | |
| Do .................... | Associate Director for Consumer Response and Operations. | ......do ..... | CA | ES | ............... | ............... | |
| Do .................... | Associate Director for Enforcement................... | ......do ..... | CA | ES | ............... | ............... | |
| Do .................... | Associate Director for Financial Practices ........ | ......do ..... | CA | ES | ............... | ............... | |
| Do .................... | Associate Director for Litigation Technology and Analysis. | ......do ..... | CA | ES | ............... | ............... | |
| Do .................... | Associate Director for Marketing Practices ....... | ......do ..... | CA | ES | ............... | ............... | |
| Do .................... | Associate Director for Privacy and Identity Protection. | ......do ..... | CA | ES | ............... | ............... | |

## FEDERAL TRADE COMMISSION—Continued

| Location | Position Title | Name of Incumbent | Type of Appt. | Pay Plan | Level, Grade, or Pay | Tenure | Expires |
|---|---|---|---|---|---|---|---|
| | **BUREAU OF ECONOMICS** | | | | | | |
| Washington, DC ...... | Director, Bureau of Economics........................... | Vacant ............................... | ............ | ES | ............... | ............... | |
| Do .................. | Deputy Director for Antitrust ......................... | Career Incumbent ............. | CA | ES | ............... | ............... | |
| Do .................. | Deputy Director for Consumer Protection ........ | ......do ............................... | CA | ES | ............... | ............... | |
| Do .................. | Assistant Director for Antitrust I...................... | ......do ............................... | CA | ES | ............... | ............... | |
| Do .................. | Assistant Director for Antitrust II..................... | ......do ............................... | CA | ES | ............... | ............... | |
| Do .................. | Assistant Director for Consumer Protection...... | ......do ............................... | CA | ES | ............... | ............... | |

## GENERAL SERVICES ADMINISTRATION

| Location | Position Title | Name of Incumbent | Type of Appt. | Pay Plan | Level, Grade, or Pay | Tenure | Expires |
|---|---|---|---|---|---|---|---|
| | **OFFICE OF THE ADMINISTRATOR** | | | | | | |
| Washington, DC ...... | Administrator of General Services ..................... | Emily Webster Murphy........ | PAS | EX | III | ............... | |
| Do .................. | Deputy Administrator ...................................... | Allison Fahrenkopf Brigati .. | NA | ES | ............... | ............... | |
| Do .................. | Chief of Staff................................................... | Robert Borden...................... | NA | ES | ............... | ............... | |
| Do .................. | Deputy Chief of Staff....................................... | Lafondra Barlow.................. | NA | ES | ............... | ............... | |
| Do .................. | Director, Service Management Office ................ | Career Incumbent .............. | CA | ES | ............... | ............... | |
| Do .................. | Senior Advisor for Technology........................... | Reynold Schweickhardt ....... | SC | SL | ............... | ............... | |
| Do .................. | White House Liaison ........................................ | Carla Sansalone .................. | SC | GS | 14 | ............... | |
| Do .................. | Special Assistant to the Administrator and Chief Scheduler. | Alexandra Petrucci.............. | SC | GS | 13 | ............... | |
| Do .................. | Deputy White House Liaison ............................ | Julia Marlowe...................... | SC | GS | 12 | ............... | |
| Do .................. | Confidential Assistant to the Administrator...... | Kevin Johnson ..................... | SC | GS | 7 | ............... | |
| | **FEDERAL ACQUISITION SERVICE** | | | | | | |
| Do .................. | Commissioner................................................... | Julie Dunne ........................ | NA | ES | ............... | ............... | |
| Do .................. | Deputy Commissioner ...................................... | Career Incumbent .............. | CA | ES | ............... | ............... | |
| Do .................. | Deputy Commissioner and Director of Technology Transformation Services. | Anil Cheriyan ...................... | NA | ES | ............... | ............... | |
| Do .................. | Assistant Commissioner for Solutions .............. | Career Incumbent .............. | CA | ES | ............... | ............... | |
| Do .................. | Deputy Director, Client Markets ...................... | Harry Lee............................ | TA | ES | ............... | ............... | 09/02/22 |
| Do .................. | Director, Centers of Excellence ....................... | Robert De Luca................... | TA | ES | ............... | ............... | 03/03/21 |
| | **PUBLIC BUILDINGS SERVICE** | | | | | | |
| Do .................. | Commissioner................................................... | Daniel Mathews .................. | NA | ES | ............... | ............... | |
| Do .................. | Deputy Commissioner ...................................... | Career Incumbent .............. | CA | ES | ............... | ............... | |
| Do .................. | Executive Assistant ......................................... | Christina Stottmann ............ | SC | GS | 13 | ............... | |
| | **OFFICE OF GENERAL COUNSEL** | | | | | | |
| Do .................. | General Counsel............................................... | John St. John...................... | NA | ES | ............... | ............... | |
| Do .................. | Deputy General Counsel .................................. | Vacant ............................... | ............ | ES | ............... | ............... | |
| Do .................. | Associate General Counsel for General Law ..... | Career Incumbent .............. | CA | ES | ............... | ............... | |
| Do .................. | Associate General Counsel for Personal Property. | ......do ............................... | CA | ES | ............... | ............... | |
| Do .................. | Associate General Counsel for Real Property.... | Vacant ............................... | ............ | ES | ............... | ............... | |
| Do .................. | Regional Counsel, National Capital Region...... | Career Incumbent .............. | CA | ES | ............... | ............... | |
| San Francisco, CA ... | Regional Counsel, Pacific Rim Region.............. | ......do ............................... | CA | ES | ............... | ............... | |
| | **OFFICE OF GOVERNMENTWIDE POLICY** | | | | | | |
| Washington, DC ...... | Associate Administrator for Governmentwide Policy. | Jessica Salmoiraghi.............. | NA | ES | ............... | ............... | |
| Do .................. | Principal Deputy Associate Administrator for Governmentwide Policy. | Career Incumbent ................ | CA | ES | ............... | ............... | |
| | **OFFICE OF ADMINISTRATIVE SERVICES** | | | | | | |
| Do .................. | Chief Administrative Services Officer................ | ......do ............................... | CA | ES | ............... | ............... | |
| Do .................. | Senior Advisor ................................................ | ......do ............................... | CA | ES | ............... | ............... | |
| Do .................. | Director, Office of Accountability and Transparency. | Susan Marshall ................... | SC | GS | 15 | ............... | |
| | **OFFICE OF CIVIL RIGHTS** | | | | | | |
| Do .................. | Associate Administrator for Civil Rights ........... | Career Incumbent ................ | CA | ES | ............... | ............... | |
| | **OFFICE OF STRATEGIC COMMUNICATION** | | | | | | |
| Do .................. | Associate Administrator for Strategic Communication. | Mark Mchale........................ | NA | ES | ............... | ............... | |
| Do .................. | Press Secretary and Deputy Associate Administrator for Media Affairs. | Pamela Pennington .............. | SC | GS | 15 | ............... | |
| Do .................. | Senior Communications Advisor......................... | Christopher Godbey ............. | SC | GS | 14 | ............... | |

## GENERAL SERVICES ADMINISTRATION—Continued

| Location | Position Title | Name of Incumbent | Type of Appt. | Pay Plan | Level, Grade, or Pay | Tenure | Expires |
|---|---|---|---|---|---|---|---|
| Washington, DC ...... | Speechwriter ...................................................... | David Keltz .......................... | SC | GS | 9 | .............. | |
| | **OFFICE OF CONGRESSIONAL AND INTERGOVERNMENTAL AFFAIRS** | | | | | | |
| Do ..................... | Associate Administrator for Congressional and Intergovernmental Affairs. | Jeffrey Post ........................... | NA | ES | .............. | .............. | |
| Do ..................... | Deputy Associate Administrator for Congressional and Intergovernmental Affairs. | Rebecca Pselos ..................... | SC | GS | 15 | .............. | |
| Do ..................... | Policy Advisor ......................................... | Kevin Ortiz .......................... | SC | GS | 13 | .............. | |
| | **OFFICE OF CUSTOMER EXPERIENCE** | | | | | | |
| Do ..................... | Chief Customer Officer..................... | Vacant ..................................... | | ES | .............. | .............. | |
| | **OFFICE OF GSA IT** | | | | | | |
| Do ..................... | Chief Information Officer................................... | Career Incumbent ................ | CA | ES | .............. | .............. | |
| Do ..................... | Deputy Chief Information Officer..................... | ...... do ................................ | CA | ES | .............. | .............. | |
| | **OFFICE OF SMALL AND DISADVANTAGED BUSINESS UTILIZATION** | | | | | | |
| Do ..................... | Associate Administrator for Small and Disadvantaged Business Utilization. | Brian Barnes ........................ | NA | ES | .............. | .............. | |
| Do ..................... | Senior Advisor ...................................... | William Pettigrew ............... | SC | GS | 15 | .............. | |
| | **REGIONAL ADMINISTRATORS** | | | | | | |
| | *National Capital Region* | | | | | | |
| Washington, DC ...... | Regional Administrator ...................... | Scott Anderson...................... | NA | ES | .............. | .............. | |
| | *New England Region* | | | | | | |
| Boston, MA .............. | ...... do .................................... | Christopher Averill.............. | NA | ES | .............. | .............. | |
| | *Northeast and Caribbean Region* | | | | | | |
| New York, NY ......... | ...... do .................................... | John Sarcone ........................ | NA | ES | .............. | .............. | |
| | *Mid-Atlantic Region* | | | | | | |
| Philadelphia, PA...... | ...... do .................................... | Joyce Haas ............................ | NA | ES | .............. | .............. | |
| | *Southeast Sunbelt Region* | | | | | | |
| Atlanta, GA ............. | ...... do .................................... | Brian Stern ........................... | NA | ES | .............. | .............. | |
| | *Great Lakes Region* | | | | | | |
| Chicago, IL............... | ...... do .................................... | Bradley Hansher .................. | NA | ES | .............. | .............. | |
| | *The Heartland Region* | | | | | | |
| Kansas City, MO ..... | ...... do .................................... | Michael Copeland.............. | NA | ES | .............. | .............. | |
| Do ..................... | Senior Advisor to the Regional Administrator... | Judith Dungan...................... | SC | GS | 14 | .............. | |
| | *Greater Southwest Region* | | | | | | |
| Fort Worth, TX........ | Regional Administrator ...................... | Vacant ..................................... | | ES | .............. | .............. | |
| | *Rocky Mountain Region* | | | | | | |
| Denver, CO .............. | ...... do .................................... | Katherine Gates .................. | SC | GS | 15 | .............. | |
| | *Pacific Rim Region* | | | | | | |
| San Francisco, CA... | ...... do .................................... | Thomas Scott........................ | NA | ES | .............. | .............. | |
| | *Northwest / Arctic Region* | | | | | | |
| Auburn, WA.............. | ...... do .................................... | Roy Atwood .......................... | SC | GS | 15 | .............. | |

## GENERAL SERVICES ADMINISTRATION OFFICE OF THE INSPECTOR GENERAL

| Location | Position Title | Name of Incumbent | Type of Appt. | Pay Plan | Level, Grade, or Pay | Tenure | Expires |
|---|---|---|---|---|---|---|---|
| Washington, DC ...... | Inspector General ............................................... | Carol A Fortine Ochoa ......... | PAS | EX | II | .............. | |

## GREAT LAKES FISHERY COMMISSION

| Location | Position Title | Name of Incumbent | Type of Appt. | Pay Plan | Level, Grade, or Pay | Tenure | Expires |
|---|---|---|---|---|---|---|---|
| Ann Arbor, MI.......... | Commissioner Member............................ | Douglas Stang ...................... | PA | WC | .............. | .............. | |
| Do ..................... | ...... do ................................................ | William Taylor ...................... | PA | WC | .............. | .............. | |
| Do ..................... | ...... do ................................................ | Charles Wooley .................... | PA | WC | .............. | .............. | |
| Do ..................... | ...... do ................................................ | Donald Pereira...................... | PA | WC | .............. | .............. | |

## GREAT LAKES FISHERY COMMISSION—Continued

| Location | Position Title | Name of Incumbent | Type of Appt. | Pay Plan | Level, Grade, or Pay | Tenure | Expires |
|---|---|---|---|---|---|---|---|
| Ann Arbor, MI......... | Commissioner Member...................................... | David A Ullrich.................... | PA | WC | .............. | ............. | |

## GULF COAST ECOSYSTEM RESTORATION COUNCIL

| Location | Position Title | Name of Incumbent | Type of Appt. | Pay Plan | Level, Grade, or Pay | Tenure | Expires |
|---|---|---|---|---|---|---|---|
| New Orleans, LA..... | Executive Director ........................................... | Vacant ................................ | ............. | ES | .............. | ............. | |
| Do ................... | Interim Executive Director ............................. | ......do ................................ | ............. | ES | .............. | ............. | |
| Tampa, FL .............. | Chief Financial Officer and Director of Administration. | Career Incumbent ................ | CA | ES | .............. | ............. | |

## HARRY S TRUMAN SCHOLARSHIP FOUNDATION

| Location | Position Title | Name of Incumbent | Type of Appt. | Pay Plan | Level, Grade, or Pay | Tenure | Expires |
|---|---|---|---|---|---|---|---|
| | **OFFICE OF EXECUTIVE SECRETARY** | | | | | | |
| Washington, DC ...... | Executive Secretary........................................ | Vacant .................................. | ............. | ES | .............. | ............. | |

## INSTITUTE OF MUSEUM AND LIBRARY SERVICES

| Location | Position Title | Name of Incumbent | Type of Appt. | Pay Plan | Level, Grade, or Pay | Tenure | Expires |
|---|---|---|---|---|---|---|---|
| Washington, DC ...... | Director, Institute of Museum and Library Services. | Rufus Crosby III Kemper .... | PAS | EX | III | .............. | |
| Do .................... | Deputy Director Museum Services.................... | Vacant ................................ | ............. | ES | .............. | ............. | |
| Do .................... | General Counsel............................................ | Career Incumbent ................ | CA | ES | .............. | ............. | |
| Do .................... | Deputy Director for Library Services ............... | Vacant ................................ | ............. | ES | .............. | ............. | |
| Do .................... | Chief of Staff ............................................... | ......do ................................ | ............. | ES | .............. | ............. | |
| Do .................... | Chief Information Officer ............................... | ......do ................................ | ............. | ES | .............. | ............. | |
| Do .................... | Chief Financial Officer .................................. | ......do ................................ | ............. | ES | .............. | ............. | |
| Do .................... | Chief Operating Officer ................................. | ......do ................................ | ............. | ES | .............. | ............. | |
| | **NATIONAL MUSEUM AND LIBRARY SERVICES BOARD** | | | | | | |
| Do .................... | Member.......................................................... | Kenneth James Schutz ........ | PAS | OT | .............. | ............. | |
| Do .................... | ......do ......................................................... | Jonathan Lee Zittrain.......... | PAS | OT | .............. | ............. | |
| Do .................... | ......do ......................................................... | Sylvia Orozco...................... | PAS | OT | .............. | ............. | |
| Do .................... | ......do ......................................................... | Annette A Evans Smith ....... | PAS | OT | .............. | ............. | |
| Do .................... | ......do ......................................................... | Lynne Ireland ...................... | PAS | OT | .............. | ............. | |
| Do .................... | ......do ......................................................... | George W Kerscher ............. | PAS | OT | .............. | ............. | |
| Do .................... | ......do ......................................................... | Nunn M Tey........................ | PAS | OT | .............. | ............. | |
| Do .................... | ......do ......................................................... | Homa S Naficy..................... | PAS | OT | .............. | ............. | |
| Do .................... | ......do ......................................................... | Hoffman F Lisa .................. | PAS | OT | .............. | ............. | |
| Do .................... | ......do ......................................................... | Mary R Minow..................... | PAS | OT | .............. | ............. | |
| Do .................... | ......do ......................................................... | Tammie J Kahn .................. | PAS | OT | .............. | ............. | |
| Do .................... | ......do ......................................................... | Morteza Sajadian ............... | PAS | OT | .............. | ............. | |
| Do .................... | ......do ......................................................... | Jacquelyn Sundstrand ........ | PAS | OT | .............. | ............. | |
| Do .................... | ......do ......................................................... | Beth Ellen Takekawa.......... | PAS | OT | .............. | ............. | |
| Do .................... | ......do ......................................................... | Robert Wedgeworth Jr ........ | PAS | OT | .............. | ............. | |
| Do .................... | ......do ......................................................... | Suzanne Elizabeth Thorin ... | PAS | OT | .............. | ............. | |
| Do .................... | ......do ......................................................... | Deborah Denise Taylor........ | PAS | OT | .............. | ............. | |
| Do .................... | ......do ......................................................... | Jane J Pickering.................. | PAS | OT | .............. | ............. | |

## INTELLECTUAL PROPERTY ENFORCEMENT COORDINATOR

| Location | Position Title | Name of Incumbent | Type of Appt. | Pay Plan | Level, Grade, or Pay | Tenure | Expires |
|---|---|---|---|---|---|---|---|
| Washington, DC ...... | Intellectual Property Enforcement Coordinator. | Vishal J Amin ...................... | PAS | EX | III | .............. | |

## INTELLECTUAL PROPERTY ENFORCEMENT COORDINATOR—Continued

| Location | Position Title | Name of Incumbent | Type of Appt. | Pay Plan | Level, Grade, or Pay | Tenure | Expires |
|---|---|---|---|---|---|---|---|
| Washington, DC ...... | Legal Advisor ................................................ | Career Incumbent ................. | CA | ES | ................ | ................ | |

## INTER-AMERICAN FOUNDATION

| Location | Position Title | Name of Incumbent | Type of Appt. | Pay Plan | Level, Grade, or Pay | Tenure | Expires |
|---|---|---|---|---|---|---|---|
| Washington, DC ...... | President and Chief Executive Officer ............... | Paloma M. Adams-Allen....... | PAS | WC | ................ | ................ | |
| Do ................... | Board Member (Chair) .............................. | Eduardo Arriola................ | PAS | WC | ................ | ................ | |
| Do ................... | Board Member (Vice Chair) ............................. | Juan Carlos Iturregui .......... | PAS | WC | ................ | ................ | |
| Do ................... | Board Member (Secretary)................................ | Jack Vaughn, Jr. ................... | PAS | WC | ................ | ................ | |
| Do ................... | Board Member .......................................... | J Kelly Ryan ...................... | PAS | WC | ................ | ................ | |
| Do ................... | ......do ..................................... | Luis Viada...................... | PAS | WC | ................ | ................ | |
| Do ................... | ......do ..................................... | Vacant ..................... | PAS | WC | ................ | ................ | |
| Do ................... | ......do ..................................... | ......do ................. | PAS | WC | ................ | ................ | |
| Do ................... | ......do ..................................... | ......do ................. | PAS | WC | ................ | ................ | |
| Do ................... | ......do ..................................... | ......do ................. | PAS | WC | ................ | ................ | |

## INTERAGENCY COUNCIL ON THE HOMELESS

| Location | Position Title | Name of Incumbent | Type of Appt. | Pay Plan | Level, Grade, or Pay | Tenure | Expires |
|---|---|---|---|---|---|---|---|
| Washington, DC ...... | Executive Director ............................................. | Robert G Marbut Jr............. | XS | AD | ................ | ................ | |

## INTERNATIONAL BOUNDARY AND WATER COMMISSION

| Location | Position Title | Name of Incumbent | Type of Appt. | Pay Plan | Level, Grade, or Pay | Tenure | Expires |
|---|---|---|---|---|---|---|---|
| Washington, DC ...... | Commissioner.................................................... | Jayne Harkins ...................... | PA | EX | ................ | ................ | |
| | **INTERNATIONAL BOUNDARY AND WATER COMMISSION: UNITED STATES AND CANADA** | | | | | | |
| Do ................... | ......do ................................................. | Kyle K. Hipsley..................... | PA | EX | ................ | ................ | |

## INTERNATIONAL JOINT COMMISSION

| Location | Position Title | Name of Incumbent | Type of Appt. | Pay Plan | Level, Grade, or Pay | Tenure | Expires |
|---|---|---|---|---|---|---|---|
| Washington, DC ...... | Commissioner.................................................... | Lance Virgil Yohe ................ | PAS | EX | ................ | ................ | |
| Do ................... | ......do .......................................... | Robert C. Sisson ................... | PAS | EX | ................ | ................ | |
| | **OFFICE OF THE CHAIR** | | | | | | |
| Minneapolis, MN ..... | Commissioner (Chair)........................................ | Jane Lewis Corwin................ | PAS | EX | IV | ................ | |

## INTERSTATE COMMISSION ON THE POTOMAC RIVER BASIN

| Location | Position Title | Name of Incumbent | Type of Appt. | Pay Plan | Level, Grade, or Pay | Tenure | Expires |
|---|---|---|---|---|---|---|---|
| | **AEGIS SOLUTIONS GROUP, LLC** | | | | | | |
| Washington, DC ...... | Principal ........................................................ | Darryl J. Madden ................. | PA | WC | ................ | ................ | |
| | **SUSSMAN AND ASSOCIATES** | | | | | | |
| Do ................... | ......do ............................................... | Robert M. Sussman .............. | PA | WC | ................ | ................ | |
| | **COMMISSIONERS OFFICE** | | | | | | |
| Do ................... | Federal Commissioner....................................... | Vacant ................................. | PA | WC | ................ | ................ | |
| Do ................... | Alternate Federal Commissioner....................... | Amy M. Guise ....................... | PA | WC | ................ | ................ | |

## JAMES MADISON MEMORIAL FELLOWSHIP FOUNDATION

| Location | Position Title | Name of Incumbent | Type of Appt. | Pay Plan | Level, Grade, or Pay | Tenure | Expires |
|---|---|---|---|---|---|---|---|
| Washington, DC ...... | President ............ | Paul A Yost Jr. ............ | XS | EX | III | .............. | |

## JAPAN UNITED STATES FRIENDSHIP COMMISSION

| Location | Position Title | Name of Incumbent | Type of Appt. | Pay Plan | Level, Grade, or Pay | Tenure | Expires |
|---|---|---|---|---|---|---|---|
| Washington, DC ...... | Executive Director ............ | Career Incumbent ............ | CA | ES | .............. | .............. | |

## MARINE MAMMAL COMMISSION

| Location | Position Title | Name of Incumbent | Type of Appt. | Pay Plan | Level, Grade, or Pay | Tenure | Expires |
|---|---|---|---|---|---|---|---|
| Lewiston, ME ......... | Chairman ............ | Daryl J Boness ............ | PAS | PD | .............. | .............. | |
| Sausalito, CA.......... | Commissioner............ | Frances M Gulland............ | PAS | PD | .............. | .............. | |
| Encinitas, CA.......... | ......do ............ | Michael F Tillman ............ | PAS | PD | .............. | .............. | |

## MEDICAID AND CHIP PAYMENT AND ACCESS COMMISSION

| Location | Position Title | Name of Incumbent | Type of Appt. | Pay Plan | Level, Grade, or Pay | Tenure | Expires |
|---|---|---|---|---|---|---|---|
| Washington, DC ...... | Commissioner............ | Leanna M George............ | XS | PD | .............. | 3 Years | |
| Do ............ | ......do ............ | Christopher P Gorton............ | XS | PD | .............. | 3 Years | |
| Do ............ | Executive Director ............ | Anne L Schwartz ............ | XS | AD | .............. | .............. | |
| Do ............ | Communications Director ............ | Kathryn S Ceja ............ | XS | AD | .............. | .............. | |
| Do ............ | Deputy Director for Operations, Finance and Management. | Ricardo P Villeta ............ | XS | AD | .............. | .............. | |
| Do ............ | Policy Director............ | Katherine M Kirchgraber .... | XS | AD | .............. | .............. | |
| Do ............ | ......do ............ | Moira Forbes............ | XS | AD | .............. | .............. | |
| Do ............ | Commissioner............ | Peter G Szilagyi ............ | XS | PD | .............. | 3 Years | |
| Do ............ | ......do ............ | Melanie Marie Bella............ | XS | PD | .............. | 3 Years | |
| Do ............ | ......do ............ | Patricia Ann Brooks ............ | XS | PD | .............. | 3 Years | |
| Do ............ | ......do ............ | Toby J Douglas ............ | XS | PD | .............. | 3 Years | |
| Do ............ | ......do ............ | William J Scanlon ............ | XS | PD | .............. | 3 Years | |
| Do ............ | ......do ............ | Martha C Carter ............ | XS | PD | .............. | 3 Years | |
| Do ............ | ......do ............ | Katherine A Weno ............ | XS | PD | .............. | 3 Years | |
| Do ............ | ......do ............ | Thomas R Barker ............ | XS | PD | .............. | 3 Years | |
| Do ............ | ......do ............ | Charles J Milligan............ | XS | PD | .............. | 3 Years | |
| Do ............ | ......do ............ | Darin J Gordon ............ | XS | PD | .............. | 3 Years | |
| Do ............ | ......do ............ | Stacey B Lampkin ............ | XS | PD | .............. | 3 Years | |
| Do ............ | ......do ............ | Kisha N Davis ............ | XS | PD | .............. | 3 Years | |
| Do ............ | ......do ............ | Frederick P Cerise............ | XS | PD | .............. | 3 Years | |
| Do ............ | ......do ............ | Brian Burwell............ | XS | PD | .............. | 3 Years | |
| Do ............ | ......do ............ | Sheldon M Retchin............ | XS | PD | .............. | 3 Years | |

## MEDICARE PAYMENT ADVISORY COMMISSION

| Location | Position Title | Name of Incumbent | Type of Appt. | Pay Plan | Level, Grade, or Pay | Tenure | Expires |
|---|---|---|---|---|---|---|---|
| Washington, DC ...... | Executive Director ............ | Mark E Miller............ | XS | AD | .............. | .............. | |
| Do ............ | Deputy Director ............ | James Edward Mathews...... | XS | AD | .............. | .............. | |
| Do ............ | Principal Policy Analyst ............ | Carol L Carter ............ | XS | AD | .............. | .............. | |

## MERIT SYSTEMS PROTECTION BOARD

| Location | Position Title | Name of Incumbent | Type of Appt. | Pay Plan | Level, Grade, or Pay | Tenure | Expires |
|---|---|---|---|---|---|---|---|
| | **OFFICE OF THE BOARD, CHAIRMAN** | | | | | | |
| Washington, DC ...... | Chairman ........................................ | Vacant ................................ | PAS | EX | III | .............. | |
| Do .................. | Executive Director ......................... | ......do ................................ | ............ | ES | | .............. | |
| Do .................. | Chief Counsel to the Chairman ........ | ......do ................................ | ............ | ES | | .............. | |
| | *Office of the Board, Vice Chairman* | | | | | | |
| Do .................. | Vice Chairman ............................... | ......do ................................ | PAS | EX | IV | .............. | |
| Do .................. | Chief Counsel to the Vice Chair........ | ......do ................................ | ............ | ES | | .............. | |
| | *Office of the Board, Member* | | | | | | |
| Do .................. | Member........................................... | ......do ................................ | PAS | EX | IV | .............. | |
| Do .................. | Chief Counsel, to the Member .......... | ......do ................................ | ............ | ES | | .............. | |
| | *Office of the General Counsel* | | | | | | |
| Do .................. | General Counsel.............................. | Tristan Leavitt ................... | NA | ES | | .............. | |
| Do .................. | Special Assistant to the General Counsel.......... | Carol J. Newell .................... | SC | GS | 15 | .............. | |
| | *Office of Appeals Counsel* | | | | | | |
| Do .................. | Director, Office of Appeals Counsel .................... | Career Incumbent ................ | CA | ES | | .............. | |

## MILLENNIUM CHALLENGE CORPORATION

| Location | Position Title | Name of Incumbent | Type of Appt. | Pay Plan | Level, Grade, or Pay | Tenure | Expires |
|---|---|---|---|---|---|---|---|
| | **DEPARTMENT OF POLICY AND EVALUATION** | | | | | | |
| Washington, DC ...... | Vice President ................................ | Vacant ................................ | PA | AD | | .............. | .............. |
| Do .................. | Senior Advisor .............................. | ......do ................................ | PA | AD | | .............. | .............. |
| | **OFFICE OF THE GENERAL COUNSEL** | | | | | | |
| Do .................. | Vice President and General Counsel................. | Jeanne M Hauch ................. | PA | AD | | .............. | .............. |
| | **DEPARTMENT OF COMPACT OPERATIONS** | | | | | | |
| Do .................. | Vice President ................................ | Anthony Welcher ............... | PA | AD | | .............. | .............. |
| Do .................. | Senior Advisor .............................. | Vacant ................................ | PA | AD | | .............. | .............. |
| Do .................. | Special Assistant............................ | Marie Danielle A Ehui ........ | PA | AD | | .............. | .............. |
| Do .................. | Deputy Vice President (Sector Operations) ...... | Vacant ................................ | PA | AD | | .............. | .............. |
| Do .................. | Regional Deputy Vice President (Europe, Asia-Pacific and Latin America). | Jonathan A Brooks.............. | PA | AD | | .............. | .............. |
| | **DEPARTMENT OF CONGRESSIONAL AND PUBLIC AFFAIRS** | | | | | | |
| Do .................. | Vice President ................................ | Emily Davis ......................... | PA | AD | | .............. | .............. |
| Do .................. | Deputy Vice President (Public Affairs).............. | Vacant ................................ | PA | AD | | .............. | .............. |
| Do .................. | Special Assistant............................ | ......do ................................ | PA | AD | | .............. | .............. |
| Do .................. | International Communications Officer .............. | ......do ................................ | PA | AD | | .............. | .............. |
| Do .................. | Digital Communications Manager.................... | Rebecca R Kepto................. | PA | AD | | .............. | .............. |
| Do .................. | Press Secretary ............................. | Vacant ................................ | PA | AD | | .............. | .............. |
| Do .................. | Deputy Vice President (Congressional Affairs).. | ......do ................................ | PA | AD | | .............. | .............. |
| Do .................. | Strategic Communications Advisor .................. | Jacob Wood........................ | PA | AD | | .............. | .............. |
| | **OFFICE OF THE CHIEF EXECUTIVE OFFICER** | | | | | | |
| Do .................. | Chief Executive Officer................... | Sean S Cairncross ............... | PAS | EX | II | .............. | |
| Do .................. | Chief of Staff................................. | Lara M Smith ..................... | PA | AD | | .............. | |
| Do .................. | Board Member ............................... | Susan McCue...................... | PAS | OT | | .............. | |
| Do .................. | ......do ........................................... | Alexander Crenshaw.......... | PAS | OT | | .............. | |
| Do .................. | ......do ........................................... | Michael O Johanns.............. | PAS | OT | | .............. | |
| Do .................. | Communications Specialist .............. | Vacant ................................ | PA | AD | | .............. | |
| Do .................. | Senior Advisor .............................. | ......do ................................ | PA | AD | | .............. | |
| Do .................. | Deputy Chief of Staff...................... | Lorrie B King...................... | PA | AD | | .............. | |
| Do .................. | Special Assistant............................ | Emily J Hardman................. | PA | AD | | .............. | |
| Do .................. | ......do ........................................... | Thaddeus C Brock .............. | PA | AD | | .............. | |
| Do .................. | ......do ........................................... | Tait A Becker ..................... | PA | AD | | .............. | |
| Do .................. | Board Member ............................... | George Marcus.................... | PAS | OT | | .............. | |
| | **DEPARTMENT OF ADMINISTRATION AND FINANCE** | | | | | | |
| Do .................. | Deputy Vice President .................... | Vacant ................................ | PA | AD | | .............. | |
| Do .................. | Vice President/Chief Financial Officer.............. | Kenneth S Jackson............. | PA | AD | | .............. | |
| Do .................. | Staff Assistant................................ | Dillon S Bullock................. | PA | OT | | .............. | |

## MORRIS K UDALL SCHOLARSHIP AND EXCELLENCE IN NATIONAL ENVIRONMENTAL POLICY FOUNDATION

| Location | Position Title | Name of Incumbent | Type of Appt. | Pay Plan | Level, Grade, or Pay | Tenure | Expires |
|---|---|---|---|---|---|---|---|
| Tucson, AZ | Member | D Michael Rappoport | PAS | OT | | 6 Years | |
| Phoenix, AZ | do | James L Huffman II | PAS | OT | | 0 Years | |
| Louisville, KY | do | Mark T Nethery | PAS | OT | | 6 Years | |
| Tucson, AZ | do | Charles Rose | PAS | OT | | 6 Years | |
| Nashville, TN | do | Lisa L Johnson-Billy | PAS | OT | | 6 Years | |
| Clackamas, OR | do | Anne J Udall M.D. | PAS | OT | | 6 Years | |
| Seattle, WA | do | Eric D Eberhard | PAS | OT | | 6 Years | |
| Nashville, TN | do | Tadd M Johnson | PAS | OT | | 6 Years | |
| Albuquerque, NM | do | Camilla C Feibelman | PAS | OT | | 6 Years | |

## NATIONAL AERONAUTICS AND SPACE ADMINISTRATION

| Location | Position Title | Name of Incumbent | Type of Appt. | Pay Plan | Level, Grade, or Pay | Tenure | Expires |
|---|---|---|---|---|---|---|---|
| | **OFFICE OF THE ADMINISTRATOR** | | | | | | |
| Washington, DC | Administrator | James F Bridenstine | PAS | EX | II | | |
| Do | Deputy Administrator | James W Morhard | PAS | EX | III | | |
| Do | Chief of Staff | Gabriel Sherman | NA | ES | | | |
| Do | Deputy Chief of Staff | Kyle Yunaska | NA | ES | | | |
| Do | Senior Advisor, International and Legal Affairs. | Michael Gold | TA | ES | | | 11/17/21 |
| Do | Special Assistant to the Administrator | Scott Masino | SC | GS | 15 | | |
| Do | Video Production Advisor | Paul Wizikowski | SC | GS | 15 | | |
| Do | Special Advisor & White House Liaison | Matthew Mcnitt | SC | GS | 12 | | |
| Do | Executive Assistant | Camden Thomas | SC | GS | 9 | | |
| | **OFFICE OF GENERAL COUNSEL** | | | | | | |
| Do | Associate General Counsel, International Law Practice Group. | Vacant | | ES | | | |
| | **OFFICE OF THE CHIEF FINANCIAL OFFICER** | | | | | | |
| Do | Chief Financial Officer | ......do | PAS | EX | IV | | |
| Do | Policy Analyst | Kristen Eichamer | SC | GS | 11 | | |
| | **OFFICE OF THE CHIEF INFORMATION OFFICER** | | | | | | |
| Do | Chief Information Officer | Vacant | | ES | | | |
| | **OFFICE OF DIVERSITY AND EQUAL OPPORTUNITY** | | | | | | |
| Do | Associate Administrator for Diversity and Equal Opportunity. | Career Incumbent | CA | ES | | | |
| | **OFFICE OF STEM ENGAGEMENT** | | | | | | |
| Do | Associate Administrator for Stem Engagement. | ......do | CA | ES | | | |
| | **OFFICE INTERNATIONAL AND INTERAGENCY RELATIONS** | | | | | | |
| Do | Associate Administrator for International and Interagency Relations. | Vacant | | ES | | | |
| | **OFFICE OF GENERAL COUNSEL** | | | | | | |
| Do | General Counsel | Career Incumbent | CA | ES | | | |
| Do | Deputy General Counsel | ......do | CA | ES | | | |
| Do | Associate General Counsel, General Law | ......do | CA | ES | | | |
| Do | Associate General Counsel, Commercial and Intellectual Property Law Practice Group. | Vacant | | ES | | | |
| Do | Associate General Counsel, Contracts and Procurement. | Career Incumbent | CA | ES | | | |
| | **OFFICE OF LEGISLATIVE AND INTERGOVERNMENTAL AFFAIRS** | | | | | | |
| Do | Associate Administrator for Legislative & Intergovernmental Affairs. | Suzanne Gillen | NA | ES | | | |
| Cuyahoga, OH | Regional Affairs Specialist | Zacchaery Ashcraft | SC | GS | 13 | | |
| Washington, DC | Intergovernmental Affairs Specialist | Megan Wenrich | SC | GS | 12 | | |
| Do | Legislative Affairs Specialist | Emily Helms | SC | GS | 11 | | |
| Do | ......do | Taylor Weeks | SC | GS | 11 | | |
| | **OFFICE OF COMMUNICATIONS** | | | | | | |
| Do | Associate Administrator for Communications | Bettina Inclan Agen | NA | ES | | | |

## NATIONAL AERONAUTICS AND SPACE ADMINISTRATION—Continued

| Location | Position Title | Name of Incumbent | Type of Appt. | Pay Plan | Level, Grade, or Pay | Tenure | Expires |
|---|---|---|---|---|---|---|---|
| Washington, DC ...... | Senior Advisor and Press Secretary .................. | Matthew Rydin...................... | SC | GS | 14 | ............... | |
| Do .................... | Deputy Press Secretary, Communications Advisor to the Deputy Administrator. | Katy Summerlin................... | SC | GS | 11 | ............... | |
| Do .................... | Executive Assistant ........................................... | Sharon Teitelbaum.............. | SC | GS | 11 | ............... | |
| Do .................... | Speechwriter ...................................................... | William Lee.......................... | SC | GS | 9 | ............... | |
| | **OFFICE OF SMALL BUSINESS PROGRAMS** | | | | | | |
| Do .................... | Associate Administrator for Small Business Programs. | Career Incumbent ................ | CA | ES | ............... | ............... | |
| | **AERONAUTICS RESEARCH MISSION DIRECTORATE** | | | | | | |
| Do .................... | Associate Administrator for Aeronautics Research Mission Directorate. | ......do ................................... | CA | ES | ............... | ............... | |
| | **HUMAN EXPLORATION AND OPERATIONS MISSION DIRECTORATE** | | | | | | |
| Do .................... | Associate Administrator for Human Exploration and Operations. | ......do ................................... | CA | ES | ............... | ............... | |
| | **SCIENCE MISSION DIRECTORATE** | | | | | | |
| Do .................... | Associate Administrator for Science Mission Directorate. | ......do ................................... | CA | ES | ............... | ............... | |
| | **SPACE TECHNOLOGY MISSION DIRECTORATE** | | | | | | |
| Do .................... | Associate Administrator for Space Technology Mission Directorate. | ......do ................................... | CA | ES | ............... | ............... | |
| | **MISSION SUPPORT DIRECTORATE** | | | | | | |
| Do .................... | Associate Administrator for Mission Support.... | ......do ................................... | CA | ES | ............... | ............... | |
| | **AMES RESEARCH CENTER** | | | | | | |
| Moffett Field, CA..... | Director, Ames Research Center ......................... | ......do ................................... | CA | ES | ............... | ............... | |
| Do .................... | Chief Counsel .................................................... | ......do ................................... | CA | ES | ............... | ............... | |
| | **ARMSTRONG FLIGHT RESEARCH CENTER** | | | | | | |
| Edwards Air Force Base, CA. | Director, Armstrong Flight Research Center ..... | ......do ................................... | CA | ES | ............... | ............... | |
| Do .................... | Chief Counsel .................................................... | ......do ................................... | CA | ES | ............... | ............... | |
| | **GLENN RESEARCH CENTER** | | | | | | |
| Cleveland, OH ........ | Director, Glenn Research Center ......................... | ......do ................................... | CA | ES | ............... | ............... | |
| Do .................... | Chief Counsel .................................................... | ......do ................................... | CA | ES | ............... | ............... | |
| | **GODDARD SPACE FLIGHT CENTER** | | | | | | |
| Greenbelt, MD........ | Director, Goddard Space Flight Center .............. | ......do ................................... | CA | ES | ............... | ............... | |
| Do .................... | Chief Counsel .................................................... | ......do ................................... | CA | ES | ............... | ............... | |
| | **JOHNSON SPACE CENTER** | | | | | | |
| Houston, TX............ | Director, Johnson Space Center ......................... | ......do ................................... | CA | ES | ............... | ............... | |
| Do .................... | Chief Counsel .................................................... | ......do ................................... | CA | ES | ............... | ............... | |
| | **KENNEDY SPACE CENTER** | | | | | | |
| Cape Canaveral, FL. | ......do ............................................................... | ......do ................................... | CA | ES | ............... | ............... | |
| Do .................... | Director, Kennedy Space Center ......................... | ......do ................................... | CA | ES | ............... | ............... | |
| | **LANGLEY RESEARCH CENTER** | | | | | | |
| Hampton, VA .......... | Director, Langley Research Center ..................... | ......do ................................... | CA | ES | ............... | ............... | |
| Do .................... | Chief Counsel .................................................... | ......do ................................... | CA | ES | ............... | ............... | |
| | **MARSHALL SPACE FLIGHT CENTER** | | | | | | |
| Huntsville, AL ........ | Director, Marshall Space Flight Center ............. | ......do ................................... | CA | ES | ............... | ............... | |
| Do .................... | Chief Counsel .................................................... | ......do ................................... | CA | ES | ............... | ............... | |
| | **STENNIS SPACE CENTER** | | | | | | |
| Bay St Louis, MS .... | Director, Stennis Space Center ......................... | ......do ................................... | CA | ES | ............... | ............... | |
| Do .................... | Chief Counsel .................................................... | ......do ................................... | CA | ES | ............... | ............... | |

## NATIONAL AERONAUTICS AND SPACE ADMINISTRATION OFFICE OF THE INSPECTOR GENERAL

| Location | Position Title | Name of Incumbent | Type of Appt. | Pay Plan | Level, Grade, or Pay | Tenure | Expires |
|---|---|---|---|---|---|---|---|
| Washington, DC ...... | Special Assistant for Audits ............................... | Vacant ................................... | ............... | ES | ............... | ............... | |

## NATIONAL AERONAUTICS AND SPACE ADMINISTRATION OFFICE OF THE INSPECTOR GENERAL—Continued

| Location | Position Title | Name of Incumbent | Type of Appt. | Pay Plan | Level, Grade, or Pay | Tenure | Expires |
|---|---|---|---|---|---|---|---|
| Washington, DC ...... | Inspector General ................................................ | Paul K Martin........................ | PAS | EX | II | ................ | |

## NATIONAL ARCHIVES AND RECORDS ADMINISTRATION

| Location | Position Title | Name of Incumbent | Type of Appt. | Pay Plan | Level, Grade, or Pay | Tenure | Expires |
|---|---|---|---|---|---|---|---|
| | **ARCHIVIST OF UNITED STATES AND DEPUTY ARCHIVIST OF THE UNITED STATES** | | | | | | |
| College Park, MD .... | Archivist of the United States ............................ | David Sean Ferriero ............ | PAS | EX | III | ................ | |
| | **OFFICE OF PRESIDENTIAL LIBRARIES** | | | | | | |
| West Branch, IA ...... | Director, Herbert Hoover Library ...................... | Thomas F Schwartz ............ | XS | SL | ............ | ............ | |
| Hyde Park, NY ........ | Director, Franklin D Roosevelt Library............. | Paul M Sparrow.................... | XS | SL | ............ | ............ | |
| Independence, MO .. | Director, Harry S Truman Library .................... | Donald Kurt Graham........... | XS | SL | ............ | ............ | |
| Abilene, KS............. | Director, Dwight D Eisenhower Library ........... | Dawn Hammatt................... | XS | SL | ............ | ............ | |
| Boston, MA ............. | Director, John F. Kennedy Library .................... | Alan Price ............................ | XS | SL | ............ | ............ | |
| Austin, TX............... | Director, Lyndon B. Johnson Library ................ | Mark A Lawrence................. | XS | SL | ............ | ............ | |
| Yorba Linda, CA...... | Director, Richard M. Nixon Library.................... | Michael D Ellzey ................. | XS | SL | ............ | ............ | |
| Ann Arbor, MI......... | Director, Gerald R. Ford Library........................ | Elaine K Didier ................... | XS | SL | ............ | ............ | |
| Atlanta, GA ............ | Director, Jimmy Carter Library.......................... | Meredith Rachelle Evans..... | XS | SL | ............ | ............ | |
| Simi Valley, CA........ | Director, Ronald Reagan Library........................ | R Duke Blackwood .............. | XS | SL | ............ | ............ | |
| College Station, TX . | Director, George Bush Library............................ | Warren Finch....................... | XS | SL | ............ | ............ | |
| Little Rock, AR ........ | Director, William J. Clinton Library.................. | Mary T Garner .................... | XS | SL | ............ | ............ | |
| Lewisville, TX.......... | Director, George W. Bush Library...................... | Patrick Xavier Mordente...... | XS | SL | ............ | ............ | |

## NATIONAL CAPITAL PLANNING COMMISSION

| Location | Position Title | Name of Incumbent | Type of Appt. | Pay Plan | Level, Grade, or Pay | Tenure | Expires |
|---|---|---|---|---|---|---|---|
| Washington, DC ...... | Chairman ................................................ | Vacant .................................... | PA | OT | ................ | 6 Years | |
| Do ..................... | Commission Member ........................................ | Thomas M. Gallas ............... | PA | OT | ................ | ................ | |
| Do ..................... | ......do ........................................... | Elizabeth Ann White............ | PA | OT | ................ | 6 Years | |

## NATIONAL COUNCIL ON DISABILITY

| Location | Position Title | Name of Incumbent | Type of Appt. | Pay Plan | Level, Grade, or Pay | Tenure | Expires |
|---|---|---|---|---|---|---|---|
| Washington, DC ...... | Chairman ................................................ | Neil Romano ........................ | PA | AD | ................ | 3 Years | |
| Do ..................... | Vice-Chairman ........................................ | James T Brett ...................... | PA | OT | ................ | 3 Years | |
| Do ..................... | Member........................................ | Clyde E Terry....................... | PA | OT | ............ | 3 Years | |
| Do ..................... | ......do ........................................... | Wendy S Harbour................. | PA | PD | ................ | 3 Years | |
| Do ..................... | ......do ........................................... | Rabia S Belt......................... | PA | PD | ............ | 3 Years | |
| Do ..................... | ......do ........................................... | Billy W Altom ...................... | PA | PD | ............ | 3 Years | |
| Do ..................... | ......do ........................................... | Andres J Gallegos ............... | PA | PD | ............ | 3 Years | |
| Do ..................... | ......do ........................................... | Jim Baldwin ........................ | PA | PD | ................ | 3 Years | |

## NATIONAL CREDIT UNION ADMINISTRATION

| Location | Position Title | Name of Incumbent | Type of Appt. | Pay Plan | Level, Grade, or Pay | Tenure | Expires |
|---|---|---|---|---|---|---|---|
| | **OFFICE OF THE CHAIRMAN** | | | | | | |
| Alexandria, VA ........ | Chairman ................................................ | Rodney Hood........................ | PAS | EX | III | 6 Years | |
| Do ..................... | Chief of Staff........................................ | Harry Lenwood Brooks ....... | SC | OT | $239,465 | ................ | |
| Do ..................... | Director, Office of External Affairs and Communications/Deputy Chief of Staff. | Gisele Roget ........................ | SC | OT | $235,001 | | |

## NATIONAL CREDIT UNION ADMINISTRATION—Continued

| Location | Position Title | Name of Incumbent | Type of Appt. | Pay Plan | Level, Grade, or Pay | Tenure | Expires |
|---|---|---|---|---|---|---|---|
| Alexandria, VA ........ | Senior Advisor to the Chairman for Communications and Engagement. | Evann Darnell Berry............ | SC | OT | $97,257 | .............. | |
| Do ..................... | Confidential Assistant ......................................... | Hallie Elizabeth Williams.... | SC | OT | $142,939 | .............. | |
| | **OFFICE OF THE BOARD** | | | | | | |
| Do ..................... | Board Member ....................................................... | John Mark Mcwatters.......... | PAS | EX | IV | .............. | |
| Do ..................... | ......do ................................................................... | Todd M Harper ...................... | PAS | EX | IV | 4 Years | |
| Do ..................... | Senior Policy Advisor............................................ | Catherine Galicia ................. | SC | OT | $204,906 | .............. | |
| Do ..................... | ......do ................................................................... | Sarah Dee Vega ..................... | SC | OT | $239,466 | .............. | |
| Do ..................... | Staff Assistant....................................................... | Jean Marter ........................... | SC | OT | $122,521 | .............. | |
| Do ..................... | ......do ................................................................... | Katie M Supples.................... | SC | OT | $128,325 | .............. | |
| | **OFFICE OF EXTERNAL AFFAIRS AND COMMUNICATIONS** | | | | | | |
| Do ..................... | Deputy Director, Office of External Affairs and Communications. | Michael Sinacore .................. | SC | OT | $190,000 | .............. | |

## NATIONAL ENDOWMENT FOR THE ARTS

| Location | Position Title | Name of Incumbent | Type of Appt. | Pay Plan | Level, Grade, or Pay | Tenure | Expires |
|---|---|---|---|---|---|---|---|
| Washington, DC ...... | Senior Deputy Chairman .................................... | Thomas Simplot..................... | NA | ES | .............. | .............. | |
| Do ..................... | Senior Advisor for Program Innovation ............. | Vacant .................................... | .............. | ES | .............. | .............. | |
| Do ..................... | Executive Director, Presidents Committee on the Arts and the Humanities. | ......do ................................... | .............. | ES | .............. | .............. | |
| Do ..................... | General Counsel...................................................... | ......do ................................... | .............. | ES | .............. | .............. | |
| Do ..................... | Deputy Chairman for Programs and Partnerships. | Tony Lynn Chauveaux.......... | NA | ES | .............. | .............. | |
| Do ..................... | Director of Strategic Communications and Public Affairs. | Vacant .................................... | .............. | ES | .............. | .............. | |
| Do ..................... | Chief of Staff ......................................................... | Michael John Griffin ............ | NA | ES | .............. | .............. | |
| Do ..................... | Director of Congressional Affairs........................ | Kelli Ripp.............................. | SC | GS | 11 | .............. | |
| Do ..................... | Director of Event Management & Development. | Caroline Harvin..................... | SC | GS | 13 | .............. | |
| Do ..................... | Senior White House Advisor ............................... | Vacant .................................... | .............. | ES | .............. | .............. | |
| Do ..................... | Confidential Assistant to the Senior Deputy Chairman. | William Maloney .................. | SC | GS | 9 | .............. | |
| Do ..................... | Senior Advisor (Creative Forces Program)........ | William O Brien .................... | SC | GS | 15 | .............. | |
| Do ..................... | Special Assistant for Events & Development .... | Phoebe Woll........................... | SC | GS | 9 | .............. | |
| Do ..................... | Director of Strategic Communications and Public Affairs. | Donald Walter....................... | SC | GS | 15 | .............. | |
| Do ..................... | Confidential Assistant to the Senior Deputy Chairman. | Hannah Elizabeth Keane .... | SC | GS | 7 | .............. | |
| Do ..................... | Deputy Director of Public Affairs ....................... | Heather Swift......................... | SC | GS | 15 | .............. | |
| Do ..................... | Director of Scheduling........................................... | Katharine Fisher.................... | SC | GS | 13 | .............. | |
| Do ..................... | Advisor to the Director of Event Management & Development. | Christine Gant....................... | SC | GS | 11 | .............. | |
| Do ..................... | Senior Advisor to the Senior Deputy Chairman. | Joshua T Mauthe................... | SC | GS | 14 | .............. | |
| | **PRESIDENTS COMMITTEE ON THE ARTS AND HUMANITIES** | | | | | | |
| Do ..................... | Executive Director ............................................... | Vacant .................................... | .............. | ES | .............. | .............. | |

## NATIONAL ENDOWMENT FOR THE HUMANITIES

| Location | Position Title | Name of Incumbent | Type of Appt. | Pay Plan | Level, Grade, or Pay | Tenure | Expires |
|---|---|---|---|---|---|---|---|
| Washington, DC ...... | Deputy Chairman ................................................. | Vacant .................................... | .............. | ES | .............. | .............. | |
| Do ..................... | Director of White House and Congressional Affairs. | ......do ................................... | .............. | ES | .............. | .............. | |
| Do ..................... | General Counsel...................................................... | Career Incumbent ................. | CA | ES | .............. | .............. | |
| Do ..................... | Assistant Chairman for Programs........................ | ......do ................................... | CA | ES | .............. | .............. | |
| Do ..................... | Chief of Staff ......................................................... | Vacant .................................... | .............. | ES | .............. | .............. | |
| Do ..................... | Director, Office of Challenge Grants.................... | ......do ................................... | .............. | ES | .............. | .............. | |
| Do ..................... | Director, Federal/State Partnership.................... | ......do ................................... | .............. | ES | .............. | .............. | |
| Do ..................... | Director, Division of Preservation and Access ... | Career Incumbent ................. | CA | ES | .............. | .............. | |
| Do ..................... | Director, Division of Public Programs ................ | Vacant .................................... | .............. | ES | .............. | .............. | |

## NATIONAL ENDOWMENT FOR THE HUMANITIES—Continued

| Location | Position Title | Name of Incumbent | Type of Appt. | Pay Plan | Level, Grade, or Pay | Tenure | Expires |
|---|---|---|---|---|---|---|---|
| Washington, DC ...... | Director, Division of Research Programs............ | Vacant ............................... | ............ | ES | ............. | ............. | |
| Do .................... | Chief Information Officer..................................... | Career Incumbent ................ | CA | ES | ............. | ............. | |
| Do .................... | Deputy Director, President's Committee on the Arts and the Humanities. | Vacant ............................... | ............ | ES | ............. | ............. | |
| Do .................... | Senior Advisor to the Chairman and White House Liaison. | Vincent Jonathan Ricardel .. | SC | GS | 15 | ............. | |
| Do .................... | Senior Deputy Chairman .................................... | Carlos Enrique Diaz-Rosillo. | NA | ES | ............. | ............. | |
| Do .................... | Supervisory Public Affairs Specialist ................ | Kathryn Wellner.................. | SC | GS | 15 | ............. | |
| Do .................... | Program Analyst ................................................. | Christine Bauserman........... | SC | GS | 14 | ............. | |
| Do .................... | Executive Assistant ........................................... | Peggy Lee Mowers................ | SC | GS | 13 | ............. | |
| Do .................... | Chief Human Capital Officer............................... | Vacant ............................... | ............ | ES | ............. | ............. | |
| Do .................... | Assistant Chairman for Partnership and Strategic Initiatives. | ......do ............................... | ............ | ES | ............. | ............. | |
| Do .................... | Chairman ........................................................... | Jon Parrish Peede............... | PAS | EX | III | 4 Years | |
| Do .................... | Director of Congressional Affairs....................... | Timothy Hoyt Robison ......... | SC | GS | 15 | ............. | |
| Do .................... | **NATIONAL ENDOWMENT FOR THE HUMANITIES OFFICE OF THE INSPECTOR GENERAL** | | | | | | |
| Do .................... | Inspector General ............................................... | Vacant ............................... | ............ | ES | ............. | ............. | |

## NATIONAL ENDOWMENT FOR THE HUMANITIES OFFICE OF THE INSPECTOR GENERAL

| Location | Position Title | Name of Incumbent | Type of Appt. | Pay Plan | Level, Grade, or Pay | Tenure | Expires |
|---|---|---|---|---|---|---|---|
| Washington, DC ...... | Inspector General ............................................... | Career Incumbent ................ | CA | ES | ............. | ............. | |

## NATIONAL LABOR RELATIONS BOARD

| Location | Position Title | Name of Incumbent | Type of Appt. | Pay Plan | Level, Grade, or Pay | Tenure | Expires |
|---|---|---|---|---|---|---|---|
| | **OFFICE OF THE BOARD MEMBERS** | | | | | | |
| Washington, DC ...... | Chief Counsel to Board Member......................... | James R Murphy ................. | NA | ES | ............. | ............. | |
| Do .................... | Deputy Chief Counsel to Board Member ........... | Career Incumbent ................ | CA | ES | ............. | ............. | |
| Do .................... | Executive Assistant to the Chairman ............... | Christine Lucy.................... | NA | ES | ............. | ............. | |
| Do .................... | Deputy Chief Counsel to Board Member ........... | Vacant ............................... | ............ | ES | ............. | ............. | |
| Do .................... | Chief Counsel to Board Member......................... | ......do ............................... | ............ | ES | ............. | ............. | |
| Do .................... | ......do ............................... | Douglas Free...................... | NA | ES | ............. | ............. | |
| Do .................... | Deputy Chief Counsel to Board Member ........... | Career Incumbent ................ | CA | ES | ............. | ............. | |
| Do .................... | Chief Counsel to Board Member......................... | Peter J Carlton .................. | NA | ES | ............. | ............. | |
| Do .................... | Deputy Chief Counsel to Board Member ........... | Career Incumbent ................ | CA | ES | ............. | ............. | |
| Do .................... | Director, Office Representation Appeals ........... | Vacant ............................... | ............ | ES | ............. | ............. | |
| Do .................... | Solicitor............................................................. | Career Incumbent ................ | CA | ES | ............. | ............. | |
| Do .................... | Special Advisor to the Deputy General Counsel. | Vacant ............................... | ............ | ES | ............. | ............. | |
| Do .................... | Congressional Liaison Specialist ....................... | Kevin Petroccione................ | SC | GS | 11 | ............. | |
| Do .................... | Assistant General Counsel................................. | Career Incumbent ................ | CA | ES | ............. | ............. | |
| Do .................... | Associate Chief Counsel to Board Member....... | Vacant ............................... | ............ | ES | ............. | ............. | |
| Do .................... | Director Congressional and Public Affairs Officer. | Edwin Egee......................... | SC | GS | 15 | ............. | |
| Do .................... | Board Member .................................................... | Vacant ............................... | PAS | EX | IV | ............. | |
| Do .................... | ......do ............................... | William J. Emanuel.............. | PAS | EX | IV | ............. | |
| Do .................... | ......do ............................... | Vacant ............................... | PAS | EX | IV | ............. | |
| Do .................... | Acting Deputy Chief Counsel to Board Member. | ......do ............................... | ............ | ES | ............. | ............. | |
| Do .................... | Acting Solicitor.................................................. | ......do ............................... | ............ | ES | ............. | ............. | |
| Do .................... | Chairman ........................................................... | John Francis Ring................ | PAS | EX | III | ............. | |
| Do .................... | Acting Deputy Chief Counsel to Board Member. | Vacant ............................... | ............ | ES | ............. | ............. | |
| Do .................... | Board Member .................................................... | Irwin Kaplan ...................... | PAS | EX | IV | ............. | |
| | **OFFICE OF THE GENERAL COUNSEL** | | | | | | |
| Do .................... | Deputy General Counsel ..................................... | Alice Stock ........................ | NA | ES | ............. | ............. | |
| Do .................... | General Counsel................................................. | Peter B Robb...................... | PAS | EX | IV | ............. | |
| Do .................... | Associate General Counsel................................. | Career Incumbent ................ | CA | ES | ............. | ............. | |
| Do .................... | Assistant General Counsel................................. | Vacant ............................... | ............ | ES | ............. | ............. | |

## NATIONAL LABOR RELATIONS BOARD—Continued

| Location | Position Title | Name of Incumbent | Type of Appt. | Pay Plan | Level, Grade, or Pay | Tenure | Expires |
|---|---|---|---|---|---|---|---|
| Washington, DC ...... | Assistant General Counsel (Legal) (Chair, National Labor Relations Board Restructuring Committee). | Vacant ................................... | ............ | ES | .............. | ............. | |
| Do .................... | Associate General Counsel................................ | ......do ................................... | ............ | ES | .............. | ............. | |
| Do .................... | ......do ................................... | ......do ................................... | ............ | ES | .............. | ............. | |
| | **NATIONAL LABOR RELATIONS BOARD** | | | | | | |
| Do .................... | Deputy Chief Counsel to Chairman ................... | Career Incumbent ................ | CA | ES | .............. | ............. | |
| Do .................... | Chief Financial Officer ....................................... | ......do ................................... | CA | ES | .............. | ............. | |
| Do .................... | Assistant General Counsel................................... | ......do ................................... | CA | ES | .............. | ............. | |
| | *Division of Administration* | | | | | | |
| Do .................... | Acting Director of Admin ................................... | Vacant ................................... | ............ | ES | .............. | ............. | |

## NATIONAL MEDIATION BOARD

| Location | Position Title | Name of Incumbent | Type of Appt. | Pay Plan | Level, Grade, or Pay | Tenure | Expires |
|---|---|---|---|---|---|---|---|
| Washington, DC ...... | General Counsel................................................. | Career Incumbent ................ | CA | ES | | .............. | |
| Do .................... | Chairman .......................................................... | Gerald W Fauth III .............. | PAS | EX | III | .............. | |
| Do .................... | Board Member ................................................... | Kyle Fortson........................ | PAS | EX | IV | .............. | |
| Do .................... | ......do ................................... | Vacant ................................... | PAS | EX | IV | .............. | |
| Do .................... | ......do ................................... | Linda A Puchala................... | PAS | EX | III | .............. | |
| Do .................... | Chief of Staff ................................................... | Vacant ................................... | ............ | ES | | .............. | |
| Do .................... | Chairman .......................................................... | ......do ................................... | PAS | EX | IV | .............. | |

## NATIONAL SCIENCE FOUNDATION

| Location | Position Title | Name of Incumbent | Type of Appt. | Pay Plan | Level, Grade, or Pay | Tenure | Expires |
|---|---|---|---|---|---|---|---|
| | **OFFICE OF THE DIRECTOR** | | | | | | |
| Alexandria, VA ........ | Director............................................................. | Sethuraman Panchanathan. | PAS | EX | II | .............. | |
| Do .................... | Deputy Director ................................................ | Vacant ................................... | PAS | EX | III | .............. | |
| Do .................... | Senior Advisor to the Director for Strategic Initiatives (Level I). | Career Incumbent ................ | CA | ES | .............. | .............. | |
| Do .................... | Chief of Staff ................................................... | ......do ................................... | CA | ES | .............. | .............. | |
| Do .................... | Chief of Research Security Strategy and Policy. | ......do ................................... | CA | ES | .............. | .............. | |
| Do .................... | Chief Officer for Research Facilities................... | ......do ................................... | CA | ES | .............. | .............. | |
| Do .................... | Chief Information Officer.................................... | ......do ................................... | CA | ES | .............. | .............. | |
| Do .................... | Assistant to the Director for Science Policy and Planning. | Vacant ................................... | ............ | ES | .............. | .............. | |
| Do .................... | Senior Advisor for Research............................... | ......do ................................... | ............ | ES | .............. | .............. | |
| Do .................... | Senior Staff Associate ....................................... | ......do ................................... | ............ | ES | .............. | .............. | |
| Do .................... | ......do ................................... | Vernon D Ross ..................... | XS | AD | .............. | .............. | |
| Do .................... | ......do ................................... | Kim Silverman .................... | XS | AD | .............. | .............. | |
| | **OFFICE OF THE GENERAL COUNSEL** | | | | | | |
| Do .................... | General Counsel................................................. | Career Incumbent ................ | CA | ES | .............. | .............. | |
| | **OFFICE OF LEGISLATIVE AND PUBLIC AFFAIRS** | | | | | | |
| Do .................... | Office Head........................................................ | ......do ................................... | CA | ES | .............. | .............. | |
| | **OFFICE OF INTEGRATIVE ACTIVITIES** | | | | | | |
| Do .................... | ......do ................................... | ......do ................................... | CA | ES | .............. | .............. | |
| Do .................... | Section Head, Integrative Activities Section...... | ......do ................................... | CA | ES | .............. | .............. | |
| Do .................... | Section Head, Established Program to Stimulate Competitive Research. | Vacant ................................... | ............ | ES | .............. | .............. | |
| Do .................... | Senior Advisor................................................... | Bernice T Anderson.............. | XS | AD | .............. | .............. | |
| Do .................... | Senior Staff Associate ....................................... | Dragana Brzakovic................ | XS | AD | .............. | .............. | |
| Do .................... | ......do ................................... | Erika Johnson Rissi ............. | XS | AD | .............. | .............. | |
| Do .................... | Office Director, Office of Convergence Accelerators. | Career Incumbent ................ | CA | ES | .............. | .............. | |
| Arlington, VA........... | Section Head for Evaluation and Assessment Capability. | Vacant ................................... | ............ | ES | .............. | .............. | |

## NATIONAL SCIENCE FOUNDATION—Continued

| Location | Position Title | Name of Incumbent | Type of Appt. | Pay Plan | Level, Grade, or Pay | Tenure | Expires |
|---|---|---|---|---|---|---|---|
| | **OFFICE OF INTERNATIONAL SCIENCE AND ENGINEERING** | | | | | | |
| Alexandria, VA ........ | Office Head................................ | Vacant ........................... | ............ | ES | ............. | ............. | |
| Do .................. | Deputy Office Head ..................... | Career Incumbent .............. | CA | ES | ............. | ............. | |
| | **NATIONAL SCIENCE BOARD** | | | | | | |
| Do .................. | Executive Officer and Director, National Science Board Office. | Vacant ........................... | ............ | ES | ............. | ............. | |
| Do .................. | Senior Counsel to the National Science Board .. | Ann E Bushmiller .............. | XS | AD | ............. | ............. | |
| | **Directorate For Biological Sciences** | | | | | | |
| Do .................. | Assistant Director........................ | Career Incumbent .............. | CA | ES | ............. | ............. | |
| | **Division of Biological Infrastructure** | | | | | | |
| Do .................. | Division Director......................... | Vacant ........................... | ............ | ES | ............. | ............. | |
| Do .................. | Deputy Division Director ................ | Career Incumbent .............. | CA | ES | ............. | ............. | |
| | **Division of Environmental Biology** | | | | | | |
| Do .................. | Division Director......................... | Vacant ........................... | ............ | ES | ............. | ............. | |
| Do .................. | Deputy Division Director ................ | Career Incumbent .............. | CA | ES | ............. | ............. | |
| | **Division of Integrative Organismal Systems** | | | | | | |
| Do .................. | Division Director......................... | Vacant ........................... | ............ | ES | ............. | ............. | |
| Do .................. | Deputy Division Director ................ | Career Incumbent .............. | CA | ES | ............. | ............. | |
| | **Division of Molecular and Cellular Biosciences** | | | | | | |
| Do .................. | Division Director......................... | Vacant ........................... | ............ | ES | ............. | ............. | |
| Do .................. | Deputy Division Director ................ | Career Incumbent .............. | CA | ES | ............. | ............. | |
| | **DIRECTORATE FOR COMPUTER AND INFORMATION SCIENCE AND ENGINEERING** | | | | | | |
| Do .................. | Assistant Director........................ | Vacant ........................... | ............ | ES | ............. | ............. | |
| Do .................. | Senior Advisor............................ | Career Incumbent .............. | CA | ES | ............. | ............. | |
| Do .................. | Senior Advisor for Strategic Engagement........... | Vacant ........................... | XS | AD | ............. | ............. | |
| | **Division of Computer and Network Systems** | | | | | | |
| Do .................. | Division Director......................... | ......do ........................... | | ES | ............. | ............. | |
| Do .................. | Deputy Division Director ................ | ......do ........................... | | ES | ............. | ............. | |
| | **Division of Computing and Communication Foundations** | | | | | | |
| Do .................. | Division Director......................... | ......do ........................... | | ES | ............. | ............. | |
| Do .................. | Deputy Division Director ................ | Career Incumbent .............. | CA | ES | ............. | ............. | |
| | **Division of Information and Intelligent Systems** | | | | | | |
| Do .................. | Division Director......................... | Vacant ........................... | ............ | ES | ............. | ............. | |
| Do .................. | Deputy Division Director ................ | Career Incumbent .............. | CA | ES | ............. | ............. | |
| | **OFFICE OF ADVANCED CYBERINFRASTRUCTURE** | | | | | | |
| Do .................. | Office Director........................... | Vacant ........................... | ............ | ES | ............. | ............. | |
| Do .................. | Deputy Office Director................... | Career Incumbent .............. | CA | ES | ............. | ............. | |
| | **DIRECTORATE FOR EDUCATION AND HUMAN RESOURCES** | | | | | | |
| Do .................. | Assistant Director........................ | Vacant ........................... | ............ | ES | ............. | ............. | |
| Do .................. | Deputy Assistant Director............... | Career Incumbent .............. | CA | ES | ............. | ............. | |
| Do .................. | Senior Advisor............................ | Sarah Kathryn Mcdonald .... | XS | AD | ............. | ............. | |
| | **Division of Graduate Education** | | | | | | |
| Do .................. | Division Director......................... | Vacant ........................... | ............ | ES | ............. | ............. | |
| Do .................. | Deputy Division Director ................ | Career Incumbent .............. | CA | ES | ............. | ............. | |
| | **Division of Human Resource Development** | | | | | | |
| Do .................. | Division Director......................... | Vacant ........................... | ............ | ES | ............. | ............. | |
| Do .................. | Deputy Division Director ................ | Career Incumbent .............. | CA | ES | ............. | ............. | |
| | **Division of Research on Learning In Formal and Informal Settings** | | | | | | |
| Do .................. | Division Director......................... | ......do ........................... | CA | ES | ............. | ............. | |
| Do .................. | Deputy Division Director ................ | ......do ........................... | CA | ES | ............. | ............. | |
| | **Division of Undergraduate Education** | | | | | | |
| Do .................. | Division Director......................... | Vacant ........................... | ............ | ES | ............. | ............. | |
| Do .................. | Deputy Division Director ................ | Career Incumbent .............. | CA | ES | ............. | ............. | |

## NATIONAL SCIENCE FOUNDATION—Continued

| Location | Position Title | Name of Incumbent | Type of Appt. | Pay Plan | Level, Grade, or Pay | Tenure | Expires |
|---|---|---|---|---|---|---|---|
| | **DIRECTORATE FOR ENGINEERING** | | | | | | |
| Alexandria, VA ....... | Assistant Director.................................................. | Vacant ...................... | ............ | ES | .............. | .............. | |
| Do .................... | Deputy Assistant Director....................... | Career Incumbent ................ | CA | ES | .............. | .............. | |
| Do .................... | Senior Advisor for Emerging Technologies and Interdisciplinary Research. | Sohi Rastegar ........................ | XS | AD | .............. | .............. | |
| Do .................... | Senior Advisor for Science and Engineering...... | Mihail C Roco ...................... | XS | AD | .............. | .............. | |
| | **Division of Engineering Education and Centers** | | | | | | |
| Do .................... | Division Director.................................. | Vacant ...................... | ............ | ES | .............. | .............. | |
| | **Division of Chemical, Bioengineering, Environmental, and Transport Systems** | | | | | | |
| Do .................... | ......do ...................................... | ......do ...................... | ............ | ES | .............. | .............. | |
| Do .................... | Deputy Division Director ...................... | Career Incumbent ................ | CA | ES | .............. | .............. | |
| | **Division of Civil, Mechanical, and Maufacturing Innovation** | | | | | | |
| Do .................... | Division Director.................................. | Vacant ...................... | ............ | ES | .............. | .............. | |
| Do .................... | Deputy Division Director ...................... | Career Incumbent ................ | CA | ES | .............. | .............. | |
| | **Division of Electrical, Communications and Cyber Systems** | | | | | | |
| Do .................... | Division Director.................................. | Vacant ...................... | ............ | ES | .............. | .............. | |
| Do .................... | Deputy Division Director ...................... | Career Incumbent ................ | CA | ES | .............. | .............. | |
| Do .................... | Senior Advisor ...................................... | Lawrence S Goldberg ............ | XS | AD | .............. | .............. | |
| | **Division of Industrial Innovation and Partnerships** | | | | | | |
| Do .................... | Division Director.................................. | Vacant ...................... | ............ | ES | .............. | .............. | |
| | **DIRECTORATE FOR GEOSCIENCES** | | | | | | |
| Do .................... | Assistant Director.................................. | ......do ...................... | ............ | ES | .............. | .............. | |
| Do .................... | Senior Advisor for Facilities Planning and Management. | Linnea M. Avallone .............. | XS | AD | .............. | .............. | |
| | **Division of Atmospheric and Geospace Sciences** | | | | | | |
| Do .................... | Division Director.................................. | Anjuli Bamzai...................... | TA | ES | .............. | .............. | 01/19/21 |
| Do .................... | Section Head, Atmosphere Section.................... | Vacant ...................... | ............ | ES | .............. | .............. | |
| Do .................... | Section Head, Geospace Section ...................... | ......do ...................... | ............ | ES | .............. | .............. | |
| | **Division of Earth Sciences** | | | | | | |
| Do .................... | Division Director.................................. | ......do ...................... | ............ | ES | .............. | .............. | |
| Do .................... | Section Head, Disciplinary Programs Section ... | ......do ...................... | ............ | ES | .............. | .............. | |
| | **Division of Ocean Sciences** | | | | | | |
| Do .................... | Division Director.................................. | ......do ...................... | ............ | ES | .............. | .............. | |
| Do .................... | Section Head, Marine Geosciences Section........ | Candace Major...................... | TA | ES | .............. | .............. | 09/04/21 |
| Do .................... | Head, Ocean Section.............................. | Career Incumbent ................ | CA | ES | .............. | .............. | |
| | **Office of Polar Programs** | | | | | | |
| Do .................... | Office Director...................................... | ......do ...................... | CA | ES | .............. | .............. | |
| Do .................... | Executive Officer.................................. | Vacant ...................... | ............ | ES | .............. | .............. | |
| Do .................... | Head, Section for Arctic Sciences........................ | Career Incumbent ................ | CA | ES | .............. | .............. | |
| Do .................... | Head, Section for Antarctic Sciences ................ | ......do ...................... | CA | ES | .............. | .............. | |
| Do .................... | Environmental Officer.............................. | Polly Ann Penhale .............. | XS | AD | .............. | .............. | |
| Do .................... | Senior Advisor for Cost Analysis and Budget Planning. | Scot A Arnold...................... | XS | AD | .............. | .............. | |
| | **DIRECTORATE FOR MATHEMATICAL AND PHYSICAL SCIENCES** | | | | | | |
| Do .................... | Assistant Director.................................. | Vacant ...................... | ............ | ES | .............. | .............. | |
| Do .................... | Head, Office of Multidisciplinary Activities and Senior Advisor for Science. | Clark V Cooper ...................... | XS | AD | .............. | .............. | |
| Do .................... | Senior Advisor for Facilities Planning and Management. | Robert Christopher Smith ... | XS | AD | .............. | .............. | |
| Do .................... | Senior Advisor...................................... | Patricia M Knezek.............. | XS | AD | .............. | .............. | |
| | **Division of Astronomical Sciences** | | | | | | |
| Do .................... | Division Director.................................. | Career Incumbent ................ | CA | ES | .............. | .............. | |
| | **Division of Chemistry** | | | | | | |
| Do .................... | ......do ...................................... | Vacant ...................... | ............ | ES | .............. | .............. | |
| Do .................... | Deputy Division Director ...................... | Career Incumbent ................ | CA | ES | .............. | .............. | |
| | **Division of Materials Research** | | | | | | |
| Do .................... | Division Director.................................. | ......do ...................... | CA | ES | .............. | .............. | |
| Do .................... | Deputy Division Director ...................... | ......do ...................... | CA | ES | .............. | .............. | |
| | **Division of Mathematical Sciences** | | | | | | |
| Do .................... | Division Director.................................. | Vacant ...................... | ............ | ES | .............. | .............. | |

## NATIONAL SCIENCE FOUNDATION—Continued

| Location | Position Title | Name of Incumbent | Type of Appt. | Pay Plan | Level, Grade, or Pay | Tenure | Expires |
|---|---|---|---|---|---|---|---|
| Alexandria, VA ........ | Deputy Division Director .................................. | Career Incumbent ............... | CA | ES | ............... | ............... | |
| Do ..................... | Senior Advisor................................................ | Henry A Warchall................ | XS | AD | ............... | | |
| | **Division of Physics** | | | | | | |
| Do ..................... | Division Director........................................... | Career Incumbent ............... | CA | ES | ............... | ............... | |
| Do ..................... | Deputy Division Director .................................. | ......do ....................... | CA | ES | ............... | ............... | |
| Do ..................... | Senior Advisor................................................ | ......do ....................... | CA | ES | ............... | ............... | |
| | **DIRECTORATE FOR SOCIAL, BEHAVIORAL AND ECONOMIC SCIENCES** | | | | | | |
| Do ..................... | Assistant Director Social Behavioral and Economic Sciences. | Vacant ....................... | ............ | ES | ............... | ............... | |
| Do ..................... | Senior Advisor................................................ | Deborah H Olster ............... | XS | AD | ............... | ............... | |
| | **Division of Behavioral and Cognitive Sciences** | | | | | | |
| Do ..................... | Division Director........................................... | Vacant ....................... | ............ | ES | ............... | ............... | |
| Arlington, VA.......... | Deputy Division Director .................................. | Antoinette Winklerprins ...... | TA | ES | ............... | ............... | 08/21/21 |
| | **NATIONAL CENTER FOR SCIENCE AND ENGINEERING STATISTICS** | | | | | | |
| Alexandria, VA ....... | ......do ....................... | Career Incumbent ............... | CA | ES | ............... | ............... | |
| Do ..................... | Chief Mathematical Statistician....................... | Samson A. Adeshiyan........... | XS | AD | ............... | ............... | |
| | **Division of Social and Economic Sciences** | | | | | | |
| Do ..................... | Division Director........................................... | Vacant ....................... | ............ | ES | ............... | ............... | |
| Do ..................... | Deputy Division Director .................................. | Career Incumbent ............... | CA | ES | ............... | ............... | |
| | **OFFICE OF BUDGET, FINANCE AND AWARD MANAGEMENT** | | | | | | |
| Do ..................... | Deputy Director Large Facilities Projects.......... | ......do ....................... | CA | ES | ............... | ............... | |
| | **Division of Institutional and Award Support** | | | | | | |
| Do ..................... | Senior Staff Associate for Policy Coordination .. | Jean Irene Feldman ............. | XS | AD | ............... | ............... | |
| Do ..................... | Senior Advisor for Oversight............................. | Michael L. Howe.................. | XS | AD | ............... | ............... | |
| | **OFFICE OF INFORMATION AND RESOURCE MANAGEMENT** | | | | | | |
| Do ..................... | Senior Advisor for Management and Planning . | Jeffrey S Rich ....................... | XS | AD | ............... | ............... | |
| | **Division of Information Systems** | | | | | | |
| Do ..................... | Division Director........................................... | Career Incumbent ............... | CA | ES | ............... | ............... | |

## NATIONAL SCIENCE FOUNDATION OFFICE OF THE INSPECTOR GENERAL

| Location | Position Title | Name of Incumbent | Type of Appt. | Pay Plan | Level, Grade, or Pay | Tenure | Expires |
|---|---|---|---|---|---|---|---|
| Alexandria, VA ........ | Senior Advisor/Ombudsman for Whistleblower Protection. | William J Kilgallin.............. | XS | AD | ............... | ............... | |

## NATIONAL TRANSPORTATION SAFETY BOARD

| Location | Position Title | Name of Incumbent | Type of Appt. | Pay Plan | Level, Grade, or Pay | Tenure | Expires |
|---|---|---|---|---|---|---|---|
| | **OFFICE OF BOARD MEMBERS** | | | | | | |
| Washington, DC ...... | Member.......................................................... | Thomas B. Chapman............ | PAS | EX | IV | ............... | |
| Do ..................... | ......do ....................... | Jennifer L Homendy ............ | PAS | EX | IV | ............... | |
| Do ..................... | ......do ....................... | Michael E. Graham ............. | PAS | EX | IV | ............... | |
| Do ..................... | Special Assistant............................................ | Thomas E. Dunlap............... | SC | GS | 15 | ............... | |
| Do ..................... | ......do ....................... | ......do ....................... | SC | GS | 15 | ............... | |
| Do ..................... | Executive Officer............................................ | Sean Dalton ...................... | NA | ES | ............... | ............... | |
| Do ..................... | Confidential Assistant ..................................... | Stephen A. Stadius............... | SC | GS | 11 | ............... | |
| Do ..................... | Communications Liaison .................................. | Michael J Hughes................ | SC | GS | 12 | 2 Years | |
| Do ..................... | Confidential Assistant ..................................... | Marsha L. Clarke ................ | SC | GS | 11 | ............... | |
| Do ..................... | Special Assistant............................................ | Erik Strickland.................... | SC | GS | 15 | ............... | |
| Do ..................... | Confidential Assistant ..................................... | Linda Mcgunigal ................ | SC | GS | 11 | ............... | |
| Do ..................... | Special Assistant............................................ | Michael M. Hampton .......... | SC | GS | 13 | ............... | |
| Do ..................... | Chairman ..................................................... | Robert L Sumwalt III........... | PAS | EX | III | ............... | |
| Do ..................... | Vice Chairman .............................................. | Bruce Landsberg ................. | PAS | EX | IV | ............... | |

## NATIONAL TRANSPORTATION SAFETY BOARD—Continued

| Location | Position Title | Name of Incumbent | Type of Appt. | Pay Plan | Level, Grade, or Pay | Tenure | Expires |
|---|---|---|---|---|---|---|---|
| Washington, DC ...... | Confidential Assistant .......................... | Anne Kerins.......................... | SC | GS | 11 | ............... | |
| Do .................. | *Office of the Managing Director*<br>Managing Director............................... | Career Incumbent ............... | CA | ES | ............... | ............... | |
| Do .................. | *Office of the General Counsel*<br>General Counsel............................... | ......do ............................ | CA | ES | ............... | ............... | |
| Do .................. | *Office of Safety Recommendations and Communications*<br>Director, Office of Safety Recommendations and Communications. | ......do ............................ | CA | ES | ............... | ............... | |

## NORTHERN BORDER REGIONAL COMMISSION

| Location | Position Title | Name of Incumbent | Type of Appt. | Pay Plan | Level, Grade, or Pay | Tenure | Expires |
|---|---|---|---|---|---|---|---|
| Concord, NH ............ | *Northern Border Regional Commission*<br>Alternate Federal Co-Chairperson .................... | Vacant .................................. | PA | EX | V | ............... | |
| Do .................. | Federal Co-Chairperson ....................................... | Harold B Parker .................. | PAS | EX | III | ............... | |

## NUCLEAR REGULATORY COMMISSION

| Location | Position Title | Name of Incumbent | Type of Appt. | Pay Plan | Level, Grade, or Pay | Tenure | Expires |
|---|---|---|---|---|---|---|---|
| Rockville, MD ......... | **OFFICE OF THE CHAIRMAN**<br>Technical Assistant for Reactors........................ | Eric Bowman ...................... | XS | OT | ............... | ............... | |
| Do .................. | Budget Policy Advisor.......................................... | Susan Kenney ...................... | XS | OT | ............... | ............... | |
| Do .................. | Chief of Staff................................................ | Alan L Frazier ...................... | XS | OT | ............... | ............... | |
| Do .................. | Chairman ................................................ | Kristine L Svinicki ............... | PAS | EX | II | 5 Years | |
| Do .................. | Legal Counsel/Deputy Chief of Staff ................. | Maxwell C Smith.................. | XS | OT | ............... | ............... | |
| Do .................. | **ADVISORY COMMITTEE ON REACTOR SAFEGUARDS**<br>Executive Director ................................................ | Career Incumbent ............... | CA | ES | ............... | ............... | |
| Do .................. | Senior Technical Advisor for Reactor Safety...... | Hossein P Nourbakhsh ........ | XS | OT | ............... | ............... | |
| Do .................. | **OFFICE OF THE SECRETARY**<br>Secretary of the Commission ............................ | Career Incumbent ............... | CA | ES | ............... | ............... | |
| Do .................. | Historian ................................................ | Thomas R Wellock ............... | XS | OT | ............... | ............... | |
| Do .................. | **OFFICE OF THE CHIEF FINANCIAL OFFICER**<br>Chief Financial Officer ...................................... | Career Incumbent ............... | CA | ES | ............... | ............... | |
| Do .................. | **OFFICE OF THE GENERAL COUNSEL**<br>Deputy General Counsel for Rulemaking and Policy. | ......do ............................ | CA | ES | ............... | ............... | |
| Do .................. | General Counsel................................................ | ......do ............................ | CA | ES | ............... | ............... | |
| Do .................. | Deputy General Counsel for Hearings and Administration. | ......do ............................ | CA | ES | ............... | ............... | |
| Do .................. | Assistant General Counsel for Reactor and Materials Rulemaking. | ......do ............................ | CA | ES | ............... | ............... | |
| Do .................. | Assistant General Counsel for Materials Litigation and Enforcement. | ......do ............................ | CA | ES | ............... | ............... | |
| Do .................. | Assistant General Counsel for New Reactor Programs. | ......do ............................ | CA | ES | ............... | ............... | |
| Do .................. | Assistant General Counsel for Legal Counsel, Legislation, and Special Projects. | ......do ............................ | CA | ES | ............... | ............... | |
| Do .................. | Assistant General Counsel for Administration.. | ......do ............................ | CA | ES | ............... | ............... | |
| Do .................. | Assistant General Counsel for Operating Reactors. | ......do ............................ | CA | ES | ............... | ............... | |
| Do .................. | Assistant General Counsel for High Level Waste, Fuel Cycle, and Nuclear Security. | Vacant .................................. | | ES | ............... | ............... | |
| Do .................. | Solicitor................................................ | Andrew P Averbach.............. | XS | OT | ............... | ............... | |
| Do .................. | Special Counsel for Litigation............................ | Sherwin E Turk.................... | XS | OT | ............... | ............... | |
| Do .................. | Special Counsel for Acquisitions....................... | Robin A Baum ...................... | XS | OT | ............... | ............... | |
| Do .................. | Special Counsel for New Reactor Licensing....... | Robert M Weisman.............. | XS | OT | ............... | ............... | |

## NUCLEAR REGULATORY COMMISSION—Continued

| Location | Position Title | Name of Incumbent | Type of Appt. | Pay Plan | Level, Grade, or Pay | Tenure | Expires |
|---|---|---|---|---|---|---|---|
| | **OFFICE OF CONGRESSIONAL AFFAIRS** | | | | | | |
| Rockville, MD ......... | Director, Office of Congressional Affairs ........... | Career Incumbent ................ | CA | ES | ................ | ................ | |
| | **OFFICE OF PUBLIC AFFAIRS** | | | | | | |
| Do .................... | Director, Office of Public Affairs ...................... | ......do ...................... | CA | ES | ................ | ................ | |
| Do .................... | Senior Level Advisor on Public Affairs.............. | Holly M Harrington ............. | XS | OT | ................ | ................ | |
| | **OFFICE OF INTERNATIONAL PROGRAMS** | | | | | | |
| Do .................... | Director, Office of International Programs........ | Career Incumbent ................ | CA | ES | ................ | ................ | |
| Do .................... | Deputy Director, Office of International Programs. | ......do ...................... | CA | ES | ................ | ................ | |
| Do .................... | Senior Level Foreign Policy Advisor ................. | Jennifer S Holzman............. | XS | OT | ................ | ................ | |
| Do .................... | Senior Level Advisor for Non-Proliferation and International Nuclear Security. | Atanasia N Fragoyannis ...... | XS | OT | ................ | ................ | |
| | **OFFICE OF THE EXECUTIVE DIRECTOR FOR OPERATIONS** | | | | | | |
| Do .................... | Executive Director for Operations ..................... | Career Incumbent ................ | CA | ES | ................ | ................ | |
| Do .................... | Deputy Executive Director for Reactor and Preparedness Programs. | ......do ...................... | CA | ES | ................ | ................ | |
| Do .................... | Deputy Executive Director for Materials, Waste, Research, State, Tribal, Compliance, Administration, and Human Capital. | ......do ...................... | CA | ES | ................ | ................ | |
| Do .................... | Assistant for Operations ................................... | ......do ...................... | CA | ES | ................ | ................ | |
| | **OFFICE OF INVESTIGATIONS** | | | | | | |
| Do .................... | Director, Office of Investigations ...................... | ......do ...................... | CA | ES | ................ | ................ | |
| | **OFFICE OF ENFORCEMENT** | | | | | | |
| Do .................... | Director Office of Enforcement ........................ | ......do ...................... | CA | ES | ................ | ................ | |
| Do .................... | Agency Allegations Advisor............................... | Lisamarie Jarriel................. | XS | OT | ................ | ................ | |
| | **OFFICE OF ADMINISTRATION** | | | | | | |
| Do .................... | Director, Office of Administration...................... | Career Incumbent ................ | CA | ES | ................ | ................ | |
| | **OFFICE OF THE CHIEF HUMAN CAPITAL OFFICER** | | | | | | |
| Do .................... | Chief Human Capital Officer ............................. | ......do ...................... | CA | ES | ................ | ................ | |
| Do .................... | Deputy Chief Human Capital Officer.............. | ......do ...................... | CA | ES | ................ | ................ | |
| Do .................... | Associate Director for Human Resources Training and Development/Chief Learning Officer. | ......do ...................... | CA | ES | ................ | ................ | |
| Do .................... | Associate Director for Human Resources Operations and Policy. | ......do ...................... | CA | ES | ................ | ................ | |
| | **OFFICE OF THE CHIEF INFORMATION OFFICER** | | | | | | |
| Do .................... | Chief Information Officer.................................. | ......do ...................... | CA | ES | ................ | ................ | |
| Do .................... | Deputy Chief Information Officer...................... | ......do ...................... | CA | ES | ................ | ................ | |
| Do .................... | Senior Information Technology Security Officer. | Paul A Ricketts.................... | XS | OT | ................ | ................ | |
| Do .................... | Senior Level Advisor for Information Security.. | Kathy L Lyons-Burke........... | XS | OT | ................ | ................ | |
| | **OFFICE OF NUCLEAR SECURITY AND INCIDENT RESPONSE** | | | | | | |
| Do .................... | Director, Office of Nuclear Security and Incident Response. | Career Incumbent ................ | CA | ES | ................ | ................ | |
| Do .................... | Senior Technical Advisor for Digital Instrumentation and Controls Cyber Security. | Vacant ...................... | XS | OT | ................ | ................ | |
| Do .................... | Senior Level Advisor for Emergency Preparedness. | Patricia A Milligan ............. | XS | OT | ................ | ................ | |
| | **OFFICE OF NUCLEAR REACTOR REGULATION** | | | | | | |
| Do .................... | Director, Office of Nuclear Reactor Regulation.. | Career Incumbent ................ | CA | ES | ................ | ................ | |
| Do .................... | Senior Level Advisor for Structural Mechanics. | Kamal A Manoly.................. | XS | OT | ................ | ................ | |
| Bethesda, MD......... | Sla for Probabilistic Assessment........................ | Sunil D Weerakkody ........... | XS | OT | ................ | ................ | |
| Rockville, MD ......... | Senior Technical Advisor for Reactor Systems .. | James A Hickey .................. | XS | OT | ................ | ................ | |
| Do .................... | Senior Technical Advisor for Nuclear Power Plant Siting. | Clifford G Munson................ | XS | OT | ................ | ................ | |
| Do .................... | Senior Technical Advisor for Human Factors Analysis and Performance Evaluation. | David R Desaulniers ............ | XS | OT | ................ | ................ | |
| Do .................... | Senior Technical Advisor for Reactor Fuel........ | Paul M Clifford................... | XS | OT | ................ | ................ | |
| Do .................... | Senior Technical Advisor for License Renewal Aging Management. | Allen L Hiser Jr................... | XS | OT | ................ | ................ | |
| Do .................... | Senior Technical Advisor for Digital Instrumentation and Control. | Steven A Arndt.................... | XS | OT | ................ | ................ | |

## NUCLEAR REGULATORY COMMISSION—Continued

| Location | Position Title | Name of Incumbent | Type of Appt. | Pay Plan | Level, Grade, or Pay | Tenure | Expires |
|---|---|---|---|---|---|---|---|
| Rockville, MD .......... | Senior Level Advisor for Nuclear Material Power Plants. | David L Rudland .................. | XS | OT | .............. | .............. | |
| Do .................... | Senior Technical Advisor for Probabilistic Risk Assessment Technology. | Martin A Stutzke.............. | XS | OT | .............. | .............. | |
| | **OFFICE OF NUCLEAR MATERIAL SAFETY AND SAFEGUARDS** | | | | | | |
| Do .................... | Deputy Director, Office of Nuclear Material Safety and Safeguards. | Career Incumbent ............... | CA | ES | .............. | .............. | |
| Do .................... | Director, Office of Nuclear Material Safety and Safeguards. | ......do ................... | CA | ES | .............. | .............. | |
| Do .................... | Senior Level Advisor for Health Physics............ | Eugene V Holahan Jr. .......... | XS | OT | .............. | .............. | |
| Do .................... | Senior Technical Advisor for Probabilistic Risk Assessment. | Donald G Harrison ............... | XS | OT | .............. | .............. | |
| Do .................... | Senior Level Advisor.............................. | Timothy J Mccartin.............. | XS | OT | .............. | .............. | |
| Do .................... | Senior Technical Advisor for Waste Management and Environmental Protection. | Rateb M Abu-Eid ................. | XS | OT | .............. | .............. | |
| Do .................... | Director, Division of Fuel Management............. | Career Incumbent ............... | CA | ES | .............. | .............. | |
| | **OFFICE OF NUCLEAR REGULATORY RESEARCH** | | | | | | |
| Do .................... | Director, Office of Nuclear Regulatory Research. | ......do ................... | CA | ES | .............. | .............. | |
| Do .................... | Deputy Director, Office of Nuclear Regulatory Research. | ......do ................... | CA | ES | .............. | .............. | |
| Do .................... | Senior Technical Advisor for Radionuclide Transport. | Thomas J Nicholson............ | XS | OT | .............. | .............. | |
| Do .................... | Senior Technical Advisor for Earth Science and Geophysical Engineering. | Jon P Ake ...................... | XS | OT | .............. | .............. | |
| Do .................... | Senior Adviser for Nuclear Safety ................. | Vacant ...................... | XS | OT | .............. | .............. | |
| Do .................... | Senior Technical Advisor for Probabilistic Risk Analysis. | Nathan O Siu..................... | XS | OT | .............. | .............. | |
| Do .................... | Senior Technical Advisor for Structural and Seismic Analysis. | Jim Xu........................... | XS | OT | .............. | .............. | |
| Do .................... | Senior Technical Advisor for Computational Fluid Dynamics. | Christopher F Boyd.............. | XS | OT | .............. | .............. | |
| Do .................... | ......do ................... | Abdelghani Zigh ................. | XS | OT | .............. | .............. | |
| Do .................... | Senior Technical Advisor for Digital Instrumentation and Control. | Sushil K Birla..................... | XS | OT | .............. | .............. | |
| Do .................... | Senior Technical Advisor for Civil/Structural Engineering Issues. | Jose A Pires ..................... | XS | OT | .............. | .............. | |
| Do .................... | Senior Technical Advisor for Materials Engineering Issues. | Robert L Tregoning .............. | XS | OT | .............. | .............. | |
| Do .................... | Senior Technical Advisor for Thermal Hydraulics and Code Development. | Stephen M Bajorek........... | XS | OT | .............. | .............. | |
| | **REGION I** | | | | | | |
| King of Prussia, PA. | Regional Administrator ........................ | Career Incumbent ............... | CA | ES | .............. | .............. | |
| | **REGION II** | | | | | | |
| Atlanta, GA ............ | ......do ................... | ......do ................... | CA | ES | .............. | .............. | |
| | **REGION III** | | | | | | |
| Lisle, IL.................. | ......do ................... | ......do ................... | CA | ES | .............. | .............. | |
| | **REGION IV** | | | | | | |
| Arlington, TX.......... | ......do ................... | ......do ................... | CA | ES | .............. | .............. | |
| | **OFFICE OF COMMISSIONER HANSON** | | | | | | |
| Rockville, MD ......... | Commissioner................................ | Christopher T Hanson ........ | PAS | EX | III | 5 Years | |
| Do .................... | Chief of Staff ............................... | Molly B Marsh.................... | XS | OT | .............. | .............. | |
| Do .................... | Legal Counsel................................ | Olivia Mikula.................... | XS | OT | .............. | .............. | |
| Do .................... | Technical Assistant for Materials ................ | Cinthya Roman-Cuevas ....... | XS | OT | .............. | .............. | |
| Do .................... | Technical Assistant for Reactors................... | Vacant ...................... | XS | OT | .............. | .............. | |
| | **OFFICE OF COMMISSIONER BARAN** | | | | | | |
| Do .................... | Commissioner................................ | Jeffery M Baran ................. | PAS | EX | III | 5 Years | |
| Do .................... | Chief of Staff ............................... | Amy Powell ...................... | XS | OT | .............. | .............. | |
| Do .................... | Legal Counsel................................ | Lisa London ...................... | XS | OT | .............. | .............. | |
| Do .................... | Technical Assistant for Materials ................ | Janelle B Jessie ................. | XS | OT | .............. | .............. | |
| Do .................... | Technical Assistant for Reactors................... | Robert G Krsek.................. | XS | OT | .............. | .............. | |
| | **ATOMIC SAFETY AND LICENSING BOARD PANEL** | | | | | | |
| Do .................... | Chief Administrative Judge ...................... | Edward R Hawkens ............ | XS | OT | .............. | .............. | |
| Bethesda, MD .......... | Administrative Judge (Technical)................... | Nicholas G Trikouros .......... | XS | OT | .............. | .............. | |
| Do .................... | Administrative Judge (Technical)................... | Vacant ...................... | XS | OT | .............. | .............. | |
| Rockville, MD .......... | Administrative Judge (Legal) .................... | George P Bollwerk.............. | XS | OT | .............. | .............. | |

## NUCLEAR REGULATORY COMMISSION—Continued

| Location | Position Title | Name of Incumbent | Type of Appt. | Pay Plan | Level, Grade, or Pay | Tenure | Expires |
|---|---|---|---|---|---|---|---|
| Rockville, MD ......... | Associate Chief Administrative Judeg (Technical). | Vacant ................... | XS | OT | .............. | ............ | |
| Do ................... | Administrative Judge (Technical)................... | Sue H Abreu ................... | XS | OT | .............. | ............ | |
| Do ................... | Associate Chief Administrative Judge (Legal)... | Paul S Ryerson ................... | XS | OT | .............. | ............ | |
| Do ................... | Administrative Judge (Legal) ........................ | Ronald M Spritzer.................... | XS | OT | .............. | ............ | |
| Do ................... | ......do ......................... | Michael M Gibson .............. | XS | OT | .............. | ............ | |
| Do ................... | Administrative Judge (Technical).................... | Gary S Arnold................... | XS | OT | .............. | ............ | |
| Do ................... | Administrative Judge (Legal) ........................ | William J Froehlich.............. | XS | OT | .............. | ............ | |
| | **OFFICE OF COMMISSIONER CAPUTO** | | | | | | |
| Do ................... | Commissioner........................ | Annie Caputo...................... | PAS | EX | III | 5 Years | |
| Do ................... | Technical Assistant for Reactors................... | William T Orders................. | XS | OT | .............. | ............ | |
| Do ................... | Budget Advisor........................ | Constance Schum ................... | XS | OT | .............. | ............ | |
| Do ................... | Legal Counsel........................ | Richard Harper................... | XS | OT | .............. | ............ | |
| Do ................... | Technical Assistant for Materials ..................... | Cynthia G Jones................ | XS | OT | .............. | ............ | |
| | **OFFICE OF COMMISSIONER WRIGHT** | | | | | | |
| Do ................... | Commissioner........................ | David A Wright.................... | PAS | EX | III | 5 Years | |
| Do ................... | Technical Assistant for Reactors....................... | Shakur Walker................... | XS | OT | .............. | ............ | |
| Do ................... | Technical Assistant for Materials...................... | Samatha Crane................... | XS | OT | .............. | ............ | |
| Do ................... | Legal Counsel........................ | Carol Lazar ................... | XS | OT | .............. | ............ | |
| Do ................... | Chief of Staff ........................ | Catherine Kanatas.............. | XS | OT | .............. | ............ | |

## NUCLEAR REGULATORY COMMISSION OFFICE OF THE INSPECTOR GENERAL

| Location | Position Title | Name of Incumbent | Type of Appt. | Pay Plan | Level, Grade, or Pay | Tenure | Expires |
|---|---|---|---|---|---|---|---|
| Rockville, MD .......... | Inspector General ................................. | Robert J. Feitel ................... | PAS | OT | .............. | ............ | |

## NUCLEAR WASTE TECHNICAL REVIEW BOARD

| Location | Position Title | Name of Incumbent | Type of Appt. | Pay Plan | Level, Grade, or Pay | Tenure | Expires |
|---|---|---|---|---|---|---|---|
| Arlington, VA........... | Executive Director ................................. | Career Incumbent ................ | CA | ES | .............. | ............ | |
| Stanford, CA........... | Member................................. | Mary L Zoback...................... | PA | AD | .............. | 4 Years | |
| Washington, DC ...... | ......do ............... | Vacant ............... | PA | AD | .............. | 4 Years | |
| Irvine, CA ............... | ......do ............... | Efi Foufoula ............... | PA | AD | .............. | 4 Years | |
| College Station, TX . | ......do ............... | Kenneth L Peddicord .......... | PA | AD | .............. | 4 Years | |
| Madison, WI ........... | ......do ............... | Jean M Bahr ...................... | PA | AD | .............. | 4 Years | |
| Washington, DC ...... | ......do ............... | Vacant ............... | PA | AD | .............. | 4 Years | |
| St. Augustine, FL .... | ......do ............... | Allen G Croff...................... | PA | AD | .............. | 4 Years | |
| Boulder, CO ........... | ......do ............... | Tissa Illangasekare .............. | PA | AD | .............. | 4 Years | |
| Norfolk, VA ............. | ......do ............... | Steven Becker ................... | PA | AD | .............. | 4 Years | |
| Raleigh, NC ............. | ......do ............... | Paul J Turinsky ................... | PA | AD | .............. | 4 Years | |
| State College, PA..... | ......do ............... | Susan L Brantley ................ | PA | AD | .............. | 4 Years | |

## OCCUPATIONAL SAFETY AND HEALTH REVIEW COMMISSION

| Location | Position Title | Name of Incumbent | Type of Appt. | Pay Plan | Level, Grade, or Pay | Tenure | Expires |
|---|---|---|---|---|---|---|---|
| Washington, DC ...... | Confidential Assistant to the Chairman ........... | Mariel C Bailey ................... | SC | GS | 12 | .............. | |
| Do ................... | Chief Counsel to the Chairman ........................ | Vacant ................... | .............. | ES | .............. | .............. | |
| | **OFFICE OF COMMISSIONERS** | | | | | | |
| Do ................... | Commission Member ...................... | Amanda Wood Laihow ......... | PAS | EX | IV | .............. | |
| Do ................... | ......do ............... | Cynthia L Attwood ................ | PAS | EX | IV | .............. | |
| Do ................... | Commission Member (Chairman)....................... | James J Sullivan Jr............. | PAS | EX | III | .............. | |
| Do ................... | Counsel to A Commissioner ............................. | Michael R Asplen ................ | SC | GS | 15 | .............. | |
| | **OFFICE OF THE GENERAL COUNSEL** | | | | | | |
| Do ................... | Special Assistant........................ | Vacant ................... | .............. | ES | .............. | .............. | |
| Do ................... | General Counsel........................ | Career Incumbent ................ | CA | ES | .............. | .............. | |

## OFFICE OF GOVERNMENT ETHICS

| Location | Position Title | Name of Incumbent | Type of Appt. | Pay Plan | Level, Grade, or Pay | Tenure | Expires |
|---|---|---|---|---|---|---|---|
| Washington, DC ...... | Director........................................................ | Emory Arthur Rounds III .... | PAS | EX | III | 5 Years | |
| Do .................... | General Counsel.......................................... | Vacant ...................................... | ............. | ES | .............. | .............. | |

## OFFICE OF NAVAJO AND HOPI INDIAN RELOCATION

| Location | Position Title | Name of Incumbent | Type of Appt. | Pay Plan | Level, Grade, or Pay | Tenure | Expires |
|---|---|---|---|---|---|---|---|
| | **OFFICE OF THE COMMISSIONER** | | | | | | |
| Flagstaff, AZ ............ | Commissioner................................................ | Vacant ...................................... | PAS | EX | IV | .............. | |
| Do .................... | Executive Director ...................................... | Career Incumbent ............... | CA | ES | .............. | .............. | |
| Do .................... | Deputy Executive Director........................ | Vacant ...................................... | ............. | ES | .............. | .............. | |

## OFFICE OF PERSONNEL MANAGEMENT

| Location | Position Title | Name of Incumbent | Type of Appt. | Pay Plan | Level, Grade, or Pay | Tenure | Expires |
|---|---|---|---|---|---|---|---|
| | **OFFICE OF THE DIRECTOR** | | | | | | |
| Washington, DC ...... | Director........................................................ | Vacant ...................................... | PAS | EX | II | .............. | |
| Do .................... | Deputy Director .......................................... | Michael Rigas ...................... | PAS | EX | III | .............. | |
| Do .................... | Chief of Staff.............................................. | Basil Parker.......................... | NA | ES | | .............. | |
| Do .................... | Deputy Chief of Staff................................ | Vacant ...................................... | ............. | ES | | .............. | |
| Do .................... | Chief Management Officer ........................ | Career Incumbent ............... | CA | ES | | .............. | |
| Do .................... | White House Liaison & Senior Advisor to the Director. | Paul Dans ............................. | NA | ES | | .............. | |
| Do .................... | Senior Advisor to the Director for Operations ... | Alexandra D Czwartacki...... | NA | ES | | .............. | |
| Do .................... | Director, Performance Accountability Council - Program Management Office. | Career Incumbent ............... | CA | ES | | .............. | |
| Do .................... | Senior Advisor to the Director .................. | George Nesterczuk ............... | NA | ES | | .............. | |
| Do .................... | Chair, Federal Prevailing Rate Advisory Committee. | Douglas Fehrer ...................... | NA | ES | | .............. | |
| Do .................... | Senior Advisor for Research and Evaluation ..... | Rebecca Thacker.................... | SC | SL | $170,800 | .............. | |
| Do .................... | Executive Secretariat & Resources Management Officer. | Peggy Grande ........................ | SC | GS | 15 | .............. | |
| Do .................... | Senior Advisor for Policy and Chco Council....... | John York .............................. | SC | GS | 14 | .............. | |
| Do .................... | Senior Advisor to the Director ............................. | Anthony Oboyle.................... | SC | GS | 15 | .............. | |
| Do .................... | Director of Advance and Speechwriter.............. | Kathryn Johnson................... | SC | GS | 13 | .............. | |
| Do .................... | Special Assistant ........................................ | Naweed Wally Tahmas......... | SC | GS | 9 | .............. | |
| Do .................... | Confidential Assistant ............................... | Reagan Hogan ...................... | SC | GS | 7 | .............. | |
| Do .................... | ......do ........................................................... | Katherine French ................. | SC | GS | 4 | .............. | |
| Do .................... | Confidential Clerk ...................................... | Bryce Liquerman................... | SC | GS | 4 | .............. | |
| | **OFFICE OF THE GENERAL COUNSEL** | | | | | | |
| Do .................... | General Counsel.......................................... | Mark A Robbins.................... | NA | ES | .............. | .............. | |
| Do .................... | Deputy General Counsel ............................ | Career Incumbent ............... | CA | ES | .............. | .............. | |
| Do .................... | Associate General Counsel ........................ | ......do ...................................... | CA | ES | .............. | .............. | |
| | **OFFICE OF COMMUNICATIONS** | | | | | | |
| Do .................... | Director, Office of Communications ................... | Anthony Marucci................... | NA | ES | .............. | .............. | |
| Do .................... | Public Affairs Specialist ........................... | Michael Cogar....................... | SC | GS | 12 | .............. | |
| Do .................... | ......do ........................................................... | Rachel Tripp ......................... | SC | GS | 12 | .............. | |
| | **CONGRESSIONAL, LEGISLATIVE, AND INTERGOVERNMENTAL AFFAIRS** | | | | | | |
| Do .................... | Director, Congressional, Legislative and Intergovernmental Affairs. | Vacant ...................................... | ............. | ES | .............. | .............. | |
| Do .................... | Deputy Director, Congressional, Legislative and Intergovernmental Affairs. | Andrew Moore ...................... | SC | GS | 14 | .............. | |
| Do .................... | Senior Congressional Relations Officer............ | Christiana Frazee.................. | SC | GS | 14 | .............. | |
| Do .................... | Congressional Relations Officer...................... | Marina Golovkina.................. | SC | GS | 12 | .............. | |
| Do .................... | Legislative Analyst ..................................... | Benjamin Steinhafel ............ | SC | GS | 12 | .............. | |
| Do .................... | ......do ........................................................... | Darin Gibbons ...................... | SC | GS | 13 | .............. | |
| Do .................... | ......do ........................................................... | Timothy Duffy Jr................... | SC | GS | 12 | .............. | |
| | **EMPLOYEE SERVICES** | | | | | | |
| Do .................... | Associate Director, Employee Services .............. | Dennis D Kirk ...................... | NA | ES | .............. | .............. | |
| Do .................... | Principal Deputy Associate Director ................. | Career Incumbent ............... | CA | ES | .............. | .............. | |
| Do .................... | Deputy Associate Director, Pay and Leave........ | ......do ...................................... | CA | ES | .............. | .............. | |

## OFFICE OF PERSONNEL MANAGEMENT—Continued

| Location | Position Title | Name of Incumbent | Type of Appt. | Pay Plan | Level, Grade, or Pay | Tenure | Expires |
|---|---|---|---|---|---|---|---|
| Washington, DC ...... | Deputy Associate Director, Outreach, Diversity, and Inclusion. | Career Incumbent ................ | CA | ES | ............... | ............... | |
| Do .................... | Deputy Associate Director, Ses and Performance Management. | ......do ......... | CA | ES | ............... | ............... | |
| Do .................... | Deputy Associate Director, Accountability and Workforce Relations. | ......do ......... | CA | ES | ............... | ............... | |
| Do .................... | Deputy Associate Director, Talent Acquisition and Workforce Shaping. | ......do ......... | CA | ES | ............... | ............... | |
| Do .................... | Senior Advisor.................................................. | Carol Matheis...................... | SC | GS | 15 | ............... | |
| Do .................... | ......do ......... | Samuel Wright................... | SC | GS | 15 | ............... | |
| Do .................... | ......do ......... | David LaCerte ............... | SC | GS | 15 | ............... | |
| Do .................... | Special Assistant................................ | Tera Dahl.......................... | SC | GS | 15 | ............... | |
| Do .................... | Senior Advisor.................................................. | Timothy Lehmann............... | SC | GS | 14 | ............... | |
| Do .................... | Executive Assistant .............................. | Oriet Hemenway ................ | SC | GS | 7 | ............... | |
| | **MERIT SYSTEM ACCOUNTABILITY AND COMPLIANCE** | | | | | | |
| Do .................... | Associate Director, Merit System Accountability and Compliance. | Career Incumbent ................ | CA | ES | ............... | ............... | |
| Do .................... | Director, Combined Federal Campaign Operations. | ......do ......... | CA | ES | ............... | ............... | |
| Do .................... | Director, Internal Oversight and Compliance.... | ......do ......... | CA | ES | ............... | ............... | |
| | **HR SOLUTIONS** | | | | | | |
| Do .................... | Associate Director, Human Resources Solutions. | Sara Ratcliff.......................... | NA | ES | ............... | ............... | |
| Do .................... | Principal Deputy Associate Director ................. | Career Incumbent ................ | CA | ES | ............... | ............... | |
| Do .................... | Senior Advisor.................................................. | Dawn Luepke...................... | NA | ES | ............... | ............... | |
| Do .................... | Deputy Associate Director, Federal Staffing Group. | Career Incumbent ................ | CA | ES | ............... | ............... | |
| Do .................... | Deputy Associate Director, HR Strategy and Evaluation Solutions. | ......do ......... | CA | ES | ............... | ............... | |
| Do .................... | Deputy Associate Director, Human Capital Industry Solutions. | ......do ......... | CA | ES | ............... | ............... | |
| Do .................... | Director, Federal Executive Institute ................. | ......do ......... | CA | ES | ............... | ............... | |
| Do .................... | Assistant Director, Leadership and Hr Development Solutions. | ......do ......... | CA | ES | ............... | ............... | |
| | **HEALTHCARE AND INSURANCE** | | | | | | |
| Do .................... | Director, Healthcare and Insurance ................... | Vacant ................................ | ............ | ES | ............... | ............... | |
| Do .................... | Deputy Director, Healthcare and Insurance ...... | Career Incumbent ................ | CA | ES | ............... | ............... | |
| Do .................... | Assistant Director, Program Development & Support. | ......do ......... | CA | ES | ............... | ............... | |
| | **OPM HUMAN RESOURCES** | | | | | | |
| Do .................... | Opm Human Resources Director...................... | ......do ......... | CA | ES | ............... | ............... | |
| | **SUITABILITY EXECUTIVE AGENT PROGRAMS** | | | | | | |
| Do .................... | Suitability Director........................................ | ......do ......... | CA | ES | ............... | ............... | |
| | **OFFICE OF THE CHIEF FINANCIAL OFFICER** | | | | | | |
| Do .................... | Associate Chief Financial Officer, Budget and Performance. | Vacant ................................ | ............ | ES | ............... | ............... | |
| Do .................... | Associate Chief Financial Officer, Financial Strategy and Operations. | Career Incumbent ................ | CA | ES | ............... | ............... | |
| | **HUMAN RESOURCES LINE OF BUSINESS** | | | | | | |
| Do .................... | Director, Human Resources Line of Business .... | David Spinale ...................... | NA | ES | ............... | ............... | |
| | **OFFICE OF THE CHIEF INFORMATION OFFICER** | | | | | | |
| Do .................... | Chief Information Officer and Transition Executive. | Vacant ................................ | ............ | ES | ............... | ............... | |
| Do .................... | Deputy Chief Information Officer...................... | ......do ......... | ............ | ES | ............... | ............... | |
| Do .................... | Associate Chief Information Office for Management and Policy. | Career Incumbent ................ | CA | ES | ............... | ............... | |
| Macon, GA ............. | Associate Chief Information Officer, Enterprise Infrastructure Systems. | ......do ......... | CA | ES | ............... | ............... | |
| | **PRESIDENTS COMMISSION ON WHITE HOUSE FELLOWSHIPS** | | | | | | |
| Washington, DC ...... | Director, Presidents Commission on White House Fellowships. | Elizabeth Pinkerton ............. | NA | ES | ............... | ............... | |
| Do .................... | Associate Director........................................ | Mckinley Scholtz ................. | SC | GS | 12 | ............... | |
| Do .................... | Special Assistant........................................ | Caroline Waller.................... | SC | GS | 9 | ............... | |

## OFFICE OF PERSONNEL MANAGEMENT—Continued

| Location | Position Title | Name of Incumbent | Type of Appt. | Pay Plan | Level, Grade, or Pay | Tenure | Expires |
|---|---|---|---|---|---|---|---|
| Washington, DC ...... | Confidential Assistant ........................................ | Hayden Combs...................... | SC | GS | 7 | .............. | |

## OFFICE OF PERSONNEL MANAGEMENT OFFICE OF THE INSPECTOR GENERAL

| Location | Position Title | Name of Incumbent | Type of Appt. | Pay Plan | Level, Grade, or Pay | Tenure | Expires |
|---|---|---|---|---|---|---|---|
| Washington, DC ...... | **OFFICE OF THE INSPECTOR GENERAL** Inspector General ................................... | Vacant ................................... | PAS | OT | .............. | .............. | |
| Do ..................... | **OFFICE OF LEGISLATIVE AND LEGAL AFFAIRS** Counsel to the Inspector General ...................... | Robin Richardson ................. | XS | SL | .............. | .............. | |

## OFFICE OF SPECIAL COUNSEL

| Location | Position Title | Name of Incumbent | Type of Appt. | Pay Plan | Level, Grade, or Pay | Tenure | Expires |
|---|---|---|---|---|---|---|---|
| Washington, DC ...... | **HEADQUARTERS, OFFICE OF SPECIAL COUNSEL** Deputy Special Counsel................................... | Vacant ................................... | .............. | ES | .............. | .............. | |
| Do ..................... | Special Counsel........................................... | ......do ................................... | PAS | EX | IV | .............. | |
| Do ..................... | Confidential Staff Assistant............................... | Jacqueline Roeder ............... | SC | GS | 9 | .............. | |
| Do ..................... | Deputy Special Counsel for Public Policy ......... | Travis G Millsaps.................. | SC | GS | 13 | .............. | |
| Do ..................... | IT Specialist ............................................... | Daniel Wallerstein................ | SC | GS | 14 | .............. | |
| Do ..................... | Special Counsel........................................... | Vacant ................................... | PAS | EX | | 5 Years | |
| Do ..................... | Principal Deputy Special Counsel ..................... | Ellen Chubin Epstein........... | NA | ES | .............. | .............. | |
| Do ..................... | ......do ...................................................... | Vacant ................................... | .............. | ES | .............. | 5 Years | |
| Do ..................... | **OFFICE OF SPECIAL COUNSEL** Associate Special Counsel for Strategic Planning. | ......do ................................... | .............. | ES | .............. | .............. | |

## OFFICE OF THE SECRETARY OF DEFENSE OFFICE OF THE INSPECTOR GENERAL

| Location | Position Title | Name of Incumbent | Type of Appt. | Pay Plan | Level, Grade, or Pay | Tenure | Expires |
|---|---|---|---|---|---|---|---|
| Alexandria, VA ........ | **OFFICE OF THE INSPECTOR GENERAL** Chief of Staff............................................... | Career Incumbent ............... | CA | ES | .............. | .............. | |
| Do ..................... | **OFFICE OF THE SECRETARY OF DEFENSE OFFICE OF THE INSPECTOR GENERAL** Inspector General ........................................ | Vacant ................................... | PAS | EX | IV | .............. | |

## PEACE CORPS

| Location | Position Title | Name of Incumbent | Type of Appt. | Pay Plan | Level, Grade, or Pay | Tenure | Expires |
|---|---|---|---|---|---|---|---|
| Washington, DC ...... | **OFFICE OF THE DIRECTOR** Director of Peace Corps ................................. | Vacant ................................... | PAS | EX | III | .............. | |
| Do ..................... | Assoiate Director, Management ....................... | Von Presnell........................ | PA | FE | .............. | .............. | |
| Do ..................... | General Counsel........................................... | Timothy Noelker.................... | PA | FE | .............. | .............. | |
| Do ..................... | Director of Gifts and Grants Management ........ | Karen J Roberts ................. | PA | FE | .............. | .............. | |
| Do ..................... | Strategic Partnerships Advisor......................... | Vacant ................................... | PA | FE | .............. | .............. | |
| Do ..................... | Special Assistant to the Director ...................... | ......do ................................... | PA | FE | .............. | .............. | |
| Do ..................... | Peace Corps Director .................................... | Jody Olsen ........................... | PA | FE | .............. | .............. | |
| Do ..................... | Director, Strategic Partnership and Intergovernment Agencies. | Shannon Kendrick................ | PA | FE | .............. | .............. | |
| Do ..................... | Gifts and Grants Management Specialist.......... | Rachel Meima....................... | PA | FE | .............. | .............. | |

## PEACE CORPS—Continued

| Location | Position Title | Name of Incumbent | Type of Appt. | Pay Plan | Level, Grade, or Pay | Tenure | Expires |
|---|---|---|---|---|---|---|---|
| Washington, DC ...... | Director of Innovation .................................... | Vacant .......................... | PA | FE | ................ | ................ | |
| Do .................... | Chief of Staff ............................................ | Michelle Brooks ................... | PAS | FE | ................ | ................ | |
| Do .................... | Deputy Chief of Staff.................................... | Robert H Mckinney ............. | PAS | FE | ................ | ................ | |
| Do .................... | White House Liaison ..................................... | Vacant .......................... | PA | FE | ................ | ................ | |
| Do .................... | Director of Office of Strategic Information, Research & Planning. | Jeffrey J Kwiecinski............. | PA | FE | ................ | ................ | |
| Do .................... | Director of Communications ......................... | Matthew T Sheehey ............ | PA | FE | ................ | ................ | |
| Do .................... | Deputy Director Peace Corps ......................... | Vacant .......................... | PAS | EX | IV | ................ | |
| | **OFFICE OF EXTERNAL AFFAIRS** | | | | | | |
| Do .................... | Director of External Affairs ........................... | Rachel Kahler...................... | PA | FE | ................ | ................ | |
| Do .................... | Director of Congressional Relations ................. | Nancy B Herbolsheimer....... | PA | FE | ................ | ................ | |
| Do .................... | Press Director ............................................ | Vacant .......................... | PA | FE | ................ | ................ | |
| Do .................... | Deputy Communications Director .................... | Jodi Kiely ........................... | PA | FE | ................ | ................ | |
| Do .................... | Deputy Director of Congressional Relations...... | Scott Rausch ........................ | PA | FE | ................ | ................ | |
| | **OFFICE OF GLOBAL OPERATION** | | | | | | |
| Do .................... | Associate Director of Global Operations ............ | Patrick John Young .............. | PA | FE | ................ | ................ | |
| | **OFFICE OF VOLUNTEER RECRUITMENT AND SELECTION** | | | | | | |
| Do .................... | Associate Director, Volunteer Recruitment and Selection. | David Walker ........................ | PA | FE | ................ | ................ | |
| | **OFFICE OF THE CHIEF FINANCIAL OFFICER** | | | | | | |
| Do .................... | Chief Financial Officer ................................. | Richard Swarttz ................... | PA | FE | ................ | ................ | |
| | **OFFICE OF THE CHIEF INFORMATION OFFICER** | | | | | | |
| Do .................... | Chief Information Officer.................................. | Scott Knell .......................... | PA | FE | ................ | ................ | |
| | **AFRICA OPERATIONS** | | | | | | |
| Do .................... | Regional Director of Africa............................... | Jonathan S Miller ................ | PA | FE | ................ | ................ | |
| | **EUROPE, MEDITARRANEAN & ASIA OPERATIONS (EMA)** | | | | | | |
| Do .................... | Regional Director of Europe, Mediterranean, and Asia. | Jeanette M Windon .............. | PA | FE | ................ | ................ | |
| | **PEACE CORPS RESPONSE** | | | | | | |
| Do .................... | Director of Peace Corps Response ..................... | Vacant ................................. | PA | FE | ................ | ................ | |
| | **OFFICE OF HEALTH SERVICES** | | | | | | |
| Do .................... | Associate Director, Office of Health Services..... | Karen Becker........................ | PA | FE | ................ | ................ | |
| | **INTER-AMERICA AND THE PACIFIC OPERATIONS (IAP)** | | | | | | |
| Do .................... | Regional Director of Inter-American and Pacific. | Gregory Huger...................... | PA | FE | ................ | ................ | |

## PENSION BENEFIT GUARANTY CORPORATION

| Location | Position Title | Name of Incumbent | Type of Appt. | Pay Plan | Level, Grade, or Pay | Tenure | Expires |
|---|---|---|---|---|---|---|---|
| | **OFFICE OF THE EXECUTIVE DIRECTOR** | | | | | | |
| Washington, DC ...... | Director................................................... | Gordon Hartogensis ............. | PAS | EX | III | ................ | |
| Do .................... | .....do ................................................... | Vacant ................................. | PAS | EX | III | ................ | |
| Do .................... | Chief of Staff ............................................. | Kristin A Chapman .............. | SC | SL | $151,373 | ................ | |
| | **OFFICE OF POLICY AND EXTERNAL AFFAIRS** | | | | | | |
| Do .................... | Chief Policy Officer....................................... | Andrew Banducci ................. | SC | SL | ................ | ................ | |

## PENSION BENEFIT GUARANTY CORPORATION OFFICE OF INSPECTOR GENERAL

| Location | Position Title | Name of Incumbent | Type of Appt. | Pay Plan | Level, Grade, or Pay | Tenure | Expires |
|---|---|---|---|---|---|---|---|
| Washington, DC ...... | Inspector General ........................................ | Vacant ................................. | XS | SL | ................ | ................ | |
| Do .................... | Deputy Inspector General ............................... | ......do ................................. | XS | SL | ................ | ................ | |

## POSTAL REGULATORY COMMISSION

| Location | Position Title | Name of Incumbent | Type of Appt. | Pay Plan | Level, Grade, or Pay | Tenure | Expires |
|---|---|---|---|---|---|---|---|
| | **OFFICE OF THE COMMISSIONERS** | | | | | | |
| Washington, DC ...... | Chairman ................................................ | Robert Taub ......................... | PAS | EX | III | 6 Years | |
| Do .................. | Commissioner.......................................... | Mark D Acton ...................... | PAS | EX | IV | 6 Years | |
| Do .................. | ......do .................... | Michael M. Kubayanda ........ | PAS | EX | IV | 6 Years | |
| Do .................. | ......do .................... | Ann C Fisher ....................... | PAS | EX | IV | .............. | |
| Do .................. | ......do .................... | Ashley J Poling.................... | PAS | EX | IV | .............. | |
| Do .................. | Chief of Staff .......................................... | April E Boston ..................... | XS | OT | .............. | .............. | |
| Do .................. | Special Assistant .................................... | David A Cooper.................... | XS | OT | .............. | .............. | |
| Do .................. | Senior Economist and Economic Advisor .......... | Viola B Stovall.................... | XS | OT | .............. | .............. | |
| Do .................. | Special Assistant .................................... | Virgil I Stanford ................. | XS | OT | .............. | .............. | |
| Do .................. | Senior Financial Economic Advisor ................... | Sharmi Dasgupta ............... | XS | OT | .............. | .............. | |
| Do .................. | Policy Analyst/Executive Assistant.................... | Jennifer A Han .................... | XS | OT | .............. | .............. | |
| Do .................. | Confidential Assistant ............................ | Anne E Landau .................... | XS | OT | .............. | .............. | |
| Do .................. | ......do .................... | Olivia K Cox ....................... | XS | OT | .............. | .............. | |
| Do .................. | ......do .................... | Michael Mcguire.................. | XS | OT | .............. | .............. | |
| | **OFFICE OF THE GENERAL COUNSEL** | | | | | | |
| Do .................. | General Counsel........................................ | Vacant ................................. | XS | OT | .............. | .............. | |
| Do .................. | Deputy General Counsel .......................... | ......do .................... | XS | OT | .............. | .............. | |
| Do .................. | ......do .................... | ......do .................... | XS | OT | .............. | .............. | |
| | **OFFICE OF ACCOUNTABILITY AND COMPLIANCE** | | | | | | |
| Do .................. | Director..................................................... | ......do .................... | XS | OT | .............. | .............. | |
| Do .................. | Deputy Director, Compliance ................... | ......do .................... | XS | OT | .............. | .............. | |
| Do .................. | Deputy Director, Accountability............... | ......do .................... | XS | OT | .............. | .............. | |
| | **OFFICE OF SECRETARY AND ADMINISTRATION** | | | | | | |
| Do .................. | Secretary and Chief Administrative Officer ..... | ......do .................... | XS | OT | .............. | .............. | |
| Do .................. | Deputy Secretary ..................................... | ......do .................... | XS | OT | .............. | .............. | |
| | **OFFICE OF PUBLIC AFFAIRS AND GOVERNMENT RELATIONS** | | | | | | |
| Do .................. | Director..................................................... | ......do .................... | XS | OT | .............. | .............. | |
| | **OFFICE OF INSPECTOR GENERAL** | | | | | | |
| Do .................. | Inspector General .................................... | ......do .................... | XS | OT | .............. | .............. | |

## PUBLIC BUILDINGS REFORM BOARD

| Location | Position Title | Name of Incumbent | Type of Appt. | Pay Plan | Level, Grade, or Pay | Tenure | Expires |
|---|---|---|---|---|---|---|---|
| | **PUBLIC BUILDINGS REFORM BOARD** | | | | | | |
| Washington, DC ...... | Member................................................... | David L Winstead................. | PA | PD | .............. | 6 Years | |
| Do .................. | ......do .................... | Nick J Rahall ....................... | PA | PD | .............. | 6 Years | |
| Do .................. | ......do .................... | Mary B Phillips ................... | PA | PD | .............. | 6 Years | |
| Do .................. | ......do .................... | David T Hocker.................... | PA | PD | .............. | 6 Years | |
| Do .................. | ......do .................... | Angela Styles ....................... | PA | PD | .............. | 6 Years | |

## RAILROAD RETIREMENT BOARD

| Location | Position Title | Name of Incumbent | Type of Appt. | Pay Plan | Level, Grade, or Pay | Tenure | Expires |
|---|---|---|---|---|---|---|---|
| | **BOARD MEMBERS** | | | | | | |
| Chicago, IL............. | Chairman ................................................ | Erhard R Chorl.................... | PAS | EX | III | .............. | |
| Do .................. | Member of Board ..................................... | Johnathan D Bragg.............. | PAS | EX | IV | .............. | |
| Do .................. | ......do .................... | Thomas R Jayne .................. | PAS | EX | IV | .............. | |

## RAILROAD RETIREMENT BOARD OFFICE OF THE INSPECTOR GENERAL

| Location | Position Title | Name of Incumbent | Type of Appt. | Pay Plan | Level, Grade, or Pay | Tenure | Expires |
|---|---|---|---|---|---|---|---|
| Chicago, IL............. | Inspector General ................................................ | Martin J Dickman................ | PAS | EX | III | ................ | |

## SECURITIES AND EXCHANGE COMMISSION

| Location | Position Title | Name of Incumbent | Type of Appt. | Pay Plan | Level, Grade, or Pay | Tenure | Expires |
|---|---|---|---|---|---|---|---|
| | **OFFICE OF THE CHAIRMAN** | | | | | | |
| Washington, DC ...... | Chairman ................................................ | Jay Clayton III ..................... | PAS | EX | III | 5 Years | |
| Do ................... | Commissioner................................................ | Vacant ................................ | PAS | EX | IV | 5 Years | |
| Do ................... | ......do ................................................ | Hester Peirce ........................ | PAS | EX | IV | 5 Years | |
| Do ................... | ......do ................................................ | Elad Roisman ........................ | PAS | EX | ................ | 5 Years | |
| Do ................... | ......do ................................................ | Allison Lee ........................ | PAS | EX | ................ | 5 Years | |
| Do ................... | Deputy Director, Office of Legislative and Intergovernmental Affairs. | Anne-Marie Kelley ................ | SC | OT | $214,480 | ................ | |
| Do ................... | Confidential Assistant ........................................ | Awilda Santiago ................... | SC | OT | $111,422 | ................ | |
| Do ................... | ......do ................................................ | Kathleen Gallagher.............. | SC | OT | $128,534 | ................ | |
| Do ................... | Information Technology Specialist..................... | Andrew D Nguyen............... | SC | OT | $90,805 | ................ | |
| Do ................... | Writer-Editor................................................ | Christopher Carofine ........... | SC | OT | $126,001 | ................ | |
| Do ................... | ......do ................................................ | Natalie Marie Strom ............ | SC | OT | $136,412 | ................ | |
| Do ................... | Senior Policy Adviser, Regulatory Reporting ..... | Manisha Kimmel.................. | SC | OT | ................ | ................ | |
| Do ................... | Confidential Assistant ........................................ | Denene Dent......................... | SC | OT | $100,001 | ................ | |
| Do ................... | ......do ................................................ | Adrien Anderson................... | SC | OT | ................ | ................ | |
| Do ................... | ......do ................................................ | Laura Spratley ..................... | SC | OT | ................ | ................ | |
| | **OFFICE OF THE CHIEF OPERATING OFFICER** | | | | | | |
| Do ................... | ......do ................................................ | Janet S Schmautz................. | SC | OT | $101,367 | ................ | |
| | **DIVISION OF TRADING AND MARKETS** | | | | | | |
| New York, NY ......... | Director, Division of Trading and Markets ........ | Brett Wilson Redfearn ......... | SC | OT | $217,000 | ................ | |

## SELECTIVE SERVICE SYSTEM

| Location | Position Title | Name of Incumbent | Type of Appt. | Pay Plan | Level, Grade, or Pay | Tenure | Expires |
|---|---|---|---|---|---|---|---|
| | **OFFICE OF THE DIRECTOR** | | | | | | |
| Arlington, VA........... | Director Selective Service System ..................... | Donald Benton...................... | PAS | EX | IV | ................ | |
| Do ................... | Chief of Staff ................................................ | Wadi A Yakhour.................... | SC | GS | 15 | ................ | |
| Do ................... | Deputy Director ................................................ | John Phillip Prigmore.......... | NA | ES | ................ | ................ | |

## SMALL BUSINESS ADMINISTRATION

| Location | Position Title | Name of Incumbent | Type of Appt. | Pay Plan | Level, Grade, or Pay | Tenure | Expires |
|---|---|---|---|---|---|---|---|
| | **OFFICE OF THE ADMINISTRATOR** | | | | | | |
| Washington, DC ...... | Administrator................................................ | Jovita Carranza.................... | PAS | EX | III | ................ | |
| Do ................... | Deputy Administrator ........................................ | Vacant ................................ | PAS | EX | IV | ................ | |
| Do ................... | Chief of Staff................................................ | William M Manger Jr.......... | NA | ES | ................ | ................ | |
| Do ................... | Deputy Chief of Staff........................................ | Christopher S Gray ............. | NA | ES | ................ | ................ | |
| Do ................... | Senior Advisor for Policy and Planning............. | Career Incumbent ................ | CA | ES | ................ | ................ | |
| Do ................... | White House Liaison ........................................ | Nancy E Prall ...................... | SC | GS | 15 | ................ | |
| Do ................... | Deputy White House Liaison ............................ | Drew L Liquerman................ | SC | GS | 9 | ................ | |
| Do ................... | Special Advisor................................................ | Kathleen Margaret Mcshane. | SC | GS | 15 | ................ | |
| Do ................... | Senior Advisor................................................ | Christopher Michael Pilkerton. | SC | GS | 15 | ................ | |
| Do ................... | ......do ................................................ | Susan Denise Acosta........... | SC | GS | 14 | ................ | |
| Do ................... | Director of Scheduling........................................ | Emily K Threadgill............... | SC | GS | 14 | ................ | |
| Do ................... | Special Assistant................................................ | Eliza W Joyner.................... | SC | GS | 9 | ................ | |
| Do ................... | Senior Advisor to the Chief of Staff.................. | David G Chiokadze.............. | SC | GS | 13 | ................ | |
| | *Office of Advocacy* | | | | | | |
| Do ................... | Chief Counsel for Advocacy................................ | Vacant ................................ | PAS | EX | IV | | |

## SMALL BUSINESS ADMINISTRATION—Continued

| Location | Position Title | Name of Incumbent | Type of Appt. | Pay Plan | Level, Grade, or Pay | Tenure | Expires |
|---|---|---|---|---|---|---|---|
| | *Office of Capital Access* | | | | | | |
| Washington, DC ...... | Deputy Associate Administrator......................... | Career Incumbent ............... | CA | ES | .............. | .............. | |
| Do ..................... | Director of Financial Assistance ...................... | ......do ...................... | CA | ES | .............. | .............. | |
| Do ..................... | Director of Financial Programs Operations....... | ......do ...................... | CA | ES | .............. | .............. | |
| Do ..................... | Director of Credit Risk Management ............... | ......do ...................... | CA | ES | .............. | .............. | |
| Do ..................... | Director of Performance and Systems Managment. | ......do ...................... | CA | ES | .............. | .............. | |
| Do ..................... | Senior Advisor...................................... | William J Briggs.................. | SC | GS | 15 | .............. | |
| | *Office of Communications and Public Liaison* | | | | | | |
| Do ..................... | Associate Administrator............................ | Jimmy F Billimoria.............. | NA | ES | .............. | .............. | |
| Do ..................... | Deputy Associate Administrator (Operations)... | Vacant ............................. | | ES | .............. | .............. | |
| Do ..................... | Deputy Aa for Communication and Public Liaison. | Erin Sayago Mccracken ....... | SC | GS | 15 | .............. | |
| Do ..................... | Senior Advisor...................................... | Patricia Mary Gibson ........... | SC | GS | 15 | .............. | |
| Do ..................... | Digital Director..................................... | Jessica Seale...................... | SC | GS | 13 | .............. | |
| Do ..................... | Deputy Press Secretary............................ | Jennifer Kelly..................... | SC | GS | 13 | .............. | |
| Do ..................... | Senior Advisor...................................... | Anna E Kopperud................. | SC | GS | 13 | .............. | |
| Do ..................... | Digital Media Manager ............................ | Gary Markam Armstrong II. | SC | GS | 12 | .............. | |
| Do ..................... | Speechwriter ....................................... | Angeline Riesterer............... | SC | GS | 11 | .............. | |
| | *Office of Congressional and Legislative Affairs* | | | | | | |
| Do ..................... | Associate Administrator for Congressional and Legislative Affairs. | Michael Scott Hershey......... | NA | ES | .............. | .............. | |
| Do ..................... | Deputy Assistant Administrator........................ | Kevin P Talley ...................... | SC | GS | 15 | .............. | |
| Do ..................... | Senior Advisor...................................... | Ryan Anthony Lambert ....... | SC | GS | 14 | .............. | |
| Do ..................... | Legislative Assistant .............................. | Tyler S Pokela ..................... | SC | GS | 9 | .............. | |
| | *Office of Disaster Assistance* | | | | | | |
| Do ..................... | Associate Administrator for Disaster Assistance. | Career Incumbent ............... | CA | ES | .............. | .............. | |
| Do ..................... | Deputy Associate Administrator for Disaster Assistance. | ......do ...................... | CA | ES | .............. | .............. | |
| | *Office of Entrepreneurial Development* | | | | | | |
| Do ..................... | Associate Administrator for Entrepreneruial Development. | Allen Gutierrez..................... | NA | ES | .............. | .............. | |
| Do ..................... | Assistant Administrator for Women Business Ownership. | Vacant ............................. | | ES | .............. | .............. | |
| Do ..................... | Senior Advisor...................................... | Jennifer Ann Lisaius............ | SC | GS | 15 | .............. | |
| Do ..................... | Director Faith Based and Community Initiatives. | Marcus C Harris.................. | SC | GS | 13 | .............. | |
| Do ..................... | Special Advisor..................................... | Andrew James Coffield ........ | SC | GS | 12 | .............. | |
| | *Office of Field Operations* | | | | | | |
| Glendale, CA............ | Associate Administrator for Field Operations/Regional Administrator, Region IX. | Michael A Vallante .............. | NA | ES | .............. | .............. | |
| Washington, DC ...... | Deputy Associate Administrator for Field Operations. | Career Incumbent ............... | CA | ES | .............. | .............. | |
| Do ..................... | District Director.................................... | ......do ...................... | CA | ES | .............. | .............. | |
| New York New York, NY. | ......do ...................... | ......do ...................... | CA | ES | .............. | .............. | |
| Boston, MA .............. | Regional Administrator, Region I ..................... | Wendell G Davis Jr............. | SC | GS | 15 | .............. | |
| New York New York, NY. | Regional Administrator, Region II ...................... | Steven James Bulger ........... | SC | GS | 15 | .............. | |
| Atlanta, GA ............. | Regional Administrator, Region IV..................... | Ashley D Bell...................... | SC | GS | 15 | .............. | |
| Columbus, OH ........ | Regional Administrator, Region V..................... | Robert Lee Scott III............. | SC | GS | 15 | .............. | |
| New Orleans, LA..... | Regional Administrator, Region VI..................... | Justin Crossie..................... | SC | GS | 15 | .............. | |
| Kansas City, MO ..... | Regional Administrator, Region VII ..................... | Thomas J Salisbury ............ | SC | GS | 15 | .............. | |
| Denver, CO ............. | Regional Administrator, Region VIII ..................... | Daniel Paul Nordberg .......... | SC | GS | 15 | .............. | |
| Boise, ID ................. | Regional Administrator, Region X ..................... | Michael Jeremy Field........... | SC | GS | 15 | .............. | |
| King of Prussia, PA. | Director of Rural Affairs............................... | Michelle Christian............... | SC | GS | 15 | .............. | |
| New York New York, NY. | Senior Advisor...................................... | Lucia Maria Castellano ....... | SC | GS | 15 | .............. | |
| Atlanta, GA ............. | ......do ...................... | Richard William Kingan ...... | SC | GS | 13 | .............. | |
| | *Office of Government Contracting and Business Development* | | | | | | |
| Washington, DC ...... | Associate Administrator for Government Contracting and Business Development. | Francis C Spampinato ......... | NA | ES | .............. | .............. | |
| Do ..................... | Associate Administrator for 8(A) Business Development. | Career Incumbent ............... | CA | ES | .............. | .............. | |
| Do ..................... | Director of Government Contracting................. | ......do ...................... | CA | ES | .............. | .............. | |
| Do ..................... | Special Advisor........................................ | Martina Ann Mutz .............. | SC | GS | 13 | .............. | |

## SMALL BUSINESS ADMINISTRATION—Continued

| Location | Position Title | Name of Incumbent | Type of Appt. | Pay Plan | Level, Grade, or Pay | Tenure | Expires |
|---|---|---|---|---|---|---|---|
| | *Office of International Trade* | | | | | | |
| Washington, DC ...... | Associate Administrator for International Trade. | Loretta Greene ..................... | NA | ES | ................ | ................ | |
| | *Office of Investment and Innovation* | | | | | | |
| Do .................... | Director of Innovation and Technology ............. | Career Incumbent ................ | CA | ES | ................ | ................ | |
| Do .................... | Associate Administrator for Investment and Innovation. | Auborn Joseph Shepard ....... | NA | ES | ................ | ................ | |
| Do .................... | Special Assistant........................................... | Ryan Newsome ..................... | SC | GS | 12 | ................ | |
| | *Office of Native American Affairs* | | | | | | |
| Do .................... | Assistant Administrator for Native American Affairs. | Shawn Pensoneau ................ | SC | GS | 15 | ................ | |
| | *Office of the Chief Financial Officer* | | | | | | |
| Denver, CO ............. | Director of Denver Finance Center ................... | Career Incumbent ................ | CA | ES | ................ | ................ | |
| Washington, DC ...... | Director Office of Financial Systems................. | ......do ........................... | CA | ES | ................ | ................ | |
| Do .................... | Director of Performance, Analysis and Evaluation. | ......do ........................... | CA | ES | ................ | ................ | |
| | *Office of the Chief Information Officer* | | | | | | |
| Do .................... | Chief Information Officer ............................... | ......do ........................... | CA | ES | ................ | ................ | |
| | *Office of the Chief Operating Officer* | | | | | | |
| Do .................... | Assistant Administrator, Office of Executive Management, Installations and Support Services. | ......do ........................... | CA | ES | ................ | ................ | |
| Do .................... | Director, Office of Disaster Strategic Planning and Operations. | Vacant ................................ | ............ | ES | ................ | ................ | |
| Do .................... | Assistant Administrator for the Office of Diversity, Inclusion and Civil Rights. | ......do ........................... | | ES | ................ | ................ | |
| | *Office of the General Counsel* | | | | | | |
| Do .................... | General Counsel............................................ | Brittany W Biles................... | NA | ES | ................ | ................ | |
| Do .................... | Senior Counsel .......................................... | John E Coleman .................... | SC | GS | 15 | ................ | |
| | *Office of the Ombudsman* | | | | | | |
| Do .................... | National Ombudsman and Assistant Administrator for Regulatory Enforcement Fairness. | Stefanie L Baker .................. | NA | ES | ................ | ................ | |
| | *Office of Veterans' Business Development* | | | | | | |
| Do .................... | Associate Administrator for Veterans Business Development. | Career Incumbent ................ | CA | ES | ................ | ................ | |

## SMALL BUSINESS ADMINISTRATION OFFICE OF THE INSPECTOR GENERAL

| Location | Position Title | Name of Incumbent | Type of Appt. | Pay Plan | Level, Grade, or Pay | Tenure | Expires |
|---|---|---|---|---|---|---|---|
| Washington, DC ...... | Inspector General .............................................. | Hannibal Ware...................... | PAS | EX | III | ................ | |

## SMITHSONIAN INSTITUTION

| Location | Position Title | Name of Incumbent | Type of Appt. | Pay Plan | Level, Grade, or Pay | Tenure | Expires |
|---|---|---|---|---|---|---|---|
| | **Woodrow Wilson International Center For Scholars** | | | | | | |
| Washington, DC ...... | Deputy Director for Planning and Management. | Dean W Anderson................. | XS | OT | ................ | ................ | |
| Do .................... | Deputy Director ........................................... | Samuel F Wells Jr. .............. | XS | OT | ................ | ................ | |

## SOCIAL SECURITY ADMINISTRATION

| Location | Position Title | Name of Incumbent | Type of Appt. | Pay Plan | Level, Grade, or Pay | Tenure | Expires |
|---|---|---|---|---|---|---|---|
| | **OFFICE OF THE COMMISSIONER** | | | | | | |
| Washington, DC ...... | Commissioner................................................... | Andrew Saul ........................ | PAS | EX | I | ................ | |

## SOCIAL SECURITY ADMINISTRATION—Continued

| Location | Position Title | Name of Incumbent | Type of Appt. | Pay Plan | Level, Grade, or Pay | Tenure | Expires |
|---|---|---|---|---|---|---|---|
| Washington, DC ...... | Deputy Commissioner of Social Security .......... | David F Black........................ | PAS | EX | II | ................ | |
| Woodlawn, MD ........ | Chief of Staff..................................... | Career Incumbent ................ | CA | ES | ................ | ................ | |
| Washington, DC ...... | Deputy Chief of Staff........................... | Vacant ...................... | ............ | ES | ................ | ................ | |
| Woodlawn, MD ........ | Counselor to the Commissioner............... | ......do ...................... | ............ | ES | ................ | ................ | |
| Washington, DC ...... | Executive Secretary.............................. | ......do ...................... | ............ | ES | ................ | ................ | |
| Woodlawn, MD ........ | Press Officer...................................... | ......do ...................... | ............ | ES | ................ | ................ | |
| Do .................... | Senior Advisor to the Commissioner............ | ......do ...................... | ............ | ES | ................ | ................ | |
| Washington, DC ...... | Senior Advisor to the Deputy Commissioner..... | Nancy A Berryhill .......... | TA | ES | ................ | ................ | 08/03/20 |
| Do .................... | Special Advisor.................................... | Shaun Kelly Kaipo Freiman. | SC | GS | 15 | ................ | |
| Do .................... | Special Assistant................................. | Victoria Rose Burnham........ | SC | GS | 11 | ................ | |
| Do .................... | Member, Social Security Advisory Board .......... | Vacant ...................... | PAS | OT | ................ | ................ | |
| Do .................... | ......do ...................... | ......do ...................... | PAS | OT | ................ | ................ | |
| | **OFFICE OF ANALYTICS AND IMPROVEMENTS** | | | | | | |
| Woodlawn, MD ........ | Associate Commissioner for Analytics and Improvements. | Career Incumbent ................ | CA | ES | ................ | ................ | |
| Do .................... | Deputy Associate Commissioner for Analytics and Improvements. | ......do ...................... | CA | ES | ................ | ................ | |
| | *Office of Quality Review* | | | | | | |
| Do .................... | Associate Commissioner for Quality Review .... | Vacant ...................... | ............ | ES | ................ | ................ | |
| Do .................... | Deputy Associate Commissioner for Quality Review. | Career Incumbent ................ | CA | ES | ................ | ................ | |
| | *Office of Budget, Finance, and Management* | | | | | | |
| Do .................... | Deputy Commissioner for Budget, Finance, and Management. | ......do ...................... | CA | ES | ................ | ................ | |
| Do .................... | Assistant Deputy Commissioner for Budget, Finance, and Management (Management). | ......do ...................... | CA | ES | ................ | ................ | |
| | *Office of Facilities and Logistics Management* | | | | | | |
| Do .................... | Associate Commissioner for Facilities and Logistics Management. | ......do ...................... | CA | ES | ................ | ................ | |
| Do .................... | Deputy Associate Commissioner for Facilities and Logistics Management. | Vacant ...................... | ............ | ES | ................ | ................ | |
| | *Office of Security and Emergency Preparedness* | | | | | | |
| Do .................... | Associate Commissioner for Security and Emergency Preparedness. | ......do ...................... | ............ | ES | ................ | ................ | |
| | *Office of Communications* | | | | | | |
| Do .................... | Deputy Commissioner for Communications ..... | Michel N Korbey.................. | NA | ES | ................ | ................ | |
| Do .................... | Assistant Deputy Commissioner for Communications. | Career Incumbent ................ | CA | ES | ................ | ................ | |
| | *Office of Public Inquiries and Communications Support* | | | | | | |
| Do .................... | Associate Commissioner for Public Inquiries and Communications Support. | ......do ...................... | CA | ES | ................ | ................ | |
| Do .................... | Associate Commissioner for Strategic and Digital Communications. | ......do ...................... | CA | ES | ................ | ................ | |
| | **OFFICE OF THE GENERAL COUNSEL** | | | | | | |
| Do .................... | Deputy General Counsel ....................... | ......do ...................... | CA | ES | ................ | ................ | |
| | **OFFICE OF PROGRAM LAW** | | | | | | |
| Do .................... | Associate General Counsel for Program Law .... | Vacant ...................... | ............ | ES | ................ | ................ | |
| | **OFFICE OF REGIONAL CHIEF COUNSELS** | | | | | | |
| Boston, MA ............. | Regional Chief Counsel ........................ | Career Incumbent ................ | CA | ES | ................ | ................ | |
| New York New York, NY. | ......do ...................... | ......do ...................... | CA | ES | ................ | ................ | |
| Philadelphia, PA...... | ......do ...................... | ......do ...................... | CA | ES | ................ | ................ | |
| Atlanta, GA ............ | ......do ...................... | ......do ...................... | CA | ES | ................ | ................ | |
| Chicago, IL.............. | ......do ...................... | ......do ...................... | CA | ES | ................ | ................ | |
| Dallas, TX ............... | ......do ...................... | Vacant ...................... | ............ | ES | ................ | ................ | |
| Kansas City, MO ..... | ......do ...................... | Career Incumbent ................ | CA | ES | ................ | ................ | |
| Denver, CO ............ | ......do ...................... | Vacant ...................... | ............ | ES | ................ | ................ | |
| Richmond, CA......... | ......do ...................... | Career Incumbent ................ | CA | ES | ................ | ................ | |
| Seattle, WA ............. | ......do ...................... | Vacant ...................... | ............ | ES | ................ | ................ | |
| | **OFFICE OF BUDGET, FACILITIES AND SECURITY** | | | | | | |
| Falls Church, VA ..... | Associate Commissioner for Budget, Facilities and Security. | Career Incumbent ................ | CA | ES | ................ | ................ | |
| Do .................... | Deputy Associate Commissioner for Budget, Facilities and Security. | Vacant ...................... | ............ | ES | ................ | ................ | |

## SOCIAL SECURITY ADMINISTRATION—Continued

| Location | Position Title | Name of Incumbent | Type of Appt. | Pay Plan | Level, Grade, or Pay | Tenure | Expires |
|---|---|---|---|---|---|---|---|
| | **OFFICE OF ELECTRONIC SERVICES AND SYSTEMS INTEGRATION** | | | | | | |
| Falls Church, VA ..... | Associate Commissioner for Electronic Services and Strategic Information. | Career Incumbent ................ | CA | ES | ............... | ............... | |
| Do ................... | Deputy Associate Commissioner for Electronic Services and Strategic Information. | ......do ...................... | CA | ES | ............... | ............... | |
| | **OFFICE OF EXECUTIVE OPERATIONS AND HUMAN RESOURCES** | | | | | | |
| Do ................... | Associate Commissioner for Executive Operations and Human Resources. | ......do ...................... | CA | ES | ............... | ............... | |
| Do ................... | Deputy Associate Commissioner for Executive Operations and Human Resources. | Vacant ...................... | | ES | ............... | ............... | |
| | **OFFICE OF HUMAN RESOURCES** | | | | | | |
| Woodlawn, MD ....... | Deputy Commissioner for Human Resources .... | Career Incumbent ................ | CA | ES | ............... | ............... | |
| Do ................... | Assistant Deputy Commissioner for Human Resources. | ......do ...................... | CA | ES | ............... | ............... | |
| Do ................... | Director for Management Support Services....... | Vacant ...................... | | ES | ............... | ............... | |
| | **OFFICE OF STRATEGY, LEARNING, AND WORKFORCE DEVELOPMENT** | | | | | | |
| Do ................... | Associate Commissioner for Strategy, Learning, and Workforce Development. | Career Incumbent ................ | CA | ES | ............... | ............... | |
| Do ................... | Deputy Associate Commissioner for Strategy, Learning, and Workforce Development. | Vacant ...................... | | ES | ............... | ............... | |
| | **OFFICE OF LEGISLATION AND CONGRESSIONAL AFFAIRS** | | | | | | |
| Washington, DC ...... | Deputy Commissioner for Legislation and Congressional Affairs. | Career Incumbent ................ | CA | ES | ............... | ............... | |
| Do ................... | Assistant Deputy Commissioner for Legislation and Congressional Affairs. | ......do ...................... | CA | ES | ............... | ............... | |
| | **OFFICE OF LEGISLATIVE DEVELOPMENT AND OPERATIONS** | | | | | | |
| Woodlawn, MD ....... | Associate Commissioner for Legislative Development and Operations. | ......do ...................... | CA | ES | ............... | ............... | |
| | **OFFICE OF OPERATIONS** | | | | | | |
| Do ................... | Deputy Commissioner for Operations ................ | ......do ...................... | CA | ES | ............... | ............... | |
| Do ................... | Assistant Deputy Commissioner for Operations. | ......do ...................... | CA | ES | ............... | ............... | |
| Do ................... | ......do ...................... | ......do ...................... | CA | ES | ............... | ............... | |
| Do ................... | Chief Business Officer (IT Modernization) ........ | ......do ...................... | CA | ES | ............... | ............... | |
| Do ................... | Deputy Chief Business Officer (IT Modernization). | Jeffrey Caplan .................. | TA | ES | ............... | ............... | 11/23/22 |
| Do ................... | Chief Program Officer (Disability Case Processing System). | Vacant ...................... | | ES | ............... | ............... | |
| Do ................... | Senior Advisor to the Deputy Commissioner for Operations. | ......do ...................... | | ES | ............... | ............... | |
| | **OFFICE OF CENTRAL OPERATIONS** | | | | | | |
| Do ................... | Associate Commissioner for Central Operations. | Career Incumbent ................ | CA | ES | ............... | ............... | |
| Do ................... | Deputy Associate Commissioner for Central Operations. | ......do ...................... | CA | ES | ............... | ............... | |
| Do ................... | Assistant Associate Commissioner for Disability Operations. | ......do ...................... | CA | ES | ............... | ............... | |
| Do ................... | Assistant Associate Commissioner for Earnings and International Operations. | Vacant ...................... | | ES | ............... | ............... | |
| Do ................... | Assistant Associate Commissioner for Management and Operations Support. | Career Incumbent ................ | CA | ES | ............... | ............... | |
| | **OFFICE OF CUSTOMER SERVICE** | | | | | | |
| Do ................... | Associate Commissioner for Customer Service.. | ......do ...................... | CA | ES | ............... | ............... | |
| Do ................... | Deputy Associate Commissioner for Customer Service. | ......do ...................... | CA | ES | ............... | ............... | |
| Do ................... | Deputy Associate Commissioner for Customer Service (Processing Centers). | ......do ...................... | CA | ES | ............... | ............... | |
| | **OFFICE OF ELECTRONIC SERVICES AND TECHNOLOGY** | | | | | | |
| Do ................... | Associate Commissioner for Electronic Services and Technology. | ......do ...................... | CA | ES | ............... | ............... | |
| Do ................... | Deputy Associate Commissioner for Electronic Services and Technology. | ......do ...................... | CA | ES | ............... | ............... | |

## SOCIAL SECURITY ADMINISTRATION—Continued

| Location | Position Title | Name of Incumbent | Type of Appt. | Pay Plan | Level, Grade, or Pay | Tenure | Expires |
|----------|---------------|-------------------|---------------|----------|---------------------|--------|---------|
| | **OFFICE OF PUBLIC SERVICE AND OPERATIONS SUPPORT** | | | | | | |
| Woodlawn, MD ........ | Associate Commissioner for Public Service and Operations Support. | Career Incumbent ................ | CA | ES | .............. | .............. | |
| Do .................... | Deputy Associate Commissioner for Public Service and Operations Support. | ......do ................................... | CA | ES | .............. | .............. | |
| Do .................... | Deputy Associate Commissioner for Public Service and Operations Support (Facilities and Security). | ......do ................................... | CA | ES | .............. | .............. | |
| | **OFFICE OF REGIONAL COMMISSIONERS** | | | | | | |
| Boston, MA ............. | Regional Commissioner Region I........................ | ......do ................................... | CA | ES | .............. | .............. | |
| Do .................... | Deputy Regional Commissioner, Region I ......... | ......do ................................... | CA | ES | .............. | .............. | |
| New York New York, NY. | Regional Commissioner Region II ...................... | ......do ................................... | CA | ES | .............. | .............. | |
| Do .................... | Deputy Regional Commissioner, Region II........ | Vacant ............................. | ............ | ES | .............. | .............. | |
| Do .................... | Assistant Regional Commissioner for Management and Operations Support. | Career Incumbent ................ | CA | ES | .............. | .............. | |
| Do .................... | Assistant Regional Commissioner for Processing Center Operations (New York). | ......do ................................... | CA | ES | .............. | .............. | |
| Philadelphia, PA...... | Regional Commissioner Region III.................... | ......do ................................... | CA | ES | .............. | .............. | |
| Do .................... | Deputy Regional Commissioner, Region III ....... | Vacant ............................. | ............ | ES | .............. | .............. | |
| Do .................... | Assistant Regional Commissioner for Management and Operations Support. | Career Incumbent ................ | CA | ES | .............. | .............. | |
| Do .................... | Assistant Regional Commissioner for Processing Center Operations (Philadelphia). | ......do ................................... | CA | ES | .............. | .............. | |
| Atlanta, GA ............. | Regional Commissioner Region IV ...................... | ......do ................................... | CA | ES | .............. | .............. | |
| Do .................... | Deputy Regional Commissioner, Region IV ....... | ......do ................................... | CA | ES | .............. | .............. | |
| Do .................... | Senior Advisor to the Regional Commissioner, Atlanta. | ......do ................................... | CA | ES | .............. | .............. | |
| Do .................... | Assistant Regional Commissioner for Management and Operations Support. | ......do ................................... | CA | ES | .............. | .............. | |
| Birmingham, AL...... | Assistant Regional Commissioner for Processing Center Operations (Atlanta). | ......do ................................... | CA | ES | .............. | .............. | |
| Chicago, IL............... | Regional Commissioner Region V ...................... | ......do ................................... | CA | ES | .............. | .............. | |
| Do .................... | Deputy Regional Commissioner, Region V ........ | Vacant ............................. | ............ | ES | .............. | .............. | |
| Do .................... | Assistant Regional Commissioner for Management and Operations Support. | ......do ................................... | ............ | ES | .............. | .............. | |
| Do .................... | Assistant Regional Commissioner for Processing Center Operations (Chicago). | Career Incumbent ................ | CA | ES | .............. | .............. | |
| Dallas, TX ............... | Regional Commissioner Region VI ...................... | Vacant ............................. | ............ | ES | .............. | .............. | |
| Do .................... | Deputy Regional Commissioner, Region VI........ | ......do ................................... | ............ | ES | .............. | .............. | |
| Do .................... | Assistant Regional Commissioner for Management and Operations Support. | Career Incumbent ................ | CA | ES | .............. | .............. | |
| Kansas City, MO ..... | Regional Commissioner Region VII .................... | ......do ................................... | CA | ES | .............. | .............. | |
| Do .................... | Deputy Regional Commissioner, Region VIII..... | Vacant ............................. | ............ | ES | .............. | .............. | |
| Do .................... | Assistant Regional Commissioner for Processing Center Operations (Kansas City). | Career Incumbent ................ | CA | ES | .............. | .............. | |
| Denver, CO ............. | Deputy Regional Commissioner, Region VIII..... | ......do ................................... | CA | ES | .............. | .............. | |
| San Francisco, CA... | Regional Commissioner Region IX ...................... | ......do ................................... | CA | ES | .............. | .............. | |
| Do .................... | Deputy Regional Commissioner, Region IX ....... | ......do ................................... | CA | ES | .............. | .............. | |
| Do .................... | Assistant Regional Commissioner for Management and Operations Support. | ......do ................................... | CA | ES | .............. | .............. | |
| Do .................... | Assistant Regional Commissioner for Processing Center Operations (San Francisco). | ......do ................................... | CA | ES | .............. | .............. | |
| Seattle, WA ............. | Regional Commissioner Region X...................... | Vacant ............................. | ............ | ES | .............. | .............. | |
| Do .................... | Assistant Regional Commissioner for Management and Operations Support. | Career Incumbent ................ | CA | ES | .............. | .............. | |
| | **OFFICE OF RETIREMENT AND DISABILITY POLICY** | | | | | | |
| Woodlawn, MD ........ | Deputy Commissioner for Retirement and Disability Policy. | Mark J Warshawsky ............ | NA | ES | .............. | .............. | |
| Do .................... | Assistant Deputy Commissioner for Retirement and Disability Policy. | Career Incumbent ................ | CA | ES | .............. | .............. | |
| Do .................... | Senior Advisor to the Deputy Commissioner ..... | Steven M Robinson .............. | SC | GS | 15 | .............. | |

## SOCIAL SECURITY ADMINISTRATION—Continued

| Location | Position Title | Name of Incumbent | Type of Appt. | Pay Plan | Level, Grade, or Pay | Tenure | Expires |
|---|---|---|---|---|---|---|---|
| | **OFFICE OF DATA EXCHANGE, POLICY PUBLICATIONS, AND INTERNATIONAL NEGOTIATIONS** | | | | | | |
| Woodlawn, MD ........ | Associate Commissioner for Data Exchange, Policy Publications, and International Negotiations. | Vacant ................ | ............ | ES | ............... | .............. | |
| | **OFFICE OF DISABILITY POLICY** | | | | | | |
| Do .................... | Associate Commissioner for Disability Policy.... | ......do ................ | ............ | ES | ............... | .............. | |
| Do .................... | Deputy Associate Commissioner for Disability Policy. | Career Incumbent ................ | CA | ES | ............... | .............. | |
| | **OFFICE OF INCOME SECURITY PROGRAMS** | | | | | | |
| Do .................... | Associate Commissioner for Income Security Programs. | ......do ................ | CA | ES | ............... | .............. | |
| Do .................... | Deputy Associate Commissioner for Income Security Programs. | Vacant ................ | ............ | ES | ............... | .............. | |
| | **OFFICE OF RESEARCH, DEMONSTRATION, AND EMPLOYMENT SUPPORT** | | | | | | |
| Do .................... | Associate Commissioner for Research, Demonstration, and Employment Support. | Career Incumbent ................ | CA | ES | ............... | .............. | |
| | **OFFICE OF RESEARCH, EVALUATION AND STATISTICS** | | | | | | |
| Washington, DC ...... | Associate Commissioner for Research, Evaluation and Statistics. | Vacant ................ | ............ | ES | ............... | .............. | |
| Do .................... | Deputy Associate Commissioner for Research, Evaluation, and Statistics. | Career Incumbent ................ | CA | ES | ............... | .............. | |
| | **OFFICE OF SYSTEMS** | | | | | | |
| Woodlawn, MD ........ | Deputy Commissioner for Systems.................... | Rajive Mathur ................ | NA | ES | ............... | .............. | |
| Do .................... | Assistant Deputy Commissioner (IT Modernization). | Career Incumbent ................ | CA | ES | ............... | .............. | |
| Do .................... | Assistant Deputy Commissioner for Systems.... | ......do ................ | CA | ES | ............... | .............. | |
| Do .................... | Chief Engineer (IT Modernization) .................. | Jian Wang ................ | TA | ES | ............... | .............. | 01/20/21 |
| Do .................... | Executive Director, Enterprise Services............ | Career Incumbent ................ | CA | ES | ............... | .............. | |
| Washington, DC ...... | Executive Director (Health Information Technology). | Jude Soundar ................ | TA | ES | ............... | .............. | 08/04/21 |
| Woodlawn, MD ........ | Senior Advisor to the Assistant Deputy Commissioner. | Career Incumbent ................ | CA | ES | ............... | .............. | |
| Do .................... | Assistant Deputy Commissioner for Systems/Deputy Chief Information Officer. | Vacant ................ | ............ | ES | ............... | .............. | |
| | **OFFICE OF THE CHIEF TECHNOLOGY OFFICER** | | | | | | |
| Do .................... | Chief Technology Officer ................................ | Career Incumbent ................ | CA | ES | ............... | .............. | |
| Do .................... | Deputy Chief Technology Officer .................... | ......do ................ | CA | ES | ............... | .............. | |
| | **OFFICE OF BENEFIT INFORMATION SYSTEMS** | | | | | | |
| Do .................... | Associate Commissioner for Benefit Information Systems. | ......do ................ | CA | ES | ............... | .............. | |
| Do .................... | Deputy Associate Commissioner for Benefit Information Systems. | ......do ................ | CA | ES | ............... | .............. | |
| | **OFFICE OF DISABILITY INFORMATION SYSTEMS** | | | | | | |
| Do .................... | Associate Commissioner for Disability Information Systems. | ......do ................ | CA | ES | ............... | .............. | |
| Do .................... | Deputy Associate Commissioner for Disability Information Systems. | ......do ................ | CA | ES | ............... | .............. | |
| | **OFFICE OF ENTERPRISE INFORMATION SYSTEMS** | | | | | | |
| Do .................... | Associate Commissioner for Enterprise Information Systems. | Vacant ................ | ............ | ES | ............... | .............. | |
| Do .................... | Deputy Associate Commissioner for Enterprise Information Systems. | Career Incumbent ................ | CA | ES | ............... | .............. | |
| | **OFFICE OF INFORMATION SECURITY** | | | | | | |
| Do .................... | Deputy Associate Commissioner for Information Security. | Vacant ................ | ............ | ES | ............... | .............. | |
| | **OFFICE OF SYSTEMS ARCHITECTURE** | | | | | | |
| Do .................... | Associate Commissioner for Systems Architecture. | ......do ................ | ............ | ES | ............... | .............. | |

## SOCIAL SECURITY ADMINISTRATION—Continued

| Location | Position Title | Name of Incumbent | Type of Appt. | Pay Plan | Level, Grade, or Pay | Tenure | Expires |
|---|---|---|---|---|---|---|---|
| Woodlawn, MD ........ | Deputy Associate Commissioner for Systems Architecture. | Career Incumbent ................ | CA | ES | ................ | ................ | |

## SOCIAL SECURITY ADMINISTRATION OFFICE OF THE INSPECTOR GENERAL

| Location | Position Title | Name of Incumbent | Type of Appt. | Pay Plan | Level, Grade, or Pay | Tenure | Expires |
|---|---|---|---|---|---|---|---|
| Woodlawn, MD ........ | **IMMEDIATE OFFICE OF THE INSPECTOR GENERAL** Inspector General ................................................ | Gail Susan Ennis ................ | PAS | EX | III | ................ | |
| Do .................... | Special Advisor to the Inspector General.......... | Vacant .................................... | ............ | ES | ................ | 3 Years | |

## SURFACE TRANSPORTATION BOARD

| Location | Position Title | Name of Incumbent | Type of Appt. | Pay Plan | Level, Grade, or Pay | Tenure | Expires |
|---|---|---|---|---|---|---|---|
| Washington, DC ...... | Chairman ................................................................ | Ann D Begeman .................... | PAS | EX | III | ................ | |
| Do .................... | Board Member ...................................................... | Patrick Fuchs........................ | PAS | EX | IV | ................ | |
| Do .................... | ......do ................................................................ | Martin Oberman ................ | PAS | EX | IV | ................ | |
| Do .................... | ......do ................................................................ | Vacant .................................... | PAS | EX | ............ | ................ | |
| Do .................... | ......do ................................................................ | ......do ................................ | PAS | EX | IV | ................ | |

## TENNESSEE VALLEY AUTHORITY

| Location | Position Title | Name of Incumbent | Type of Appt. | Pay Plan | Level, Grade, or Pay | Tenure | Expires |
|---|---|---|---|---|---|---|---|
| Knoxville, TN.......... | **BOARD OF DIRECTORS** Chairman of the Board of Directors .................. | John Ryder........................... | PAS | EX | III | ................ | |
| Do .................... | Director................................................................ | Kenneth Allen...................... | PAS | EX | ................ | ................ | |
| Do .................... | ......do ................................................................ | Adolphus Frazier.................. | PAS | EX | ................ | ................ | |
| Do .................... | ......do ................................................................ | William Kilbride.................. | PAS | EX | ................ | ................ | |
| Do .................... | ......do ................................................................ | Jeffrey Smith ...................... | PAS | EX | ................ | ................ | |
| Do .................... | ......do ................................................................ | Vacant .................................... | PAS | EX | ................ | ................ | |
| Do .................... | ......do ................................................................ | ......do ................................ | PAS | EX | ................ | ................ | |
| Do .................... | **OFFICE OF THE INSPECTOR GENERAL** Inspector General ................................................ | ......do ................................ | PAS | EX | ............ | ................ | |

## TRADE AND DEVELOPMENT AGENCY

| Location | Position Title | Name of Incumbent | Type of Appt. | Pay Plan | Level, Grade, or Pay | Tenure | Expires |
|---|---|---|---|---|---|---|---|
| Arlington, VA.......... | **OFFICE OF THE DIRECTOR** Director................................................................ | Vacant .................................... | PAS | EX | III | ................ | |
| Do .................... | Senior Advisor...................................................... | Todd Joseph Abrajano.......... | SC | GS | 15 | ............ | |
| Do .................... | Director of Public Engagement.......................... | Dianne Quebral .................... | SC | GS | 15 | ................ | |
| Do .................... | Senior Advisor for Communications .................. | Jonathan Wilcox .................. | SC | GS | 15 | ................ | |

## U.S. AGENCY FOR GLOBAL MEDIA

| Location | Position Title | Name of Incumbent | Type of Appt. | Pay Plan | Level, Grade, or Pay | Tenure | Expires |
|---|---|---|---|---|---|---|---|
| Washington, DC ...... | Chief Executive Officer....................................... | Michael Pack........................ | PAS | EX | III | ............ | |
| Do .................... | General Counsel.................................................... | Career Incumbent ................ | CA | ES | ................ | ................ | |
| Do .................... | Chief Strategy Officer......................................... | ......do ................................ | CA | ES | ................ | ................ | |

## U.S. AGENCY FOR GLOBAL MEDIA—Continued

| Location | Position Title | Name of Incumbent | Type of Appt. | Pay Plan | Level, Grade, or Pay | Tenure | Expires |
|---|---|---|---|---|---|---|---|
| Washington, DC | Associate Director for Program Support | Career Incumbent | CA | ES | | | |
| Do | Director, Office of Technology Services and Innovation. | ......do | CA | ES | | | |
| Do | Deputy for Resources and Project Management. | ......do | CA | ES | | | |
| Do | Director, Voice of America | Vacant | | ES | | | |
| Do | Deputy Director, Voice of America | ......do | | ES | | | |
| Do | Program Director | Career Incumbent | CA | ES | | | |
| Do | Chief Information Officer | ......do | CA | ES | | | |
| Miami, FL | Director Office of Cuba Broadcasting | Vacant | | ES | | | |

## UNITED STATES – CHINA ECONOMIC AND SECURITY REVIEW COMMISSION

| Location | Position Title | Name of Incumbent | Type of Appt. | Pay Plan | Level, Grade, or Pay | Tenure | Expires |
|---|---|---|---|---|---|---|---|
| Washington, DC | Chairman | Robin Cleveland | XS | AD | | 2 Years | |
| Do | Vice Chairman | Carolyn Bartholomew | XS | AD | | 2 Years | |
| Charleston, WV | Commissioner | Carte P Goodwin | XS | AD | | 2 Years | |
| Falls Church, VA | ......do | Michael R Wessel | XS | AD | | 2 Years | |
| Washington, DC | ......do | Larry M Wortzel | XS | AD | | 2 Years | |
| Do | ......do | Jeffrey L Fiedler | XS | AD | | 2 Years | |
| Do | ......do | James M Talent | XS | AD | | 2 Years | |
| Do | ......do | Kenneth Lewis | XS | PD | | 2 Years | |
| Do | ......do | Andreas A Borgeas | XS | PD | | 2 Years | |
| Do | ......do | Thea M Lee | XS | PD | | 2 Years | |
| Do | ......do | Robert Ivan Borochoff | XS | PD | | 2 Years | |
| Do | ......do | Roy David Kamphausen | XS | PD | | 2 Years | |

## UNITED STATES AGENCY FOR INTERNATIONAL DEVELOPMENT

| Location | Position Title | Name of Incumbent | Type of Appt. | Pay Plan | Level, Grade, or Pay | Tenure | Expires |
|---|---|---|---|---|---|---|---|
| | **OFFICE OF THE ADMINISTRATOR** | | | | | | |
| Washington, DC | Administrator, Agency for International Development. | Vacant | PAS | EX | II | | |
| Do | Deputy Administrator, Agency for International Development. | Bonnie Glick | PAS | EX | III | | |
| Do | Chief of Staff | William Steiger | NA | ES | | | |
| Do | Deputy Chief of Staff | Bethany Kozma | XS | AD | | | |
| Do | National Security Advisor and Chief Legislative Strategist. | Edward Acevedo | NA | ES | | | |
| Do | Director, Center for Faith and Opportunity Initiatives. | Kirsten Evans | XS | AD | | | |
| Do | Deputy Director, Center for Faith and Opportunity Initiatives. | Brian Klotz | XS | AD | | | |
| Do | White House Liaison | William Maloney | XS | AD | | | |
| Do | Deputy White House Liaison | Merritt Corrigan | XS | AD | | | |
| Do | Senior Advisor | Jennifer Arangio | XS | AD | | | |
| Do | Advisor | Mark Lloyd | XS | AD | | | |
| Do | Special Assistant | Graham Higgins | XS | AD | | | |
| Do | ......do | Julia Lee | XS | AD | | | |
| Do | ......do | Dore Feith | XS | AD | | | |
| Do | ......do | Serena Allison Frechter | XS | AD | | | |
| Do | ......do | Camille Solberg | XS | AD | | | |
| | *Office of Budget and Resource Management* | | | | | | |
| Do | Director | Career Incumbent | CA | ES | | | |
| Do | Advisor, Office of Budget and Resources Management. | Nicholas Rigas | XS | AD | | | |
| | *Office of Civil Rights and Diversity* | | | | | | |
| Do | Equal Opportunity Officer | Career Incumbent | CA | ES | | | |
| | *Office of the Executive Secretariat* | | | | | | |
| Do | Executive Secretary | Vacant | | ES | | | |
| Do | Program Analyst | Ashley Danielle Depriest | XS | AD | | | |

## UNITED STATES AGENCY FOR INTERNATIONAL DEVELOPMENT—Continued

| Location | Position Title | Name of Incumbent | Type of Appt. | Pay Plan | Level, Grade, or Pay | Tenure | Expires |
|---|---|---|---|---|---|---|---|
| | *Office of the General Counsel* | | | | | | |
| Washington, DC | General Counsel | Mitchell Craig Wolf | NA | ES | | | |
| Do | Senior Advisor | Frederick Guy Sr. | XS | AD | | | |
| Do | ......do | Career Incumbent | CA | ES | | | |
| | **BUREAU FOR LEGISLATIVE AND PUBLIC AFFAIRS** | | | | | | |
| Do | Assistant Administrator for Legislative and Public Affairs. | Richard Parker | PAS | EX | IV | | |
| Do | Deputy Assistant Administrator | Jennifer Hazelton | XS | AD | | | |
| Do | Chief Speech Writer and Communications Advisor. | Scot Alan Montrey | XS | AD | | | |
| Do | Speech Writer and Communications Senior Advisor. | Russell N Newell | XS | AD | | | |
| Do | Supervisory Congressional Liaison Specialist | Brian Fauls | XS | AD | | | |
| Do | Congressional Liaison Specialist | Daniel Henke | XS | AD | | | |
| Do | ......do | John Pezzullo | XS | AD | | | |
| Do | ......do | Lindsay Schneider Barsky | XS | AD | | | |
| Do | ......do | Gefen Golan Kabik | XS | AD | | | |
| Do | Advisor | Alexander Titus | XS | AD | | | |
| Do | Public Affairs Specialist | Lauren Westcott | XS | AD | | | |
| Do | ......do | Joseph William Molieri | XS | AD | | | |
| | **BUREAU FOR MANAGEMENT** | | | | | | |
| Do | Assistant Administrator | Frederick Nutt | PA | EX | IV | | |
| Do | Deputy Assistant Administrator | Albert Georg Bullock | XS | AD | | | |
| Do | ......do | Career Incumbent | CA | ES | | | |
| Do | Deputy Chief Information Officer | ......do | CA | ES | | | |
| Do | Deputy Director, Office of Management Services Organization. | ......do | CA | ES | | | |
| Do | Deputy Director, Office of Management, Policy, Budget, and Performance. | ......do | CA | ES | | | |
| Do | Senior Advisor, Office of Acquisition and Assistance. | Maria T Paul | XS | AD | | | |
| Do | Senior Advisor, Office of Acquisition and Assistance. | James Tift | XS | AD | | | |
| Do | Senior Advisor | Nancy Dudiak Hibbs | XS | AD | | | |
| Do | ......do | Alan R Swendiman | XS | AD | | | |
| Do | Advisor | Harriett Swarttz | XS | AD | | | |
| Do | Management and Program Analyst | Hallam Overton | XS | AD | | | |
| Do | Chief Technology Officer | Vacant | | ES | | | |
| | **BUREAU FOR POLICY, PLANNING AND LEARNING** | | | | | | |
| Do | Deputy Assistant Administrator | ......do | | ES | | | |
| Do | ......do | Ramsey C Day | XS | AD | | | |
| Do | Special Advisor | Robert Powers | XS | AD | | | |
| Do | Program Advisor | Megan Asdorian | XS | AD | | | |
| Do | Senior Advisor | Brynn Barnett | XS | AD | | | |
| Do | ......do | Laura Cunliffe | XS | AD | | | |
| Do | ......do | Kaushalendra Arha | XS | AD | | | |
| Do | Advisor | Kevin Eck | XS | AD | | | |
| Do | Policy Analyst | Russel Kopley | XS | AD | | | |
| Do | Donor Coordinator | Marilyn Baker | XS | AD | | | |
| Do | Program Manager | Meghan Hanson | XS | AD | | | |
| Do | Trip Content Coordinator | Elizabeth Saady | XS | AD | | | |
| | **GLOBAL DEVELOPMENT LAB** | | | | | | |
| Do | Deputy Executive Director | Career Incumbent | CA | ES | | | |
| Do | Senior Advisor | Douglas Britt | XS | AD | | | |
| Do | Program Advisor | Leah Pedersen | XS | AD | | | |
| | **OFFICE OF HUMAN CAPITAL AND TALENT MANAGEMENT** | | | | | | |
| Do | Advisor, Office of the Chief Human Capital Officer. | Monica Filyaw | XS | AD | | | |
| | **BUREAU FOR DEMOCRACY, CONFLICT, AND HUMANITARIAN ASSISTANCE** | | | | | | |
| Do | Assistant Administrator, Democracy, Conflict, and Humanitarian Assistance. | Vacant | PAS | EX | IV | | |
| Do | Deputy Assistant Administrator | Career Incumbent | CA | ES | | | |
| Do | Director, Democracy and Governance | Timothy Meisburger | XS | AD | | | |
| Do | Director, Office of Transition Initiatives | Owen Kirby | XS | AD | | | |
| Do | Special Advisor, Office of Food for Peace | Mary Vigil | XS | AD | | | |
| Do | Senior Advisor | Adam J Killian | XS | AD | | | |

## UNITED STATES AGENCY FOR INTERNATIONAL DEVELOPMENT—Continued

| Location | Position Title | Name of Incumbent | Type of Appt. | Pay Plan | Level, Grade, or Pay | Tenure | Expires |
|---|---|---|---|---|---|---|---|
| Washington, DC ...... | Advisor, the Center of Excellence on Democracy, Human Rights and Governance. | Sarah Gesiriech.................... | XS | AD | ............. | ............. | |
| Do .................. | Advisor........................................ | Patrina Mosley .................... | XS | AD | ............. | ............. | |
| Do .................. | Operations Assistant ............................. | Megan McCormick .............. | XS | AD | ............. | ............. | |
| Do .................. | Adjunct Professor of International Affairs........ | Career Incumbent ................ | CA | ES | ............. | ............. | |
| | **BUREAU FOR ECONOMIC GROWTH, EDUCATION AND ENVIRONMENT** | | | | | | |
| Do .................. | Assistant Administrator........................... | Michelle Bekkering .............. | PAS | EX | IV | ............. | |
| Do .................. | Deputy Assistant Administrator...................... | Julie Cram ...................... | XS | AD | ............. | ............. | |
| Do .................. | ......do ...................................... | Vacant .......................... | ............. | ES | ............. | ............. | |
| Do .................. | Senior Advisor, Office of Private Capital and Microenterprise. | Jack M Hawkins.................. | XS | AD | ............. | ............. | |
| Do .................. | Senior Advisor................................. | Charlotte Florence................ | XS | AD | ............. | ............. | |
| Do .................. | ......do ...................................... | Bernardo Rico .................... | XS | AD | ............. | ............. | |
| Do .................. | Program Analyst................................ | Elizabeth Montgomery......... | XS | AD | ............. | ............. | |
| | **BUREAU FOR GLOBAL HEALTH** | | | | | | |
| Do .................. | Assistant Administrator........................... | Alma Golden .................... | PAS | EX | IV | ............. | |
| Do .................. | Deputy Assistant Administrator...................... | Monique Wubbenhorst ........ | XS | AD | ............. | ............. | |
| Do .................. | ......do ...................................... | Vacant .......................... | ............. | ES | ............. | ............. | |
| Do .................. | Malaria Coordinator ............................. | Kenneth William Staley........ | NA | ES | ............. | ............. | |
| Do .................. | Executive Director ............................. | Robert Siedlecki.................. | XS | AD | ............. | ............. | |
| Do .................. | Senior Advisor................................. | Dorothy Narvaez-Woods ...... | XS | AD | ............. | ............. | |
| Do .................. | Advisor........................................ | Dianna Lightfoot ................ | XS | AD | ............. | ............. | |
| Do .................. | Special Assistant............................... | Thomas Degraba ................ | XS | AD | ............. | ............. | |
| Do .................. | ......do ...................................... | Joseph Guy ...................... | XS | AD | ............. | ............. | |
| | **BUREAU FOR HUMANITARIAN ASSISTANCE** | | | | | | |
| Do .................. | Assistant to the Administrator...................... | Clyde Hicks...................... | XS | AD | ............. | ............. | |
| Do .................. | Deputy Assistant Administrator...................... | Max Primorac .................... | XS | AD | ............. | ............. | |
| | **BUREAU FOR RESILIENCE AND FOOD SECURITY** | | | | | | |
| Do .................. | ......do ...................................... | Jennifer Key Mcgillicuddy ... | XS | AD | ............. | ............. | |
| Do .................. | ......do ...................................... | Career Incumbent ................ | CA | ES | ............. | ............. | |
| Do .................. | Program Advisor ............................... | Kevin Mulligan.................. | XS | AD | ............. | ............. | |
| | **BUREAU FOR AFRICA** | | | | | | |
| Do .................. | Assistant Administrator........................... | Vacant .......................... | PAS | EX | IV | ............. | |
| Do .................. | Deputy Assistant Administrator...................... | Christopher Maloney ........... | XS | AD | ............. | ............. | |
| Do .................. | ......do ...................................... | Career Incumbent ................ | CA | ES | ............. | ............. | |
| Do .................. | Chief Operating Officer ......................... | Victoria Whitney ................ | XS | AD | ............. | ............. | |
| Do .................. | Senior Advisor................................. | Gregory Simpkins................ | XS | AD | ............. | ............. | |
| Do .................. | Program Specialist............................. | Michael Drager.................. | XS | AD | ............. | ............. | |
| Do .................. | Special Assistant............................... | Mary Bridgid Joyce ............. | XS | AD | ............. | ............. | |
| Do .................. | ......do ...................................... | Jeffery Aaron Kempler......... | XS | AD | ............. | ............. | |
| | **BUREAU FOR ASIA** | | | | | | |
| Do .................. | Assistant Administrator........................... | Vacant .......................... | PAS | EX | IV | ............. | |
| Do .................. | Deputy Assistant Administrator...................... | Javier Piedra .................... | XS | AD | ............. | ............. | |
| Do .................. | Deputy Assistant Administrator...................... | Career Incumbent ................ | CA | ES | ............. | ............. | |
| Do .................. | Program Technology Specialist ..................... | Tanner Mastaw.................. | XS | AD | ............. | ............. | |
| Do .................. | Special Assistant............................... | Kevin Wang...................... | XS | AD | ............. | ............. | |
| | **BUREAU FOR EUROPE AND EURASIA** | | | | | | |
| Do .................. | Assistant Administrator........................... | Brock Bierman.................... | PAS | EX | IV | ............. | |
| Do .................. | Deputy Assistant Administrator...................... | Gretchen Birkle.................. | XS | AD | ............. | ............. | |
| Do .................. | ......do ...................................... | Career Incumbent ................ | CA | ES | ............. | ............. | |
| Do .................. | Special Assistant............................... | Kevin Edward Monson......... | XS | AD | ............. | ............. | |
| | **BUREAU FOR LATIN AMERICA AND THE CARIBBEAN** | | | | | | |
| Do .................. | Assistant Administrator........................... | John Barsa...................... | PAS | EX | IV | ............. | |
| Do .................. | Deputy Assistant Administrator...................... | Joshua Hodges.................. | XS | AD | ............. | ............. | |
| Do .................. | ......do ...................................... | Career Incumbent ................ | CA | ES | ............. | ............. | |
| Do .................. | Advisor........................................ | Jon Perdue ...................... | XS | AD | ............. | ............. | |
| | **BUREAU FOR MIDDLE EAST** | | | | | | |
| Do .................. | Assistant Administrator for Middle East.......... | Michael Harvey ................ | PAS | EX | IV | ............. | |
| Do .................. | Deputy Assistant Administrator...................... | Hallam Ferguson................ | XS | AD | ............. | ............. | |
| Do .................. | ......do ...................................... | Career Incumbent ................ | CA | ES | ............. | ............. | |
| Do .................. | Senior Advisor................................. | Brian Moore...................... | XS | AD | ............. | ............. | |
| Do .................. | ......do ...................................... | Jeanne Pryor...................... | TA | ES | ............. | ............. | 03/14/23 |
| Do .................. | ......do ...................................... | Samah Norquist .................. | XS | AD | ............. | ............. | |
| Do .................. | Advisor, Office of North African Affairs ............. | Scott B Shiller.................... | XS | AD | ............. | ............. | |

## UNITED STATES AGENCY FOR INTERNATIONAL DEVELOPMENT—Continued

| Location | Position Title | Name of Incumbent | Type of Appt. | Pay Plan | Level, Grade, or Pay | Tenure | Expires |
|---|---|---|---|---|---|---|---|
| Washington, DC ...... | Special Assistant | Abigail Berg | XS | AD | | | |

## UNITED STATES AGENCY FOR INTERNATIONAL DEVELOPMENT OFFICE OF THE INSPECTOR GENERAL

| Location | Position Title | Name of Incumbent | Type of Appt. | Pay Plan | Level, Grade, or Pay | Tenure | Expires |
|---|---|---|---|---|---|---|---|
| Washington, DC ...... | Inspector General | Ann Calvaresi Barr | PAS | OT | | | |

## UNITED STATES COMMISSION FOR THE PRESERVATION OF AMERICA'S HERITAGE ABROAD

| Location | Position Title | Name of Incumbent | Type of Appt. | Pay Plan | Level, Grade, or Pay | Tenure | Expires |
|---|---|---|---|---|---|---|---|
| Washington, DC ...... | Member | Harriet Rotter | PA | WC | | 3 Years | |
| Do | ......do | John Horne | PA | WC | | 3 Years | |
| Do | ......do | Michael Levy | PA | WC | | 3 Years | |
| Do | ......do | Lee R Seeman | PA | WC | | 3 Years | |
| Do | ......do | Warren L Miller | PA | WC | | 3 Years | |
| Do | ......do | Abba Cohen | PA | WC | | 3 Years | |
| Do | ......do | Julie A Strauss | PA | WC | | 3 Years | |
| Do | ......do | Ned W Bandler | PA | WC | | 3 Years | |
| Do | ......do | Marjorie Margolies | PA | WC | | 3 Years | |
| Do | ......do | A Emil Fish | PA | WC | | 3 Years | |
| Do | ......do | Jules Fleischer | PA | WC | | 3 Years | |
| Do | ......do | Martin B Gold | PA | WC | | 3 Years | |
| Do | ......do | Elie Hirschfeld | PA | WC | | 3 Years | |
| Do | ......do | Lesley Israel | PA | WC | | 3 Years | |
| Do | ......do | Mark Levenson | PA | WC | | 3 Years | |
| Do | ......do | Joseph Douek | PA | WC | | 3 Years | |
| Do | ......do | Tyrone C Fahner | PA | WC | | 3 Years | |
| Do | ......do | Jonathan J Rikoon | PA | WC | | 3 Years | |
| Do | Chair | Paul Packer | PA | WC | | 3 Years | |
| Do | Member | Harley Lippman | PA | WC | | 3 Years | |
| Do | ......do | Heshie Billet | PA | WC | | 3 Years | |

## UNITED STATES COMMISSION ON INTERNATIONAL RELIGIOUS FREEDOM

| Location | Position Title | Name of Incumbent | Type of Appt. | Pay Plan | Level, Grade, or Pay | Tenure | Expires |
|---|---|---|---|---|---|---|---|
| Washington, DC ...... | Member | Anthony R Perkins | XS | WC | | 2 Years | |
| Do | ......do | Gary L Bauer | PA | WC | | 2 Years | |
| Washington, CO ...... | ......do | Anurima Bhargava | XS | WC | | 2 Years | |
| Washington, DC ...... | ......do | Gayle C Manchin | XS | WC | | 2 Years | |
| Do | ......do | James W Carr | XS | WC | | 2 Years | |
| Do | ......do | Nury A Turkel | XS | WC | | 2 Years | |
| Do | ......do | Nadine B Maenza | PA | WC | | 2 Years | |
| Do | ......do | Frederick A Davie | XS | WC | | 2 Years | |
| Do | ......do | Johnnie R Moore | PA | WC | | 2 Years | |

## UNITED STATES ELECTION ASSISTANCE COMMISSION

| Location | Position Title | Name of Incumbent | Type of Appt. | Pay Plan | Level, Grade, or Pay | Tenure | Expires |
|---|---|---|---|---|---|---|---|
| Silver Spring, MD ... | Member | Benjamin W Hovland | PAS | EX | IV | 4 Years | |
| Williamsburg, VA .... | ......do | Christy A McCormick | PAS | EX | IV | 4 Years | |
| Silver Spring, MD ... | General Counsel | Kevin M Rayburn | XS | AD | | 4 Years | |
| Do | Member | Thomas Hicks | PAS | EX | IV | 4 Years | |
| Do | Executive Director | Mona M Harrington | XS | AD | | 4 Years | |

## UNITED STATES ELECTION ASSISTANCE COMMISSION—Continued

| Location | Position Title | Name of Incumbent | Type of Appt. | Pay Plan | Level, Grade, or Pay | Tenure | Expires |
|---|---|---|---|---|---|---|---|
| Jacksonville, FL | Member | Donald L Palmer | PAS | EX | IV | 4 Years | |

## UNITED STATES HOLOCAUST MEMORIAL COUNCIL

| Location | Position Title | Name of Incumbent | Type of Appt. | Pay Plan | Level, Grade, or Pay | Tenure | Expires |
|---|---|---|---|---|---|---|---|
| | **UNITED STATES HOLOCAUST MEMORIAL COUNCIL STAFF** | | | | | | |
| Washington, DC | Chief of Staff | William S Parsons | XS | SL | | | |
| Do | Associate Museum Director, Museum Programs. | Alice M Greenwald | XS | SL | | | |
| Do | Chair 10 | Vacant | PA | WC | | | |

## UNITED STATES INSTITUTE OF PEACE

| Location | Position Title | Name of Incumbent | Type of Appt. | Pay Plan | Level, Grade, or Pay | Tenure | Expires |
|---|---|---|---|---|---|---|---|
| Washington, DC | Chairman, Board of Directors | Stephen J Hadley | PAS | EX | | | |
| Do | Vice Chair, Board of Directors | George E Moose | PAS | EX | | | |
| Do | Member, Board of Directors | Ikram Khan | PAS | EX | | | |
| Do | ......do | Joseph T Eldridge | PAS | EX | | | |
| Do | ......do | John Lancaster | PAS | EX | | | |
| Do | ......do | Judy Ansley | PAS | EX | | | |
| Do | ......do | Nancy M Zirkin | PAS | EX | | | |
| Do | ......do | J Robinson West | PAS | EX | | | |
| Do | ......do | Eric S Edelman | PAS | EX | | | |
| Do | ......do | Stephen D Krasner | PAS | EX | | | |
| Do | ......do | Jeremy A Rabkin | PAS | EX | | | |
| Do | ......do | Kerry Kennedy | PAS | EX | | | |

## UNITED STATES INTERNATIONAL DEVELOPMENT FINANCE CORPORATION

| Location | Position Title | Name of Incumbent | Type of Appt. | Pay Plan | Level, Grade, or Pay | Tenure | Expires |
|---|---|---|---|---|---|---|---|
| | **OVERSEAS PRIVATE INVESTMENT CORPORATION** | | | | | | |
| Washington, DC | Vice President, Investment Funds | Vacant | XS | AD | | | |
| Do | Vice President and General Counsel | Kevin L Turner | XS | AD | | | |
| Do | Chief Operating Officer | Vacant | XS | AD | | | |
| Do | Special Assistant to the President and Ceo and Front Office Manager. | ......do | XS | AD | | | |
| Do | Chief of Staff | Stewart Ackerly | XS | AD | | | |
| Do | Board Member | Vacant | PAS | EX | IV | | |
| Do | ......do | ......do | PAS | EX | IV | | |
| Do | ......do | Irving Widmer Bailey | PAS | EX | IV | | |
| Do | Vice President, Investment Policy | Vacant | XS | AD | | | |
| Do | Managing Director, Cngressional Affairs | ......do | XS | AD | | | |
| Do | Special Assistant to the Executive Vice President and Projects and Events Coordinator. | ......do | XS | AD | | | |
| Do | Senior Advisor | ......do | XS | AD | | | |
| Do | Special Assistant and Advisor to the President and CEO. | ......do | XS | AD | | | |
| Do | Communications Director | ......do | XS | AD | | | |
| Do | Special Assistant | Owen M. Dorney | XS | AD | | | |
| Do | Board Member | Christopher P Vincze | PAS | EX | IV | | |
| Do | Deputy Vice President and Managing Director for Development Effectiveness. | Anne Anne Lesser | XS | AD | | | |
| Do | Chief Operating Officer | Austin Smith | XS | AD | | | |
| Do | Associate Director | Kerry Wisdom Dittmeier | SC | GS | 11 | | |
| Do | Senior Adviser | Nathan John Miller | XS | OT | | | |
| Do | Managing Director, External Affairs | Lara M. Driscoe | XS | AD | | | |

## UNITED STATES INTERNATIONAL DEVELOPMENT FINANCE CORPORATION—Continued

| Location | Position Title | Name of Incumbent | Type of Appt. | Pay Plan | Level, Grade, or Pay | Tenure | Expires |
|---|---|---|---|---|---|---|---|
| Washington, DC ...... | Senior Adviser | Kristie Pellecchia | XS | AD | | | |
| Do | Counsel to the Chief Executive Officer | Caleb Mccarry | XS | OT | | | |
| Do | Special Assistant | Jacob Daniel Ashendorf | SC | GS | 13 | | |
| Do | Confidential Assistant | Vacant | XS | AD | | | |
| Do | Managing Director, Communications | Molly Millerwise Meiners | XS | OT | | | |
| Do | Special Assistant | Majorie Cecile Reed | SC | GS | 9 | | |
| Do | .....do | Vacant | XS | AD | | | |
| Do | Deputy Chief of Staff | Rachel Baitel | XS | AD | | | |
| Do | Advisor, Office the Chief Executive | Tyler Levin | SC | GS | 13 | | |
| Do | Special Assistant | Vacant | XS | AD | | | |
| Do | Senior Adviser | .....do | XS | AD | | | |
| Do | .....do | Charity N Wallace | XS | AD | | | |
| Do | .....do | Eric Reece Jones | SC | AD | $175,218 | | |
| Do | Vice President, Office of Strategic Initiatives and Senior Advisor for National Security. | Garrett Marquis | XS | AD | | | |
| Do | Associate Director, Office of Strategic Initiatives. | Natalie Monica Szmyd | SC | GS | 11 | | |
| Do | Special Assistant | Adriana Kania | SC | GS | 13 | | |
| Do | Senior Adviser | Vacant | XS | AD | | | |
| Do | .....do | Worku Gachou | XS | AD | | | |
| Do | Chief Executive Officer | Adam Seth Boehler | PAS | EX | II | | |
| Do | Senior Adviser | Vacant | XS | AD | | | |
| Do | Counselor to the Chief Executive Officer | Frank Miller Dunlevy | XS | AD | | | |
| Do | Senior Adviser, Policy and Procedures | Christopher S. Siddall | XS | AD | | | |
| Do | Development Specialist | Amana Tanii Bawa | XS | AD | | | |
| Do | Managing Director, Western Hemisphere and Senior Adviser to the Chief Executive Officer. | Jessica L Bedoya Herman | XS | AD | | | |
| Do | Director, Office of Accountability | William Vincent Kennedy | XS | AD | | | |
| Do | Chief Risk Officer | Miller Mcnutt Alice | XS | AD | | | |
| Do | Director, Covid19 and Energy | Brian Thomas Gilmore | XS | AD | | | |
| Do | Vice President for Operations, Counsel to the Chief Executive Officer. | Vacant | XS | AD | | | |
| Do | Deputy Vice President Office of External Affairs. | Amanda M. Burke | XS | AD | | | |
| Do | Director, Europe and Health Care | Hayden Woodruff Stone | SC | GS | 15 | | |
| Do | Executive Vice President Strategy | Edward Burrier | XS | AD | | | |
| Do | Senior Vice President, Office of Strategic Initiatives. | David James Penna | XS | AD | | | |
| Do | Senior Adviser | Vibhuti Jain | XS | AD | | | |
| Do | Managing Director, Middle East | Allison Dale Minor | XS | AD | | | |
| Do | Vice President, Office of Development Policy | Vacant | XS | AD | | | |
| Do | .....do | Claire Foster Avett | XS | AD | | | |
| Do | Deputy Chief Executive Officer | Vacant | PAS | EX | | | |
| Do | Counselor to the Chief Executive Officer | David Glaccum | XS | AD | | | |

## UNITED STATES INTERNATIONAL TRADE COMMISSION

| Location | Position Title | Name of Incumbent | Type of Appt. | Pay Plan | Level, Grade, or Pay | Tenure | Expires |
|---|---|---|---|---|---|---|---|
| | **OFFICE OF THE CHAIRMAN** | | | | | | |
| Washington, DC ...... | Chairman | Jason E. Kearns | PAS | EX | | | |
| Do | Chief of Staff | Vacant | | ES | | | |
| Do | Confidential Assistant | Gwendolyn Diggs | SC | GS | 13 | | |
| Do | .....do | Samira I. Howard | SC | GS | 11 | | |
| Do | Staff Assistant | Roop K. Bhatti | SC | GS | 15 | | |
| Do | Staff Assistant (Legal) | Stuart M. Weiser | SC | GS | 15 | | |
| Do | .....do | William T. Kane | SC | GS | 15 | | |
| | **OFFICE OF VICE CHAIRMAN STAYIN** | | | | | | |
| Do | Confidential Assistant | Sally E. Knight | SC | GS | 13 | | |
| Do | Vice Chairman | Randolph Stayin | PAS | EX | | 7 Years | |
| Do | Staff Assistant (Legal) | Mark Douglas Beatty | SC | GS | 13 | | |
| Do | .....do | Lane Steven Hurewitz | SC | GS | 15 | | |
| Do | .....do | Erin Joffre | SC | GS | 15 | | |
| | **OFFICE OF COMMISSIONER JOHANSON** | | | | | | |
| Do | Commissioner | David Stanley Johanson | PAS | EX | IV | 7 Years | |
| Do | Staff Assistant (Legal) | Mark B. Rees | SC | GS | 15 | | |

## UNITED STATES INTERNATIONAL TRADE COMMISSION—Continued

| Location | Position Title | Name of Incumbent | Type of Appt. | Pay Plan | Level, Grade, or Pay | Tenure | Expires |
|---|---|---|---|---|---|---|---|
| Washington, DC ...... | Staff Assistant (Legal) | Michael Joseph Robbins | SC | GS | 14 | ............... | |
| | **OFFICE OF COMMISSIONER KARPEL** | | | | | | |
| Do .................. | ......do | Juliana M. Cofrancesco | SC | GS | 15 | ............. | |
| | **OFFICE OF COMMISSIONER JOHANSON** | | | | | | |
| Do .................. | Commissioner | Vacant | PAS | EX | IV | 7 Years | |
| | **OFFICE OF COMMISSIONER SCHMIDTLEIN** | | | | | | |
| Do .................. | ......do | Rhonda Kay Schmidtlein | PAS | EX | IV | 7 Years | |
| Do .................. | Confidential Assistant | Cordelia Odessa Stroman | SC | GS | 13 | ............. | |
| Do .................. | Staff Assistant (Legal) | Elizabeth Argenti | SC | GS | 15 | ............. | |
| Do .................. | ......do | Rowan Morris Dougherty | SC | GS | 15 | ............. | |
| Do .................. | ......do | Michael J. Leib Esq. | SC | GS | 15 | ............. | |
| | **OFFICE OF COMMISSIONER KARPEL** | | | | | | |
| Do .................. | Commissioner | Amy A. Karpel | PAS | EX | IV | 7 Years | |
| Do .................. | Staff Assistant (Legal) | James H. Ahrens II | SC | GS | 15 | ............. | |
| Do .................. | Staff Assistant (Economist) | Fay M. Johnson | SC | GS | 15 | ............. | |

## UNITED STATES INTERNATIONAL TRADE COMMISSION OFFICE OF THE INSPECTOR GENERAL

| Location | Position Title | Name of Incumbent | Type of Appt. | Pay Plan | Level, Grade, or Pay | Tenure | Expires |
|---|---|---|---|---|---|---|---|
| Washington, DC ...... | Inspector General | Vacant | ............ | ES | ............... | ............. | |

## UNITED STATES POSTAL SERVICE

| Location | Position Title | Name of Incumbent | Type of Appt. | Pay Plan | Level, Grade, or Pay | Tenure | Expires |
|---|---|---|---|---|---|---|---|
| Alexandria, VA ........ | Deputy Assistant Inspector General (Investigations). | Lavan Griffith | XS | OT | ............... | ............. | |
| Arlington, VA........... | Deputy Assistant Inspector General for Investigations. | Vacant | ............ | ES | ............... | ............. | |
| Do ..................... | ......do | ......do | XS | OT | ............... | ............. | |

## UNITED STATES SEMIQUINCENTENNIAL COMMISSION

| Location | Position Title | Name of Incumbent | Type of Appt. | Pay Plan | Level, Grade, or Pay | Tenure | Expires |
|---|---|---|---|---|---|---|---|
| Philadelphia, PA...... | Chairman | Daniel M Dilella | PA | WC | ............... | ............. | |

## VIETNAM EDUCATION FOUNDATION

| Location | Position Title | Name of Incumbent | Type of Appt. | Pay Plan | Level, Grade, or Pay | Tenure | Expires |
|---|---|---|---|---|---|---|---|
| Arlington, VA........... | Executive Director | Sandy Hoa Dang | XS | AD | ............... | ............. | |
| Do .................... | Member | Edmund Malesky | PA | AD | ............... | ............. | |
| Do .................... | Chairman | Vacant | PA | OT | ............... | ............. | |
| Do .................... | Member | ......do | PA | OT | ............... | ............. | |
| Do .................... | ......do | ......do | PA | OT | ............... | ............. | |
| Do .................... | ......do | ......do | PA | OT | ............... | ............. | |
| Do .................... | ......do | ......do | PA | OT | ............... | ............. | |

## WOMEN'S SUFFRAGE CENTENNIAL COMMISSION

| Location | Position Title | Name of Incumbent | Type of Appt. | Pay Plan | Level, Grade, or Pay | Tenure | Expires |
|---|---|---|---|---|---|---|---|
| Washington, DC ...... | Board Member .................................................. | Kay C James......................... | PA | WC | .............. | ............... | |

## WOODROW WILSON INTERNATIONAL CENTER FOR SCHOLARS

| Location | Position Title | Name of Incumbent | Type of Appt. | Pay Plan | Level, Grade, or Pay | Tenure | Expires |
|---|---|---|---|---|---|---|---|
| Washington, DC ...... | Director............................................................. | Vacant .................................. | XS | OT | .............. | .............. | |
| Do .................. | Senior Advisor................................................ | ......do .................................. | XS | OT | .............. | .............. | |
| Do .................. | ......do .............................................................. | Meghann K Ritcheson........... | XS | OT | .............. | .............. | |
| Do .................. | Vice Chair, Board of Trustees (Private Citizen). | Drew Maloney....................... | PA | AD | .............. | .............. | |
| Do .................. | Trustee, Wilson Center (Private Citizen).......... | Louis Susman ....................... | PA | AD | .............. | .............. | |
| Do .................. | ......do .............................................................. | Nathalie Rayes .................... | PA | AD | .............. | .............. | |
| Do .................. | ......do .............................................................. | Thelma Duggin.................... | PA | AD | .............. | .............. | |
| Do .................. | ......do .............................................................. | Barry S Jackson ................... | PA | AD | .............. | .............. | |
| Do .................. | ......do .............................................................. | David Jacobson..................... | PA | AD | .............. | .............. | |
| Do .................. | ......do .............................................................. | Earl Stafford........................ | PA | AD | .............. | .............. | |
| Do .................. | ......do .............................................................. | Peter Beshar ......................... | PA | AD | .............. | .............. | |

## WORLD WAR I CENTENNIAL COMMISSION

| Location | Position Title | Name of Incumbent | Type of Appt. | Pay Plan | Level, Grade, or Pay | Tenure | Expires |
|---|---|---|---|---|---|---|---|
| Washington, DC ...... | Commissioner..................................................... | Debra L Anderson ............... | PA | WC | .............. | .............. | |
| Do .................. | Chairman ......................................................... | Terry W Hamby.................... | PA | WC | .............. | .............. | |
| Do .................. | Commissioner..................................................... | John D Monahan.................. | PA | WC | .............. | .............. | |
| Do .................. | Executive Director ............................................. | Daniel S Dayton .................. | XS | AD | .............. | .............. | |

# APPENDICES

## APPENDIX NO. 1

### SUMMARY OF POSITIONS SUBJECT TO NONCOMPETITIVE APPOINTMENT

PAS = Positions Subject to Presidential Appointment with Senate Confirmation
PA  = Positions Subject to Presidential Appointment without Senate Confirmation
GEN = Positions Designated as Senior Executive Service "General"
NA  = Senior Executive Service General Positions Filled by Noncareer Appointment
TA  = Senior Executive Service Positions Filled by Limited Emergency or Limited Term Appointment
SC  = Positions Filled by Schedule C Excepted Appointment
XS  = Positions Subject to Statutory Excepted Appointment

| Agency or Department | PAS | PA | GEN | NA | TA | SC | XS |
|---|---|---|---|---|---|---|---|
| ADVISORY COUNCIL ON HISTORIC PRESERVATION | 1 | 10 | 0 | 0 | 0 | 0 | 0 |
| AFRICAN DEVELOPMENT FOUNDATION | 5 | 0 | 0 | 0 | 0 | 0 | 0 |
| AMERICAN BATTLE MONUMENTS COMMISSION | 0 | 1 | 0 | 0 | 0 | 0 | 0 |
| APPALACHIAN REGIONAL COMMISSION | 2 | 0 | 0 | 0 | 0 | 2 | 0 |
| ARCTIC RESEARCH COMMISSION | 1 | 7 | 1 | 0 | 0 | 0 | 0 |
| ARMED FORCES RETIREMENT HOME | 0 | 2 | 0 | 0 | 0 | 0 | 0 |
| BARRY GOLDWATER SCHOLARSHIP AND EXCELLENCE IN EDUCATION FOUNDATION | 1 | 0 | 0 | 1 | 0 | 0 | 0 |
| CENTRAL INTELLIGENCE AGENCY | 3 | 0 | 0 | 0 | 0 | 0 | 0 |
| CHEMICAL SAFETY AND HAZARD INVESTIGATION BOARD | 4 | 0 | 2 | 0 | 0 | 0 | 0 |
| CHRISTOPHER COLUMBUS FELLOWSHIP FOUNDATION | 0 | 13 | 0 | 0 | 0 | 0 | 0 |
| COMMISSION OF FINE ARTS | 0 | 7 | 1 | 0 | 0 | 0 | 0 |
| COMMISSION ON CIVIL RIGHTS | 0 | 7 | 0 | 1 | 0 | 5 | 4 |
| COMMITTEE FOR PURCHASE FROM PEOPLE WHO ARE BLIND OR SEVERELY DISABLED | 0 | 2 | 0 | 0 | 0 | 0 | 0 |
| COMMODITY FUTURES TRADING COMMISSION | 5 | 0 | 0 | 0 | 0 | 9 | 0 |
| CONSUMER FINANCIAL PROTECTION BUREAU | 1 | 0 | 0 | 0 | 0 | 0 | 0 |
| CONSUMER PRODUCT SAFETY COMMISSION | 6 | 0 | 4 | 0 | 0 | 9 | 0 |
| CORPORATION FOR NATIONAL AND COMMUNITY SERVICE | 17 | 0 | 0 | 0 | 0 | 0 | 18 |
| COUNCIL OF ECONOMIC ADVISERS | 3 | 0 | 1 | 0 | 0 | 0 | 1 |
| COUNCIL OF INSPECTORS GENERAL ON INTEGRITY AND EFFICIENCY | 0 | 0 | 2 | 0 | 0 | 0 | 0 |
| COUNCIL ON ENVIRONMENTAL QUALITY | 4 | 0 | 0 | 0 | 0 | 1 | 5 |
| COURT SERVICES AND OFFENDER SUPERVISION AGENCY FOR THE DISTRICT OF COLUMBIA | 1 | 0 | 1 | 0 | 0 | 0 | 0 |
| DEFENSE NUCLEAR FACILITIES SAFETY BOARD | 5 | 0 | 2 | 0 | 0 | 0 | 1 |
| DELAWARE RIVER BASIN COMMISSION | 0 | 1 | 0 | 0 | 0 | 0 | 0 |
| DELTA REGIONAL AUTHORITY | 1 | 1 | 0 | 0 | 0 | 0 | 0 |
| DENALI COMMISSION | 0 | 0 | 0 | 0 | 0 | 0 | 1 |
| DEPARTMENT OF AGRICULTURE | 14 | 3 | 130 | 46 | 1 | 157 | 1 |
| DEPARTMENT OF COMMERCE | 23 | 1 | 82 | 36 | 7 | 96 | 3 |
| DEPARTMENT OF COMMERCE OFFICE OF THE INSPECTOR GENERAL | 0 | 0 | 1 | 0 | 0 | 0 | 0 |
| DEPARTMENT OF EDUCATION | 15 | 1 | 35 | 21 | 1 | 73 | 1 |
| DEPARTMENT OF EDUCATION OFFICE OF THE INSPECTOR GENERAL | 1 | 0 | 0 | 0 | 0 | 0 | 0 |
| DEPARTMENT OF ENERGY | 22 | 0 | 133 | 25 | 1 | 123 | 1 |
| DEPARTMENT OF ENERGY OFFICE OF THE INSPECTOR GENERAL | 1 | 0 | 0 | 0 | 0 | 0 | 0 |
| DEPARTMENT OF HEALTH AND HUMAN SERVICES | 18 | 2 | 237 | 78 | 11 | 92 | 1 |
| DEPARTMENT OF HEALTH AND HUMAN SERVICES OFFICE OF THE INSPECTOR GENERAL | 1 | 0 | 0 | 0 | 0 | 0 | 0 |

| Agency or Department | PAS | PA | GEN | NA | TA | SC | XS |
|---|---|---|---|---|---|---|---|
| DEPARTMENT OF HOMELAND SECURITY .................................. | 17 | 4 | 82 | 57 | 9 | 72 | 158 |
| DEPARTMENT OF HOMELAND SECURITY OFFICE OF THE INSPEC-TOR GENERAL .................................................................................. | 1 | 0 | 1 | 0 | 0 | 0 | 0 |
| DEPARTMENT OF HOUSING AND URBAN DEVELOPMENT ............... | 12 | 1 | 44 | 23 | 3 | 81 | 0 |
| DEPARTMENT OF HOUSING AND URBAN DEVELOPMENT OFFICE OF THE INSPECTOR GENERAL ............................................... | 1 | 0 | 0 | 0 | 1 | 0 | 0 |
| DEPARTMENT OF JUSTICE ....................................................... | 218 | 8 | 96 | 57 | 6 | 60 | 1 |
| DEPARTMENT OF JUSTICE OFFICE OF THE INSPECTOR GENERAL ........................................................................................ | 1 | 0 | 0 | 0 | 0 | 0 | 0 |
| DEPARTMENT OF LABOR ............................................................. | 15 | 2 | 32 | 23 | 0 | 108 | 0 |
| DEPARTMENT OF LABOR OFFICE OF INSPECTOR GENERAL ........... | 1 | 0 | 0 | 0 | 0 | 0 | 0 |
| DEPARTMENT OF STATE ............................................................. | 254 | 3 | 130 | 36 | 2 | 86 | 0 |
| DEPARTMENT OF STATE OFFICE OF THE INSPECTOR GENERAL ..... | 1 | 0 | 0 | 0 | 0 | 0 | 2 |
| DEPARTMENT OF THE AIR FORCE ............................................. | 7 | 0 | 16 | 3 | 0 | 5 | 1 |
| DEPARTMENT OF THE ARMY ...................................................... | 8 | 0 | 29 | 10 | 6 | 10 | 1 |
| DEPARTMENT OF THE INTERIOR .............................................. | 17 | 0 | 158 | 35 | 0 | 42 | 4 |
| DEPARTMENT OF THE INTERIOR OFFICE OF THE INSPECTOR GENERAL ........................................................................................ | 1 | 0 | 0 | 0 | 0 | 0 | 0 |
| DEPARTMENT OF THE NAVY ...................................................... | 7 | 0 | 11 | 1 | 0 | 4 | 0 |
| DEPARTMENT OF THE TREASURY ............................................. | 32 | 3 | 90 | 25 | 3 | 33 | 0 |
| DEPARTMENT OF THE TREASURY OFFICE OF THE INSPECTOR GENERAL ........................................................................................ | 1 | 0 | 1 | 0 | 0 | 0 | 0 |
| DEPARTMENT OF THE TREASURY SPECIAL INSPECTOR GENERAL FOR THE TROUBLED ASSET RELIEF PROGRAM ............................. | 1 | 0 | 1 | 0 | 0 | 0 | 0 |
| DEPARTMENT OF THE TREASURY TAX ADMINISTRATION OFFICE OF THE INSPECTOR GENERAL ............................................... | 1 | 0 | 0 | 0 | 0 | 0 | 0 |
| DEPARTMENT OF TRANSPORTATION ....................................... | 17 | 2 | 136 | 41 | 1 | 61 | 4 |
| DEPARTMENT OF TRANSPORTATION OFFICE OF THE INSPECTOR GENERAL ........................................................................................ | 1 | 0 | 0 | 0 | 0 | 0 | 0 |
| DEPARTMENT OF VETERANS AFFAIRS ..................................... | 11 | 3 | 281 | 16 | 9 | 12 | 147 |
| DEPARTMENT OF VETERANS AFFAIRS OFFICE OF THE INSPECTOR GENERAL ........................................................................................ | 1 | 0 | 0 | 0 | 0 | 0 | 0 |
| DWIGHT D EISENHOWER MEMORIAL COMMISSION ...................... | 0 | 0 | 0 | 0 | 0 | 0 | 1 |
| ENVIRONMENTAL PROTECTION AGENCY .................................. | 12 | 0 | 88 | 30 | 0 | 62 | 0 |
| ENVIRONMENTAL PROTECTION AGENCY OFFICE OF THE INSPEC-TOR GENERAL .................................................................................. | 1 | 0 | 0 | 0 | 0 | 0 | 0 |
| EQUAL EMPLOYMENT OPPORTUNITY COMMISSION ...................... | 6 | 0 | 13 | 2 | 0 | 1 | 0 |
| EXECUTIVE OFFICE OF THE PRESIDENT ................................. | 5 | 1 | 0 | 0 | 0 | 0 | 1 |
| EXPORT-IMPORT BANK .............................................................. | 5 | 0 | 0 | 0 | 0 | 23 | 0 |
| EXPORT-IMPORT BANK OFFICE OF THE INSPECTOR GENERAL ...... . | 1 | 0 | 0 | 0 | 0 | 0 | 0 |
| FARM CREDIT ADMINISTRATION .............................................. | 3 | 0 | 0 | 0 | 0 | 3 | 0 |
| FEDERAL COMMUNICATIONS COMMISSION ................................ | 5 | 0 | 42 | 1 | 0 | 0 | 6 |
| FEDERAL DEPOSIT INSURANCE CORPORATION ......................... | 4 | 0 | 0 | 0 | 0 | 2 | 0 |
| FEDERAL ELECTION COMMISSION ............................................. | 6 | 0 | 0 | 0 | 0 | 0 | 18 |
| FEDERAL ELECTION COMMISSION OFFICE OF THE INSPECTOR GENERAL ........................................................................................ | 0 | 0 | 0 | 0 | 0 | 0 | 1 |
| FEDERAL ENERGY REGULATORY COMMISSION ........................... | 5 | 0 | 44 | 1 | 0 | 4 | 0 |
| FEDERAL HOUSING FINANCE AGENCY ...................................... | 1 | 0 | 0 | 0 | 0 | 1 | 0 |
| FEDERAL HOUSING FINANCE BOARD ....................................... | 0 | 0 | 0 | 0 | 0 | 3 | 0 |
| FEDERAL LABOR RELATIONS AUTHORITY ................................ | 4 | 7 | 0 | 0 | 0 | 0 | 2 |
| FEDERAL MARITIME COMMISSION ........................................... | 5 | 0 | 2 | 0 | 0 | 2 | 0 |
| FEDERAL MEDIATION AND CONCILIATION SERVICE .................... | 0 | 0 | 3 | 0 | 0 | 0 | 1 |
| FEDERAL MINE SAFETY AND HEALTH REVIEW COMMISSION ........ | 6 | 0 | 1 | 0 | 0 | 3 | 0 |
| FEDERAL PERMITTING IMPROVEMENT STEERING COUNCIL .......... | 0 | 0 | 0 | 1 | 0 | 2 | 0 |
| FEDERAL RESERVE SYSTEM ...................................................... | 7 | 0 | 0 | 0 | 0 | 0 | 0 |
| FEDERAL RETIREMENT THRIFT INVESTMENT BOARD .................... | 5 | 0 | 4 | 0 | 0 | 0 | 1 |
| FEDERAL TRADE COMMISSION ................................................. | 5 | 0 | 25 | 5 | 1 | 4 | 0 |
| GENERAL SERVICES ADMINISTRATION ................................... | 1 | 0 | 14 | 19 | 2 | 16 | 0 |

| Agency or Department | PAS | PA | GEN | NA | TA | SC | XS |
|---|---|---|---|---|---|---|---|
| GENERAL SERVICES ADMINISTRATION OFFICE OF THE INSPECTOR GENERAL | 1 | 0 | 0 | 0 | 0 | 0 | 0 |
| GREAT LAKES FISHERY COMMISSION | 0 | 5 | 0 | 0 | 0 | 0 | 0 |
| GULF COAST ECOSYSTEM RESTORATION COUNCIL | 0 | 0 | 1 | 0 | 0 | 0 | 0 |
| INSTITUTE OF MUSEUM AND LIBRARY SERVICES | 19 | 0 | 1 | 0 | 0 | 0 | 0 |
| INTELLECTUAL PROPERTY ENFORCEMENT COORDINATOR | 1 | 0 | 1 | 0 | 0 | 0 | 0 |
| INTER-AMERICAN FOUNDATION | 10 | 0 | 0 | 0 | 0 | 0 | 0 |
| INTERAGENCY COUNCIL ON THE HOMELESS | 0 | 0 | 0 | 0 | 0 | 0 | 1 |
| INTERNATIONAL BOUNDARY AND WATER COMMISSION | 0 | 2 | 0 | 0 | 0 | 0 | 0 |
| INTERNATIONAL JOINT COMMISSION | 3 | 0 | 0 | 0 | 0 | 0 | 0 |
| INTERSTATE COMMISSION ON THE POTOMAC RIVER BASIN | 0 | 4 | 0 | 0 | 0 | 0 | 0 |
| JAMES MADISON MEMORIAL FELLOWSHIP FOUNDATION | 0 | 0 | 0 | 0 | 0 | 0 | 1 |
| JAPAN UNITED STATES FRIENDSHIP COMMISSION | 0 | 0 | 1 | 0 | 0 | 0 | 0 |
| MARINE MAMMAL COMMISSION | 3 | 0 | 0 | 0 | 0 | 0 | 0 |
| MEDICAID AND CHIP PAYMENT AND ACCESS COMMISSION | 0 | 0 | 0 | 0 | 0 | 0 | 22 |
| MEDICARE PAYMENT ADVISORY COMMISSION | 0 | 0 | 0 | 0 | 0 | 0 | 3 |
| MERIT SYSTEMS PROTECTION BOARD | 3 | 0 | 1 | 1 | 0 | 1 | 0 |
| MILLENNIUM CHALLENGE CORPORATION | 5 | 26 | 0 | 0 | 0 | 0 | 0 |
| MORRIS K UDALL SCHOLARSHIP AND EXCELLENCE IN NATIONAL ENVIRONMENTAL POLICY FOUNDATION | 9 | 0 | 0 | 0 | 0 | 0 | 0 |
| NATIONAL AERONAUTICS AND SPACE ADMINISTRATION | 3 | 0 | 30 | 4 | 1 | 13 | 0 |
| NATIONAL AERONAUTICS AND SPACE ADMINISTRATION OFFICE OF THE INSPECTOR GENERAL | 1 | 0 | 0 | 0 | 0 | 0 | 0 |
| NATIONAL ARCHIVES AND RECORDS ADMINISTRATION | 1 | 0 | 0 | 0 | 0 | 0 | 13 |
| NATIONAL CAPITAL PLANNING COMMISSION | 0 | 3 | 0 | 0 | 0 | 0 | 0 |
| NATIONAL COUNCIL ON DISABILITY | 0 | 8 | 0 | 0 | 0 | 0 | 0 |
| NATIONAL CREDIT UNION ADMINISTRATION | 3 | 0 | 0 | 0 | 0 | 9 | 0 |
| NATIONAL ENDOWMENT FOR THE ARTS | 0 | 0 | 0 | 3 | 0 | 11 | 0 |
| NATIONAL ENDOWMENT FOR THE HUMANITIES | 1 | 0 | 4 | 1 | 0 | 5 | 0 |
| NATIONAL ENDOWMENT FOR THE HUMANITIES OFFICE OF THE INSPECTOR GENERAL | 0 | 0 | 1 | 0 | 0 | 0 | 0 |
| NATIONAL LABOR RELATIONS BOARD | 6 | 0 | 9 | 5 | 0 | 2 | 0 |
| NATIONAL MEDIATION BOARD | 5 | 0 | 1 | 0 | 0 | 0 | 0 |
| NATIONAL SCIENCE FOUNDATION | 2 | 0 | 46 | 0 | 3 | 0 | 23 |
| NATIONAL SCIENCE FOUNDATION OFFICE OF THE INSPECTOR GENERAL | 0 | 0 | 0 | 0 | 0 | 0 | 1 |
| NATIONAL SECURITY COUNCIL | 0 | 1 | 0 | 0 | 0 | 0 | 0 |
| NATIONAL SPACE COUNCIL | 0 | 1 | 0 | 0 | 0 | 0 | 3 |
| NATIONAL TRANSPORTATION SAFETY BOARD | 5 | 0 | 3 | 1 | 0 | 9 | 0 |
| NORTHERN BORDER REGIONAL COMMISSION | 1 | 1 | 0 | 0 | 0 | 0 | 0 |
| NUCLEAR REGULATORY COMMISSION | 5 | 0 | 40 | 0 | 0 | 0 | 70 |
| NUCLEAR REGULATORY COMMISSION OFFICE OF THE INSPECTOR GENERAL | 1 | 0 | 0 | 0 | 0 | 0 | 0 |
| NUCLEAR WASTE TECHNICAL REVIEW BOARD | 0 | 11 | 1 | 0 | 0 | 0 | 0 |
| OCCUPATIONAL SAFETY AND HEALTH REVIEW COMMISSION | 3 | 0 | 1 | 0 | 0 | 2 | 0 |
| OFFICE OF ADMINISTRATION | 0 | 11 | 0 | 0 | 0 | 0 | 0 |
| OFFICE OF GOVERNMENT ETHICS | 1 | 0 | 0 | 0 | 0 | 0 | 0 |
| OFFICE OF MANAGEMENT AND BUDGET | 7 | 0 | 7 | 16 | 0 | 26 | 0 |
| OFFICE OF NATIONAL DRUG CONTROL POLICY | 1 | 1 | 4 | 3 | 1 | 4 | 0 |
| OFFICE OF NAVAJO AND HOPI INDIAN RELOCATION | 1 | 0 | 1 | 0 | 0 | 0 | 0 |
| OFFICE OF PERSONNEL MANAGEMENT | 2 | 0 | 26 | 12 | 0 | 25 | 0 |
| OFFICE OF PERSONNEL MANAGEMENT OFFICE OF THE INSPECTOR GENERAL | 1 | 0 | 0 | 0 | 0 | 0 | 1 |
| OFFICE OF POLICY DEVELOPMENT | 0 | 8 | 0 | 0 | 0 | 0 | 0 |
| OFFICE OF SCIENCE AND TECHNOLOGY POLICY | 7 | 1 | 0 | 1 | 0 | 2 | 0 |
| OFFICE OF SPECIAL COUNSEL | 2 | 0 | 0 | 1 | 0 | 3 | 0 |
| OFFICE OF THE SECRETARY OF DEFENSE | 44 | 1 | 211 | 58 | 9 | 96 | 0 |
| OFFICE OF THE SECRETARY OF DEFENSE OFFICE OF THE INSPECTOR GENERAL | 1 | 0 | 1 | 0 | 0 | 0 | 0 |

| Agency or Department | PAS | PA | GEN | NA | TA | SC | XS |
|---|---|---|---|---|---|---|---|
| OFFICE OF THE UNITED STATES TRADE REPRESENTATIVE ............. | 6 | 0 | 15 | 5 | 0 | 4 | 12 |
| OFFICIAL RESIDENCE OF THE VICE PRESIDENT ................................. | 0 | 0 | 0 | 0 | 0 | 1 | 0 |
| PEACE CORPS ................................................................................................ | 4 | 26 | 0 | 0 | 0 | 0 | 0 |
| PENSION BENEFIT GUARANTY CORPORATION ..................................... | 2 | 0 | 0 | 0 | 0 | 2 | 0 |
| PENSION BENEFIT GUARANTY CORPORATION OFFICE OF INSPEC-TOR GENERAL ................................................................................................ | 0 | 0 | 0 | 0 | 0 | 0 | 2 |
| POSTAL REGULATORY COMMISSION ..................................................... | 5 | 0 | 0 | 0 | 0 | 0 | 19 |
| PUBLIC BUILDINGS REFORM BOARD ....................................................... | 0 | 5 | 0 | 0 | 0 | 0 | 0 |
| RAILROAD RETIREMENT BOARD ............................................................. | 3 | 0 | 0 | 0 | 0 | 0 | 0 |
| RAILROAD RETIREMENT BOARD OFFICE OF THE INSPECTOR GENERAL ........................................................................................................ | 1 | 0 | 0 | 0 | 0 | 0 | 0 |
| SECURITIES AND EXCHANGE COMMISSION ......................................... | 5 | 0 | 0 | 0 | 0 | 12 | 0 |
| SELECTIVE SERVICE SYSTEM ................................................................. | 1 | 0 | 0 | 1 | 0 | 1 | 0 |
| SMALL BUSINESS ADMINISTRATION ..................................................... | 3 | 0 | 20 | 11 | 0 | 37 | 0 |
| SMALL BUSINESS ADMINISTRATION OFFICE OF THE INSPECTOR GENERAL ........................................................................................................ | 1 | 0 | 0 | 0 | 0 | 0 | 0 |
| SMITHSONIAN INSTITUTION ................................................................. | 0 | 0 | 0 | 0 | 0 | 0 | 2 |
| SOCIAL SECURITY ADMINISTRATION ................................................... | 4 | 0 | 85 | 3 | 4 | 3 | 0 |
| SOCIAL SECURITY ADMINISTRATION OFFICE OF THE INSPECTOR GENERAL ........................................................................................................ | 1 | 0 | 0 | 0 | 0 | 0 | 0 |
| SURFACE TRANSPORTATION BOARD ..................................................... | 5 | 0 | 0 | 0 | 0 | 0 | 0 |
| TENNESSEE VALLEY AUTHORITY .......................................................... | 8 | 0 | 0 | 0 | 0 | 0 | 0 |
| TRADE AND DEVELOPMENT AGENCY ..................................................... | 1 | 0 | 0 | 0 | 0 | 3 | 0 |
| U.S. AGENCY FOR GLOBAL MEDIA ........................................................ | 1 | 0 | 7 | 0 | 0 | 0 | 0 |
| UNITED STATES—CHINA ECONOMIC AND SECURITY REVIEW COMMISSION ............................................................................................... | 0 | 0 | 0 | 0 | 0 | 0 | 12 |
| UNITED STATES AGENCY FOR INTERNATIONAL DEVELOPMENT ..... | 11 | 1 | 16 | 4 | 1 | 0 | 87 |
| UNITED STATES AGENCY FOR INTERNATIONAL DEVELOPMENT OFFICE OF THE INSPECTOR GENERAL ............................................... | 1 | 0 | 0 | 0 | 0 | 0 | 0 |
| UNITED STATES COMMISSION FOR THE PRESERVATION OF AMERI-CA'S HERITAGE ABROAD ......................................................................... | 0 | 21 | 0 | 0 | 0 | 0 | 0 |
| UNITED STATES COMMISSION ON INTERNATIONAL RELIGIOUS FREEDOM .................................................................................................. | 0 | 3 | 0 | 0 | 0 | 0 | 6 |
| UNITED STATES ELECTION ASSISTANCE COMMISSION ................... | 4 | 0 | 0 | 0 | 0 | 0 | 2 |
| UNITED STATES HOLOCAUST MEMORIAL COUNCIL ......................... | 0 | 1 | 0 | 0 | 0 | 0 | 2 |
| UNITED STATES INSTITUTE OF PEACE ................................................ | 12 | 0 | 0 | 0 | 0 | 0 | 0 |
| UNITED STATES INTERNATIONAL DEVELOPMENT FINANCE CORPORATION ........................................................................................... | 6 | 0 | 0 | 0 | 0 | 8 | 45 |
| UNITED STATES INTERNATIONAL TRADE COMMISSION ................... | 6 | 0 | 0 | 0 | 0 | 20 | 0 |
| TOTAL      (7078) ................................................................ | 1118 | 354 | 2510 | 724 | 83 | 1566 | 723 |

# APPENDIX NO. 2

## SENIOR EXECUTIVE SERVICE

The Senior Executive Service (SES) is a personnel system covering top level policy, supervisory, and managerial positions in most Federal agencies. Positions in Government corporations, the FBI and Drug Enforcement Administration, certain intelligence agencies, certain financial regulatory agencies, and the Foreign Service are exempt from the SES.

The SES includes most Civil Service positions above grade 15 of the General Schedule. An agency may establish an SES position only within an allocation approved by the U.S. Office of Personnel Management (OPM). Currently, there are 8328 SES positions allocated by OPM to agencies.

*Types of SES Positions*

There are two types of SES positions: Career Reserved and General. About half of the SES positions are designated in each category. Once a position is designated by an agency, the designation may not be changed without prior OPM approval.

SES positions are designated Career Reserved when the need to ensure impartiality, or the public's confidence in the impartiality of the Government, requires that they be filled only by career employees (e.g., law enforcement and audit positions).

The remaining SES positions are designated General. A General position may be filled by a career appointee, a noncareer appointee, or, if the position meets the criteria described below, by a limited term or limited emergency appointee. Because of the limitations on the number of limited appointees, most General positions are filled by career appointees.

A given General position may be filled at one time by a career appointee and at another time by a noncareer or limited appointee, or vice versa. Because of the limitations on the number of noncareer and limited appointees, as discussed below, most General positions are filled by career appointees. This publication lists only General positions since Career Reserved positions must be filled by a career appointee.

*Appointments to SES Positions*

The legislation establishing the SES provides three methods of appointment. Veterans' preference is not applicable in the SES.

(1) Career appointment: Career appointments are made through a Governmentwide or an "all sources" merit staffing (competitive) process, including recruitment through a published announcement, rating and ranking of eligible candidates, approval by the agency of the professional qualifications of the selected candidate, and a further review and approval of the executive/managerial qualifications of the proposed selectee by an OPM-administered SES Qualifications Review Board.

A career appointee serves a 1-year probationary period. Upon completion, the appointee acquires tenure rights and may be removed from the SES only for cause or for poor performance. (A performance appraisal for a career appointee may not be made, however, within 120 days after the beginning of a new Presidential Administration, i.e., one where the President changes.)

When a career appointee is reassigned within an agency, he or she must be given at least a 15-day advance written notice. If the reassignment is to another commuting area, the notice period is 60 days; the agency first must consult with the individual as to the reasons and the individual's preferences.

A career appointee may not be involuntarily reassigned within 120 days after the appointment of a new agency head, or during the same period after the appointment of a noncareer supervisor who has the authority to make an initial appraisal of the career appointee's performance. A career appointee may not be involuntarily transferred to another agency.

Like all career Federal employees, a career SES appointee is entitled to protection against retaliatory or politically motivated personnel actions and may lodge a complaint with the Office of the Special Counsel if a prohibited personnel practice has occurred.

(2) Noncareer appointment: By law, no more than 10 percent of total SES positions Governmentwide may be filled by noncareer appointees. The proportion of noncareer appointees may, however, vary from

agency to agency, generally up to a limit of 25 percent of the agency's number of SES positions. OPM approves each use of a noncareer authority by an agency, and the authority reverts to OPM when the noncareer appointee leaves the position.

Noncareer appointees may be appointed to any SES General position. There is no requirement for competitive staffing, but the agency head must certify that the appointee meets the qualifications requirements for the position.

Any noncareer appointee may be removed by the appointing authority (e.g., for loss of confidence or change in policy). There is no appeal right.

(3) Limited appointment: Limited appointments are used in situations where the position is not continuing (e.g., to head a special project), or where the position is established to meet a bona fide, unanticipated, urgent need. Limited term appointments may not exceed 3 years; limited emergency appointments, 18 months.

By law, limited appointments Governmentwide may not exceed 5 percent of total SES positions. The appointments may be made only to General positions. Generally, OPM allocates limited appointment authorities on a case-by-case basis. However, each agency has a small pool of limited authorities equal to 3 percent of their total SES position allocation from OPM. Such pool authorities may be used only for appointment of career or career-type Federal civil service employees. Selection procedures and qualification requirements are determined by the agency, and the incumbent serves at the pleasure of the appointing authority.

By law, the appointment to or removal from any SES position in an independent regulatory commission shall not be subject, directly or indirectly, to review or approval by an officer or entity within the Executive Office of the President.

# APPENDIX NO. 3

## SCHEDULE C POSITIONS

———

Schedule C positions are excepted from the competitive service because of their confidential or policy-determining character. Most such positions are at grade 15 of the General Schedule or lower. Schedule C positions above the GS–15 level are either in the Senior Level (SL) personnel system or are specifically authorized in law.

The decision concerning whether to place a position in Schedule C is made by the Director, U.S. Office of Personnel Management, upon agency request. Such requests are considered on a case-by-case basis. In addition to consideration of the justification submitted by the agency, OPM may conduct an independent review and analysis. In addition to the Schedule C positions authorized by the OPM Director, a limited number of positions may be placed under Schedule C by Executive Order of the President or by legislation.

Requests for Schedule C exception are appropriate when:

(1) The position involves making or approving substantive policy recommendations; or

(2) The work of the position can be performed successfully only by someone with a thorough knowledge of and sympathy with the goals, priorities, and preferences of an official who has a confidential or policy determining relationship with the President or the agency head. There are special requirements for the types of superiors who are eligible for Schedule C secretaries.

The immediate supervisor of a Schedule C position must be a Presidential appointee, a Senior Executive Service appointee (career or noncareer) occupying a General position, or a Schedule C appointee. The immediate supervisor may not occupy a position in the competitive service or a Career Reserved position in the Senior Executive Service.

The only time when OPM approval is not required for a Schedule C position is when a position is filled by a temporary Schedule C appointment during a Presidential transition, a change of agency head, or establishment of a new agency. Temporary Schedule C positions may be established for 120 days, with one extension of 120 days, under conditions prescribed by OPM. There is a limit on the number of such positions that can be established by an agency. New appointments may be made only during the 1-year period beginning on the date of the agency head's appointment, a new Administration or establishment of a new agency.

By law, the agency head must certify to OPM that both Schedule C and temporary Schedule C positions are not being requested for the sole purpose of detailing the incumbent to the White House.

Agencies may fill Schedule C positions noncompetitively. Because of the confidential or policy-determining nature of Schedule C positions, the incumbents serve at the pleasure of the appointing authority (usually the agency head) and may be removed at any time. They are not covered under conduct-based or performance-removal procedures that apply to certain other excepted Service appointees.

Schedule C positions authorized by OPM are automatically revoked when the incumbent leaves the position (i.e., there is no such thing as a "vacant" Schedule C position).

# APPENDIX NO. 4

## FEDERAL SALARY SCHEDULES FOR 2020

The information in the body of this report reflects grades or salaries in effect on the first pay period on or after January 1, 2020.

### EXECUTIVE SCHEDULE (EX)

| | |
|---|---|
| Level I | $219,200 |
| Level II | $197,300 |
| Level III | $181,500 |
| Level IV | $170,800 |
| Level V | $160,100 |

### SENIOR EXECUTIVE SERVICE SCHEDULE (ES)

Pay ranges for the Senior Executive Service (SES) are established by law. The minimum is 120 percent of the rate of basic pay for GS–15, step 1. For agencies without a certified SES performance appraisal system, SES members' pay may not exceed the rate payable for level III of the Executive Schedule. For agencies with a certified SES performance appraisal system, SES members' pay may not exceed the rate payable for level II of the Executive Schedule. SES members are not entitled to locality-based comparability payments.**

| Structure of the SES Pay System | Minimum | Maximum |
|---|---|---|
| Agencies with a Certified SES Performance Appraisal System | $131,240 | $197,300 |
| Agencies without a Certified SES Performance Appraisal System | $131,240 | $181,500 |

### SENIOR LEVEL (SL)

Pay for SL positions ranges from 120 percent of the rate of basic pay for GS–15, step 1 to the rate payable for level III of the Executive Schedule. For agencies without a certified SL performance appraisal system, SL members' pay may not exceed the rate payable for level III of the Executive Schedule. For agencies with a certified SL performance appraisal system, SL members' pay may not exceed the rate payable for level II of the Executive Schedule. SL members are not entitled to locality-based comparability payments. **

| Structure of the SL Pay System | Minimum | Maximum |
|---|---|---|
| Agencies with a Certified SES Performance Appraisal System | $131,239 | $197,300 |
| Agencies without a Certified SES Performance Appraisal System | $131,239 | $181,500 |

**Certain SES and SL employees in Non-Foreign Areas receive locality pay under provisions of the Non-Foreign Area Retirement Equity Assurance (AREA) Act (as contained in the National Defense Authorization Act for Fiscal Year 2010 (Pub. L. 111–84, October 28, 2009).

## GENERAL SCHEDULE (GS)

Initial appointments to positions under the General Schedule are normally made at the minimum rate of the grade, although under certain circumstances, individuals with superior qualifications or fulfilling a special agency need may be paid at a rate above the minimum rate.

Step increases are granted to GS employees at the end of 52 weeks of service in steps 1, 2, and 3 of each grade; at the end of 104 weeks of service in steps 4, 5, and 6; and at the end of 156 weeks of service in steps 7, 8, and 9. An employee's work must be determined to be of an acceptable level of competence before granting a step increase. In addition to the periodic step increase, an employee whose work is outstanding may be advanced to the next higher step rate no more than once every 52 weeks. In addition to the 2020 basic pay rates listed below, GS employees are entitled to locality-based comparability payments for their respective locality pay area. The employee's locality rate of pay may not exceed the rate payable for level IV of the Executive Schedule. Certain GS employees may receive higher special rates instead of locality rates established to address significant recruitment or retention problems.

GENERAL SCHEDULE

| Grade | 2020 Annual Rates and Steps | | | | | | | | | |
|---|---|---|---|---|---|---|---|---|---|---|
| | 1 | 2 | 3 | 4 | 5 | 6 | 7 | 8 | 9 | 10 |
| GS–1 ........................ | $19,543 | $20,198 | $20,848 | $21,494 | $22,144 | $22,524 | $23,166 | $23,814 | $23,840 | $24,448 |
| GS–2 ........................ | 21,974 | 22,497 | 23,225 | 23,840 | 24,108 | 24,817 | 25,526 | 26,235 | 26,944 | 27,653 |
| GS–3 ........................ | 23,976 | 24,775 | 25,574 | 26,373 | 27,172 | 27,971 | 28,770 | 29,569 | 30,368 | 31,167 |
| GS–4 ........................ | 26,915 | 27,812 | 28,709 | 29,606 | 30,503 | 31,400 | 32,297 | 33,194 | 34,091 | 34,988 |
| GS–5 ........................ | 30,113 | 31,117 | 32,121 | 33,125 | 34,129 | 35,133 | 36,137 | 37,141 | 38,145 | 39,149 |
| GS–6 ........................ | 33,567 | 34,686 | 35,805 | 36,924 | 38,043 | 39,162 | 40,281 | 41,400 | 42,519 | 43,638 |
| GS–7 ........................ | 37,301 | 38,544 | 39,787 | 41,030 | 42,273 | 43,516 | 44,759 | 46,002 | 47,245 | 48,488 |
| GS–8 ........................ | 41,310 | 42,687 | 44,064 | 45,441 | 46,818 | 48,195 | 49,572 | 50,949 | 52,326 | 53,703 |
| GS–9 ........................ | 45,627 | 47,148 | 48,669 | 50,190 | 51,711 | 53,232 | 54,753 | 56,274 | 57,795 | 59,316 |
| GS–10 ...................... | 50,246 | 51,921 | 53,596 | 55,271 | 56,946 | 58,621 | 60,296 | 61,971 | 63,646 | 65,321 |
| GS–11 ...................... | 55,204 | 57,044 | 58,884 | 60,724 | 62,564 | 64,404 | 66,244 | 68,084 | 69,924 | 71,764 |
| GS–12 ...................... | 66,167 | 68,373 | 70,579 | 72,785 | 74,991 | 77,197 | 79,403 | 81,609 | 83,815 | 86,021 |
| GS–13 ...................... | 78,681 | 81,304 | 83,927 | 86,550 | 89,173 | 91,796 | 94,419 | 97,042 | 99,665 | 102,288 |
| GS–14 ...................... | 92,977 | 96,076 | 99,175 | 102,274 | 105,373 | 108,472 | 111,571 | 114,670 | 117,769 | 120,868 |
| GS–15 ...................... | 109,366 | 113,012 | 116,658 | 120,304 | 123,950 | 127,596 | 131,242 | 134,888 | 138,534 | 142,180 |

218

FEDERAL SALARY SCHEDULES

## 2020 LOCALITY PAY AREAS AND RATES

| | |
|---|---|
| ALBANY–SCHENECTADY, NY | 17.88% |
| ALBUQUERQUE–SANTA FE–LAS VEGAS, NM | 16.68% |
| ATLANTA—ATHENS–CLARKE COUNTY—SANDY SPRINGS, GA–AL | 22.16% |
| AUSTIN–ROUND ROCK, TX | 18.17% |
| BOSTON–WORCESTER–PROVIDENCE, MA–RI–NH–CT–ME | 29.11% |
| BUFFALO–CHEEKTOWAGA, NY | 20.20% |
| CHARLOTTE–CONCORD, NC–SC | 17.44% |
| CHICAGO–NAPERVILLE, IL–IN–WI | 28.59% |
| CINCINNATI–WILMINGTON–MAYSVILLE, OH–KY–IN | 20.55% |
| CLEVELAND–AKRON–CANTON, OH | 20.82% |
| COLORADO SPRINGS, CO | 17.78% |
| COLUMBUS–MARION–ZANESVILLE, OH | 20.02% |
| DALLAS–FORT WORTH, TX–OK | 24.98% |
| DAVENPORT–MOLINE, IA–IL | 17.04% |
| DAYTON–SPRINGFIELD–SIDNEY, OH | 19.18% |
| DENVER–AURORA, CO | 27.13% |
| DETROIT–WARREN–ANN ARBOR, MI | 27.32% |
| HARRISBURG–LEBANON, PA | 17.20% |
| HARTFORD–WEST HARTFORD, CT–MA | 29.49% |
| HOUSTON–THE WOODLANDS, TX | 33.32% |
| HUNTSVILLE–DECATUR–ALBERTVILLE, AL | 19.85% |
| INDIANAPOLIS–CARMEL–MUNCIE, IN | 16.92% |
| KANSAS CITY–OVERLAND PARK–KANSAS CITY, MO–KS | 17.13% |
| LAREDO, TX | 18.88% |
| LAS VEGAS–HENDERSON, NV–AZ | 17.68% |
| LOS ANGELES–LONG BEACH, CA | 32.41% |
| MIAMI–FORT LAUDERDALE–PORT ST. LUCIE, FL | 23.51% |
| MILWAUKEE–RACINE–WAUKESHA, WI | 20.96% |
| MINNEAPOLIS–ST. PAUL, MN–WI | 24.66% |
| NEW YORK–NEWARK, NY–NJ–CT–PA | 33.98% |
| PALM BAY–MELBOURNE–TITUSVILLE, FL | 16.73% |
| PHILADELPHIA–READING–CAMDEN, PA–NJ–DE–MD | 26.04% |
| PHOENIX–MESA–SCOTTSDALE, AZ | 20.12% |
| PITTSBURGH–NEW CASTLE–WEIRTON, PA–OH–WV | 19.40% |
| PORTLAND–VANCOUVER–SALEM, OR–WA | 23.74% |
| RALEIGH–DURHAM–CHAPEL HILL, NC | 20.49% |
| RICHMOND, VA | 19.95% |
| SACRAMENTO–ROSEVILLE, CA–NV | 26.37% |
| SAN DIEGO–CARLSBAD, CA | 29.77% |
| SAN JOSE–SAN FRANCISCO–OAKLAND, CA | 41.44% |
| SEATTLE–TACOMA, WA | 27.02% |
| ST. LOUIS–ST. CHARLES–FARMINGTON, MO–IL | 17.65% |
| TUCSON–NOGALES, AZ | 17.19% |
| WASHINGTON–BALTIMORE–ARLINGTON, DC–MD–VA–WV–PA | 30.48% |
| REST OF UNITED STATES (Consisting of those portions of the United States and its territories and possessions as listed in 5 CFR 591.205 not located within another locality pay area.) | 15.95% |
| STATE OF ALASKA | 29.67% |
| STATE OF HAWAII | 19.56% |

Note: Locality pay areas are defined in 5 CFR 531.603(b) and are available on the Office of Personnel Management Website at https://www.opm.gov/policy-data-oversight/pay-leave/salaries-wages/salary-tables/pdf/2016/saltbl.pdf.

# WASHINGTON–BALTIMORE–NORTHERN VIRGINIA, DC–MD–VA–WV–PA
## LOCALITY PAY SCHEDULE

The following salary tables reflect the locality pay rates for the Washington–Baltimore–Northern Virginia, DC–MD–VA–WV–PA locality pay area in 2020. The tables incorporate a locality payment of 30.48 percent.

GENERAL SCHEDULE

| Grade | 2020 Annual Rates and Steps | | | | | | | | | |
|---|---|---|---|---|---|---|---|---|---|---|
| | 1 | 2 | 3 | 4 | 5 | 6 | 7 | 8 | 9 | 10 |
| GS–1 | $25,500 | $26,354 | $27,202 | $28,045 | $28,893 | $29,389 | $30,227 | $31,073 | $31,106 | $31,900 |
| GS–2 | 28,672 | 29,354 | 30,304 | 31,106 | 31,456 | 32,381 | 33,306 | 34,231 | 35,157 | 36,082 |
| GS–3 | 31,284 | 32,326 | 33,369 | 34,411 | 35,454 | 36,497 | 37,539 | 38,582 | 39,624 | 40,667 |
| GS–4 | 35,119 | 36,289 | 37,460 | 38,630 | 39,800 | 40,971 | 42,141 | 43,312 | 44,482 | 45,652 |
| GS–5 | 39,291 | 40,601 | 41,911 | 43,222 | 44,532 | 45,842 | 47,152 | 48,462 | 49,772 | 51,082 |
| GS–6 | 43,798 | 45,258 | 46,718 | 48,178 | 49,639 | 51,099 | 52,559 | 54,019 | 55,479 | 56,939 |
| GS–7 | 48,670 | 50,292 | 51,914 | 53,536 | 55,158 | 56,780 | 58,402 | 60,023 | 61,645 | 63,267 |
| GS–8 | 53,901 | 55,698 | 57,495 | 59,291 | 61,088 | 62,885 | 64,682 | 66,478 | 68,275 | 70,072 |
| GS–9 | 59,534 | 61,519 | 63,503 | 65,488 | 67,473 | 69,457 | 71,442 | 73,426 | 75,411 | 77,396 |
| GS–10 | 65,561 | 67,747 | 69,932 | 72,118 | 74,303 | 76,489 | 78,674 | 80,860 | 83,045 | 85,231 |
| GS–11 | 72,030 | 74,431 | 76,832 | 79,233 | 81,634 | 84,034 | 86,435 | 88,836 | 91,237 | 93,638 |
| GS–12 | 86,335 | 89,213 | 92,091 | 94,970 | 97,848 | 100,727 | 103,605 | 106,483 | 109,362 | 112,240 |
| GS–13 | 102,663 | 106,085 | 109,508 | 112,930 | 116,353 | 119,775 | 123,198 | 126,620 | 130,043 | 133,465 |
| GS–14 | 121,316 | 125,360 | 129,404 | 133,447 | 137,491 | 141,534 | 145,578 | 149,621 | 153,665 | 157,709 |
| GS–15 | 142,701 | 147,458 | 152,215 | 156,973 | 161,730 | 166,487 | 170,800* | 170,800* | 170,800* | 170,800* |

# SPECIAL LAW ENFORCEMENT OFFICER (LEO) PAY SCHEDULES

Law enforcement officers at grades GS–3 through GS–10 are entitled to special base rates that are higher than General Schedule base rates. Such LEOs receive the locality payments applicable in their locality pay area on top of these special base rates. The locality pay area definitions and pay percentages are the same as those used for regular General Schedule employees.

SPECIAL SALARY RATES FOR LEOS

| Grade | 2020 Annual Rates and Steps | | | | | | | | | | |
|---|---|---|---|---|---|---|---|---|---|---|---|
| | 1 | 2 | 3 | 4 | 5 | 6 | 7 | 8 | 9 | 10 | WGI |
| GS–3 | $28,770 | $29,569 | $30,368 | $31,167 | $31,966 | $32,765 | $33,564 | $34,363 | $35,162 | $35,961 | $799 |
| GS–4 | 32,297 | 33,194 | 34,091 | 34,988 | 35,885 | 36,782 | 37,679 | 38,576 | 39,473 | 40,370 | 897 |
| GS–5 | 37,141 | 38,145 | 39,149 | 40,153 | 41,157 | 42,161 | 43,165 | 44,169 | 45,173 | 46,177 | 1,004 |
| GS–6 | 39,162 | 40,281 | 41,400 | 42,519 | 43,638 | 44,757 | 45,876 | 46,995 | 48,114 | 49,233 | 1,119 |
| GS–7 | 42,273 | 43,516 | 44,759 | 46,002 | 47,245 | 48,488 | 49,731 | 50,974 | 52,217 | 53,460 | 1,243 |
| GS–8 | 44,064 | 45,441 | 46,818 | 48,195 | 49,572 | 50,949 | 52,326 | 53,703 | 55,080 | 56,457 | 1,377 |
| GS–9 | 47,148 | 48,669 | 50,190 | 51,711 | 53,232 | 54,753 | 56,274 | 57,795 | 59,316 | 60,837 | 1,521 |
| GS–10 | 51,921 | 53,596 | 55,271 | 56,949 | 58,621 | 60,296 | 61,971 | 63,646 | 65,321 | 66,996 | 1,675 |

NOTE: These special base rates for law enforcement officers (as defined in 5 U.S.C. 5541(3) and 5 CFR 550.103) are authorized by section 403 of the Federal Employees Pay Comparability Act of 1990, as amended. By law, these rates must be the basis for computing locality payments. (5 CFR part 531, subpart F.)

## THE FOREIGN SERVICE SCHEDULE

| | Class | | | | | | | | |
|---|---|---|---|---|---|---|---|---|---|
| | **1** | **2** | **3** | **4** | **5** | **6** | **7** | **8** | **9** |
| Step 1 | $109,366 | $88,619 | $71,808 | $58,186 | $47,148 | $42,149 | $37,680 | $33,685 | $30,113 |
| Step 2 | 112,647 | 91,278 | 73,962 | 59,932 | 48,562 | 43,413 | 38,810 | 34,696 | 31,016 |
| Step 3 | 116,026 | 94,016 | 76,181 | 61,730 | 50,019 | 44,716 | 39,975 | 35,736 | 31,947 |
| Step 4 | 119,507 | 96,836 | 78,467 | 63,581 | 51,520 | 46,057 | 41,174 | 36,809 | 32,905 |
| Step 5 | 123,092 | 99,741 | 80,821 | 65,489 | 53,065 | 47,439 | 42,409 | 37,913 | 33,892 |
| Step 6 | 126,785 | 102,734 | 83,245 | 67,454 | 54,657 | 48,862 | 43,681 | 39,050 | 34,909 |
| Step 7 | 130,589 | 105,816 | 85,743 | 69,477 | 56,297 | 50,328 | 44,992 | 40,222 | 35,956 |
| Step 8 | 134,506 | 108,990 | 88,315 | 71,561 | 57,986 | 51,838 | 46,342 | 41,428 | 37,035 |
| Step 9 | 138,542 | 112,260 | 90,964 | 73,708 | 59,726 | 53,393 | 47,732 | 42,671 | 38,146 |
| Step 10 | 142,180 | 115,628 | 93,693 | 75,920 | 61,517 | 54,995 | 49,164 | 43,951 | 39,291 |
| Step 11 | 142,180 | 119,097 | 96,504 | 78,197 | 63,363 | 56,645 | 50,639 | 45,270 | 40,469 |
| Step 12 | 142,180 | 122,669 | 99,399 | 80,543 | 65,264 | 58,344 | 52,158 | 46,628 | 41,683 |
| Step 13 | 142,180 | 126,350 | 102,381 | 82,959 | 67,222 | 60,094 | 53,723 | 48,027 | 42,934 |
| Step 14 | 142,180 | 130,140 | 105,452 | 85,448 | 69,238 | 61,897 | 55,334 | 49,468 | 44,222 |

## SENIOR FOREIGN SERVICE SCHEDULE

The Senior Foreign Service (SFS) pay system is an open-range, performance-based pay system that is linked to the SES pay system. SFS members, like SES members, are not entitled to automatic across-the-board increases and locality-based comparability payments. Instead, pay adjustments are based on a member's individual performance and/or contribution to the agency's performance.

The Executive order prescribes three SFS salary classes that are linked to the SES as follows:

(1) Career Minister (CM). with a range from 94 percent of the rate payable to level III of the Executive Schedule to 100 percent of the rate payable to level III of the Executive Schedule (Note: Career Ambassador (CA) SFS members are also paid within the CM rate range);

(2) Minister-Counselor (MC) with a range from 90 percent of the rate payable to level III of the Executive Schedule to 100 percent of the rate payable to level III of the Executive Schedule; and

(3) Counselor (OC), with a range from 120 percent of the rate payable to GS–15, step 1 to 100 percent of the rate payable to level III of the Executive Schedule.

The 2020 pay ranges for the SFS classes are:

| SFS Class | Minimum | Maximum |
|---|---|---|
| OC | $131,239 | $185,130 |
| MC | $131,239 | $194,205 |
| CM, CA | $131,239 | $197,300 |

# DEPARTMENT OF VETERANS AFFAIRS, VETERANS HEALTH ADMINISTRATION FEDERAL SALARY SCHEDULES EFFECTIVE ON THE FIRST DAY OF THE FIRST APPLICABLE PAY PERIOD BEGINNING ON OR AFTER JANUARY 1, 2020

### SCHEDULE FOR THE OFFICE OF THE UNDER SECRETARY FOR HEALTH

(38 U.S.C. 7306)*

| | Minimum | Maximum |
|---|---|---|
| Assistant Under Secretaries for Health | | $157,279* |
| (Only applies to incumbents who are not physicians or dentists) | | |
| Service Directors | $116,844 | $ 145,113 |
| Director, National Center for Preventive Health | 98,654 | 164,974 |

### Physician and Dentist Base and Longevity Schedule***

| | Minimum | Maximum |
|---|---|---|
| Physician Grade | $107,569 | $ 157,773 |
| Dentist Grade | 107,569 | 157,773 |

### Clinical Podiatrist, Chiropractor, and Optometrist Schedule

| | Minimum | Maximum |
|---|---|---|
| Chief Grade | $142,701 | $170,800* |
| Senior Grade | 121,316 | 157,709 |
| Intermediate Grade | 102,663 | 133,465 |
| Full Grade | 86,335 | 112,240 |
| Associate Grade | 72,030 | 93,638 |

*Rate limited to level IV of the Executive Schedule

### Physician Assistant and Expanded-Function Dental Auxiliary Schedule****

| | Minimum | Maximum |
|---|---|---|
| Director Grade | $102,646 | $ 133,444 |
| Assistant Director Grade | 87,263 | 113,444 |
| Chief Grade | 73,846 | 96,004 |
| Senior Grade | 62,101 | 80,731 |
| Intermediate Grade | 51,811 | 67,354 |
| Full Grade | 42,823 | 55,666 |
| Associate Grade | 36,850 | 47,902 |
| Junior Grade | 31,504 | 40,954 |

*This schedule does not apply to the Deputy Under Secretary for Health, the Associate Deputy Under Secretary for Health, Assistant Under Secretaries for Health who are physicians or dentists, Medical Directors, the Assistant Under Secretary for Nursing Programs, or the Director of Nursing Services.

**Pursuant to 38 U.S.C. 7404(d), the rate of basic pay payable to these employees is limited to the rate for level V of the Executive Schedule, which is $150,200.

***Pursuant to section 3 of Public Law 108–445 and 38 U.S.C. 7431, Veterans Health Administration physicians and dentists may also be paid market pay and performance pay.

****Pursuant to section 301(a) of Public Law 102–40, these positions are paid according to the Nurse Schedule in 38 U.S.C. 4107(b), as in effect on August 14, 1990, with subsequent adjustments.

Made in United States
Troutdale, OR
10/05/2024

23439794R00131